UNIVERSITY CASEBOOK SERIES

STATUTORY AND
DOCUMENTARY SUPPLEMENT

DOMESTIC
RELATIONS

SELECTED UNIFORM LAWS,
MODEL LEGISLATION, FEDERAL
STATUTES, STATE STATUTES,
AND INTERNATIONAL TREATIES

2017 EDITION

WALTER WADLINGTON
James Madison Professor of Law Emeritus
University of Virginia

RAYMOND C. O'BRIEN
Professor of Law
Columbus School of Law
The Catholic University of America

ROBIN FRETWELL WILSON
Roger and Stephany Joslin Professor of Law
and Director, Family Law and Policy Program
University of Illinois College of Law

FOUNDATION
PRESS

University Casebook Series is a trademark registered in the U.S. Patent and Trademark Office.

© 2017 LEG, Inc. d/b/a West Academic
    444 Cedar Street, Suite 700
    St. Paul, MN 55101
    1-877-888-1330

Printed in the United States of America

ISBN: 978-1-62810-200-0

INTRODUCTION

The Fifth Edition of this book of selected code provisions is, like the previous editions, meant to be a companion book to the family law casebook published by the same authors. There are fewer pages in the majority of casebooks used in American law schools today. This development is in response to the increasing number of innovations that must be addressed so as to provide students with a comprehensive picture of what has occurred, is occurring, and likely to occur in the future. Code provisions, together with the common law, continue to evolve too, but including all of the pertinent statutes in casebooks would increase the number of pages to an unmanageable length. In addition, simply providing an Internet citation in the casebook prompts time consumption and requires connectivity. Therefore, this book is meant as a supplement to cases and materials provided in the casebook, an easily managed compendium of what we consider to be pertinent to any modern course on family law.

This Fifth Edition is divided into four parts. The first part, *Uniform Laws and Model Legislation* contains Model Rules of Professional Conduct, and Principles of the Law of Family Dissolution, neither of which was in previous editions. We added these because of the increasing number of references made to them in cases and state legislation. In addition, we have added the newly enacted Uniform Premarital and Marital Agreement Act, and the Uniform Arbitration Act because of their pertinence to modern practice. And finally, we added the Uniform Child Witness Testimony by Alternative Methods Act, the Uniform Interstate Enforcement of Domestic-Violence Protection Orders Act, and the Uniform Representation of Children in Abuse, Neglect, and Custody Proceedings Act in response to continuing concern over abusive conduct. These statutes are meant to illustrate current responses to these issues.

The second part, *Federal Statutes*, is notable because of the lack of increasing federal legislation in the area of family law. Most notable is the deletion of the federal Defense of Marriage Act, held to be unconstitutional in 2013. This decision by the Supreme Court of the United States was a prelude to the 2015 holding of the Court that same sex marriage be made available and be recognized throughout the United States. Updates were made to the Violence Against Women Act, but mandated federal legislation was relatively dormant. But this is not the case with the third part, *State Statutes*. We have added a North Dakota statute pertaining to ABA Standards of Practice for Family and Divorce Mediation because of its pertinence to family law practice. Likewise, we favor the Illinois alimony statute and suggest it be compared to the New York and California statutes on spousal support appearing in the casebook. Also, we offer the Illinois statute on allocation of parental responsibility and invite a comparison with child custody statutes from California and West Virginia. We think the court ordered parenting plan illustrated in the Oregon statute deserves attention too, as does the

Oregon family law mediation statute. And increasingly families are incorporating older members into a younger family member's household. Accordingly, we have added the California statute on elder abuse and protection, plus the Illinois Statutory Custodial Claim for Incapacitated Relative's Care.

In the fourth part, *International Treaties*, we have retained existing code provisions, but added two additional ones: the United Nations Declaration on the Elimination of Discrimination Against Women, and the United Nations Declaration on Social and Leal Principles Relating to the Protection and Welfare of Children, with Special Reference to Foster Placement and Adoption Nationally and Internationally. Both of these new provisions complement state and federal legislation and offer comparison. The other provisions call attention to child abuse and protection internationally.

There have been significant developments in family law since the publication of the previous edition to this book. Most notable is the availability of same sex marriage throughout the United States. As a result, we have eliminated an illustration of a same sex marriage statute. In addition, we have eliminated illustrations of domestic partnership, reciprocal beneficiaries, and civil unions. But there is added emphasis on other areas of law. Particular attention is being paid to practice-ready materials, hence we have purposefully included material on professional responsibility, mediation, and arbitration. Likewise, older and younger family members' interaction is increasing with greater longevity among Americans. Hence we have added materials on elder protection, assisted suicide, and statutory monetary claims for caring for an incapacitated relative. Assisted reproductive technology continues to advance and mindful of this we have included material on scientific proof of paternity, surrogacy, and the parental presumptions provided by the Uniform Parentage Act.

As we have done in previous editions, we provide a list of legal articles pertaining to each of the code provisions we include in this book. We have attempted to provide commentary from a range of authors, academics, students and practitioners. We suggest consulting these articles for insights into the history of the legislation and for suggestions as to what may follow.

Finally, we express our sincere appreciation to the National Conference of Commissioners on Uniform State Laws for their permission to reprint the text of selected Uniform Laws. And we gratefully acknowledge the research and editorial assistance of Daniel B. O'Connell, Samuel Mott and Elaina Valtierra in the preparation of this book.

WALTER WADLINGTON
RAYMOND C. O'BRIEN
ROBIN FRETWELL WILSON

TABLE OF CONTENTS

PART III. STATE STATUTES

PART IV. INTERNATIONAL TREATIES

UNIVERSITY CASEBOOK SERIES®

STATUTORY AND
DOCUMENTARY SUPPLEMENT

DOMESTIC RELATIONS

SELECTED UNIFORM LAWS,
MODEL LEGISLATION, FEDERAL
STATUTES, STATE STATUTES,
AND INTERNATIONAL TREATIES

2017 EDITION

PART I

UNIFORM LAWS AND
MODEL LEGISLATION

MODEL RULES OF PROFESSIONAL CONDUCT

American Bar Association (2016)*

[EDITORS' INTRODUCTION: Todd A. Berger, *The Constitutional Limits of Client-Centered Decision Making,* 50 U. RICH. L. REV. 1089 (2016); Alex B. Long, *Employment Discrimination in the Legal Profession: A Question of Ethics?,* 2016 U. ILL. L. REV. 445 (2016); Deborah Jones Merritt, *Hippocrates and Socrates: Professional Obligations to Educate the Next Generation,* 51 WAKE FOREST L. REV. 403 (2016); Antigone Peyton, *The Connected State of Things: A Lawyer's Survival Guide in an Internet of Things World,* 24 CATH. U. J. L. & TECH. 369 (2016); Evan G. Zuckerman, *Justicecorps: Helping Pro Se Litigants Bridge a Divide,* 49 COLUM. J.L. & SOC. PROBS. 551 (2016).]

* * *

RULE 1.2. SCOPE OF REPRESENTATION AND ALLOCATION OF AUTHORITY BETWEEN CLIENT AND LAWYER

(a) Subject to paragraphs (c) and (d), a lawyer shall abide by a client's decisions concerning the objectives of representation and, as required by Rule 1.4, shall consult with the client as to the means by which they are to be pursued. A lawyer may take such action on behalf of the client as is impliedly authorized to carry out the representation. A lawyer shall abide by a client's decision whether to settle a matter. In a criminal case, the lawyer shall abide by the client's decision, after consultation with the lawyer, as to a plea to be entered, whether to waive jury trial and whether the client will testify.

(b) A lawyer's representation of a client, including representation by appointment, does not constitute an endorsement of the client's political, economic, social or moral views or activities.

(c) A lawyer may limit the scope of the representation if the limitation is reasonable under the circumstances and the client gives informed consent.

(d) A lawyer shall not counsel a client to engage, or assist a client, in conduct that the lawyer knows is criminal or fraudulent, but a lawyer may discuss the legal consequences of any proposed course of conduct with a client and may counsel or assist a client to make a good faith effort to determine the validity, scope, meaning or application of the law.

RULE 1.3. DILIGENCE

A lawyer shall act with reasonable diligence and promptness in representing a client.

* * *

RULE 1.5. FEES

(a)   A lawyer shall not make an agreement for, charge, or collect an unreasonable fee or an unreasonable amount for expenses. The factors to be considered in determining the reasonableness of a fee include the following:

(1)   the time and labor required, the novelty and difficulty of the questions involved, and the skill requisite to perform the legal service properly;

(2)   the likelihood, if apparent to the client, that the acceptance of the particular employment will preclude other employment by the lawyer;

(3)   the fee customarily charged in the locality for similar legal services;

(4)   the amount involved and the results obtained;

(5)   the time limitations imposed by the client or by the circumstances;

(6)   the nature and length of the professional relationship with the client;

(7)   the experience, reputation, and ability of the lawyer or lawyers performing the services; and

(8)   whether the fee is fixed or contingent.

(b)   The scope of the representation and the basis or rate of the fee and expenses for which the client will be responsible shall be communicated to the client, preferably in writing, before or within a reasonable time after commencing the representation, except when the lawyer will charge a regularly represented client on the same basis or rate. Any changes in the basis or rate of the fee or expenses shall also be communicated to the client.

(c)   A fee may be contingent on the outcome of the matter for which the service is rendered, except in a matter in which a contingent fee is prohibited by paragraph (d) or other law. A contingent fee agreement shall be in a writing signed by the client and shall state the method by which the fee is to be determined, including the percentage or percentages that shall accrue to the lawyer in the event of settlement, trial or appeal; litigation and other expenses to be deducted from the recovery; and whether such expenses are to be deducted before or after the contingent fee is calculated. The agreement must clearly notify the client of any expenses for which the client will be liable whether or not the client is the prevailing party. Upon conclusion of a contingent fee matter, the lawyer shall provide the client with a written statement stating the outcome of the matter and, if there is a recovery, showing the remittance to the client and the method of its determination.

(d) A lawyer shall not enter into an arrangement for, charge, or collect:

>   (1) any fee in a domestic relations matter, the payment or amount of which is contingent upon the securing of a divorce or upon the amount of alimony or support, or property settlement in lieu thereof; or

>   (2) a contingent fee for representing a defendant in a criminal case.

(e) A division of a fee between lawyers who are not in the same firm may be made only if:

>   (1) the division is in proportion to the services performed by each lawyer or each lawyer assumes joint responsibility for the representation;

>   (2) the client agrees to the arrangement, including the share each lawyer will receive, and the agreement is confirmed in writing; and

>   (3) the total fee is reasonable.

RULE 1.6. CONFIDENTIALITY OF INFORMATION

(a) A lawyer shall not reveal information relating to the representation of a client unless the client gives informed consent, the disclosure is impliedly authorized in order to carry out the representation or the disclosure is permitted by paragraph (b).

(b) A lawyer may reveal information relating to the representation of a client to the extent the lawyer reasonably believes necessary:

>   (1) to prevent reasonably certain death or substantial bodily harm;

>   (2) to prevent the client from committing a crime or fraud that is reasonably certain to result in substantial injury to the financial interests or property of another and in furtherance of which the client has used or is using the lawyer's services;

>   (3) to prevent, mitigate or rectify substantial injury to the financial interests or property of another that is reasonably certain to result or has resulted from the client's commission of a crime or fraud in furtherance of which the client has used the lawyer's services;

>   (4) to secure legal advice about the lawyer's compliance with these Rules;

>   (5) to establish a claim or defense on behalf of the lawyer in a controversy between the lawyer and the client, to establish a defense to a criminal charge or civil claim against the lawyer based upon conduct in which the client was involved, or to respond to allegations

in any proceeding concerning the lawyer's representation of the client;

(6)   to comply with other law or a court order; or

(7)   to detect and resolve conflicts of interest arising from the lawyer's change of employment or from changes in the composition or ownership of a firm, but only if the revealed information would not compromise the attorney-client privilege or otherwise prejudice the client.

(c)   A lawyer shall make reasonable efforts to prevent the inadvertent or unauthorized disclosure of, or unauthorized access to, information relating to the representation of a client.

* * *

RULE 1.8. CONFLICT OF INTEREST: CURRENT CLIENTS: SPECIFIC RULES

(a)   A lawyer shall not enter into a business transaction with a client or knowingly acquire an ownership, possessory, security or other pecuniary interest adverse to a client unless:

(1)   the transaction and terms on which the lawyer acquires the interest are fair and reasonable to the client and are fully disclosed and transmitted in writing in a manner that can be reasonably understood by the client;

(2)   the client is advised in writing of the desirability of seeking and is given a reasonable opportunity to seek the advice of independent legal counsel on the transaction; and

(3)   the client gives informed consent, in a writing signed by the client, to the essential terms of the transaction and the lawyer's role in the transaction, including whether the lawyer is representing the client in the transaction.

(b)   A lawyer shall not use information relating to representation of a client to the disadvantage of the client unless the client gives informed consent, except as permitted or required by these Rules.

(c)   A lawyer shall not solicit any substantial gift from a client, including a testamentary gift, or prepare on behalf of a client an instrument giving the lawyer or a person related to the lawyer any substantial gift unless the lawyer or other recipient of the gift is related to the client. For purposes of this paragraph, related persons include a spouse, child, grandchild, parent, grandparent or other relative or individual with whom the lawyer or the client maintains a close, familial relationship.

(d)   Prior to the conclusion of representation of a client, a lawyer shall not make or negotiate an agreement giving the lawyer literary or media rights to a portrayal or account based in substantial part on information relating to the representation.

(e) A lawyer shall not provide financial assistance to a client in connection with pending or contemplated litigation, except that:

(1) a lawyer may advance court costs and expenses of litigation, the repayment of which may be contingent on the outcome of the matter; and

(2) a lawyer representing an indigent client may pay court costs and expenses of litigation on behalf of the client.

(f) A lawyer shall not accept compensation for representing a client from one other than the client unless:

(1) the client gives informed consent;

(2) there is no interference with the lawyer's independence of professional judgment or with the client-lawyer relationship; and

(3) information relating to representation of a client is protected as required by Rule 1.6.

(g) A lawyer who represents two or more clients shall not participate in making an aggregate settlement of the claims of or against the clients, or in a criminal case an aggregated agreement as to guilty or nolo contendere pleas, unless each client gives informed consent, in a writing signed by the client. The lawyer's disclosure shall include the existence and nature of all the claims or pleas involved and of the participation of each person in the settlement.

(h) A lawyer shall not:

(1) make an agreement prospectively limiting the lawyer's liability to a client for malpractice unless the client is independently represented in making the agreement; or

(2) settle a claim or potential claim for such liability with an unrepresented client or former client unless that person is advised in writing of the desirability of seeking and is given a reasonable opportunity to seek the advice of independent legal counsel in connection therewith.

(i) A lawyer shall not acquire a proprietary interest in the cause of action or subject matter of litigation the lawyer is conducting for a client, except that the lawyer may:

(1) acquire a lien authorized by law to secure the lawyer's fee or expenses; and

(2) contract with a client for a reasonable contingent fee in a civil case.

(j) A lawyer shall not have sexual relations with a client unless a consensual sexual relationship existed between them when the client-lawyer relationship commenced.

(k) While lawyers are associated in a firm, a prohibition in the foregoing paragraphs (a) through (i) that applies to any one of them shall apply to all of them.

RULE 1.9. DUTIES TO FORMER CLIENTS

(a) A lawyer who has formerly represented a client in a matter shall not thereafter represent another person in the same or a substantially related matter in which that person's interests are materially adverse to the interests of the former client unless the former client gives informed consent, confirmed in writing.

(b) A lawyer shall not knowingly represent a person in the same or a substantially related matter in which a firm with which the lawyer formerly was associated had previously represented a client

(1) whose interests are materially adverse to that person; and

(2) about whom the lawyer had acquired information protected by Rules 1.6 and 1.9(c) that is material to the matter; unless the former client gives informed consent, confirmed in writing.

(c) A lawyer who has formerly represented a client in a matter or whose present or former firm has formerly represented a client in a matter shall not thereafter:

(1) use information relating to the representation to the disadvantage of the former client except as these Rules would permit or require with respect to a client, or when the information has become generally known; or

(2) reveal information relating to the representation except as these Rules would permit or require with respect to a client.

* * *

RULE 2.1. ADVISOR

In representing a client, a lawyer shall exercise independent professional judgment and render candid advice. In rendering advice, a lawyer may refer not only to law but to other considerations such as moral, economic, social and political factors that may be relevant to the client's situation.

* * *

RULE 4.3. DEALING WITH UNREPRESENTED PERSON

In dealing on behalf of a client with a person who is not represented by counsel, a lawyer shall not state or imply that the lawyer is disinterested. When the lawyer knows or reasonably should know that the unrepresented person misunderstands the lawyer's role in the matter, the lawyer shall make reasonable efforts to correct the misunderstanding. The lawyer shall not give legal advice to an unrepresented person, other than the advice to secure counsel, if the lawyer knows or reasonably should know that the interests of such a person are or have a reasonable possibility of being in conflict with the interests of the client.

* * *

RULE 8.4. MISCONDUCT

It is professional misconduct for a lawyer to:

(a) violate or attempt to violate the Rules of Professional Conduct, knowingly assist or induce another to do so, or do so through the acts of another;

(b) commit a criminal act that reflects adversely on the lawyer's honesty, trustworthiness or fitness as a lawyer in other respects;

(c) engage in conduct involving dishonesty, fraud, deceit or misrepresentation;

(d) engage in conduct that is prejudicial to the administration of justice;

(e) state or imply an ability to influence improperly a government agency or official or to achieve results by means that violate the Rules of Professional Conduct or other law; or

(f) knowingly assist a judge or judicial officer in conduct that is a violation of applicable rules of judicial conduct or other law.

PRINCIPLES OF THE LAW OF FAMILY DISSOLUTION

American Law Institute (2002)

[EDITORS' INTRODUCTION: Erez Aloni, *Deprivative Recognition*, 61 UCLA L. REV. 1276 (2014); Susan Frelich Appleton, *Restating Childhood*, 79 BROOK. L. REV. 525 (2014); Yitshak Cohen, *Extramarital Relationships and the Theoretical Rationales for the Joint Property Rules—A New Model*, 80 MO. L. REV. 131 (2015); Josh Gupta-Kagan, *Non-Exclusive Adoption and Child Welfare*, 66 ALA. L. REV. 715 (2015); Jeffrey A. Parness, *Parentage Prenups and Midnups*, 31 GA. ST. U. L. REV. 343 (2015); Danaya C. Wright, *Inheritance Equity: Reforming the Inheritance Penalties Facing Children in Nontraditional Families*, 25 CORNELL J.L. & PUB. POL'Y 1 (2015); Brittanie Wagnon, Comment, *From Wedding Bells to Working Women: Unmasking the Sexism Resulting from "Illicit Concubinage" in Louisiana's Jurisprudence*, 76 LA. L. REV. 1383 (2016).]

CHAPTER 2.   THE ALLOCATION OF CUSTODIAL AND DECISIONMAKING RESPONSIBILITY FOR CHILDREN

TOPIC 2.   PARENTING PLAN

SECTION 2.05. PARENTING PLAN: PROPOSED, TEMPORARY, AND FINAL

(1) An individual seeking a judicial allocation of custodial responsibility or decisionmaking responsibility under this Chapter should be required to file with the court a proposed parenting plan containing proposals for each of the provisions specified in Paragraph (5). Individuals should be allowed to file a joint plan.

(2) Each parenting plan filed under Paragraph (1) should be required to be supported by an affidavit containing, to the extent known or reasonably discoverable by the filing individual or individuals, all of the following:

(a)   the name and address of any individual who has a right to participate in the action under § 2.04;

(b)   the name, address, and length of co-residence of any individuals with whom the child has lived for one year or more, or in the case of a child less than one year old, any individuals with whom the child has lived for any significant period of time since birth;

(c)   a description of the past allocation of caretaking and other parenting functions performed by each individual identified under Paragraph (2)(a) or (2)(b), including at a minimum during the 24 months preceding the filing of an action under this Chapter;

(d)   a description of the employment and child-care schedules of any individual seeking an allocation of custodial responsibility, and any expected changes to these schedules in the future;

(e) a schedule of the child's school and extracurricular activities;

(f) a description of any of the limiting factors specified in § 2.11 that are present in the case, including any restraining orders to prevent child abuse or domestic violence, with case number and issuing court;

(g) financial information required to be disclosed under Chapter 3;

(h) a description of the known areas of agreement and disagreement with any other parenting plan submitted in the case.

The court should maintain the confidentiality of information required to be filed under this section if the individual providing the information demonstrates a reasonable fear of child abuse or domestic violence and disclosure of the information would increase safety risks.

(3) The court should have a process to identify cases in which there is credible information that child abuse, as defined by state law, or domestic violence as defined in § 2.03(7), has occurred. The process should include assistance for possible victims of domestic violence in complying with Paragraph (2), referral to appropriate resources for safe shelter, counseling, safety planning, information regarding the potential impact of domestic violence on children, and information regarding civil and criminal remedies for domestic violence. The process should include a system for ensuring the court review mandated in § 2.06(2) when there is credible information that child abuse or domestic violence has occurred.

(4) Prior to a decision on a final parenting plan and upon motion of a party, the court may order a temporary allocation of custodial responsibility or decisionmaking responsibility as the court determines is in the child's best interests, considering the factors in §§ 2.08 and 2.09. A temporary allocation order ordinarily should not preclude access to the child by a parent who has been exercising a reasonable share of parenting functions. Upon credible information of one or more of the circumstances set forth in § 2.11(1) and pending adjudication of the underlying facts, the court should issue a temporary order limiting or denying access to the child as required by that section, in order to protect the child or other family member.

(5) After consideration of any proposed parenting plans submitted in the case and any evidence presented in support thereof, the court should order a parenting plan that is consistent with the provisions of §§ 2.08–2.12 and contains the following provisions:

(a) a provision for the child's living arrangements and for each parent's custodial responsibility, which should include either

(i) a custodial schedule that designates in which parent's home each minor child will reside on given days of the year; or

(ii) a formula or method for determining such a schedule in sufficient detail that, if necessary, the schedule can be enforced in a subsequent proceeding.

(b) an allocation of decisionmaking responsibility as to significant matters reasonably likely to arise with respect to the child; and

(c) a provision consistent with § 2.07 for resolution of disputes that arise under the plan, and a provision establishing remedies for violations of the plan.

(6) The court may provide in the parenting plan for how issues relating to a party's future relocation will be resolved, and it may provide for future modifications of the parenting plan if specified contingencies occur.

(7) Expedited procedures should facilitate the prompt issuance of a parenting plan.

SECTION 2.06. PARENTAL AGREEMENTS

(1) The court should order provisions of a parenting plan agreed to by the parents, unless the agreement

(a) is not knowing or voluntary, or

(b) would be harmful to the child.

(2) The court, on any basis it deems sufficient, may conduct an evidentiary hearing to determine whether there is a factual basis under Paragraph (1) to find that the court should not be bound by an agreement. If credible information is presented to the court that child abuse as defined by state law or domestic violence as defined by § 2.03(7) has occurred, the court should hold a hearing and, if the court determines that child abuse or domestic violence has occurred, it should order appropriate protective measures under § 2.11.

(3) If the court rejects an agreement, in whole or in part, under the standards set forth in Paragraph (1), it should allow the parents the opportunity to negotiate another agreement.

SECTION 2.07. COURT-ORDERED SERVICES

(1) The court may inform the parents, or require them to be informed, about any of the following:

(a) how to prepare a parenting plan;

(b) the impact of family dissolution on children and how the needs of children facing family dissolution can best be met;

(c) the impact of conflict and domestic violence on children, and the availability of resources for addressing these issues;

(d) mediation or other nonjudicial procedures designed to help them reach agreement.

(2) A mediator should screen for domestic violence and for other conditions or circumstances that may impede a party's capacity to participate in the mediation process. If there is credible evidence of such circumstances, the mediation should not occur, unless reasonable steps are taken both

    (a) to ensure meaningful consent of each party to participate in the mediation and to any results reached through the mediation process; and

    (b) to protect the safety of the victim.

(3) The court should not compel any services under Paragraph (1) that would require a parent to have a face-to-face meeting with the other parent.

(4) A mediator should not be allowed to make a recommendation to the court in a case in which the mediator has provided mediation services.

(5) A mediator should not be allowed to reveal information that a parent has disclosed during mediation under a reasonable expectation of confidentiality, except such information as is necessary to factfinding under § 2.06 or § 2.11.

(6) A court should be prohibited from ordering services authorized under Paragraph (1) unless available at no cost or at a cost that is reasonable in light of the financial circumstances of each parent. When one parent's ability to pay for such services is significantly greater than the other's, the court should have discretion to order that parent to pay some or all of the expenses of the other.

SECTION 2.08. ALLOCATION OF CUSTODIAL RESPONSIBILITY

(1) Unless otherwise resolved by agreement of the parents under § 2.06, the court should allocate custodial responsibility so that the proportion of custodial time the child spends with each parent approximates the proportion of time each parent spent performing caretaking functions for the child prior to the parents' separation or, if the parents never lived together, before the filing of the action, except to the extent required under § 2.11 or necessary to achieve one or more of the following objectives:

    (a) to permit the child to have a relationship with each parent which, in the case of a legal parent or a parent by estoppel who has performed a reasonable share of parenting functions, should be not less than a presumptive amount of custodial time set by a uniform rule of statewide application;

    (b) to accommodate the firm and reasonable preferences of a child who has reached a specific age, set by a uniform rule of statewide application;

(c)   to keep siblings together when the court finds that doing so is necessary to their welfare;

(d)   to protect the child's welfare when the presumptive allocation under this section would harm the child because of a gross disparity in the quality of the emotional attachment between each parent and the child or in each parent's demonstrated ability or availability to meet the child's needs;

(e)   to take into account any prior agreement, other than one under § 2.06, that would be appropriate to consider in light of the circumstances as a whole, including the reasonable expectations of the parties, the extent to which they could have reasonably anticipated the events that occurred and their significance, and the interests of the child;

(f)   to avoid an allocation of custodial responsibility that would be extremely impractical or that would interfere substantially with the child's need for stability in light of economic, physical, or other circumstances, including the distance between the parents' residences, the cost and difficulty of transporting the child, each parent's and the child's daily schedules, and the ability of the parents to cooperate in the arrangement;

(g)   to apply the Principles set forth in § 2.17(4) if one parent relocates or proposes to relocate at a distance that will impair the ability of a parent to exercise the presumptive amount of custodial responsibility under this section;

(h)   to avoid substantial and almost certain harm to the child.

(2)   In determining the proportion of caretaking functions each parent previously performed for the child under Paragraph (1), the court should not consider the division of functions arising from temporary arrangements after the parents' separation, whether those arrangements are consensual or by court order. The court may take into account information relating to the temporary arrangements in determining other issues under this section.

(3)   If the court is unable to allocate custodial responsibility under Paragraph (1) because there is no history of past performance of caretaking functions, as in the case of a newborn, or because the history does not establish a sufficiently clear pattern of caretaking, the court should allocate custodial responsibility based on the child's best interests, taking into account the factors and considerations that are set forth in this Chapter, preserving to the extent possible this section's priority on the share of past caretaking functions each parent performed.

(4)   In determining how to schedule the custodial time allocated to each parent, the court should take account of economic, physical, and other practical circumstances, such as those listed in Paragraph (1)(f).

SECTION 2.09. ALLOCATION OF SIGNIFICANT DECISIONMAKING RESPONSIBILITY

(1) Unless otherwise resolved by agreement of the parents under § 2.06, the court should allocate responsibility for making significant life decisions on behalf of the child, including decisions regarding the child's education and health care, to one parent or to two parents jointly, in accordance with the child's best interests, in light of the following:

(a) the allocation of custodial responsibility under § 2.08;

(b) the level of each parent's participation in past decisionmaking on behalf of the child;

(c) the wishes of the parents;

(d) the level of ability and cooperation the parents have demonstrated in past decisionmaking on behalf of the child;

(e) a prior agreement, other than one agreed to under § 2.06, that would be appropriate to consider under the circumstances as a whole including the reasonable expectations of the parents and the interests of the child;

(f) the existence of any limiting factors, as set forth in § 2.11.

(2) The court should presume that an allocation of decisionmaking responsibility jointly to each legal parent or parent by estoppel who has been exercising a reasonable share of parenting functions is in the child's best interests. The presumption is overcome if there is a history of domestic violence or child abuse, or if it is shown that joint allocation of decisionmaking responsibility is not in the child's best interests.

(3) Unless otherwise provided or agreed by the parents, a parent should have sole responsibility for day-to-day decisions for the child while the child is in that parent's custodial care and control, including emergency decisions affecting the health and safety of the child.

(4) Even if not allocated decisionmaking responsibility under this section, any legal parent and any parent by estoppel should have access to the child's school and health-care records to which legal parents have access by other law, except insofar as access is not in the best interests of the child or when the provision of such information might endanger an individual who has been the victim of child abuse or domestic violence.

SECTION 2.10. CRITERIA FOR PARENTING PLAN-DISPUTE RESOLUTION

(1) Unless otherwise resolved by agreement of the parents under § 2.06, and subject to the limitations set forth in § 2.07, the court should include in the parenting plan a process for resolving future disputes that will serve the chil0nce of any limiting factor set forth in § 2.11.

(2) The court may order a nonjudicial process of dispute resolution, by designating with particularity the person or organization to conduct the process or the method for selecting such a person or organization.

(3) The disposition of a dispute through a nonjudicial process of dispute resolution that was ordered by the court without prior parental agreement is subject to de novo judicial review. However, if the parents have agreed in a parenting plan or by agreement thereafter to a binding resolution of future disputes by nonjudicial process, a decision resulting from such process is binding upon the parents, unless the court finds it will result in harm to the child or is the result of fraud, misconduct, corruption, or other serious irregularity in the dispute-resolution process.

SECTION 2.11. CRITERIA FOR PARENTING PLAN-LIMITING FACTORS

(1) If e0interfering parent or another family member, pending adjudication of the facts underlying that belief which the interfering parent should be required to initiate as soon as reasonably possible.

(2) If a parent is found to have engaged in any activity specified by Paragraph (1), the court should impose limits that are reasonably calculated to protect the child, child's parent, or other member of the household from harm. The limitations available to the court to consider include, but are not restricted to, the following:

(a) an adjustment, including a reduction or the elimination, of the custodial responsibility of a parent;

(b) supervision of the custodial time between a parent and the child;

(c) exchange of the child between parents through an intermediary, or in a protected setting;

(d) restraints on a parent's communication with or proximity to the other parent or the child;

(e) a requirement that a parent abstain from possession or consumption of alcohol or nonprescribed drugs while exercising custodial responsibility and within a specified period immediately preceding such exercise;

(f) denial of overnight custodial responsibility;

(g) restrictions on the presence of specific persons while a parent is with the child;

(h) a requirement that a parent post a bond to secure return of the child following a period in which the parent is exercising custodial responsibility or to secure other performance required by the court;

(i) a requirement that a parent complete a treatment program for perpetrators of domestic violence, for drug or alcohol abuse, or for other behavior addressed in this section;

(j) any other constraints or conditions that the court deems necessary to provide for the safety of the child, a child's parent, or any other person whose safety immediately affects the child's welfare.

(3) If a parent is found to have engaged in any activity specified in Paragraph (1), the court should not allocate custodial responsibility or decisionmaking responsibility to that parent without making special written findings under § 1.02 that the child, other parent, or other household member can be adequately protected from harm by the limits imposed under Paragraph (2). A parent found to have engaged in the behavior specified in Paragraph (1) should have the burden of proving that an allocation of custodial responsibility or decisionmaking responsibility to that parent will not endanger the child, other parent, or other household member.

SECTION 2.12. CRITERIA FOR PARENTING PLAN-PROHIBITED FACTORS

(1) In issuing orders under this Chapter, the court should not consider any of the following factors:

(a)   the race or ethnicity of the child, a parent, or other member of the household;

(b)   the sex of a parent or the child;

(c)   the religious practices of a parent or the child, except to the minimum degree necessary to protect the child from severe and almost certain harm or to protect the child's ability to practice a religion that has been a significant part of the child's life;

(d)   the sexual orientation of a parent;

(e)   the extramarital sexual conduct of a parent, except upon a showing that it causes harm to the child;

(f)   the parents' relative earning capacities or financial circumstances, except the court may take account of the degree to which the combined financial resources of the parents set practical limits on the custodial arrangements.

(2) Nothing in this section should preclude the court's consideration of a parent's ability to care for the child, including meeting the child's needs for a positive self-image.

UNIFORM ADOPTION ACT (1994)

9 U.L.A. Pt. IA 11 et seq. (1999)

[EDITORS' INTRODUCTION: Jack Darcher, *Market Forces in Domestic Adoptions: Advocating a Quantitative Limit on Private Agency Adoption Fees*, 8 SEATTLE J. SOC. JUST. 729 (2010); Erin E. Gibbs, *Preserving Your Right To Parent: The Supreme Court of North Carolina Addresses Unmarried Fathers' Due Process Rights in* In re Adoption of S.D.W., 94 N.C. L. REV. 723 (2016); Olga Grosh, *A Call of Duty: Preventing Adoption Disruption by Expanding Adoption Providers' Responsibility to Investigate and Disclose Adoptive Children's Medical History*, 11 WHITTIER J. CHILD & FAM. ADVOC. 149 (2011); Josh Gupta-Kagan, *Non-Exclusive Adoption and Child Welfare*, 66 ALA. L. REV. 715 (2015); J. Savannah Lengsfelder, *Who is a "Suitable" Adoptive Parent*, 5 HARV. L. & POL'Y REV. 433 (2011); Sara C. Mills, *Perpetuating Ageism via Adoption Standards and Practices*, 26 WIS. J.L. GENDER & SOC'Y 69 (2011); Jennie Rischbieter, *Addendum to Adoption: Adjusting the Adoption Statutes in South Carolina*, 66 S.C. L. REV. 841 (2015); Deborah E. Crum, Note, *Uniform Adoption Laws: A Public Health Perspective*, 7 PITT. J. ENVTL PUB. HEALTH L. 127 (2012); Pamela K. Terry, Note, *E Pluribus Unum? The Full Faith and Credit Clause and Meaningful Recognition of Out-of-State Adoptions*, 80 FORDHAM L. REV. 3093 (2012).]

[ARTICLE] 1. GENERAL PROVISIONS

§ 1–101. DEFINITIONS.

In this [Act]:

(1) "Adoptee" means an individual who is adopted or is to be adopted.

(2) "Adult" means an individual who has attained 18 years of age.

(3) "Agency" means a public or private entity, including the department, that is authorized by the law of this State to place individuals for adoption.

(4) "Child" means a minor or adult son or daughter, by birth or adoption.

(5) "Court," with reference to a court of this State, means the [appropriate court].

(6) "Department" means the [department of social services, or health services, or children's services].

(7) "Guardian" means an individual, other than a parent, appointed by an appropriate court as general guardian or guardian of the person of a minor.

(8) "Legal custody" means the right and duty to exercise continuing general supervision of a minor as authorized by law. The term includes the right and duty to protect, educate, nurture, and discipline the minor and to provide the minor with food, clothing, shelter, medical care, and a supportive environment.

(9) "Minor" means an individual who has not attained 18 years of age.

(10) "Parent" means an individual who is legally recognized as a mother or father or whose consent to the adoption of a minor is required under Section 2–401(a)(1). The term does not include an individual whose parental relationship to a child has been terminated judicially or by operation of law.

(11) "Person" means an individual, corporation, limited liability company, business trust, estate, trust, partnership, association, agency, joint venture, government, governmental subdivision or instrumentality, public corporation, or any other legal or commercial entity.

(12) "Physical custody" means the physical care and supervision of a minor.

(13) "Place for adoption" means to select a prospective adoptive parent for a minor and transfer physical custody of the minor to the prospective adoptive parent.

(14) "Relative" means a grandparent, great grandparent, sibling, first cousin, aunt, uncle, great-aunt, great-uncle, niece, or nephew of an individual, whether related to the individual by the whole or the half blood, affinity, or adoption. The term does not include an individual's stepparent.

(15) "Relinquishment" means the voluntary surrender to an agency by a minor's parent or guardian, for purposes of the minor's adoption, of the rights of the parent or guardian with respect to the minor, including legal and physical custody of the minor.

(16) "State" means a State of the United States, the District of Columbia, the Commonwealth of Puerto Rico, or any territory or insular possession subject to the jurisdiction of the United States.

(17) "Stepparent" means an individual who is the spouse or surviving spouse of a parent of a child but who is not a parent of the child.

§ 1–102. WHO MAY ADOPT OR BE ADOPTED.

Subject to this [Act], any individual may adopt or be adopted by another individual for the purpose of creating the relationship of parent and child between them.

§ 1–103. NAME OF ADOPTEE AFTER ADOPTION.

The name of an adoptee designated in a decree of adoption takes effect as specified in the decree.

§ 1–104. LEGAL RELATIONSHIP BETWEEN ADOPTEE AND ADOPTIVE PARENT AFTER ADOPTION.

After a decree of adoption becomes final, each adoptive parent and the adoptee have the legal relationship of parent and child and have all the rights and duties of that relationship.

§ 1–105. LEGAL RELATIONSHIP BETWEEN ADOPTEE AND FORMER PARENT AFTER ADOPTION.

Except as otherwise provided in Section 4–103, when a decree of adoption becomes final:

(1) the legal relationship of parent and child between each of the adoptee's former parents and the adoptee terminates, except for a former parent's duty to pay arrearages for child support; and

(2) any previous court order for visitation or communication with an adoptee terminates.

§ 1–106. OTHER RIGHTS OF ADOPTEE.

A decree of adoption does not affect any right or benefit vested in the adoptee before the decree becomes final.

§ 1–107. PROCEEDINGS SUBJECT TO INDIAN CHILD WELFARE ACT.

A proceeding under this [Act] which pertains to an Indian child, as defined in the Indian Child Welfare Act, 25 U.S.C. Sections 1901 et seq., is subject to that Act.

§ 1–108. RECOGNITION OF ADOPTION IN ANOTHER JURISDICTION.

A decree or order of adoption issued by a court of any other State which is entitled to full faith and credit in this State, or a decree or order of adoption entered by a court or administrative entity in another country acting pursuant to that country's law or to any convention or treaty on intercountry adoption which the United States has ratified, has the same effect as a decree or order of adoption issued by a court of this State. The rights and obligations of the parties as to matters within the jurisdiction of this State must be determined as though the decree or order were issued by a court of this State.

[ARTICLE] 2. ADOPTION OF MINORS

[PART] 1. PLACEMENT OF MINOR FOR ADOPTION

§ 2–101.   WHO MAY PLACE MINOR FOR ADOPTION.

(a) The only persons who may place a minor for adoption are:

(1) a parent having legal and physical custody of the minor, as provided in subsections (b) and (c);

(2) a guardian expressly authorized by the court to place the minor for adoption;

(3) an agency to which the minor has been relinquished for purposes of adoption; or

(4) an agency expressly authorized to place the minor for adoption by a court order terminating the relationship between the minor and the minor's parent or guardian.

(b) Except as otherwise provided in subsection (c), a parent having legal and physical custody of a minor may place the minor for adoption, even if the other parent has not executed a consent or a relinquishment or the other parent's relationship to the minor has not been terminated.

(c) A parent having legal and physical custody of a minor may not place the minor for adoption if the other parent has legal custody or a right of visitation with the minor and that parent's whereabouts are known, unless that parent agrees in writing to the placement or, before the placement, the parent who intends to place the minor sends notice of the intended placement by certified mail to the other parent's last known address.

(d) An agency authorized under this [Act] to place a minor for adoption may place the minor for adoption, even if only one parent has executed a relinquishment or has had his or her parental relationship to the minor terminated.

§ 2–102.   DIRECT PLACEMENT FOR ADOPTION BY PARENT OR GUARDIAN.

(a) A parent or guardian authorized to place a minor directly for adoption may place the minor only with a prospective adoptive parent for whom a favorable preplacement evaluation has been prepared pursuant to Sections 2–201 through 2–206 or for whom a preplacement evaluation is not required under Section 2–201(b) or (c).

(b) A parent or guardian shall personally select a prospective adoptive parent for the direct placement of a minor. Subject to [Article] 7, the parent or guardian may be assisted by another person, including a lawyer, health-care provider, or agency, in locating or transferring legal and physical custody of the minor to a prospective adoptive parent.

(c) A prospective adoptive parent shall furnish a copy of the preplacement evaluation to the parent or guardian and may provide additional information requested by the parent or guardian. The evaluation and any additional information must be edited to exclude identifying information, but information identifying a prospective adoptive parent need not be edited if the individual agrees to its disclosure. Subject to [Article] 7, a prospective adoptive parent may be assisted by another person in locating a minor who is available for adoption.

(d) If a consent to a minor's adoption is not executed at the time the minor is placed for adoption, the parent or guardian who places the minor shall furnish to the prospective adoptive parent a signed writing stating that the transfer of physical custody is for purposes of adoption and that the parent or guardian has been informed of the provisions of this [Act] relevant to placement for adoption, consent, relinquishment, and termination of parental rights. The writing must authorize the prospective adoptive parent to provide support and medical and other care for the minor pending execution of the consent within a time specified in the writing. The prospective adoptive parent shall acknowledge in a signed writing responsibility for the minor's support and medical and other care and for returning the minor to the custody of the parent or guardian if the consent is not executed within the time specified.

(e) A person who provides services with respect to direct placements for adoption shall furnish to an individual who inquires about the person's services a written statement of the person's services and a schedule of fees.

§ 2–103. PLACEMENT FOR ADOPTION BY AGENCY.

(a) An agency authorized to place a minor for adoption shall furnish to an individual who inquires about its services a written statement of its services, including the agency's procedure for selecting a prospective adoptive parent for a minor and a schedule of its fees.

(b) An agency that places a minor for adoption shall authorize in writing the prospective adoptive parent to provide support and medical and other care for the minor pending entry of a decree of adoption. The prospective adoptive parent shall acknowledge in writing responsibility for the minor's support and medical and other care.

(c) Upon request by a parent who has relinquished a minor child pursuant to [Part] 4, the agency shall promptly inform the parent as to whether the minor has been placed for adoption, whether a petition for adoption has been granted, denied, or withdrawn, and, if the petition was not granted, whether another placement has been made.

§ 2–104. PREFERENCES FOR PLACEMENT WHEN AGENCY PLACES MINOR.

(a) An agency may place a minor for adoption only with an individual for whom a favorable preplacement evaluation has been prepared pursuant to Sections 2–201 through 2–206. Placement must be made:

(1) if the agency has agreed to place the minor with a prospective adoptive parent selected by the parent or guardian, with the individual selected by the parent or guardian;

(2) if the agency has not so agreed, with an individual selected by the agency in accordance with the best interest of the minor.

(b) In determining the best interest of the minor under subsection (a)(2), the agency shall consider the following individuals in order of preference:

(1) an individual who has previously adopted a sibling of the minor and who makes a written request to adopt the minor;

(2) an individual with characteristics requested by a parent or guardian, if the agency agrees to comply with the request and locates the individual within a time agreed to by the parent or guardian and the agency;

(3) an individual who has had physical custody of the minor for six months or more within the preceding 24 months or for half of the minor's life, whichever is less, and makes a written request to adopt the minor;

(4) a relative with whom the minor has established a positive emotional relationship and who makes a written request to adopt the minor; and

(5) any other individual selected by the agency.

(c) Unless necessary to comply with a request under subsection (b)(2), an agency may not delay or deny a minor's placement for adoption solely on the basis of the minor's race, national origin, or ethnic background. A guardian ad litem of a minor or an individual with a favorable preplacement evaluation who makes a written request to an agency to adopt the minor may maintain an action or proceeding for equitable relief against an agency that violates this subsection.

(d) If practicable and in the best interest of minors who are siblings, an agency shall place siblings with the same prospective adoptive parent selected in accordance with subsections (a) through (c).

(e) If an agency places a minor pursuant to subsection (a)(2), an individual described in subsection (b)(3) may commence an action or proceeding within 30 days after the placement to challenge the agency's placement. If the individual proves by a preponderance of the evidence that the minor has substantial emotional ties to the individual and that an adoptive placement of the minor with the individual would be in the best interest of the minor, the court shall place the minor with the individual.

§ 2–105. RECRUITMENT OF ADOPTIVE PARENTS BY AGENCY.

An agency receiving public funds pursuant to Title IV-E of the federal Adoption Assistance and Child Welfare Act, 42 U.S.C. Sections 670 et seq., or pursuant to [the State's adoption subsidy program], shall make a diligent search for and actively recruit prospective adoptive parents for minors in the agency's custody who are entitled to funding from those sources and who are difficult to place for adoption because of a special need as described in [the applicable law on minors with special needs]. The department shall prescribe the procedure for recruiting prospective adoptive parents pursuant to this section.

§ 2–106. DISCLOSURE OF INFORMATION ON BACKGROUND.

(a) As early as practicable before a prospective adoptive parent accepts physical custody of a minor, a person placing the minor for adoption shall furnish to the prospective adoptive parent a written report containing all of the following information reasonably available from any person who has had legal or physical custody of the minor or who has provided medical, psychological, educational, or similar services to the minor:

(1) a current medical and psychological history of the minor, including an account of the minor's prenatal care, medical condition at birth, any drug or medication taken by the minor's mother during pregnancy, any subsequent medical, psychological, or psychiatric examination and diagnosis, any physical, sexual, or emotional abuse suffered by the minor, and a record of any immunizations and health care received while in foster or other care;

(2) relevant information concerning the medical and psychological history of the minor's genetic parents and relatives, including any known disease or hereditary predisposition to disease, any addiction to drugs or alcohol, the health of the minor's mother during her pregnancy, and the health of each parent at the minor's birth; and

(3) relevant information concerning the social history of the minor and the minor's parents and relatives, including:

(i) the minor's enrollment and performance in school, results of educational testing, and any special educational needs;

(ii) the minor's racial, ethnic, and religious background, tribal affiliation, and a general description of the minor's parents;

(iii) an account of the minor's past and existing relationship with any individual with whom the minor has regularly lived or visited; and

(iv) the level of educational and vocational achievement of the minor's parents and relatives and any noteworthy accomplishments;

(4) information concerning a criminal conviction of a parent for a felony, a judicial order terminating the parental rights of a parent, and a proceeding in which the parent was alleged to have abused, neglected, abandoned, or otherwise mistreated the minor, a sibling of the minor, or the other parent;

(5) information concerning a criminal conviction or delinquency adjudication of the minor; and

(6) information necessary to determine the minor's eligibility for state or federal benefits, including subsidies for adoption and other financial, medical, or similar assistance.

(b) Before a hearing on a petition for adoption, the person who placed a minor for adoption shall furnish to the prospective adoptive parent a supplemental written report containing information required by subsection (a) which was unavailable before the minor was placed for adoption but becomes reasonably available to the person after the placement.

(c) The court may request that a respondent in a proceeding under [Article] 3, [Part] 5, supply the information required by this section.

(d) A report furnished under this section must indicate who prepared the report and, unless confidentiality has been waived, be edited to exclude the identity of any individual who furnished information or about whom information is reported.

(e) Information furnished under this section may not be used as evidence in any civil or criminal proceeding against an individual who is the subject of the information.

(f) The department shall prescribe forms designed to obtain the specific information sought under this section and shall furnish the forms to a person who is authorized to place a minor for adoption or who provides services with respect to placements for adoption.

§ 2–107.   INTERSTATE PLACEMENT.

An adoption in this State of a minor brought into this State from another State by a prospective adoptive parent, or by a person who places the minor for adoption in this State, is governed by the laws of this State, including this [Act] and the Interstate Compact on the Placement of Children.

§ 2–108. INTERCOUNTRY PLACEMENT.

An adoption in this State of a minor brought into this State from another country by a prospective adoptive parent, or by a person who places the minor for adoption in this State, is governed by this [Act], subject to any convention or treaty on intercountry adoption which the United States has ratified and any relevant federal law.

[PART] 2. PREPLACEMENT EVALUATION

§ 2–201. PREPLACEMENT EVALUATION REQUIRED.

(a) Except as otherwise provided in subsections (b) and (c), only an individual for whom a current, favorable written preplacement evaluation has been prepared may accept custody of a minor for purposes of adoption. An evaluation is current if it is prepared or updated within the 18 months next preceding the placement of the minor with the individual for adoption. An evaluation is favorable if it contains a finding that the individual is suited to be an adoptive parent, either in general or for a particular minor.

(b) A court may excuse the absence of a preplacement evaluation for good cause shown, but the prospective adoptive parent so excused must be evaluated during the pendency of the proceeding for adoption.

(c) A preplacement evaluation is not required if a parent or guardian places a minor directly with a relative of the minor for purposes of adoption, but an evaluation of the relative is required during the pendency of a proceeding for adoption.

§ 2–202. PREPLACEMENT EVALUATOR.

(a) Only an individual qualified by [a state-approved licensing, certifying, or other procedure] to make a preplacement evaluation may do so.

(b) An agency from which an individual is seeking to adopt a minor may require the individual to be evaluated by its own qualified employee or independent contractor, even if the individual has received a favorable preplacement evaluation from another qualified evaluator.

§ 2–203. TIMING AND CONTENT OF PREPLACEMENT EVALUATION.

(a) An individual requesting a preplacement evaluation need not have located a prospective minor adoptee when the request is made, and the individual may request more than one evaluation.

(b) A preplacement evaluation must be completed within 45 days after it is requested. An evaluator shall expedite an evaluation for an individual who has located a prospective adoptee.

(c) A preplacement evaluation must be based upon a personal interview and visit at the residence of the individual being evaluated, personal interviews with others who know the individual and may have information relevant to the evaluation, and the information required by subsection (d).

(d) A preplacement evaluation must contain the following information about the individual being evaluated:

(1) age and date of birth, nationality, racial or ethnic background, and any religious affiliation;

(2) marital status and family history, including the age and location of any child of the individual and the identity of and relationship to anyone else living in the individual's household;

(3) physical and mental health, and any history of abuse of alcohol or drugs;

(4) educational and employment history and any special skills;

(5) property and income, including outstanding financial obligations as indicated in a current credit report or financial statement furnished by the individual;

(6) any previous request for an evaluation or involvement in an adoptive placement and the outcome of the evaluation or placement;

(7) whether the individual has been charged with having committed domestic violence or a violation of [the State's child protection statute], and the disposition of the charges, or whether the individual is subject to a court order restricting the individual's right to custody or visitation with a child;

(8) whether the individual has been convicted of a crime other than a minor traffic violation;

(9) whether the individual has located a parent interested in placing a minor with the individual for adoption and, if so, a brief description of the parent and the minor; and

(10) any other fact or circumstance that may be relevant in determining whether the individual is suited to be an adoptive parent, including the quality of the environment in the individual's home and the functioning of other children in the individual's household.

(e) An individual being evaluated must submit to fingerprinting and sign a release permitting the evaluator to obtain from an appropriate law enforcement agency any record indicating that the individual has been convicted of a crime other than a minor traffic violation.

(f) An individual being evaluated shall, at the request of the evaluator, sign any release necessary for the evaluator to obtain information required by subsection (d).

§ 2–204. DETERMINING SUITABILITY TO BE ADOPTIVE PARENT.

(a) An evaluator shall assess the information required by Section 2–203 to determine whether it raises a specific concern that placement of any minor, or a particular minor, in the home of the individual would pose a significant risk of harm to the physical or psychological well-being of the minor.

(b) If an evaluator determines that the information assessed does not raise a specific concern, the evaluator shall find that the individual is suited to be an adoptive parent. The evaluator may comment about any factor that in the evaluator's opinion makes the individual suited in general or for a particular minor.

(c) If an evaluator determines that the information assessed raises a specific concern, the evaluator, on the basis of the original or any further investigation, shall find that the individual is or is not suited to be an adoptive parent. The evaluator shall support the finding with a written explanation.

§ 2–205. FILING AND COPIES OF PREPLACEMENT EVALUATION.

(a) If a preplacement evaluation contains a finding that an individual is suited to be an adoptive parent, the evaluator shall give the individual a signed copy of the evaluation. At the individual's request, the evaluator shall furnish a copy of the evaluation to a person authorized under this [Act] to place a minor for adoption and, unless the individual requests otherwise, edit the copy to exclude identifying information.

(b) If a preplacement evaluation contains a finding that an individual is not suited to be an adoptive parent of any minor, or a particular minor, the evaluator shall immediately give a signed copy of the evaluation to the individual and to the department. The department shall retain for 10 years the copy and a copy of any court order concerning the evaluation issued pursuant to Section 2–206 or 2–207.

(c) An evaluator shall retain for two years the original of a completed or incomplete preplacement evaluation and a list of every source for each item of information in the evaluation.

(d) An evaluator who conducted an evaluation in good faith is not subject to civil liability for anything contained in the evaluation.

§ 2–206. REVIEW OF EVALUATION.

(a) Within 90 days after an individual receives a preplacement evaluation with a finding that he or she is not suited to be an adoptive parent, the individual may petition a court for review of the evaluation.

(b) If the court determines that the petitioner has failed to prove suitability by a preponderance of the evidence, it shall order that the petitioner not be permitted to adopt a minor and shall send a copy of the order to the department to be retained with the copy of the original evaluation. If, at the time of the court's determination, the petitioner has custody of a minor for purposes of adoption, the court shall make an appropriate order for the care and custody of the minor.

(c) If the court determines that the petitioner has proved suitability, the court shall find the petitioner suitable to be an adoptive parent and the petitioner may commence or continue a proceeding for adoption of a minor. The court shall send a copy of its order to the department to be retained with the copy of the original evaluation.

§ 2–207. ACTION BY DEPARTMENT.

If, before a decree of adoption is issued, the department learns from an evaluator or another person that a minor has been placed for adoption with an individual who is the subject of a preplacement evaluation on file with the department containing a finding of unsuitability, the department shall immediately review the evaluation and investigate the circumstances of the placement and may request that the individual return the minor to the custody of the person who placed the minor or to the department. If the individual refuses to return the minor, the department shall immediately commence an action or proceeding to remove the minor from the home of the individual pursuant to [the State's child protection statute] and, pending a hearing, the court shall make an appropriate order for the care and custody of the minor.

[PART] 3. TRANSFER OF PHYSICAL CUSTODY OF MINOR BY HEALTH-CARE FACILITY FOR PURPOSES OF ADOPTION

§ 2–301. "HEALTH-CARE FACILITY" DEFINED.

In this [part], "health-care facility" means a hospital, clinic, or other facility authorized by this State to provide services related to birth and neonatal care.

§ 2–302. AUTHORIZATION TO TRANSFER PHYSICAL CUSTODY.

(a) A health-care facility shall release a minor for the purpose of adoption to an individual or agency not otherwise legally entitled to the physical custody of the minor if, in the presence of an employee authorized by the health-care facility, the woman who gave birth to the minor signs an authorization of the transfer of physical custody.

(b) An authorized employee in whose presence the authorization required under subsection (a) is signed shall attest the signing in writing.

§ 2–303. REPORTS TO DEPARTMENT.

(a) No later than 72 hours after a release pursuant to Section 2–302, a health-care facility that releases a minor for purposes of adoption shall transmit to the department a copy of the authorization required by Section 2–302 and shall report:

(1) the name, address, and telephone number of the person who authorized the release;

(2) the name, address, and telephone number of the person to whom physical custody was transferred; and

(3) the date of the transfer.

(b) No later than 30 days after a release pursuant to Section 2–302, the person to whom physical custody of a minor was transferred shall report to the department which, if any, of the following has occurred:

(1) the filing of a petition for adoption with the name and address of the petitioner;

(2) the acquisition of custody of the minor by an agency and the name and address of the agency;

(3) the return of the minor to a parent or other person having legal custody and the name and address of the parent or other person; or

(4) the transfer of physical custody of the minor to another individual and the name and address of the individual.

§ 2–304. ACTION BY DEPARTMENT.

(a) If the department receives a report required under Section 2–303(a) from a health-care facility, but does not receive the report required under Section 2–303(b) within 45 days after the transfer of a minor, the department shall immediately investigate to determine the whereabouts of the minor.

(b) If none of the dispositions listed in Section 2–303(b)(1) through (3) has occurred, or the minor has been transferred to an individual described in Section 2–303(b)(4) who has not filed a petition to adopt, the department shall immediately take appropriate action to remove the minor from the individual to whom the minor has been transferred.

(c) The department may also review and investigate compliance with Sections 2–101 through 2–106 and may maintain an action in the [appropriate] court to compel compliance.

[PART] 4. CONSENT TO AND RELINQUISHMENT FOR ADOPTION

§ 2–401.   PERSONS WHOSE CONSENT REQUIRED.

(a) Unless consent is not required or is dispensed with by Section 2–402, in a direct placement of a minor for adoption by a parent or guardian authorized under this [Act] to place the minor, a petition to adopt the minor may be granted only if consent to the adoption has been executed by:

(1)   the woman who gave birth to the minor and the man, if any, who:

(i)   is or has been married to the woman if the minor was born during the marriage or within 300 days after the marriage was terminated or a court issued a decree of separation;

(ii) attempted to marry the woman before the minor's birth by a marriage solemnized in apparent compliance with law, although the attempted marriage is or could be declared invalid, if the minor was born during the attempted marriage or within 300 days after the attempted marriage was terminated;

(iii) has been judicially determined to be the father of the minor, or has signed a document that has the effect of establishing his parentage of the minor, and:

(A) has provided, in accordance with his financial means, reasonable and consistent payments for the support of the minor and has visited or communicated with the minor; or

(B) after the minor's birth, but before the minor's placement for adoption, has married the woman who gave birth to the minor or attempted to marry her by a marriage solemnized in apparent compliance with law, although the attempted marriage is or could be declared invalid; or

(iv) has received the minor into his home and openly held out the minor as his child;

(2)   the minor's guardian if expressly authorized by a court to consent to the minor's adoption; or

(3)   the current adoptive or other legally recognized mother and father of the minor.

(b) Unless consent is not required under Section 2–402, in a placement of a minor for adoption by an agency authorized under this [Act] to place the minor, a petition to adopt the minor may be granted only if consent to the adoption has been executed by:

(1)   the agency that placed the minor for adoption; and

(2)   any individuals described in subsection (a) who have not relinquished the minor.

(c)   Unless the court dispenses with the minor's consent, a petition to adopt a minor who has attained 12 years of age may be granted only if, in addition to any consent required by subsections (a) and (b), the minor has executed an informed consent to the adoption.

§ 2–402.   PERSONS WHOSE CONSENT NOT REQUIRED.

(a)   Consent to an adoption of a minor is not required of:

(1)   an individual who has relinquished the minor to an agency for purposes of adoption;

(2)   an individual whose parental relationship to the minor has been judicially terminated or determined not to exist;

(3)   a parent who has been judicially declared incompetent;

(4)   a man who has not been married to the woman who gave birth to the minor and who, after the conception of the minor, executes a verified statement denying paternity or disclaiming any interest in the minor and acknowledging that his statement is irrevocable when executed;

(5)   the personal representative of a deceased parent's estate; or

(6)   a parent or other person who has not executed a consent or a relinquishment and who fails to file an answer or make an appearance in a proceeding for adoption or for termination of a parental relationship within the requisite time after service of notice of the proceeding.

(b)   The court may dispense with the consent of:

(1)   a guardian or an agency whose consent is otherwise required upon a finding that the consent is being withheld contrary to the best interest of a minor adoptee; or

(2)   a minor adoptee who has attained 12 years of age upon a finding that it is not in the best interest of the minor to require the consent.

§ 2–403.   INDIVIDUALS WHO MAY RELINQUISH MINOR.

A parent or guardian whose consent to the adoption of a minor is required by Section 2–401 may relinquish to an agency all rights with respect to the minor, including legal and physical custody and the right to consent to the minor's adoption.

§ 2–404. TIME AND PREREQUISITES FOR EXECUTION OF CONSENT OR RELINQUISHMENT.

(a) A parent whose consent to the adoption of a minor is required by Section 2–401 may execute a consent or a relinquishment only after the minor is born. A parent who executes a consent or relinquishment may revoke the consent or relinquishment within 192 hours after the birth of the minor.

(b) A guardian may execute a consent to the adoption of a minor or a relinquishment at any time after being authorized by a court to do so.

(c) An agency that places a minor for adoption may execute its consent at any time before or during the hearing on the petition for adoption.

(d) A minor adoptee whose consent is required may execute a consent at any time before or during the hearing on the petition for adoption.

(e) Before executing a consent or relinquishment, a parent must have been informed of the meaning and consequences of adoption, the availability of personal and legal counseling, the consequences of misidentifying the other parent, the procedure for releasing information about the health and other characteristics of the parent which may affect the physical or psychological well-being of the adoptee, and the procedure for the consensual release of the parent's identity to an adoptee, an adoptee's direct descendant, or an adoptive parent pursuant to [Article] 6. The parent must have had an opportunity to indicate in a signed document whether and under what circumstances the parent is or is not willing to release identifying information, and must have been informed of the procedure for changing the document at a later time.

§ 2–405. PROCEDURE FOR EXECUTION OF CONSENT OR RELINQUISHMENT.

(a) A consent or relinquishment executed by a parent or guardian must be signed or confirmed in the presence of:

(1) a judge of a court of record;

(2) an individual whom a judge of a court of record designates to take consents or relinquishments;

(3) an employee other than an employee of an agency to which a minor is relinquished whom an agency designates to take consents or relinquishments;

(4) a lawyer other than a lawyer who is representing an adoptive parent or the agency to which a minor is relinquished;

(5) a commissioned officer on active duty in the military service of the United States, if the individual executing the consent or relinquishment is in military service; or

(6)   an officer of the foreign service or a consular officer of the United States in another country, if the individual executing the consent or relinquishment is in that country.

(b)   A consent executed by a minor adoptee must be signed or confirmed in the presence of the court in the proceeding for adoption or in a manner the court directs.

(c)   A parent who is a minor is competent to execute a consent or relinquishment if the parent has had access to counseling and has had the advice of a lawyer who is not representing an adoptive parent or the agency to which the parent's child is relinquished.

(d)   An individual before whom a consent or relinquishment is signed or confirmed under subsection (a) shall certify in writing that he or she orally explained the contents and consequences of the consent or relinquishment, and to the best of his or her knowledge or belief, the individual executing the consent or relinquishment:

(1)   read or was read the consent or relinquishment and understood it;

(2)   signed the consent or relinquishment voluntarily and received or was offered a copy of it;

(3)   was furnished the information and afforded an opportunity to sign the document described by Section 2–404(e);

(4)   received or was offered counseling services and information about adoption; and

(5)   if a parent who is a minor, was advised by a lawyer who is not representing an adoptive parent or the agency to which the parent's child is being relinquished, or, if an adult, was informed of the right to have a lawyer who is not representing an adoptive parent or an agency to which the parent's child is being relinquished.

(e)   A prospective adoptive parent named or described in a consent to the adoption of a minor shall sign a statement indicating an intention to adopt the minor, acknowledging an obligation to return legal and physical custody of the minor to the minor's parent if the parent revokes the consent within the time specified in Section 2–404(a), and acknowledging responsibility for the minor's support and medical and other care if the consent is not revoked.

(f)   If an agency accepts a relinquishment, an employee of the agency shall sign a statement accepting the relinquishment, acknowledging its obligation to return legal and physical custody of the child to the minor's parent if the parent revokes the relinquishment within the time indicated in Section 2–404(a), and acknowledging responsibility for the minor's support and medical and other care if the relinquishment is not revoked.

(g) An individual before whom a consent or a relinquishment is signed or confirmed shall certify having received the statements required by subsections (e) and (f).

(h) A consent by an agency to the adoption of a minor in the agency's legal custody must be executed by the head or an individual authorized by the agency and must be signed or confirmed under oath in the presence of an individual authorized to take acknowledgments.

(i) A consent or relinquishment executed and signed or confirmed in another State or country is valid if in accordance with this [Act] or with the law and procedure prevailing where executed.

§ 2–406.   CONTENT OF CONSENT OR RELINQUISHMENT.

(a) A consent or relinquishment required from a parent or guardian must be in writing and contain, in plain English or, if the native language of the parent or guardian is a language other than English, in that language:

(1) the date, place, and time of the execution of the consent or relinquishment;

(2) the name, date of birth, and current mailing address of the individual executing the consent or relinquishment;

(3) the date of birth and the name or pseudonym of the minor adoptee;

(4) if a consent, the name, address, and telephone and telecopier numbers of the lawyer representing the prospective adoptive parent with whom the individual executing the consent has placed or intends to place the minor for adoption;

(5) if a relinquishment, the name, address, and telephone and telecopier numbers of the agency to which the minor is being relinquished; and

(6) specific instructions as to how to revoke the consent or relinquishment and how to commence an action to set it aside.

(b) A consent must state that the parent or guardian executing the document is voluntarily and unequivocally consenting to the transfer of legal and physical custody to, and the adoption of the minor by, a specific adoptive parent whom the parent or guardian has selected.

(c) A relinquishment must state that the individual executing the relinquishment voluntarily consents to the permanent transfer of legal and physical custody of the minor to the agency for the purposes of adoption.

(d) A consent or relinquishment must state:

(1) an understanding that after the consent or relinquishment is signed or confirmed in substantial compliance with Section 2–405, it is final and, except under a circumstance stated in Section 2–408

or 2–409, may not be revoked or set aside for any reason, including the failure of an adoptive parent to permit the individual executing the consent or relinquishment to visit or communicate with the minor adoptee;

(2) an understanding that the adoption will extinguish all parental rights and obligations the individual executing the consent or relinquishment has with respect to the minor adoptee, except for arrearages of child support, and will remain valid whether or not any agreement for visitation or communication with the minor adoptee is later performed;

(3) that the individual executing the consent or relinquishment has:

(i) received a copy of the consent or relinquishment;

(ii) received or been offered counseling services and information about adoption which explains the meaning and consequences of an adoption;

(iii) been advised, if a parent who is a minor, by a lawyer who is not representing an adoptive parent or the agency to which the minor adoptee is being relinquished, or, if an adult, has been informed of the right to have a lawyer who is not representing an adoptive parent or the agency;

(iv) been provided the information and afforded an opportunity to sign the document described in Section 2–404(e); and

(v) been advised of the obligation to provide the information required under Section 2–106;

(4) that the individual executing the consent or relinquishment has not received or been promised any money or anything of value for the consent or the relinquishment, except for payments authorized by [Article] 7;

(5) that the minor is not an Indian child as defined in the Indian Child Welfare Act, 25 U.S.C. Sections 1901 et seq.;

(6) that the individual believes the adoption of the minor is in the minor's best interest; and

(7) if a consent, that the individual who is consenting waives further notice unless the adoption is contested, appealed, or denied.

(e) A relinquishment may provide that the individual who is relinquishing waives notice of any proceeding for adoption, or waives notice unless the adoption is contested, appealed, or denied.

(f) A consent or relinquishment may provide for its revocation if:

(1) another consent or relinquishment is not executed within a specified period;

(2) a court decides not to terminate another individual's parental relationship to the minor; or

(3) in a direct placement for adoption, a petition for adoption by a prospective adoptive parent, named or described in the consent, is denied or withdrawn.

§ 2–407. CONSEQUENCES OF CONSENT OR RELINQUISHMENT.

(a) Except under a circumstance stated in Section 2–408, a consent to the adoption of a minor which is executed by a parent or guardian in substantial compliance with Sections 2–405 and 2–406 is final and irrevocable, and:

(1) unless a court orders otherwise to protect the welfare of the minor, entitles the prospective adoptive parent named or described in the consent to the legal and physical custody of the minor and imposes on that individual responsibility for the support and medical and other care of the minor;

(2) terminates any duty of a parent who executed the consent with respect to the minor, except for arrearages of child support; and

(3) terminates any right of a parent or guardian who executed the consent to object to the minor's adoption by the prospective adoptive parent and any right to notice of the proceeding for adoption unless the adoption is contested, appealed, or denied.

(b) Except under a circumstance stated in Section 2–409, a relinquishment of a minor to an agency which is executed by a parent or guardian in substantial compliance with Sections 2–405 and 2–406 is final and irrevocable and:

(1) unless a court orders otherwise to protect the welfare of the minor, entitles the agency to the legal custody of the minor until a decree of adoption becomes final;

(2) empowers the agency to place the minor for adoption, consent to the minor's adoption, and delegate to a prospective adoptive parent responsibility for the support and medical and other care of the minor;

(3) terminates any duty of the individual who executed the relinquishment with respect to the minor, except for arrearages of child support; and

(4) terminates any right of the individual who executed the relinquishment to object to the minor's adoption and, unless otherwise provided in the relinquishment, any right to notice of the proceeding for adoption.

§ 2–408.   REVOCATION OF CONSENT.

(a) In a direct placement of a minor for adoption by a parent or guardian, a consent is revoked if:

    (1) within 192 hours after the birth of the minor, a parent who executed the consent notifies in writing the prospective adoptive parent, or the adoptive parent's lawyer, that the parent revokes the consent, or the parent complies with any other instructions for revocation specified in the consent; or

    (2) the individual who executed the consent and the prospective adoptive parent named or described in the consent agree to its revocation.

(b) In a direct placement of a minor for adoption by a parent or guardian, the court shall set aside the consent if the individual who executed the consent establishes:

    (1) by clear and convincing evidence, before a decree of adoption is issued, that the consent was obtained by fraud or duress;

    (2) by a preponderance of the evidence before a decree of adoption is issued that, without good cause shown, a petition to adopt was not filed within 60 days after the minor was placed for adoption; or

    (3) by a preponderance of the evidence, that a condition permitting revocation has occurred, as expressly provided for in the consent pursuant to Section 2–406.

(c) If the consent of an individual who had legal and physical custody of a minor when the minor was placed for adoption or when the consent was executed is revoked, the prospective adoptive parent shall immediately return the minor to the individual's custody and move to dismiss a proceeding for adoption or termination of the individual's parental relationship to the minor. If the minor is not returned immediately, the individual may petition the court named in the consent for appropriate relief. The court shall hear the petition expeditiously.

(d) If the consent of an individual who had legal and physical custody of a minor when the minor was placed for adoption or the consent was executed is set aside under subsection (b)(1), the court shall order the return of the minor to the custody of the individual and dismiss a proceeding for adoption.

(e) If the consent of an individual who had legal and physical custody of a minor when the minor was placed for adoption or the consent was executed is set aside under subsection (b)(2) or (3) and no ground exists under [Article] 3, [Part] 5, for terminating the relationship of parent and child between the individual and the minor, the court shall dismiss a proceeding for adoption and order the return of the minor to the custody of the individual unless the court finds that return will be detrimental to the minor.

(f)   If the consent of an individual who did not have physical custody of a minor when the minor was placed for adoption or when the consent was executed is revoked or set aside and no ground exists under [Article] 3, [Part] 5, for terminating the relationship of parent and child between the individual and the minor, the court shall dismiss a proceeding for adoption and issue an order providing for the care and custody of the minor according to the best interest of the minor.

§ 2–409.   REVOCATION OF RELINQUISHMENT.

(a)   A relinquishment is revoked if:

(1)   within 192 hours after the birth of the minor, a parent who executed the relinquishment gives written notice to the agency that accepted it, that the parent revokes the relinquishment, or the parent complies with any other instructions for revocation specified in the relinquishment; or

(2)   the individual who executed the relinquishment and the agency that accepted it agree to its revocation.

(b)   The court shall set aside a relinquishment if the individual who executed the relinquishment establishes:

(1)   by clear and convincing evidence, before a decree of adoption is issued, that the relinquishment was obtained by fraud or duress; or

(2)   by a preponderance of the evidence, that a condition permitting revocation has occurred, as expressly provided for in the relinquishment pursuant to Section 2–406.

(c)   If a relinquishment by an individual who had legal and physical custody of a minor when the relinquishment was executed is revoked, the agency shall immediately return the minor to the individual's custody and move to dismiss a proceeding for adoption. If the minor is not returned immediately, the individual may petition the court named in the relinquishment for appropriate relief. The court shall hear the petition expeditiously.

(d)   If a relinquishment by an individual who had legal and physical custody of a minor when the relinquishment was executed is set aside under subsection (b)(1), the court shall dismiss a proceeding for adoption and order the return of the minor to the custody of the individual.

(e)   If a relinquishment by an individual who had legal and physical custody of a minor when the relinquishment was executed is set aside under subsection (b)(2) and no ground exists under [Article] 3, [Part] 5, for terminating the relationship of parent and child between the individual and the minor, the court shall dismiss a proceeding for adoption and order the return of the minor to the custody of the individual unless the court finds that return will be detrimental to the minor.

(f)   If a relinquishment by an individual who did not have physical custody of a minor when the relinquishment was executed is revoked or set aside and no ground exists under [Article] 3, [Part] 5, for terminating the relationship of parent and child between the individual and the minor, the court shall dismiss a proceeding for adoption and shall issue an order providing for the care and custody of the minor according to the best interest of the minor.

[ARTICLE] 3. GENERAL PROCEDURE FOR ADOPTION OF MINORS

[PART] 1. JURISDICTION AND VENUE

§ 3–101.   JURISDICTION.

(a)   Except as otherwise provided in subsections (b) and (c), a court of this State has jurisdiction over a proceeding for the adoption of a minor commenced under this [Act] if:

(1)   immediately before commencement of the proceeding, the minor lived in this State with a parent, a guardian, a prospective adoptive parent, or another person acting as parent, for at least six consecutive months, excluding periods of temporary absence, or, in the case of a minor under six months of age, lived in this State from soon after birth with any of those individuals and there is available in this State substantial evidence concerning the minor's present or future care;

(2)   immediately before commencement of the proceeding, the prospective adoptive parent lived in this State for at least six consecutive months, excluding periods of temporary absence, and there is available in this State substantial evidence concerning the minor's present or future care;

(3)   the agency that placed the minor for adoption is located in this State and it is in the best interest of the minor that a court of this State assume jurisdiction because:

(i)   the minor and the minor's parents, or the minor and the prospective adoptive parent, have a significant connection with this State; and

(ii)   there is available in this State substantial evidence concerning the minor's present or future care;

(4)   the minor and the prospective adoptive parent are physically present in this State and the minor has been abandoned or it is necessary in an emergency to protect the minor because the minor has been subjected to or threatened with mistreatment or abuse or is otherwise neglected; or

(5)   it appears that no other State would have jurisdiction under prerequisites substantially in accordance with paragraphs (1) through (4), or another State has declined to exercise jurisdiction on the ground that this State is the more appropriate forum to hear a petition for adoption of the minor, and it is in the best interest of the minor that a court of this State assume jurisdiction.

(b)   A court of this State may not exercise jurisdiction over a proceeding for adoption of a minor if at the time the petition for adoption is filed a proceeding concerning the custody or adoption of the minor is pending in a court of another State exercising jurisdiction substantially in conformity with [the Uniform Child Custody Jurisdiction Act] or this [Act] unless the proceeding is stayed by the court of the other State.

(c)   If a court of another State has issued a decree or order concerning the custody of a minor who may be the subject of a proceeding for adoption in this State, a court of this State may not exercise jurisdiction over a proceeding for adoption of the minor unless:

(1)   the court of this State finds that the court of the State which issued the decree or order:

(i)   does not have continuing jurisdiction to modify the decree or order under jurisdictional prerequisites substantially in accordance with [the Uniform Child Custody Jurisdiction Act] or has declined to assume jurisdiction to modify the decree or order; or

(ii)   does not have jurisdiction over a proceeding for adoption substantially in conformity with subsection (a)(1) through (4) or has declined to assume jurisdiction over a proceeding for adoption; and

(2)   the court of this State has jurisdiction over the proceeding.

§ 3–102. VENUE.

A petition for adoption of a minor may be filed in the court in the [county] in which a petitioner lives, the minor lives, or an office of the agency that placed the minor is located.

[PART] 2. GENERAL PROCEDURAL PROVISIONS

§ 3–201. APPOINTMENT OF LAWYER OR GUARDIAN AD LITEM.

(a)   In a proceeding under this [Act] which may result in the termination of a relationship of parent and child, the court shall appoint a lawyer for any indigent, minor, or incompetent individual who appears in the proceeding and whose parental relationship to a child may be terminated, unless the court finds that the minor or incompetent individual has sufficient financial means to hire a lawyer, or the indigent individual declines to be represented by a lawyer.

(b)   The court shall appoint a guardian ad litem for a minor adoptee in a contested proceeding under this [Act] and may appoint a guardian ad litem for a minor adoptee in an uncontested proceeding.

§ 3–202.   NO RIGHT TO JURY.

A proceeding under this [Act] for adoption or termination of a parental relationship must be heard by the court without a jury.

§ 3–203.   CONFIDENTIALITY OF PROCEEDINGS.

Except for a proceeding pursuant to [Article] 7, a civil proceeding under this [Act] must be heard in closed court.

§ 3–204.   CUSTODY DURING PENDENCY OF PROCEEDING.

In order to protect the welfare of the minor, the court shall make an interim order for custody of a minor adoptee according to the best interest of the minor in a contested proceeding under this [Act] for adoption or termination of a parental relationship and may make an interim order for custody in an uncontested proceeding.

§ 3–205.   REMOVAL OF ADOPTEE FROM STATE.

Before a decree of adoption is issued, a petitioner may not remove a minor adoptee for more than 30 consecutive days from the State in which the petitioner resides without the permission of the court, if the minor was placed directly for adoption, or, if an agency placed the minor for adoption, the permission of the agency.

[PART] 3.   PETITION FOR ADOPTION OF MINOR

§ 3–301.   STANDING TO PETITION TO ADOPT.

(a)   Except as otherwise provided in subsection (c), the only individuals who have standing to petition to adopt a minor under this [article] are:

(1)   an individual with whom a minor has been placed for adoption or who has been selected as a prospective adoptive parent by a person authorized under this [Act] to place the minor for adoption; or

(2)   an individual with whom a minor has not been placed for adoption or who has not been selected or rejected as a prospective adoptive parent pursuant to [Article] 2, [Parts] 1 through 3, but who has had physical custody of the minor for at least six months immediately before seeking to file a petition for adoption and is allowed to file the petition by the court for good cause shown.

(b)   The spouse of a petitioner must join in the petition unless legally separated from the petitioner or judicially declared incompetent.

(c)   A petition for adoption of a minor stepchild by a stepparent may be filed under [Article] 4 and a petition for adoption of an emancipated minor may be filed under [Article] 5.

§ 3–302.   TIME FOR FILING PETITION.

Unless the court allows a later filing, a prospective adoptive parent with standing under Section 3–301(a)(1) shall file a petition for adoption no later than 30 days after a minor is placed for adoption with that individual.

§ 3–303.   CAPTION OF PETITION.

The caption of a petition for adoption of a minor must contain the name of or a pseudonym for the minor adoptee. The caption may not contain the name of the petitioner.

§ 3–304.   CONTENT OF PETITION.

(a)   A petition for adoption of a minor must be signed and verified by the petitioner and contain the following information or state why any of the information omitted is not contained in the petition:

(1)   the full name, age, and place and duration of residence of the petitioner;

(2)   the current marital status of the petitioner, including the date and place of any marriage, the date of any legal separation or divorce, and the date of any judicial determination that a petitioner's spouse is incompetent;

(3)   that the petitioner has facilities and resources to provide for the care and support of the minor;

(4)   that a preplacement evaluation containing a finding that the petitioner is suited to be an adoptive parent has been prepared or updated within the 18 months next preceding the placement, or that the absence of a preplacement evaluation has been excused by a court for good cause shown or is not required under Section 2–201;

(5)   the first name, sex, and date, or approximate date, and place of birth of the minor adoptee and a statement that the minor is or is not an Indian child as defined in the Indian Child Welfare Act, 25 U.S.C. Sections 1901 et seq.;

(6)   the circumstances under which the petitioner obtained physical custody of the minor, including the date of placement of the minor with the petitioner for adoption and the name of the agency or the name or relationship to the minor of the individual that placed the minor;

(7)   the length of time the minor has been in the custody of the petitioner and, if the minor is not in the physical custody of the petitioner, the reason why the petitioner does not have custody and

the date and manner in which the petitioner intends to obtain custody;

(8) a description and estimate of the value of any property of the minor;

(9) that any law governing interstate or intercountry placement was complied with;

(10) the name or relationship to the minor of any individual who has executed a consent or relinquishment to the adoption or a disclaimer of paternal interest, and the name or relationship to the minor of any individual whose consent or relinquishment may be required, but whose parental relationship has not been terminated, and any fact or circumstance that may excuse the lack of consent;

(11) that a previous petition by the petitioner to adopt has or has not been made in any court, and its disposition; and

(12) a description of any previous court order or pending proceeding known to the petitioner concerning custody of or visitation with the minor and any other fact known to the petitioner and needed to establish the jurisdiction of the court.

(b) The petitioner shall request in the petition:

(1) that the petitioner be permitted to adopt the minor as the petitioner's child;

(2) that the court approve the full name by which the minor is to be known if the petition is granted; and

(3) any other relief sought by the petitioner.

§ 3–305. REQUIRED DOCUMENTS.

(a) Before the hearing on a petition for adoption, the following must be filed:

(1) a certified copy of the birth certificate or other record of the date and place of birth of the minor adoptee;

(2) any consent, relinquishment, or disclaimer of paternal interest with respect to the minor that has been executed, and any written certifications required by Section 2–405(d) and (g) from the individual before whom a consent or relinquishment was executed;

(3) a certified copy of any court order terminating the rights and duties of the minor's parents or guardian;

(4) a certified copy of each parent's or former parent's marriage certificate, decree of divorce, annulment, or dissolution, or agreement or decree of legal separation, and a certified copy of any court order determining the parent's or former parent's incompetence;

(5)   a certified copy of any existing court order or the petition in any pending proceeding concerning custody of or visitation with the minor;

(6)   a copy of the preplacement evaluation and of the evaluation during the pendency of the proceeding for adoption;

(7)   a copy of any report containing the information required by Section 2–106;

(8)   a document signed pursuant to Section 2–404(e);

(9)   a certified copy of the petitioner's marriage certificate, decree of divorce, annulment, or dissolution, or agreement or decree of legal separation, and a certified copy of any court order determining the incompetence of the petitioner's spouse;

(10) a copy of any agreement with a public agency to provide a subsidy for the benefit of a minor adoptee with a special need;

(11) if an agency placed the minor adoptee, a verified document from the agency stating:

(i)   the circumstances under which it obtained custody of the minor for purposes of adoption;

(ii)   that it complied with any provision of law governing an interstate or intercountry placement of the minor;

(iii)   the name or relationship to the minor of any individual whose consent is required, but who has not executed a consent or a relinquishment or whose parental relationship has not been terminated, and any fact or circumstance that may excuse the lack of consent or relinquishment; and

(iv)   whether it has executed its consent to the proposed adoption and whether it waives notice of the proceeding; and

(12) the name and address, if known, of any person who is entitled to receive notice of the proceeding for adoption.

(b)   If an item required by subsection (a) is not available, the person responsible for furnishing the item shall file an affidavit explaining its absence.

[PART] 4. NOTICE OF PENDENCY OF PROCEEDING

§ 3–401.   SERVICE OF NOTICE.

(a)   Unless notice has been waived, notice of a proceeding for adoption of a minor must be served, within 20 days after a petition for adoption is filed, upon:

(1)   an individual whose consent to the adoption is required under Section 2–401, but notice need not be served upon an individual whose parental relationship to the minor or whose status as a guardian has been terminated;

(2) an agency whose consent to the adoption is required under Section 2–401;

(3) an individual whom the petitioner knows is claiming to be or who is named as the father or possible father of the minor adoptee and whose paternity of the minor has not been judicially determined, but notice need not be served upon a man who has executed a verified statement, as described in Section 2–402(a)(4), denying paternity or disclaiming any interest in the minor;

(4) an individual other than the petitioner who has legal or physical custody of the minor adoptee or who has a right of visitation with the minor under an existing court order issued by a court in this or another State;

(5) the spouse of the petitioner if the spouse has not joined in the petition; and

(6) a grandparent of a minor adoptee if the grandparent's child is a deceased parent of the minor and, before death, the deceased parent had not executed a consent or relinquishment or the deceased parent's parental relationship to the minor had not been terminated.

(b) The court shall require notice of a proceeding for adoption of a minor to be served upon any person the court finds, at any time during the proceeding, is:

(1) a person described in subsection (a) who has not been given notice;

(2) an individual who has revoked a consent or relinquishment pursuant to Section 2–408(a) or 2–409(a) or is attempting to have a consent or relinquishment set aside pursuant to Section 2–408(b) or 2–409(b); or

(3) a person who, on the basis of a previous relationship with the minor adoptee, a parent, an alleged parent, or the petitioner, can provide information that is relevant to the proposed adoption and that the court in its discretion wants to hear.

§ 3–402. CONTENT OF NOTICE.

A notice required by Section 3–401 must use a pseudonym for a petitioner or any individual named in the petition for adoption who has not waived confidentiality and must contain:

(1) the caption of the petition;

(2) the address and telephone number of the court where the petition is pending;

(3) a concise summary of the relief requested in the petition;

(4) the name, mailing address, and telephone number of the petitioner or petitioner's lawyer;

(5)   a conspicuous statement of the method of responding to the notice of the proceeding for adoption and the consequences of failure to respond; and

(6)   any statement required by [other applicable law or rule].

§ 3–403.   MANNER AND EFFECT OF SERVICE.

(a)   Personal service of the notice required by Section 3–401 must be made in a manner appropriate under [the rules of civil procedure for the service of process in a civil action in this State] unless the court otherwise directs.

(b)   Except as otherwise provided in subsection (c), a person who fails to respond to the notice within 20 days after its service may not appear in or receive further notice of the proceeding for adoption.

(c)   An individual who is a respondent in a petition to terminate the relationship of parent and child pursuant to [Part] 5 which is served upon the individual with the notice required by Section 3–401 may not appear in or receive further notice of the proceeding for adoption or for termination unless the individual responds to the notice as required by Section 3–504.

§ 3–404.   INVESTIGATION AND NOTICE TO UNKNOWN FATHER.

(a)   If, at any time in a proceeding for adoption or for termination of a relationship of parent and child under [Part] 5, the court finds that an unknown father of a minor adoptee may not have received notice, the court shall determine whether he can be identified. The determination must be based on evidence that includes inquiry of appropriate persons in an effort to identify an unknown father for the purpose of providing notice.

(b)   The inquiry required by subsection (a) must include whether:

(1)   the woman who gave birth to the minor adoptee was married at the probable time of conception of the minor, or at a later time;

(2)   the woman was cohabiting with a man at the probable time of conception of the minor;

(3)   the woman has received payments or promises of support, other than from a governmental agency, with respect to the minor or because of her pregnancy;

(4)   the woman has named any individual as the father on the birth certificate of the minor or in connection with applying for or receiving public assistance; and

(5)   any individual has formally or informally acknowledged or claimed paternity of the minor in a jurisdiction in which the woman

resided during or since her pregnancy, or in which the minor has resided or resides, at the time of the inquiry.

(c)   If inquiry pursuant to subsection (b) identifies as the father of the minor an individual who has not received notice of the proceeding, the court shall require notice to be served upon him pursuant to Section 3–403 unless service is not possible because his whereabouts are unknown.

(d)   If, after inquiry pursuant to subsection (b), the court finds that personal service cannot be made upon the father of the minor because his identity or whereabouts is unknown, the court shall order publication or public posting of the notice only if, on the basis of all information available, the court determines that publication or posting is likely to lead to receipt of notice by the father. If the court determines that publication or posting is not likely to lead to receipt of notice, the court may dispense with the publication or posting of a notice.

(e)   If, in an inquiry pursuant to this section, the woman who gave birth to the minor adoptee fails to disclose the identity of a possible father or reveal his whereabouts, she must be advised that the proceeding for adoption may be delayed or subject to challenge if a possible father is not given notice of the proceeding, that the lack of information about the father's medical and genetic history may be detrimental to the adoptee, and that she is subject to a civil penalty if she knowingly misidentified the father.

§ 3–405.   WAIVER OF NOTICE.

(a)   A person entitled to receive notice required under this [Act] may waive the notice before the court or in a consent, relinquishment, or other document signed by the person.

(b)   Except for the purpose of moving to revoke a consent or relinquishment on the ground that it was obtained by fraud or duress, a person who has waived notice may not appear in the proceeding for adoption.

[PART] 5. PETITION TO TERMINATE RELATIONSHIP BETWEEN PARENT AND CHILD

§ 3–501.   AUTHORIZATION.

A petition to terminate the relationship between a parent or an alleged parent and a minor child may be filed in a proceeding for adoption under this [Act] by:

(1)   a parent or a guardian who has selected a prospective adoptive parent for a minor and who intends to place, or has placed, the minor with that individual;

(2) a parent whose spouse has filed a petition under [Article] 4 to adopt the parent's minor child;

(3) a prospective adoptive parent of the minor who has filed a petition to adopt under this [article] or [Article] 4; or

(4) an agency that has selected a prospective adoptive parent for the minor and intends to place, or has placed, the minor with that individual.

§ 3–502.   TIMING AND CONTENT OF PETITION.

(a) A petition under this [part] may be filed at any time after a petition for adoption has been filed under this [article] or [Article] 4 and before entry of a decree of adoption.

(b) A petition under this [part] must be signed and verified by the petitioner, be filed with the court, and state:

(1) the name or pseudonym of the petitioner;

(2) the name of the minor;

(3) the name and last known address of the parent or alleged parent whose parental relationship to the minor is to be terminated;

(4) the facts and circumstances forming the basis for the petition and the grounds on which termination of a parental relationship is sought;

(5) if the petitioner is a prospective adoptive parent, that the petitioner intends to proceed with the petition to adopt the minor if the petition to terminate is granted; and

(6) if the petitioner is a parent, a guardian, or an agency, that the petitioner has selected the prospective adoptive parent who is the petitioner in the proceeding for adoption.

§ 3–503.   SERVICE OF PETITION AND NOTICE.

(a) A petition to terminate under this [part] and a notice of hearing on the petition must be served upon the respondent, with notice of the proceeding for adoption, in the manner prescribed in Sections 3–403 and 3–404.

(b) The notice of a hearing must inform the respondent of the method for responding and that:

(1) the respondent has a right to be represented by a lawyer and may be entitled to have a lawyer appointed by the court; and

(2) failure to respond within 20 days after service and, in the case of an alleged father, failure to file a claim of paternity within 20 days after service unless a claim of paternity is pending, will result in termination of the relationship of parent and child between the respondent and the minor unless the proceeding for adoption is dismissed.

§ 3–504.   GROUNDS FOR TERMINATING RELATIONSHIP.

(a)   If the respondent is served with a petition to terminate under this [part] and the accompanying notice and does not respond and, in the case of an alleged father, file a claim of paternity within 20 days after the service unless a claim of paternity is pending, the court shall order the termination of any relationship of parent and child between the respondent and the minor unless the proceeding for adoption is dismissed.

(b)   If, under Section 3–404, the court dispenses with service of the petition upon the respondent, the court shall order the termination of any relationship of parent and child between the respondent and the minor unless the proceeding for adoption is dismissed.

(c)   If the respondent responds and asserts parental rights, the court shall proceed with the hearing expeditiously. If the court finds, upon clear and convincing evidence, that one of the following grounds exists, and, by a preponderance of the evidence, that termination is in the best interest of the minor, the court shall terminate any relationship of parent and child between the respondent and the minor:

(1)   in the case of a minor who has not attained six months of age at the time the petition for adoption is filed, unless the respondent proves by a preponderance of the evidence a compelling reason for not complying with this paragraph, the respondent has failed to:

(i)   pay reasonable prenatal, natal, and postnatal expenses in accordance with the respondent's financial means;

(ii)   make reasonable and consistent payments, in accordance with the respondent's financial means, for the support of the minor;

(iii)   visit regularly with the minor; and

(iv)   manifest an ability and willingness to assume legal and physical custody of the minor, if, during this time, the minor was not in the physical custody of the other parent;

(2)   in the case of a minor who has attained six months of age at the time a petition for adoption is filed, unless the respondent proves by a preponderance of the evidence a compelling reason for not complying with this paragraph, the respondent, for a period of at least six consecutive months immediately preceding the filing of the petition, has failed to:

(i)   make reasonable and consistent payments, in accordance with the respondent's means, for the support of the minor;

(ii)   communicate or visit regularly with the minor; and

(iii) manifest an ability and willingness to assume legal and physical custody of the minor, if, during this time, the minor was not in the physical custody of the other parent;

(3) the respondent has been convicted of a crime of violence or of violating a restraining or protective order, and the facts of the crime or violation and the respondent's behavior indicate that the respondent is unfit to maintain a relationship of parent and child with the minor;

(4) the respondent is a man who was not married to the minor's mother when the minor was conceived or born and is not the genetic or adoptive father of the minor; or

(5) termination is justified on a ground specified in [the State's statute for involuntary termination of parental rights].

(d) If the respondent proves by a preponderance of the evidence that he or she had a compelling reason for not complying with subsection (c)(1) or (2) and termination is not justified on a ground stated in subsection (c)(3) through (5), the court may terminate the relationship of parent and child between the respondent and a minor only if it finds, upon clear and convincing evidence, that one of the following grounds exists, and, by a preponderance of the evidence, that termination is in the best interest of the minor:

(1) if the minor is not in the legal and physical custody of the other parent, the respondent is not able or willing promptly to assume legal and physical custody of the minor, and to pay for the minor's support, in accordance with the respondent's financial means;

(2) if the minor is in the legal and physical custody of the other parent and a stepparent, and the stepparent is the prospective adoptive parent, the respondent is not able or willing promptly to establish and maintain contact with the minor and to pay for the minor's support, in accordance with the respondent's financial means;

(3) placing the minor in the respondent's legal and physical custody would pose a risk of substantial harm to the physical or psychological well-being of the minor because the circumstances of the minor's conception, the respondent's behavior during the mother's pregnancy or since the minor's birth, or the respondent's behavior with respect to other minors, indicates that the respondent is unfit to maintain a relationship of parent and child with the minor; or

(4) failure to terminate the relationship of parent and child would be detrimental to the minor.

(e) In making a determination under subsection (d)(4), the court shall consider any relevant factor, including the respondent's efforts to obtain or maintain legal and physical custody of the minor, the role of other persons in thwarting the respondent's efforts to assert parental rights, the respondent's ability to care for the minor, the age of the minor, the quality of any previous relationship between the respondent and the minor and between the respondent and any other minor children, the duration and suitability of the minor's present custodial environment, and the effect of a change of physical custody on the minor.

§ 3–505. EFFECT OF ORDER GRANTING PETITION.

An order issued under this [part] granting the petition:

(1) terminates the relationship of parent and child between the respondent and the minor, except an obligation for arrearages of child support;

(2) extinguishes any right the respondent had to withhold consent to a proposed adoption of the minor or to further notice of a proceeding for adoption; and

(3) is a final order for purposes of appeal.

§ 3–506. EFFECT OF ORDER DENYING PETITION.

(a) If the court denies the petition to terminate a relationship of parent and child, the court shall dismiss the proceeding for adoption and shall determine the legal and physical custody of the minor according to the criteria stated in Section 3–704.

(b) An order issued under this [part] denying a petition to terminate a relationship of parent and child is a final order for purposes of appeal.

[PART] 6. EVALUATION OF ADOPTEE AND PROSPECTIVE ADOPTIVE PARENT

§ 3–601. EVALUATION DURING PROCEEDING FOR ADOPTION.

(a) After a petition for adoption of a minor is filed, the court shall order that an evaluation be made by an individual qualified under Section 2–202.

(b) The court shall provide the evaluator with copies of the petition for adoption and of the items filed with the petition.

§ 3–602. CONTENT OF EVALUATION.

(a) An evaluation must be based on a personal interview with the petitioner in the petitioner's residence and observation of the relationship between the minor adoptee and the petitioner.

(b) An evaluation must be in writing and contain:

(1) an account of any change in the petitioner's marital status or family history, physical or mental health, home environment, property, income, or financial obligations since the filing of the preplacement evaluation;

(2) all reasonably available information concerning the physical, mental, and emotional condition of the minor adoptee which is not included in any report on the minor's health, genetic, and social history filed in the proceeding for adoption;

(3) copies of any court order, judgment, decree, or pending legal proceeding affecting the minor adoptee, the petitioner, or any child of the petitioner;

(4) a list of the expenses, fees, or other charges incurred, paid, or to be paid, and anything of value exchanged or to be exchanged, in connection with the adoption;

(5) any behavior or characteristics of the petitioner which raise a specific concern, as described in Section 2–204(a), about the petitioner or the petitioner's home; and

(6) a finding by the evaluator concerning the suitability of the petitioner and the petitioner's home for the minor adoptee and a recommendation concerning the granting of the petition for adoption.

§ 3–603. TIME AND FILING OF EVALUATION.

(a) The evaluator shall complete a written evaluation and file it with the court within 60 days after receipt of the court's order for an evaluation, unless the court for good cause allows a later filing.

(b) If an evaluation produces a specific concern, as described in Section 2–204(a), the evaluation must be filed immediately, and must explain why the concern poses a significant risk of harm to the physical or psychological well-being of the minor.

(c) An evaluator shall give the petitioner a copy of an evaluation when filed with the court and for two years shall retain a copy and a list of every source for each item of information in the evaluation.

[PART] 7. DISPOSITIONAL HEARING: DECREE OF ADOPTION

§ 3–701. TIME FOR HEARING ON PETITION.

The court shall set a date and time for hearing the petition, which must be no sooner than 90 days and no later than 180 days after the petition for adoption has been filed, unless the court for good cause sets an earlier or later date and time.

§ 3–702.   DISCLOSURE OF FEES AND CHARGES.

At least 10 days before the hearing:

(1)   the petitioner shall file with the court a signed and verified accounting of any payment or disbursement of money or anything of value made or agreed to be made by or on behalf of the petitioner in connection with the adoption, or pursuant to [Article] 7. The accounting must include the date and amount of each payment or disbursement made, the name and address of each recipient, and the purpose of each payment or disbursement;

(2)   the lawyer for a petitioner shall file with the court an affidavit itemizing any fee, compensation, or other thing of value received by, or agreed to be paid to, the lawyer incidental to the placement and adoption of the minor;

(3)   the lawyer for each parent of the minor or for the guardian of the minor shall file with the court an affidavit itemizing any fee, compensation, or other thing of value received by, or agreed to be paid to, the lawyer incidental to the placement and adoption of the minor;

(4)   if an agency placed the minor for adoption, the agency shall file with the court an affidavit itemizing any fee, compensation, or other thing of value received by the agency for, or incidental to, the placement and adoption of the minor; and

(5)   if a guardian placed the minor for adoption, the guardian shall file with the court an affidavit itemizing any fee, compensation, or other thing of value received by the guardian for, or incidental to, the placement and adoption of the minor.

§ 3–703.   GRANTING PETITION FOR ADOPTION.

(a)   The court shall grant a petition for adoption if it determines that the adoption will be in the best interest of the minor, and that:

(1)   at least 90 days have elapsed since the filing of the petition for adoption unless the court for good cause shown waives this requirement;

(2)   the adoptee has been in the physical custody of the petitioner for at least 90 days unless the court for good cause shown waives this requirement;

(3)   notice of the proceeding for adoption has been served or dispensed with as to any person entitled to receive notice under [Part] 4;

(4)   every necessary consent, relinquishment, waiver, disclaimer of paternal interest, or judicial order terminating parental rights, including an order issued under [Part] 5, has been obtained and filed with the court;

(5) any evaluation required by this [Act] has been filed with and considered by the court;

(6) the petitioner is a suitable adoptive parent for the minor;

(7) if applicable, any requirement of this [Act] governing an interstate or intercountry placement for adoption has been met;

(8) the Indian Child Welfare Act, 25 U.S.C. Sections 1901 et seq., is not applicable to the proceeding or, if applicable, its requirements have been met;

(9) an accounting and affidavit required by Section 3–702 have been reviewed by the court, and the court has denied, modified, or ordered reimbursement of any payment or disbursement that is not authorized by [Article] 7 or is unreasonable or unnecessary when compared with the expenses customarily incurred in connection with an adoption;

(10) the petitioner has received each report required by Section 2–106; and

(11) any document signed pursuant to Section 2–404(e) concerning the release of a former parent's identity to the adoptee after the adoptee attains 18 years of age has been filed with the court.

(b) Notwithstanding a finding by the court that an activity prohibited by this [Act] has occurred, if the court makes the determinations required by subsection (a), the court shall grant the petition for adoption and report the violation to the appropriate authorities.

(c) Except as otherwise provided in [Article] 4, the court shall inform the petitioner and any other individual affected by an existing order for visitation or communication with the minor adoptee that the decree of adoption terminates any existing order for visitation or communication.

§ 3–704. DENIAL OF PETITION FOR ADOPTION.

If a court denies a petition for adoption, it shall dismiss the proceeding and issue an appropriate order for the legal and physical custody of the minor. If the reason for the denial is that a consent or relinquishment is revoked or set aside pursuant to Section 2–408 or 2–409, the court shall determine the minor's custody according to the criteria stated in those sections. If the petition for adoption is denied for any other reason, the court shall determine the minor's custody according to the best interest of the minor.

§ 3–705. DECREE OF ADOPTION.

(a) A decree of adoption must state or contain:

(1)   the original name of the minor adoptee, if the adoption is by a stepparent or relative and, in all other adoptions, the original name or a pseudonym;

(2)   the name of the petitioner for adoption;

(3)   whether the petitioner is married or unmarried;

(4)   whether the petitioner is a stepparent of the adoptee;

(5)   the name by which the adoptee is to be known and when the name takes effect;

(6)   information to be incorporated into a new birth certificate to be issued by the [State Registrar of Vital Records], unless the petitioner or an adoptee who has attained 12 years of age requests that a new certificate not be issued;

(7)   the adoptee's date and place of birth, if known, or in the case of an adoptee born outside the United States, as determined pursuant to subsection (b);

(8)   the effect of the decree of adoption as stated in Sections 1–104 through 1–106; and

(9)   that the adoption is in the best interest of the adoptee.

(b)   In determining the date and place of birth of an adoptee born outside the United States, the court shall:

(1)   enter the date and place of birth as stated in the birth certificate from the country of origin, the United States Department of State's report of birth abroad, or the documents of the United States Immigration and Naturalization Service;

(2)   if the exact place of birth is unknown, enter the information that is known and designate a place of birth according to the best information known with respect to the country of origin;

(3)   if the exact date of birth is unknown, determine a date of birth based upon medical evidence as to the probable age of the adoptee and other evidence the court considers appropriate; and

(4)   if documents described in paragraph (1) are not available, determine the date and place of birth based upon evidence the court finds appropriate to consider.

(c)   Unless a petitioner requests otherwise and the former parent agrees, the decree of adoption may not name a former parent of the adoptee.

(d)   Except for a decree of adoption of a minor by a stepparent which is issued pursuant to [Article] 4, a decree of adoption of a minor must contain a statement that the adoption terminates any order for visitation or communication with the minor that was in effect before the decree is issued.

(e) A decree that substantially complies with the requirements of this section is not subject to challenge solely because one or more items required by this section are not contained in the decree.

§ 3–706. FINALITY OF DECREE.

A decree of adoption is a final order for purposes of appeal when it is issued and becomes final for other purposes upon the expiration of the time for filing an appeal, if no appeal is filed, or upon the denial or dismissal of any appeal filed within the requisite time.

§ 3–707. CHALLENGES TO DECREE.

(a) An appeal from a decree of adoption or other appealable order issued under this [Act] must be heard expeditiously.

(b) A decree or order issued under this [Act] may not be vacated or annulled upon application of a person who waived notice, or who was properly served with notice pursuant to this [Act] and failed to respond or appear, file an answer, or file a claim of paternity within the time allowed.

(c) The validity of a decree of adoption issued under this [Act] may not be challenged for failure to comply with an agreement for visitation or communication with an adoptee.

(d) A decree of adoption or other order issued under this [Act] is not subject to a challenge begun more than six months after the decree or order is issued. If a challenge is brought by an individual whose parental relationship to an adoptee is terminated by a decree or order under this [Act], the court shall deny the challenge, unless the court finds by clear and convincing evidence that the decree or order is not in the best interest of the adoptee.

[PART] 8. BIRTH CERTIFICATE

§ 3–801. REPORT OF ADOPTION.

(a) Within 30 days after a decree of adoption becomes final, the clerk of the court shall prepare a report of adoption on a form furnished by the [State Registrar of Vital Records] and certify and send the report to the [Registrar]. The report must include:

(1) information in the court's record of the proceeding for adoption which is necessary to locate and identify the adoptee's birth certificate or, in the case of an adoptee born outside the United States, evidence the court finds appropriate to consider as to the adoptee's date and place of birth;

(2) information in the court's record of the proceeding for adoption which is necessary to issue a new birth certificate for the adoptee and a request that a new certificate be issued, unless the

court, the adoptive parent, or an adoptee who has attained 12 years of age requests that a new certificate not be issued; and

(3) the file number of the decree of adoption and the date on which the decree became final.

(b) Within 30 days after a decree of adoption is amended or vacated, the clerk of the court shall prepare a report of that action on a form furnished by the [Registrar] and shall certify and send the report to the [Registrar]. The report must include information necessary to identify the original report of adoption, and shall also include information necessary to amend or withdraw any new birth certificate that was issued pursuant to the original report of adoption.

§ 3–802. ISSUANCE OF NEW BIRTH CERTIFICATE.

(a) Except as otherwise provided in subsection (d), upon receipt of a report of adoption prepared pursuant to Section 3–801, a report of adoption prepared in accordance with the law of another State or country, a certified copy of a decree of adoption together with information necessary to identify the adoptee's original birth certificate and to issue a new certificate, or a report of an amended adoption, the [Registrar] shall:

(1) issue a new birth certificate for an adoptee born in this State and furnish a certified copy of the new certificate to the adoptive parent and to an adoptee who has attained 12 years of age;

(2) forward a certified copy of a report of adoption for an adoptee born in another State to the [Registrar] of the State of birth;

(3) issue a certificate of foreign birth for an adoptee adopted in this State and who was born outside the United States and was not a citizen of the United States at the time of birth, and furnish a certified copy of the certificate to the adoptive parent and to an adoptee who has attained 12 years of age;

(4) notify an adoptive parent of the procedure for obtaining a revised birth certificate through the United States Department of State for an adoptee born outside the United States who was a citizen of the United States at the time of birth; or

(5) in the case of an amended decree of adoption, issue an amended birth certificate according to the procedure in paragraph (1) or (3) or follow the procedure in paragraph (2) or (4).

(b) Unless otherwise specified by the court, a new birth certificate issued pursuant to subsection (a)(1) or (3) or an amended certificate issued pursuant to subsection (a)(5) must include the date and place of birth of the adoptee, substitute the name of the adoptive parent for the name of the individual listed as the adoptee's parent on the original birth certificate, and contain any other information prescribed by [the State's vital records law or regulations].

(c) The [Registrar] shall substitute the new or amended birth certificate for the original birth certificate in the [Registrar's] files. The original certificate and all copies of the certificate in the files of the [Registrar] or any other custodian of vital records in the State must be sealed and are not subject to inspection until 99 years after the adoptee's date of birth, but may be inspected as provided in this [Act].

(d) If the court, the adoptive parent, or an adoptee who has attained 12 years of age requests that a new or amended birth certificate not be issued, the [Registrar] may not issue a new or amended certificate for an adoptee pursuant to subsection (a), but shall forward a certified copy of the report of adoption or of an amended decree of adoption for an adoptee who was born in another State to the appropriate office in the adoptee's State of birth.

(e) Upon receipt of a report that an adoption has been vacated, the [Registrar] shall:

(1) restore the original birth certificate for an individual born in this State to its place in the files, seal any new or amended birth certificate issued pursuant to subsection (a), and not allow inspection of a sealed certificate except upon court order or as otherwise provided in this [Act];

(2) forward the report with respect to an individual born in another State to the appropriate office in the State of birth; or

(3) notify the individual who is granted legal custody of a former adoptee after an adoption is vacated of the procedure for obtaining an original birth certificate through the United States Department of State for a former adoptee born outside the United States who was a citizen of the United States at the time of birth.

(f) Upon request by an individual who was listed as a parent on a child's original birth certificate and who furnishes appropriate proof of the individual's identity, the [Registrar] shall give the individual a noncertified copy of the original birth certificate.

[ARTICLE] 4. ADOPTION OF MINOR STEPCHILD BY STEPPARENT

§ 4–101. OTHER PROVISIONS APPLICABLE TO ADOPTION OF STEPCHILD.

Except as otherwise provided by this [article], [Article] 3 applies to an adoption of a minor stepchild by a stepparent.

§ 4–102. STANDING TO ADOPT MINOR STEPCHILD.

(a) A stepparent has standing under this [article] to petition to adopt a minor stepchild who is the child of the stepparent's spouse if:

(1)   the spouse has sole legal and physical custody of the child and the child has been in the physical custody of the spouse and the stepparent during the 60 days next preceding the filing of a petition for adoption;

(2)   the spouse has joint legal custody of the child with the child's other parent and the child has resided primarily with the spouse and the stepparent during the 12 months next preceding the filing of the petition;

(3)   the spouse is deceased or mentally incompetent, but before dying or being judicially declared mentally incompetent, had legal and physical custody of the child, and the child has resided primarily with the stepparent during the 12 months next preceding the filing of the petition; or

(4)   an agency placed the child with the stepparent pursuant to Section 2–104.

(b)   For good cause shown, a court may allow an individual who does not meet the requirements of subsection (a), but has the consent of the custodial parent of a minor to file a petition for adoption under this [article]. A petition allowed under this subsection must be treated as if the petitioner were a stepparent.

(c)   A petition for adoption by a stepparent may be joined with a petition under [Article] 3, [Part] 5, to terminate the relationship of parent and child between a minor adoptee and the adoptee's parent who is not the stepparent's spouse.

§ 4–103. LEGAL   CONSEQUENCES   OF   ADOPTION   OF STEPCHILD.

(a)   Except as otherwise provided in subsections (b) and (c), the legal consequences of an adoption of a stepchild by a stepparent are the same as under Sections 1–103 through 1–106.

(b)   An adoption by a stepparent does not affect:

(1)   the relationship between the adoptee and the adoptee's parent who is the adoptive stepparent's spouse or deceased spouse;

(2)   an existing court order for visitation or communication with a minor adoptee by an individual related to the adoptee through the parent who is the adoptive stepparent's spouse or deceased spouse;

(3)   the right of the adoptee or a descendant of the adoptee to inheritance or intestate succession through or from the adoptee's former parent; or

(4)   a court order or agreement for visitation or communication with a minor adoptee which is approved by the court pursuant to Section 4–113.

(c)   Failure to comply with an agreement or order is not a ground for challenging the validity of an adoption by a stepparent.

§ 4–104.   CONSENT TO ADOPTION.

Unless consent is not required under Section 2–402, a petition to adopt a minor stepchild may be granted only if consent to the adoption has been executed by a stepchild who has attained 12 years of age; and

(1)   the minor's parents as described in Section 2–401(a);

(2)   the minor's guardian if expressly authorized by a court to consent to the minor's adoption; or

(3)   an agency that placed the minor for adoption by the stepparent.

§ 4–105.   CONTENT OF CONSENT BY STEPPARENT'S SPOUSE.

(a)   A consent executed by a parent who is the stepparent's spouse must be signed or confirmed in the presence of an individual specified in Section 2–405, or an individual authorized to take acknowledgements.

(b)   A consent under subsection (a) must be in writing, must contain the required statements described in Section 2–406(a)(1) through (3) and (d)(3) through (6), may contain the optional statements described in Section 2–406(f), and must state that:

(1)   the parent executing the consent has legal and physical custody of the parent's minor child and voluntarily and unequivocally consents to the adoption of the minor by the stepparent;

(2)   the adoption will not terminate the parental relationship between the parent executing the consent and the minor child; and

(3)   the parent executing the consent understands and agrees that the adoption will terminate the relationship of parent and child between the minor's other parent and the minor, and will terminate any existing court order for custody, visitation, or communication with the minor, but:

(i)   the minor and any descendant of the minor will retain rights of inheritance from or through the minor's other parent;

(ii)   a court order for visitation or communication with the minor by an individual related to the minor through the parent executing the consent, or an agreement or order concerning another individual which is approved by the court pursuant to Section 4–113 survives the decree of adoption, but failure to comply with the terms of the order or agreement is not a ground for revoking or setting aside the consent or the adoption; and

(iii) the other parent remains liable for arrearages of child support unless released from that obligation by the parent executing the consent and by a governmental entity providing public assistance to the minor.

(c) A consent may not waive further notice of the proceeding for adoption of the minor by the stepparent.

§ 4–106. CONTENT OF CONSENT BY MINOR'S OTHER PARENT.

(a) A consent executed by a minor's parent who is not the stepparent's spouse must be signed or confirmed in the presence of an individual specified in Section 2–405.

(b) A consent under subsection (a) must be in writing, must contain the required statements described in Section 2–406(a)(1) through (3) and (d)(3) through (6), may contain the optional statements described in Section 2–406(f), and must state that:

(1) the parent executing the consent voluntarily and unequivocally consents to the adoption of the minor by the stepparent and the transfer to the stepparent's spouse and the adoptive stepparent of any right the parent executing the consent has to legal or physical custody of the minor;

(2) the parent executing the consent understands and agrees that the adoption will terminate his or her parental relationship to the minor and will terminate any existing court order for custody, visitation, or communication with the minor, but:

(i) the minor and any descendant of the minor will retain rights of inheritance from or through the parent executing the consent;

(ii) a court order for visitation or communication with the minor by an individual related to the minor through the minor's other parent, or an agreement or order concerning another individual which is approved by the court pursuant to Section 4–113 survives the decree of adoption, but failure to comply with the terms of the order or agreement is not a ground for revoking or setting aside the consent or the adoption; and

(iii) the parent executing the consent remains liable for arrearages of child support unless released from that obligation by the other parent and any guardian ad litem of the minor and by a governmental entity providing public assistance to the minor; and

(3) the parent executing the consent has provided the adoptive stepparent with the information required by Section 2–106.

(c) A consent under subsection (a) may waive notice of the proceeding for adoption of the minor by the stepparent unless the adoption is contested, appealed, or denied.

§ 4–107.   CONTENT OF CONSENT BY OTHER PERSONS.

(a)   A consent executed by the guardian of a minor stepchild or by an agency must be in writing and signed or confirmed in the presence of the court, or in a manner the court directs, and:

> (1)   must state the circumstances under which the guardian or agency obtained the authority to consent to the adoption of the minor by a stepparent;

> (2)   must contain the statements required by Sections 4–104 and 4–105, except for any that can be made only by a parent of the minor; and

> (3)   may waive notice of the proceeding for adoption, unless the adoption is contested, appealed, or denied.

(b)   A consent executed by a minor stepchild in a proceeding for adoption by a stepparent must be signed or confirmed in the presence of the court or in a manner the court directs.

§ 4–108.   PETITION TO ADOPT.

(a)   A petition by a stepparent to adopt a minor stepchild must be signed and verified by the petitioner and contain the following information or state why any of the information is not contained in the petition:

> (1)   the information required by Section 3–304(a) (1), (3), (5), and (8) through (12) and (b);

> (2)   the current marital status of the petitioner, including the date and place of marriage, the name and date and place of birth of the petitioner's spouse and, if the spouse is deceased, the date, place, and cause of death and, if the spouse is incompetent, the date on which a court declared the spouse incompetent;

> (3)   the length of time the minor has been residing with the petitioner and the petitioner's spouse and, if the minor is not in the physical custody of the petitioner and the petitioner's spouse, the reason why they do not have custody and when they intend to obtain custody; and

> (4)   the length of time the petitioner's spouse or the petitioner has had legal custody of the minor and the circumstances under which legal custody was obtained.

§ 4–109.   REQUIRED DOCUMENTS.

(a)   After a petition to adopt a minor stepchild is filed, the following must be filed in the proceeding:

> (1)   any item required by Section 3–305(a) which is relevant to an adoption by a stepparent; and

(2) a copy of any agreement to waive arrearages of child support.

(b) If any of the items required by subsection (a) is not available, the person responsible for furnishing the item shall file an affidavit explaining its absence.

§ 4–110. NOTICE OF PENDENCY OF PROCEEDING.

(a) Within 30 days after a petition to adopt a minor stepchild is filed, the petitioner shall serve notice of the proceeding upon:

(1) the petitioner's spouse;

(2) any other person whose consent to the adoption is required under this [article];

(3) any person described in Section 3–401(a)(3), (4), and (6) and (b); and

(4) the parents of the minor's parent whose parental relationship will be terminated by the adoption unless the identity or the whereabouts of those parents are unknown.

§ 4–111. EVALUATION OF STEPPARENT.

(a) After a petition for adoption of a minor stepchild is filed, the court may order that an evaluation be made by an individual qualified under Section 2–202 to assist the court in determining whether the proposed adoption is in the best interest of the minor.

(b) The court shall provide an evaluator with copies of the petition for adoption and of the items filed with the petition.

(c) Unless otherwise directed by the court, an evaluator shall base the evaluation on a personal interview with the petitioner and the petitioner's spouse in the petitioner's residence, observation of the relationship between the minor and the petitioner, personal interviews with others who know the petitioner and may have information relevant to the examination, and any information received pursuant to subsection (d).

(d) An evaluation under this section must be in writing and contain the following:

(1) the information required by Section 2–203(d) and (e);

(2) the information required by Section 3–602(b)(2) through (5); and

(3) the finding required by Section 3–602(b)(6).

(e) An evaluator shall complete an evaluation and file it with the court within 60 days after being asked for the evaluation under this section, unless the court allows a later filing.

(f) Section 3–603(b) and (c) apply to an evaluation under this section.

§ 4–112. DISPOSITIONAL HEARING; DECREE OF ADOPTION.

Sections 3–701 through 3–707 apply to a proceeding for adoption of a minor stepchild by a stepparent, but the court may waive the requirements of section 3–702.

§ 4–113. VISITATION AGREEMENT AND ORDER.

(a) Upon the request of the petitioner in a proceeding for adoption of a minor stepchild, the court shall review a written agreement that permits another individual to visit or communicate with the minor after the decree of adoption becomes final, which must be signed by the individual, the petitioner, the petitioner's spouse, the minor if 12 years of age or older, and, if an agency placed the minor for adoption, an authorized employee of the agency.

(b) The court may enter an order approving the agreement only upon determining that the agreement is in the best interest of the minor adoptee. In making this determination, the court shall consider:

(1) the preference of the minor, if the minor is mature enough to express a preference;

(2) any special needs of the minor and how they would be affected by performance of the agreement;

(3) the length and quality of any existing relationship between the minor and the individual who would be entitled to visit or communicate, and the likely effect on the minor of allowing this relationship to continue;

(4) the specific terms of the agreement and the likelihood that the parties to the agreement will cooperate in performing its terms;

(5) the recommendation of the minor's guardian ad litem, lawyer, social worker, or other counselor; and

(6) any other factor relevant to the best interest of the minor.

(c) In addition to any agreement approved pursuant to subsections (a) and (b), the court may approve the continuation of an existing order or issue a new order permitting the minor adoptee's former parent, grandparent, or sibling to visit or communicate with the minor if:

(1) the grandparent is the parent of a deceased parent of the minor or the parent of the adoptee's parent whose parental relationship to the minor is terminated by the decree of adoption;

(2) the former parent, grandparent, or sibling requests that an existing order be permitted to survive the decree of adoption or that a new order be issued; and

(3) the court determines that the requested visitation or communication is in the best interest of the minor.

(d) In making a determination under subsection (c)(3), the court shall consider the factors listed in subsection (b) and any objections to the requested order by the adoptive stepparent and the stepparent's spouse.

(e) An order issued under this section may be enforced in a civil action only if the court finds that enforcement is in the best interest of a minor adoptee.

(f) An order issued under this section may not be modified unless the court finds that modification is in the best interest of a minor adoptee and:

(1) the individuals subject to the order request the modification; or

(2) exceptional circumstances arising since the order was issued justify the modification.

(g) Failure to comply with the terms of an order approved under this section or with any other agreement for visitation or communication is not a ground for revoking, setting aside, or otherwise challenging the validity of a consent, relinquishment, or adoption pertaining to a minor stepchild, and the validity of the consent, relinquishment, and adoption is not affected by any later action to enforce, modify, or set aside the order or agreement.

[ARTICLE] 5. ADOPTION OF ADULTS AND EMANCIPATED MINORS

§ 5–101. WHO MAY ADOPT ADULT OR EMANCIPATED MINOR.

(a) An adult may adopt another adult or an emancipated minor pursuant to this [article], but:

(1) an adult may not adopt his or her spouse; and

(2) an incompetent individual of any age may be adopted only pursuant to [Articles] 2, 3, and 4.

(b) An individual who has adopted an adult or emancipated minor may not adopt another adult or emancipated minor within one year after the adoption unless the prospective adoptee is a sibling of the adoptee.

§ 5–102. LEGAL CONSEQUENCES OF ADOPTION.

The legal consequences of an adoption of an adult or emancipated minor are the same as under Sections 1–103 through 1–106, but the legal consequences of adoption of an adult stepchild by an adult stepparent are the same as under Section 4–103.

§ 5–103. CONSENT TO ADOPTION.

(a) Consent to the adoption of an adult or emancipated minor is required only of:

(1) the adoptee;

(2) the prospective adoptive parent; and

(3) the spouse of the prospective adoptive parent, unless they are legally separated, or the court finds that the spouse is not capable of giving consent or is withholding consent contrary to the best interest of the adoptee and the prospective adoptive parent.

(b) The consent of the adoptee and the prospective adoptive parent must:

(1) be in writing and be signed or confirmed by each of them in the presence of the court or an individual authorized to take acknowledgments;

(2) state that they agree to assume toward each other the legal relationship of parent and child and to have all of the rights and be subject to all of the duties of that relationship; and

(3) state that they understand the consequences the adoption may have for any right of inheritance, property, or support each has.

(c) The consent of the spouse of the prospective adoptive parent:

(1) must be in writing and be signed or confirmed in the presence of the court or an individual authorized to take acknowledgments;

(2) must state that the spouse:

(i) consents to the proposed adoption; and

(ii) understands the consequences the adoption may have for any right of inheritance, property, or support the spouse has; and

(3) may contain a waiver of any proceeding for adoption.

§ 5–104. JURISDICTION AND VENUE.

(a) The court has jurisdiction over a proceeding for the adoption of an adult or emancipated minor under this [article] if a petitioner lived in this State for at least 90 days immediately preceding the filing of a petition for adoption.

(b) A petition for adoption may be filed in the court in the [county] in which a petitioner lives.

§ 5–105. PETITION FOR ADOPTION.

(a) A prospective adoptive parent and an adoptee under this [article] must jointly file a petition for adoption.

(b)   The petition must be signed and verified by each petitioner and state:

(1)   the full name, age, and place and duration of residence of each petitioner;

(2)   the current marital status of each petitioner, including the date and place of marriage, if married;

(3)   the full name by which the adoptee is to be known if the petition is granted;

(4)   the duration and nature of the relationship between the prospective adoptive parent and the adoptee;

(5)   that the prospective adoptive parent and the adoptee desire to assume the legal relationship of parent and child and to have all of the rights and be subject to all of the duties of that relationship;

(6)   that the adoptee understands that a consequence of the adoption will be to terminate the adoptee's relationship as the child of an existing parent, but if the adoptive parent is the adoptee's stepparent, the adoption will not affect the adoptee's relationship with a parent who is the stepparent's spouse, but will terminate the adoptee's relationship to the adoptee's other parent, except for the right to inherit from or through that parent;

(7)   the name and last known address of any other individual whose consent is required;

(8)   the name, age, and last known address of any child of the prospective adoptive parent, including a child previously adopted by the prospective adoptive parent or his or her spouse, and the date and place of the adoption; and

(9)   the name, age, and last known address of any living parent or child of the adoptee.

(c)   The petitioners shall attach to the petition:

(1)   a certified copy of the birth certificate or other evidence of the date and place of birth of the adoptee and the prospective adoptive parent, if available; and

(2)   any required consent that has been executed.

§ 5–106.   NOTICE AND TIME OF HEARING.

(a)   Within 30 days after a petition for adoption is filed, the petitioners shall serve notice of hearing the petition upon any individual whose consent to the adoption is required under Section 5–103, and who has not waived notice, by sending a copy of the petition and notice of hearing to the individual at the address stated in the petition, or according to the manner of service provided in Section 3–403.

(b)   The court shall set a date and time for hearing the petition, which must be at least 30 days after the notice is served.

§ 5–107. DISPOSITIONAL HEARING.

(a) Both petitioners shall appear in person at the hearing unless an appearance is excused for good cause shown. In the latter event an appearance may be made for either or both of them by a lawyer authorized in writing to make the appearance, or a hearing may be conducted by telephone or other electronic medium.

(b) The court shall examine the petitioners, or the lawyer for a petitioner not present in person, and shall grant the petition for adoption if it determines that:

> (1) at least 30 days have elapsed since the service of notice of hearing the petition for adoption;

> (2) notice has been served, or dispensed with, as to any person whose consent is required under Section 5–103;

> (3) every necessary consent, waiver, document, or judicial order has been obtained and filed with the court;

> (4) the adoption is for the purpose of creating the relationship of parent and child between the petitioners and the petitioners understand the consequences of the relationship; and

> (5) there has been substantial compliance with this [Act].

§ 5–108. DECREE OF ADOPTION.

(a) A decree of adoption issued under this [article] must substantially conform to the relevant requirements of Section 3–705 and appeals from a decree, or challenges to it, are governed by Sections 3–706 and 3–707.

(b) The court shall send a copy of the decree to each individual named in the petition at the address stated in the petition.

(c) Within 30 days after a decree of adoption becomes final, the clerk of the court shall prepare a report of the adoption for the [State Registrar of Vital Records], and, if the petitioners have requested it, the report shall instruct the [Registrar] to issue a new birth certificate to the adoptee, as provided in [Article] 3, [Part] 8.

[ARTICLE] 6. RECORDS OF ADOPTION PROCEEDING: RETENTION, CONFIDENTIALITY, AND ACCESS

§ 6–101. RECORDS DEFINED.

Unless the context requires otherwise, for purposes of this [article], "records" includes all documents, exhibits, and data pertaining to an adoption.

§ 6–102. RECORDS CONFIDENTIAL, COURT RECORDS SEALED.

(a) All records, whether on file with the court, or in the possession of an agency, the [Registrar of Vital Records or Statistics], a lawyer, or another provider of professional services in connection with an adoption, are confidential and may not be inspected except as provided in this [Act].

(b) During a proceeding for adoption, records are not open to inspection except as directed by the court.

(c) Within 30 days after a decree of adoption becomes final, the clerk of the court shall send to the [Registrar], in addition to the report of adoption required by Section 3–801, a certified copy of any document signed pursuant to Section 2–404(e) and filed in the proceeding for adoption.

(d) All records on file with the court must be retained permanently and sealed for 99 years after the date of the adoptee's birth. Sealed records and indices of the records are not open to inspection by any person except as provided in this [Act].

(e) Any additional information about an adoptee, the adoptee's former parents, and the adoptee's genetic history that is submitted to the court within the 99-year period, must be added to the sealed records of the court. Any additional information that is submitted to an agency, lawyer, or other professional provider of services within the 99-year period must be kept confidential.

§ 6–103. RELEASE OF NONIDENTIFYING INFORMATION.

(a) An adoptive parent or guardian of an adoptee, an adoptee who has attained 18 years of age, an emancipated adoptee, a deceased adoptee's direct descendant who has attained 18 years of age, or the parent or guardian of a direct descendant who has not attained 18 years of age may request the court that granted the adoption or the agency that placed the adoptee for adoption, to furnish the nonidentifying information about the adoptee, the adoptee's former parents, and the adoptee's genetic history that has been retained by the court or agency, including the information required by Section 2–106.

(b) The court or agency shall furnish the individual who makes the request with a detailed summary of any relevant report or information that is included in the sealed records of the court or the confidential records of the agency. The summary must exclude identifying information concerning an individual who has not filed a waiver of confidentiality with the court or agency. The department or the court shall prescribe forms and a procedure for summarizing any report or information released under this section.

(c) An individual who is denied access to nonidentifying information to which the individual is entitled under this [article] or Section 2–106 may petition the court for relief.

(d) If a court receives a certified statement from a physician which explains in detail how a health condition may seriously affect the health of the adoptee or a direct descendant of the adoptee, the court shall make a diligent effort to notify an adoptee who has attained 18 years of age, an adoptive parent or guardian of an adoptee who has not attained 18 years of age, or a direct descendant of a deceased adoptee that the nonidentifying information is available and may be requested from the court.

(e) If a court receives a certified statement from a physician which explains in detail why a serious health condition of the adoptee or a direct descendant of the adoptee should be communicated to the adoptee's genetic parent or sibling to enable them to make an informed reproductive decision, the court shall make a diligent effort to notify those individuals that the nonidentifying information is available and may be requested from the court.

(f) If the [Registrar] receives a request or any additional information from an individual pursuant to this section, the [Registrar] shall give the individual the name and address of the court or agency having the records, and if the court or agency is in another State, shall assist the individual in locating the court or agency. The [Registrar] shall prescribe a reasonable procedure for verifying the identity, age, or other relevant characteristics of an individual who requests or furnishes information under this section.

§ 6–104.   DISCLOSURE OF IDENTIFYING INFORMATION.

(a) Except as otherwise provided in this [article], identifying information about an adoptee's former parent, an adoptee, or an adoptive parent which is contained in records, including original birth certificates, required by this [Act] to be confidential or sealed, may not be disclosed to any person.

(b) Identifying information about an adoptee's former parent must be disclosed by the [Registrar] to an adoptee who has attained 18 years of age, an adoptive parent or guardian of an adoptee who has not attained 18 years of age, a deceased adoptee's direct descendant who has attained 18 years of age, or the parent or guardian of a direct descendant who has not attained 18 years of age if one of these individuals requests the information and:

(1) the adoptee's former parent or, if the former parent is deceased or has been judicially declared incompetent, an adult descendant of the former parent authorizes the disclosure of his or her name, date of birth, or last known address, or other identifying information, either in a document signed pursuant to Section 2–

404(e) and filed in the proceeding for adoption or in another signed document filed with the court, an agency, or the [Registrar]; or

(2) the adoptee's former parent authorizes the disclosure of the requested information only if the adoptee, adoptive parent, or direct descendant agrees to release similar identifying information about the adoptee, adoptive parent, or direct descendant and this individual authorizes the disclosure of the information in a signed document kept by the court, an agency, or the [Registrar].

(c) Identifying information about an adoptee or a deceased adoptee's direct descendant must be disclosed by the [Registrar] to an adoptee's former parent if that individual requests the information and:

(1) an adoptee who has attained 18 years of age, an adoptive parent or guardian of an adoptee who has not attained 18 years of age, a deceased adoptee's direct descendant who has attained 18 years of age, or the parent or guardian of a direct descendant who has not attained 18 years of age authorizes the disclosure of the requested information in a signed document kept by the court, an agency, or the [Registrar]; or

(2) one of the individuals listed in paragraph (1) authorizes the disclosure of the requested information only if the adoptee's former parent agrees to release similar information about himself or herself, and the former parent authorizes the disclosure of the information in a signed document kept by the court, an agency, or the [Registrar].

(d) Identifying information about an adult sibling of an adoptee who has attained 18 years of age must be disclosed by the [Registrar] to an adoptee if the sibling is also an adoptee and both the sibling and the adoptee authorize the disclosure.

(e) Subsection (d) does not permit disclosure of a former parent's identity unless that parent has authorized disclosure under this [Act].

§ 6–105. ACTION FOR NONDISCLOSURE OF INFORMATION.

(a) To obtain information not otherwise available under Section 6–103 or 6–104, an adoptee who has attained 18 years of age, an adoptee who has not attained 18 years of age and has the permission of an adoptive parent or guardian, an adoptive parent or guardian of an adoptee who has not attained 18 years of age, a deceased adoptee's direct descendant who has attained 18 years of age, the parent or guardian of a direct descendant who has not attained 18 years of age, or an adoptee's former parent may file a petition in the court to obtain information about another individual described in this section which is contained in records, including original birth certificates, required by this [Act] to be confidential or sealed.

(b) In determining whether to grant a petition under this section, the court shall review the sealed records of the relevant proceeding for adoption and shall make specific findings concerning:

(1)   the reason the information is sought;

(2)   whether the individual about whom information is sought has filed a signed document described in Section 2–404(e) or 6–104 requesting that his or her identity not be disclosed, or has not filed any document;

(3)   whether the individual about whom information is sought is alive;

(4)   whether it is possible to satisfy the petitioner's request without disclosing the identity of another individual;

(5)   the likely effect of disclosure on the adoptee, the adoptive parents, the adoptee's former parents, and other members of the adoptee's original and adoptive families; and

(6)   the age, maturity, and expressed needs of the adoptee.

(c)   The court may order the disclosure of the requested information only upon a determination that good cause exists for the release based on the findings required by subsection (b) and a conclusion that:

(1)   there is a compelling reason for disclosure of the information; and

(2)   the benefit to the petitioner will be greater than the harm to any other individual of disclosing the information.

§ 6–106.   STATEWIDE REGISTRY.

The [Registrar] shall:

(1)   establish a statewide confidential registry for receiving, filing, and retaining documents requesting, authorizing, or not authorizing, the release of identifying information;

(2)   prescribe and distribute forms or documents on which an individual may request, authorize, or refuse to authorize the release of identifying information;

(3)   devise a procedure for releasing identifying information in the [Registrar's] possession upon receipt of an appropriate request and authorization;

(4)   cooperate with registries in other States to facilitate the matching of documents filed pursuant to this [article] by individuals in different States; and

(5)   announce and publicize to the general public the existence of the registry and the procedure for the consensual release of identifying information.

§ 6–107.   RELEASE OF ORIGINAL BIRTH CERTIFICATE.

(a)   In addition to any copy of an adoptee's original birth certificate authorized for release by a court order issued pursuant to Section 6–105, the [Registrar] shall furnish a copy of the original birth certificate upon the request of an adoptee who has attained 18 years of age, the direct descendant of a deceased adoptee, or an adoptive parent or guardian of an adoptee who has not attained 18 years of age, if the individual who makes the request furnishes a consent to disclosure signed by each individual who was named as a parent on the adoptee's original birth certificate.

(b) When 99 years have elapsed after the date of birth of an adoptee whose original birth certificate is sealed under this [Act], the [Registrar] shall unseal the original certificate and file it with any new or amended certificate that has been issued. The unsealed certificates become public information in accordance with any statute or regulation applicable to the retention and disclosure of records by the [Registrar].

§ 6–108. CERTIFICATE OF ADOPTION.

Upon the request of an adoptive parent or an adoptee who has attained 18 years of age, the clerk of the court that entered a decree of adoption shall issue a certificate of adoption which states the date and place of adoption, the date of birth of the adoptee, the name of each adoptive parent, and the name of the adoptee as provided in the decree.

§ 6–109. DISCLOSURE AUTHORIZED IN COURSE OF EMPLOYMENT.

This [article] does not preclude an employee or agent of a court, agency, or the [Registrar] from:

(1) inspecting permanent, confidential, or sealed records for the purpose of discharging any obligation under this [Act];

(2) disclosing the name of the court where a proceeding for adoption occurred, or the name of an agency that placed an adoptee, to an individual described in Sections 6–103 through 6–105, who can verify his or her identity; or

(3) disclosing nonidentifying information contained in confidential or sealed records in accordance with any other applicable state or federal law.

§ 6–110. FEE FOR SERVICES.

A court, an agency, or the [Registrar] may charge a reasonable fee for services, including copying services, it performs pursuant to this [article].

[ARTICLE] 7. PROHIBITED AND PERMISSIBLE ACTIVITIES IN CONNECTION WITH ADOPTION

§ 7–101.   PROHIBITED ACTIVITIES IN PLACEMENT.

(a)   Except as otherwise provided in [Article] 2, [Part] 1:

(1)   a person, other than a parent, guardian, or agency, as specified in Sections 2–101 through 2–103, may not place a minor for adoption or advertise in any public medium that the person knows of a minor who is available for adoption;

(2)   a person, other than an agency or an individual with a favorable preplacement evaluation, as required by Sections 2–201 through 2–207, may not advertise in any public medium that the person is willing to accept a minor for adoption;

(3)   an individual, other than a relative or stepparent of a minor, who does not have a favorable preplacement evaluation or a court-ordered waiver of the evaluation, or who has an unfavorable evaluation, may not obtain legal or physical custody of a minor for purposes of adoption; and

(4)   a person may not place or assist in placing a minor for adoption with an individual, other than a relative or stepparent, unless the person knows that the individual has a favorable preplacement evaluation or a waiver pursuant to Section 2–201.

(b)   A person who violates subsection (a) is liable for a [civil penalty] not to exceed [$5,000] for the first violation, and not to exceed [$10,000] for each succeeding violation in an action brought by the [appropriate official]. The court may enjoin from further violations any person who violates subsection (a) and shall inform any appropriate licensing authority or other official of the violation.

§ 7–102.   UNLAWFUL PAYMENTS RELATED TO ADOPTION.

(a)   Except as otherwise provided in Sections 7–103 and 7–104, a person may not pay or give or offer to pay or give to any other person, or request, receive, or accept any money or anything of value, directly or indirectly, for:

(1)   the placement of a minor for adoption;

(2)   the consent of a parent, a guardian, or an agency to the adoption of a minor; or

(3)   the relinquishment of a minor to an agency for the purpose of adoption.

(b)   The following persons are liable for a [civil penalty] not to exceed [$5,000] for the first violation, and not to exceed [$10,000] for each succeeding violation in an action brought by the [appropriate official]:

(1)   a person who knowingly violates subsection (a);

(2) a person who knowingly makes a false report to the court about a payment prohibited by this section or authorized by Section 7–103 or 7–104; and

(3) a parent or guardian who knowingly receives or accepts a payment authorized by Section 7–103 or 7–104 with the intent not to consent to an adoption or to relinquish a minor for adoption.

(c) The court may enjoin from further violations any person described in subsection (b) and shall inform any appropriate licensing authority or other official of the violation.

§ 7–103. LAWFUL PAYMENTS RELATED TO ADOPTION.

(a) Subject to the requirements of Sections 3–702 and 3–703 for an accounting and judicial approval of fees and charges related to an adoption, an adoptive parent, or a person acting on behalf of an adoptive parent, may pay for:

(1) the services of an agency in connection with an adoption;

(2) advertising and similar expenses incurred in locating a minor for adoption;

(3) medical, hospital, nursing, pharmaceutical, travel, or other similar expenses incurred by a mother or her minor child in connection with the birth or any illness of the minor;

(4) counseling services for a parent or a minor for a reasonable time before and after the minor's placement for adoption;

(5) living expenses of a mother for a reasonable time before the birth of her child and for no more than six weeks after the birth;

(6) expenses incurred in ascertaining the information required by Section 2–106;

(7) legal services, court costs, and travel or other administrative expenses connected with an adoption, including any legal services performed for a parent who consents to the adoption of a minor or relinquishes the minor to an agency;

(8) expenses incurred in obtaining a preplacement evaluation and an evaluation during the proceeding for adoption; and

(9) any other service the court finds is reasonably necessary.

(b) A parent or a guardian, a person acting on the parent's or guardian's behalf, or a provider of a service listed in subsection (a), may receive or accept a payment authorized by subsection (a). The payment may not be made contingent on the placement of a minor for adoption, relinquishment of the minor, or consent to the adoption. If the adoption is not completed, a person who is authorized to make a specific payment by subsection (a) is not liable for that payment unless the person has agreed in a signed writing with a provider of a service to make the payment regardless of the outcome of the proceeding for adoption.

§ 7–104.   CHARGES BY AGENCY.

Subject to the requirements of Sections 3–702 and 3–703 for an accounting and judicial approval of fees and charges related to an adoption, an agency may charge or accept a fee or other reasonable compensation from a prospective adoptive parent for:

(1)   medical, hospital, nursing, pharmaceutical, travel, or other similar expenses incurred by a mother or her minor child in connection with the birth or any illness of the minor;

(2)   a percentage of the annual cost the agency incurs in locating and providing counseling services for minor adoptees, parents, and prospective parents;

(3)   living expenses of a mother for a reasonable time before the birth of a child and for no more than six weeks after the birth;

(4)   expenses incurred in ascertaining the information required by Section 2–106;

(5)   legal services, court costs, and travel or other administrative expenses connected with an adoption, including the legal services performed for a parent who relinquishes a minor child to the agency;

(6)   preparation of a preplacement evaluation and an evaluation during the proceeding for adoption; and

(7)   any other service the court finds is reasonably necessary.

§ 7–105.   FAILURE TO DISCLOSE INFORMATION.

(a)   A person, other than a parent, who has a duty to furnish the nonidentifying information required by Section 2–106, or authorized for release under [Article] 6, and who intentionally refuses to provide the information is subject to a [civil penalty] not to exceed [$5,000] for the first violation, and not to exceed [$10,000] for each succeeding violation in an action brought by the [appropriate official]. The court may enjoin the person from further violations of the duty to furnish nonidentifying information.

(b)   An employee or agent of an agency, the court, or the [State Registrar of Vital Records] who intentionally destroys any information or report compiled pursuant to Section 2–106, or authorized for release under [Article] 6, is guilty of a [misdemeanor] [punishable upon conviction by a fine of not more than [$] or imprisonment for not more than [ ], or both].

(c)   In addition to the penalties provided in subsections (a) and (b), an adoptive parent, an adoptee, or any person who is the subject of any information required by Section 2–106, or authorized for release under [Article] 6, may maintain an action for damages or equitable relief against a person, other than a parent who placed a minor for adoption, who fails to perform the duties required by Section 2–106 or [Article] 6.

(d) A prospective adoptive parent who knowingly fails to furnish information or knowingly furnishes false information to an evaluator preparing an evaluation pursuant to [Article] 2, [Part] 2 or [Article] 3, [Part] 6, with the intent to deceive the evaluator, is guilty of a [misdemeanor] [punishable upon conviction by a fine of not more than [$] or imprisonment for not more than [ ], or both].

(e) An evaluator who prepares an evaluation pursuant to [Article] 2, [Part] 2 or [Article] 3, [Part] 6 and who knowingly omits or misrepresents information about the individual being evaluated with the intent to deceive a person authorized under this [Act] to place a minor for adoption is guilty of a [misdemeanor] [punishable upon conviction by a fine of not more than [$] or imprisonment for not more than [ ], or both].

(f) A parent of a minor child who knowingly misidentifies the minor's other parent with an intent to deceive the other parent, an agency, or a prospective adoptive parent is subject to a [civil penalty] not to exceed [$5,000] in an action brought by the [appropriate official].

§ 7–106.   UNAUTHORIZED DISCLOSURE OF INFORMATION.

(a) Except as authorized in this [Act], a person who furnishes or retains a report or records pursuant to this [Act] may not disclose any identifying or nonidentifying information contained in the report or records.

(b) A person who knowingly gives or offers to give or who accepts or agrees to accept anything of value for an unauthorized disclosure of identifying information made confidential by this [Act] is guilty of a [misdemeanor] [punishable upon conviction by a fine of not more than [$] or imprisonment for not more than [ ], or both,] for the first violation and of a [felony] [punishable upon conviction by a fine of not more than [$] or imprisonment for not more than [ ], or both,] for each succeeding violation.

(c) A person who knowingly gives or offers to give or who accepts or agrees to accept anything of value for an unauthorized disclosure of nonidentifying information made confidential by this [Act] is subject to a [civil penalty] not to exceed [$5,000] for the first violation, and not to exceed [$10,000] for each succeeding violation in an action brought by the [appropriate official].

(d) A person who makes a disclosure, that the person knows is unauthorized, of identifying or nonidentifying information from a report or record made confidential by this [Act] is subject to a [civil penalty] not to exceed [$2,500] for the first violation, and not to exceed [$5,000] for each succeeding violation in an action brought by the [appropriate official].

(e) The court may enjoin from further violations any person who makes or obtains an unauthorized disclosure and shall inform any appropriate licensing authority or other official of the violation.

(f) In addition to the penalties provided in subsections (b) through (e), an individual who is the subject of any of the information contained in a report or records made confidential by this [Act] may maintain an action for damages or equitable relief against any person who makes or obtains, or is likely to make or obtain, an unauthorized disclosure of the information.

(g) Identifying information contained in a report or records required by this [Act] to be kept confidential or sealed may not be disclosed under any other law of this State.

§ 7–107. ACTION BY DEPARTMENT.

The department may review and investigate compliance with this [Act] and may maintain an action in the [appropriate court] to compel compliance.

[ARTICLE] 8. MISCELLANEOUS PROVISIONS

§ 8–101. UNIFORMITY OF APPLICATION AND CONSTRUCTION.

This [Act] shall be applied and construed to effectuate its general purpose to make uniform the law with respect to the subject of this [Act] among the States enacting it.

§ 8–102. SHORT TITLE.

This [Act] may be cited as the Uniform Adoption Act (1994).

§ 8–103. SEVERABILITY CLAUSE.

If any provision of this [Act] or its application to any person or circumstance is held invalid, the invalidity does not affect other provisions or application of this [Act] which can be given effect without the invalid provision or application, and to this end the provisions of this [Act] are severable.

* * *

UNIFORM ARBITRATION ACT (2000)

7 U.L.A. Pt. IA 1 et seq. (2009)

[EDITORS' INTRODUCTION: Jana Douglas, Kirk Eby & (Zhiying) Mikaela Feng, *Marriage and Divorce*, 17 GEO. J. GENDER & L. 325 (2016); Jack M. Graves, *Arbitration as Contract: The Need for a Fully Developed and Comprehensive Set of Statutory Default Legal Rules*, 2 WM. & MARY BUS. L. REV. 227 (2011); L. Ali Khan, *Arbitral Autonomy*, 74 LA. L. REV. 1 (2013); Lindsay Melworm, *Biased? Prove It: Addressing Arbitrator Bias and the Merits of Implementing Broad Disclosure Standards*, 22 CARDOZO J. INT'L & COMP. L. 431 (2014); E. Gary Spitko, *The Will as an Implied Unilateral Arbitration Contract,* 68 FLA. L. REV. 49 (2016); Patrick Sweeney, Note, *Exceeding Their Powers: A Critique of Stolt-Nielsen and Manifest Disregard, and a Proposal for Substantive Arbitral Award Review*, 71 WASH. & LEE L. REV. 1571 (2014).]

§ 1. DEFINITIONS.

In this [Act]:

(1) "Arbitration organization" means an association, agency, board, commission, or other entity that is neutral and initiates, sponsors, or administers an arbitration proceeding or is involved in the appointment of an arbitrator.

(2) "Arbitrator" means an individual appointed to render an award, alone or with others, in a controversy that is subject to an agreement to arbitrate.

(3) "Court" means [a court of competent jurisdiction in this State].

(4) "Knowledge" means actual knowledge.

(5) "Person" means an individual, corporation, business trust, estate, trust, partnership, limited liability company, association, joint venture, government; governmental subdivision, agency, or instrumentality; public corporation; or any other legal or commercial entity.

(6) "Record" means information that is inscribed on a tangible medium or that is stored in an electronic or other medium and is retrievable in perceivable form.

§ 2. NOTICE.

(a) Except as otherwise provided in this [Act], a person gives notice to another person by taking action that is reasonably necessary to inform the other person in ordinary course, whether or not the other person acquires knowledge of the notice.

(b) A person has notice if the person has knowledge of the notice or has received notice.

(c)   A person receives notice when it comes to the person's attention or the notice is delivered at the person's place of residence or place of business, or at another location held out by the person as a place of delivery of such communications.

§ 3.   WHEN [ACT] APPLIES.

(a)   This [Act] governs an agreement to arbitrate made on or after [the effective date of this [Act]].

(b)   This [Act] governs an agreement to arbitrate made before [the effective date of this [Act]] if all the parties to the agreement or to the arbitration proceeding so agree in a record.

(c)   On or after [a delayed date], this [Act] governs an agreement to arbitrate whenever made.

§ 4.   EFFECT   OF   AGREEMENT   TO   ARBITRATE;   NONWAIVABLE PROVISIONS.

(a)   Except as otherwise provided in subsections (b) and (c), a party to an agreement to arbitrate or to an arbitration proceeding may waive or, the parties may vary the effect of, the requirements of this [Act] to the extent permitted by law.

(b)   Before a controversy arises that is subject to an agreement to arbitrate, a party to the agreement may not:

(1)   waive or agree to vary the effect of the requirements of Section 5(a), 6(a), 8, 17(a), 17(b), 26, or 28;

(2)   agree to unreasonably restrict the right under Section 9 to notice of the initiation of an arbitration proceeding;

(3)   agree to unreasonably restrict the right under Section 12 to disclosure of any facts by a neutral arbitrator; or

(4)   waive the right under Section 16 of a party to an agreement to arbitrate to be represented by a lawyer at any proceeding or hearing under this [Act], but an employer and a labor organization may waive the right to representation by a lawyer in a labor arbitration.

(c)   A party to an agreement to arbitrate or arbitration proceeding may not waive, or the parties may not vary the effect of, the requirements of this section or Section 3(a) or (c), 7, 14, 18, 20(d) or (e), 22, 23, 24, 25(a) or (b), 29, 30, 31, or 32.

§ 5.   [APPLICATION] FOR JUDICIAL RELIEF.

(a)   Except as otherwise provided in Section 28, an [application] for judicial relief under this [Act] must be made by [motion] to the court and heard in the manner provided by law or rule of court for making and hearing [motions].

(b) Unless a civil action involving the agreement to arbitrate is pending, notice of an initial [motion] to the court under this [Act] must be served in the manner provided by law for the service of a summons in a civil action. Otherwise, notice of the motion must be given in the manner provided by law or rule of court for serving [motions] in pending cases.

§ 6. VALIDITY OF AGREEMENT TO ARBITRATE.

(a) An agreement contained in a record to submit to arbitration any existing or subsequent controversy arising between the parties to the agreement is valid, enforceable, and irrevocable except upon a ground that exists at law or in equity for the revocation of a contract.

(b) The court shall decide whether an agreement to arbitrate exists or a controversy is subject to an agreement to arbitrate.

(c) An arbitrator shall decide whether a condition precedent to arbitrability has been fulfilled and whether a contract containing a valid agreement to arbitrate is enforceable.

(d) If a party to a judicial proceeding challenges the existence of, or claims that a controversy is not subject to, an agreement to arbitrate, the arbitration proceeding may continue pending final resolution of the issue by the court, unless the court otherwise orders.

§ 7. [MOTION] TO COMPEL OR STAY ARBITRATION.

(a) On [motion] of a person showing an agreement to arbitrate and alleging another person's refusal to arbitrate pursuant to the agreement:

(1) if the refusing party does not appear or does not oppose the [motion], the court shall order the parties to arbitrate; and

(2) if the refusing party opposes the [motion], the court shall proceed summarily to decide the issue and order the parties to arbitrate unless it finds that there is no enforceable agreement to arbitrate.

(b) On [motion] of a person alleging that an arbitration proceeding has been initiated or threatened but that there is no agreement to arbitrate, the court shall proceed summarily to decide the issue. If the court finds that there is an enforceable agreement to arbitrate, it shall order the parties to arbitrate.

(c) If the court finds that there is no enforceable agreement, it may not pursuant to subsection (a) or (b) order the parties to arbitrate.

(d) The court may not refuse to order arbitration because the claim subject to arbitration lacks merit or grounds for the claim have not been established.

(e) If a proceeding involving a claim referable to arbitration under an alleged agreement to arbitrate is pending in court, a [motion] under this section must be made in that court. Otherwise a [motion] under this section may be made in any court as provided in Section 27.

(f)   If a party makes a [motion] to the court to order arbitration, the court on just terms shall stay any judicial proceeding that involves a claim alleged to be subject to the arbitration until the court renders a final decision under this section.

(g)   If the court orders arbitration, the court on just terms shall stay any judicial proceeding that involves a claim subject to the arbitration. If a claim subject to the arbitration is severable, the court may limit the stay to that claim.

§ 8. PROVISIONAL REMEDIES.

(a)   Before an arbitrator is appointed and is authorized and able to act, the court, upon [motion] of a party to an arbitration proceeding and for good cause shown, may enter an order for provisional remedies to protect the effectiveness of the arbitration proceeding to the same extent and under the same conditions as if the controversy were the subject of a civil action.

(b)   After an arbitrator is appointed and is authorized and able to act:

(1)   the arbitrator may issue such orders for provisional remedies, including interim awards, as the arbitrator finds necessary to protect the effectiveness of the arbitration proceeding and to promote the fair and expeditious resolution of the controversy, to the same extent and under the same conditions as if the controversy were the subject of a civil action and

(2)   a party to an arbitration proceeding may move the court for a provisional remedy only if the matter is urgent and the arbitrator is not able to act timely or the arbitrator cannot provide an adequate remedy.

(c)   A party does not waive a right of arbitration by making a [motion] under subsection (a) or (b).

§ 9. INITIATION OF ARBITRATION.

(a)   A person initiates an arbitration proceeding by giving notice in a record to the other parties to the agreement to arbitrate in the agreed manner between the parties or, in the absence of agreement, by certified or registered mail, return receipt requested and obtained, or by service as authorized for the commencement of a civil action. The notice must describe the nature of the controversy and the remedy sought.

(b)   Unless a person objects for lack or insufficiency of notice under Section 15(c) not later than the beginning of the arbitration hearing, the person by appearing at the hearing waives any objection to lack of or insufficiency of notice.

§ 10. CONSOLIDATION OF SEPARATE ARBITRATION PROCEEDINGS.

(a)   Except as otherwise provided in subsection (c), upon [motion] of a party to an agreement to arbitrate or to an arbitration proceeding, the court may order consolidation of separate arbitration proceedings as to all or some of the claims if:

(1)   there are separate agreements to arbitrate or separate arbitration proceedings between the same persons or one of them is a party to a separate agreement to arbitrate or a separate arbitration proceeding with a third person;

(2)   the claims subject to the agreements to arbitrate arise in substantial part from the same transaction or series of related transactions;

(3)   the existence of a common issue of law or fact creates the possibility of conflicting decisions in the separate arbitration proceedings; and

(4)   prejudice resulting from a failure to consolidate is not outweighed by the risk of undue delay or prejudice to the rights of or hardship to parties opposing consolidation.

(b)   The court may order consolidation of separate arbitration proceedings as to some claims and allow other claims to be resolved in separate arbitration proceedings.

(c)   The court may not order consolidation of the claims of a party to an agreement to arbitrate if the agreement prohibits consolidation.

§ 11. APPOINTMENT OF ARBITRATOR; SERVICE AS A NEUTRAL ARBITRATOR.

(a)   If the parties to an agreement to arbitrate agree on a method for appointing an arbitrator, that method must be followed, unless the method fails. If the parties have not agreed on a method, the agreed method fails, or an arbitrator appointed fails or is unable to act and a successor has not been appointed, the court, on [motion] of a party to the arbitration proceeding, shall appoint the arbitrator. An arbitrator so appointed has all the powers of an arbitrator designated in the agreement to arbitrate or appointed pursuant to the agreed method.

(b)   An individual who has a known, direct, and material interest in the outcome of the arbitration proceeding or a known, existing, and substantial relationship with a party may not serve as an arbitrator required by an agreement to be neutral.

§ 12. DISCLOSURE BY ARBITRATOR.

(a)   Before accepting appointment, an individual who is requested to serve as an arbitrator, after making a reasonable inquiry, shall disclose to all parties to the agreement to arbitrate and arbitration proceeding and to any other arbitrators any known facts that a reasonable person would consider likely to affect the impartiality of the arbitrator in the arbitration proceeding, including:

(1) a financial or personal interest in the outcome of the arbitration proceeding; and

(2) an existing or past relationship with any of the parties to the agreement to arbitrate or the arbitration proceeding, their counsel or representatives, a witness, or another arbitrators.

(b) An arbitrator has a continuing obligation to disclose to all parties to the agreement to arbitrate and arbitration proceeding and to any other arbitrators any facts that the arbitrator learns after accepting appointment which a reasonable person would consider likely to affect the impartiality of the arbitrator.

(c) If an arbitrator discloses a fact required by subsection (a) or (b) to be disclosed and a party timely objects to the appointment or continued service of the arbitrator based upon the fact disclosed, the objection may be a ground under Section 23(a)(2) for vacating an award made by the arbitrator.

(d) If the arbitrator did not disclose a fact as required by subsection (a) or (b), upon timely objection by a party, the court under Section 23(a)(2) may vacate an award.

(e) An arbitrator appointed as a neutral arbitrator who does not disclose a known, direct, and material interest in the outcome of the arbitration proceeding or a known, existing, and substantial relationship with a party is presumed to act with evident partiality under Section 23(a)(2).

(f) If the parties to an arbitration proceeding agree to the procedures of an arbitration organization or any other procedures for challenges to arbitrators before an award is made, substantial compliance with those procedures is a condition precedent to a [motion] to vacate an award on that ground under Section 23(a)(2).

§ 13. ACTION BY MAJORITY.

If there is more than one arbitrator, the powers of an arbitrator must be exercised by a majority of the arbitrators, but all of them shall conduct the hearing under Section 15(C).

§ 14. IMMUNITY OF ARBITRATOR; COMPETENCY TO TESTIFY; ATTORNEY'S FEES AND COSTS.

(a) An arbitrator or an arbitration organization acting in that capacity is immune from civil liability to the same extent as a judge of a court of this State acting in a judicial capacity.

(b) The immunity afforded by this section supplements any immunity under other law.

(c) The failure of an arbitrator to make a disclosure required by Section 12 does not cause any loss of immunity under this section.

(d) In a judicial, administrative, or similar proceeding, an arbitrator or representative of an arbitration organization is not competent to testify, and may not be required to produce records as to any statement, conduct, decision, or ruling occurring during the arbitration proceeding, to the same extent as a judge of a court of this State acting in a judicial capacity. This subsection does not apply:

(1) to the extent necessary to determine the claim of an arbitrator, arbitration organization, or representative of the arbitration organization against a party to the arbitration proceeding; or

(2) to a hearing on a [motion] to vacate an award under Section 23(a)(1) or (2) if the [movant] establishes prima facie that a ground for vacating the award exists.

(e) If a person commences a civil action against an arbitrator, arbitration organization, or representative of an arbitration organization arising from the services of the arbitrator, organization, or representative or if a person seeks to compel an arbitrator or a representative of an arbitration organization to testify or produce records in violation of subsection (d), and the court decides that the arbitrator, arbitration organization, or representative of an arbitration organization is immune from civil liability or that the arbitrator or representative of the organization is not competent to testify, the court shall award to the arbitrator, organization, or representative reasonable attorney's fees and other reasonable expenses of litigation.

§ 15. ARBITRATION PROCESS.

(a) An arbitrator may conduct an arbitration in such manner as the arbitrator considers appropriate for a fair and expeditious disposition of the proceeding. The authority conferred upon the arbitrator includes the power to hold conferences with the parties to the arbitration proceeding before the hearing and, among other matters, determine the admissibility, relevance, materiality and weight of any evidence.

(b) An arbitrator may decide a request for summary disposition of a claim or particular issue:

(1) if all interested parties agree; or

(2) upon request of one party to the arbitration proceeding if that party gives notice to all other parties to the proceeding, and the other parties have a reasonable opportunity to respond.

(c) If an arbitrator orders a hearing, the arbitrator shall set a time and place and give notice of the hearing not less than five days before the hearing begins. Unless a party to the arbitration proceeding makes an objection to lack or insufficiency of notice not later than the beginning of the hearing, the party's appearance at the hearing waives the objection. Upon request of a party to the arbitration proceeding and for good cause shown, or upon the arbitrator's own initiative, the arbitrator may adjourn the hearing from time to time as necessary but may not postpone the hearing to a time later than that fixed by the agreement to arbitrate for making the award unless the parties to the arbitration proceeding consent to a later date. The arbitrator may hear and decide the controversy upon the evidence produced although a party who was duly notified of the arbitration proceeding did not appear. The court, on request, may direct the arbitrator to conduct the hearing promptly and render a timely decision.

(d) At a hearing under subsection (c), a party to the arbitration proceeding has a right to be heard, to present evidence material to the controversy, and to cross-examine witnesses appearing at the hearing.

(e) If an arbitrator ceases or is unable to act during the arbitration proceeding, a replacement arbitrator must be appointed in accordance with Section 11 to continue the proceeding and to resolve the controversy.

§ 16. REPRESENTATION BY LAWYER.

A party to an arbitration proceeding may be represented by a lawyer.

§ 17. WITNESSES; SUBPOENAS; DEPOSITIONS; DISCOVERY.

(a) An arbitrator may issue a subpoena for the attendance of a witness and for the production of records and other evidence at any hearing and may administer oaths. A subpoena must be served in the manner for service of subpoenas in a civil action and, upon [motion] to the court by a party to the arbitration proceeding or the arbitrator, enforced in the manner for enforcement of subpoenas in a civil action.

(b) In order to make the proceedings fair, expeditious, and cost effective, upon request of a party to or a witness in an arbitration proceeding, an arbitrator may permit a deposition of any witness to be taken for use as evidence at the hearing, including a witness who cannot be subpoenaed for or is unable to attend a hearing. The arbitrator shall determine the conditions under which the deposition is taken.

(c) An arbitrator may permit such discovery as the arbitrator decides is appropriate in the circumstances, taking into account the needs of the parties to the arbitration proceeding and other affected persons and the desirability of making the proceeding fair, expeditious, and cost effective.

(d) If an arbitrator permits discovery under subsection (c), the arbitrator may order a party to the arbitration proceeding to comply with the arbitrator's discovery-related orders, issue subpoenas for the attendance of a witness and for the production of records and other evidence at a discovery proceeding, and take action against a noncomplying party to the extent a court could if the controversy were the subject of a civil action in this State.

(e) An arbitrator may issue a protective order to prevent the disclosure of privileged information, confidential information, trade secrets, and other information protected from disclosure to the extent a court could if the controversy were the subject of a civil action in this State.

(f) All laws compelling a person under subpoena to testify and all fees for attending a judicial proceeding, a deposition, or a discovery proceeding as a witness apply to an arbitration proceeding as if the controversy were the subject of a civil action in this State.

(g) The court may enforce a subpoena or discovery-related order for the attendance of a witness within this State and for the production of records and other evidence issued by an arbitrator in connection with an arbitration proceeding in another State upon conditions determined by the court so as to make the arbitration proceeding fair, expeditious, and cost effective. A subpoena or discovery-related order issued by an arbitrator in another State must be served in the manner provided by law for service of subpoenas in a civil action in this State and, upon [motion] to the court by a party to the arbitration proceeding or the arbitrator, enforced in the manner provided by law for enforcement of subpoenas in a civil action in this State.

§ 18. JUDICIAL ENFORCEMENT OF PREAWARD RULING BY ARBITRATOR.

If an arbitrator makes a preaward ruling in favor of a party to the arbitration proceeding, the party may request the arbitrator to incorporate the ruling into an award under Section 19. A prevailing party may make a [motion] to the court for an expedited order to confirm the award under Section 22, in which case the court shall summarily decide the [motion]. The court shall issue an order to confirm the award unless the court vacates, modifies, or corrects the award under Section 23 or 24.

§ 19. AWARD.

(a) An arbitrator shall make a record of an award. The record must be signed or otherwise authenticated by any arbitrator who concurs with the award. The arbitrator or the arbitration organization shall give notice of the award, including a copy of the award, to each party to the arbitration proceeding.

(b) An award must be made within the time specified by the agreement to arbitrate or, if not specified therein, within the time ordered by the court. The court may extend or the parties to the arbitration proceeding may agree in a record to extend the time. The court or the parties may do so within or after the time specified or ordered. A party waives any objection that an award was not timely made unless the party gives notice of the objection to the arbitrator before receiving notice of the award.

§ 20. CHANGE OF AWARD BY ARBITRATOR.

(a)   On [motion] to an arbitrator by a party to an arbitration proceeding, the arbitrator may modify or correct an award:

  (1)   upon a ground stated in Section 24(a)(1) or (3);

  (2)   because the arbitrator has not made a final and definite award upon a claim submitted by the parties to the arbitration proceeding; or

  (3)   to clarify the award.

(b)   A [motion] under subsection (a) must be made and notice given to all parties within 20 days after the movant receives notice of the award.

(c)   A party to the arbitration proceeding must give notice of any objection to the [motion] within 10 days after receipt of the notice.

(d)   If a [motion] to the court is pending under Section 22, 23, or 24, the court may submit the claim to the arbitrator to consider whether to modify or correct the award:

  (1)   upon a ground stated in Section 24(a)(1) or (3);

  (2)   because the arbitrator has not made a final and definite award upon a claim submitted by the parties to the arbitration proceeding; or

  (3)   to clarify the award.

(e)   An award modified or corrected pursuant to this section is subject to Sections 19(a), 22, 23, and 24.

§ 21. REMEDIES; FEES AND EXPENSES OF ARBITRATION PROCEEDING.

(a)   An arbitrator may award punitive damages or other exemplary relief if such an award is authorized by law in a civil action involving the same claim and the evidence produced at the hearing justifies the award under the legal standards otherwise applicable to the claim.

(b)   An arbitrator may award reasonable attorney's fees and other reasonable expenses of arbitration if such an award is authorized by law in a civil action involving the same claim or by the agreement of the parties to the arbitration proceeding.

(c)   As to all remedies other than those authorized by subsections (a) and (b), an arbitrator may order such remedies as the arbitrator considers just and appropriate under the circumstances of the arbitration proceeding. The fact that such a remedy could not or would not be granted by the court is not a ground for refusing to confirm an award under Section 22 or for vacating an award under Section 23.

(d) An arbitrator's expenses and fees, together with other expenses, must be paid as provided in the award.

(e) If an arbitrator awards punitive damages or other exemplary relief under subsection (a), the arbitrator shall specify in the award the basis in fact justifying and the basis in law authorizing the award and state separately the amount of the punitive damages or other exemplary relief.

§ 22. CONFIRMATION OF AWARD.

After a party to an arbitration proceeding receives notice of an award, the party may make a [motion] to the court for an order confirming the award at which time the court shall issue a confirming order unless the award is modified or corrected pursuant to Section 20 or 24 or is vacated pursuant to Section 23.

§ 23. VACATING AWARD.

(a) Upon [motion] to the court by a party to an arbitration proceeding, the court shall vacate an award made in the arbitration proceeding if:

(1) the award was procured by corruption, fraud, or other undue means;

(2) there was:

(A) evident partiality by an arbitrator appointed as a neutral arbitrator;

(B) corruption by an arbitrator; or

(C) misconduct by an arbitrator prejudicing the rights of a party to the arbitration proceeding;

(3) an arbitrator refused to postpone the hearing upon showing of sufficient cause for postponement, refused to consider evidence material to the controversy, or otherwise conducted the hearing contrary to Section 15, so as to prejudice substantially the rights of a party to the arbitration proceeding;

(4) an arbitrator exceeded the arbitrator's powers;

(5) there was no agreement to arbitrate, unless the person participated in the arbitration proceeding without raising the objection under Section 15(c) not later than the beginning of the arbitration hearing; or

(6) the arbitration was conducted without proper notice of the initiation of an arbitration as required in Section 9 so as to prejudice substantially the rights of a party to the arbitration proceeding.

(b) A [motion] under this section must be filed within 90 days after the [movant] receives notice of the award pursuant to Section 19 or within 90 days after the [movant] receives notice of a modified or corrected award pursuant to Section 20, unless the [movant] alleges that the award was procured by corruption, fraud, or other undue means, in which case the [motion] must be made within 90 days after the ground is known or by the exercise of reasonable care would have been known by the [movant].

(c) If the court vacates an award on a ground other than that set forth in subsection (a)(5), it may order a rehearing. If the award is vacated on a ground stated in subsection (a)(1) or (2), the rehearing must be before a new arbitrator. If the award is vacated on a ground stated in subsection (a)(3), (4), or (6), the rehearing may be before the arbitrator who made the award or the arbitrator's successor. The arbitrator must render the decision in the rehearing within the same time as that provided in Section 19(b) for an award.

(d) If the court denies a [motion] to vacate an award, it shall confirm the award unless a [motion] to modify or correct the award is pending.

§ 24. Modification or Correction of Award.

(a) Upon [motion] made within 90 days after the [movant] receives notice of the award pursuant to Section 19 or within 90 days after the [movant] receives notice of a modified or corrected award pursuant to Section 20, the court shall modify or correct the award if:

(1) there was an evident mathematical miscalculation or an evident mistake in the description of a person, thing, or property referred to in the award;

(2) the arbitrator has made an award on a claim not submitted to the arbitrator and the award may be corrected without affecting the merits of the decision upon the claims submitted; or

(3) the award is imperfect in a matter of form not affecting the merits of the decision on the claims submitted.

(b) If a [motion] made under subsection (a) is granted, the court shall modify or correct and confirm the award as modified or corrected. Otherwise, unless a motion to vacate is pending, the court shall confirm the award.

(c) A [motion] to modify or correct an award pursuant to this section may be joined with a [motion] to vacate the award.

§ 25. Judgment on Award; Attorney's Fees and Litigation Expenses.

(a) Upon granting an order confirming, vacating without directing a rehearing, modifying, or correcting an award, the court shall enter a judgment in conformity therewith. The judgment may be recorded, docketed, and enforced as any other judgment in a civil action.

(b) A court may allow reasonable costs of the [motion] and subsequent judicial proceedings.

(c) On [application] of a prevailing party to a contested judicial proceeding under Section 22, 23, or 24, the court may add reasonable attorney's fees and other reasonable expenses of litigation incurred in a judicial proceeding after the award is made to a judgment confirming, vacating without directing a rehearing, modifying, or correcting an award.

§ 26. JURISDICTION.

(a) A court of this State having jurisdiction over the controversy and the parties may enforce an agreement to arbitrate.

(b) An agreement to arbitrate providing for arbitration in this State confers exclusive jurisdiction on the court to enter judgment on an award under this [Act].

§ 27. VENUE.

A [motion] pursuant to Section 5 must be made in the court of the [county] in which the agreement to arbitrate specifies the arbitration hearing is to be held or, if the hearing has been held, in the court of the [county] in which it was held. Otherwise, the [motion] may be made in the court of any [county] in which an adverse party resides or has a place of business or, if no adverse party has a residence or place of business in this state, in the court of any [county] in this state. All subsequent [motions] must be made in the court hearing the initial [motion] unless the court otherwise directs.

§ 28. APPEALS.

(a) An appeal may be taken from:

(1) an order denying a [motion] to compel arbitration;

(2) an order granting a [motion] to stay arbitration;

(3) an order confirming or denying confirmation of an award;

(4) an order modifying or correcting an award;

(5) an order vacating an award without directing a rehearing; or

(6) a final judgment entered pursuant to this [Act].

(b) An appeal under this section must be taken as from an order or a judgment in a civil action.

§ 29. UNIFORMITY OF APPLICATION AND CONSTRUCTION.

In applying and construing this uniform act, consideration must be given to the need to promote uniformity of the law with respect to its subject matter among States that enact it.

§ 30. RELATIONSHIP TO ELECTRONIC SIGNATURES IN GLOBAL AND NATIONAL COMMERCE ACT.

The provisions of this Act governing the legal effect, validity, and enforceability of electronic records or electronic signatures, and of contracts performed with the use of such records or signatures conform to the requirements of Section 102 of the Electronic Signatures in Global and National Commerce Act.

§ 31. EFFECTIVE DATE.

This [Act] takes effect on [effective date].

§ 32. REPEAL.

Effective on [delayed date should be the same as that in Section 3(C)], the [Uniform Arbitration Act] is repealed.

§ 33. SAVINGS CLAUSE.

This [Act] does not affect an action or proceeding commenced or right accrued before this [Act] takes effect. Subject to Section 3 of this [Act], an arbitration agreement made before the effective date of this [Act] is governed by the [Uniform Arbitration Act].

UNIFORM CHILD ABDUCTION PREVENTION ACT (2006)

9 U.L.A. Pt. IA 49 (Supp. 2015)

[EDITORS' INTRODUCTION: Katrina M. Parra, *The Need for Exit Controls to Prevent International Child Abduction from the United States*, 31 WHITTIER L. REV. 817 (2010); Blake Sherer, *The Maturation of International Child Abduction Law: From the Hague Convention to the Uniform Abduction Prevention Act*, 26 J. AM. ACAD. MATRIM. LAW. 137 (2013); Robert A. Stein, *Strengthening Federalism: The Uniform State Law Movement in the United States*, 99 MINN. L. REV. 2253 (2015).]

§ 1. SHORT TITLE

This [act] may be cited as the Uniform Child Abduction Prevention Act.

§ 2. DEFINITIONS

In this [act]:

(1) "Abduction" means the wrongful removal or wrongful retention of a child.

(2) "Child" means an unemancipated individual who is less than 18 years of age.

(3) "Child-custody determination" means a judgment, decree, or other order of a court providing for the legal custody, physical custody, or visitation with respect to a child. The term includes a permanent, temporary, initial, and modification order.

(4) "Child-custody proceeding" means a proceeding in which legal custody, physical custody, or visitation with respect to a child is at issue. The term includes a proceeding for divorce, dissolution of marriage, separation, neglect, abuse, dependency, guardianship, paternity, termination of parental rights, or protection from domestic violence.

(5) "Court" means an entity authorized under the law of a state to establish, enforce, or modify a child-custody determination.

(6) "Petition" includes a motion or its equivalent.

(7) "Record" means information that is inscribed on a tangible medium or that is stored in an electronic or other medium and is retrievable in perceivable form.

(8) "State" means a state of the United States, the District of Columbia, Puerto Rico, the United States Virgin Islands, or any territory or insular possession subject to the jurisdiction of the United States. The term includes a federally recognized Indian tribe or nation.

(9) "Travel document" means records relating to a travel itinerary, including travel tickets, passes, reservations for

transportation, or accommodations. The term does not include a passport or visa.

(10) "Wrongful removal" means the taking of a child that breaches rights of custody or visitation given or recognized under the law of this state.

(11) "Wrongful retention" means the keeping or concealing of a child that breaches rights of custody or visitation given or recognized under the law of this state.

§ 3.   COOPERATION AND COMMUNICATION AMONG COURTS

Sections [110], [111], and [112] of [insert citation to the provisions of the Uniform Child Custody Jurisdiction and Enforcement Act or its equivalent in the state] apply to cooperation and communications among courts in proceedings under this [act].

§ 4.   ACTIONS FOR ABDUCTION PREVENTION MEASURES

(a) A court on its own motion may order abduction prevention measures in a child-custody proceeding if the court finds that the evidence establishes a credible risk of abduction of the child.

(b) A party to a child-custody determination or another individual or entity having a right under the law of this state or any other state to seek a child-custody determination for the child may file a petition seeking abduction prevention measures to protect the child under this [act].

(c) A prosecutor or public authority designated under [insert citation to Section 315 of the Uniform Child Custody Jurisdiction and Enforcement Act or applicable law of this state] may seek a warrant to take physical custody of a child under Section 9 or other appropriate prevention measures.

§ 5.   JURISDICTION

(a) A petition under this [act] may be filed only in a court that has jurisdiction to make a child-custody determination with respect to the child at issue under [insert citation to Uniform Child Custody Jurisdiction and Enforcement Act or the Uniform Child Custody Jurisdiction Act].

(b) A court of this state has temporary emergency jurisdiction under [insert citation to Section 204 of the Uniform Child Custody Jurisdiction and Enforcement Act or Section 3(a)(3) of the Uniform Child Custody Jurisdiction Act] if the court finds a credible risk of abduction.

§ 6.   CONTENTS OF PETITION

A petition under this [act] must be verified and include a copy of any existing child-custody determination, if available. The petition must specify the risk factors for abduction, including the relevant factors described in Section 7. Subject to [insert citation to Section 209(e) of the Uniform Child Custody Jurisdiction and Enforcement Act or cite the law of this state providing for the confidentiality of procedures, addresses, and other identifying information], if reasonably ascertainable, the petition must contain:

(1)   the name, date of birth, and gender of the child;

(2)   the customary address and current physical location of the child;

(3)   the identity, customary address, and current physical location of the respondent;

(4)   a statement of whether a prior action to prevent abduction or domestic violence has been filed by a party or other individual or entity having custody of the child, and the date, location, and disposition of the action;

(5)   a statement of whether a party to the proceeding has been arrested for a crime related to domestic violence, stalking, or child abuse or neglect, and the date, location, and disposition of the case; and

(6)   any other information required to be submitted to the court for a child-custody determination under [insert citation to Section 209 of the Uniform Child Custody Jurisdiction and Enforcement Act or applicable law of this state].

§ 7.   FACTORS TO DETERMINE RISK OF ABDUCTION

(a)   In determining whether there is a credible risk of abduction of a child, the court shall consider any evidence that the petitioner or respondent:

(1)   has previously abducted or attempted to abduct the child;

(2)   has threatened to abduct the child;

(3)   has recently engaged in activities that may indicate a planned abduction, including:

(A)   abandoning employment;

(B)   selling a primary residence;

(C)   terminating a lease;

(D)   closing bank or other financial management accounts, liquidating assets, hiding or destroying financial documents, or conducting any unusual financial activities;

(E)   applying for a passport or visa or obtaining travel documents for the respondent, a family member, or the child; or

(F)   seeking to obtain the child's birth certificate or school or medical records;

(4) has engaged in domestic violence, stalking, or child abuse or neglect;

(5) has refused to follow a child-custody determination;

(6) lacks strong familial, financial, emotional, or cultural ties to the state or the United States;

(7) has strong familial, financial, emotional, or cultural ties to another state or country;

(8) is likely to take the child to a country that:

(A) is not a party to the Hague Convention on the Civil Aspects of International Child Abduction and does not provide for the extradition of an abducting parent or for the return of an abducted child;

(B) is a party to the Hague Convention on the Civil Aspects of International Child Abduction but:

(i) the Hague Convention on the Civil Aspects of International Child Abduction is not in force between the United States and that country;

(ii) is noncompliant according to the most recent compliance report issued by the United States Department of State; or

(iii) lacks legal mechanisms for immediately and effectively enforcing a return order under the Hague Convention on the Civil Aspects of International Child Abduction;

(C) poses a risk that the child's physical or emotional health or safety would be endangered in the country because of specific circumstances relating to the child or because of human rights violations committed against children;

(D) has laws or practices that would:

(i) enable the respondent, without due cause, to prevent the petitioner from contacting the child;

(ii) restrict the petitioner from freely traveling to or exiting from the country because of the petitioner's gender, nationality, marital status, or religion; or

(iii) restrict the child's ability legally to leave the country after the child reaches the age of majority because of a child's gender, nationality, or religion;

(E) is included by the United States Department of State on a current list of state sponsors of terrorism;

(F) does not have an official United States diplomatic presence in the country; or

(G) is engaged in active military action or war, including a civil war, to which the child may be exposed;

(9) is undergoing a change in immigration or citizenship status that would adversely affect the respondent's ability to remain in the United States legally;

(10) has had an application for United States citizenship denied;

(11) has forged or presented misleading or false evidence on government forms or supporting documents to obtain or attempt to obtain a passport, a visa, travel documents, a Social Security card, a driver's license, or other government-issued identification card or has made a misrepresentation to the United States government;

(12) has used multiple names to attempt to mislead or defraud; or

(13) has engaged in any other conduct the court considers relevant to the risk of abduction.

(b) In the hearing on a petition under this [act], the court shall consider any evidence that the respondent believed in good faith that the respondent's conduct was necessary to avoid imminent harm to the child or respondent and any other evidence that may be relevant to whether the respondent may be permitted to remove or retain the child.

§ 8.   Provisions and Measures to Prevent Abduction

(a) If a petition is filed under this [act], the court may enter an order that must include:

(1) the basis for the court's exercise of jurisdiction;

(2) the manner in which notice and opportunity to be heard were given to the persons entitled to notice of the proceeding;

(3) a detailed description of each party's custody and visitation rights and residential arrangements for the child;

(4) a provision stating that a violation of the order may subject the party in violation to civil and criminal penalties; and

(5) identification of the child's country of habitual residence at the time of the issuance of the order.

(b) If, at a hearing on a petition under this [act] or on the court's own motion, the court after reviewing the evidence finds a credible risk of abduction of the child, the court shall enter an abduction prevention order. The order must include the provisions required by subsection (a) and measures and conditions, including those in subsections (c), (d), and (e), that are reasonably calculated to prevent abduction of the child, giving due consideration to the custody and visitation rights of the parties. The court shall consider the age of the child, the potential harm to the child from an abduction, the legal and practical difficulties of returning the child to the jurisdiction if abducted, and the reasons for the potential abduction, including evidence of domestic violence, stalking, or child abuse or neglect.

(c) An abduction prevention order may include one or more of the following:

(1) an imposition of travel restrictions that require that a party traveling with the child outside a designated geographical area provide the other party with the following:

(A) the travel itinerary of the child;

(B) a list of physical addresses and telephone numbers at which the child can be reached at specified times; and

(C) copies of all travel documents;

(2) a prohibition of the respondent directly or indirectly:

(A) removing the child from this state, the United States, or another geographic area without permission of the court or the petitioner's written consent;

(B) removing or retaining the child in violation of a child-custody determination;

(C) removing the child from school or a child-care or similar facility; or

(D) approaching the child at any location other than a site designated for supervised visitation;

(3) a requirement that a party register the order in another state as a prerequisite to allowing the child to travel to that state;

(4) with regard to the child's passport:

(A) a direction that the petitioner place the child's name in the United States Department of State's Child Passport Issuance Alert Program;

(B) a requirement that the respondent surrender to the court or the petitioner's attorney any United States or foreign passport issued in the child's name, including a passport issued in the name of both the parent and the child; and

(C) a prohibition upon the respondent from applying on behalf of the child for a new or replacement passport or visa;

(5) as a prerequisite to exercising custody or visitation, a requirement that the respondent provide:

(A) to the United States Department of State Office of Children's Issues and the relevant foreign consulate or embassy, an authenticated copy of the order detailing passport and travel restrictions for the child;

(B) to the court:

(i) proof that the respondent has provided the information in subparagraph (A); and

(ii) an acknowledgment in a record from the relevant foreign consulate or embassy that no passport application has been made, or passport issued, on behalf of the child;

(C) to the petitioner, proof of registration with the United States Embassy or other United States diplomatic presence in the destination country and with the Central Authority for the Hague Convention on the Civil Aspects of International Child Abduction, if that Convention is in effect between the United States and the destination country, unless one of the parties objects; and

(D) a written waiver under the Privacy Act, 5 U.S.C. Section 552a [as amended], with respect to any document, application, or other information pertaining to the child authorizing its disclosure to the court and the petitioner; and

(6) upon the petitioner's request, a requirement that the respondent obtain an order from the relevant foreign country containing terms identical to the child-custody determination issued in the United States.

(d) In an abduction prevention order, the court may impose conditions on the exercise of custody or visitation that:

(1) limit visitation or require that visitation with the child by the respondent be supervised until the court finds that supervision is no longer necessary and order the respondent to pay the costs of supervision;

(2) require the respondent to post a bond or provide other security in an amount sufficient to serve as a financial deterrent to abduction, the proceeds of which may be used to pay for the reasonable expenses of recovery of the child, including reasonable attorneys fees and costs if there is an abduction; and

(3) require the respondent to obtain education on the potentially harmful effects to the child from abduction.

(e) To prevent imminent abduction of a child, a court may:

(1) issue a warrant to take physical custody of the child under Section 9 or the law of this state other than this [act];

(2) direct the use of law enforcement to take any action reasonably necessary to locate the child, obtain return of the child, or enforce a custody determination under this [act] or the law of this state other than this [act]; or

(3) grant any other relief allowed under the law of this state other than this [act].

(f)   The remedies provided in this [act] are cumulative and do not affect the availability of other remedies to prevent abduction.

§ 9.   WARRANT TO TAKE PHYSICAL CUSTODY OF CHILD

(a)   If a petition under this [act] contains allegations, and the court finds that there is a credible risk that the child is imminently likely to be wrongfully removed, the court may issue an ex parte warrant to take physical custody of the child.

(b)   The respondent on a petition under subsection (a) must be afforded an opportunity to be heard at the earliest possible time after the ex parte warrant is executed, but not later than the next judicial day unless a hearing on that date is impossible. In that event, the court shall hold the hearing on the first judicial day possible.

(c)   An ex parte warrant under subsection (a) to take physical custody of a child must:

(1)   recite the facts upon which a determination of a credible risk of imminent wrongful removal of the child is based;

(2)   direct law enforcement officers to take physical custody of the child immediately;

(3)   state the date and time for the hearing on the petition; and

(4)   provide for the safe interim placement of the child pending further order of the court.

(d)   If feasible, before issuing a warrant and before determining the placement of the child after the warrant is executed, the court may order a search of the relevant databases of the National Crime Information Center system and similar state databases to determine if either the petitioner or respondent has a history of domestic violence, stalking, or child abuse or neglect.

(e)   The petition and warrant must be served on the respondent when or immediately after the child is taken into physical custody.

(f)   A warrant to take physical custody of a child, issued by this state or another state, is enforceable throughout this state. If the court finds that a less intrusive remedy will not be effective, it may authorize law enforcement officers to enter private property to take physical custody of the child. If required by exigent circumstances, the court may authorize law enforcement officers to make a forcible entry at any hour.

(g)   If the court finds, after a hearing, that a petitioner sought an ex parte warrant under subsection (a) for the purpose of harassment or in bad faith, the court may award the respondent reasonable attorney's fees, costs, and expenses.

(h)   This [act] does not affect the availability of relief allowed under the law of this state other than this [act].

§ 10. DURATION OF ABDUCTION PREVENTION ORDER

An abduction prevention order remains in effect until the earliest of:

(1) the time stated in the order;

(2) the emancipation of the child;

(3) the child's attaining 18 years of age; or

(4) the time the order is modified, revoked, vacated, or superseded by a court with jurisdiction under [insert citation to Sections 201 through 203 of the Uniform Child Custody Jurisdiction and Enforcement Act or Section 3 of the Uniform Child Custody Jurisdiction Act and applicable law of this state].

§ 11. UNIFORMITY OF APPLICATION AND CONSTRUCTION

In applying and construing this uniform act, consideration must be given to the need to promote uniformity of the law with respect to its subject matter among states that enact it.

§ 12. RELATION TO ELECTRONIC SIGNATURES IN GLOBAL AND NATIONAL COMMERCE ACT

This [act] modifies, limits, and supersedes the federal Electronic Signatures in Global and National Commerce Act, 15 U.S.C. Section 7001, et seq., but does not modify, limit, or supersede Section 101(c) of the act, 15 U.S.C. Section 7001(c), of that act or authorize electronic delivery of any of the notices described in Section 103(b) of that act, 15 U.S.C. Section 7003(b).

* * *

UNIFORM CHILD-CUSTODY JURISDICTION AND ENFORCEMENT ACT (1997)

9 U.L.A. Pt. IA 649 et seq. (1999)

[EDITORS' INTRODUCTION: Andrea Charlow, *There's No Place Like Home: Temporary Absences in the UCCJEA Home State*, 28 J. AM. ACAD. MATRIM. LAW. 25 (2015); Ann Laquer Estin, *Where (in the World) Do Children Belong*, 25 BYU J. PUB. L. 217 (2011); Amy C. Gromek, *Military Child Custody Disputes: The Need for Federal Encouragement for the States' Adoption of the Uniform Deployed Parents Custody and Visitation Act*, 44 SETON HALL L. REV. 873 (2014); Barry B. McGough, Elinor H. Hitt & Katherine S. Cornwell, *Domestic Relations*, 67 MERCER L. REV. 47 (2015); Joan M. Shaughnessy, *The Other Side of the Rabbit Hole: Reconciling Recent Supreme Court Personal Jurisdiction Jurisprudence with Jurisdiction to Terminate Parental Rights*, 19 LEWIS & CLARK L. REV. 811 (2015); Robert G. Spector, *International Abduction of Children: Why the UCCJEA is Usually a Better Remedy than the Abduction Convention*, 49 FAM. L.Q. 385 (2015); Robert G. Spector, *Memorandum: Accommodating the UCCJEA and the 1996 Hague Convention*, 63 OKLA. L. REV. 615 (2011); Merle H. Weiner, *Uprooting Children in the Name of Equity*, 33 FORDHAM INT'L L.J. 409 (2010); Kevin Wessel, *Home Is Where the Court Is: Determining Residence for Child Custody Matters Under the UCCJEA*, 79 U. CHI. L. REV. 1141 (2012).]

[ARTICLE] 1 GENERAL PROVISIONS

§ 101. SHORT TITLE.

This [Act] may be cited as the Uniform Child-Custody Jurisdiction and Enforcement Act.

§ 102. DEFINITIONS.

In this [Act]:

(1) "Abandoned" means left without provision for reasonable and necessary care or supervision.

(2) "Child" means an individual who has not attained 18 years of age.

(3) "Child-custody determination" means a judgment, decree, or other order of a court providing for the legal custody, physical custody, or visitation with respect to a child. The term includes a permanent, temporary, initial, and modification order. The term does not include an order relating to child support or other monetary obligation of an individual.

(4) "Child-custody proceeding" means a proceeding in which legal custody, physical custody, or visitation with respect to a child is an issue. The term includes a proceeding for divorce, separation,

neglect, abuse, dependency, guardianship, paternity, termination of parental rights, and protection from domestic violence, in which the issue may appear. The term does not include a proceeding involving juvenile delinquency, contractual emancipation, or enforcement under [Article] 3.

(5) "Commencement" means the filing of the first pleading in a proceeding.

(6) "Court" means an entity authorized under the law of a State to establish, enforce, or modify a child-custody determination.

(7) "Home State" means the State in which a child lived with a parent or a person acting as a parent for at least six consecutive months immediately before the commencement of a child-custody proceeding. In the case of a child less than six months of age, the term means the State in which the child lived from birth with any of the persons mentioned. A period of temporary absence of any of the mentioned persons is part of the period.

(8) "Initial determination" means the first child-custody determination concerning a particular child.

(9) "Issuing court" means the court that makes a child-custody determination for which enforcement is sought under this [Act].

(10) "Issuing State" means the State in which a child-custody determination is made.

(11) "Modification" means a child-custody determination that changes, replaces, supersedes, or is otherwise made after a previous determination concerning the same child, whether or not it is made by the court that made the previous determination.

(12) "Person" means an individual, corporation, business trust, estate, trust, partnership, limited liability company, association, joint venture, government; governmental subdivision, agency, or instrumentality; public corporation; or any other legal or commercial entity.

(13) "Person acting as a parent" means a person, other than a parent, who:

> (A) has physical custody of the child or has had physical custody for a period of six consecutive months, including any temporary absence, within one year immediately before the commencement of a child-custody proceeding; and

> (B) has been awarded legal custody by a court or claims a right to legal custody under the law of this State.

(14) "Physical custody" means the physical care and supervision of a child.

(15) "State" means a State of the United States, the District of Columbia, Puerto Rico, the United States Virgin Islands, or any

territory or insular possession subject to the jurisdiction of the United States.

(16) "Tribe" means an Indian tribe or band, or Alaskan Native village, which is recognized by federal law or formally acknowledged by a State.

(17) "Warrant" means an order issued by a court authorizing law enforcement officers to take physical custody of a child.

§ 103. PROCEEDINGS GOVERNED BY OTHER LAW.

This [Act] does not govern an adoption proceeding or a proceeding pertaining to the authorization of emergency medical care for a child.

§ 104. APPLICATION TO INDIAN TRIBES.

(a) A child-custody proceeding that pertains to an Indian child as defined in the Indian Child Welfare Act, 25 U.S.C. § 1901 et seq., is not subject to this [Act] to the extent that it is governed by the Indian Child Welfare Act.

[(b) A court of this State shall treat a tribe as if it were a State of the United States for the purpose of applying [Articles] 1 and 2.]

[(c) A child-custody determination made by a tribe under factual circumstances in substantial conformity with the jurisdictional standards of this [Act] must be recognized and enforced under [Article] 3.]

§ 105. INTERNATIONAL APPLICATION OF [ACT].

(a) A court of this State shall treat a foreign country as if it were a State of the United States for the purpose of applying [Articles] 1 and 2.

(b) Except as otherwise provided in subsection (c), a child-custody determination made in a foreign country under factual circumstances in substantial conformity with the jurisdictional standards of this [Act] must be recognized and enforced under [Article] 3.

(c) A court of this State need not apply this [Act] if the child custody law of a foreign country violates fundamental principles of human rights.

§ 106. EFFECT OF CHILD-CUSTODY DETERMINATION.

A child-custody determination made by a court of this State that had jurisdiction under this [Act] binds all persons who have been served in accordance with the laws of this State or notified in accordance with Section 108 or who have submitted to the jurisdiction of the court, and who have been given an opportunity to be heard. As to those persons, the determination is conclusive as to all decided issues of law and fact except to the extent the determination is modified.

§ 107. PRIORITY.

If a question of existence or exercise of jurisdiction under this [Act] is raised in a child-custody proceeding, the question, upon request of a party, must be given priority on the calendar and handled expeditiously.

§ 108. NOTICE TO PERSONS OUTSIDE STATE.

(a)   Notice required for the exercise of jurisdiction when a person is outside this State may be given in a manner prescribed by the law of this State for service of process or by the law of the State in which the service is made. Notice must be given in a manner reasonably calculated to give actual notice but may be by publication if other means are not effective.

(b)   Proof of service may be made in the manner prescribed by the law of this state or by the law of the state in which the service is made.

(c)   Notice is not required for the exercise of jurisdiction with respect to a person who submits to the jurisdiction of the court.

§ 109. APPEARANCE AND LIMITED IMMUNITY.

(a)   A party to a child-custody proceeding, including a modification proceeding, or a petitioner or respondent in a proceeding to enforce or register a child-custody determination, is not subject to personal jurisdiction in this State for another proceeding or purpose solely by reason of having participated, or of having been physically present for the purpose of participating, in the proceeding.

(b)   A person who is subject to personal jurisdiction in this State on a basis other than physical presence is not immune from service of process in this State. A party present in this State who is subject to the jurisdiction of another State is not immune from service of process allowable under the laws of that State.

(c)   The immunity granted by subsection (a) does not extend to civil litigation based on acts unrelated to the participation in a proceeding under this [Act] committed by an individual while present in this State.

§ 110. COMMUNICATION BETWEEN COURTS.

(a)   A court of this State may communicate with a court in another State concerning a proceeding arising under this [Act].

(b)   The court may allow the parties to participate in the communication. If the parties are not able to participate in the communication, they must be given the opportunity to present facts and legal arguments before a decision on jurisdiction is made.

(c)   Communication between courts on schedules, calendars, court records, and similar matters may occur without informing the parties. A record need not be made of the communication.

(d) Except as otherwise provided in subsection (c), a record must be made of a communication under this section. The parties must be informed promptly of the communication and granted access to the record.

(e) For the purposes of this section, "record" means information that is inscribed on a tangible medium or that is stored in an electronic or other medium and is retrievable in perceivable form.

§ 111. TAKING TESTIMONY IN ANOTHER STATE.

(a) In addition to other procedures available to a party, a party to a child-custody proceeding may offer testimony of witnesses who are located in another State, including testimony of the parties and the child, by deposition or other means allowable in this State for testimony taken in another State. The court on its own motion may order that the testimony of a person be taken in another State and may prescribe the manner in which and the terms upon which the testimony is taken.

(b) A court of this State may permit an individual residing in another State to be deposed or to testify by telephone, audiovisual means, or other electronic means before a designated court or at another location in that State. A court of this State shall cooperate with courts of other States in designating an appropriate location for the deposition or testimony.

(c) Documentary evidence transmitted from another State to a court of this State by technological means that do not produce an original writing may not be excluded from evidence on an objection based on the means of transmission.

§ 112. COOPERATION BETWEEN COURTS; PRESERVATION OF RECORDS.

(a) A court of this State may request the appropriate court of another State to:

(1) hold an evidentiary hearing;

(2) order a person to produce or give evidence pursuant to procedures of that State;

(3) order that an evaluation be made with respect to the custody of a child involved in a pending proceeding;

(4) forward to the court of this State a certified copy of the transcript of the record of the hearing, the evidence otherwise presented, and any evaluation prepared in compliance with the request; and

(5) order a party to a child-custody proceeding or any person having physical custody of the child to appear in the proceeding with or without the child.

(b)   Upon request of a court of another State, a court of this State may hold a hearing or enter an order described in subsection (a).

(c)   Travel and other necessary and reasonable expenses incurred under subsections (a) and (b) may be assessed against the parties according to the law of this State.

(d)   A court of this State shall preserve the pleadings, orders, decrees, records of hearings, evaluations, and other pertinent records with respect to a child-custody proceeding until the child attains 18 years of age. Upon appropriate request by a court or law enforcement official of another State, the court shall forward a certified copy of those records.

[ARTICLE] 2 JURISDICTION

§ 201. INITIAL CHILD-CUSTODY JURISDICTION.

(a)   Except as otherwise provided in Section 204, a court of this State has jurisdiction to make an initial child-custody determination only if:

(1)   this State is the home State of the child on the date of the commencement of the proceeding, or was the home State of the child within six months before the commencement of the proceeding and the child is absent from this State but a parent or person acting as a parent continues to live in this State;

(2)   a court of another State does not have jurisdiction under paragraph (1), or a court of the home State of the child has declined to exercise jurisdiction on the ground that this State is the more appropriate forum under Section 207 or 208, and:

(A)   the child and the child's parents, or the child and at least one parent or a person acting as a parent, have a significant connection with this State other than mere physical presence; and

(B)   substantial evidence is available in this State concerning the child's care, protection, training, and personal relationships;

(3)   all courts having jurisdiction under paragraph (1) or (2) have declined to exercise jurisdiction on the ground that a court of this State is the more appropriate forum to determine the custody of the child under Section 207 or 208; or

(4)   no court of any other State would have jurisdiction under the criteria specified in paragraph (1), (2), or (3).

(b)   Subsection (a) is the exclusive jurisdictional basis for making a child-custody determination by a court of this State.

(c)   Physical presence of, or personal jurisdiction over, a party or a child is not necessary or sufficient to make a child-custody determination.

§ 202. EXCLUSIVE, CONTINUING JURISDITION.

(a)   Except as otherwise provided in Section 204, a court of this State which has made a child-custody determination consistent with Section 201 or 203 has exclusive, continuing jurisdiction over the determination until:

> (1)   a court of this State determines that neither the child, nor the child and one parent, nor the child and a person acting as a parent have a significant connection with this State and that substantial evidence is no longer available in this State concerning the child's care, protection, training, and personal relationships; or

> (2)   a court of this State or a court of another State determines that the child, the child's parents, and any person acting as a parent do not presently reside in this State.

(b) A court of this State which has made a child-custody determination and does not have exclusive, continuing jurisdiction under this section may modify that determination only if it has jurisdiction to make an initial determination under Section 201.

§ 203. JURISDICTION TO MODIFY DETERMINATION.

Except as otherwise provided in Section 204, a court of this State may not modify a child-custody determination made by a court of another State unless a court of this State has jurisdiction to make an initial determination under Section 201(a)(1) or (2) and:

> (1)   the court of the other State determines it no longer has exclusive, continuing jurisdiction under Section 202 or that a court of this State would be a more convenient forum under Section 207; or

> (2)   a court of this State or a court of the other State determines that the child, the child's parents, and any person acting as a parent do not presently reside in the other State.

§ 204. TEMPORARY EMERGENCY JURISDICTION.

(a)   A court of this State has temporary emergency jurisdiction if the child is present in this State and the child has been abandoned or it is necessary in an emergency to protect the child because the child, or a sibling or parent of the child, is subjected to or threatened with mistreatment or abuse.

(b) If there is no previous child-custody determination that is entitled to be enforced under this [Act] and a child-custody proceeding has not been commenced in a court of a State having jurisdiction under Sections 201 through 203, a child-custody determination made under this section remains in effect until an order is obtained from a court of a State having jurisdiction under Sections 201 through 203. If a child-custody proceeding has not been or is not commenced in a court of a State having jurisdiction under Sections 201 through 203, a child-custody determination made under this section becomes a final determination, if it so provides and this State becomes the home State of the child.

(c) If there is a previous child-custody determination that is entitled to be enforced under this [Act], or a child-custody proceeding has been commenced in a court of a State having jurisdiction under Sections 201 through 203, any order issued by a court of this State under this section must specify in the order a period that the court considers adequate to allow the person seeking an order to obtain an order from the State having jurisdiction under Sections 201 through 203. The order issued in this State remains in effect until an order is obtained from the other State within the period specified or the period expires.

(d) A court of this State which has been asked to make a child-custody determination under this section, upon being informed that a child-custody proceeding has been commenced in, or a child-custody determination has been made by, a court of a State having jurisdiction under Sections 201 through 203, shall immediately communicate with the other court. A court of this State which is exercising jurisdiction pursuant to Sections 201 through 203, upon being informed that a child-custody proceeding has been commenced in, or a child-custody determination has been made by, a court of another State under a statute similar to this section shall immediately communicate with the court of that State to resolve the emergency, protect the safety of the parties and the child, and determine a period for the duration of the temporary order.

§ 205. NOTICE; OPPORTUNITY TO BE HEARD; JOINDER.

(a) Before a child-custody determination is made under this [Act], notice and an opportunity to be heard in accordance with the standards of Section 108 must be given to all persons entitled to notice under the law of this State as in child-custody proceedings between residents of this State, any parent whose parental rights have not been previously terminated, and any person having physical custody of the child.

(b) This [Act] does not govern the enforceability of a child-custody determination made without notice or an opportunity to be heard.

(c) The obligation to join a party and the right to intervene as a party in a child-custody proceeding under this [Act] are governed by the law of this State as in child-custody proceedings between residents of this State.

§ 206. SIMULTANEOUS PROCEEDINGS.

(a) Except as otherwise provided in Section 204, a court of this State may not exercise its jurisdiction under this [article] if, at the time of the commencement of the proceeding, a proceeding concerning the custody of the child has been commenced in a court of another State having jurisdiction substantially in conformity with this [Act], unless the proceeding has been terminated or is stayed by the court of the other State because a court of this State is a more convenient forum under Section 207.

(b) Except as otherwise provided in Section 204, a court of this State, before hearing a child-custody proceeding, shall examine the court documents and other information supplied by the parties pursuant to Section 209. If the court determines that a child-custody proceeding has been commenced in a court in another State having jurisdiction substantially in accordance with this [Act], the court of this State shall stay its proceeding and communicate with the court of the other State. If the court of the State having jurisdiction substantially in accordance with this [Act] does not determine that the court of this State is a more appropriate forum, the court of this State shall dismiss the proceeding.

(c) In a proceeding to modify a child-custody determination, a court of this State shall determine whether a proceeding to enforce the determination has been commenced in another State. If a proceeding to enforce a child-custody determination has been commenced in another State, the court may:

(1) stay the proceeding for modification pending the entry of an order of a court of the other State enforcing, staying, denying, or dismissing the proceeding for enforcement;

(2) enjoin the parties from continuing with the proceeding for enforcement; or

(3) proceed with the modification under conditions it considers appropriate.

§ 207. INCONVENIENT FORUM.

(a) A court of this State which has jurisdiction under this [Act] to make a child-custody determination may decline to exercise its jurisdiction at any time if it determines that it is an inconvenient forum under the circumstances and that a court of another State is a more appropriate forum. The issue of inconvenient forum may be raised upon motion of a party, the court's own motion, or request of another court.

(b) Before determining whether it is an inconvenient forum, a court of this State shall consider whether it is appropriate for a court of another State to exercise jurisdiction. For this purpose, the court shall allow the parties to submit information and shall consider all relevant factors, including:

(1) whether domestic violence has occurred and is likely to continue in the future and which State could best protect the parties and the child;

(2) the length of time the child has resided outside this State;

(3) the distance between the court in this State and the court in the State that would assume jurisdiction;

(4)   the relative financial circumstances of the parties;

(5)   any agreement of the parties as to which State should assume jurisdiction;

(6)   the nature and location of the evidence required to resolve the pending litigation, including testimony of the child;

(7)   the ability of the court of each State to decide the issue expeditiously and the procedures necessary to present the evidence; and

(8)   the familiarity of the court of each State with the facts and issues in the pending litigation.

(c)   If a court of this State determines that it is an inconvenient forum and that a court of another State is a more appropriate forum, it shall stay the proceedings upon condition that a child-custody proceeding be promptly commenced in another designated State and may impose any other condition the court considers just and proper.

(d)   A court of this State may decline to exercise its jurisdiction under this [Act] if a child-custody determination is incidental to an action for divorce or another proceeding while still retaining jurisdiction over the divorce or other proceeding.

§ 208. JURISDICTION DECLINED BY REASON OF CONDUCT.

(a)   Except as otherwise provided in Section 204 [or by other law of this State], if a court of this State has jurisdiction under this [Act] because a person seeking to invoke its jurisdiction has engaged in unjustifiable conduct, the court shall decline to exercise its jurisdiction unless:

(1)   the parents and all persons acting as parents have acquiesced in the exercise of jurisdiction;

(2)   a court of the State otherwise having jurisdiction under Sections 201 through 203 determines that this State is a more appropriate forum under Section 207; or

(3)   no court of any other State would have jurisdiction under the criteria specified in Sections 201 through 203.

(b)   If a court of this State declines to exercise its jurisdiction pursuant to subsection (a), it may fashion an appropriate remedy to ensure the safety of the child and prevent a repetition of the unjustifiable conduct, including staying the proceeding until a child-custody proceeding is commenced in a court having jurisdiction under Sections 201 through 203.

(c)   If a court dismisses a petition or stays a proceeding because it declines to exercise its jurisdiction pursuant to subsection (a), it shall assess against the party seeking to invoke its jurisdiction necessary and reasonable expenses including costs, communication expenses, attorney's fees, investigative fees, expenses for witnesses, travel expenses, and child care during the course of the proceedings, unless the party from whom fees are sought establishes that the assessment would be clearly inappropriate. The court may not assess fees, costs, or expenses against this State unless authorized by law other than this [Act].

§ 209. INFORMATION TO BE SUBMITTED TO COURT.

(a) [Subject to [local law providing for the confidentiality of procedures, addresses, and other identifying information], in] [In] a child-custody proceeding, each party, in its first pleading or in an attached affidavit, shall give information, if reasonably ascertainable, under oath as to the child's present address or whereabouts, the places where the child has lived during the last five years, and the names and present addresses of the persons with whom the child has lived during that period. The pleading or affidavit must state whether the party:

(1) has participated, as a party or witness or in any other capacity, in any other proceeding concerning the custody of or visitation with the child and, if so, identify the court, the case number, and the date of the child-custody determination, if any;

(2) knows of any proceeding that could affect the current proceeding, including proceedings for enforcement and proceedings relating to domestic violence, protective orders, termination of parental rights, and adoptions and, if so, identify the court, the case number, and the nature of the proceeding; and

(3) knows the names and addresses of any person not a party to the proceeding who has physical custody of the child or claims rights of legal custody or physical custody of, or visitation with, the child and, if so, the names and addresses of those persons.

(b) If the information required by subsection (a) is not furnished, the court, upon motion of a party or its own motion, may stay the proceeding until the information is furnished.

(c) If the declaration as to any of the items described in subsection (a)(1) through (3) is in the affirmative, the declarant shall give additional information under oath as required by the court. The court may examine the parties under oath as to details of the information furnished and other matters pertinent to the court's jurisdiction and the disposition of the case.

(d) Each party has a continuing duty to inform the court of any proceeding in this or any other State that could affect the current proceeding.

[(e) If a party alleges in an affidavit or a pleading under oath that the health, safety, or liberty of a party or child would be jeopardized by disclosure of identifying information, the information must be sealed and may not be disclosed to the other party or the public unless the court orders the disclosure to be made after a hearing in which the court takes into consideration the health, safety, or liberty of the party or child and determines that the disclosure is in the interest of justice.]

§ 210. APPEARANCE OF PARTIES AND CHILD.

(a)   In a child-custody proceeding in this State, the court may order a party to the proceeding who is in this State to appear before the court in person with or without the child. The court may order any person who is in this State and who has physical custody or control of the child to appear in person with the child.

(b)   If a party to a child-custody proceeding whose presence is desired by the court is outside this State, the court may order that a notice given pursuant to Section 108 include a statement directing the party to appear in person with or without the child and informing the party that failure to appear may result in a decision adverse to the party.

(c)   The court may enter any orders necessary to ensure the safety of the child and of any person ordered to appear under this section.

(d)   If a party to a child-custody proceeding who is outside this State is directed to appear under subsection (b) or desires to appear personally before the court with or without the child, the court may require another party to pay reasonable and necessary travel and other expenses of the party so appearing and of the child.

[ARTICLE] 3 ENFORCEMENT

§ 301. DEFINITIONS.

In this [article]:

(1)   "Petitioner" means a person who seeks enforcement of an order for return of a child under the Hague Convention on the Civil Aspects of International Child Abduction or enforcement of a child-custody determination.

(2)   "Respondent" means a person against whom a proceeding has been commenced for enforcement of an order for return of a child under the Hague Convention on the Civil Aspects of International Child Abduction or enforcement of a child-custody determination.

§ 302.   ENFORCEMENT UNDER HAGUE CONVENTION.

Under this [article] a court of this State may enforce an order for the return of the child made under the Hague Convention on the Civil Aspects of International Child Abduction as if it were a child-custody determination.

§ 303. DUTY TO ENFORCE.

(a)   A court of this State shall recognize and enforce a child-custody determination of a court of another State if the latter court exercised jurisdiction in substantial conformity with this [Act] or the determination was made under factual circumstances meeting the jurisdictional standards of this [Act] and the determination has not been modified in accordance with this [Act].

(b) A court of this State may utilize any remedy available under other law of this State to enforce a child-custody determination made by a court of another State. The remedies provided in this [article] are cumulative and do not affect the availability of other remedies to enforce a child-custody determination.

§ 304. TEMPORARY VISITATION.

(a) A court of this State which does not have jurisdiction to modify a child-custody determination, may issue a temporary order enforcing:

(1) a visitation schedule made by a court of another State; or

(2) the visitation provisions of a child-custody determination of another State that does not provide for a specific visitation schedule.

(b) If a court of this State makes an order under subsection (a)(2), it shall specify in the order a period that it considers adequate to allow the petitioner to obtain an order from a court having jurisdiction under the criteria specified in [Article] 2. The order remains in effect until an order is obtained from the other court or the period expires.

§ 305. REGISTRATION OF CHILD-CUSTODY DETERMINATION.

(a) A child-custody determination issued by a court of another State may be registered in this State, with or without a simultaneous request for enforcement, by sending to [the appropriate court] in this State:

(1) a letter or other document requesting registration;

(2) two copies, including one certified copy, of the determination sought to be registered, and a statement under penalty of perjury that to the best of the knowledge and belief of the person seeking registration the order has not been modified; and

(3) except as otherwise provided in Section 209, the name and address of the person seeking registration and any parent or person acting as a parent who has been awarded custody or visitation in the child-custody determination sought to be registered.

(b) On receipt of the documents required by subsection (a), the registering court shall:

(1) cause the determination to be filed as a foreign judgment, together with one copy of any accompanying documents and information, regardless of their form; and

(2) serve notice upon the persons named pursuant to subsection (a)(3) and provide them with an opportunity to contest the registration in accordance with this section.

(c)   The notice required by subsection (b)(2) must state that:

(1)   a registered determination is enforceable as of the date of the registration in the same manner as a determination issued by a court of this State;

(2)   a hearing to contest the validity of the registered determination must be requested within 20 days after service of notice; and

(3)   failure to contest the registration will result in confirmation of the child-custody determination and preclude further contest of that determination with respect to any matter that could have been asserted.

(d)   A person seeking to contest the validity of a registered order must request a hearing within 20 days after service of the notice. At that hearing, the court shall confirm the registered order unless the person contesting registration establishes that:

(1)   the issuing court did not have jurisdiction under [Article] 2;

(2)   the child-custody determination sought to be registered has been vacated, stayed, or modified by a court having jurisdiction to do so under [Article] 2; or

(3)   the person contesting registration was entitled to notice, but notice was not given in accordance with the standards of Section 108, in the proceedings before the court that issued the order for which registration is sought.

(e)   If a timely request for a hearing to contest the validity of the registration is not made, the registration is confirmed as a matter of law and the person requesting registration and all persons served must be notified of the confirmation.

(f)   Confirmation of a registered order, whether by operation of law or after notice and hearing, precludes further contest of the order with respect to any matter that could have been asserted at the time of registration.

§ 306. ENFORCEMENT OF REGISTERED DETERMINATION.

(a)   A court of this State may grant any relief normally available under the law of this State to enforce a registered child-custody determination made by a court of another State.

(b)   A court of this State shall recognize and enforce, but may not modify, except in accordance with [Article] 2, a registered child-custody determination of a court of another State.

§ 307. SIMULTANEOUS PROCEEDINGS.

If a proceeding for enforcement under this [article] is commenced in a court of this State and the court determines that a proceeding to modify the determination is pending in a court of another State having jurisdiction to modify the determination under [Article] 2, the enforcing court shall immediately communicate with the modifying court. The proceeding for enforcement continues unless the enforcing court, after consultation with the modifying court, stays or dismisses the proceeding.

§ 308. EXPEDITED ENFORCEMENT OF CHILD-CUSTODY DETERMINATION.

(a) A petition under this [article] must be verified. Certified copies of all orders sought to be enforced and of any order confirming registration must be attached to the petition. A copy of a certified copy of an order may be attached instead of the original.

(b) A petition for enforcement of a child-custody determination must state:

(1) whether the court that issued the determination identified the jurisdictional basis it relied upon in exercising jurisdiction and, if so, what the basis was;

(2) whether the determination for which enforcement is sought has been vacated, stayed, or modified by a court whose decision must be enforced under this [Act] and, if so, identify the court, the case number, and the nature of the proceeding;

(3) whether any proceeding has been commenced that could affect the current proceeding, including proceedings relating to domestic violence, protective orders, termination of parental rights, and adoptions and, if so, identify the court, the case number, and the nature of the proceeding;

(4) the present physical address of the child and the respondent, if known;

(5) whether relief in addition to the immediate physical custody of the child and attorney's fees is sought, including a request for assistance from [law enforcement officials] and, if so, the relief sought; and

(6) if the child-custody determination has been registered and confirmed under Section 305, the date and place of registration.

(c) Upon the filing of a petition, the court shall issue an order directing the respondent to appear in person with or without the child at a hearing and may enter any order necessary to ensure the safety of the parties and the child. The hearing must be held on the next judicial day after service of the order unless that date is impossible. In that event, the court shall hold the hearing on the first judicial day possible. The court may extend the date of hearing at the request of the petitioner.

(d) An order issued under subsection (c) must state the time and place of the hearing and advise the respondent that at the hearing the court will order that the petitioner may take immediate physical custody of the child and the payment of fees, costs, and expenses under Section 312, and may schedule a hearing to determine whether further relief is appropriate, unless the respondent appears and establishes that:

(1) the child-custody determination has not been registered and confirmed under Section 305 and that:

(A) the issuing court did not have jurisdiction under [Article] 2;

(B) the child-custody determination for which enforcement is sought has been vacated, stayed, or modified by a court having jurisdiction to do so under [Article] 2;

(C) the respondent was entitled to notice, but notice was not given in accordance with the standards of Section 108, in the proceedings before the court that issued the order for which enforcement is sought; or

(2) the child-custody determination for which enforcement is sought was registered and confirmed under Section 304, but has been vacated, stayed, or modified by a court of a State having jurisdiction to do so under [Article] 2.

§ 309. SERVICE OF PETITION AND ORDER.

Except as otherwise provided in Section 311, the petition and order must be served, by any method authorized [by the law of this State], upon respondent and any person who has physical custody of the child.

§ 310. HEARING AND ORDER.

(a) Unless the court issues a temporary emergency order pursuant to Section 204, upon a finding that a petitioner is entitled to immediate physical custody of the child, the court shall order that the petitioner may take immediate physical custody of the child unless the respondent establishes that:

(1) the child-custody determination has not been registered and confirmed under Section 305 and that:

(A) the issuing court did not have jurisdiction under [Article] 2;

(B) the child-custody determination for which enforcement is sought has been vacated, stayed, or modified by a court of a State having jurisdiction to do so under [Article] 2; or

(C) the respondent was entitled to notice, but notice was not given in accordance with the standards of Section 108, in the proceedings before the court that issued the order for which enforcement is sought; or

(2) the child-custody determination for which enforcement is sought was registered and confirmed under Section 305 but has been

vacated, stayed, or modified by a court of a State having jurisdiction to do so under [Article] 2.

(b) The court shall award the fees, costs, and expenses authorized under Section 312 and may grant additional relief, including a request for the assistance of [law enforcement officials], and set a further hearing to determine whether additional relief is appropriate.

(c) If a party called to testify refuses to answer on the ground that the testimony may be self-incriminating, the court may draw an adverse inference from the refusal.

(d) A privilege against disclosure of communications between spouses and a defense of immunity based on the relationship of husband and wife or parent and child may not be invoked in a proceeding under this [article].

§ 311. WARRANT TO TAKE PHYSICAL CUSTODY OF CHILD.

(a) Upon the filing of a petition seeking enforcement of a child-custody determination, the petitioner may file a verified application for the issuance of a warrant to take physical custody of the child if the child is immediately likely to suffer serious physical harm or be removed from this State.

(b) If the court, upon the testimony of the petitioner or other witness, finds that the child is imminently likely to suffer serious physical harm or be removed from this State, it may issue a warrant to take physical custody of the child. The petition must be heard on the next judicial day after the warrant is executed unless that date is impossible. In that event, the court shall hold the hearing on the first judicial day possible. The application for the warrant must include the statements required by Section 308(b).

(c) A warrant to take physical custody of a child must:

(1) recite the facts upon which a conclusion of imminent serious physical harm or removal from the jurisdiction is based;

(2) direct law enforcement officers to take physical custody of the child immediately; and

(3) provide for the placement of the child pending final relief.

(d) The respondent must be served with the petition, warrant, and order immediately after the child is taken into physical custody.

(e) A warrant to take physical custody of a child is enforceable throughout this State. If the court finds on the basis of the testimony of the petitioner or other witness that a less intrusive remedy is not effective, it may authorize law enforcement officers to enter private property to take physical custody of the child. If required by exigent circumstances of the case, the court may authorize law enforcement officers to make a forcible entry at any hour.

(f)   The court may impose conditions upon placement of a child to ensure the appearance of the child and the child's custodian.

§ 312. COSTS, FEES, AND EXPENSES.

(a)   The court shall award the prevailing party, including a State, necessary and reasonable expenses incurred by or on behalf of the party, including costs, communication expenses, attorney's fees, investigative fees, expenses for witnesses, travel expenses, and child care during the course of the proceedings, unless the party from whom fees or expenses are sought establishes that the award would be clearly inappropriate.

(b)   The court may not assess fees, costs, or expenses against a State unless authorized by law other than this [Act].

§ 313. RECOGNITION AND ENFORCEMENT.

A court of this State shall accord full faith and credit to an order issued by another State and consistent with this [Act] which enforces a child-custody determination by a court of another State unless the order has been vacated, stayed, or modified by a court having jurisdiction to do so under [Article] 2.

§ 314. APPEALS.

An appeal may be taken from a final order in a proceeding under this [article] in accordance with [expedited appellate procedures in other civil cases]. Unless the court enters a temporary emergency order under Section 204, the enforcing court may not stay an order enforcing a child-custody determination pending appeal.

§ 315. ROLE OF [PROSECUTOR OR PUBLIC OFFICIAL].

(a)   In a case arising under this [Act] or involving the Hague Convention on the Civil Aspects of International Child Abduction, the [prosecutor or other appropriate public official] may take any lawful action, including resort to a proceeding under this [article] or any other available civil proceeding to locate a child, obtain the return of a child, or enforce a child-custody determination if there is:

(1)   an existing child-custody determination;

(2)   a request to do so from a court in a pending child-custody proceeding;

(3)   a reasonable belief that a criminal statute has been violated; or

(4)   a reasonable belief that the child has been wrongfully removed or retained in violation of the Hague Convention on the Civil Aspects of International Child Abduction.

(b)   A [prosecutor or appropriate public official] acting under this section acts on behalf of the court and may not represent any party.

§ 316. ROLE OF [LAW ENFORCEMENT].

At the request of a [prosecutor or other appropriate public official] acting under Section 315, a [law enforcement officer] may take any lawful action reasonably necessary to locate a child or a party and assist [a prosecutor or appropriate public official] with responsibilities under Section 315.

§ 317. COSTS AND EXPENSES.

If the respondent is not the prevailing party, the court may assess against the respondent all direct expenses and costs incurred by the [prosecutor or other appropriate public official] and [law enforcement officers] under Section 315 or 316.

[ARTICLE] 4 MISCELLANEOUS PROVISIONS

§ 401. APPLICATION AND CONSTRUCTION.

In applying and construing this Uniform Act, consideration must be given to the need to promote uniformity of the law with respect to its subject matter among States that enact it.

§ 402. SEVERABILITY CLAUSE.

If any provision of this [Act] or its application to any person or circumstance is held invalid, the invalidity does not affect other provisions or applications of this [Act] which can be given effect without the invalid provision or application, and to this end the provisions of this [Act] are severable.

* * *

UNIFORM CHILD WITNESS TESTIMONY BY ALTERNATIVE METHODS ACT (2002)

12 U.L.A. 80 (2008)

[EDITORS' INTRODUCTION: Tanya Asim Cooper, *Sacrificing the Child to Convict the Defendant: Secondary Traumatization of Child Witnesses by Prosecutors, Their Inherent Conflict of Interest, and the Need for Child Witness Counsel,* 9 CARDOZO PUB. L. POL'Y & ETHICS J. 239 (2011); Andrea L. Dennis, *Prosecutorial Discretion and the Neglect of Juvenile Shielding Statutes,* 90 NEB. L. REV. 341 (2011); Casey Holder, Comment, *All Dogs Go to Court: The Impact of Court Facility Dogs as Comfort for Child Witnesses on a Defendant's Right to a Fair Trial,* 50 HOUS. L. REV. 1155 (2013); Kelsey Marie Ellen Till, Comment, *Empowering Voices: Working Toward a Children's Right to Participatory Agency in Their Courtroom Experience,* 64 BUFF. L. REV. 609 (2016).]

§ 1.   SHORT TITLE.

This [Act] may be cited as the Uniform Child Witness Testimony by Alternative Methods Act.

§ 2.   DEFINITIONS.

In this [Act]:

(1) "Alternative method" means a method by which a child witness testifies which does not include all of the following:

(A) having the child testify in person in an open forum;

(B) having the child testify in the presence and full view of the finder of fact and presiding officer; and

(C) allowing all of the parties to be present, to participate, and to view and be viewed by the child.

(2) "Child witness" means an individual under the age of [13] who has been or will be called to testify in a proceeding.

(3) "Criminal proceeding" means a trial or hearing before a court in a prosecution of a person charged with violating a criminal law of this State or a [insert term for a juvenile delinquency proceeding] involving conduct that if engaged in by an adult would constitute a violation of a criminal law of this State.

(4) "Noncriminal proceeding" means a trial or hearing before a court or an administrative agency of this State having judicial or quasi-judicial powers, other than a criminal proceeding.

§ 3.   APPLICABILITY.

This [Act] applies to the testimony of a child witness in a criminal or noncriminal proceeding. However, this [Act] does not preclude, in a noncriminal proceeding, any other procedure permitted by law for a child witness to testify[, or in a [*insert the term for a juvenile delinquency proceeding*] involving conduct that if engaged in by an adult would constitute a violation of a criminal law of this State, testimony by a child witness in a closed forum as [*authorized or required*] by [*cite the law of this State that permits or requires closed juvenile hearings*]].

§ 4. HEARING WHETHER TO ALLOW TESTIMONY BY ALTERNATIVE METHOD.

(a) The presiding officer in a criminal or noncriminal proceeding may order a hearing to determine whether to allow a child witness to testify by an alternative method. The presiding officer, for good cause shown, shall order the hearing upon motion of a party, a child witness, or an individual determined by the presiding officer to have sufficient standing to act on behalf of the child.

(b) A hearing to determine whether to allow a child witness to testify by an alternative method must be conducted on the record after reasonable notice to all parties, any nonparty movant, and any other person the presiding officer specifies. The child's presence is not required at the hearing unless ordered by the presiding officer. In conducting the hearing, the presiding officer is not bound by rules of evidence except the rules of privilege.

§ 5. STANDARDS FOR DETERMINING WHETHER CHILD WITNESS MAY TESTIFY BY ALTERNATIVE METHOD.

(a) In a criminal proceeding, the presiding officer may allow a child witness to testify by an alternative method only in the following situations:

(1) The child may testify otherwise than in an open forum in the presence and full view of the finder of fact if the presiding officer finds by clear and convincing evidence that the child would suffer serious emotional trauma that would substantially impair the child's ability to communicate with the finder of fact if required to testify in the open forum.

(2) The child may testify other than face-to-face with the defendant if the presiding officer finds by clear and convincing evidence that the child would suffer serious emotional trauma that would substantially impair the child's ability to communicate with the finder of fact if required to be confronted face-to-face by the defendant.

(b) In a noncriminal proceeding, the presiding officer may allow a child witness to testify by an alternative method if the presiding officer finds by a preponderance of the evidence that allowing the child to testify by an alternative method is necessary to serve the best interests of the child or enable the child to communicate with the finder of fact. In making this finding, the presiding officer shall consider:

(1)   the nature of the proceeding;

(2)   the age and maturity of the child;

(3)   the relationship of the child to the parties in the proceeding;

(4)   the nature and degree of emotional trauma that the child may suffer in testifying; and

(5)   any other relevant factor.

§ 6.   FACTORS FOR DETERMINING WHETHER TO PERMIT ALTERNATIVE METHOD.

If the presiding officer determines that a standard under Section 5 has been met, the presiding officer shall determine whether to allow a child witness to testify by an alternative method and in doing so shall consider:

(1)   alternative methods reasonably available;

(2)   available means for protecting the interests of or reducing emotional trauma to the child without resort to an alternative method;

(3)   the nature of the case;

(4)   the relative rights of the parties;

(5)   the importance of the proposed testimony of the child;

(6)   the nature and degree of emotional trauma that the child may suffer if an alternative method is not used; and

(7)   any other relevant factor.

§ 7.   ORDER REGARDING TESTIMONY BY ALTERNATIVE METHOD.

(a)   An order allowing or disallowing a child witness to testify by an alternative method must state the findings of fact and conclusions of law that support the presiding officer's determination.

(b)   An order allowing a child witness to testify by an alternative method must:

(1)   state the method by which the child is to testify;

(2)   list any individual or category of individuals allowed to be in, or required to be excluded from, the presence of the child during the testimony;

(3)   state any special conditions necessary to facilitate a party's right to examine or cross-examine the child;

(4)   state any condition or limitation upon the participation of individuals present during the testimony of the child;

(5)   state any other condition necessary for taking or presenting the testimony.

(c) The alternative method ordered by the presiding officer may be no more restrictive of the rights of the parties than is necessary under the circumstances to serve the purposes of the order.

§ 8. RIGHT OF PARTY TO EXAMINE CHILD WITNESS.

An alternative method ordered by the presiding officer must permit a full and fair opportunity for examination or cross-examination of the child witness by each party.

§ 9. UNIFORMITY OF APPLICATION AND CONSTRUCTION.

In applying and construing this Uniform Act, consideration must be given to the need to promote uniformity of the law with respect to its subject matter among states that enact it.

§ 10. SEVERABILITY CLAUSE.

If any provision of this [Act] or the application to any person or circumstance is held invalid, the invalidity does not affect other provisions or applications of this [Act] which can be given effect without the invalid provision or application, and to this end the provisions of this [Act] are severable.

§ 11. EFFECTIVE DATE.

This [Act] takes effect [ ].

§ 12. REPEALS.

The following acts and parts of acts are repealed:

    (1) . . .

    (2) . . .

UNIFORM INTERSTATE ENFORCEMENT OF DOMESTIC-VIOLENCE PROTECTION ORDERS ACT (2002)

9 U.L.A. Pt. IB 133 et seq. (2005)

[EDITORS' INTRODUCTION: Adeola Olagunju & Christine Reynolds, *Domestic Violence*, 13 GEO. J. GENDER & L. 203 (2012); Jane K. Stoever, *Enjoining Abuse: The Case for Indefinite Domestic Violence Protection Orders*, 67 VAND. L. REV. 1015 (2014); Jessica Miles, *We are Never Ever Getting Back Together: Domestic Violence Victims, Defendants, and Due Process*, 35 CARDOZO L. REV. 141 (2013).]

§ 1. SHORT TITLE.

This [Act] may be cited as the Uniform Interstate Enforcement of Domestic-Violence Protection Orders Act.

§ 2. DEFINITIONS.

In this [Act]:

(1) "Foreign protection order" means a protection order issued by a tribunal of another State.

(2) "Issuing State" means the State whose tribunal issues a protection order.

(3) "Mutual foreign protection order" means a foreign protection order that includes provisions in favor of both the protected individual seeking enforcement of the order and the respondent.

(4) "Protected individual" means an individual protected by a protection order.

(5) "Protection order" means an injunction or other order, issued by a tribunal under the domestic-violence, family-violence, or anti-stalking laws of the issuing State, to prevent an individual from engaging in violent or threatening acts against, harassment of, contact or communication with, or physical proximity to, another individual.

(6) "Respondent" means the individual against whom enforcement of a protection order is sought.

(7) "State" means a State of the United States, the District of Columbia, Puerto Rico, the United States Virgin Islands, or any territory or insular possession subject to the jurisdiction of the United States. The term includes an Indian tribe or band that has jurisdiction to issue protection orders.

(8) "Tribunal" means a court, agency, or other entity authorized by law to issue or modify a protection order.

§ 3. JUDICIAL ENFORCEMENT OF ORDER.

(a)   A person authorized by the law of this State to seek enforcement of a protection order may seek enforcement of a valid foreign protection order in a tribunal of this State. The tribunal shall enforce the terms of the order, including terms that provide relief that a tribunal of this State would lack power to provide but for this section. The tribunal shall enforce the order, whether the order was obtained by independent action or in another proceeding, if it is an order issued in response to a complaint, petition, or motion filed by or on behalf of an individual seeking protection. In a proceeding to enforce a foreign protection order, the tribunal shall follow the procedures of this State for the enforcement of protection orders.

(b)   A tribunal of this State may not enforce a foreign protection order issued by a tribunal of a State that does not recognize the standing of a protected individual to seek enforcement of the order.

(c)   A tribunal of this State shall enforce the provisions of a valid foreign protection order which govern custody and visitation, if the order was issued in accordance with the jurisdictional requirements governing the issuance of custody and visitation orders in the issuing State.

(d)   A foreign protection order is valid if it:

(1)   identifies the protected individual and the respondent;

(2)   is currently in effect;

(3)   was issued by a tribunal that had jurisdiction over the parties and subject matter under the law of the issuing State; and

(4)   was issued after the respondent was given reasonable notice and had an opportunity to be heard before the tribunal issued the order or, in the case of an order ex parte, the respondent was given notice and has had or will have an opportunity to be heard within a reasonable time after the order was issued, in a manner consistent with the rights of the respondent to due process.

(e)   A foreign protection order valid on its face is prima facie evidence of its validity.

(f)   Absence of any of the criteria for validity of a foreign protection order is an affirmative defense in an action seeking enforcement of the order.

(g)   A tribunal of this State may enforce provisions of a mutual foreign protection order which favor a respondent only if:

(1)   the respondent filed a written pleading seeking a protection order from the tribunal of the issuing State; and

(2)   the tribunal of the issuing State made specific findings in favor of the respondent.

§ 4. NONJUDICIAL ENFORCEMENT OF ORDER.

(a) A law enforcement officer of this State, upon determining that there is probable cause to believe that a valid foreign protection order exists and that the order has been violated, shall enforce the order as if it were the order of a tribunal of this State. Presentation of a protection order that identifies both the protected individual and the respondent and, on its face, is currently in effect constitutes probable cause to believe that a valid foreign protection order exists. For the purposes of this section, the protection order may be inscribed on a tangible medium or may have been stored in an electronic or other medium if it is retrievable in perceivable form. Presentation of a certified copy of a protection order is not required for enforcement.

(b) If a foreign protection order is not presented, a law enforcement officer of this State may consider other information in determining whether there is probable cause to believe that a valid foreign protection order exists.

(c) If a law enforcement officer of this State determines that an otherwise valid foreign protection order cannot be enforced because the respondent has not been notified or served with the order, the officer shall inform the respondent of the order, make a reasonable effort to serve the order upon the respondent, and allow the respondent a reasonable opportunity to comply with the order before enforcing the order.

(d) Registration or filing of an order in this State is not required for the enforcement of a valid foreign protection order pursuant to this [Act].

§ 5. REGISTRATION OF ORDER.

(a) Any individual may register a foreign protection order in this State. To register a foreign protection order, an individual shall:

(1) present a certified copy of the order to [the state agency responsible for the registration of such orders]; or

(2) present a certified copy of the order to [an agency designated by the State] and request that the order be registered with [the agency responsible for the registration of such orders].

(b) Upon receipt of a foreign protection order, [the agency responsible for the registration of such orders] shall register the order in accordance with this section. After the order is registered, [the responsible agency] shall furnish to the individual registering the order a certified copy of the registered order.

(c) [The agency responsible for the registration of foreign protection orders] shall register an order upon presentation of a copy of a protection order which has been certified by the issuing State. A registered foreign protection order that is inaccurate or is not currently in effect must be corrected or removed from the registry in accordance with the law of this State.

(d)   An individual registering a foreign protection order shall file an affidavit by the protected individual stating that, to the best of the protected individual's knowledge, the order is currently in effect.

(e)   A foreign protection order registered under this [Act] may be entered in any existing state or federal registry of protection orders, in accordance with applicable law.

(f)   A fee may not be charged for the registration of a foreign protection order.]

§ 6. IMMUNITY.

This State or a local governmental agency, or a law enforcement officer, prosecuting attorney, clerk of court, or any state or local governmental official acting in an official capacity, is immune from civil and criminal liability for an act or omission arising out of the registration or enforcement of a foreign protection order or the detention or arrest of an alleged violator of a foreign protection order if the act or omission was done in good faith in an effort to comply with this [Act].

§ 7. OTHER REMEDIES.

A protected individual who pursues remedies under this [Act] is not precluded from pursuing other legal or equitable remedies against the respondent.

§ 8. UNIFORMITY OF APPLICATION AND CONSTRUCTION.

In applying and construing this Uniform Act, consideration must be given to the need to promote uniformity of the law with respect to its subject matter among States that enact it.

§ 9. SEVERABILITY CLAUSE.

If any provision of this [Act] or its application to any person or circumstance is held invalid, the invalidity does not affect other provisions or applications of this [Act] which can be given effect without the invalid provision or application, and to this end the provisions of this [Act] are severable.

§ 10. EFFECTIVE DATE.

This [Act] takes effect on . . . .

§ 11. TRANSITIONAL PROVISION.

This [Act] applies to protection orders issued before [the effective date of this [Act]] and to continuing actions for enforcement of foreign protection orders commenced before [the effective date of this [Act]]. A request for enforcement of a foreign protection order made on or after [the effective date of this [Act]] for violations of a foreign protection order occurring before [the effective date of this [Act]] is governed by this [Act].

UNIFORM INTERSTATE FAMILY SUPPORT ACT (2

9 U.L.A. Pt. IB 100 et seq. (Supp. 2015)

[EDITORS' INTRODUCTION: Kimball Denton, *A Brief Uniform Laws for Private Interstate Support Enforcem* CONTEMP. LEGAL ISSUES 323 (2012); Linda D. Elrod & Robert *A Review of the year in Family Law 2011–2012: "DOMA" Cha Federal Courts and Abduction Cases Increase*, 46 FAM. L.Q. 4 Jill C. Engle, *Promoting the General Welfare: Legal Reform to Lift Women and Children in the United States of Poverty*, 16 J. GENDER RACE & JUST. 1 (2013); Eric M. Fish, *The Uniform Interstate Family Support Act (UIFSA) 2008: Enforcing International Obligations Through Cooperative Federalism*, 24 J. AM. ACAD. MATRIM. LAW. 33 (2011); Margaret Campbell Haynes & Susan Friedman Paikin, *"Reconciling" FFCCSOA and UIFSA*, 49 FAM. L.Q. 331 (2015); William H. Henning, *The Uniform Law Commission and Cooperative Federalism: Implementing Private International Law Conventions Through Uniform State Laws*, 2 ELON L. REV. 39 (2011); Jeffrey A. Parness, *Choosing Among Imprecise American State Parentage Laws*, 76 LA. L. REV. 481 (2015); John J. Sampson & Barry J. Brooks, *Integrating UIFSA (2008) with the Hague Convention of 23 November 2007 on the International Recovery of Child Support and Other Forms of Family Maintenance*, 49 FAM. L.Q. 179 (2015); Laura W. Morgan, Note, *Pre-Emption or Abdication? Courts Rule Federal Law Trumps State Law in Child Support Jurisdiction*, 24 J. AM. ACAD. MATRIM. LAW. 217 (2011).]

ARTICLE 1: GENERAL PROVISIONS

§ 101. SHORT TITLE.

This [act] may be cited as the Uniform Interstate Family Support Act.

§ 102. DEFINITIONS.

In this [act]:

(1) "Child" means an individual, whether over or under the age of majority, who is or is alleged to be owed a duty of support by the individual's parent or who is or is alleged to be the beneficiary of a support order directed to the parent.

(2) "Child-support order" means a support order for a child, including a child who has attained the age of majority under the law of the issuing state or foreign country.

(3) "Convention" means the Convention on the International Recovery of Child Support and Other Forms of Family Maintenance, concluded at The Hague on November 23, 2007.

(4) "Duty of support" means an obligation imposed or imposable by law to provide support for a child, spouse, or former spouse, including an unsatisfied obligation to provide support.

(5) "Foreign country" means a country, including a political subdivision thereof, other than the United States, that authorizes the issuance of support orders and:

> (A) which has been declared under the law of the United States to be a foreign reciprocating country;

> (B) which has established a reciprocal arrangement for child support with this state as provided in Section 308;

> (C) which has enacted a law or established procedures for the issuance and enforcement of support orders which are substantially similar to the procedures under this [act]; or

> (D) in which the Convention is in force with respect to the United States.

(6) "Foreign support order" means a support order of a foreign tribunal.

(7) "Foreign tribunal" means a court, administrative agency, or quasi-judicial entity of a foreign country which is authorized to establish, enforce, or modify support orders or to determine parentage of a child. The term includes a competent authority under the Convention.

(8) "Home state" means the state or foreign country in which a child lived with a parent or a person acting as parent for at least six consecutive months immediately preceding the time of filing of a [petition] or comparable pleading for support and, if a child is less than six months old, the state or foreign country in which the child lived from birth with any of them. A period of temporary absence of any of them is counted as part of the six-month or other period.

(9) "Income" includes earnings or other periodic entitlements to money from any source and any other property subject to withholding for support under the law of this state.

(10) "Income-withholding order" means an order or other legal process directed to an obligor's [employer] [or other debtor], as defined by [the income-withholding law of this state], to withhold support from the income of the obligor.

(11) "Initiating tribunal" means the tribunal of a state or foreign country from which a [petition] or comparable pleading is forwarded or in which a [petition] or comparable pleading is filed for forwarding to another state or foreign country.

(12) "Issuing foreign country" means the foreign country in which a tribunal issues a support order or a judgment determining parentage of a child.

(13) "Issuing state" means the state in which a tribunal issues a support order or a judgment determining parentage of a child.

(14) "Issuing tribunal" means the tribunal of a state or foreign country that issues a support order or a judgment determining parentage of a child.

(15) "Law" includes decisional and statutory law and rules and regulations having the force of law.

(16) "Obligee" means:

(A) an individual to whom a duty of support is or is alleged to be owed or in whose favor a support order or a judgment determining parentage of a child has been issued;

(B) a foreign country, state, or political subdivision of a state to which the rights under a duty of support or support order have been assigned or which has independent claims based on financial assistance provided to an individual obligee in place of child support;

(C) an individual seeking a judgment determining parentage of the individual's child; or

(D) a person that is a creditor in a proceeding under [Article] 7.

(17) "Obligor" means an individual, or the estate of a decedent that:

(A) owes or is alleged to owe a duty of support;

(B) is alleged but has not been adjudicated to be a parent of a child;

(C) is liable under a support order; or

(D) is a debtor in a proceeding under [Article] 7.

(18) "Outside this state" means a location in another state or a country other than the United States, whether or not the country is a foreign country.

(19) "Person" means an individual, corporation, business trust, estate, trust, partnership, limited liability company, association, joint venture, public corporation, government or governmental subdivision, agency, or instrumentality, or any other legal or commercial entity.

(20) "Record" means information that is inscribed on a tangible medium or that is stored in an electronic or other medium and is retrievable in perceivable form.

(21) "Register" means to [record; file] in a tribunal of this state a support order or judgment determining parentage of a child issued in another state or a foreign country].

(22) "Registering tribunal" means a tribunal in which a support order or judgment determining parentage of a child is registered.

(23) "Responding state" means a state in which a [petition] or comparable pleading for support or to determine parentage of a child is filed or to which a [petition] or comparable pleading is forwarded for filing from another state or a foreign country.

(24) "Responding tribunal" means the authorized tribunal in a responding state or foreign country.

(25) "Spousal-support order" means a support order for a spouse or former spouse of the obligor.

(26) "State" means a state of the United States, the District of Columbia, Puerto Rico, the United States Virgin Islands, or any territory or insular possession under the jurisdiction of the United States. The term includes an Indian nation or tribe.

(27) "Support enforcement agency" means a public official, governmental entity, or private agency authorized to:

(A) seek enforcement of support orders or laws relating to the duty of support;

(B) seek establishment or modification of child support;

(C) request determination of parentage of a child;

(D) attempt to locate obligors or their assets; or

(E) request determination of the controlling child-support order.

(28) "Support order" means a judgment, decree, order, decision, or directive, whether temporary, final, or subject to modification, issued in a state or foreign country for the benefit of a child, a spouse, or a former spouse, which provides for monetary support, health care, arrearages, retroactive support, or reimbursement for financial assistance provided to an individual obligee in place of child support. The term may include related costs and fees, interest, income withholding, automatic adjustment, reasonable attorney's fees, and other relief.

(29) "Tribunal" means a court, administrative agency, or quasi-judicial entity authorized to establish, enforce, or modify support orders or to determine parentage of a child.

§ 103. STATE TRIBUNAL AND SUPPORT ENFORCEMENT AGENCY.

(a) The [court, administrative agency, or quasi-judicial entity, or combination] [is the tribunal] [are the tribunals] of this state.

(b) The [public official, governmental entity, or private agency] [is] [are] the support enforcement [agency] [agencies] of this state.

§ 104. REMEDIES CUMULATIVE.

(a) Remedies provided by this [act] are cumulative and do not affect the availability of remedies under other law or the recognition of a foreign support order on the basis of comity.

(b) This [act] does not:

(1) provide the exclusive method of establishing or enforcing a support order under the law of this state; or

(2) grant a tribunal of this state jurisdiction to render judgment or issue an order relating to [child custody or visitation] in a proceeding under this [act].

§ 105. APPLICATION OF [ACT] TO RESIDENT OF FOREIGN COUNTRY AND FOREIGN SUPPORT PROCEEDING.

(a) A tribunal of this state shall apply [Articles] 1 through 6 and, as applicable, [Article] 7, to a support proceeding involving:

(1) a foreign support order;

(2) a foreign tribunal; or

(3) an obligee, obligor, or child residing in a foreign country.

(b) A tribunal of this state that is requested to recognize and enforce a support order on the basis of comity may apply the procedural and substantive provisions of [Articles] 1 through 6.

(c) [Article] 7 applies only to a support proceeding under the Convention. In such a proceeding, if a provision of [Article] 7 is inconsistent with [Articles] 1 through 6, [Article] 7 controls.

ARTICLE 2: JURISDICTION

§ 201. BASES FOR JURISDICTION OVER NONRESIDENT.

(a) In a proceeding to establish or enforce a support order or to determine parentage of a child, a tribunal of this state may exercise personal jurisdiction over a nonresident individual [or the individual's guardian or conservator] if:

(1) the individual is personally served with [citation, summons, notice] within this state;

(2) the individual submits to the jurisdiction of this state by consent in a record, by entering a general appearance, or by filing a responsive document having the effect of waiving any contest to personal jurisdiction;

(3) the individual resided with the child in this state;

(4) the individual resided in this state and provided prenatal expenses or support for the child;

(5) the child resides in this state as a result of the acts or directives of the individual;

(6) the individual engaged in sexual intercourse in this state and the child may have been conceived by that act of intercourse;

(7) [the individual asserted parentage of a child in the [putative father registry] maintained in this state by the [appropriate agency]; or

(8)] there is any other basis consistent with the constitutions of this state and the United States for the exercise of personal jurisdiction.

(b) The bases of personal jurisdiction set forth in subsection (a) or in any other law of this state may not be used to acquire personal jurisdiction for a tribunal of this state to modify a child-support order of another state unless the requirements of Section 611 are met, or, in the case of a foreign support order, unless the requirements of Section 615 are met.

§ 202. DURATION OF PERSONAL JURISDICTION.

Personal jurisdiction acquired by a tribunal of this state in a proceeding under this [act] or other law of this state relating to a support order continues as long as a tribunal of this state has continuing, exclusive jurisdiction to modify its order or continuing jurisdiction to enforce its order as provided by Sections 205, 206, and 211.

§ 203. INITIATING AND RESPONDING TRIBUNAL OF STATE.

Under this [act], a tribunal of this state may serve as an initiating tribunal to forward proceedings to a tribunal of another state, and as a responding tribunal for proceedings initiated in another state or a foreign country.

§ 204. SIMULTANEOUS PROCEEDINGS.

(a) A tribunal of this state may exercise jurisdiction to establish a support order if the [petition] or comparable pleading is filed after a pleading is filed in another state or a foreign country only if:

(1) the [petition] or comparable pleading in this state is filed before the expiration of the time allowed in the other state or the foreign country for filing a responsive pleading challenging the exercise of jurisdiction by the other state or the foreign country;

(2) the contesting party timely challenges the exercise of jurisdiction in the other state or the foreign country; and

(3) if relevant, this state is the home state of the child.

(b) A tribunal of this state may not exercise jurisdiction to establish a support order if the [petition] or comparable pleading is filed before a [petition] or comparable pleading is filed in another state or a foreign country if:

    (1) the [petition] or comparable pleading in the other state or foreign country is filed before the expiration of the time allowed in this state for filing a responsive pleading challenging the exercise of jurisdiction by this state;

    (2) the contesting party timely challenges the exercise of jurisdiction in this state; and

    (3) if relevant, the other state or foreign country is the home state of the child.

§ 205. CONTINUING, EXCLUSIVE JURISDICTION TO MODIFY CHILD-SUPPORT ORDER.

(a) A tribunal of this state that has issued a child-support order consistent with the law of this state has and shall exercise continuing, exclusive jurisdiction to modify its child-support order if the order is the controlling order and:

    (1) at the time of the filing of a request for modification this state is the residence of the obligor, the individual obligee, or the child for whose benefit the support order is issued; or

    (2) even if this state is not the residence of the obligor, the individual obligee, or the child for whose benefit the support order is issued, the parties consent in a record or in open court that the tribunal of this state may continue to exercise jurisdiction to modify its order.

(b) A tribunal of this state that has issued a child-support order consistent with the law of this state may not exercise continuing, exclusive jurisdiction to modify the order if:

    (1) all of the parties who are individuals file consent in a record with the tribunal of this state that a tribunal of another state that has jurisdiction over at least one of the parties who is an individual or that is located in the state of residence of the child may modify the order and assume continuing, exclusive jurisdiction; or

    (2) its order is not the controlling order.

(c) If a tribunal of another state has issued a child-support order pursuant to the Uniform Interstate Family Support Act or a law substantially similar to that Act which modifies a child-support order of a tribunal of this state, tribunals of this state shall recognize the continuing, exclusive jurisdiction of the tribunal of the other state.

(d) A tribunal of this state that lacks continuing, exclusive jurisdiction to modify a child-support order may serve as an initiating tribunal to request a tribunal of another state to modify a support order issued in that state.

(e)   A temporary support order issued ex parte or pending resolution of a jurisdictional conflict does not create continuing, exclusive jurisdiction in the issuing tribunal.

§ 206. CONTINUING JURISDICTION TO ENFORCE CHILD-SUPPORT ORDER.

(a)   A tribunal of this state that has issued a child-support order consistent with the law of this state may serve as an initiating tribunal to request a tribunal of another state to enforce:

> (1)   the order if the order is the controlling order and has not been modified by a tribunal of another state that assumed jurisdiction pursuant to the Uniform Interstate Family Support Act; or

> (2)   a money judgment for arrears of support and interest on the order accrued before a determination that an order of a tribunal of another state is the controlling order.

(b)   A tribunal of this state having continuing jurisdiction over a support order may act as a responding tribunal to enforce the order.

§ 207. DETERMINATION OF CONTROLLING CHILD-SUPPORT ORDER.

(a)   If a proceeding is brought under this [act] and only one tribunal has issued a child-support order, the order of that tribunal controls and must be recognized.

(b)   If a proceeding is brought under this [act], and two or more child-support orders have been issued by tribunals of this state, another state, or a foreign country with regard to the same obligor and same child, a tribunal of this state having personal jurisdiction over both the obligor and individual obligee shall apply the following rules and by order shall determine which order controls and must be recognized:

> (1)   If only one of the tribunals would have continuing, exclusive jurisdiction under this [act], the order of that tribunal controls.

> (2)   If more than one of the tribunals would have continuing, exclusive jurisdiction under this [act]:

>> (A)   an order issued by a tribunal in the current home state of the child controls; or

>> (B)   if an order has not been issued in the current home state of the child, the order most recently issued controls.

> (3)   If none of the tribunals would have continuing, exclusive jurisdiction under this [act], the tribunal of this state shall issue a child-support order, which controls.

(c)   If two or more child-support orders have been issued for the same obligor and same child, upon request of a party who is an individual or that is a support enforcement agency, a tribunal of this state having personal jurisdiction over both the obligor and the obligee who is an individual shall determine which order controls under subsection (b). The request may be filed with a registration for enforcement or registration for modification pursuant to [Article] 6, or may be filed as a separate proceeding.

(d) A request to determine which is the controlling order must be accompanied by a copy of every child-support order in effect and the applicable record of payments. The requesting party shall give notice of the request to each party whose rights may be affected by the determination.

(e) The tribunal that issued the controlling order under subsection (a), (b), or (c) has continuing jurisdiction to the extent provided in Section 205 or 206.

(f) A tribunal of this state that determines by order which is the controlling order under subsection (b)(1) or (2) or (c), or that issues a new controlling order under subsection (b)(3), shall state in that order:

(1) the basis upon which the tribunal made its determination;

(2) the amount of prospective support, if any; and

(3) the total amount of consolidated arrears and accrued interest, if any, under all of the orders after all payments made are credited as provided by Section 209.

(g) Within [30] days after issuance of an order determining which is the controlling order, the party obtaining the order shall file a certified copy of it in each tribunal that issued or registered an earlier order of child support. A party or support enforcement agency obtaining the order that fails to file a certified copy is subject to appropriate sanctions by a tribunal in which the issue of failure to file arises. The failure to file does not affect the validity or enforceability of the controlling order.

(h) An order that has been determined to be the controlling order, or a judgment for consolidated arrears of support and interest, if any, made pursuant to this section must be recognized in proceedings under this [act].

§ 208. CHILD-SUPPORT ORDERS FOR TWO OR MORE OBLIGEES.

In responding to registrations or [petitions] for enforcement of two or more child-support orders in effect at the same time with regard to the same obligor and different individual obligees, at least one of which was issued by a tribunal of another state or a foreign country, a tribunal of this state shall enforce those orders in the same manner as if the orders had been issued by a tribunal of this state.

§ 209. CREDIT FOR PAYMENTS.

A tribunal of this state shall credit amounts collected for a particular period pursuant to any child-support order against the amounts owed for the same period under any other child-support order for support of the same child issued by a tribunal of this state, another state, or a foreign country.

§ 210. APPLICATION OF [ACT] TO NONRESIDENT SUBJECT TO PERSONAL JURISDICTION.

A tribunal of this state exercising personal jurisdiction over a nonresident in a proceeding under this [act], under other law of this state relating to a support order, or recognizing a foreign support order may receive evidence from outside this state pursuant to Section 316, communicate with a tribunal outside this state pursuant to Section 317, and obtain discovery through a tribunal outside this state pursuant to Section 318. In all other respects, [Articles] 3 through 6 do not apply, and the tribunal shall apply the procedural and substantive law of this state.

§ 211. CONTINUING, EXCLUSIVE JURISDICTION TO MODIFY SPOUSAL-SUPPORT ORDER.

(a) A tribunal of this state issuing a spousal-support order consistent with the law of this state has continuing, exclusive jurisdiction to modify the spousal-support order throughout the existence of the support obligation.

(b) A tribunal of this state may not modify a spousal-support order issued by a tribunal of another state or a foreign country having continuing, exclusive jurisdiction over that order under the law of that state or foreign country.

(c) A tribunal of this state that has continuing, exclusive jurisdiction over a spousal-support order may serve as:

(1) an initiating tribunal to request a tribunal of another state to enforce the spousal-support order issued in this state; or

(2) a responding tribunal to enforce or modify its own spousal-support order.

ARTICLE 3: CIVIL PROVISIONS OF GENERAL APPLICATION

§ 301. PROCEEDINGS UNDER [ACT].

(a) Except as otherwise provided in this [act], this [article] applies to all proceedings under this [act].

(b) An individual [petitioner] or a support enforcement agency may initiate a proceeding authorized under this [act] by filing a [petition] in an initiating tribunal for forwarding to a responding tribunal or by filing a [petition] or a comparable pleading directly in a tribunal of another state or a foreign country which has or can obtain personal jurisdiction over the [respondent].

§ 302. PROCEEDING BY MINOR PARENT.

A minor parent, or a guardian or other legal representative of a minor parent, may maintain a proceeding on behalf of or for the benefit of the minor's child.

§ 303. APPLICATION OF LAW OF STATE.

Except as otherwise provided in this [act], a responding tribunal of this state shall:

(1) apply the procedural and substantive law generally applicable to similar proceedings originating in this state and may exercise all powers and provide all remedies available in those proceedings; and

(2) determine the duty of support and the amount payable in accordance with the law and support guidelines of this state.

§ 304. DUTIES OF INITIATING TRIBUNAL.

(a) Upon the filing of a [petition] authorized by this [act], an initiating tribunal of this state shall forward the [petition] and its accompanying documents:

(1) to the responding tribunal or appropriate support enforcement agency in the responding state; or

(2) if the identity of the responding tribunal is unknown, to the state information agency of the responding state with a request that they be forwarded to the appropriate tribunal and that receipt be acknowledged.

(b) If requested by the responding tribunal, a tribunal of this state shall issue a certificate or other document and make findings required by the law of the responding state. If the responding tribunal is in a foreign country, upon request the tribunal of this state shall specify the amount of support sought, convert that amount into the equivalent amount in the foreign currency under applicable official or market exchange rate as publicly reported, and provide any other documents necessary to satisfy the requirements of the responding foreign tribunal.

§ 305. DUTIES AND POWERS OF RESPONDING TRIBUNAL.

(a) When a responding tribunal of this state receives a [petition] or comparable pleading from an initiating tribunal or directly pursuant to Section 301(b), it shall cause the [petition] or pleading to be filed and notify the [petitioner] where and when it was filed.

(b) A responding tribunal of this state, to the extent not prohibited by other law, may do one or more of the following:

(1) establish or enforce a support order, modify a child-support order, determine the controlling child-support order, or determine parentage of a child;

(2) order an obligor to comply with a support order, specifying the amount and the manner of compliance;

(3) order income withholding;

(4) determine the amount of any arrearages, and specify a method of payment;

(5) enforce orders by civil or criminal contempt, or both;

(6) set aside property for satisfaction of the support order;

(7) place liens and order execution on the obligor's property;

(8) order an obligor to keep the tribunal informed of the obligor's current residential address, electronic-mail address, telephone number, employer, address of employment, and telephone number at the place of employment;

(9) issue a [bench warrant; capias] for an obligor who has failed after proper notice to appear at a hearing ordered by the tribunal and enter the [bench warrant; capias] in any local and state computer systems for criminal warrants;

(10) order the obligor to seek appropriate employment by specified methods;

(11) award reasonable attorney's fees and other fees and costs; and

(12) grant any other available remedy.

(c) A responding tribunal of this state shall include in a support order issued under this [act], or in the documents accompanying the order, the calculations on which the support order is based.

(d) A responding tribunal of this state may not condition the payment of a support order issued under this [act] upon compliance by a party with provisions for visitation.

(e) If a responding tribunal of this state issues an order under this [act], the tribunal shall send a copy of the order to the [petitioner] and the [respondent] and to the initiating tribunal, if any.

(f) If requested to enforce a support order, arrears, or judgment or modify a support order stated in a foreign currency, a responding tribunal of this state shall convert the amount stated in the foreign currency to the equivalent amount in dollars under the applicable official or market exchange rate as publicly reported.

§ 306. INAPPROPRIATE TRIBUNAL.

If a [petition] or comparable pleading is received by an inappropriate tribunal of this state, the tribunal shall forward the pleading and accompanying documents to an appropriate tribunal of this state or another state and notify the [petitioner] where and when the pleading was sent.

§ 307. DUTIES OF SUPPORT ENFORCEMENT AGENCY.

Alternative A

(a) A support enforcement agency of this state, upon request, shall provide services to a [petitioner] in a proceeding under this [act].

Alternative B

(a) In a proceeding under this [act], a support enforcement agency of this state, upon request:

(1) shall provide services to a [petitioner] residing in a state;

(2) shall provide services to a [petitioner] requesting services through a central authority of a foreign country as described in Section 102(5)(A) or (D); and

(3) may provide services to a [petitioner] who is an individual not residing in a state.

End of Alternatives

(b) A support enforcement agency of this state that is providing services to the [petitioner] shall:

(1) take all steps necessary to enable an appropriate tribunal of this state, another state, or a foreign country to obtain jurisdiction over the [respondent];

(2) request an appropriate tribunal to set a date, time, and place for a hearing;

(3) make a reasonable effort to obtain all relevant information, including information as to income and property of the parties;

(4) within [two] days, exclusive of Saturdays, Sundays, and legal holidays, after receipt of notice in a record from an initiating, responding, or registering tribunal, send a copy of the notice to the [petitioner];

(5) within [two] days, exclusive of Saturdays, Sundays, and legal holidays, after receipt of communication in a record

from the [respondent] or the [respondent's] attorney, send a copy of the communication to the [petitioner]; and

(6) notify the [petitioner] if jurisdiction over the [respondent] cannot be obtained.

(c) A support enforcement agency of this state that requests registration of a child-support order in this state for enforcement or for modification shall make reasonable efforts:

(1) to ensure that the order to be registered is the controlling order; or

(2) if two or more child-support orders exist and the identity of the controlling order has not been determined, to ensure that a request for such a determination is made in a tribunal having jurisdiction to do so.

(d) A support enforcement agency of this state that requests registration and enforcement of a support order, arrears, or judgment stated in a foreign currency shall convert the amounts stated in the foreign currency into the equivalent amounts in dollars under the applicable official or market exchange rate as publicly reported.

(e) A support enforcement agency of this state shall [issue or] request a tribunal of this state to issue a child-support order and an income-withholding order that redirect payment of current support, arrears, and interest if requested to do so by a support enforcement agency of another state pursuant to Section 319.

(f) This [act] does not create or negate a relationship of attorney and client or other fiduciary relationship between a support enforcement agency or the attorney for the agency and the individual being assisted by the agency.

§ 308. DUTY OF [STATE OFFICIAL OR AGENCY].

(a) If the [appropriate state official or agency] determines that the support enforcement agency is neglecting or refusing to provide services to an individual, the [state official or agency] may order the agency to perform its duties under this [act] or may provide those services directly to the individual.

(b) The [appropriate state official or agency] may determine that a foreign country has established a reciprocal arrangement for child support with this state and take appropriate action for notification of the determination.

§ 309. PRIVATE COUNSEL.

An individual may employ private counsel to represent the individual in proceedings authorized by this [act].

§ 310. DUTIES OF [STATE INFORMATION AGENCY].

(a) The [Attorney General's Office, State Attorney's Office, State Central Registry or other information agency] is the state information agency under this [act].

(b) The state information agency shall:

(1) compile and maintain a current list, including addresses, of the tribunals in this state which have jurisdiction under this [act] and any support enforcement agencies in this state and transmit a copy to the state information agency of every other state;

(2) maintain a register of names and addresses of tribunals and support enforcement agencies received from other states;

(3) forward to the appropriate tribunal in the [county] in this state in which the obligee who is an individual or the obligor resides, or in which the obligor's property is believed to be located, all documents concerning a proceeding under this [act] received from another state or a foreign country; and

(4) obtain information concerning the location of the obligor and the obligor's property within this state not exempt from execution, by such means as postal verification and federal or state locator services, examination of telephone directories, requests for the obligor's address from employers, and examination of governmental records, including, to the extent not prohibited by other law, those relating to real property, vital statistics, law enforcement, taxation, motor vehicles, driver's licenses, and social security.

§ 311. PLEADINGS AND ACCOMPANYING DOCUMENTS.

(a) In a proceeding under this [act], a [petitioner] seeking to establish a support order, to determine parentage of a child, or to register and modify a support order of a tribunal of another state or a foreign country must file a [petition]. Unless otherwise ordered under Section 312, the [petition] or accompanying documents must provide, so far as known, the name, residential address, and social security numbers of the obligor and the obligee or the parent and alleged parent, and the name, sex, residential address, social security number, and date of birth of each child for whose benefit support is sought or whose parentage is to be determined. Unless filed at the time of registration, the [petition] must be accompanied by a copy of any support order known to have been issued by another tribunal. The [petition] may include any other information that may assist in locating or identifying the [respondent].

(b) The [petition] must specify the relief sought. The [petition] and accompanying documents must conform substantially with the requirements imposed by the forms mandated by federal law for use in cases filed by a support enforcement agency.

§ 312. NONDISCLOSURE OF INFORMATION IN EXCEPTIONAL CIRCUMSTANCES.

If a party alleges in an affidavit or a pleading under oath that the health, safety, or liberty of a party or child would be jeopardized by disclosure of specific identifying information, that information must be sealed and may not be disclosed to the other party or the public. After a hearing in which a tribunal takes into consideration the health, safety, or liberty of the party or child, the tribunal may order disclosure of information that the tribunal determines to be in the interest of justice.

§ 313. COSTS AND FEES.

(a) The [petitioner] may not be required to pay a filing fee or other costs.

(b) If an obligee prevails, a responding tribunal of this state may assess against an obligor filing fees, reasonable attorney's fees, other costs, and necessary travel and other reasonable expenses incurred by the obligee and the obligee's witnesses. The tribunal may not assess fees, costs, or expenses against the obligee or the support enforcement agency of either the initiating or responding state or foreign country, except as provided by other law. Attorney's fees may be taxed as costs, and may be ordered paid directly to the attorney, who may enforce the order in the attorney's own name. Payment of support owed to the obligee has priority over fees, costs, and expenses.

(c) The tribunal shall order the payment of costs and reasonable attorney's fees if it determines that a hearing was requested primarily for delay. In a proceeding under [Article] 6, a hearing is presumed to have been requested primarily for delay if a registered support order is confirmed or enforced without change.

§ 314. LIMITED IMMUNITY OF [PETITIONER].

(a) Participation by a [petitioner] in a proceeding under this [act] before a responding tribunal, whether in person, by private attorney, or through services provided by the support enforcement agency, does not confer personal jurisdiction over the [petitioner] in another proceeding.

(b) A [petitioner] is not amenable to service of civil process while physically present in this state to participate in a proceeding under this [act].

(c) The immunity granted by this section does not extend to civil litigation based on acts unrelated to a proceeding under this [act] committed by a party while physically present in this state to participate in the proceeding.

§ 315. NONPARENTAGE AS DEFENSE.

A party whose parentage of a child has been previously determined by or pursuant to law may not plead nonparentage as a defense to a proceeding under this [act].

§ 316. SPECIAL RULES OF EVIDENCE AND PROCEDURE.

(a) The physical presence of a nonresident party who is an individual in a tribunal of this state is not required for the establishment, enforcement, or modification of a support order or the rendition of a judgment determining parentage of a child.

(b) An affidavit, a document substantially complying with federally mandated forms, or a document incorporated by reference in any of them, which would not be excluded under the hearsay rule if given in person, is admissible in evidence if given under penalty of perjury by a party or witness residing outside this state.

(c) A copy of the record of child-support payments certified as a true copy of the original by the custodian of the record may be forwarded to a responding tribunal. The copy is evidence of facts asserted in it, and is admissible to show whether payments were made.

(d) Copies of bills for testing for parentage of a child, and for prenatal and postnatal health care of the mother and child, furnished to the adverse party at least [10] days before trial, are admissible in evidence to prove the amount of the charges billed and that the charges were reasonable, necessary, and customary.

(e) Documentary evidence transmitted from outside this state to a tribunal of this state by telephone, telecopier, or other electronic means that do not provide an original record may not be excluded from evidence on an objection based on the means of transmission.

(f) In a proceeding under this [act], a tribunal of this state shall permit a party or witness residing outside this state to be deposed or to testify under penalty of perjury by telephone, audiovisual means, or other electronic means at a designated tribunal or other location. A tribunal of this state shall cooperate with other tribunals in designating an appropriate location for the deposition or testimony.

(g) If a party called to testify at a civil hearing refuses to answer on the ground that the testimony may be self-incriminating, the trier of fact may draw an adverse inference from the refusal.

(h) A privilege against disclosure of communications between spouses does not apply in a proceeding under this [act].

(i) The defense of immunity based on the relationship of husband and wife or parent and child does not apply in a proceeding under this [act].

(j)   A voluntary acknowledgment of paternity, certified as a true copy, is admissible to establish parentage of the child.

§ 317. COMMUNICATIONS BETWEEN TRIBUNALS.

A tribunal of this state may communicate with a tribunal outside this state in a record or by telephone, electronic mail, or other means, to obtain information concerning the laws, the legal effect of a judgment, decree, or order of that tribunal, and the status of a proceeding. A tribunal of this state may furnish similar information by similar means to a tribunal outside this state.

§ 318. ASSISTANCE WITH DISCOVERY.

A tribunal of this state may:

(1)   request a tribunal outside this state to assist in obtaining discovery; and

(2)   upon request, compel a person over which it has jurisdiction to respond to a discovery order issued by a tribunal outside this state.

§ 319. RECEIPT AND DISBURSEMENT OF PAYMENTS.

(a)   A support enforcement agency or tribunal of this state shall disburse promptly any amounts received pursuant to a support order, as directed by the order. The agency or tribunal shall furnish to a requesting party or tribunal of another state or a foreign country a certified statement by the custodian of the record of the amounts and dates of all payments received.

(b)   If neither the obligor, nor the obligee who is an individual, nor the child resides in this state, upon request from the support enforcement agency of this state or another state, [the support enforcement agency of this state or] a tribunal of this state shall:

(1)   direct that the support payment be made to the support enforcement agency in the state in which the obligee is receiving services; and

(2)   issue and send to the obligor's employer a conforming income-withholding order or an administrative notice of change of payee, reflecting the redirected payments.

(c)   The support enforcement agency of this state receiving redirected payments from another state pursuant to a law similar to subsection (b) shall furnish to a requesting party or tribunal of the other state a certified statement by the custodian of the record of the amount and dates of all payments received.

ARTICLE 4: ESTABLISHMENT OF SUPPORT ORDER OR DETERMINATION OF PARENTAGE

§ 401. ESTABLISHMENT OF SUPPORT ORDER.

(a) If a support order entitled to recognition under this [act] has not been issued, a responding tribunal of this state with personal jurisdiction over the parties may issue a support order if:

(1) the individual seeking the order resides outside this state; or

(2) the support enforcement agency seeking the order is located outside this state.

(b) The tribunal may issue a temporary child-support order if the tribunal determines that such an order is appropriate and the individual ordered to pay is:

(1) a presumed father of the child;

(2) petitioning to have his paternity adjudicated;

(3) identified as the father of the child through genetic testing;

(4) an alleged father who has declined to submit to genetic testing;

(5) shown by clear and convincing evidence to be the father of the child;

(6) an acknowledged father as provided by [applicable state law];

(7) the mother of the child; or

(8) an individual who has been ordered to pay child support in a previous proceeding and the order has not been reversed or vacated.

(c) Upon finding, after notice and opportunity to be heard, that an obligor owes a duty of support, the tribunal shall issue a support order directed to the obligor and may issue other orders pursuant to Section 305.

§ 402. PROCEEDING TO DETERMINE PARENTAGE.

A tribunal of this state authorized to determine parentage of a child may serve as a responding tribunal in a proceeding to determine parentage of a child brought under this [act] or a law or procedure substantially similar to this [act].

ARTICLE 5:   ENFORCEMENT OF SUPPORT ORDER WITHOUT REGISTRATION

§ 501. EMPLOYER'S RECEIPT OF INCOME-WITHHOLDING ORDER OF ANOTHER STATE.

An income-withholding order issued in another state may be sent by or on behalf of the obligee, or by the support enforcement agency, to the person defined as the obligor's employer under [the income-withholding law of this state] without first filing a [petition] or comparable pleading or registering the order with a tribunal of this state.

§ 502. EMPLOYER'S COMPLIANCE WITH INCOME-WITHHOLDING ORDER OF ANOTHER STATE.

(a) Upon receipt of an income-withholding order, the obligor's employer shall immediately provide a copy of the order to the obligor.

(b) The employer shall treat an income-withholding order issued in another state which appears regular on its face as if it had been issued by a tribunal of this state.

(c) Except as otherwise provided in subsection (d) and Section 503, the employer shall withhold and distribute the funds as directed in the withholding order by complying with terms of the order which specify:

(1) the duration and amount of periodic payments of current child support, stated as a sum certain;

(2) the person designated to receive payments and the address to which the payments are to be forwarded;

(3) medical support, whether in the form of periodic cash payment, stated as a sum certain, or ordering the obligor to provide health insurance coverage for the child under a policy available through the obligor's employment;

(4) the amount of periodic payments of fees and costs for a support enforcement agency, the issuing tribunal, and the obligee's attorney, stated as sums certain; and

(5) the amount of periodic payments of arrearages and interest on arrearages, stated as sums certain.

(d) An employer shall comply with the law of the state of the obligor's principal place of employment for withholding from income with respect to:

(1) the employer's fee for processing an income-withholding order;

(2) the maximum amount permitted to be withheld from the obligor's income; and

(3) the times within which the employer must implement the withholding order and forward the child-support payment.

§ 503. EMPLOYER'S COMPLIANCE WITH TWO OR MORE INCOME-WITHHOLDING ORDERS.

If an obligor's employer receives two or more income-withholding orders with respect to the earnings of the same obligor, the employer satisfies the terms of the orders if the employer complies with the law of the state of the obligor's principal place of employment to establish the priorities for withholding and allocating income withheld for two or more child-support obligees.

§ 504. IMMUNITY FROM CIVIL LIABILITY.

An employer that complies with an income-withholding order issued in another state in accordance with this [article] is not subject to civil liability to an individual or agency with regard to the employer's withholding of child support from the obligor's income.

§ 505. PENALTIES FOR NONCOMPLIANCE.

An employer that willfully fails to comply with an income-withholding order issued in another state and received for enforcement is subject to the same penalties that may be imposed for noncompliance with an order issued by a tribunal of this state.

§ 506. CONTEST BY OBLIGOR.

(a) An obligor may contest the validity or enforcement of an income-withholding order issued in another state and received directly by an employer in this state by registering the order in a tribunal of this state and filing a contest to that order as provided in [Article] 6, or otherwise contesting the order in the same manner as if the order had been issued by a tribunal of this state.

(b) The obligor shall give notice of the contest to:

(1) a support enforcement agency providing services to the obligee;

(2) each employer that has directly received an income-withholding order relating to the obligor; and

(3) the person designated to receive payments in the income-withholding order or, if no person is designated, to the obligee.

§ 507. ADMINISTRATIVE ENFORCEMENT OF ORDERS.

(a) A party or support enforcement agency seeking to enforce a support order or an income-withholding order, or both, issued in another state or a foreign support order may send the documents required for registering the order to a support enforcement agency of this state.

(b) Upon receipt of the documents, the support enforcement agency, without initially seeking to register the order, shall consider and, if appropriate, use any administrative procedure authorized by the law of this state to enforce a support order or an income-withholding order, or both. If the obligor does not contest administrative enforcement, the order need not be registered. If the obligor contests the validity or administrative enforcement of the order, the support enforcement agency shall register the order pursuant to this [act].

ARTICLE 6:   REGISTRATION, ENFORCEMENT, AND MODIFICATION OF SUPPORT ORDER

PART 1.   REGISTRATION FOR ENFORCEMENT OF SUPPORT ORDER

§ 601. REGISTRATION OF ORDER FOR ENFORCEMENT.

A support order or income-withholding order issued in another state or a foreign support order may be registered in this state for enforcement.

§ 602. PROCEDURE   TO   REGISTER   ORDER   FOR ENFORCEMENT.

(a) Except as otherwise provided in Section 706, a support order or income-withholding order of another state or a foreign support order may be registered in this state by sending the following records to the [appropriate tribunal] in this state:

(1) a letter of transmittal to the tribunal requesting registration and enforcement;

(2) two copies, including one certified copy, of the order to be registered, including any modification of the order;

(3) a sworn statement by the person requesting registration or a certified statement by the custodian of the records showing the amount of any arrearage;

(4) the name of the obligor and, if known:

(A) the obligor's address and social security number;

(B) the name and address of the obligor's employer and any other source of income of the obligor; and

(C) a description and the location of property of the obligor in this state not exempt from execution; and

(5) except as otherwise provided in Section 312, the name and address of the obligee and, if applicable, the person to whom support payments are to be remitted.

(b) On receipt of a request for registration, the registering tribunal shall cause the order to be filed as an order of a tribunal of another state or a foreign support order, together with one copy of the documents and information, regardless of their form.

(c) A [petition] or comparable pleading seeking a remedy that must be affirmatively sought under other law of this state may be filed at the same time as the request for registration or later. The pleading must specify the grounds for the remedy sought.

(d) If two or more orders are in effect, the person requesting registration shall:

> (1) furnish to the tribunal a copy of every support order asserted to be in effect in addition to the documents specified in this section;

> (2) specify the order alleged to be the controlling order, if any; and

> (3) specify the amount of consolidated arrears, if any.

(e) A request for a determination of which is the controlling order may be filed separately or with a request for registration and enforcement or for registration and modification. The person requesting registration shall give notice of the request to each party whose rights may be affected by the determination.

§ 603. EFFECT OF REGISTRATION FOR ENFORCEMENT.

(a) A support order or income-withholding order issued in another state or a foreign support order is registered when the order is filed in the registering tribunal of this state.

(b) A registered support order issued in another state or a foreign country is enforceable in the same manner and is subject to the same procedures as an order issued by a tribunal of this state.

(c) Except as otherwise provided in this [act], a tribunal of this state shall recognize and enforce, but may not modify, a registered support order if the issuing tribunal had jurisdiction.

§ 604. CHOICE OF LAW.

(a) Except as otherwise provided in subsection (d), the law of the issuing state or foreign country governs:

> (1) the nature, extent, amount, and duration of current payments under a registered support order;

> (2) the computation and payment of arrearages and accrual of interest on the arrearages under the support order; and

> (3) the existence and satisfaction of other obligations under the support order.

(b) In a proceeding for arrears under a registered support order, the statute of limitation of this state, or of the issuing state or foreign country, whichever is longer, applies.

(c) A responding tribunal of this state shall apply the procedures and remedies of this state to enforce current support and collect arrears and interest due on a support order of another state or a foreign country registered in this state.

(d)   After a tribunal of this state or another state determines which is the controlling order and issues an order consolidating arrears, if any, a tribunal of this state shall prospectively apply the law of the state or foreign country issuing the controlling order, including its law on interest on arrears, on current and future support, and on consolidated arrears.

PART 2.   CONTEST OF VALIDITY OR ENFORCEMENT

§ 605. NOTICE OF REGISTRATION OF ORDER.

(a)   When a support order or income-withholding order issued in another state or a foreign support order is registered, the registering tribunal of this state shall notify the nonregistering party. The notice must be accompanied by a copy of the registered order and the documents and relevant information accompanying the order.

(b)   A notice must inform the nonregistering party:

(1)   that a registered support order is enforceable as of the date of registration in the same manner as an order issued by a tribunal of this state;

(2)   that a hearing to contest the validity or enforcement of the registered order must be requested within [20] days after notice unless the registered order is under Section 707;

(3)   that failure to contest the validity or enforcement of the registered order in a timely manner will result in confirmation of the order and enforcement of the order and the alleged arrearages; and

(4)   of the amount of any alleged arrearages.

(c)   If the registering party asserts that two or more orders are in effect, a notice must also:

(1)   identify the two or more orders and the order alleged by the registering party to be the controlling order and the consolidated arrears, if any;

(2)   notify the nonregistering party of the right to a determination of which is the controlling order;

(3)   state that the procedures provided in subsection (b) apply to the determination of which is the controlling order; and

(4)   state that failure to contest the validity or enforcement of the order alleged to be the controlling order in a timely manner may result in confirmation that the order is the controlling order.

(d) Upon registration of an income-withholding order for enforcement, the support enforcement agency or the registering tribunal shall notify the obligor's employer pursuant to [the income-withholding law of this state].

§ 606. PROCEDURE TO CONTEST VALIDITY OR ENFORCEMENT OF REGISTERED SUPPORT ORDER.

(a) A nonregistering party seeking to contest the validity or enforcement of a registered support order in this state shall request a hearing within the time required by Section 605. The nonregistering party may seek to vacate the registration, to assert any defense to an allegation of noncompliance with the registered order, or to contest the remedies being sought or the amount of any alleged arrearages pursuant to Section 607.

(b) If the nonregistering party fails to contest the validity or enforcement of the registered support order in a timely manner, the order is confirmed by operation of law.

(c) If a nonregistering party requests a hearing to contest the validity or enforcement of the registered support order, the registering tribunal shall schedule the matter for hearing and give notice to the parties of the date, time, and place of the hearing.

§ 607. CONTEST OF REGISTRATION OR ENFORCEMENT.

(a) A party contesting the validity or enforcement of a registered support order or seeking to vacate the registration has the burden of proving one or more of the following defenses:

(1) the issuing tribunal lacked personal jurisdiction over the contesting party;

(2) the order was obtained by fraud;

(3) the order has been vacated, suspended, or modified by a later order;

(4) the issuing tribunal has stayed the order pending appeal;

(5) there is a defense under the law of this state to the remedy sought;

(6) full or partial payment has been made;

(7) the statute of limitation under Section 604 precludes enforcement of some or all of the alleged arrearages; or

(8) the alleged controlling order is not the controlling order.

(b) If a party presents evidence establishing a full or partial defense under subsection (a), a tribunal may stay enforcement of a registered support order, continue the proceeding to permit production of additional relevant evidence, and issue other appropriate orders. An uncontested portion of the registered support order may be enforced by all remedies available under the law of this state.

(c) If the contesting party does not establish a defense under subsection (a) to the validity or enforcement of a registered support order, the registering tribunal shall issue an order confirming the order.

§ 608. CONFIRMED ORDER.

Confirmation of a registered support order, whether by operation of law or after notice and hearing, precludes further contest of the order with respect to any matter that could have been asserted at the time of registration.

PART 3.   REGISTRATION AND MODIFICATION OF CHILD-SUPPORT ORDER OF ANOTHER STATE

§ 609. PROCEDURE TO REGISTER CHILD-SUPPORT ORDER OF ANOTHER STATE FOR MODIFICATION.

A party or support enforcement agency seeking to modify, or to modify and enforce, a child-support order issued in another state shall register that order in this state in the same manner provided in Sections 601 through 608 if the order has not been registered. A [petition] for modification may be filed at the same time as a request for registration, or later. The pleading must specify the grounds for modification.

§ 610. EFFECT OF REGISTRATION FOR MODIFICATION.

A tribunal of this state may enforce a child-support order of another state registered for purposes of modification, in the same manner as if the order had been issued by a tribunal of this state, but the registered support order may be modified only if the requirements of Section 611 or 613 have been met.

§ 611. MODIFICATION OF CHILD-SUPPORT ORDER OF ANOTHER STATE.

(a) If Section 613 does not apply, upon [petition] a tribunal of this state may modify a child-support order issued in another state which is registered in this state if, after notice and hearing, the tribunal finds that:

(1)   the following requirements are met:

(A) neither the child, nor the obligee who is an individual, nor the obligor resides in the issuing state;

(B) a [petitioner] who is a nonresident of this state seeks modification; and

(C) the [respondent] is subject to the personal jurisdiction of the tribunal of this state; or

(2)   this state is the residence of the child, or a party who is an individual is subject to the personal jurisdiction of the tribunal of this state, and all of the parties who are individuals have filed

consents in a record in the issuing tribunal for a tribunal of this state to modify the support order and assume continuing, exclusive jurisdiction.

(b) Modification of a registered child-support order is subject to the same requirements, procedures, and defenses that apply to the modification of an order issued by a tribunal of this state and the order may be enforced and satisfied in the same manner.

(c) A tribunal of this state may not modify any aspect of a child-support order that may not be modified under the law of the issuing state, including the duration of the obligation of support. If two or more tribunals have issued child-support orders for the same obligor and same child, the order that controls and must be so recognized under Section 207 establishes the aspects of the support order which are nonmodifiable.

(d) In a proceeding to modify a child-support order, the law of the state that is determined to have issued the initial controlling order governs the duration of the obligation of support. The obligor's fulfillment of the duty of support established by that order precludes imposition of a further obligation of support by a tribunal of this state.

(e) On the issuance of an order by a tribunal of this state modifying a child-support order issued in another state, the tribunal of this state becomes the tribunal having continuing, exclusive jurisdiction.

(f) Notwithstanding subsections (a) through (e) and Section 201(b), a tribunal of this state retains jurisdiction to modify an order issued by a tribunal of this state if:

(1) one party resides in another state; and

(2) the other party resides outside the United States.

§ 612. RECOGNITION OF ORDER MODIFIED IN ANOTHER STATE.

If a child-support order issued by a tribunal of this state is modified by a tribunal of another state which assumed jurisdiction pursuant to the Uniform Interstate Family Support Act, a tribunal of this state:

(1) may enforce its order that was modified only as to arrears and interest accruing before the modification;

(2) may provide appropriate relief for violations of its order which occurred before the effective date of the modification; and

(3) shall recognize the modifying order of the other state, upon registration, for the purpose of enforcement.

§ 613. JURISDICTION TO MODIFY CHILD-SUPPORT ORDER OF ANOTHER STATE WHEN INDIVIDUAL PARTIES RESIDE IN THIS STATE.

(a) If all of the parties who are individuals reside in this state and the child does not reside in the issuing state, a tribunal of this state has jurisdiction to enforce and to modify the issuing state's child-support order in a proceeding to register that order.

(b) A tribunal of this state exercising jurisdiction under this section shall apply the provisions of [Articles] 1 and 2, this [article], and the procedural and substantive law of this state to the proceeding for enforcement or modification. [Articles] 3, 4, 5, 7, and 8 do not apply.

§ 614. NOTICE TO ISSUING TRIBUNAL OF MODIFICATION.

Within [30] days after issuance of a modified child-support order, the party obtaining the modification shall file a certified copy of the order with the issuing tribunal that had continuing, exclusive jurisdiction over the earlier order, and in each tribunal in which the party knows the earlier order has been registered. A party who obtains the order and fails to file a certified copy is subject to appropriate sanctions by a tribunal in which the issue of failure to file arises. The failure to file does not affect the validity or enforceability of the modified order of the new tribunal having continuing, exclusive jurisdiction.

PART 4.   REGISTRATION AND MODIFICATION OF FOREIGN CHILD-SUPPORT ORDER

§ 615. JURISDICTION TO MODIFY CHILD-SUPPORT ORDER OF FOREIGN COUNTRY.

(a) Except as otherwise provided in Section 711, if a foreign country lacks or refuses to exercise jurisdiction to modify its child-support order pursuant to its laws, a tribunal of this state may assume jurisdiction to modify the child-support order and bind all individuals subject to the personal jurisdiction of the tribunal whether the consent to modification of a child-support order otherwise required of the individual pursuant to Section 611 has been given or whether the individual seeking modification is a resident of this state or of the foreign country.

(b) An order issued by a tribunal of this state modifying a foreign child-support order pursuant to this section is the controlling order.

§ 616. PROCEDURE TO REGISTER CHILD-SUPPORT ORDER OF FOREIGN COUNTRY FOR MODIFICATION.

A party or support enforcement agency seeking to modify, or to modify and enforce, a foreign child-support order not under the Convention may register that order in this state under Sections 601 through 608 if the order has not been registered. A [petition] for modification may be filed at the same time as a request for registration, or at another time. The [petition] must specify the grounds for modification.

ARTICLE 7: SUPPORT PROCEEDING UNDER CONVENTION

§ 701. DEFINITIONS.

In this [article]:

(1) "Application" means a request under the Convention by an obligee or obligor, or on behalf of a child, made through a central authority for assistance from another central authority.

(2) "Central authority" means the entity designated by the United States or a foreign country described in Section 102(5)(D) to perform the functions specified in the Convention.

(3) "Convention support order" means a support order of a tribunal of a foreign country described in Section 102(5)(D).

(4) "Direct request" means a [petition] filed by an individual in a tribunal of this state in a proceeding involving an obligee, obligor, or child residing outside the United States.

(5) "Foreign central authority" means the entity designated by a foreign country described in Section 102(5)(D) to perform the functions specified in the Convention.

(6) "Foreign support agreement":

(A) means an agreement for support in a record that:

(i) is enforceable as a support order in the country of origin;

(ii) has been:

(I) formally drawn up or registered as an authentic instrument by a foreign tribunal; or

(II) authenticated by, or concluded, registered, or filed with a foreign tribunal; and

(iii) may be reviewed and modified by a foreign tribunal; and

(B) includes a maintenance arrangement or authentic instrument under the Convention.

(7) "United States central authority" means the Secretary of the United States Department of Health and Human Services.

§ 702. APPLICABILITY.

This [article] applies only to a support proceeding under the Convention. In such a proceeding, if a provision of this [article] is inconsistent with [Articles] 1 through 6, this [article] controls.

§ 703. RELATIONSHIP OF [GOVERNMENTAL ENTITY] TO UNITED STATES CENTRAL AUTHORITY.

The [governmental entity] of this state is recognized as the agency designated by the United States central authority to perform specific functions under the Convention.

§ 704. INITIATION BY [GOVERNMENTAL ENTITY] OF SUPPORT PROCEEDING UNDER CONVENTION.

(a) In a support proceeding under this [article], the [governmental entity] of this state shall:

(1) transmit and receive applications; and

(2) initiate or facilitate the institution of a proceeding regarding an application in a tribunal of this state.

(b) The following support proceedings are available to an obligee under the Convention:

(1) recognition or recognition and enforcement of a foreign support order;

(2) enforcement of a support order issued or recognized in this state;

(3) establishment of a support order if there is no existing order, including, if necessary, determination of parentage of a child;

(4) establishment of a support order if recognition of a foreign support order is refused under Section 708(b)(2), (4), or (9);

(5) modification of a support order of a tribunal of this state; and

(6) modification of a support order of a tribunal of another state or a foreign country.

(c) The following support proceedings are available under the Convention to an obligor against which there is an existing support order:

(1) recognition of an order suspending or limiting enforcement of an existing support order of a tribunal of this state;

(2) modification of a support order of a tribunal of this state; and

(3) modification of a support order of a tribunal of another state or a foreign country.

(d) A tribunal of this state may not require security, bond, or deposit, however described, to guarantee the payment of costs and expenses in proceedings under the Convention.

§ 705. DIRECT REQUEST.

(a) A [petitioner] may file a direct request seeking establishment or modification of a support order or determination of parentage of a child. In the proceeding, the law of this state applies.

(b) A [petitioner] may file a direct request seeking recognition and enforcement of a support order or support agreement. In the proceeding, Sections 706 through 713 apply.

(c) In a direct request for recognition and enforcement of a Convention support order or foreign support agreement:

(1) a security, bond, or deposit is not required to guarantee the payment of costs and expenses; and

(2) an obligee or obligor that in the issuing country has benefited from free legal assistance is entitled to benefit, at least to the same extent, from any free legal assistance provided for by the law of this state under the same circumstances.

(d) A [petitioner] filing a direct request is not entitled to assistance from the [governmental entity].

(e) This [article] does not prevent the application of laws of this state that provide simplified, more expeditious rules regarding a direct request for recognition and enforcement of a foreign support order or foreign support agreement.

§ 706. REGISTRATION OF CONVENTION SUPPORT ORDER.

(a) Except as otherwise provided in this [article], a party who is an individual or a support enforcement agency seeking recognition of a Convention support order shall register the order in this state as provided in [Article] 6.

(b) Notwithstanding Sections 311 and 602(a), a request for registration of a Convention support order must be accompanied by:

(1) a complete text of the support order [or an abstract or extract of the support order drawn up by the issuing foreign tribunal, which may be in the form recommended by the Hague Conference on Private International Law];

(2) a record stating that the support order is enforceable in the issuing country;

(3) if the respondent did not appear and was not represented in the proceedings in the issuing country, a record attesting, as appropriate, either that the respondent had proper notice of the proceedings and an opportunity to be heard or that the respondent

had proper notice of the support order and an opportunity to be heard in a challenge or appeal on fact or law before a tribunal;

(4) a record showing the amount of arrears, if any, and the date the amount was calculated;

(5) a record showing a requirement for automatic adjustment of the amount of support, if any, and the information necessary to make the appropriate calculations; and

(6) if necessary, a record showing the extent to which the applicant received free legal assistance in the issuing country.

(c) A request for registration of a Convention support order may seek recognition and partial enforcement of the order.

(d) A tribunal of this state may vacate the registration of a Convention support order without the filing of a contest under Section 707 only if, acting on its own motion, the tribunal finds that recognition and enforcement of the order would be manifestly incompatible with public policy.

(e) The tribunal shall promptly notify the parties of the registration or the order vacating the registration of a Convention support order.

§ 707. CONTEST OF REGISTERED CONVENTION SUPPORT ORDER.

(a) Except as otherwise provided in this [article], Sections 605 through 608 apply to a contest of a registered Convention support order.

(b) A party contesting a registered Convention support order shall file a contest not later than 30 days after notice of the registration, but if the contesting party does not reside in the United States, the contest must be filed not later than 60 days after notice of the registration.

(c) If the nonregistering party fails to contest the registered Convention support order by the time specified in subsection (b), the order is enforceable.

(d) A contest of a registered Convention support order may be based only on grounds set forth in Section 708. The contesting party bears the burden of proof.

(e) In a contest of a registered Convention support order, a tribunal of this state:

(1) is bound by the findings of fact on which the foreign tribunal based its jurisdiction; and

(2) may not review the merits of the order.

(f) A tribunal of this state deciding a contest of a registered Convention support order shall promptly notify the parties of its decision.

(g) A challenge or appeal, if any, does not stay the enforcement of a Convention support order unless there are exceptional circumstances.

§ 708. RECOGNITION AND ENFORCEMENT OF REGISTERED CONVENTION SUPPORT ORDER.

(a) Except as otherwise provided in subsection (b), a tribunal of this state shall recognize and enforce a registered Convention support order.

(b) The following grounds are the only grounds on which a tribunal of this state may refuse recognition and enforcement of a registered Convention support order:

(1) recognition and enforcement of the order is manifestly incompatible with public policy, including the failure of the issuing tribunal to observe minimum standards of due process, which include notice and an opportunity to be heard;

(2) the issuing tribunal lacked personal jurisdiction consistent with Section 201;

(3) the order is not enforceable in the issuing country;

(4) the order was obtained by fraud in connection with a matter of procedure;

(5) a record transmitted in accordance with Section 706 lacks authenticity or integrity;

(6) a proceeding between the same parties and having the same purpose is pending before a tribunal of this state and that proceeding was the first to be filed;

(7) the order is incompatible with a more recent support order involving the same parties and having the same purpose if the more recent support order is entitled to recognition and enforcement under this [act] in this state;

(8) payment, to the extent alleged arrears have been paid in whole or in part;

(9) in a case in which the respondent neither appeared nor was represented in the proceeding in the issuing foreign country:

(A) if the law of that country provides for prior notice of proceedings, the respondent did not have proper notice of the proceedings and an opportunity to be heard; or

(B) if the law of that country does not provide for prior notice of the proceedings, the respondent did not have proper notice of the order and an opportunity to be heard in a challenge or appeal on fact or law before a tribunal; or

(10) the order was made in violation of Section 711.

(c) If a tribunal of this state does not recognize a Convention support order under subsection (b)(2), (4), or (9):

(1) the tribunal may not dismiss the proceeding without allowing a reasonable time for a party to request the establishment of a new Convention support order; and

(2) the [governmental entity] shall take all appropriate measures to request a child-support order for the obligee if the application for recognition and enforcement was received under Section 704.

§ 709. PARTIAL ENFORCEMENT.

If a tribunal of this state does not recognize and enforce a Convention support order in its entirety, it shall enforce any severable part of the order. An application or direct request may seek recognition and partial enforcement of a Convention support order.

§ 710. FOREIGN SUPPORT AGREEMENT.

(a) Except as otherwise provided in subsections (c) and (d), a tribunal of this state shall recognize and enforce a foreign support agreement registered in this state.

(b) An application or direct request for recognition and enforcement of a foreign support agreement must be accompanied by:

(1) a complete text of the foreign support agreement; and

(2) a record stating that the foreign support agreement is enforceable as an order of support in the issuing country.

(c) A tribunal of this state may vacate the registration of a foreign support agreement only if, acting on its own motion, the tribunal finds that recognition and enforcement would be manifestly incompatible with public policy.

(d) In a contest of a foreign support agreement, a tribunal of this state may refuse recognition and enforcement of the agreement if it finds:

(1) recognition and enforcement of the agreement is manifestly incompatible with public policy;

(2) the agreement was obtained by fraud or falsification;

(3) the agreement is incompatible with a support order involving the same parties and having the same purpose in this state, another state, or a foreign country if the support order is entitled to recognition and enforcement under this [act] in this state; or

(4) the record submitted under subsection (b) lacks authenticity or integrity.

(e) A proceeding for recognition and enforcement of a foreign support agreement must be suspended during the pendency of a challenge to or appeal of the agreement before a tribunal of another state or a foreign country.

§ 711. MODIFICATION OF CONVENTION CHILD-SUPPORT ORDER.

(a) A tribunal of this state may not modify a Convention child-support order if the obligee remains a resident of the foreign country where the support order was issued unless:

(1) the obligee submits to the jurisdiction of a tribunal of this state, either expressly or by defending on the merits of the case without objecting to the jurisdiction at the first available opportunity; or

(2) the foreign tribunal lacks or refuses to exercise jurisdiction to modify its support order or issue a new support order.

(b) If a tribunal of this state does not modify a Convention child-support order because the order is not recognized in this state, Section 708(c) applies.

§ 712. PERSONAL INFORMATION; LIMIT ON USE.

Personal information gathered or transmitted under this [article] may be used only for the purposes for which it was gathered or transmitted.

§ 713. RECORD IN ORIGINAL LANGUAGE; ENGLISH TRANSLATION.

A record filed with a tribunal of this state under this [article] must be in the original language and, if not in English, must be accompanied by an English translation.

ARTICLE 8: INTERSTATE RENDITION

§ 801. GROUNDS FOR RENDITION.

(a) For purposes of this [article], "governor" includes an individual performing the functions of governor or the executive authority of a state covered by this [act].

(b) The governor of this state may:

(1) demand that the governor of another state surrender an individual found in the other state who is charged criminally in this state with having failed to provide for the support of an obligee; or

(2) on the demand of the governor of another state, surrender an individual found in this state who is charged criminally in the other state with having failed to provide for the support of an obligee.

(c) A provision for extradition of individuals not inconsistent with this [act] applies to the demand even if the individual whose surrender is demanded was not in the demanding state when the crime was allegedly committed and has not fled therefrom.

§ 802. CONDITIONS OF RENDITION.

(a) Before making a demand that the governor of another state surrender an individual charged criminally in this state with having failed to provide for the support of an obligee, the governor of this state may require a prosecutor of this state to demonstrate that at least [60] days previously the obligee had initiated proceedings for support pursuant to this [act] or that the proceeding would be of no avail.

(b) If, under this [act] or a law substantially similar to this [act], the governor of another state makes a demand that the governor of this state surrender an individual charged criminally in that state with having failed to provide for the support of a child or other individual to whom a duty of support is owed, the governor may require a prosecutor to investigate the demand and report whether a proceeding for support has been initiated or would be effective. If it appears that a proceeding would be effective but has not been initiated, the governor may delay honoring the demand for a reasonable time to permit the initiation of a proceeding.

(c) If a proceeding for support has been initiated and the individual whose rendition is demanded prevails, the governor may decline to honor the demand. If the [petitioner] prevails and the individual whose rendition is demanded is subject to a support order, the governor may decline to honor the demand if the individual is complying with the support order.

ARTICLE 9:   MISCELLANEOUS PROVISIONS

§ 901. UNIFORMITY OF APPLICATION AND CONSTRUCTION.

In applying and construing this uniform act, consideration must be given to the need to promote uniformity of the law with respect to its subject matter among states that enact it.

§ 902. TRANSITIONAL PROVISION.

This [act] applies to proceedings begun on or after [the effective date of this act] to establish a support order or determine parentage of a child or to register, recognize, enforce, or modify a prior support order, determination, or agreement, whenever issued or entered.]

§ 903. SEVERABILITY CLAUSE.

If any provision of this [act] or its application to any person or circumstance is held invalid, the invalidity does not affect other provisions or applications of this [act] which can be given effect without the invalid provision or application, and to this end the provisions of this [act] are severable.]

UNIFORM MARRIAGE AND DIVORCE ACT (1973)

9A U.L.A. Pt. I 159 et seq. (1998)

[EDITORS' INTRODUCTION: Hon. Karen S. Adam & Stacey N. Brady, *Fifty Years of Judging in Family Law: The Cleavers Have Left the Building*, 51 FAM. CT. REV. 28 (2013); Rebecca Aviel, *A New Formalism for Family Law*, 55 WM. & MARY L. REV. 2003 (2014); Lauren Barth, *Consultant Conduct in Anticipation of a Child Custody Evaluation: Ethical and Social Dilemmas and the Need for Neutral Parent Education*, 49 FAM. CT. REV. 155 (2011); Yitshak Cohen, *Extramarital Relationships and the Theoretical Rationales for the Joint Property Rules—A New Model*, 80 MO. L. REV. 131 (2015); Deborah Dinner, *The Divorce Bargain: The Fathers' Rights Movement and Family Inequalities*, 102 VA. L. REV. 79 (2016); Vivian E. Hamilton, *The Age of Marital Capacity: Reconsidering Civil Recognition of Adolescent Marriage*, 92 B.U. L. REV. 1817 (2012); Raymond C. O'Brien, *Integrating Marital Property into a Spouse's Elective Share*, 59 Cath. U. L. Rev. 617 (2010); Cynthia Lee Starnes, *Lovers, Parents, and Partners: Disentangling Spousal and Co-Parenting Commitments*, 54 ARIZ. L. REV. 197 (2012); Allison Anna Tait, *Divorce Equality*, 90 WASH. L. REV. 1245 (2015); Richard A. Warshak, *Parenting by the Clock: The Best-Interest-of-the-Child Standard, Judicial Discretion, and the American Law Institute's "Approximate Rule"*, 41 U. BALT. L. REV. 83 (2011); Deborah A. Widiss, *Changing the Marriage Equation*, 89 WASH. U. L. REV. 721 (2012); Emily Gleiss, Note, *The Due Process Rights of Parents to Cross-Examine Guardians Ad Litem in Custody Disputes: The Reality and the Ideal*, 94 MINN. L. REV. 2103 (2010); Emma J. Cone-Roddy, Comment, *Payments to Not Parent? Noncustodial Parents as the Recipients of Child Support*, 81 U. CHI. L. REV. 1749 (2014).]

[PART] I. GENERAL PROVISIONS

§ 101. [SHORT TITLE].

This Act may be cited as the "Uniform Marriage and Divorce Act."

§ 102. [PURPOSES: RULES OF CONSTRUCTION].

This Act shall be liberally construed and applied to promote its underlying purposes, which are to:

> (1) provide adequate procedures for the solemnization and registration of marriage;

> (2) strengthen and preserve the integrity of marriage and safeguard family relationships;

> (3) promote the amicable settlement of disputes that have arisen between parties to a marriage;

(4) mitigate the potential harm to the spouses and their children caused by the process of legal dissolution of marriage;

(5) make reasonable provision for spouse and minor children during and after litigation; and

(6) make the law of legal dissolution of marriage effective for dealing with the realities of matrimonial experience by making irretrievable breakdown of the marriage relationship the sole basis for its dissolution.

§ 103. [UNIFORMITY OF APPLICATION AND CONSTRUCTION].

This Act shall be so applied and construed as to effectuate its general purpose to make uniform the law with respect to the subject of this Act among those states which enact it.

[PART] II. MARRIAGE

§ 201. [FORMALITIES].

Marriage is a personal relationship between a man and a woman arising out of a civil contract to which the consent of the parties is essential. A marriage licensed, solemnized, and registered as provided in this Act is valid in this State. A marriage may be contracted, maintained, invalidated, or dissolved only as provided by law.

§ 202. [MARRIAGE LICENSE AND MARRIAGE CERTIFICATE].

(a) The [Secretary of State, Commissioner of Public Health] shall prescribe the form for an application for a marriage license, which shall include the following information:

(1) name, sex, occupation, address, social security number, date and place of birth of each party to the proposed marriage;

(2) if either party was previously married, his name, and the date, place, and court in which the marriage was dissolved or declared invalid or the date and place of death of the former spouse;

(3) name and address of the parents or guardian of each party; and

(4) whether the parties are related to each other and, if so, their relationship.

(5) the name and date of birth of any child of which both parties are parents, born before the making of the application, unless their parental rights and the parent and child relationship with respect to the child have been terminated.

(b) The [Secretary of State, Commissioner of Public Health] shall prescribe the forms for the marriage license, the marriage certificate, and the consent to marriage.

§ 203. [LICENSE TO MARRY].

When a marriage application has been completed and signed by both parties to a prospective marriage and at least one party has appeared before the [marriage license] clerk and paid the marriage license fee of [$_____], the [marriage license] clerk shall issue a license to marry and a marriage certificate form upon being furnished:

 (1) satisfactory proof that each party to the marriage will have attained the age of 18 years at the time the marriage license is effective, or will have attained the age of 16 years and has either the consent to the marriage of both parents or his guardian, or judicial approval; [or, if under the age of 16 years, has both the consent of both parents or his guardian and judicial approval;] and

 (2) satisfactory proof that the marriage is not prohibited; [and]

 [(3) a certificate of the results of any medical examination required by the laws of this State].

§ 204. [LICENSE, EFFECTIVE DATE].

A license to marry becomes effective throughout this state 3 days after the date of issuance, unless the [_____] court orders that the license is effective when issued, and expires 180 days after it becomes effective.

§ 205. [JUDICIAL APPROVAL].

(a) The [_____] court, after a reasonable effort has been made to notify the parents or guardian of each underaged party, may order the [marriage license] clerk to issue a marriage license and a marriage certificate form:

 [(1)] to a party aged 16 or 17 years who has no parent capable of consenting to his marriage, or whose parent or guardian has not consented to his marriage; [or

 (2) to a party under the age of 16 years who has the consent of both parents to his marriage, if capable of giving consent, or his guardian].

(b) A marriage license and a marriage certificate form may be issued under this section only if the court finds that the underaged party is capable of assuming the responsibilities of marriage and the marriage will serve his best interest. Pregnancy alone does not establish that the best interest of the party will be served.

(c) The [_____] court shall authorize performance of a marriage by proxy upon the showing required by the provisions on solemnization.

§ 206. [SOLEMNIZATION AND REGISTRATION].

(a) A marriage may be solemnized by a judge of a court of record, by a public official whose powers include solemnization of marriages, or in accordance with any mode of solemnization recognized by any religious denomination, Indian Nation or Tribe, or Native Group. Either the person solemnizing the marriage, or, if no individual acting alone solemnized the marriage, a party to the marriage, shall complete the marriage certificate form and forward it to the [marriage license] clerk.

(b) If a party to a marriage is unable to be present at the solemnization, he may authorize in writing a third person to act as his proxy. If the person solemnizing the marriage is satisfied that the absent party is unable to be present and has consented to the marriage, he may solemnize the marriage by proxy. If he is not satisfied, the parties may petition the [_____] court for an order permitting the marriage to be solemnized by proxy.

(c) Upon receipt of the marriage certificate, the [marriage license] clerk shall register the marriage.

(d) The solemnization of the marriage is not invalidated by the fact that the person solemnizing the marriage was not legally qualified to solemnize it, if neither party to the marriage believed him to be so qualified.

§ 207. [PROHIBITED MARRIAGES].

(a) The following marriages are prohibited:

(1) a marriage entered into prior to the dissolution of an earlier marriage of one of the parties;

(2) a marriage between an ancestor and a descendant, or between a brother and a sister, whether the relationship is by the half or the whole blood, or by adoption;

(3) a marriage between an uncle and a niece or between an aunt and a nephew, whether the relationship is by the half or the whole blood, except as to marriages permitted by the established customs of aboriginal cultures.

(b) Parties to a marriage prohibited under this section who cohabit after removal of the impediment are lawfully married as of the date of the removal of the impediment.

(c) Children born of a prohibited marriage are legitimate.

§ 208. [DECLARATION OF INVALIDITY].

(a) The [____] court shall enter its decree declaring the invalidity of a marriage entered into under the following circumstances:

(1) a party lacked capacity to consent to the marriage at the time the marriage was solemnized, either because of mental incapacity or infirmity or because of the influence of alcohol, drugs, or other incapacitating substances, or a party was induced to enter into a marriage by force or duress, or by fraud involving the essentials of marriage;

(2) a party lacks the physical capacity to consummate the marriage by sexual intercourse, and at the time the marriage was solemnized the other party did not know of the incapacity;

(3) a party [was under the age of 16 years and did not have the consent of his parents or guardian and judicial approval or] was aged 16 or 17 years and did not have the consent of his parents or guardian or judicial approval; or

(4) the marriage is prohibited.

(b) A declaration of invalidity under subsection (a)(1) through (3) may be sought by any of the following persons and must be commenced within the times specified, but in no event may a declaration of invalidity be sought after the death of either party to the marriage:

(1) for a reason set forth in subsection (a)(1), by either party or by the legal representative of the party who lacked capacity to consent, no later than 90 days after the petitioner obtained knowledge of the described condition;

(2) for the reason set forth in subsection (a)(2), by either party, no later than one year after the petitioner obtained knowledge of the described condition;

(3) for the reason set forth in subsection (a)(3), by the underaged party, his parent or guardian, prior to the time the underaged party reaches the age at which he could have married without satisfying the omitted requirement.

Alternative A

[(c) A declaration of invalidity for the reason set forth in subsection (a)(4) may be sought by either party, the legal spouse in case of a bigamous marriage, the [appropriate state official], or a child of either party, at any time prior to the death of one of the parties.]

Alternative B

[(c) A declaration of invalidity for the reason set forth in subsection (a)(4) may be sought by either party, the legal spouse in case of a bigamous marriage, the [appropriate state official] or a child of either party, at any time, not to exceed 5 years following the death of either party.]

(d) Children born of a marriage declared invalid are legitimate.

(e) Unless the court finds, after a consideration of all relevant circumstances, including the effect of a retroactive decree on third parties, that the interests of justice would be served by making the decree not retroactive, it shall declare the marriage invalid as of the date of the marriage. The provisions of this Act relating to property rights of the spouses, maintenance, support, and custody of children on dissolution of marriage are applicable to non-retroactive decrees of invalidity.

§ 209. [PUTATIVE SPOUSE].

Any person who has cohabited with another to whom he is not legally married in the good faith belief that he was married to that person is a putative spouse until knowledge of the fact that he is not legally married terminates his status and prevents acquisition of further rights. A putative spouse acquires the rights conferred upon a legal spouse, including the right to maintenance following termination of his status, whether or not the marriage is prohibited (Section 207) or declared invalid (Section 208). If there is a legal spouse or other putative spouses, rights acquired by a putative spouse do not supersede the rights of the legal spouse or those acquired by other putative spouses, but the court shall apportion property, maintenance, and support rights among the claimants as appropriate in the circumstances and in the interests of justice.

§ 210. [APPLICATION].

All marriages contracted within this State prior to the effective date of this Act, or outside this State, that were valid at the time of the contract or subsequently validated by the laws of the place in which they were contracted or by the domicil of the parties, are valid in this State.

§ 211. [VALIDITY OF COMMON LAW MARRIAGE] [ALTERNATIVE A].

Common law marriages are not invalidated by this Act.]

§ 211. [INVALIDITY OF COMMON LAW MARRIAGE] [ALTERNATIVE B].

Common law marriages contracted in this State after the effective date of this Act are invalid.]

PART III. DISSOLUTION

§ 301. [APPLICATION   OF   [RULES   OF   CIVIL   PROCEDURE]   TO   PROCEEDINGS UNDER THIS ACT].

(a) The [Rules of Civil Practice] apply to all proceedings under this Act, except as otherwise provided in this Act.

(b) A proceeding for dissolution of marriage, legal separation, or declaration of invalidity of marriage shall be entitled "In re the Marriage of ____ and ____." A custody or support proceeding shall be entitled "In re the (Custody) (Support) of ____."

(c) The initial pleading in all proceedings under this Act shall be denominated a petition. A responsive pleading shall be denominated a response. Other pleadings, and all pleadings in other matters under this Act, shall be denominated as provided in the [Rules of Civil Practice].

(d) In this Act, "decree" includes "judgment."

(e) A decree of dissolution or of legal separation, if made, shall not be awarded to one of the parties, but shall provide that it affects the status previously existing between the parties in the manner decreed.

§ 302. [DISSOLUTION OF MARRIAGE; LEGAL SEPARATION].

(a) The [____] court shall enter a decree of dissolution of marriage if:

(1) the court finds that one of the parties, at the time the action was commenced, was domiciled in this State, or was stationed in this State while a member of the armed services, and that the domicil or military presence has been maintained for 90 days next preceding the making of the findings;

(2) the court finds that the marriage is irretrievably broken, if the finding is supported by evidence that (i) the parties have lived separate and apart for a period of more than 180 days next preceding the commencement of the proceeding, or (ii) there is serious marital discord adversely affecting the attitude of one or both of the parties toward the marriage;

(3) the court finds that the conciliation provisions of Section 305 either do not apply or have been met;

(4) to the extent it has jurisdiction to do so, the court has considered, approved, or provided for child custody, the support of any child entitled to support, the maintenance of either spouse, and the disposition of property; or has provided for a separate, later hearing to complete these matters.

(b) If a party requests a decree of legal separation rather than a decree of dissolution of marriage, the court shall grant the decree in that form unless the other party objects.

§ 303. [PROCEDURE; COMMENCEMENT; PLEADINGS; ABOLITION OF EXISTING DEFENSES].

(a) All proceedings under this Act are commenced in the manner provided by the [Rules of Civil Practice].

(b) The verified petition in a proceeding for dissolution of marriage or legal separation shall allege that the marriage is irretrievably broken and shall set forth:

(1) the age, occupation, and residence of each party and his length of residence in this State;

(2) the date of the marriage and the place at which it was registered;

(3) that the jurisdictional requirements of Section 302 exist and the marriage is irretrievably broken in that either (i) the parties have lived separate and apart for a period of more than 180 days next preceding the commencement of the proceeding or (ii) there is

serious marital discord adversely affecting the attitude of one or both of the parties toward the marriage, and there is no reasonable prospect of reconciliation;

(4) the names, ages, and addresses of all living children of the marriage, and whether the wife is pregnant;

(5) any arrangements as to support, custody, and visitation of the children and maintenance of a spouse; and

(6) the relief sought.

(c) Either or both parties to the marriage may initiate the proceeding.

(d) If a proceeding is commenced by one of the parties, the other party must be served in the manner provided by the [Rules of Civil Practice] and may within [30] days after the date of service file a verified response.

(e) Previously existing defenses to divorce and legal separation, including but not limited to condonation, connivance, collusion, recrimination, insanity, and lapse of time, are abolished.

(f) The court may join additional parties proper for the exercise of its authority to implement this Act.

§ 304. [TEMPORARY ORDER OR TEMPORARY INJUNCTION].

(a) In a proceeding for dissolution of marriage or for legal separation, or in a proceeding for disposition of property or for maintenance or support following dissolution of the marriage by a court which lacked personal jurisdiction over the absent spouse, either party may move for temporary maintenance or temporary support of a child of the marriage entitled to support. The motion shall be accompanied by an affidavit setting forth the factual basis for the motion and the amounts requested.

(b) As a part of a motion for temporary maintenance or support or by independent motion accompanied by affidavit, either party may request the court to issue a temporary injunction for any of the following relief:

(1) restraining any person from transferring, encumbering, concealing, or otherwise disposing of any property except in the usual course of business or for the necessities of life, and, if so restrained, requiring him to notify the moving party of any proposed extraordinary expenditures made after the order is issued;

(2) enjoining a party from molesting or disturbing the peace of the other party or of any child;

(3) excluding a party from the family home or from the home of the other party upon a showing that physical or emotional harm would otherwise result;

(4) enjoining a party from removing a child from the jurisdiction of the court; and

(5) providing other injunctive relief proper in the circumstances.

(c) The court may issue a temporary restraining order without requiring notice to the other party only if it finds on the basis of the moving affidavit or other evidence that irreparable injury will result to the moving party if no order is issued until the time for responding has elapsed.

(d) A response may be filed within [20] days after service of notice of motion or at the time specified in the temporary restraining order.

(e) On the basis of the showing made and in conformity with Sections 308 and 309, the court may issue a temporary injunction and an order for temporary maintenance or support in amounts and on terms just and proper in the circumstance.

(f) A temporary order or temporary injunction:

(1) does not prejudice the rights of the parties or the child which are to be adjudicated at subsequent hearings in the proceeding;

(2) may be revoked or modified before final decree on a showing by affidavit of the facts necessary to revocation or modification of a final decree under Section 316; and

(3) terminates when the final decree is entered or when the petition for dissolution or legal separation is voluntarily dismissed.

§ 305. [IRRETRIEVABLE BREAKDOWN].

(a) If both of the parties by petition or otherwise have stated under oath or affirmation that the marriage is irretrievably broken, or one of the parties has so stated and the other has not denied it, the court, after hearing, shall make a finding whether the marriage is irretrievably broken.

(b) If one of the parties has denied under oath or affirmation that the marriage is irretrievably broken, the court shall consider all relevant factors, including the circumstances that gave rise to filing the petition and the prospect of reconciliation, and shall:

(1) make a finding whether the marriage is irretrievably broken; or

(2) continue the matter for further hearing not fewer than 30 nor more than 60 days later, or as soon thereafter as the matter may be reached on the court's calendar, and may suggest to the parties that they seek counseling. The court, at the request of either party shall, or on its own motion may, order a conciliation conference. At

the adjourned hearing the court shall make a finding whether the marriage is irretrievably broken.

(c) A finding of irretrievable breakdown is a determination that there is no reasonable prospect of reconciliation.

§ 306. [SEPARATION AGREEMENT].

(a) To promote amicable settlement of disputes between parties to a marriage attendant upon their separation or the dissolution of their marriage, the parties may enter into a written separation agreement containing provisions for disposition of any property owned by either of them, maintenance of either of them, and support, custody, and visitation of their children.

(b) In a proceeding for dissolution of marriage or for legal separation, the terms of the separation agreement, except those providing for the support, custody, and visitation of children, are binding upon the court unless it finds, after considering the economic circumstances of the parties and any other relevant evidence produced by the parties, on their own motion or on request of the court, that the separation agreement is unconscionable.

(c) If the court finds the separation agreement unconscionable, it may request the parties to submit a revised separation agreement or may make orders for the disposition of property, maintenance, and support.

(d) If the court finds that the separation agreement is not unconscionable as to disposition of property or maintenance, and not unsatisfactory as to support:

(1) unless the separation agreement provides to the contrary, its terms shall be set forth in the decree of dissolution or legal separation and the parties shall be ordered to perform them, or

(2) if the separation agreement provides that its terms shall not be set forth in the decree, the decree shall identify the separation agreement and state that the court has found the terms not unconscionable.

(e) Terms of the agreement set forth in the decree are enforceable by all remedies available for enforcement of a judgment, including contempt, and are enforceable as contract terms.

(f) Except for terms concerning the support, custody, or visitation of children, the decree may expressly preclude or limit modification of terms set forth in the decree if the separation agreement so provides. Otherwise, terms of a separation agreement set forth in the decree are automatically modified by modification of the decree.

§ 307. [DISPOSITION OF PROPERTY] [ALTERNATIVE A].

(a) In a proceeding for dissolution of a marriage, legal separation, or disposition of property following a decree of dissolution of marriage or legal separation by a court which lacked personal jurisdiction over the absent spouse or lacked jurisdiction to dispose of the property, the court, without regard to marital misconduct, shall, and in a proceeding for legal separation may, finally equitably apportion between the parties the property and assets belonging to either or both however and whenever acquired, and whether the title thereto is in the name of the husband or wife or both. In making apportionment the court shall consider the duration of the marriage, and prior marriage of either party, antenuptial agreement of the parties, the age, health, station, occupation, amount and sources of income, vocational skills, employability, estate, liabilities, and needs of each of the parties, custodial provisions, whether the apportionment is in lieu of or in addition to maintenance, and the opportunity of each for future acquisition of capital assets and income. The court shall also consider the contribution or dissipation of each party in the acquisition, preservation, depreciation, or appreciation in value of the respective estates, and the contribution of a spouse as a homemaker or to the family unit.

(b) In a proceeding, the court may protect and promote the best interests of the children by setting aside a portion of the jointly and separately held estates of the parties in a separate fund or trust for the support, maintenance, education, and general welfare of any minor, dependent, or incompetent children of the parties.

§ 307. [DISPOSITION OF PROPERTY] [ALTERNATIVE B].

In a proceeding for dissolution of the marriage, legal separation, or disposition of property following a decree of dissolution of the marriage or legal separation by a court which lacked personal jurisdiction over the absent spouse or lacked jurisdiction to dispose of the property, the court shall assign each spouse's separate property to that spouse. It also shall divide community property, without regard to marital misconduct, in just proportions after considering all relevant factors including:

(1) contribution of each spouse to acquisition of the marital property, including contribution of a spouse as homemaker;

(2) value of the property set apart to each spouse;

(3) duration of the marriage; and

(4) economic circumstances of each spouse when the division of property is to become effective, including the desirability of awarding the family home or the right to live therein for a reasonable period to the spouse having custody of any children.

§ 308. [MAINTENANCE].

(a) In a proceeding for dissolution of marriage, legal separation, or maintenance following a decree of dissolution of the marriage by a court which lacked personal jurisdiction over the absent spouse, the court may grant a maintenance order for either spouse only if it finds that the spouse seeking maintenance:

(1) lacks sufficient property to provide for his reasonable needs; and

(2) is unable to support himself through appropriate employment or is the custodian of a child whose condition or circumstances make it appropriate that the custodian not be required to seek employment outside the home.

(b) The maintenance order shall be in amounts and for periods of time the court deems just, without regard to marital misconduct, and after considering all relevant factors including:

(1) the financial resources of the party seeking maintenance, including marital property apportioned to him, his ability to meet his needs independently, and the extent to which a provision for support of a child living with the party includes a sum for that party as custodian;

(2) the time necessary to acquire sufficient education or training to enable the party seeking maintenance to find appropriate employment;

(3) the standard of living established during the marriage;

(4) the duration of the marriage;

(5) the age and the physical and emotional condition of the spouse seeking maintenance; and

(6) the ability of the spouse from whom maintenance is sought to meet his needs while meeting those of the spouse seeking maintenance.

§ 309. [CHILD SUPPORT].

In a proceeding for dissolution of marriage, legal separation, maintenance, or child support, the court may order either or both parents owing a duty of support to a child to pay an amount reasonable or necessary for his support, without regard to marital misconduct, after considering all relevant factors including:

(1) the financial resources of the child;

(2) the financial resources of the custodial parent;

(3) the standard of living the child would have enjoyed had the marriage not been dissolved;

(4) the physical and emotional condition of the child and his educational needs; and

(5) the financial resources and needs of the noncustodial parent.

§ 310. [REPRESENTATION OF CHILD].

The court may appoint an attorney to represent the interests of a minor or dependent child with respect to his support, custody, and visitation. The court shall enter an order for costs, fees, and disbursements in favor of the child's attorney. The order shall be made against either or both parents, except that, if the responsible party is indigent, the costs, fees, and disbursements shall be borne by the [appropriate agency].

§ 311. [PAYMENT OF MAINTENANCE OR SUPPORT TO COURT].

(a) Upon its own motion or upon motion of either party, the court may order at any time that maintenance or support payments be made to the [clerk of court, court trustee, probation officer] as trustee for remittance to the person entitled to receive the payments.

(b) The [clerk of court, court trustee, probation officer] shall maintain records listing the amount of payments, the date payments are required to be made, and the names and addresses of the parties affected by the order.

(c) The parties affected by the order shall inform the [clerk of court, court trustee, probation officer] of any change of address or of other condition that may affect the administration of the order.

(d) If a party fails to make a required payment, the [clerk of court, court trustee, probation officer] shall send by registered or certified mail notice of the arrearage to the obligor. If payment of the sum due is not made to the [clerk of court, court trustee, probation officer] within 10 days after sending notice, the [clerk of court, court trustee, probation officer] shall certify the amount due to the [prosecuting attorney]. The [prosecuting attorney] shall promptly initiate contempt proceedings against the obligator.

(e) The [prosecuting attorney] shall assist the court on behalf of a person entitled to receive maintenance or support in all proceedings initiated under this section to enforce compliance with the order. The person to whom maintenance or support is awarded may also initiate action to collect arrearages.

(f) If the person obligated to pay support has left or is beyond the jurisdiction of the court, the [prosecuting attorney] may institute any other proceeding available under the laws of this State for enforcement of the duties of support and maintenance.

§ 312. [ASSIGNMENT].

The court may order the person obligated to pay support or maintenance to make an assignment of a part of his periodic earnings or trust income to the person entitled to receive the payments. The assignment is binding on the employer, trustee, or other payor of the funds 2 weeks after service upon him of notice that it has been made. The payor shall withhold from the earnings or trust income payable to the person obligated to support the amount specified in the assignment and shall transmit the payments to the person specified in the order. The payor may deduct from each payment a sum not exceeding [$1.00] as reimbursement for costs. An employer shall not discharge or otherwise discipline an employee as a result of a wage or salary assignment authorized by this section.

§ 313. [ATTORNEY'S FEES].

The court from time to time after considering the financial resources of both parties may order a party to pay a reasonable amount for the cost to the other party of maintaining or defending any proceeding under this Act and for attorney's fees, including sums for legal services rendered and costs incurred prior to the commencement of the proceeding or after entry of judgment. The court may order that the amount be paid directly to the attorney, who may enforce the order in his name.

§ 314. [DECREE].

(a) A decree of dissolution of marriage or of legal separation is final when entered, subject to the right of appeal. An appeal from the decree of dissolution that does not challenge the finding that the marriage is irretrievably broken does not delay the finality of that provision of the decree which dissolves the marriage beyond the time for appealing from that provision, and either of the parties may remarry pending appeal.

(b) No earlier than 6 months after entry of a decree of legal separation, the court on motion of either party shall convert the decree to a decree of dissolution of marriage.

(c) The Clerk of Court shall give notice of the entry of a decree of dissolution or legal separation:

(1) if the marriage is registered in this State, to the [marriage license] clerk of the [county, judicial district] where the marriage is registered who shall enter the fact of dissolution or separation in the [Registry of Marriage]; or

(2) if the marriage is registered in another jurisdiction, to the appropriate official of that jurisdiction, with the request that he enter the fact of dissolution in the appropriate record.

(d) Upon request by a wife whose marriage is dissolved or declared invalid, the court may, and if there are no children of the parties shall, order her maiden name or a former name restored.

§ 315. [INDEPENDENCE OF PROVISIONS OF DECREE OR TEMPORARY ORDER].

If a party fails to comply with a provision of a decree or temporary order or injunction, the obligation of the other party to make payments for support or maintenance or to permit visitation is not suspended; but he may move the court to grant an appropriate order.

§ 316. [MODIFICATION AND TERMINATION OF PROVISIONS FOR MAINTENANCE, SUPPORT AND PROPERTY DISPOSITION].

(a)   Except as otherwise provided in subsection (f) of Section 306, the provisions of any decree respecting maintenance or support may be modified only as to installments accruing subsequent to the motion for modification and only upon a showing of changed circumstances so substantial and continuing as to make the terms unconscionable. The provisions as to property disposition may not be revoked or modified, unless the court finds the existence of conditions that justify the reopening of a judgment under the laws of this state.

(b)   Unless otherwise agreed in writing or expressly provided in the decree, the obligation to pay future maintenance is terminated upon the death of either party or the remarriage of the party receiving maintenance.

(c)   Unless otherwise agreed in writing or expressly provided in the decree, provisions for the support of a child are terminated by emancipation of the child but not by the death of a parent obligated to support the child. When a parent obligated to pay support dies, the amount of support may be modified, revoked, or commuted to a lump sum payment, to the extent just and appropriate in the circumstances.

PART IV. CUSTODY

§ 401. [JURISDICTION; COMMENCEMENT OF PROCEEDING].

(a)   A court of this State competent to decide child custody matters has jurisdiction to make a child custody determination by initial or modification decree if:

(1)   this State (i) is the home state of the child at the time of commencement of the proceeding, or (ii) had been the child's home state within 6 months before commencement of the proceeding and the child is absent from this State because of his removal or retention by a person claiming his custody or for other reason, and a parent or person acting as parent continues to live in this State; or

(2)   it is in the best interest of the child that a court of this State assume jurisdiction because (i) the child and his parents, or the child and at least one contestant, have a significant connection with this State, and (ii) there is available in this State substantial evidence concerning the child's present or future care, protection, training, and personal relationships; or

(3)   the child is physically present in this State and (i) has been abandoned or (ii) it is necessary in an emergency to protect him

because he has been subjected to or threatened with mistreatment or abuse or is neglected or dependent; or

(4)(i)   no other state has jurisdiction under prerequisites substantially in accordance with paragraphs (1), (2) or (3), or another state has declined to exercise jurisdiction on the ground that this State is the more appropriate forum to determine custody of the child, and (ii) it is in his best interest that the court assume jurisdiction.

(b) Except under paragraphs (3) and (4) of subsection (a), physical presence in this State of the child, or of the child and one of the contestants, is not alone sufficient to confer jurisdiction on a court of this State to make a child custody determination.

(c) Physical presence of the child, while desirable, is not a prerequisite for jurisdiction to determine his custody.

(d) A child custody proceeding is commenced in the [_____] court:

(1) by a parent, by filing a petition

(i) for dissolution or legal separation; or

(ii) for custody of the child in the [county, judicial district] in which he is permanently resident or found; or

(2) by a person other than a parent, by filing a petition for custody of the child in the [county, judicial district] in which he is permanently resident or found, but only if he is not in the physical custody of one of his parents.

(e) Notice of a child custody proceeding shall be given to the child's parent, guardian, and custodian, who may appear, be heard, and file a responsive pleading. The court, upon a showing of good cause, may permit intervention of other interested parties.

§ 402. [BEST INTEREST OF CHILD].

The court shall determine custody in accordance with the best interest of the child. The court shall consider all relevant factors including:

(1) the wishes of the child's parent or parents as to his custody;

(2) the wishes of the child as to his custodian;

(3) the interaction and interrelationship of the child with his parent or parents, his siblings, and any other person who may significantly affect the child's best interest;

(4) the child's adjustment to his home, school, and community; and

(5) the mental and physical health of all individuals involved. The court shall not consider conduct of a proposed custodian that does not affect his relationship to the child.

§ 403. [TEMPORARY ORDERS].

(a) A party to a custody proceeding may move for a temporary custody order. The motion must be supported by an affidavit as provided in Section 410. The court may award temporary custody under the standards of Section 402 after a hearing, or, if there is no objection, solely on the basis of the affidavits.

(b) If a proceeding for dissolution of marriage or legal separation is dismissed, any temporary custody order is vacated unless a parent or the child's custodian moves that the proceeding continue as a custody proceeding and the court finds, after a hearing, that the circumstances of the parents and the best interest of the child requires that a custody decree be issued.

(c) If a custody proceeding commenced in the absence of a petition for dissolution of marriage or legal separation under subsection (1)(ii) or (2) of Section 401 is dismissed, any temporary custody order is vacated.

§ 404. [INTERVIEWS].

(a) The court may interview the child in chambers to ascertain the child's wishes as to his custodian and as to visitation. The court may permit counsel to be present at the interview. The court shall cause a record of the interview to be made and to be part of the record in the case.

(b) The court may seek the advice of professional personnel, whether or not employed by the court on a regular basis. The advice given shall be in writing and made available by the court to counsel upon request. Counsel may examine as a witness any professional personnel consulted by the court.

§ 405. [INVESTIGATIONS AND REPORTS].

(a) In contested custody proceedings, and in other custody proceedings if a parent or the child's custodian so requests, the court may order an investigation and report concerning custodial arrangements for the child. The investigation and report may be made by [the court social service agency, the staff of the juvenile court, the local probation or welfare department, or a private agency employed by the court for the purpose].

(b) In preparing his report concerning a child, the investigator may consult any person who may have information about the child and his potential custodial arrangements. Upon order of the court, the investigator may refer the child to professional personnel for diagnosis. The investigator may consult with and obtain information from medical, psychiatric, or other expert persons who have served the child in the past without obtaining the consent of the parent or the child's custodian; but the child's consent must be obtained if he has reached the age of 16, unless the court finds that he lacks mental capacity to consent. If the requirements of subsection (c) are fulfilled, the investigator's report may be received in evidence at the hearing.

(c) The court shall mail the investigator's report to counsel and to any party not represented by counsel at least 10 days prior to the hearing. The investigator shall make available to counsel and to any party not represented by counsel the investigator's file of underlying data, and reports, complete texts of diagnostic reports made to the investigator pursuant to the provisions of subsection (b), and the names and addresses of all persons whom the investigator has consulted. Any party to the proceeding may call the investigator and any person whom he has consulted for cross-examination. A party may not waive his right of cross-examination prior to the hearing.

§ 406. [HEARINGS].

(a) Custody proceedings shall receive priority in being set for hearing.

(b) The court may tax as costs the payment of necessary travel and other expenses incurred by any person whose presence at the hearing the court deems necessary to determine the best interest of the child.

(c) The court without a jury shall determine questions of law and fact. If it finds that a public hearing may be detrimental to the child's best interest, the court may exclude the public from a custody hearing, but may admit any person who has a direct and legitimate interest in the particular case or a legitimate educational or research interest in the work of the court.

(d) If the court finds it necessary to protect the child's welfare that the record of any interview, report, investigation, or testimony in a custody proceeding be kept secret, the court may make an appropriate order sealing the record.

§ 407. [VISITATION].

(a) A parent not granted custody of the child is entitled to reasonable visitation rights unless the court finds, after a hearing, that visitation would endanger seriously the child's physical, mental, moral, or emotional health.

(b) The court may modify an order granting or denying visitation rights whenever modification would serve the best interest of the child; but the court shall not restrict a parent's visitation rights unless it finds that the visitation would endanger seriously the child's physical, mental, moral, or emotional health.

§ 408. [JUDICIAL SUPERVISION].

(a) Except as otherwise agreed by the parties in writing at the time of the custody decree, the custodian may determine the child's upbringing, including his education, health care, and religious training, unless the court after hearing, finds, upon motion by the noncustodial parent, that in the absence of a specific limitation of the custodian's authority, the child's physical health would be endangered or his emotional development significantly impaired.

(b) If both parents or all contestants agree to the order, or if the court finds that in the absence of the order the child's physical health would be endangered or his emotional development significantly impaired, the court may order the [local probation or welfare department, court social service agency] to exercise continuing supervision over the case to assure that the custodial or visitation terms of the decree are carried out.

§ 409. [MODIFICATION].

(a) No motion to modify a custody decree may be made earlier than 2 years after its date, unless the court permits it to be made on the basis of affidavits that there is reason to believe the child's present environment may endanger seriously his physical, mental, moral, or emotional health.

(b) If a court of this State has jurisdiction pursuant to the Uniform Child Custody Jurisdiction Act, the court shall not modify a prior custody decree unless it finds, upon the basis of facts that have arisen since the prior decree or that were unknown to the court at the time of entry of the prior decree, that a change has occurred in the circumstances of the child or his custodian, and that the modification is necessary to serve the best interest of the child. In applying these standards the court shall retain the custodian appointed pursuant to the prior decree unless:

(1) the custodian agrees to the modification;

(2) the child has been integrated into the family of the petitioner with consent of the custodian; or

(3) the child's present environment endangers seriously his physical, mental, moral, or emotional health, and the harm likely to be caused by a change of environment is outweighed by its advantages to him.

(c) Attorney fees and costs shall be assessed against a party seeking modification if the court finds that the modification action is vexatious and constitutes harassment.

§ 410. [AFFIDAVIT PRACTICE].

A party seeking a temporary custody order or modification of a custody decree shall submit together with his moving papers an affidavit setting forth facts supporting the requested order or modification and shall give notice, together with a copy of his affidavit, to other parties to the proceeding, who may file opposing affidavits. The court shall deny the motion unless it finds that adequate cause for hearing the motion is established by the affidavits, in which case it shall set a date for hearing on an order to show cause why the requested order or modification should not be granted.

PART V.   EFFECTIVE DATE AND REPEALER

§ 501. [TIME OF TAKING EFFECT].

This Act shall take effect [_____]

§ 502. [APPLICATION].

(a) This Act applies to all proceedings commenced on or after its effective date.

(b) This Act applies to all pending actions and proceedings commenced prior to its effective date with respect to issues on which a judgment has not been entered. Pending actions for divorce or separation are deemed to have been commenced on the basis of irretrievable breakdown. Evidence adduced after the effective date of this Act shall be in compliance with this Act.

(c) This Act applies to all proceedings commenced after its effective date for the modification of a judgment or order entered prior to the effective date of this Act.

(d) In any action or proceeding in which an appeal was pending or a new trial was ordered prior to the effective date of this Act, the law in effect at the time of the order sustaining the appeal or the new trial governs the appeal, the new trial, and any subsequent trial or appeal.

§ 503. [SEVERABILITY].

If any provision of this Act or application thereof to any person or circumstance is held invalid, the invalidity does not affect other provisions or applications of the Act which can be given effect without the invalid provision or application, and to this end the provisions of this Act are severable.

§ 504. [SPECIFIC REPEALER].

The following acts and all other acts and parts of acts inconsistent herewith are hereby repealed: [Here should follow the acts to be specifically repealed, including any acts regulating:

(1) marriage, including grounds for annulment and provisions for void marriages;

(2) existing grounds for divorce and legal separation;

(3) existing defenses to divorce and legal separation, including but not limited to condonation, connivance, collusion, recrimination, insanity, and lapse of time; and

(4) alimony, child support, custody, and division of spouses' property in the event of a divorce and judicial proceedings designed to modify the financial or custody provisions of divorce decrees].

§ 505. [GENERAL REPEALER].

Except as provided in Section 506, all acts and parts of acts inconsistent with this Act are hereby repealed.

§ 506. [LAWS NOT REPEALED].

This Act does not repeal: [Here should follow the acts not to be repealed, including any acts regulating or prescribing:

(1) the contents of and forms for marriage licenses and methods of registering marriages and providing for license or registration fees;

(2) the validity of premarital agreements between spouses concerning their marital property rights;

(3) marital property rights during a marriage or when the marriage terminates by the death of one of the spouses;

(4) the scope and extent of the duty of a parent to support a child of the marriage;

(5) custody of and support duty owed to an illegitimate child;

(6) the Uniform Child Custody Jurisdiction Act; and

(7) any applicable laws relating to wage assignments, garnishments, and exemptions other than those providing for family support and maintenance].

UNIFORM PARENTAGE ACT (2002)

9B U.L.A. 295 et seq. (2001 & Supp. 2015)

[EDITORS' INTRODUCTION: Naomi Cahn, *The New Kinship*, 100 GEO. L.J. 367 (2012); Linda D. Elrod, *A Child's Perspective of Defining a Parent: The Case for Intended Parenthood*, 25 BYU J. PUB. L. 245 (2011); Deborah L. Forman, *Embryo Disposition, Divorce & Family Law Contracting: A Model for Enforceability*, 24 COLUM. J. GENDER & L. 378 (2013); Joanna L Grossman, *Parentage Without Gender*, 17 CARDOZO J. CONFLICT RESOL. 717 (2016); Myrisha S. Lewis, *Biology, Genetics, Nurture, and the Law: The Expansion of the Legal Definition of Family to Include Three or More Parents*, 16 NEV. L.J. 743 (2016); Paula A. Monopoli, *Toward Equality: Nonmarital Children and the Uniform Probate Code*, 45 U. MICH. J.L. REFORM 995 (2012); Melissa Murray, *Family Law's Doctrines*, 163 U. PA. L. REV. 1985 (2015); Nancy D. Polikoff, *Response: And Baby Makes. . .How Many? Using* In re M.C. *to Consider Parentage of a Child Conceived Through Sexual Intercourse and Born to a Lesbian Couple*, 100 GEO. L.J. 2015 (2012); Jennifer Sroka, *A Mother Yesterday, But Not Today: Deficiencies of the Uniform Parentage Act for Non-Biological Parents in Same-Sex Relationships*, 47 VAL. U. L. REV. 537 (2013); Benjamin T. Forman, Note, *Statutory Requirements for Artificial Insemination: A Sperm Donor's Fight to Let Go of His Rights*, 9 PITT. J. ENVTL PUB. HEALTH L. 66 (2014); Ann E. Kinsey, Comment, *A Modern King Solomon's Dilemma: Why State Legislatures Should Give Courts the Discretion to Find that a Child Has More than Two Legal Parents*, 51 SAN DIEGO L. REV. 295 (2014); Elizabeth A. Pfenson, Note, *Too Many Cooks in the Kitchen?: The Potential Concerns of Finding More Parents and Fewer Legal Strangers in California's Recently-Proposed Multiple-Parents Bill*, 88 NOTRE DAME L. REV. 2023 (2013); Elizabeth Traylor, Note, *Protecting the Rights of Children of Same-Sex Parents in Indiana by Adopting a Version of the Uniform Parentage Act*, 48 IND. L. REV. 695 (2015).]

ARTICLE 1: GENERAL PROVISIONS

§ 101. SHORT TITLE.

This [Act] may be cited as the Uniform Parentage Act (2000).

§ 102. DEFINITIONS.

In this [Act]:

(1) "Acknowledged father" means a man who has established a father-child relationship under [Article] 3.

(2) "Adjudicated father" means a man who has been adjudicated by a court of competent jurisdiction to be the father of a child.

(3) "Alleged father" means a man who alleges himself to be, or is alleged to be, the genetic father or a possible genetic father of a child, but whose paternity has not been determined. The term does not include:

(A) a presumed father;

(B) a man whose parental rights have been terminated or declared not to exist; or

(C) a male donor.

(4) "Assisted reproduction" means a method of causing pregnancy other than sexual intercourse. The term includes:

(A) intrauterine insemination;

(B) donation of eggs;

(C) donation of embryos;

(D) in-vitro fertilization and transfer of embryos; and

(E) intracytoplasmic sperm injection.

(5) "Child" means an individual of any age whose parentage may be determined under this [Act].

(6) "Commence" means to file the initial pleading seeking an adjudication of parentage in [the appropriate court] of this State.

(7) "Determination of parentage" means the establishment of the parent-child relationship by the signing of a valid acknowledgment of paternity under [Article] 3 or adjudication by the court.

(8) "Donor" means an individual who produces eggs or sperm used for assisted reproduction, whether or not for consideration. The term does not include:

(A) a husband who provides sperm, or a wife who provides eggs, to be used for assisted reproduction by the wife;

(B) a woman who gives birth to a child by means of assisted reproduction [, except as otherwise provided in [Article] 8]; or

(C) a parent under Article 7 [or an intended parent under Article 8].

(9) "Ethnic or racial group" means, for purposes of genetic testing, a recognized group that an individual identifies as all or part of the individual's ancestry or that is so identified by other information.

(10) "Genetic testing" means an analysis of genetic markers to exclude or identify a man as the father or a woman as the mother of a child. The term includes an analysis of one or a combination of the following:

(A) deoxyribonucleic acid; and

(B) blood-group antigens, red-cell antigens, human-leukocyte antigens, serum enzymes, serum proteins, or red-cell enzymes.

[(11)   "Gestational mother" means an adult woman who gives birth to a child under a gestational agreement.]

(12) "Man" means a male individual of any age.

(13) "Parent" means an individual who has established a parent-child relationship under Section 201.

(14) "Parent-child relationship" means the legal relationship between a child and a parent of the child. The term includes the mother-child relationship and the father-child relationship.

(15) "Paternity index" means the likelihood of paternity calculated by computing the ratio between:

(A) the likelihood that the tested man is the father, based on the genetic markers of the tested man, mother, and child, conditioned on the hypothesis that the tested man is the father of the child; and

(B) the likelihood that the tested man is not the father, based on the genetic markers of the tested man, mother, and child, conditioned on the hypothesis that the tested man is not the father of the child and that the father is of the same ethnic or racial group as the tested man.

(16) "Presumed father" means a man who, by operation of law under Section 204, is recognized as the father of a child until that status is rebutted or confirmed in a judicial proceeding.

(17) "Probability of paternity" means the measure, for the ethnic or racial group to which the alleged father belongs, of the probability that the man in question is the father of the child, compared with a random, unrelated man of the same ethnic or racial group, expressed as a percentage incorporating the paternity index and a prior probability.

(18) "Record" means information that is inscribed on a tangible medium or that is stored in an electronic or other medium and is retrievable in perceivable form.

(19) "Signatory" means an individual who authenticates a record and is bound by its terms.

(20) "State" means a State of the United States, the District of Columbia, Puerto Rico, the United States Virgin Islands, or any territory or insular possession subject to the jurisdiction of the United States.

(21) "Support-enforcement agency" means a public official or agency authorized to seek:

(A) enforcement of support orders or laws relating to the duty of support;

(B) establishment or modification of child support;

(C) determination of parentage; or

(D) location of child-support obligors and their income and assets.

§ 103. SCOPE OF [ACT]; CHOICE OF LAW.

(a) This [Act] applies to determination of parentage in this State.

(b) The court shall apply the law of this State to adjudicate the parent-child relationship. The applicable law does not depend on:

(1) the place of birth of the child; or

(2) the past or present residence of the child.

(c) This [Act] does not create, enlarge, or diminish parental rights or duties under other law of this State.

[(d) This [Act] does not authorize or prohibit an agreement between a woman and a man and another woman in which the woman relinquishes all rights as a parent of a child conceived by means of assisted reproduction, and which provides that the man and other woman become the parents of the child. If a birth results under such an agreement and the agreement is unenforceable under [the law of this State], the parent-child relationship is determined as provided in [Article] 2.]

§ 104. COURT OF THIS STATE.

The [designate] court is authorized to adjudicate parentage under this [Act].

§ 105. PROTECTION OF PARTICIPANTS.

Proceedings under this [Act] are subject to other law of this State governing the health, safety, privacy, and liberty of a child or other individual who could be jeopardized by disclosure of identifying information, including address, telephone number, place of employment, social security number, and the child's day-care facility and school.

§ 106. DETERMINATION OF MATERNITY.

Provisions of this [Act] relating to determination of paternity apply to determinations of maternity.

ARTICLE 2:   PARENT-CHILD RELATIONSHIP

§ 201. ESTABLISHMENT OF PARENT-CHILD RELATIONSHIP.

(a) The mother-child relationship is established between a woman and a child by:

(1) the woman's having given birth to the child [, except as otherwise provided in [Article] 8];

(2) an adjudication of the woman's maternity; [or]

(3) adoption of the child by the woman [; or

(4) an adjudication confirming the woman as a parent of a child born to a gestational mother if the agreement was validated under [Article] 8 or is enforceable under other law].

(b) The father-child relationship is established between a man and a child by:

(1) an unrebutted presumption of the man's paternity of the child under Section 204;

(2) an effective acknowledgment of paternity by the man under [Article] 3, unless the acknowledgment has been rescinded or successfully challenged;

(3) an adjudication of the man's paternity;

(4) adoption of the child by the man; [or]

(5) the man's having consented to assisted reproduction by a woman under [Article] 7 which resulted in the birth of the child [; or

(6) an adjudication confirming the man as a parent of a child born to a gestational mother if the agreement was validated under [Article] 8 or is enforceable under other law].

§ 202. NO DISCRIMINATION BASED ON MARITAL STATUS.

A child born to parents who are not married to each other has the same rights under the law as a child born to parents who are married to each other.

§ 203. CONSEQUENCES OF ESTABLISHMENT OF PARENTAGE.

Unless parental rights are terminated, a parent-child relationship established under this [Act] applies for all purposes, except as otherwise specifically provided by other law of this State.

§ 204. PRESUMPTION OF PATERNITY.

(a) A man is presumed to be the father of a child if:

(1) he and the mother of the child are married to each other and the child is born during the marriage;

(2)   he and the mother of the child were married to each other and the child is born within 300 days after the marriage is terminated by death, annulment, declaration of invalidity, or divorce [, or after a decree of separation];

(3)   before the birth of the child, he and the mother of the child married each other in apparent compliance with law, even if the attempted marriage is or could be declared invalid, and the child is born during the invalid marriage or within 300 days after its termination by death, annulment, declaration of invalidity, or divorce [, or after a decree of separation];

(4)   after the birth of the child, he and the mother of the child married each other in apparent compliance with law, whether or not the marriage is or could be declared invalid, and he voluntarily asserted his paternity of the child, and:

(A)   the assertion is in a record filed with [state agency maintaining birth records];

(B)   he agreed to be and is named as the child's father on the child's birth certificate; or

(C)   he promised in a record to support the child as his own; or

(5)   for the first two years of the child's life, he resided in the same household with the child and openly held out the child as his own.

(b)   A presumption of paternity established under this section may be rebutted only by an adjudication under [Article] 6.

ARTICLE 3:   VOLUNTARY ACKNOWLEDGMENT OF PATERNITY

§ 301. ACKNOWLEDGMENT OF PATERNITY.

The mother of a child and a man claiming to be the genetic father of the child may sign an acknowledgment of paternity with intent to establish the man's paternity.

§ 302. EXECUTION OF ACKNOWLEDGMENT OF PATERNITY.

(a)   An acknowledgment of paternity must:

(1)   be in a record;

(2)   be signed, or otherwise authenticated, under penalty of perjury by the mother and by the man seeking to establish his paternity;

(3)   state that the child whose paternity is being acknowledged:

(A)   does not have a presumed father, or has a presumed father whose full name is stated; and

(B) does not have another acknowledged or adjudicated father;

(4) state whether there has been genetic testing and, if so, that the acknowledging man's claim of paternity is consistent with the results of the testing; and

(5) state that the signatories understand that the acknowledgment is the equivalent of a judicial adjudication of paternity of the child and that a challenge to the acknowledgment is permitted only under limited circumstances and is barred after two years.

(b) An acknowledgment of paternity is void if it:

(1) states that another man is a presumed father, unless a denial of paternity signed or otherwise authenticated by the presumed father is filed with the [agency maintaining birth records];

(2) states that another man is an acknowledged or adjudicated father; or

(3) falsely denies the existence of a presumed, acknowledged, or adjudicated father of the child.

(c) A presumed father may sign or otherwise authenticate an acknowledgment of paternity.

§ 303. DENIAL OF PATERNITY.

A presumed father may sign a denial of his paternity. The denial is valid only if:

(1) an acknowledgment of paternity signed, or otherwise authenticated, by another man is filed pursuant to Section 305;

(2) the denial is in a record, and is signed, or otherwise authenticated, under penalty of perjury; and

(3) the presumed father has not previously:

(A) acknowledged his paternity, unless the previous acknowledgment has been rescinded pursuant to Section 307 or successfully challenged pursuant to Section 308; or

(B) been adjudicated to be the father of the child.

§ 304. RULES FOR ACKNOWLEDGMENT AND DENIAL OF PATERNITY.

(a) An acknowledgment of paternity and a denial of paternity may be contained in a single document or may be signed in counterparts, and may be filed separately or simultaneously. If the acknowledgement and denial are both necessary, neither is valid until both are filed.

(b) An acknowledgment of paternity or a denial of paternity may be signed before the birth of the child.

(c) Subject to subsection (a), an acknowledgment of paternity or denial of paternity takes effect on the birth of the child or the filing of the document with the [agency maintaining birth records], whichever occurs later.

(d) An acknowledgment of paternity or denial of paternity signed by a minor is valid if it is otherwise in compliance with this [Act].

§ 305. EFFECT OF ACKNOWLEDGMENT OR DENIAL OF PATERNITY.

(a) Except as otherwise provided in Sections 307 and 308, a valid acknowledgment of paternity filed with the [agency maintaining birth records] is equivalent to an adjudication of paternity of a child and confers upon the acknowledged father all of the rights and duties of a parent.

(b) Except as otherwise provided in Sections 307 and 308, a valid denial of paternity by a presumed father filed with the [agency maintaining birth records] in conjunction with a valid acknowledgment of paternity is equivalent to an adjudication of the nonpaternity of the presumed father and discharges the presumed father from all rights and duties of a parent.

§ 306. NO FILING FEE.

The [agency maintaining birth records] may not charge for filing an acknowledgment of paternity or denial of paternity.

§ 307. PROCEEDING FOR RESCISSION.

A signatory may rescind an acknowledgment of paternity or denial of paternity by commencing a proceeding to rescind before the earlier of:

(1) 60 days after the effective date of the acknowledgment or denial, as provided in Section 304; or

(2) the date of the first hearing, in a proceeding to which the signatory is a party, before a court to adjudicate an issue relating to the child, including a proceeding that establishes support.

§ 308. CHALLENGE AFTER EXPIRATION OF PERIOD FOR RESCISSION.

(a) After the period for rescission under Section 307 has expired, a signatory of an acknowledgment of paternity or denial of paternity may commence a proceeding to challenge the acknowledgment or denial only:

(1) on the basis of fraud, duress, or material mistake of fact; and

(2) within two years after the acknowledgment or denial is filed with the [agency maintaining birth records].

(b) A party challenging an acknowledgment of paternity or denial of paternity has the burden of proof.

§ 309. PROCEDURE FOR RESCISSION OF CHALLENGE.

(a) Every signatory to an acknowledgment of paternity and any related denial of paternity must be made a party to a proceeding to rescind or challenge the acknowledgment or denial.

(b) For the purpose of rescission of, or challenge to, an acknowledgment of paternity or denial of paternity, a signatory submits to personal jurisdiction of this State by signing the acknowledgment or denial, effective upon the filing of the document with the [agency maintaining birth records].

(c) Except for good cause shown, during the pendency of a proceeding to rescind or challenge an acknowledgment of paternity or denial of paternity, the court may not suspend the legal responsibilities of a signatory arising from the acknowledgment, including the duty to pay child support.

(d) A proceeding to rescind or to challenge an acknowledgment of paternity or denial of paternity must be conducted in the same manner as a proceeding to adjudicate parentage under [Article] 6.

(e) At the conclusion of a proceeding to rescind or challenge an acknowledgment of paternity or denial of paternity, the court shall order the [agency maintaining birth records] to amend the birth record of the child, if appropriate.

§ 310. RATIFICATION BARRED.

A court or administrative agency conducting a judicial or administrative proceeding is not required or permitted to ratify an unchallenged acknowledgment of paternity.

§ 311. FULL FAITH AND CREDIT.

A court of this State shall give full faith and credit to an acknowledgment of paternity or denial of paternity effective in another State if the acknowledgment or denial has been signed and is otherwise in compliance with the law of the other State.

§ 312. FORMS FOR ACKNOWLEDGMENT AND DENIAL OF PATERNITY.

(a) To facilitate compliance with this [article], the [agency maintaining birth records] shall prescribe forms for the acknowledgment of paternity and the denial of paternity.

(b) A valid acknowledgment of paternity or denial of paternity is not affected by a later modification of the prescribed form.

§ 313. RELEASE OF INFORMATION.

The [agency maintaining birth records] may release information relating to the acknowledgment of paternity or denial of paternity to a signatory of the acknowledgment or denial and to courts and [appropriate state or federal agencies] of this or another State.

§ 314. ADOPTION OF RULES.

The [agency maintaining birth records] may adopt rules to implement this [article].]

ARTICLE 4:   REGISTRY OF PATERNITY

PART 1.   GENERAL PROVISIONS

§ 401. ESTABLISHMENT OF REGISTRY.

A registry of paternity is established in the [agency maintaining the registry].

§ 402. REGISTRATION FOR NOTIFICATION.

(a)   Except as otherwise provided in subsection (b) or Section 405, a man who desires to be notified of a proceeding for adoption of, or termination of parental rights regarding, a child that he may have fathered must register in the registry of paternity before the birth of the child or within 30 days after the birth.

(b)   A man is not required to register if [:

(1)] a father-child relationship between the man and the child has been established under this [Act] or other law [; or

(2) the man commences a proceeding to adjudicate his paternity before the court has terminated his parental rights].

(c)   A registrant shall promptly notify the registry in a record of any change in the information registered. The [agency maintaining the registry] shall incorporate all new information received into its records but need not affirmatively seek to obtain current information for incorporation in the registry.

§ 403. NOTICE OF PROCEEDING.

Notice of a proceeding for the adoption of, or termination of parental rights regarding, a child must be given to a registrant who has timely registered. Notice must be given in a manner prescribed for service of process in a civil action.

§ 404. TERMINATION OF PARENTAL RIGHTS: CHILD UNDER ONE YEAR OF AGE.

The parental rights of a man who may be the father of a child may be terminated without notice if:

(1)   the child has not attained one year of age at the time of the termination of parental rights;

(2) the man did not register timely with the [agency maintaining the registry]; and

(3) the man is not exempt from registration under Section 402.

§ 405. TERMINATION OF PARENTAL RIGHTS: CHILD AT LEAST ONE YEAR OF AGE.

(a) If a child has attained one year of age, notice of a proceeding for adoption of, or termination of parental rights regarding, the child must be given to every alleged father of the child, whether or not he has registered with the [agency maintaining the registry].

(b) Notice must be given in a manner prescribed for service of process in a civil action.

PART 2. OPERATION OF REGISTRY

§ 411. REQUIRED FORM.

The [agency maintaining the registry] shall prepare a form for registering with the agency. The form must require the signature of the registrant. The form must state that the form is signed under penalty of perjury. The form must also state that:

(1) a timely registration entitles the registrant to notice of a proceeding for adoption of the child or termination of the registrant's parental rights;

(2) a timely registration does not commence a proceeding to establish paternity;

(3) the information disclosed on the form may be used against the registrant to establish paternity;

(4) services to assist in establishing paternity are available to the registrant through the support-enforcement agency;

(5) the registrant should also register in another State if conception or birth of the child occurred in the other State;

(6) information on registries of other States is available from [appropriate state agency or agencies]; and

(7) procedures exist to rescind the registration of a claim of paternity.

§ 412. FURNISHING OF INFORMATION; CONFIDENTIALITY.

(a) The [agency maintaining the registry] need not seek to locate the mother of a child who is the subject of a registration, but the [agency maintaining the registry] shall send a copy of the notice of registration to a mother if she has provided an address.

(b) Information contained in the registry is confidential and may be released on request only to:

(1) a court or a person designated by the court;

(2) the mother of the child who is the subject of the registration;

(3) an agency authorized by other law to receive the information;

(4) a licensed child-placing agency;

(5) a support-enforcement agency;

(6) a party or the party's attorney of record in a proceeding under this [Act] or in a proceeding for adoption of, or for termination of parental rights regarding, a child who is the subject of the registration; and

(7) the registry of paternity in another State.

§ 413. PENALTY FOR RELEASING INFORMATION.

An individual commits a [appropriate level misdemeanor] if the individual intentionally releases information from the registry to another individual or agency not authorized to receive the information under Section 412.

§ 414. RESCISSION OF REGISTRATION.

A registrant may rescind his registration at any time by sending to the registry a rescission in a record signed or otherwise authenticated by him, and witnessed or notarized.

§ 415. UNTIMELY REGISTRATION.

If a man registers more than 30 days after the birth of the child, the [agency] shall notify the registrant that on its face his registration was not filed timely.

§ 416. FEES FOR REGISTRY.

(a) A fee may not be charged for filing a registration or a rescission of registration.

(b) [Except as otherwise provided in subsection (c), the] [The] [agency maintaining the registry] may charge a reasonable fee for making a search of the registry and for furnishing a certificate.

[(c) A support-enforcement agency [is] [and other appropriate agencies, if any, are] not required to pay a fee authorized by subsection (b).]

PART 3.   SEARCH OF REGISTRIES

§ 421. SEARCH OF APPROPRIATE REGISTRY.

(a) If a father-child relationship has not been established under this [Act] for a child under one year of age, a [petitioner] for adoption of, or termination of parental rights regarding, the child, must obtain a certificate of search of the registry of paternity.

(b) If a [petitioner] for adoption of, or termination of parental rights regarding, a child has reason to believe that the conception or birth of the child may have occurred in another State, the [petitioner] must also obtain a certificate of search from the registry of paternity, if any, in that State.

§ 422. CERTIFICATE OF SEARCH OF REGISTRY.

(a) The [agency maintaining the registry] shall furnish to the requester a certificate of search of the registry on request of an individual, court, or agency identified in Section 412.

(b) A certificate provided by the [agency maintaining the registry] must be signed on behalf of the [agency] and state that:

(1) a search has been made of the registry; and

(2) a registration containing the information required to identify the registrant:

(A) has been found and is attached to the certificate of search; or

(B) has not been found.

(c) A [petitioner] must file the certificate of search with the court before a proceeding for adoption of, or termination of parental rights regarding, a child may be concluded.

§ 423. ADMISSIBILITY OF REGISTERED INFORMATION.

A certificate of search of the registry of paternity in this or another State is admissible in a proceeding for adoption of, or termination of parental rights regarding, a child and, if relevant, in other legal proceedings.

ARTICLE 5:   GENETIC TESTING

§ 501. SCOPE OF ARTICLE.

This [article] governs genetic testing of an individual to determine parentage, whether the individual:

(1) voluntarily submits to testing; or

(2) is tested pursuant to an order of the court or a support-enforcement agency.

§ 502. ORDER FOR TESTING.

(a) Except as otherwise provided in this [article] and [Article] 6, the court shall order the child and other designated individuals to submit to genetic testing if the request for testing is supported by the sworn statement of a party to the proceeding:

   (1) alleging paternity and stating facts establishing a reasonable probability of the requisite sexual contact between the individuals; or

   (2) denying paternity and stating facts establishing a possibility that sexual contact between the individuals, if any, did not result in the conception of the child.

   (b) A support-enforcement agency may order genetic testing only if there is no presumed, acknowledged, or adjudicated father.

   (c) If a request for genetic testing of a child is made before birth, the court or support-enforcement agency may not order in-utero testing.

   (d) If two or more men are subject to court-ordered genetic testing, the testing may be ordered concurrently or sequentially.

§ 503. REQUIREMENTS FOR GENETIC TESTING.

   (a) Genetic testing must be of a type reasonably relied upon by experts in the field of genetic testing and performed in a testing laboratory accredited by:

   (1) the American Association of Blood Banks, or a successor to its functions;

   (2) the American Society for Histocompatibility and Immunogenetics, or a successor to its functions; or

   (3) an accrediting body designated by the federal Secretary of Health and Human Services.

   (b) A specimen used in genetic testing may consist of one or more samples, or a combination of samples, of blood, buccal cells, bone, hair, or other body tissue or fluid. The specimen used in the testing need not be of the same kind for each individual undergoing genetic testing.

   (c) Based on the ethnic or racial group of an individual, the testing laboratory shall determine the databases from which to select frequencies for use in calculation of the probability of paternity. If there is disagreement as to the testing laboratory's choice, the following rules apply:

   (1) The individual objecting may require the testing laboratory, within 30 days after receipt of the report of the test, to recalculate the probability of paternity using an ethnic or racial group different from that used by the laboratory.

   (2) The individual objecting to the testing laboratory's initial choice shall:

      (A) if the frequencies are not available to the testing laboratory for the ethnic or racial group requested, provide the requested frequencies compiled in a manner recognized by accrediting bodies; or

(B) engage another testing laboratory to perform the calculations.

(3) The testing laboratory may use its own statistical estimate if there is a question regarding which ethnic or racial group is appropriate. If available, the testing laboratory shall calculate the frequencies using statistics for any other ethnic or racial group requested.

(d) If, after recalculation using a different ethnic or racial group, genetic testing does not rebuttably identify a man as the father of a child under Section 505, an individual who has been tested may be required to submit to additional genetic testing.

§ 504. REPORT OF GENETIC TESTING.

(a) A report of genetic testing must be in a record and signed under penalty of perjury by a designee of the testing laboratory. A report made under the requirements of this [article] is self-authenticating.

(b) Documentation from the testing laboratory of the following information is sufficient to establish a reliable chain of custody that allows the results of genetic testing to be admissible without testimony:

(1) the names and photographs of the individuals whose specimens have been taken;

(2) the names of the individuals who collected the specimens;

(3) the places and dates the specimens were collected;

(4) the names of the individuals who received the specimens in the testing laboratory; and

(5) the dates the specimens were received.

§ 505. GENETIC TESTING RESULTS; REBUTTAL.

(a) Under this [Act], a man is rebuttably identified as the father of a child if the genetic testing complies with this [article] and the results disclose that:

(1) the man has at least a 99 percent probability of paternity, using a prior probability of 0.50, as calculated by using the combined paternity index obtained in the testing; and

(2) a combined paternity index of at least 100 to 1.

(b) A man identified under subsection (a) as the father of the child may rebut the genetic testing results only by other genetic testing satisfying the requirements of this [article] which:

(1) excludes the man as a genetic father of the child; or

(2) identifies another man as the possible father of the child.

(c)   Except as otherwise provided in Section 510, if more than one man is identified by genetic testing as the possible father of the child, the court shall order them to submit to further genetic testing to identify the genetic father.

§ 506. COSTS OF GENETIC TESTING.

(a)   Subject to assessment of costs under [Article] 6, the cost of initial genetic testing must be advanced:

(1)   by a support-enforcement agency in a proceeding in which the support-enforcement agency is providing services;

(2)   by the individual who made the request;

(3)   as agreed by the parties; or

(4)   as ordered by the court.

(b)   In cases in which the cost is advanced by the support-enforcement agency, the agency may seek reimbursement from a man who is rebuttably identified as the father.

§ 507. ADDITIONAL GENETIC TESTING.

The court or the support-enforcement agency shall order additional genetic testing upon the request of a party who contests the result of the original testing. If the previous genetic testing identified a man as the father of the child under Section 505, the court or agency may not order additional testing unless the party provides advance payment for the testing.

§ 508. GENETIC TESTING WHEN SPECIMENS NOT AVAILABLE.

(a)   Subject to subsection (b), if a genetic-testing specimen is not available from a man who may be the father of a child, for good cause and under circumstances the court considers to be just, the court may order the following individuals to submit specimens for genetic testing:

(1)   the parents of the man;

(2)   brothers and sisters of the man;

(3)   other children of the man and their mothers; and

(4)   other relatives of the man necessary to complete genetic testing.

(b)   Issuance of an order under this section requires a finding that a need for genetic testing outweighs the legitimate interests of the individual sought to be tested.

§ 509. DECEASED INDIVIDUAL.

For good cause shown, the court may order genetic testing of a deceased individual.

§ 510. IDENTICAL BROTHERS.

(a) The court may order genetic testing of a brother of a man identified as the father of a child if the man is commonly believed to have an identical brother and evidence suggests that the brother may be the genetic father of the child.

(b) If each brother satisfies the requirements as the identified father of the child under Section 505 without consideration of another identical brother being identified as the father of the child, the court may rely on nongenetic evidence to adjudicate which brother is the father of the child.

§ 511. CONFIDENTIALITY OF GENETIC TESTING.

(a) Release of the report of genetic testing for parentage is controlled by [applicable state law].

(b) An individual who intentionally releases an identifiable specimen of another individual for any purpose other than that relevant to the proceeding regarding parentage without a court order or the written permission of the individual who furnished the specimen commits a [appropriate level misdemeanor].

ARTICLE 6:   PROCEEDING TO ADJUDICATE PARENTAGE

PART 1.   NATURE OF PROCEEDING

§ 601. PROCEEDING AUTHORIZED.

A civil proceeding may be maintained to adjudicate the parentage of a child. The proceeding is governed by the [rules of civil procedure].

§ 602. STANDING TO MAINTAIN PROCEEDING.

Subject to [Article] 3 and Sections 607 and 609, a proceeding to adjudicate parentage may be maintained by:

(1)   the child;

(2)   the mother of the child;

(3)   a man whose paternity of the child is to be adjudicated;

(4)   the support-enforcement agency [or other governmental agency authorized by other law];

(5)   an authorized adoption agency or licensed child-placing agency; [or]

(6)   a representative authorized by law to act for an individual who would otherwise be entitled to maintain a proceeding but who is deceased, incapacitated, or a minor [; or

(7)   an intended parent under [Article] 8].

§ 603. PARTIES TO PROCEEDING.

The following individuals must be joined as parties in a proceeding to adjudicate parentage:

 (1) the mother of the child; and

 (2) a man whose paternity of the child is to be adjudicated.

§ 604. PERSONAL JURISDICTION.

(a) An individual may not be adjudicated to be a parent unless the court has personal jurisdiction over the individual.

(b) A court of this State having jurisdiction to adjudicate parentage may exercise personal jurisdiction over a nonresident individual, or the guardian or conservator of the individual, if the conditions prescribed in [Section 201 of the Uniform Interstate Family Support Act] are fulfilled.

(c) Lack of jurisdiction over one individual does not preclude the court from making an adjudication of parentage binding on another individual over whom the court has personal jurisdiction.

§ 605. VENUE.

Venue for a proceeding to adjudicate parentage is in the [county] of this State in which:

 (1) the child resides or is found;

 (2) the [respondent] resides or is found if the child does not reside in this State; or

 (3) a proceeding for probate or administration of the presumed or alleged father's estate has been commenced.

§ 606. NO   LIMITATION: CHILD   HAVING   NO   PRESUMED, ACKNOWLEDGED, OR ADJUDICATED FATHER.

A proceeding to adjudicate the parentage of a child having no presumed, acknowledged, or adjudicated father may be commenced at any time, even after:

 (1) the child becomes an adult, but only if the child initiates the proceeding; or

 (2) an earlier proceeding to adjudicate paternity has been dismissed based on the application of a statute of limitation then in effect.

§ 607. LIMITATION: CHILD HAVING PRESUMED FATHER.

(a) Except as otherwise provided in subsection (b), a proceeding brought by a presumed father, the mother, or another individual to adjudicate the parentage of a child having a presumed father must be commenced not later than two years after the birth of the child.

(b) A proceeding seeking to disprove the father-child relationship between a child and the child's presumed father may be maintained at any time if the court determines that:

(1) the presumed father and the mother of the child neither cohabited nor engaged in sexual intercourse with each other during the probable time of conception; and

(2) the presumed father never openly held out the child as his own.

§ 608. AUTHORITY TO DENY MOTION FOR GENETIC TESTING.

(a) In a proceeding to adjudicate the parentage of a child having a presumed father or to challenge the paternity of a child having an acknowledged father, the court may deny a motion seeking an order for genetic testing of the mother, the child, and the presumed or acknowledged father if the court determines that:

(1) the conduct of the mother or the presumed or acknowledged father estops that party from denying parentage; and

(2) it would be inequitable to disprove the father-child relationship between the child and the presumed or acknowledged father.

(b) In determining whether to deny a motion seeking an order for genetic testing under this section, the court shall consider the best interest of the child, including the following factors:

(1) the length of time between the proceeding to adjudicate parentage and the time that the presumed or acknowledged father was placed on notice that he might not be the genetic father;

(2) the length of time during which the presumed or acknowledged father has assumed the role of father of the child;

(3) the facts surrounding the presumed or acknowledged father's discovery of his possible nonpaternity;

(4) the nature of the relationship between the child and the presumed or acknowledged father;

(5) the age of the child;

(6) the harm that may result to the child if presumed or acknowledged paternity is successfully disproved;

(7) the nature of the relationship between the child and any alleged father;

(8) the extent to which the passage of time reduces the chances of establishing the paternity of another man and a child-support obligation in favor of the child; and

(9) other factors that may affect the equities arising from the disruption of the father-child relationship between the child and the

presumed or acknowledged father or the chance of other harm to the child.

(c)   In a proceeding involving the application of this section, a minor or incapacitated child must be represented by a guardian ad litem.

(d)   Denial of a motion seeking an order for genetic testing must be based on clear and convincing evidence.

(e)   If the court denies a motion seeking an order for genetic testing, it shall issue an order adjudicating the presumed or acknowledged father to be the father of the child.

§ 609. LIMITATION: CHILD HAVING ACKNOWLEDGED OR ADJUDICATED FATHER.

(a)   If a child has an acknowledged father, a signatory to the acknowledgment of paternity or denial of paternity may commence a proceeding seeking to rescind the acknowledgement or denial or challenge the paternity of the child only within the time allowed under Section 307 or 308.

(b)   If a child has an acknowledged father or an adjudicated father, an individual, other than the child, who is neither a signatory to the acknowledgment of paternity nor a party to the adjudication and who seeks an adjudication of paternity of the child must commence a proceeding not later than two years after the effective date of the acknowledgment or adjudication.

(c)   A proceeding under this section is subject to the application of the principles of estoppel established in Section 608.

§ 610. JOINDER OF PROCEEDINGS.

(a)   Except as otherwise provided in subsection (b), a proceeding to adjudicate parentage may be joined with a proceeding for adoption, termination of parental rights, child custody or visitation, child support, divorce, annulment, [legal separation or separate maintenance,] probate or administration of an estate, or other appropriate proceeding.

(b)   A [respondent] may not join a proceeding described in subsection (a) with a proceeding to adjudicate parentage brought under [the Uniform Interstate Family Support Act].

§ 611. PROCEEDING BEFORE BIRTH.

A proceeding to determine parentage may be commenced before the birth of the child, but may not be concluded until after the birth of the child. The following actions may be taken before the birth of the child:

(1)   service of process;

(2)   discovery; and

(3) except as prohibited by Section 502, collection of specimens for genetic testing.

§ 612. CHILD AS PARTY; REPRESENTATION.

(a) A minor child is a permissible party, but is not a necessary party to a proceeding under this [article].

(b) The court shall appoint an [attorney ad litem] to represent a minor or incapacitated child if the child is a party or the court finds that the interests of the child are not adequately represented.

PART 2.   SPECIAL RULES FOR PROCEEDING TO ADJUDICATE PARENTAGE

§ 621. ADMISSIBILITY OF RESULTS OF GENETIC TESTING; EXPENSES.

(a) Except as otherwise provided in subsection (c), a record of a genetic-testing expert is admissible as evidence of the truth of the facts asserted in the report unless a party objects to its admission within [14] days after its receipt by the objecting party and cites specific grounds for exclusion. The admissibility of the report is not affected by whether the testing was performed:

(1) voluntarily or pursuant to an order of the court or a support-enforcement agency; or

(2) before or after the commencement of the proceeding.

(b) A party objecting to the results of genetic testing may call one or more genetic-testing experts to testify in person or by telephone, videoconference, deposition, or another method approved by the court. Unless otherwise ordered by the court, the party offering the testimony bears the expense for the expert testifying.

(c) If a child has a presumed, acknowledged, or adjudicated father, the results of genetic testing are inadmissible to adjudicate parentage unless performed:

(1) with the consent of both the mother and the presumed, acknowledged, or adjudicated father; or

(2) pursuant to an order of the court under Section 502.

(d) Copies of bills for genetic testing and for prenatal and postnatal health care for the mother and child which are furnished to the adverse party not less than 10 days before the date of a hearing are admissible to establish:

(1) the amount of the charges billed; and

(2) that the charges were reasonable, necessary, and customary.

§ 622. CONSEQUENCES OF DECLINING GENETIC TESTING.

(a) An order for genetic testing is enforceable by contempt.

(b) If an individual whose paternity is being determined declines to submit to genetic testing ordered by the court, the court for that reason may adjudicate parentage contrary to the position of that individual.

(c) Genetic testing of the mother of a child is not a condition precedent to testing the child and a man whose paternity is being determined. If the mother is unavailable or declines to submit to genetic testing, the court may order the testing of the child and every man whose paternity is being adjudicated.

§ 623. ADMISSION OF PATERNITY AUTHORIZED.

(a) A [respondent] in a proceeding to adjudicate parentage may admit to the paternity of a child by filing a pleading to that effect or by admitting paternity under penalty of perjury when making an appearance or during a hearing.

(b) If the court finds that the admission of paternity satisfies the requirements of this section and finds that there is no reason to question the admission, the court shall issue an order adjudicating the child to be the child of the man admitting paternity.

§ 624. TEMPORARY ORDER.

(a) In a proceeding under this [article], the court shall issue a temporary order for support of a child if the order is appropriate and the individual ordered to pay support is:

(1) a presumed father of the child;

(2) petitioning to have his paternity adjudicated;

(3) identified as the father through genetic testing under Section 505;

(4) an alleged father who has declined to submit to genetic testing;

(5) shown by clear and convincing evidence to be the father of the child; or

(6) the mother of the child.

(b) A temporary order may include provisions for custody and visitation as provided by other law of this State.

PART 3.   HEARINGS OF ADJUDICATION

§ 631. RULES FOR ADJUDICATION OF PATERNITY.

The court shall apply the following rules to adjudicate the paternity of a child:

(1) The paternity of a child having a presumed, acknowledged, or adjudicated father may be disproved only by admissible results of genetic testing excluding that man as the father of the child or identifying another man as the father of the child.

(2) Unless the results of genetic testing are admitted to rebut other results of genetic testing, a man identified as the father of a child under Section 505 must be adjudicated the father of the child.

(3) If the court finds that genetic testing under Section 505 neither identifies nor excludes a man as the father of a child, the court may not dismiss the proceeding. In that event, the results of genetic testing, and other evidence, are admissible to adjudicate the issue of paternity.

(4) Unless the results of genetic testing are admitted to rebut other results of genetic testing, a man excluded as the father of a child by genetic testing must be adjudicated not to be the father of the child.

§ 632. JURY PROHIBITED.

The court, without a jury, shall adjudicate paternity of a child.

§ 633. HEARINGS; INSPECTION OF RECORDS.

(a) On request of a party and for good cause shown, the court may close a proceeding under this [article].

(b) A final order in a proceeding under this [article] is available for public inspection. Other papers and records are available only with the consent of the parties or on order of the court for good cause.

§ 634. ORDER ON DEFAULT.

The court shall issue an order adjudicating the paternity of a man who:

(1) after service of process, is in default; and

(2) is found by the court to be the father of a child.

§ 635. DISMISSAL FOR WANT OF PROSECUTION.

The court may issue an order dismissing a proceeding commenced under this [Act] for want of prosecution only without prejudice. An order of dismissal for want of prosecution purportedly with prejudice is void and has only the effect of a dismissal without prejudice.

§ 636. ORDER ADJUDICATING PARENTAGE.

(a) The court shall issue an order adjudicating whether a man alleged or claiming to be the father is the parent of the child.

(b) An order adjudicating parentage must identify the child by name and date of birth.

(c) Except as otherwise provided in subsection (d), the court may assess filing fees, reasonable attorney's fees, fees for genetic testing, other costs, and necessary travel and other reasonable expenses incurred in a proceeding under this [article]. The court may award attorney's fees, which may be paid directly to the attorney, who may enforce the order in the attorney's own name.

(d) The court may not assess fees, costs, or expenses against the support-enforcement agency of this State or another State, except as provided by other law.

(e) On request of a party and for good cause shown, the court may order that the name of the child be changed.

(f) If the order of the court is at variance with the child's birth certificate, the court shall order [agency maintaining birth records] to issue an amended birth registration.

§ 637. BINDING EFFECT OF DETERMINATION OF PARENTAGE.

(a) Except as otherwise provided in subsection (b), a determination of parentage is binding on:

(1) all signatories to an acknowledgement or denial of paternity as provided in [Article] 3; and

(2) all parties to an adjudication by a court acting under circumstances that satisfy the jurisdictional requirements of [Section 201 of the Uniform Interstate Family Support Act].

(b) A child is not bound by a determination of parentage under this [Act] unless:

(1) the determination was based on an unrescinded acknowledgment of paternity and the acknowledgement is consistent with the results of genetic testing;

(2) the adjudication of parentage was based on a finding consistent with the results of genetic testing and the consistency is declared in the determination or is otherwise shown; or

(3) the child was a party or was represented in the proceeding determining parentage by an [attorney ad litem].

(c) In a proceeding to dissolve a marriage, the court is deemed to have made an adjudication of the parentage of a child if the court acts under circumstances that satisfy the jurisdictional requirements of [Section 201 of the Uniform Interstate Family Support Act], and the final order:

(1) expressly identifies a child as a "child of the marriage," "issue of the marriage," or similar words indicating that the husband is the father of the child; or

(2) provides for support of the child by the husband unless paternity is specifically disclaimed in the order.

(d) Except as otherwise provided in subsection (b), a determination of parentage may be a defense in a subsequent proceeding seeking to adjudicate parentage by an individual who was not a party to the earlier proceeding.

(e) A party to an adjudication of paternity may challenge the adjudication only under law of this State relating to appeal, vacation of judgments, or other judicial review.

ARTICLE 7:   CHILD OF ASSISTED REPRODUCTION

§ 701. SCOPE OF ARTICLE.

This [article] does not apply to the birth of a child conceived by means of sexual intercourse [, or as the result of a gestational agreement as provided in [Article] 8].

§ 702. PARENTAL STATUS OF DONOR.

A donor is not a parent of a child conceived by means of assisted reproduction.

§ 703. PATERNITY OF CHILD OF ASSISTED REPRODUCTION.

A man who provides sperm for, or consents to, assisted reproduction by a woman as provided in Section 704 with the intent to be the parent of her child, is a parent of the resulting child.

§ 704. CONSENT TO ASSISTED REPRODUCTION.

(a) Consent by a woman, and a man who intends to be a parent of a child born to the woman by assisted reproduction must be in a record signed by the woman and the man. This requirement does not apply to a donor.

(b) Failure a man to sign a consent required by subsection (a), before or after birth of the child, does not preclude a finding of paternity if the woman and the man, during the first two years of the child's life resided together in the same household with the child and openly held out the child as their own.

§ 705. LIMITATION ON HUSBAND'S DISPUTE OF PATERNITY.

(a) Except as otherwise provided in subsection (b), the husband of a wife who gives birth to a child by means of assisted reproduction may not challenge his paternity of the child unless:

(1) within two years after learning of the birth of the child he commences a proceeding to adjudicate his paternity; and

(2) the court finds that he did not consent to the assisted reproduction, before or after birth of the child.

(b) A proceeding to adjudicate paternity may be maintained at any time if the court determines that:

(1) the husband did not provide sperm for, or before or after the birth of the child consent to, assisted reproduction by his wife;

(2) the husband and the mother of the child have not cohabited since the probable time of assisted reproduction; and

(3) the husband never openly held out the child as his own.

(c) The limitation provided in this section applies to a marriage declared invalid after assisted reproduction.

§ 706. EFFECT OF DISSOLUTION OF MARRIAGE OR WITHDRAWAL OF CONSENT.

(a) If a marriage is dissolved before placement of eggs, sperm, or embryos, the former spouse is not a parent of the resulting child unless the former spouse consented in a record that if assisted reproduction were to occur after a divorce, the former spouse would be a parent of the child.

(b) The consent of a woman or a man to assisted reproduction may be withdrawn by that individual in a record at any time before placement of eggs, sperm, or embryos. An individual who withdraws consent under this section is not a parent of the resulting child.

§ 707. PARENTAL STATUS OF DECEASED INDIVIDUAL.

If an individual who consented in a record to be a parent by assisted reproduction dies before placement of eggs, sperm, or embryos, the deceased individual is not a parent of the resulting child unless the deceased spouse consented in a record that if assisted reproduction were to occur after death, the deceased individual would be a parent of the child.

ARTICLE 8:   GESTATIONAL AGREEMENT

§ 801. GESTATIONAL AGREEMENT AUTHORIZED.

(a) A prospective gestational mother, her husband if she is married, a donor or the donors, and the intended parents may enter into a written agreement providing that:

(1) the prospective gestational mother agrees to pregnancy by means of assisted reproduction;

(2) the prospective gestational mother, her husband if she is married, and the donors relinquish all rights and duties as the parents of a child conceived through assisted reproduction; and

(3)   the intended parents become the parents of the child.

(b)   The man and the woman who are the intended parents must both be parties to the gestational agreement.

(c)   A gestational agreement is enforceable only if validated as provided in Section 803.

(d)   A gestational agreement does not apply to the birth of a child conceived by means of sexual intercourse.

(e)   A gestational agreement may provide for payment of consideration.

(f)   A gestational agreement may not limit the right of the gestational mother to make decisions to safeguard her health or that of the embryos or fetus.

§ 802.   REQUIREMENTS OF PETITION.

(a)   The intended parents and the prospective gestational mother may commence a proceeding in the [appropriate court] to validate a gestational agreement.

(b)   A proceeding to validate a gestational agreement may not be maintained unless:

(1)   the mother or the intended parents have been residents of this State for at least 90 days;

(2)   the prospective gestational mother's husband, if she is married, is joined in the proceeding; and

(3)   a copy of the gestational agreement is attached to the [petition].

§ 803.   HEARING TO VALIDATE GESTATIONAL AGREEMENT.

(a)   If the requirements of subsection (b) are satisfied, a court may issue an order validating the gestational agreement and declaring that the intended parents will be the parents of a child born during the term of the of the agreement.

(b)   The court may issue an order under subsection (a) only on finding that:

(1)   the residence requirements of Section 802 have been satisfied and the parties have submitted to the jurisdiction of the court under the jurisdictional standards of this [Act];

(2)   unless waived by the court, the [relevant child-welfare agency] has made a home study of the intended parents and the intended parents meet the standards of suitability applicable to adoptive parents;

(3)   all parties have voluntarily entered into the agreement and understand its terms;

(4) adequate provision has been made for all reasonable health-care expense associated with the gestational agreement until the birth of the child, including responsibility for those expenses if the agreement is terminated; and

(5) the consideration, if any, paid to the prospective gestational mother is reasonable.

§ 804. INSPECTION OF RECORDS.

The proceedings, records, and identities of the individual parties to a gestational agreement under this [article] are subject to inspection under the standards of confidentiality applicable to adoptions as provided under other law of this State.

§ 805. EXCLUSIVE, CONTINUING JURISDICTION.

Subject to the jurisdictional standards of [Section 201 of the Uniform Child Custody Jurisdiction and Enforcement Act], the court conducting a proceeding under this [article] has exclusive, continuing jurisdiction of all matters arising out of the gestational agreement until a child born to the gestational mother during the period governed by the agreement attains the age of 180 days.

§ 806. TERMINATION OF GESTATIONAL AGREEMENT.

(a) After issuance of an order under this [article], but before the prospective gestational mother becomes pregnant by means of assisted reproduction, the prospective gestational mother, her husband, or either of the intended parents may terminate the gestational agreement by giving written notice of termination to all other parties.

(b) The court for good cause shown may terminate the gestational agreement.

(c) An individual who terminates a gestational agreement shall file notice of the termination with the court. On receipt of the notice, the court shall vacate the order issued under this [article]. An individual who does not notify the court of the termination of the agreement is subject to appropriate sanctions.

(d) Neither a prospective gestational mother nor her husband, if any, is liable to the intended parents for terminating a gestational agreement pursuant to this section.

§ 807. PARENTAGE UNDER VALIDATED GESTATIONAL AGREEMENT.

(a) Upon birth of a child to a gestational mother, the intended parents shall file notice with the court that a child has been born to the gestational mother within 300 days after assisted reproduction. Thereupon, the court shall issue an order:

(1) confirming that the intended parents are the parents of the child;

(2) if necessary, ordering that the child be surrendered to the intended parents; and

(3) directing the [agency maintaining birth records] to issue a birth certificate naming the intended parents as parents of the child.

(b) If the parentage of a child born to a gestational mother is alleged not to be the result of assisted reproduction, the court shall order genetic testing to determine the parentage of the child.

(c) If the intended parents fail to file notice required under subsection (a), the gestational mother or the appropriate State agency may file notice with the court that a child has been born to the gestational mother within 300 days after assisted reproduction. Upon proof of a court order issued pursuant to Section 803 validating the gestational agreement, the court shall order the intended parents are the parents of the child and are financially responsible for the child.

§ 808. GESTATIONAL AGREEMENT: EFFECT OF SUBSEQUENT MARRIAGE.

After the issuance of an order under this [article], subsequent marriage of the gestational mother does not affect the validity of a gestational agreement, her husband's consent to the agreement is not required, and her husband is not a presumed father of the resulting child.

§ 809. EFFECT OF NONVALIDATED GESTATIONAL AGREEMENT.

(a) A gestational agreement, whether in a record or not, that is not judicially validated is not enforceable.

(b) If a birth results under a gestational agreement that is not judicially validated as provided in this [article], the parent-child relationship is determined as provided in [Article] 2.

(c) Individuals who are parties to a nonvalidated gestational agreement as intended parents may be held liable for support of the resulting child, even if the agreement is otherwise unenforceable. The liability under this subsection includes assessing all expenses and fees as provided in Section 636.]

ARTICLE 9: MISCELLANEOUS PROVISIONS

§ 901. UNIFORMITY OF APPLICATION AND CONSTRUCTION.

In applying and construing this Uniform Act, consideration must be given to the need to promote uniformity of the law with respect to its subject matter among States that enact it.

§ 902. SEVERABILITY CLAUSE.

If any provision of this [Act] or its application to an individual or circumstance is held invalid, the invalidity does not affect other provisions or applications of this [Act] which can be given effect without the invalid provision or application, and to this end the provisions of this [Act] are severable.

§ 903. TIME OF TAKING EFFECT.

This [Act] takes effect on _____.

§ 904. REPEAL.

The following acts and parts of acts are repealed:

(1)   [Uniform Act on Paternity, 1960]

(2)   [Uniform Parentage Act, 1973]

(3)   [Uniform Putative and Unknown Fathers Act, 1988]

(4)   [Uniform Status of Children of Assisted Conception Act, 1988]

(5)   [other inconsistent statutes]

§ 905. TRANSITIONAL PROVISION.

A proceeding to adjudicate parentage which was commenced before the effective date of this [Act] is governed by the law in effect at the time the proceeding was commenced.

UNIFORM PREMARITAL AND MARITAL AGREEMENT ACT (2012)

9C U.L.A. 12 et seq. (Supp. 2015)

[EDITORS' INTRODUCTION: Barbara A. Atwood & Brian H. Bix, *A New Uniform Law for Premarital and Marital Agreements*, 46 FAM. L.Q. 313 (2012); Chelsea Biemiller, *The Uncertain Enforceability of Prenuptial Agreements: Why the "Extreme" Approach in Pennsylvania is the Right Approach for Review*, 6 DREXEL L. REV. 133 (2013); Benjamin Means, *The Contractual Foundation Of Family-Business Law*, 75 OHIO ST. L.J. 675 (2014); J. Thomas Oldham, *Would Enactment of the Uniform Premarital and Marital Agreements Act in all Fifty States Change U.S. Law Regarding Premarital Agreements?*, 46 FAM. L.Q. 367 (2012); Madeleine M. Plasencia, *No Right to Lie, Cheat, or Steal: Public Good v. Private Order*, 68 U. MIAMI L. REV. 677 (2014); Christopher Kirt Ulfers, Comment, *Is a Postmarital Agreement in Your Best Interest? Why Louisiana Civil Code Article 2329 Should Let You Decide*, 75 LA. L. REV. 1399 (2016).]

§ 1.   SHORT TITLE.

This [act] may be cited as the Uniform Premarital and Marital Agreements Act.

§ 2.   DEFINITIONS.

In this [act]:

(1) "Amendment" means a modification or revocation of a premarital agreement or marital agreement.

(2) "Marital agreement" means an agreement between spouses who intend to remain married which affirms, modifies, or waives a marital right or obligation during the marriage or at separation, marital dissolution, death of one of the spouses, or the occurrence or nonoccurrence of any other event. The term includes an amendment, signed after the spouses marry, of a premarital agreement or marital agreement.

(3) "Marital dissolution" means the ending of a marriage by court decree. The term includes a divorce, dissolution, and annulment.

(4) "Marital right or obligation" means any of the following rights or obligations arising between spouses because of their marital status:

(A) spousal support;

(B) a right to property, including characterization, management, and ownership;

(C) responsibility for a liability;

(D) a right to property and responsibility for liabilities at separation, marital dissolution, or death of a spouse; or

(E) award and allocation of attorney's fees and costs.

(5) "Premarital agreement" means an agreement between individuals who intend to marry which affirms, modifies, or waives a marital right or obligation during the marriage or at separation, marital dissolution, death of one of the spouses, or the occurrence or nonoccurrence of any other event. The term includes an amendment, signed before the individuals marry, of a premarital agreement.

(6) "Property" means anything that may be the subject of ownership, whether real or personal, tangible or intangible, legal or equitable, or any interest therein.

(7) "Record" means information that is inscribed on a tangible medium or that is stored in an electronic or other medium and is retrievable in perceivable form.

(8) "Sign" means with present intent to authenticate or adopt a record:

(A) to execute or adopt a tangible symbol; or

(B) to attach to or logically associate with the record an electronic symbol, sound, or process.

(9) "State" means a state of the United States, the District of Columbia, Puerto Rico, the United States Virgin Islands, or any territory or insular possession subject to the jurisdiction of the United States.

§ 3. SCOPE.

(a) This [act] applies to a premarital agreement or marital agreement signed on or after [the effective date of this [act]].

(b) This [act] does not affect any right, obligation, or liability arising under a premarital agreement or marital agreement signed before [the effective date of this [act]].

(c) This [act] does not apply to:

(1) an agreement between spouses which affirms, modifies, or waives a marital right or obligation and requires court approval to become effective; or

(2) an agreement between spouses who intend to obtain a marital dissolution or court-decreed separation which resolves their marital rights or obligations and is signed when a proceeding for marital dissolution or court-decreed separation is anticipated or pending.

(d) This [act] does not affect adversely the rights of a bona fide purchaser for value to the extent that this [act] applies to a waiver of a marital right or obligation in a transfer or conveyance of property by a spouse to a third party.

§ 4. GOVERNING LAW.

The validity, enforceability, interpretation, and construction of a premarital agreement or marital agreement are determined:

    (1) by the law of the jurisdiction designated in the agreement if the jurisdiction has a significant relationship to the agreement or either party and the designated law is not contrary to a fundamental public policy of this state; or

    (2) absent an effective designation described in paragraph (1), by the law of this state, including the choice-of-law rules of this state.

§ 5. PRINCIPLES OF LAW AND EQUITY.

Unless displaced by a provision of this [act], principles of law and equity supplement this [act].

§ 6. FORMATION REQUIREMENTS.

A premarital agreement or marital agreement must be in a record and signed by both parties. The agreement is enforceable without consideration.

§ 7. WHEN AGREEMENT EFFECTIVE.

A premarital agreement is effective on marriage. A marital agreement is effective on signing by both parties.

§ 8. VOID MARRIAGE.

If a marriage is determined to be void, a premarital agreement or marital agreement is enforceable to the extent necessary to avoid an inequitable result.

§ 9. ENFORCEMENT.

    (a) A premarital agreement or marital agreement is unenforceable if a party against whom enforcement is sought proves:

    (1) the party's consent to the agreement was involuntary or the result of duress;

    (2) the party did not have access to independent legal representation under subsection (b);

    (3) unless the party had independent legal representation at the time the agreement was signed, the agreement did not include a notice of waiver of rights under subsection (c) or an explanation in plain language of the marital rights or obligations being modified or waived by the agreement; or

(4) before signing the agreement, the party did not receive adequate financial disclosure under subsection (d).

(b) A party has access to independent legal representation if:

(1) before signing a premarital or marital agreement, the party has a reasonable time to:

(A) decide whether to retain a lawyer to provide independent legal representation; and

(B) locate a lawyer to provide independent legal representation, obtain the lawyer's advice, and consider the advice provided; and

(2) the other party is represented by a lawyer and the party has the financial ability to retain a lawyer or the other party agrees to pay the reasonable fees and expenses of independent legal representation.

(c) A notice of waiver of rights under this section requires language, conspicuously displayed, substantially similar to the following, as applicable to the premarital agreement or marital agreement:

"If you sign this agreement, you may be:

Giving up your right to be supported by the person you are marrying or to whom you are married.

Giving up your right to ownership or control of money and property.

Agreeing to pay bills and debts of the person you are marrying or to whom you are married.

Giving up your right to money and property if your marriage ends or the person to whom you are married dies.

Giving up your right to have your legal fees paid."

(d) A party has adequate financial disclosure under this section if the party:

(1) receives a reasonably accurate description and good-faith estimate of value of the property, liabilities, and income of the other party;

(2) expressly waives, in a separate signed record, the right to financial disclosure beyond the disclosure provided; or

(3) has adequate knowledge or a reasonable basis for having adequate knowledge of the information described in paragraph (1).

(e) If a premarital agreement or marital agreement modifies or eliminates spousal support and the modification or elimination causes a party to the agreement to be eligible for support under a program of public assistance at the time of separation or marital dissolution, a court, on request of that party, may require the other party to provide support to the extent necessary to avoid that eligibility.

(f)   A court may refuse to enforce a term of a premarital agreement or marital agreement if, in the context of the agreement taken as a whole[:]

[(1)] the term was unconscionable at the time of signing[; or

(2) enforcement of the term would result in substantial hardship for a party because of a material change in circumstances arising after the agreement was signed].

(g) The court shall decide a question of unconscionability [or substantial hardship] under subsection (f) as a matter of law.

§ 10. UNENFORCEABLE TERMS.

(a) In this section, "custodial responsibility" means physical or legal custody, parenting time, access, visitation, or other custodial right or duty with respect to a child.

(b) A term in a premarital agreement or marital agreement is not enforceable to the extent that it:

(1)   adversely affects a child's right to support;

(2)   limits or restricts a remedy available to a victim of domestic violence under law of this state other than this [act];

(3) purports to modify the grounds for a court-decreed separation or marital dissolution available under law of this state other than this [act]; or

(4)   penalizes a party for initiating a legal proceeding leading to a court-decreed separation or marital dissolution.

(c) A term in a premarital agreement or marital agreement which defines the rights or duties of the parties regarding custodial responsibility is not binding on the court.

§ 11. LIMITATION OF ACTION.

A statute of limitations applicable to an action asserting a claim for relief under a premarital agreement or marital agreement is tolled during the marriage of the parties to the agreement, but equitable defenses limiting the time for enforcement, including laches and estoppel, are available to either party.

§ 12. UNIFORMITY OF APPLICATION AND CONSTRUCTION.

In applying and construing this uniform act, consideration must be given to the need to promote uniformity of the law with respect to its subject matter among states that enact it.

§ 13. RELATION TO ELECTRONIC SIGNATURES IN GLOBAL AND NATIONAL COMMERCE ACT.

This [act] modifies, limits, or supersedes the Electronic Signatures in Global and National Commerce Act, 15 U.S.C. Section 7001 et seq., but does not modify, limit, or supersede Section 101(c) of that act, 15 U.S.C. Section 7001(c), or authorize electronic delivery of any of the notices described in Section 103(b) of that act, 15 U.S.C. Section 7003(b).

§ 14. REPEALS; CONFORMING AMENDMENTS.

(a)   [Uniform Premarital Agreement Act] is repealed.

(b)   [Uniform Probate Code Section 2–213 (Waiver of Right to Elect and of Other Rights)] is repealed.

(c)   [. . . .]

§ 15. EFFECTIVE DATE.

This [act] takes effect . . . .

UNIFORM PROBATE CODE (2010)

8 U.L.A. Pt. I 1 et seq. (2013)

[EDITORS' INTRODUCTION: Lynda Wray Black, *The Birth of a Parent: Defining Parentage for Lenders of Genetic Material*, 92 NEB. L. REV. 799 (2014); Kelsey Brown, *Posthumously Conceived Children and Social Security Survivors' Benefits*, 13 U. MD. L.J. RACE, RELIGION, GENDER & CLASS 257 (2013); Susan N. Gary, *The Probate Definition of Family: A Proposal for Guided Discretion Intestacy*, 45 U. MICH. J.L. REFORM 787 (2012); Charles P. Kindregan, Jr., *Dead Soldiers and Their Posthumously Conceived Children*, 31 J. CONTEMP. HEALTH L. & POL'Y 74 (2015); Kristine S. Knaplund, *Children of Assisted Reproduction*, 45 U. MICH. J.L. REFORM 899 (2012); Kristine S. Knaplund, *The New Uniform Probate Code's Surprising Gender Inequities*, 18 DUKE J. GENDER L. & POL'Y 335 (2011); Heather Lacount, *Dead Money: A Posthumously Conceived Child's Inheritance Rights Under the Social Security Act & State Intestacy Law*, 20 SUFFOLK J. TRIAL & APP. ADVOC. 219 (2015); Jennifer Matystik, *Posthumously Conceived Children: Why States Should Update Their Intestacy Laws After* Astrue v. Capato, 28 BERKELEY J. GENDER L. & JUST. 269 (2013); Andrew T. Peebles, *Challenges and Inconsistencies Facing the Posthumously Conceived Child*, 79 MO. L. REV. 497 (2014); Danaya C. Wright, *Inheritance Equity: Reforming the Inheritance Penalties Facing Children in Nontraditional Families*, 25 CORNELL J.L. & PUB. POL'Y 1 (2015).]

§ 2–111. ALIENAGE.

No individual is disqualified to take as an heir because the individual or an individual through whom he [or she] claims is or has been an alien.

    * * *

§ 2–115. DEFINITIONS.

In this [subpart]:

    (1) "Adoptee" means an individual who is adopted.

    (2) "Assisted reproduction" means a method of causing pregnancy other than sexual intercourse.

    (3) "Divorce" includes an annulment, dissolution, and declaration of invalidity of a marriage.

    (4) "Functioned as a parent of the child" means behaving toward a child in a manner consistent with being the child's parent and performing functions that are customarily performed by a parent, including fulfilling parental responsibilities toward the child, recognizing or holding out the child as the individual's child, materially participating in the child's upbringing, and residing with

the child in the same household as a regular member of that household.

(5) "Genetic father" means the man whose sperm fertilized the egg of a child's genetic mother. If the father-child relationship is established under the presumption of paternity under [insert applicable state law], the term means only the man for whom that relationship is established.

(6) "Genetic mother" means the woman whose egg was fertilized by the sperm of a child's genetic father.

(7) "Genetic parent" means a child's genetic father or genetic mother.

(8) "Incapacity" means the inability of an individual to function as a parent of a child because of the individual's physical or mental condition.

(9) "Relative" means a grandparent or a descendant of a grandparent.

* * *

§ 2–118. ADOPTEE AND ADOPTEE'S ADOPTIVE PARENT OR PARENTS.

(a) [Parent-Child Relationship Between Adoptee and Adoptive Parent or Parents.] A parent-child relationship exists between an adoptee and the adoptee's adoptive parent or parents.

(b) [Individual in Process of Being Adopted by Married Couple; Stepchild in Process of Being Adopted by Stepparent.] For purposes of subsection (a):

(1) an individual who is in the process of being adopted by a married couple when one of the spouses dies is treated as adopted by the deceased spouse if the adoption is subsequently granted to the decedent's surviving spouse; and

(2) a child of a genetic parent who is in the process of being adopted by a genetic parent's spouse when the spouse dies is treated as adopted by the deceased spouse if the genetic parent survives the deceased spouse by 120 hours.

(c) [Child of Assisted Reproduction or Gestational Child in Process of Being Adopted.] If, after a parent-child relationship is established between a child of assisted reproduction and a parent under Section 2–120 or between a gestational child and a parent under Section 2–121, the child is in the process of being adopted by the parent's spouse when that spouse dies, the child is treated as adopted by the deceased spouse for the purpose of subsection (b)(2).

§ 2–119. ADOPTEE AND ADOPTEE'S GENETIC PARENTS.

(a) [Parent-Child Relationship Between Adoptee and Genetic Parents.] Except as otherwise provided in subsections (b) through (e), a parent-child relationship does not exist between an adoptee and the adoptee's genetic parents.

(b) [Stepchild Adopted by Stepparent.] A parent-child relationship exists between an individual who is adopted by the spouse of either genetic parent and:

    (1) the genetic parent whose spouse adopted the individual; and

    (2) the other genetic parent, but only for the purpose of the right of the adoptee or a descendant of the adoptee to inherit from or through the other genetic parent.

(c) [Individual Adopted by Relative of Genetic Parent.] A parent-child relationship exists between both genetic parents and an individual who is adopted by a relative of a genetic parent, or by the spouse or surviving spouse of a relative of a genetic parent, but only for the purpose of the right of the adoptee or a descendant of the adoptee to inherit from or through either genetic parent.

(d) [Individual Adopted after Death of Both Genetic Parents.] A parent-child relationship exists between both genetic parents and an individual who is adopted after the death of both genetic parents, but only for the purpose of the right of the adoptee or a descendant of the adoptee to inherit through either genetic parent.

(e) [Child of Assisted Reproduction or Gestational Child Who Is Subsequently Adopted.] If, after a parent-child relationship is established between a child of assisted reproduction and a parent or parents under Section 2–120 or between a gestational child and a parent or parents under Section 2–121, the child is adopted by another or others, the child's parent or parents under Section 2–120 or 2–121 are treated as the child's genetic parent or parents for the purpose of this section.

§ 2–120. CHILD CONCEIVED BY ASSISTED REPRODUCTION OTHER THAN CHILD BORN TO GESTATIONAL CARRIER.

(a) [Definitions.] In this section:

    (1) "Birth mother" means a woman, other than a gestational carrier under Section 2–121, who gives birth to a child of assisted reproduction. The term is not limited to a woman who is the child's genetic mother.

    (2) "Child of assisted reproduction" means a child conceived by means of assisted reproduction by a woman other than a gestational carrier under Section 2–121.

(3) "Third-party donor" means an individual who produces eggs or sperm used for assisted reproduction, whether or not for consideration. The term does not include:

(A) a husband who provides sperm, or a wife who provides eggs, that are used for assisted reproduction by the wife;

(B) the birth mother of a child of assisted reproduction; or

(C) an individual who has been determined under subsection (e) or (f) to have a parent-child relationship with a child of assisted reproduction.

(b) [Third-Party Donor.] A parent-child relationship does not exist between a child of assisted reproduction and a third-party donor.

(c) [Parent-Child Relationship with Birth Mother.] A parent-child relationship exists between a child of assisted reproduction and the child's birth mother.

(d) [Parent-Child Relationship with Husband Whose Sperm Were Used During His Lifetime by His Wife for Assisted Reproduction.] Except as otherwise provided in subsections (i) and (j), a parent-child relationship exists between a child of assisted reproduction and the husband of the child's birth mother if the husband provided the sperm that the birth mother used during his lifetime for assisted reproduction.

(e) [Birth Certificate: Presumptive Effect.] A birth certificate identifying an individual other than the birth mother as the other parent of a child of assisted reproduction presumptively establishes a parent-child relationship between the child and that individual.

(f) [Parent-Child Relationship with Another.] Except as otherwise provided in subsections (g), (i), and (j), and unless a parent-child relationship is established under subsection (d) or (e), a parent-child relationship exists between a child of assisted reproduction and an individual other than the birth mother who consented to assisted reproduction by the birth mother with intent to be treated as the other parent of the child. Consent to assisted reproduction by the birth mother with intent to be treated as the other parent of the child is established if the individual:

(1) before or after the child's birth, signed a record that, considering all the facts and circumstances, evidences the individual's consent; or

(2) in the absence of a signed record under paragraph (1):

(A) functioned as a parent of the child no later than two years after the child's birth;

(B) intended to function as a parent of the child no later than two years after the child's birth but was prevented from carrying out that intent by death, incapacity, or other circumstances; or

(C) intended to be treated as a parent of a posthumously conceived child, if that intent is established by clear and convincing evidence.

(g) [Record Signed More than Two Years after the Birth of the Child: Effect.] For the purpose of subsection (f)(1), neither an individual who signed a record more than two years after the birth of the child, nor a relative of that individual who is not also a relative of the birth mother, inherits from or through the child unless the individual functioned as a parent of the child before the child reached [18] years of age.

(h) [Presumption: Birth Mother Is Married or Surviving Spouse.] For the purpose of subsection (f)(2), the following rules apply:

(1) If the birth mother is married and no divorce proceeding is pending, in the absence of clear and convincing evidence to the contrary, her spouse satisfies subsection (f)(2)(A) or (B).

(2) If the birth mother is a surviving spouse and at her deceased spouse's death no divorce proceeding was pending, in the absence of clear and convincing evidence to the contrary, her deceased spouse satisfies subsection (f)(2)(B) or (C).

(i) [Divorce Before Placement of Eggs, Sperm, or Embryos.] If a married couple is divorced before placement of eggs, sperm, or embryos, a child resulting from the assisted reproduction is not a child of the birth mother's former spouse, unless the former spouse consented in a record that if assisted reproduction were to occur after divorce, the child would be treated as the former spouse's child.

(j) [Withdrawal of Consent Before Placement of Eggs, Sperm, or Embryos.] If, in a record, an individual withdraws consent to assisted reproduction before placement of eggs, sperm, or embryos, a child resulting from the assisted reproduction is not a child of that individual, unless the individual subsequently satisfies subsection (f).

(k) [When Posthumously Conceived Child Treated as in Gestation.] If, under this section, an individual is a parent of a child of assisted reproduction who is conceived after the individual's death, the child is treated as in gestation at the individual's death for purposes of Section 2–104(a)(2) if the child is:

(1) in utero not later than 36 months after the individual's death; or

(2) born not later than 45 months after the individual's death.

§ 2–121. CHILD BORN TO GESTATIONAL CARRIER.

(a) [Definitions.] In this section:

(1) "Gestational agreement" means an enforceable or unenforceable agreement for assisted reproduction in which a woman agrees to carry a child to birth for an intended parent, intended parents, or an individual described in subsection (e).

(2) "Gestational carrier" means a woman who is not an intended parent who gives birth to a child under a gestational agreement. The term is not limited to a woman who is the child's genetic mother.

(3) "Gestational child" means a child born to a gestational carrier under a gestational agreement.

(4) "Intended parent" means an individual who entered into a gestational agreement providing that the individual will be the parent of a child born to a gestational carrier by means of assisted reproduction. The term is not limited to an individual who has a genetic relationship with the child.

(b) [Court Order Adjudicating Parentage: Effect.] A parent-child relationship is conclusively established by a court order designating the parent or parents of a gestational child.

(c) [Gestational Carrier.] A parent-child relationship between a gestational child and the child's gestational carrier does not exist unless the gestational carrier is:

(1) designated as a parent of the child in a court order described in subsection (b); or

(2) the child's genetic mother and a parent-child relationship does not exist under this section with an individual other than the gestational carrier.

(d) [Parent-Child Relationship with Intended Parent or Parents.] In the absence of a court order under subsection (b), a parent-child relationship exists between a gestational child and an intended parent who:

(1) functioned as a parent of the child no later than two years after the child's birth; or

(2) died while the gestational carrier was pregnant if:

(A) there were two intended parents and the other intended parent functioned as a parent of the child no later than two years after the child's birth;

(B) there were two intended parents, the other intended parent also died while the gestational carrier was pregnant, and a relative of either deceased intended parent or the spouse or surviving spouse of a relative of either deceased intended parent functioned as a parent of the child no later than two years after the child's birth; or

(C) there was no other intended parent and a relative of or the spouse or surviving spouse of a relative of the deceased intended parent functioned as a parent of the child no later than two years after the child's birth.

(e) [Gestational Agreement after Death or Incapacity.] In the absence of a court order under subsection (b), a parent-child relationship exists between a gestational child and an individual whose sperm or eggs were used after the individual's death or incapacity to conceive a child under a gestational agreement entered into after the individual's death or incapacity if the individual intended to be treated as the parent of the child. The individual's intent may be shown by:

(1) a record signed by the individual which considering all the facts and circumstances evidences the individual's intent; or

(2) other facts and circumstances establishing the individual's intent by clear and convincing evidence.

(f) [Presumption: Gestational Agreement after Spouse's Death or Incapacity.] Except as otherwise provided in subsection (g), and unless there is clear and convincing evidence of a contrary intent, an individual is deemed to have intended to be treated as the parent of a gestational child for purposes of subsection (e)(2) if:

(1) the individual, before death or incapacity, deposited the sperm or eggs that were used to conceive the child;

(2) when the individual deposited the sperm or eggs, the individual was married and no divorce proceeding was pending; and

(3) the individual's spouse or surviving spouse functioned as a parent of the child no later than two years after the child's birth.

(g) [Subsection (f) Presumption Inapplicable.] The presumption under subsection (f) does not apply if there is:

(1) a court order under subsection (b); or

(2) a signed record that satisfies subsection (e)(1).

(h) [When Posthumously Conceived Gestational Child Treated as in Gestation.] If, under this section, an individual is a parent of a gestational child who is conceived after the individual's death, the child is treated as in gestation at the individual's death for purposes of Section 2–104(a)(2) if the child is:

(1) in utero not later than 36 months after the individual's death; or

(2) born not later than 45 months after the individual's death.

(i) [No Effect on Other Law.] This section does not affect law of this state other than this [code] regarding the enforceability or validity of a gestational agreement.

* * *

§ 2–705. CLASS GIFTS CONSTRUED TO ACCORD WITH INTESTATE SUCCESSION; EXCEPTIONS.

* * *

(b) [Terms of Relationship.] A class gift that uses a term of relationship to identify the class members includes a child of assisted reproduction, a gestational child, and, except as otherwise provided in subsections (e) and (f), an adoptee and a child born to parents who are not married to each other, and their respective descendants if appropriate to the class, in accordance with the rules for intestate succession regarding parent-child relationships.

* * *

(c) [Relatives by Marriage.] Terms of relationship in a governing instrument that do not differentiate relationships by blood from those by marriage, such as uncles, aunts, nieces, or nephews, are construed to exclude relatives by marriage, unless:

(1) when the governing instrument was executed, the class was then and foreseeably would be empty; or

(2) the language or circumstances otherwise establish that relatives by marriage were intended to be included.

(d) [Half-Blood Relatives.] Terms of relationship in a governing instrument that do not differentiate relationships by the half blood from those by the whole blood, such as brothers, sisters, nieces, or nephews, are construed to include both types of relationships.

(e) [Transferor Not Genetic Parent.] In construing a dispositive provision of a transferor who is not the genetic parent, a child of a genetic parent is not considered the child of that genetic parent unless the genetic parent, a relative of the genetic parent, or the spouse or surviving spouse of the genetic parent or of a relative of the genetic parent functioned as a parent of the child before the child reached [18] years of age.

(f) [Transferor Not Adoptive Parent.] In construing a dispositive provision of a transferor who is not the adoptive parent, an adoptee is not considered the child of the adoptive parent unless:

(1) the adoption took place before the adoptee reached [18] years of age;

(2) the adoptive parent was the adoptee's stepparent or foster parent; or

(3) the adoptive parent functioned as a parent of the adoptee before the adoptee reached [18] years of age.

(g) [Class-Closing Rules.] The following rules apply for purposes of the class-closing rules:

(1) A child in utero at a particular time is treated as living at that time if the child lives 120 hours after birth.

(2) If a child of assisted reproduction or a gestational child is conceived posthumously and the distribution date is the deceased parent's death, the child is treated as living on the distribution date if the child lives 120 hours after birth and was in utero not later than 36 months after the deceased parent's death or born not later than 45 months after the deceased parent's death.

(3) An individual who is in the process of being adopted when the class closes is treated as adopted when the class closes if the adoption is subsequently granted.

* * *

UNIFORM REPRESENTATION OF CHILDREN IN ABUSE, NEGLECT, AND CUSTODY PROCEEDINGS ACT (2007)

9C U.L.A. 56 et seq. (Supp. 2015)

[EDITORS' INTRODUCTION: MICHAEL T. FLANNERY & RAYMOND C. O'BRIEN, THE SEXUAL EXPLOITATION OF CHILDREN (2016); Barbara A. Atwood, *Representing Children Who Can't or Won't Direct Counsel: Best Interests Lawyering or No Lawyer at All*, 53 ARIZ. L. REV. 381 (2011); Donald N. Duquette & Julian Darwall, *Child Representation in America: Progress Report from the National Quality Improvement Center*, 46 FAM. L.Q. 87 (2012); Katherine Hunt Federle, *Righting Wrongs: A Reply to the Uniform Law Commission's Uniform Representation of Children in Abuse, Neglect, and Custody Proceedings Act*, 42 FAM. L.Q. 103 (2008); Suparna Malempati, *Beyond Paternalism: The Role of Counsel for Children in Abuse and Neglect Proceedings*, 11 U. N.H. L. REV. 97 (2013); Elizabeth Weyer, Note, *Respecting Uncustomary Family Traditions: Reforming The Role Of Guardians Ad Litem*, 17 J. GENDER RACE & JUST. 197 (2014).]

§ 1. SHORT TITLE.

This [act] may be cited as the Uniform Representation of Children in Abuse, Neglect, and Custody Proceedings Act.

§ 2. DEFINITIONS.

In this [act]:

(1) "Abuse or neglect proceeding" means a court proceeding under [cite state statute] for protection of a child from abuse or neglect or a court proceeding under [cite state statute] in which termination of parental rights is at issue.

(2) "Best interests advocate" means an individual, not functioning as an attorney, appointed to assist the court in determining the best interests of a child.

(3) "Best interests attorney" means an attorney who provides legal representation for a child to protect the child's best interests without being bound by the child's directives or objectives.

(4) "Child's attorney" means an attorney who provides legal representation for a child.

(5) "Custody proceeding" means a court proceeding other than an abuse or neglect proceeding in which legal or physical custody of, access to, or visitation or parenting time with a child is at issue. The term does not include a proceeding initiated against a child for [adjudication of delinquency or status offense under [cite state statute]].

(6) "Developmental level" means the ability to understand and communicate, taking into account such factors as age, mental capacity,

level of education, cultural background, and degree of language acquisition.

§ 3. APPLICABILITY AND RELATIONSHIP TO OTHER LAW.

(a) This [act] applies to an abuse or neglect or custody proceeding [pending on or] commenced on or after [the effective date of this act].

(b) This [act] does not affect children's rights or standing under law other than this [act] or give standing or party status not provided under law other than this [act].

§ 4. MANDATORY APPOINTMENT IN ABUSE OR NEGLECT PROCEEDING.

(a) In an abuse or neglect proceeding, the court shall appoint either a child's attorney or a best interests attorney. The appointment must be made as soon as practicable to ensure adequate representation of the child and, in any event, before the first court hearing that may substantially affect the interests of the child.

(b) In determining whether to appoint a child's attorney or a best interests attorney, the court may consider such factors as the child's age and developmental level, any desire for an attorney expressed by the child, whether the child has expressed objectives in the proceeding, and the value of an independent advocate for the child's best interests.

(c) The court may appoint one attorney to represent siblings if there is no conflict of interest, even if the attorney serves in different capacities with respect to two or more siblings.

(d) Neither the child nor a representative of the child, whether or not appointed by the court, may waive representation of the child under this section or Section 5.

§ 5. APPOINTMENT OF BEST INTERESTS ADVOCATE IN ABUSE OR NEGLECT PROCEEDING.

Alternative A

(a) In an abuse or neglect proceeding:

(1) if the court does not appoint a best interests attorney, the court shall appoint a best interests advocate before the first court hearing that may substantially affect the interests of the child; or

(2) if the court appoints a best interests attorney, the court may appoint a best interests advocate if the court determines that a best interests advocate is necessary to assist the court in determining the best interests of the child.

(b) In determining whether a best interests advocate is necessary under subsection (a)(2), the court shall consider such factors as the court's need for information and assistance, the circumstances and needs of the child, the value of a best interests advocate's expertise and experience, and any request for the appointment of a best interests advocate.

(c) If the court determines to make an appointment under subsection (a)(2), the court shall make the appointment as soon as practicable.

Alternative B

(a) In an abuse or neglect proceeding, whether the court appoints a child's attorney or a best interests attorney, the court may appoint a best interests advocate if the court determines that a best interests advocate is necessary to assist the court in determining the child's best interests.

(b) In determining whether a best interests advocate is necessary under subsection (a), the court shall consider such factors as the court's need for information and assistance, the circumstances and needs of the child, the value of a best interests advocate's expertise and experience, and any request for the appointment of a best interests advocate.

(c) If the court determines to make an appointment under subsection (a), the court shall make the appointment as soon as practicable.

§ 6. DISCRETIONARY APPOINTMENT IN CUSTODY PROCEEDING.

(a) In a custody proceeding, the court, on its own or on motion, may appoint either a child's attorney or a best interests attorney. Whether or not the court appoints an attorney, the court may appoint a best interests advocate. An appointment may be made at any stage of the proceeding and the appointment order must designate the role of the appointee.

(b) In determining whether an appointment under subsection (a) is appropriate, the court shall consider the circumstances and needs of the child, the court's need for information and assistance, the financial burden on the parties and the cost of available alternatives for resolving the issues in the proceeding, and any factors indicating a particularized need for representation, including:

(1) any desire for representation or participation expressed by the child;

(2) any inappropriate adult influence on or manipulation of the child;

(3) the likelihood that the child will be called as a witness or be questioned by the court in chambers and the need to minimize harm to the child from the processes of litigation;

(4) any level of acrimony that indicates a lack of objectivity of the parties regarding the needs of the child;

(5) any interference, or threatened interference, with custody, access, visitation, or parenting time, including abduction or risk of abduction of the child;

(6) the likelihood of a geographic relocation of the child that could substantially reduce the child's time with:

(A) a parent;

(B) a sibling; or

(C) another individual with whom the child has a close relationship;

(7) any conduct by a party or an individual with whom a party associates which raises serious concerns for the safety of the child during periods of custody, visitation, or parenting time with that party;

(8) any special physical, educational, or mental-health needs of the child that require investigation or advocacy; and

(9) any dispute as to paternity of the child.

(c) If the court determines to make an appointment under subsection (a), in deciding whether a child's attorney, best interests attorney, or best interests advocate is appropriate, the court shall consider such factors as the child's age and developmental level, any desire for an attorney expressed by the child, whether the child has expressed objectives in the proceeding, the value of an independent representative for the child's best interests, and the value of a best interests advocate's expertise and experience.

§ 7. QUALIFICATIONS OF CHILD'S ATTORNEY OR BEST INTERESTS ATTORNEY.

The court may appoint as a child's attorney or best interests attorney only an individual who is qualified through training or experience in the type of proceeding in which the appointment is made [, according to standards established by [insert reference to source of standards]].

§ 8. BEST INTERESTS ADVOCATE: QUALIFICATIONS AND LIMITATIONS.

(a) The court may appoint as a best interests advocate only an individual who is qualified through training or experience in the type of proceeding in which the appointment is made [, according to standards established by [insert reference to standards]].

(b) An attorney appointed as a best interests advocate may take only those actions that may be taken by a best interests advocate who is not an attorney.

(c) The appointment of a best interests advocate does not create a professional relationship between the advocate and the child unless such a relationship is expressly established in the order of appointment.

§ 9. APPOINTMENT ORDER.

(a)   Subject to subsection (b), an appointment of a child's attorney, best interests attorney, or best interests advocate must be in a record, identify the individual who will act in that capacity, and clearly set forth the terms of the appointment, including the grounds for the appointment, rights of access as provided under Section 15, and applicable terms of compensation. In a custody proceeding, the appointment order must also specify the duration of the appointment.

(b)   In the appointment order under subsection (a), the court may identify a private organization or governmental program through which a child's attorney, best interests attorney, or best interests advocate will be provided. The organization or program shall designate an individual who will act in that capacity and submit to the court the name of the individual as soon as practicable, at which time the court shall amend the appointment order to identify the designated individual.

(c)   If appropriate in light of information not available to the court at the time of the original appointment, changed circumstances, or a request by the appointee, the court may modify the appointment order to:

(1)   redesignate as a child's attorney an individual originally appointed as a best interests attorney;

(2)   add the appointment of a child's attorney if the original or amended appointment was a best interests attorney; or

(3)   add the appointment of a best interests attorney if the original or amended appointment was a child's attorney.

§ 10. DURATION OF APPOINTMENT.

(a)   In an abuse or neglect proceeding, unless otherwise provided by a court order, an appointment of a child's attorney, best interests attorney, or best interests advocate continues in effect until the individual is discharged by court order at the conclusion of the proceeding.

(b)   In a custody proceeding, an appointment of a child's attorney, best interests attorney, or best interests advocate continues in effect only for the duration provided in the appointment order or any subsequent order.

§ 11. COMMON DUTIES OF CHILD'S ATTORNEY AND BEST INTERESTS ATTORNEY.

Alternative A

(a) A child's attorney or best interests attorney shall participate in the proceeding to the full extent necessary to represent the child.

(b) The duties of a child's attorney or best interests attorney include:

(1) meeting with the child and ascertaining, in a manner appropriate to the child's developmental level, the child's needs, circumstances, and views;

(2) consulting with any best interests advocate for the child;

(3) investigating the facts relevant to the proceeding to the extent the attorney considers appropriate, including interviewing persons with significant knowledge of the child's history and condition and reviewing copies of relevant records;

(4) providing advice and counsel to the child;

(5) informing the child of the status of the proceeding and the opportunity to participate and, if appropriate, facilitating the child's participation in the proceeding;

(6) reviewing and accepting or declining to accept any proposed stipulation for an order affecting the child and explaining to the court the basis for any opposition;

(7) taking action the attorney considers appropriate to expedite the proceeding and the resolution of contested issues; and

(8) if the attorney considers it appropriate, encouraging settlement and the use of alternative forms of dispute resolution and participating in such processes to the extent permitted under the law of this state.

(c) When the court has appointed both a child's attorney and a best interests attorney for a child under Section 9(c), the court and the attorneys shall confer to determine how the attorneys will perform their common duties under this [act].

Alternative B

The common duties of the child's attorney and the best interests attorney are set forth in [insert reference to court rule or administrative guideline].

§ 12. SEPARATE DUTIES OF CHILD'S ATTORNEY.

(a) A child's attorney owes to the child the duties imposed by the law of this state in an attorney-client relationship, including duties of individual loyalty, confidentiality, and competent representation.

Alternative A

(b) A child's attorney, in a manner appropriate to the child's developmental level, shall explain the nature of the attorney-client relationship to the child, including the requirements of confidentiality.

(c) Subject to subsections (d) and (e), once a child has formed an attorney-client relationship with a child's attorney, the attorney shall advocate any objectives of representation expressed by the child unless they are prohibited by law or without factual foundation.

(d) If a child's attorney reasonably believes that the child lacks the capacity or refuses to direct the attorney with respect to a particular issue, the attorney shall:

(1) present to the court a position that the attorney determines will serve the child's best interests if the position is not inconsistent with the child's expressed objectives;

(2) take no position as to the issue in question; or

(3) request appointment of a best interests attorney or best interests advocate if one has not been appointed.

(e) If, despite appropriate legal counseling, the child expresses objectives of representation that the child's attorney reasonably believes would place the child at risk of substantial harm, the attorney shall:

(1) request the appointment of a best interests advocate, if a best interests advocate has not been appointed;

(2) withdraw from representation and request the appointment of a best interests attorney; or

(3) continue the representation and request the appointment of a best interests attorney.

(f) The child's attorney may not disclose the reasons for requesting a best interests advocate or best interests attorney under subsection (e) except as permitted by [insert reference to this state's rules of professional conduct].

Alternative B

(b) The separate duties of a child's attorney are set forth in [insert reference to court rule or administrative guideline containing the duties].

§ 13. SEPARATE DUTIES OF BEST INTERESTS ATTORNEY.

(a) Except as otherwise provided in [this section] [court rule] [administrative guideline], a best interests attorney owes to the child the duties imposed by the law of this state in an attorney-client relationship, including duties of individual loyalty, confidentiality, and competent representation.

(b)   A best interests attorney shall advocate for the best interests of the child according to criteria established by law and based on the circumstances and needs of the child and other facts relevant to the proceeding.

Alternative A

(c)   A best interests attorney, in a manner appropriate to the child's developmental level, shall:

(1)   explain the role of the attorney to the child; and

(2)   inform the child that, in providing assistance to the court, the attorney may use information that the child gives to the attorney.

(d)   If the child desires, the best interests attorney shall present any expressed objectives of the child in the proceeding to the court by a method that is appropriate in light of the purpose of the proceeding and the impact on the child.

(e)   A best interests attorney is not bound by the child's expressed objectives but shall consider the child's objectives, the reasons underlying those objectives, and the child's developmental level, in determining what to advocate.

(f)   A best interests attorney may not disclose or be compelled to disclose information relating to the representation of the child except as permitted by [insert reference to this state's rules of professional conduct], but the attorney may use such information for the purpose of performing the duties of a best interests attorney without disclosing that the child was the source of the information.

Alternative B

(c)   The separate duties of a best interests attorney are set forth in [insert reference to rule of court or administrative guideline].

§ 14. DUTIES OF BEST INTERESTS ADVOCATE.

A best interests advocate shall:

(1)   within a reasonable time after the appointment:

(A)   meet with the child and, in a manner appropriate to the child's developmental level:

(i)   explain the role of the best interests advocate; and

(ii)   ascertain the child's needs, circumstances, and views;

(B)   investigate the facts relevant to the proceeding to the extent the advocate considers appropriate, including interviewing persons with significant knowledge of the child's history and condition;

(C) obtain and review copies of relevant records relating to the child to the extent the advocate considers appropriate; and

(D) consult with any child's attorney or best interests attorney appointed in the proceeding;

(2) determine, in a manner appropriate to the child's developmental level, the child's expressed objectives in the proceeding;

(3) present the child's expressed objectives to the court, if the child desires, by report or other submission;

(4) consider the child's expressed objectives in the proceeding without being bound by them;

(5) maintain the confidentiality of information relating to the proceeding except as necessary to perform the duties of best interests advocate or as may be specifically provided by law of this state other than this [act];

(6) if the advocate considers it appropriate, and subject to the requirements of Section 16(e), present recommendations to the court by testimony or written report or both regarding the child's best interests and the bases of those recommendations;

(7) provide to the parties and to any attorney for the child copies of any report or other document submitted to the court by the advocate; and

(8) if the advocate considers it appropriate, encourage settlement and the use of any alternative forms of dispute resolution and participate in such processes to the extent permitted under the law of this state.

§ 15. ACCESS TO CHILD AND INFORMATION RELATING TO CHILD.

(a) Subject to subsections (b) and (c), when the court makes an appointment under this [act], it shall issue an order, with notice to all parties, authorizing the individual appointed to have access to:

(1) the child; and

(2) confidential information regarding the child, including the child's educational, medical, and mental health records, any agency or court files involving allegations of abuse or neglect of the child, any delinquency records involving the child, and other information relevant to the issues in the proceeding.

(b) A child's record that is privileged or confidential under law other than this [act] may be released to an individual appointed under this [act] only in accordance with that law, including any requirements in that law for notice and opportunity to object to release of records. Information that is privileged under the attorney-client relationship may not be disclosed except as otherwise permitted by law of this state other than this [act].

(c)   An order issued pursuant to subsection (a) must require that a child's attorney, best interests attorney, or best interests advocate maintain the confidentiality of information released, except as necessary for the resolution of the issues in the proceeding. The court may impose any other condition or limitation on an order of access which is required by law, rules of professional conduct, the child's needs, or the circumstances of the proceeding.

(d)   The custodian of any record regarding the child shall provide access to the record to an individual authorized access by order issued pursuant to subsection (a).

Alternative A

(e)   Subject to subsection (b), an order issued pursuant to subsection (a) takes effect upon issuance.

Alternative B

(e)   An order issued pursuant to subsection (a)(1) takes effect upon issuance. Except as otherwise provided in subsection (g), an order issued pursuant to subsection (a)(2) does not take effect until [10] days after notice of the order has been sent to all parties. The notice must inform the individual to whom it is sent that any objection to the release of records must be filed with the court by a specified date.

(f)   If no objection to an order issued pursuant to subsection (a)(2) is filed with the court by the date specified in the notice, the order takes effect the day after the specified date. If an objection is filed with the court, the court shall conduct a hearing on a priority basis. Any appeal from the court's order granting or denying access must be processed in accordance with [insert reference to expedited appellate procedures in other civil cases].

(g)   Subject to subsection (b), if the court finds that immediate access to a specific record is necessary to protect the child from harm, the court shall specify the record in the order issued pursuant to subsection (a)(2) and, as to that record, the order takes effect upon issuance.

§ 16. PARTICIPATION IN PROCEEDING.

(a)   A child's attorney, best interests attorney, or best interests advocate appointed under this [act] is entitled to:

(1)   receive a copy of each pleading or other record filed with the court in the proceeding;

(2)   receive notice of and participate in each hearing in the proceeding [and participate and receive copies of all records in any appeal that may be filed in the proceeding]; and

(3) participate in any case staffing or case management conference regarding the child in an abuse or neglect proceeding.

(b) A child's attorney, best interests attorney, or best interests advocate appointed under this [act] may not engage in ex parte contact with the court except as authorized by law other than this [act].

(c) A best interests advocate may not take any action that may be taken only by an attorney licensed in this state, including making opening and closing statements, examining witnesses in court, and engaging in discovery other than as a witness.

(d) The court, a child's attorney, or a best interests attorney may compel any best interests advocate for a child to attend a trial or hearing relating to the child and to testify as necessary for the proper disposition of the proceeding.

(e) The court shall ensure that any best interests advocate for a child has an opportunity to testify or, if present at the hearing and available for cross-examination, submit a report setting forth:

(1) the advocate's recommendations regarding the best interests of the child; and

(2) the reasons for the advocate's recommendations.

(f) A party may call any best interests advocate for the child as a witness for the purpose of cross-examination regarding the advocate's report even if the advocate is not listed as a witness by a party.

[(g) In a jury trial, disclosure to the jury of the contents of a best interests advocate's report is subject to this state's rules of evidence.]

§ 17. ATTORNEY WORK PRODUCT AND TESTIMONY.

[(a)] Except as authorized by [insert reference to this state's rules of professional conduct] or court rule, a child's attorney or best interests attorney may not:

(1) be compelled to produce the attorney's work product developed during the appointment;

(2) be required to disclose the source of information obtained as a result of the appointment;

(3) introduce into evidence a report prepared by the attorney; or

(4) testify in court.

[(b) Subsection (a) does not alter the duty of an attorney to report child abuse or neglect under [insert reference to applicable state law]].

§ 18. CHILD'S RIGHT OF ACTION.

(a) Only the child has a right of action for money damages against a child's attorney, best interests attorney, or best interests advocate for inaction or action taken in the capacity of child's attorney, best interests attorney, or best interests advocate.

(b) A [best interests attorney or] best interests advocate appointed pursuant to this [act] is not liable for money damages because of inaction or action taken in the capacity of [best interests attorney or] best interests advocate unless the inaction or action taken constituted willful misconduct or gross negligence.

§ 19. FEES AND EXPENSES IN ABUSE OR NEGLECT PROCEEDING.

(a) In an abuse or neglect proceeding, an individual appointed pursuant to this [act], other than a volunteer, is entitled to reasonable and timely fees and expenses in an amount set by the court to be paid from [authorized public funds].

(b) To receive payment under this section, the payee must complete and submit to the court a written claim for payment, whether interim or final, justifying the fees and expenses charged.

(c) If the court, after hearing, determines that a party whose conduct gave rise to a finding of abuse or neglect is able to defray all or part of the fees and expenses set pursuant to subsection (a), the court shall enter a judgment in favor of [the state, state agency, or political subdivision] against the party in an amount the court determines is reasonable.

§ 20. FEES AND EXPENSES IN CUSTODY PROCEEDING.

(a) In a custody proceeding, an individual appointed pursuant to this [act], other than a volunteer, is entitled to reasonable and timely fees and expenses in an amount set by the court by reference to the reasonable and customary fees and expenses for similar services in the jurisdiction.

(b) The court may do one or more of the following:

    (1) allocate fees and expenses among the parties;

    (2) order a deposit to be made into an account designated by the court for the use and benefit of the individual appointed under this [act];

    (3) before the final hearing, order an amount in addition to the amount ordered deposited under paragraph (2) to be paid into the account.

(c) To receive payment under this section, the individual must complete and submit to the court a written claim for payment, whether interim or final, justifying the fees and expenses charged.

(d)   [Except as otherwise authorized by [insert reference to state law authorizing payment of fees or expenses], a] [A] court may not award fees or expenses under this section against the state, a state agency, or a political subdivision of the state.

§ 21. UNIFORMITY OF APPLICATION AND CONSTRUCTION.

In applying and construing this uniform act, consideration must be given to the need to promote uniformity of the law with respect to its subject matter among states that enact it.

§ 22. REPEALS.

The following acts and parts of acts are repealed:

(1)   . . . .

(2)   . . . .

(3)   . . . .

§ 23. CONFORMING AMENDMENTS.

The following acts or parts of acts are amended to conform to the terminology used in this act:

. . .

§ 24. EFFECTIVE DATE.

This [act] takes effect on _____.

UNIFORM STATUS OF CHILDREN OF ASSISTED CONCEPTION ACT (1988)

9C U.L.A. 363 et seq. (2001)

[EDITORS' INTRODUCTION: Linda S. Anderson, *Legislative Oppression: Restricting Gestational Surrogacy to Married Couples is an Attempt to Legislate Morality*, 42 U. BALT. L. REV. 611 (2013); Andrea B. Carroll, *Discrimination in Baby Making: The Unconstitutional Treatment of Prospective Parents Through Surrogacy*, 88 IND. L.J. 1187 (2013); Linda Choe, *What in the Name of Conception? A Comparative Analysis of the Inheritance Rights of Posthumously Conceived Children in the United States and United Kingdom*, 25 SYRACUSE SCI. & TECH. L. REP. 53 (2011); Craig Dashiell, *From Louise Brown to* Baby M *and Beyond: A Proposed Framework for Understanding Surrogacy*, 65 RUTGERS L. REV. 851 (2013); Stephanie Liu, *And Baby Makes Two: Posthumously Conceived Children and the Eight Circuit's Denial of Survivors Benefits*, 77 MO. L. REV. 829 (2012); Yehezkel Margalit, *In Defense of Surrogacy Agreements: A Modern Contract Law Perspective*, 20 WM. & MARY J. WOMEN & L. 423 (2014); Dominque Ladomato, Note, *Protecting Traditional Surrogacy Contracting Through Fee Payment Regulation*, 23 HASTINGS WOMEN'S L.J. 245 (2012); Lane Thomasson, Comment, Burns v. Astrue*: "Born in Peculiar Circumstances," Posthumously Conceived Children and the Adequacy of State Intestacy Laws*, 91 DENV. U. L. REV. 715 (2014).]

§ 1. DEFINITIONS.

In this [Act]:

(1) "Assisted conception" means a pregnancy resulting from (i) fertilizing an egg of a woman with sperm of a man by means other than sexual intercourse or (ii) implanting an embryo, but the term does not include the pregnancy of a wife resulting from fertilizing her egg with sperm of her husband.

(2) "Donor" means an individual [other than a surrogate] who produces egg or sperm used for assisted conception, whether or not a payment is made for the egg or sperm used, but does not include a woman who gives birth to a resulting child.

[(3) "Intended parents" means a man and woman, married to each other, who enter into an agreement under this [Act] providing that they will be the parents of a child born to a surrogate through assisted conception using egg or sperm of one or both of the intended parents.]

(4) "Surrogate" means an adult woman who enters into an agreement to bear a child conceived through assisted conception for intended parents.

§ 2. MATERNITY.

[Except as provided in Sections 5 through 9,] a woman who gives birth to a child is the child's mother.

§ 3. ASSISTED CONCEPTION BY MARRIED WOMAN.

[Except as provided in Sections 5 through 9,] the husband of a woman who bears a child through assisted conception is the father of the child, notwithstanding a declaration of invalidity or annulment of the marriage obtained after the assisted conception, unless within two years after learning of the child's birth he commences an action in which the mother and child are parties and in which it is determined that he did not consent to the assisted conception.

§ 4. PARENTAL STATUS OF DONORS AND DECEASED INDIVIDUALS.

[Except as otherwise provided in Sections 5 through 9:]

(a) A donor is not a parent of a child conceived through assisted conception.

(b) An individual who dies before implantation of an embryo, or before a child is conceived other than through sexual intercourse, using the individual's egg or sperm, is not a parent of the resulting child.

ALTERNATIVE A

§ 5. SURROGACY AGREEMENT.

(a) A surrogate, her husband, if she is married, and intended parents may enter into a written agreement whereby the surrogate relinquishes all her rights and duties as a parent of a child to be conceived through assisted conception, and the intended parents may become the parents of the child pursuant to Section 8.

(b) If the agreement is not approved by the court under Section 6 before conception, the agreement is void and the surrogate is the mother of a resulting child and the surrogate's husband, if a party to the agreement, is the father of the child. If the surrogate's husband is not a party to the agreement or the surrogate is unmarried, paternity of the child is governed by [the Uniform Parentage Act].

§ 6. PETITION AND HEARING FOR APPROVAL OF SURROGACY AGREEMENT.

(a) The intended parents and the surrogate may file a petition in the [appropriate court] to approve a surrogacy agreement if one of them is a resident of this State. The surrogate's husband, if she is married, must join in the petition. A copy of the agreement must be attached to the petition. The court shall name a [guardian ad litem] to represent the interests of a child to be conceived by the surrogate through assisted conception and [shall] [may] appoint counsel to represent the surrogate.

(b)   The court shall hold a hearing on the petition and shall enter an order approving the surrogacy agreement, authorizing assisted conception for a period of 12 months after the date of the order, declaring the intended parents to be the parents of a child to be conceived through assisted conception pursuant to the agreement and discharging the guardian ad litem and attorney for the surrogate, upon finding that:

(1)   the court has jurisdiction and all parties have submitted to its jurisdiction under subsection (e) and have agreed that the law of this State governs all matters arising under this [Act] and the agreement;

(2)   the intended mother is unable to bear a child or is unable to do so without unreasonable risk to an unborn child or to the physical or mental health of the intended mother or child, and the finding is supported by medical evidence;

(3)   the [relevant child-welfare agency] has made a home study of the intended parents and the surrogate and a copy of the report of the home study has been filed with the court;

(4)   the intended parents, the surrogate, and the surrogate's husband, if she is married, meet the standards of fitness applicable to adoptive parents in this State;

(5)   all parties have voluntarily entered into the agreement and understand its terms, nature, and meaning, and the effect of the proceeding;

(6)   the surrogate has had at least one pregnancy and delivery and bearing another child will not pose an unreasonable risk to the unborn child or to the physical or mental health of the surrogate or the child, and this finding is supported by medical evidence;

(7)   all parties have received counseling concerning the effect of the surrogacy by [a qualified health-care professional or social worker] and a report containing conclusions about the capacity of the parties to enter into and fulfill the agreement has been filed with the court;

(8)   a report of the results of any medical or psychological examination or genetic screening agreed to by the parties or required by law has been filed with the court and made available to the parties;

(9)   adequate provision has been made for all reasonable health-care costs associated with the surrogacy until the child's birth including responsibility for those costs if the agreement is terminated pursuant to Section 7; and

(10) the agreement will not be substantially detrimental to the interest of any of the affected individuals.

(c)   Unless otherwise provided in the surrogacy agreement, all court costs, attorney's fees, and other costs and expenses associated with the proceeding must be assessed against the intended parents.

(d)   Notwithstanding any other law concerning judicial proceedings or vital statistics, the court shall conduct all hearings and proceedings under this section in camera. The court shall keep all records of the proceedings confidential and subject to inspection under the same standards applicable to adoptions. At the request of any party, the court shall take steps necessary to ensure that the identities of the parties are not disclosed.

(e)   The court conducting the proceedings has exclusive and continuing jurisdiction of all matters arising out of the surrogacy until a child born after entry of an order under this section is 180 days old.

§ 7. TERMINATION OF SURROGACY AGREEMENT.

(a)   After entry of an order under Section 6, but before the surrogate becomes pregnant through assisted conception, the court for cause, or the surrogate, her husband, or the intended parents may terminate the surrogacy agreement by giving written notice of termination to all other parties and filing notice of the termination with the court. Thereupon, the court shall vacate the order entered under Section 6.

(b)   A surrogate who has provided an egg for the assisted conception pursuant to an agreement approved under Section 6 may terminate the agreement by filing written notice with the court within 180 days after the last insemination pursuant to the agreement. Upon finding, after notice to the parties to the agreement and hearing, that the surrogate has voluntarily terminated the agreement and understands the nature, meaning, and effect of the termination, the court shall vacate the order entered under Section 6.

(c)   The surrogate is not liable to the intended parents for terminating the agreement pursuant to this section.

§ 8. PARENTAGE UNDER APPROVED SURROGACY AGREEMENT.

(a)   The following rules of parentage apply to surrogacy agreements approved under Section 6:

(1)   Upon birth of a child to the surrogate, the intended parents are the parents of the child and the surrogate and her husband, if she is married, are not parents of the child unless the court vacates the order pursuant to Section 7(b).

(2)   If, after notice of termination by the surrogate, the court vacates the order under Section 7(b) the surrogate is the mother of a resulting child, and her husband, if a party to the agreement, is the father. If the surrogate's husband is not a party to the agreement or the surrogate is unmarried, paternity of the child is governed by [the Uniform Parentage Act].

(b)   Upon birth of the child, the intended parents shall file a written notice with the court that a child has been born to the surrogate within 300 days after assisted conception. Thereupon, the court shall enter an order directing the [Department of Vital Statistics] to issue a new birth certificate naming the intended parents as parents and to seal the original birth certificate in the records of the [Department of Vital Statistics].

§ 9. SURROGACY; MISCELLANEOUS PROVISIONS.

(a)   A surrogacy agreement that is the basis of an order under Section 6 may provide for the payment of consideration.

(b)   A surrogacy agreement may not limit the right of the surrogate to make decisions regarding her health care or that of the embryo or fetus.

(c)   After the entry of an order under Section 6, marriage of the surrogate does not affect the validity of the order, and her husband's consent to the surrogacy agreement is not required, nor is he the father of a resulting child.

(d)   A child born to a surrogate within 300 days after assisted conception pursuant to an order under Section 6 is presumed to result from the assisted conception. The presumption is conclusive as to all persons who have notice of the birth and who do not commence within 180 days after notice, an action to assert the contrary in which the child and the parties to the agreement are named as parties. The action must be commenced in the court that issued the order under Section 6.

(e)   A health-care provider is not liable for recognizing the surrogate as the mother before receipt of a copy of the order entered under Section 6 or for recognizing the intended parents as parents after receipt of an order entered under Section 6.]

[END OF ALTERNATIVE A]

ALTERNATIVE B

§ 5. SURROGATE AGREEMENTS.

An agreement in which a woman agrees to become a surrogate or to relinquish her rights and duties as parent of a child thereafter conceived through assisted conception is void. However, she is the mother of a resulting child, and her husband, if a party to the agreement, is the father of the child. If her husband is not a party to the agreement or the surrogate is unmarried, paternity of the child is governed by [the Uniform Parentage Act].]

[END OF ALTERANTIVE B]

§ 10. PARENT AND CHILD RELATIONSHIP; STATUS OF CHILD.

(a) A child whose status as a child is declared or negated by this [Act] is the child only of his or her parents as determined under this [Act].

(b) Unless superseded by later events forming or terminating a parent and child relationship, the status of parent and child declared or negated by this [Act] as to a given individual and a child born alive controls for purposes of:

(1) intestate succession;

(2) probate law exemptions, allowances, or other protections for children in a parent's estate; and

(3) determining eligibility of the child or its descendants to share in a donative transfer from any person as a member of a class determined by reference to the relationship.

§ 11. UNIFORMITY OF APPLICATION AND CONSTRUCTION.

This [Act] shall be applied and construed to effectuate its general purpose to make uniform the law with respect to the subject of this [Act] among states enacting it.

§ 12. SHORT TITLE.

This [Act] may be cited as the Uniform Status of Children of Assisted Conception Act.

§ 13. SEVERABILITY.

If any provision of this [Act] or its application to any person or circumstance is held invalid, the invalidity does not affect other provisions or applications of this [Act] which can be given effect without the invalid provision or application, and to this end the provisions of this [Act] are severable.

* * *

PART II

FEDERAL STATUTES

ADOPTION AND SAFE FAMILIES ACT OF 1997

Pub. L. No. 105–89, 111 Stat. 2115
(codified as amended in scattered sections of 2, 42 U.S.C.)

[EDITORS' INTRODUCTION: Josh Gupta-Kagan, *The New Permanency*, 19 U.C. DAVIS J. JUV. L. & POL'Y 1 (2015); Sarah Katz, *The Value of Permanency: State Implementation of Legal Guardianship Under the Adoption and Safe Families Act of 1997*, 2013 MICH. ST. L. REV. 1079 (2013); Kelli M. Mulder-Westrate, *Waiting for the Justice League: Motivating Child Welfare Agencies to Save Children*, 88 NOTRE DAME L. REV. 523 (2012); Miriam C. Meyer-Thompson, *Wanted: Forever Home Achieving Permanent Outcomes for Nevada's Foster Children*, 14 NEV. L.J. 268 (2013); Kele Stewart, *The Connection Between Permanency and Education in Child Welfare Policy*, 9 HASTINGS RACE & POVERTY L. J. 511 (2012); Samantha Williams & Lior Haas, *Child Custody, Visitation & Termination of Parental Rights*, 15 GEO. J. GENDER & L. 365 (2014); Heather A. Bartel, Note, *From Orphan Trains to Underground Networks: The Need to get on Board with Adoption Reform*, 48 SUFFOLK U. L. REV. 823 (2015).]

TITLE I—REASONABLE EFFORTS AND SAFETY REQUIREMENTS FOR FOSTER CARE AND ADOPTION PLACEMENTS

§ 101. CLARIFICATION OF THE REASONABLE EFFORTS REQUIREMENT.

(a) IN GENERAL.—Section 471(a)(15) of the Social Security Act (42 U.S.C. 671(a)(15)) is amended to read as follows:

* * *

(A) in determining reasonable efforts to be made with respect to a child, as described in this paragraph, and in making such reasonable efforts, the child's health and safety shall be the paramount concern;

(B) except as provided in subparagraph (D), reasonable efforts shall be made to preserve and reunify families—

(i) prior to the placement of a child in foster care, to prevent or eliminate the need for removing the child from the child's home; and

(ii) to make it possible for a child to safely return to the child's home;

(C) if continuation of reasonable efforts of the type described in subparagraph (B) is determined to be inconsistent with the permanency plan for the child, reasonable efforts shall be made to place the child in a timely manner in accordance with the permanency plan, and to complete whatever steps are necessary to finalize the permanent placement of the child;

(D) reasonable efforts of the type described in subparagraph (B) shall not be required to be made with respect to a parent of a child if a court of competent jurisdiction has determined that—

(i) the parent has subjected the child to aggravated circumstances (as defined in State law, which definition may include but need not be limited to abandonment, torture, chronic abuse, and sexual abuse);

(ii) the parent has—

(I) committed murder (which would have been an offense under section 1111(a) of title 18, United States Code, if the offense had occurred in the special maritime or territorial jurisdiction of the United States) of another child of the parent;

(II) committed voluntary manslaughter (which would have been an offense under section 1112(a) of title 18, United States Code, if the offense had occurred in the special maritime or territorial jurisdiction of the United States) of another child of the parent;

(III) aided or abetted, attempted, conspired, or solicited to commit such a murder or such a voluntary manslaughter; or

(IV) committed a felony assault that results in serious bodily injury to the child or another child of the parent; or

(iii) the parental rights of the parent to a sibling have been terminated involuntarily;

(E) if reasonable efforts of the type described in subparagraph (B) are not made with respect to a child as a result of a determination made by a court of competent jurisdiction in accordance with subparagraph (D)—

(i) a permanency hearing (as described in section 475(5)(C)) shall be held for the child within 30 days after the determination; and

(ii) reasonable efforts shall be made to place the child in a timely manner in accordance with the permanency plan, and to complete whatever steps are necessary to finalize the permanent placement of the child; and

(F) reasonable efforts to place a child for adoption or with a legal guardian may be made concurrently with reasonable efforts of the type described in subparagraph (B);

* * *

§ 103. STATES REQUIRED TO INITIATE OR JOIN PROCEEDINGS TO TERMINATE PARENTAL RIGHTS FOR CERTAIN CHILDREN IN FOSTER CARE.

(a) REQUIREMENT FOR PROCEEDINGS.—Section 475(5) of the Social Security Act (42 U.S.C. 675(5)) is amended—

* * *

(E) in the case of a child who has been in foster care under the responsibility of the State for 15 of the most recent 22 months, or, if a court of competent jurisdiction has determined a child to be an abandoned infant (as defined under State law) or has made a determination that the parent has committed murder of another child of the parent, committed voluntary manslaughter of another child of the parent, aided or abetted, attempted, conspired, or solicited to commit such a murder or such a voluntary manslaughter, or committed a felony assault that has resulted in serious bodily injury to the child or to another child of the parent, the State shall file a petition to terminate the parental rights of the child's parents (or, if such a petition has been filed by another party, seek to be joined as a party to the petition), and, concurrently, to identify, recruit, process, and approve a qualified family for an adoption, unless—

(i) at the option of the State, the child is being cared for by a relative;

(ii) a State agency has documented in the case plan (which shall be available for court review) a compelling reason for determining that filing such a petition would not be in the best interests of the child; or

(iii) the State has not provided to the family of the child, consistent with the time period in the State case plan, such services as the State deems necessary for the safe return of the child to the child's home, if reasonable efforts of the type described in section 471(a)(15)(B)(ii) are required to be made with respect to the child.

* * *

(c) TRANSITION RULES.—

(1) NEW FOSTER CHILDREN.—In the case of a child who enters foster care (within the meaning of section 475(5)(F) of the Social Security Act) under the responsibility of a State after the date of the enactment of this Act—

(A) if the State comes into compliance with the amendments made by subsection (a) of this section before the child has been in such foster care for 15 of the most recent 22 months, the State shall comply with section 475(5)(E) of the

Social Security Act with respect to the child when the child has been in such foster care for 15 of the most recent 22 months; and

(B) if the State comes into such compliance after the child has been in such foster care for 15 of the most recent 22 months, the State shall comply with such section 475(5)(E) with respect to the child not later than 3 months after the end of the first regular session of the State legislature that begins after such date of enactment.

(2) CURRENT FOSTER CHILDREN.—In the case of children in foster care under the responsibility of the State on the date of the enactment of this Act, the State shall—

(A) not later than 6 months after the end of the first regular session of the State legislature that begins after such date of enactment, comply with section 475(5)(E) of the Social Security Act with respect to not less than ⅓ of such children as the State shall select, giving priority to children for whom the permanency plan (within the meaning of part E of title IV of the Social Security Act) is adoption and children who have been in foster care for the greatest length of time;

(B) not later than 12 months after the end of such first regular session, comply with such section 475(5)(E) with respect to not less than ⅔ of such children as the State shall select; and

(C) not later than 18 months after the end of such first regular session, comply with such section 475(5)(E) with respect to all of such children.

* * *

(d) RULE OF CONSTRUCTION.—Nothing in this section or in part E of title IV of the Social Security Act (42 U.S.C. 670 et seq.), as amended by this Act, shall be construed as precluding State courts or State agencies from initiating the termination of parental rights for reasons other than, or for timelines earlier than, those specified in part E of title IV of such Act, when such actions are determined to be in the best interests of the child, including cases where the child has experienced multiple foster care placements of varying durations.

§ 104. NOTICE OF REVIEWS AND HEARINGS; OPPORTUNITY TO BE HEARD.

Section 475(5) of the Social Security Act (42 U.S.C. 675(5)), as amended by section 103, is amended—

* * *

(G) the foster parents (if any) of a child and any preadoptive parent or relative providing care for the child are provided with notice of, and an opportunity to be heard in, any review or hearing to be held with respect to the child, except that this subparagraph shall not be construed to require that any foster parent, preadoptive parent, or relative providing care for the child be made a party to such a review or hearing solely on the basis of such notice and opportunity to be heard.

* * *

§ 107. DOCUMENTATION OF EFFORTS FOR ADOPTION OR LOCATION OF A PERMANENT HOME.

Section 475(1) of the Social Security Act (42 U.S.C. 675(1)) is amended—

* * *

(E) In the case of a child with respect to whom the permanency plan is adoption or placement in another permanent home, documentation of the steps the agency is taking to find an adoptive family or other permanent living arrangement for the child, to place the child with an adoptive family, a fit and willing relative, a legal guardian, or in another planned permanent living arrangement, and to finalize the adoption or legal guardianship. At a minimum, such documentation shall include child specific recruitment efforts such as the use of State, regional, and national adoption exchanges including electronic exchange systems.

TITLE II—INCENTIVES FOR PROVIDING PERMANENT FAMILIES FOR CHILDREN

§ 201. ADOPTION INCENTIVE PAYMENTS.

* * *

(a) GRANT AUTHORITY.—Subject to the availability of such amounts as may be provided in advance in appropriations Acts for this purpose, the Secretary shall make a grant to each State that is an incentive-eligible State for a fiscal year in an amount equal to the adoption incentive payment payable to the State under this section for the fiscal year, which shall be payable in the immediately succeeding fiscal year.

(b) INCENTIVE–ELIGIBLE STATE.—A State is an incentive-eligible State for a fiscal year if—

(1) the State has a plan approved under this part for the fiscal year;

(2) the number of foster child adoptions in the State during the fiscal year exceeds the base number of foster child adoptions for the State for the fiscal year;

(3) the State is in compliance with subsection (c) for the fiscal year;

(4)   in the case of fiscal years 2001 and 2002, the State provides health insurance coverage to any child with special needs (as determined under section 473(c)) for whom there is in effect an adoption assistance agreement between a State and an adoptive parent or parents; and

(5)   the fiscal year is any of fiscal years 1998 through 2002.

* * *

§ 202. ADOPTIONS ACROSS STATE AND COUNTY JURISDICTIONS.

* * *

(b)   CONDITION OF ASSISTANCE.—Section 474 of such Act (42 U.S.C. 674) is amended by adding at the end the following:

(e)   Notwithstanding subsection (a), a State shall not be eligible for any payment under this section if the Secretary finds that, after the date of the enactment of this subsection, the State has—

(1)   denied or delayed the placement of a child for adoption when an approved family is available outside of the jurisdiction with responsibility for handling the case of the child; or

(2)   failed to grant an opportunity for a fair hearing, as described in section 471(a)(12), to an individual whose allegation of a violation of paragraph (1) of this subsection is denied by the State or not acted upon by the State with reasonable promptness.

(c)   STUDY OF INTERJURISDICTIONAL ADOPTION ISSUES.—

(1)   IN GENERAL.—The Comptroller General of the United States shall—

(A)   study and consider how to improve procedures and policies to facilitate the timely and permanent adoptions of children across State and county jurisdictions; and

(B)   examine, at a minimum, interjurisdictional adoption issues—

(i)   concerning the recruitment of prospective adoptive families from other States and counties;

(ii)   concerning the procedures to grant reciprocity to prospective adoptive family home studies from other States and counties;

(iii)   arising from a review of the comity and full faith and credit provided to adoption decrees and termination of parental rights orders from other States; and

(iv) concerning the procedures related to the administration and implementation of the Interstate Compact on the Placement of Children.

(2) REPORT TO THE CONGRESS.—Not later than 1 year after the date of the enactment of this Act, the Comptroller General shall submit to the appropriate committees of the Congress a report that includes—

(A) the results of the study conducted under paragraph (1); and

(B) recommendations on how to improve procedures to facilitate the interjurisdictional adoption of children, including interstate and intercounty adoptions, so that children will be assured timely and permanent placements.

§ 203. PERFORMANCE OF STATES IN PROTECTING CHILDREN.

* * *

The Secretary, in consultation with Governors, State legislatures, State and local public officials responsible for administering child welfare programs, and child welfare advocates, shall—

(1) develop a set of outcome measures (including length of stay in foster care, number of foster care placements, and number of adoptions) that can be used to assess the performance of States in operating child protection and child welfare programs pursuant to parts B and E to ensure the safety of children;

(2) to the maximum extent possible, the outcome measures should be developed from data available from the Adoption and Foster Care Analysis and Reporting System;

(3) develop a system for rating the performance of States with respect to the outcome measures, and provide to the States an explanation of the rating system and how scores are determined under the rating system;

(4) prescribe such regulations as may be necessary to ensure that States provide to the Secretary the data necessary to determine State performance with respect to each outcome measure, as a condition of the State receiving funds under this part; and

(5) on May 1, 1999, and annually thereafter, prepare and submit to the Congress a report on the performance of each State on each outcome measure, which shall examine the reasons for high performance and low performance and, where possible, make recommendations as to how State performance could be improved.

(b) DEVELOPMENT OF PERFORMANCE–BASED INCENTIVE SYSTEM.—The Secretary of Health and Human Services, in consultation with State and local public officials responsible for administering child welfare programs and child welfare advocates, shall study, develop, and recommend to Congress an incentive system to provide payments under parts B and E of title IV of the Social Security Act (42 U.S.C. 620 et seq., 670 et seq.) to any State based on the State's performance under such a system. Such a system shall, to the extent the Secretary determines feasible and appropriate, be based on the annual report required by section 479A of the Social Security Act (as added by subsection (a) of this section) or on any proposed modifications of the annual report. Not later than 6 months after the date of the enactment of this Act, the Secretary shall submit to the Committee on Ways and Means of the House of Representatives and the Committee on Finance of the Senate a progress report on the feasibility, timetable, and consultation process for conducting such a study. Not later than 15 months after such date of enactment, the Secretary shall submit to the Committee on Ways and Means of the House of Representatives and the Committee on Finance of the Senate the final report on a performance-based incentive system. The report may include other recommendations for restructuring the program and payments under parts B and E of title IV of the Social Security Act.

TITLE III—ADDITIONAL IMPROVEMENTS AND REFORMS

* * *

§ 303. KINSHIP CARE.

(a) REPORT.—

(1) IN GENERAL.—The Secretary of Health and Human Services shall—

(A) not later than June 1, 1998, convene the advisory panel provided for in subsection (b)(1) and prepare and submit to the advisory panel an initial report on the extent to which children in foster care are placed in the care of a relative (in this section referred to as "kinship care"); and

(B) not later than June 1, 1999, submit to the Committee on Ways and Means of the House of Representatives and the Committee on Finance of the Senate a final report on the matter described in subparagraph (A), which shall—

(i) be based on the comments submitted by the advisory panel pursuant to subsection (b)(2) and other information and considerations; and

(ii) include the policy recommendations of the Secretary with respect to the matter.

(2) REQUIRED CONTENTS.—Each report required by paragraph (1) shall—

(A) include, to the extent available for each State, information on—

(i) the policy of the State regarding kinship care;

(ii) the characteristics of the kinship care providers (including age, income, ethnicity, and race, and the relationship of the kinship care providers to the children);

(iii) the characteristics of the household of such providers (such as number of other persons in the household and family composition);

(iv) how much access to the child is afforded to the parent from whom the child has been removed;

(v) the cost of, and source of funds for, kinship care (including any subsidies such as medicaid and cash assistance);

(vi) the permanency plan for the child and the actions being taken by the State to achieve the plan;

(vii) the services being provided to the parent from whom the child has been removed; and

(viii) the services being provided to the kinship care provider; and

(B) specifically note the circumstances or conditions under which children enter kinship care.

(b) ADVISORY PANEL.—

(1) ESTABLISHMENT.—The Secretary of Health and Human Services, in consultation with the Chairman of the Committee on Ways and Means of the House of Representatives and the Chairman of the Committee on Finance of the Senate, shall convene an advisory panel which shall include parents, foster parents, relative caregivers, former foster children, State and local public officials responsible for administering child welfare programs, private persons involved in the delivery of child welfare services, representatives of tribal governments and tribal courts, judges, and academic experts.

(2) DUTIES.—The advisory panel convened pursuant to paragraph (1) shall review the report prepared pursuant to subsection (a), and, not later than October 1, 1998, submit to the Secretary comments on the report.

* * *

§ 305. REAUTHORIZATION AND EXPANSION OF FAMILY PRESERVATION AND SUPPORT SERVICES.

* * *

(2) DEFINITIONS OF TIME–LIMITED FAMILY REUNIFICATION SERVICES AND ADOPTION PROMOTION AND SUPPORT SERVICES.—Section 431(a) of the Social Security Act (42 U.S.C. 629a(a)) is amended by adding at the end the following:

* * *

(A) IN GENERAL.—The term 'time-limited family reunification services' means the services and activities described in subparagraph (B) that are provided to a child that is removed from the child's home and placed in a foster family home or a child care institution and to the parents or primary caregiver of such a child, in order to facilitate the reunification of the child safely and appropriately within a timely fashion, but only during the 15–month period that begins on the date that the child, pursuant to section 475(5)(F), is considered to have entered foster care.

(B) SERVICES AND ACTIVITIES DESCRIBED.—The services and activities described in this subparagraph are the following:

(i) Individual, group, and family counseling.

(ii) Inpatient, residential, or outpatient substance abuse treatment services.

(iii) Mental health services.

(iv) Assistance to address domestic violence.

(v) Services designed to provide temporary child care and therapeutic services for families, including crisis nurseries.

(vi) Transportation to or from any of the services and activities described in this subparagraph.

* * *

TITLE IV—MISCELLANEOUS

§ 401. PRESERVATION OF REASONABLE PARENTING.

Nothing in this Act is intended to disrupt the family unnecessarily or to intrude inappropriately into family life, to prohibit the use of reasonable methods of parental discipline, or to prescribe a particular method of parenting.

* * *

§ 403. SENSE OF CONGRESS REGARDING STANDBY GUARDIANSHIP.

It is the sense of Congress that the States should have in effect laws and procedures that permit any parent who is chronically ill or near death, without surrendering parental rights, to designate a standby guardian for the parent's minor children, whose authority would take effect upon—

(1) the death of the parent;

(2) the mental incapacity of the parent; or

(3) the physical debilitation and consent of the parent.

* * *

§ 405. COORDINATION OF SUBSTANCE ABUSE AND CHILD PROTECTION SERVICES.

Within 1 year after the date of the enactment of this Act, the Secretary of Health and Human Services, based on information from the Substance Abuse and Mental Health Services Administration and the Administration for Children and Families in the Department of Health of Human Services, shall prepare and submit to the Committee on Ways and Means of the House of Representatives and the Committee on Finance of the Senate a report which describes the extent and scope of the problem of substance abuse in the child welfare population, the types of services provided to such population, and the outcomes resulting from the provision of such services to such population. The report shall include recommendations for any legislation that may be needed to improve coordination in providing such services to such population.

* * *

Bankruptcy Abuse Prevention and Consumer Protection Act of 2005

11 U.S.C.A. 523 (West 2016)

[EDITORS' INTRODUCTION: Linda Coco, *Visible Women: Locating Women in Financial Failure, Bankruptcy Law, and Bankruptcy Reform*, 8 CHARLESTON L. REV. 191 (2013); Joseph W. McKnight, *Family Law: Husband and Wife*, 64 SMU L. REV. 253 (2011); Amanda Moreno, *The Effect of Bankruptcy on a Spouse in a Divorce*, 20 J. CONTEMP. LEGAL ISSUES 81 (2012); Jeffrey Traczynski, *Divorce Rates and Bankruptcy Exemption Levels in the United States*, 54 J.L. & ECON. 751 (2011); Becker McKay Wyckoff, Comment, *They're Just Letting Anyone in These Days: The Expansion of § 523(A)(5)'s "Domestic Support Obligation" Exception to Discharge*, 28 EMORY BANKR. DEV. J. 637 (2012).]

§ 523. EXCEPTIONS TO DISCHARGE

(a) A discharge under section 727, 1141, 1228(a), 1228(b), or 1328(b) of this title does not discharge an individual debtor from any debt—

. . .

(5) for a domestic support obligation;

. . .

(15) to a spouse, former spouse, or child of the debtor and not of the kind described in paragraph (5) that is incurred by the debtor in the course of a divorce or separation or in connection with a separation agreement, divorce decree or other order of a court of record, or a determination made in accordance with State or territorial law by a governmental unit;

. . .

(b) Notwithstanding subsection (a) of this section, a debt that was excepted from discharge under subsection (a)(1), (a)(3), or (a)(8) of this section, under section 17a(1), 17a(3), or 17a(5) of the Bankruptcy Act, under section 439A of the Higher Education Act of 1965, or under section 733(g) of the Public Health Service Act in a prior case concerning the debtor under this title, or under the Bankruptcy Act, is dischargeable in a case under this title unless, by the terms of subsection (a) of this section, such debt is not dischargeable in the case under this title.

(c)(1) Except as provided in subsection (a)(3)(B) of this section, the debtor shall be discharged from a debt of a kind specified in paragraph (2), (4), or (6) of subsection (a) of this section, unless, on request of the creditor to whom such debt is owed, and after notice and a hearing, the court determines such debt to be excepted from discharge under paragraph (2), (4), or (6), as the case may be, of subsection (a) of this section.

(2) Paragraph (1) shall not apply in the case of a Federal depository institutions regulatory agency seeking, in its capacity as conservator, receiver, or liquidating agent for an insured depository institution, to recover a debt described in subsection (a)(2), (a)(4), (a)(6), or (a)(11) owed to such institution by an institution-affiliated party unless the receiver, conservator, or liquidating agent was appointed in time to reasonably comply, or for a Federal depository institutions regulatory agency acting in its corporate capacity as a successor to such receiver, conservator, or liquidating agent to reasonably comply, with subsection (a)(3)(B) as a creditor of such institution-affiliated party with respect to such debt.

(d) If a creditor requests a determination of dischargeability of a consumer debt under subsection (a)(2) of this section, and such debt is discharged, the court shall grant judgment in favor of the debtor for the costs of, and a reasonable attorney's fee for, the proceeding if the court finds that the position of the creditor was not substantially justified, except that the court shall not award such costs and fees if special circumstances would make the award unjust.

(e) Any institution-affiliated party of an insured depository institution shall be considered to be acting in a fiduciary capacity with respect to the purposes of subsection (a)(4) or (11).

BORN ALIVE INFANT PROTECTION ACT OF 2002

Pub. L. No. 107–207, 116 Stat. 926, 1 U.S.C.A. 8 (West 2016)

[EDITORS' INTRODUCTION: Samuel W. Calhoun, *"Partial-Birth Abortion" is Not Abortion:* Carhart II's *Fundamental Misapplication of Roe,* 79 MISS. L.J. 775 (2010); Samuel W. Calhoun, *Stopping Philadelphia Abortion Provider Kermit Gosnell and Preventing Others Like Him: An Outcome That Both Pro-Choicers and Pro-Lifers Should Support,* 57 VILL. L. REV. 1 (2012).]

§ 1. SHORT TITLE.

This Act may be cited as the "Born–Alive Infants Protection Act of 2002".

§ 2. DEFINITION OF BORN-ALIVE INFANT.

(a) IN GENERAL.—Chapter 1 of title 1, United States Code, is amended by adding at the end the following:

§ 8. 'Person', 'human being', 'child', and 'individual' as including born-alive infant

"(a) In determining the meaning of any Act of Congress, or of any ruling, regulation, or interpretation of the various administrative bureaus and agencies of the United States, the words 'person', 'human being', 'child', and 'individual', shall include every infant member of the species homo sapiens who is born alive at any stage of development.

"(b) As used in this section, the term 'born alive', with respect to a member of the species homo sapiens, means the complete expulsion or extraction from his or her mother of that member, at any stage of development, who after such expulsion or extraction breathes or has a beating heart, pulsation of the umbilical cord, or definite movement of voluntary muscles, regardless of whether the umbilical cord has been cut, and regardless of whether the expulsion or extraction occurs as a result of natural or induced labor, cesarean section, or induced abortion.

"(c) Nothing in this section shall be construed to affirm, deny, expand, or contract any legal status or legal right applicable to any member of the species homo sapiens at any point prior to being 'born alive' as defined in this section."

CHILD SUPPORT RECOVERY ACT OF 1992

18 U.S.C.A. § 228 (West 2016)

[EDITORS' INTRODUCTION: Nicole K. Bridges, Note, *The "Strengthen and Vitalize Enforcement of Child Support (Save Child Support) Act": Can the Save Child Support Act Save Child Support from the Recent Economic Downturn?*, 36 OKLA. CITY U. L. REV. 679 (2011).]

18 U.S.C.A. § 228

(a) Offense.—Any person who—

(1) willfully fails to pay a support obligation with respect to a child who resides in another State, if such obligation has remained unpaid for a period longer than 1 year, or is greater than $5,000;

(2) travels in interstate or foreign commerce with the intent to evade a support obligation, if such obligation has remained unpaid for a period longer than 1 year, or is greater than $5,000; or

(3) willfully fails to pay a support obligation with respect to a child who resides in another State, if such obligation has remained unpaid for a period longer than 2 years, or is greater than $10,000;

shall be punished as provided in subsection (c).

(b) Presumption.—The existence of a support obligation that was in effect for the time period charged in the indictment or information creates a rebuttable presumption that the obligor has the ability to pay the support obligation for that time period.

(c) Punishment.—The punishment for an offense under this section is—

(1) in the case of a first offense under subsection (a)(1), a fine under this title, imprisonment for not more than 6 months, or both; and

(2) in the case of an offense under paragraph (2) or (3) of subsection (a), or a second or subsequent offense under subsection (a)(1), a fine under this title, imprisonment for not more than 2 years, or both.

(d) Mandatory restitution.—Upon a conviction under this section, the court shall order restitution under section 3663A in an amount equal to the total unpaid support obligation as it exists at the time of sentencing.

(e) Venue.—With respect to an offense under this section, an action may be inquired of and prosecuted in a district court of the United States for—

(1) the district in which the child who is the subject of the support obligation involved resided during a period during which a

person described in subsection (a) (referred to in this subsection as an "obliger") failed to meet that support obligation;

(2) the district in which the obliger resided during a period described in paragraph (1); or

(3) any other district with jurisdiction otherwise provided for by law.

(f) Definitions.—As used in this section—

(1) the term "Indian tribe" has the meaning given that term in section 102 of the Federally Recognized Indian Tribe List Act of 1994 (25 U.S.C. 479a);

(2) the term "State" includes any State of the United States, the District of Columbia, and any commonwealth, territory, or possession of the United States; and

(3) the term "support obligation" means any amount determined under a court order or an order of an administrative process pursuant to the law of a State or of an Indian tribe to be due from a person for the support and maintenance of a child or of a child and the parent with whom the child is living.

PARENTAL KIDNAPPING PREVENTION ACT

Pub. L. No. 96–611, 94 Stat. 3568 (1980)
(codified in scattered sections of 18, 28, 42 U.S.C.)

[EDITORS' INTRODUCTION: Amy C. Gromek, *Military Child Custody Disputes: The Need for Federal Encouragement for the States' Adoption of the Uniform Deployed Parents Custody and Visitation Act*, 44 SETON HALL L. REV. 873 (2014); Cassandra R. Hewlings, *With* Adar v. Smith, *the Fifth Circuit Opens a Hole in the Full Faith and Credit Clause*, 86 TUL. L. REV. 1359 (2012); Thomas M. Joraanstad, *Half Faith and Credit?: The Fifth Circuit Upholds Louisiana's Refusal to Issue a Revised Birth Certificate*, 19 WM. & MARY J. WOMEN & L. 421 (2013); Kevin Wessel, *Home Is Where the Court Is: Determining Residence for Child Custody Matters Under the UCCJEA*, 79 U. CHI. L. REV. 1141 (2012); Brittany A. Jenkins, Comment, *My Country or My Child?: How State Enactment of the Uniform Deployed Parents Custody and Visitation Act Will Allow Service Members to Protect Their Country & Fight for Their Children*, 45 TEX. TECH L. REV. 1011 (2013); Rebecca Miller, Note, *The Parental Kidnapping Prevention Act: Thirty Years Later and No Effect? Where Can the Unwed Father Turn?*, 40 PEPP. L. REV. 735 (2013); Pamela K. Terry, Note, *E Pluribus Unum? The Full Faith and Credit Clause and Meaningful Recognition of Out-of-State Adoptions*, 80 FORDHAM L. REV. 3093 (2012).]

28 U.S.C. § 1738A

(a) The appropriate authorities of every State shall enforce according to its terms, and shall not modify except as provided in subsections (f), (g), and (h) of this section, any custody determination or visitation determination made consistently with the provisions of this section by a court of another State.

(b) As used in this section, the term—

(1) "child" means a person under the age of eighteen;

(2) "contestant" means a person, including a parent or grandparent, who claims a right to custody or visitation of a child;

(3) "custody determination" means a judgment, decree, or other order of a court providing for the custody of a child, and includes permanent and temporary orders, and initial orders and modifications;

(4) "home State" means the State in which, immediately preceding the time involved, the child lived with his parents, a parent, or a person acting as parent, for at least six consecutive months, and in the case of a child less than six months old, the State in which the child lived from birth with any of such persons. Periods of temporary absence of any of such persons are counted as part of the six-month or other period;

(5) "modification" and "modify" refer to a custody or visitation determination which modifies, replaces, supersedes, or otherwise is made subsequent to, a prior custody or visitation determination concerning the same child, whether made by the same court or not;

(6) "person acting as a parent" means a person, other than a parent, who has physical custody of a child and who has either been awarded custody by a court or claims a right to custody;

(7) "physical custody" means actual possession and control of a child;

(8) "State" means a State of the United States, the District of Columbia, the Commonwealth of Puerto Rico, or a territory or possession of the United States; and

(9) "visitation determination" means a judgment, decree, or other order of a court providing for the visitation of a child and includes permanent and temporary orders and initial orders and modifications.

(c) A child custody or visitation determination made by a court of a State is consistent with the provisions of this section only if—

(1) such court has jurisdiction under the law of such State; and

(2) one of the following conditions is met:

(A) such State (i) is the home State of the child on the date of the commencement of the proceeding, or (ii) had been the child's home State within six months before the date of the commencement of the proceeding and the child is absent from such State because of his removal or retention by a contestant or for other reasons, and a contestant continues to live in such State;

(B) (i) it appears that no other State would have jurisdiction under subparagraph (A), and (ii) it is in the best interest of the child that a court of such State assume jurisdiction because (I) the child and his parents, or the child and at least one contestant, have a significant connection with such State other than mere physical presence in such State, and (II) there is available in such State substantial evidence concerning the child's present or future care, protection, training, and personal relationships;

(C) the child is physically present in such State and (i) the child has been abandoned, or (ii) it is necessary in an emergency to protect the child because the child, a sibling, or parent of the child has been subjected to or threatened with mistreatment or abuse;

(D) (i) it appears that no other State would have jurisdiction under subparagraph (A), (B), (C), or (E), or another State has declined to exercise jurisdiction on the ground that the

State whose jurisdiction is in issue is the more appropriate forum to determine the custody or visitation of the child, and (ii) it is in the best interest of the child that such court assume jurisdiction; or

(E) the court has continuing jurisdiction pursuant to subsection (d) of this section.

(d) The jurisdiction of a court of a State which has made a child custody or visitation determination consistently with the provisions of this section continues as long as the requirement of subsection (c)(1) of this section continues to be met and such State remains the residence of the child or of any contestant.

(e) Before a child custody or visitation determination is made, reasonable notice and opportunity to be heard shall be given to the contestants, any parent whose parental rights have not been previously terminated and any person who has physical custody of a child.

(f) A court of a State may modify a determination of the custody of the same child made by a court of another State, if—

(1) it has jurisdiction to make such a child custody determination; and

(2) the court of the other State no longer has jurisdiction, or it has declined to exercise such jurisdiction to modify such determination.

(g) A court of a State shall not exercise jurisdiction in any proceeding for a custody or visitation determination commenced during the pendency of a proceeding in a court of another State where such court of that other State is exercising jurisdiction consistently with the provisions of this section to make a custody or visitation determination.

(h) A court of a State may not modify a visitation determination made by a court of another State unless the court of the other State no longer has jurisdiction to modify such determination or has declined to exercise jurisdiction to modify such determination.

FULL FAITH AND CREDIT FOR CHILD SUPPORT ORDERS ACT

28 U.S.C.A. § 1738B (West 2016)

[EDITORS' INTRODUCTION: Jeffrey A. Parness, *Choosing Among Imprecise American State Parentage Laws*, 76 LA. L. REV. 481 (2015); Jill C. Engle, *Promoting the General Welfare: Legal Reform to Lift Women and Children in the United States Out of Poverty*, 97 MARQ. L. REV. 215 (2013); Margaret Campbell Haynes & Susan Friedman Paikin, *"Reconciling" FFCCSOA and UIFSA*, 49 FAM. L.Q. 331 (2015); Joseph A. Fraioli, Note, *Having Faith in Full Faith & Credit:* Finstuen, Adar, *and the Quest for Interstate Same-Sex Parental Recognition*, 98 IOWA L. REV. 365 (2012).]

28 U.S.C.A. § 1738B

(a) General rule.—The appropriate authorities of each State—

(1) shall enforce according to its terms a child support order made consistently with this section by a court of another State; and

(2) shall not seek or make a modification of such an order except in accordance with subsections (e), (f), and (i).

(b) Definitions.—In this section:

(1) The term "child" means—

(A) a person under 18 years of age; and

(B) a person 18 or more years of age with respect to whom a child support order has been issued pursuant to the laws of a State.

(2) The term "child's State" means the State in which a child resides.

(3) The term "child's home State" means the State in which a child lived with a parent or a person acting as parent for at least 6 consecutive months immediately preceding the time of filing of a petition or comparable pleading for support and, if a child is less than 6 months old, the State in which the child lived from birth with any of them. A period of temporary absence of any of them is counted as part of the 6-month period.

(4) The term "child support" means a payment of money, continuing support, or arrearages or the provision of a benefit (including payment of health insurance, child care, and educational expenses) for the support of a child.

(5) The term "child support order"—

(A) means a judgment, decree, or order of a court requiring the payment of child support in periodic amounts or in a lump sum; and

(B) includes—

(i)   a permanent or temporary order; and

(ii)   an initial order or a modification of an order.

(6)   The term "contestant" means—

(A)   a person (including a parent) who—

(i)   claims a right to receive child support;

(ii)   is a party to a proceeding that may result in the issuance of a child support order; or

(iii)   is under a child support order; and

(B)   a State or political subdivision of a State to which the right to obtain child support has been assigned.

(7)   The term "court" means a court or administrative agency of a State that is authorized by State law to establish the amount of child support payable by a contestant or make a modification of a child support order.

(8)   The term "modification" means a change in a child support order that affects the amount, scope, or duration of the order and modifies, replaces, supersedes, or otherwise is made subsequent to the child support order.

(9)   The term "State" means a State of the United States, the District of Columbia, the Commonwealth of Puerto Rico, the territories and possessions of the United States, and Indian country (as defined in section 1151 of title 18).

(c)   Requirements of child support orders.—A child support order made by a court of a State is made consistently with this section if—

(1)   a court that makes the order, pursuant to the laws of the State in which the court is located and subsections (e), (f), and (g)—

(A)   has subject matter jurisdiction to hear the matter and enter such an order; and

(B)   has personal jurisdiction over the contestants; and

(2)   reasonable notice and opportunity to be heard is given to the contestants.

(d)   Continuing jurisdiction.—A court of a State that has made a child support order consistently with this section has continuing, exclusive jurisdiction over the order if the State is the child's State or the residence of any individual contestant unless the court of another State, acting in accordance with subsections (e) and (f), has made a modification of the order.

(e)   Authority to modify orders.—A court of a State may modify a child support order issued by a court of another State if—

(1) the court has jurisdiction to make such a child support order pursuant to subsection (i); and

(2)(A)   the court of the other State no longer has continuing, exclusive jurisdiction of the child support order because that State no longer is the child's State or the residence of any individual contestant; or

(B) each individual contestant has filed written consent with the State of continuing, exclusive jurisdiction for a court of another State to modify the order and assume continuing, exclusive jurisdiction over the order.

(f)   Recognition of child support orders.—If 1 or more child support orders have been issued with regard to an obligor and a child, a court shall apply the following rules in determining which order to recognize for purposes of continuing, exclusive jurisdiction and enforcement:

(1) If only 1 court has issued a child support order, the order of that court must be recognized.

(2) If 2 or more courts have issued child support orders for the same obligor and child, and only 1 of the courts would have continuing, exclusive jurisdiction under this section, the order of that court must be recognized.

(3) If 2 or more courts have issued child support orders for the same obligor and child, and more than 1 of the courts would have continuing, exclusive jurisdiction under this section, an order issued by a court in the current home State of the child must be recognized, but if an order has not been issued in the current home State of the child, the order most recently issued must be recognized.

(4) If 2 or more courts have issued child support orders for the same obligor and child, and none of the courts would have continuing, exclusive jurisdiction under this section, a court having jurisdiction over the parties shall issue a child support order, which must be recognized.

(5) The court that has issued an order recognized under this subsection is the court having continuing, exclusive jurisdiction under subsection (d).

(g) Enforcement of modified orders.—A court of a State that no longer has continuing, exclusive jurisdiction of a child support order may enforce the order with respect to nonmodifiable obligations and unsatisfied obligations that accrued before the date on which a modification of the order is made under subsections (e) and (f).

(h) Choice of law.—

(1) In general.—In a proceeding to establish, modify, or enforce a child support order, the forum State's law shall apply except as provided in paragraphs (2) and (3).

(2) Law of State of issuance of order.—In interpreting a child support order including the duration of current payments and other obligations of support, a court shall apply the law of the State of the court that issued the order.

(3) Period of limitation.—In an action to enforce arrears under a child support order, a court shall apply the statute of limitation of the forum State or the State of the court that issued the order, whichever statute provides the longer period of limitation.

(i) Registration for modification.—If there is no individual contestant or child residing in the issuing State, the party or support enforcement agency seeking to modify, or to modify and enforce, a child support order issued in another State shall register that order in a State with jurisdiction over the nonmovant for the purpose of modification.

INCOME TAX CREDIT AND EXCLUSION FOR ADOPTION ASSISTANCE

26 U.S.C.A. §§ 23, 137 (West 2016)

[EDITORS' INTRODUCTION: Bethany R. Berger, *In the Name of the Child: Race, Gender, and Economics in* Adoptive Couple v. Baby Girl, 67 FLA. L. REV. 295 (2015); Marie A. Fallinger, *Moving Toward Human Rights Principles for Intercountry Adoption*, 39 N.C. J. INT'L L. & COM. REG. 523 (2014); Edward L. Metzger, *Falling Fertility Rates: The Offspring of the Contraceptive Mentality*, 24 NOTRE DAME J.L. ETHICS & PUB. POL'Y 425 (2010); Deleith Duke Gossett, *If Charity Begins at Home, Why Do We Go Searching Abroad? Why the Federal Adoption Tax Credit Should Not Subsidize International Adoptions*, 17 LEWIS & CLARK L. REV. 839 (2013); Carolyn J. Head, *Adopting the Right Incentives: Encouraging People to Adopt in the Medical Age*, 9 J.L. ECON. & POL'Y 717 (2013); Melissa B. Jacoby, *Credit for Motherhood*, 88 N.C. L. REV. 1715 (2010); Leah Carson Kanoy, *The Effectiveness of the Internal Revenue Code's Adoption Tax Credit: Fostering the Nation's Future*, 21 U. FLA. J.L. & PUB. POL'Y 201 (2010).]

26 U.S.C.A. § 23 ADOPTION EXPENSES

(a) Allowance of credit.—

(1) In general.—In the case of an individual, there shall be allowed as a credit against the tax imposed by this chapter the amount of the qualified adoption expenses paid or incurred by the taxpayer.

(2) Year credit allowed.—The credit under paragraph (1) with respect to any expense shall be allowed—

(A) in the case of any expense paid or incurred before the taxable year in which such adoption becomes final, for the taxable year following the taxable year during which such expense is paid or incurred, and

(B) in the case of an expense paid or incurred during or after the taxable year in which such adoption becomes final, for the taxable year in which such expense is paid or incurred.

(3) $10,000 credit for adoption of child with special needs regardless of expenses.—In the case of an adoption of a child with special needs which becomes final during a taxable year, the taxpayer shall be treated as having paid during such year qualified adoption expenses with respect to such adoption in an amount equal to the excess (if any) of $10,000 over the aggregate qualified adoption expenses actually paid or incurred by the taxpayer with respect to such adoption during such taxable year and all prior taxable years.

(b) Limitations.—

(1) Dollar limitation.—The aggregate amount of qualified adoption expenses which may be taken into account under subsection (a) for all taxable years with respect to the adoption of a child by the taxpayer shall not exceed $10,000.

(2) Income limitation.—

(A) In general.—The amount allowable as a credit under subsection (a) for any taxable year (determined without regard to subsection (c)) shall be reduced (but not below zero) by an amount which bears the same ratio to the amount so allowable (determined without regard to this paragraph but with regard to paragraph (1)) as—

(i) the amount (if any) by which the taxpayer's adjusted gross income exceeds $150,000, bears to

(ii) $40,000.

(B) Determination of adjusted gross income.—For purposes of subparagraph (A), adjusted gross income shall be determined without regard to section 911, 931, and 933.

(3) Denial of double benefit.—

(A) In general.—No credit shall be allowed under subsection (a) for any expense for which a deduction or credit is allowed under any other provision of this chapter.

(B) Grants.—No credit shall be allowed under subsection (a) for any expense to the extent that funds for such expense are received under any Federal, State, or local program.

* * *

(d) Definitions.—For purposes of this section—

(1) Qualified adoption expenses.—The term "qualified adoption expenses" means reasonable and necessary adoption fees, court costs, attorney fees, and other expenses—

(A) which are directly related to, and the principal purpose of which is for, the legal adoption of an eligible child by the taxpayer,

(B) which are not incurred in violation of State or Federal law or in carrying out any surrogate parenting arrangement,

(C) which are not expenses in connection with the adoption by an individual of a child who is the child of such individual's spouse, and

(D) which are not reimbursed under an employer program or otherwise.

(2) Eligible child.—The term "eligible child" means any individual who—

(A) has not attained age 18, or

(B) is physically or mentally incapable of caring for himself.

(3) Child with special needs.—The term "child with special needs" means any child if—

(A) a State has determined that the child cannot or should not be returned to the home of his parents,

(B) such State has determined that there exists with respect to the child a specific factor or condition (such as his ethnic background, age, or membership in a minority or sibling group, or the presence of factors such as medical conditions or physical, mental, or emotional handicaps) because of which it is reasonable to conclude that such child cannot be placed with adoptive parents without providing adoption assistance, and

(C) such child is a citizen or resident of the United States (as defined in section 217(h)(3)).

(e) Special rules for foreign adoptions.—In the case of an adoption of a child who is not a citizen or resident of the United States (as defined in section 217(h)(3))—

(1) subsection (a) shall not apply to any qualified adoption expense with respect to such adoption unless such adoption becomes final, and

(2) any such expense which is paid or incurred before the taxable year in which such adoption becomes final shall be taken into account under this section as if such expense were paid or incurred during such year.

(f) Filing requirements.—

(1) Married couples must file joint returns.—Rules similar to the rules of paragraphs (2), (3), and (4) of section 21(e) shall apply for purposes of this section.

(2) Taxpayer must include TIN.—

(A) In general.—No credit shall be allowed under this section with respect to any eligible child unless the taxpayer includes (if known) the name, age, and TIN of such child on the return of tax for the taxable year.

(B) Other methods.—The Secretary may, in lieu of the information referred to in subparagraph (A), require other information meeting the purposes of subparagraph (A), including identification of an agent assisting with the adoption.

(g) Basis adjustments.—For purposes of this subtitle, if a credit is allowed under this section for any expenditure with respect to any property, the increase in the basis of such property which would (but for this subsection) result from such expenditure shall be reduced by the amount of the credit so allowed.

(h) Adjustments for inflation.—In the case of a taxable year beginning after December 31, 2002, each of the dollar amounts in subsection (a)(3) and paragraphs (1) and (2)(A)(i) of subsection (b) shall be increased by an amount equal to—

(1) such dollar amount, multiplied by

(2) the cost-of-living adjustment determined under section 1(f)(3) for the calendar year in which the taxable year begins, determined by substituting "calendar year 2001" for "calendar year 1992" in subparagraph (B) thereof.

If any amount as increased under the preceding sentence is not a multiple of $10, such amount shall be rounded to the nearest multiple of $10.

(i) Regulations.—The Secretary shall prescribe such regulations as may be appropriate to carry out this section and section 137, including regulations which treat unmarried individuals who pay or incur qualified adoption expenses with respect to the same child as 1 taxpayer for purposes of applying the dollar amounts in subsections (a)(3) and (b)(1) of this section and in section 137(b)(1).

26 U.S.C.A. § 137 ADOPTION ASSISTANCE PROGRAMS

(a) Exclusion.—

(1) In general.—Gross income of an employee does not include amounts paid or expenses incurred by the employer for qualified adoption expenses in connection with the adoption of a child by an employee if such amounts are furnished pursuant to an adoption assistance program.

(2) $10,000 exclusion for adoption of child with special needs regardless of expenses.—In the case of an adoption of a child with special needs which becomes final during a taxable year, the qualified adoption expenses with respect to such adoption for such year shall be increased by an amount equal to the excess (if any) of $10,000 over the actual aggregate qualified adoption expenses with respect to such adoption during such taxable year and all prior taxable years.

(b) Limitations—

(1) Dollar limitation.—The aggregate of the amounts paid or expenses incurred which may be taken into account under subsection (a) for all taxable years with respect to the adoption of a child by the taxpayer shall not exceed $10,000.

(2) Income limitation.—The amount excludable from gross income under subsection (a) for any taxable year shall be reduced (but not below zero) by an amount which bears the same ratio to the

amount so excludable (determined without regard to this paragraph but with regard to paragraph (1)) as—

(A) the amount (if any) by which the taxpayer's adjusted gross income exceeds $150,000, bears to

(B) $40,000.

(3) Determination of adjusted gross income.—For purposes of paragraph (2), adjusted gross income shall be determined—

(A) without regard to this section and sections 199, 221, 222, 911, 931, and 933, and

(B) after the application of sections 86, 135, 219, and 469.

(c) Adoption assistance program.—For purposes of this section, an adoption assistance program is a separate written plan of an employer for the exclusive benefit of such employer's employees—

(1) under which the employer provides such employees with adoption assistance, and

(2) which meets requirements similar to the requirements of paragraphs (2), (3), (5), and (6) of section 127(b).

An adoption reimbursement program operated under section 1052 of title 10, United States Code (relating to armed forces) or section 514 of title 14, United States Code (relating to members of the Coast Guard) shall be treated as an adoption assistance program for purposes of this section.

(d) Qualified adoption expenses.—For purposes of this section, the term "qualified adoption expenses" has the meaning given such term by section 23(d) (determined without regard to reimbursements under this section).

(e) Certain rules to apply.—Rules similar to the rules of subsections (e), (f), and (g) of section 23 shall apply for purposes of this section.

(f) Adjustments for inflation.—In the case of a taxable year beginning after December 31, 2002, each of the dollar amounts in subsection (a)(2) and paragraphs (1) and (2)(A) of subsection (b) shall be increased by an amount equal to—

(1) such dollar amount, multiplied by

(2) the cost-of-living adjustment determined under section 1(f)(3) for the calendar year in which the taxable year begins, determined by substituting "calendar year 2001" for "calendar year 1992" in subparagraph (B) thereof.

If any amount as increased under the preceding sentence is not a multiple of $10, such amount shall be rounded to the nearest multiple of $10.

Indian Child Welfare Act of 1978

Pub. L. No. 95–608, 92 Stat. 3069
(codified in scattered sections of 25 U.S.C.)
25 U.S.C.A. §§ 1911–1923 (West 2016)

[EDITORS' INTRODUCTION: Christopher Deluzio, *Tribes and Race: The Court's Missed Opportunity in* Adoptive Couple v. Baby Girl, 34 PACE L. REV. 509 (2014); Jessica Di Palma, Adoptive Couple v. Baby Girl: *The Supreme Courts Distorted Interpretation of the Indian Child Welfare Act of 1978*, 47 LOY. L.A. L. REV. 523 (2014); Kathryn E. Fort, *Waves of Education: Tribal-State Court Cooperation and the Indian Child Welfare Act*, 47 TULSA L. REV. 529 (2012); Thalia Gonzalez, *Reclaiming the Promise of the Indian Child Welfare Act: A study of State Incorporation and Adoption of Legal Protections for Indian Status Offenders*, 42 N.M. L. REV. 131 (2012); Phillip McCarthy, *The Oncoming Storm: State Indian Child Welfare Act Laws and the Clash of Tribal, Parental, and Child Rights*, 2013 UTAH L. REV. 1027 (2013); Shawn L. Murphy, *The Supreme Court's Revitalization of the Dying "Existing Indian Family" Exception*, 46 MCGEORGE L. REV. 629 (2014); Addie Rolnick, *Untangling the Web: Juvenile Justice in Indian Country*, 19 N.Y.U. J. LEGIS. & PUB. POL'Y 49 (2016); Christina Lewis, Note, *Born Native, Raised White: The Divide Between Federal and Tribal Jurisdiction with Extra-Tribal Native American Adoption*, 7 GEO. J. L. & MOD. CRITICAL RACE PERSP. 245 (2015).]

§ 1911. INDIAN TRIBE JURISDICTION OVER INDIAN CHILD CUSTODY PROCEEDINGS

(a) Exclusive jurisdiction

An Indian tribe shall have jurisdiction exclusive as to any State over any child custody proceeding involving an Indian child who resides or is domiciled within the reservation of such tribe, except where such jurisdiction is otherwise vested in the State by existing Federal law. Where an Indian child is a ward of a tribal court, the Indian tribe shall retain exclusive jurisdiction, notwithstanding the residence or domicile of the child.

(b) Transfer of proceedings; declination by tribal court

In any State court proceeding for the foster care placement of, or termination of parental rights to, an Indian child not domiciled or residing within the reservation of the Indian child's tribe, the court, in the absence of good cause to the contrary, shall transfer such proceeding to the jurisdiction of the tribe, absent objection by either parent, upon the petition of either parent or the Indian custodian or the Indian child's tribe: *Provided*, That such transfer shall be subject to declination by the tribal court of such tribe.

(c)   State court proceedings; intervention

In any State court proceeding for the foster care placement of, or termination of parental rights to, an Indian child, the Indian custodian of the child and the Indian child's tribe shall have a right to intervene at any point in the proceeding.

(d)   Full faith and credit to public acts, records, and judicial proceedings of Indian tribes

The United States, every State, every territory or possession of the United States, and every Indian tribe shall give full faith and credit to the public acts, records, and judicial proceedings of any Indian tribe applicable to Indian child custody proceedings to the same extent that such entities give full faith and credit to the public acts, records, and judicial proceedings of any other entity.

§ 1912.   PENDING COURT PROCEEDINGS

(a)   Notice; time for commencement of proceedings; additional time for preparation

In any involuntary proceeding in a State court, where the court knows or has reason to know that an Indian child is involved, the party seeking the foster care placement of, or termination of parental rights to, an Indian child shall notify the parent or Indian custodian and the Indian child's tribe, by registered mail with return receipt requested, of the pending proceedings and of their right of intervention. If the identity or location of the parent or Indian custodian and the tribe cannot be determined, such notice shall be given to the Secretary in like manner, who shall have fifteen days after receipt to provide the requisite notice to the parent or Indian custodian and the tribe. No foster care placement or termination of parental rights proceeding shall be held until at least ten days after receipt of notice by the parent or Indian custodian and the tribe or the Secretary: *Provided*, That the parent or Indian custodian or the tribe shall, upon request, be granted up to twenty additional days to prepare for such proceeding.

(b)   Appointment of counsel

In any case in which the court determines indigency, the parent or Indian custodian shall have the right to court-appointed counsel in any removal, placement, or termination proceeding. The court may, in its discretion, appoint counsel for the child upon a finding that such appointment is in the best interest of the child. Where State law makes no provision for appointment of counsel in such proceedings, the court shall promptly notify the Secretary upon appointment of counsel, and the Secretary, upon certification of the presiding judge, shall pay reasonable fees and expenses out of funds which may be appropriated pursuant to section 13 of this title.

(c)   Examination of reports or other documents

Each party to a foster care placement or termination of parental rights proceeding under State law involving an Indian child shall have the right to examine all reports or other documents filed with the court upon which any decision with respect to such action may be based.

(d) Remedial services and rehabilitative programs; preventive measures

Any party seeking to effect a foster care placement of, or termination of parental rights to, an Indian child under State law shall satisfy the court that active efforts have been made to provide remedial services and rehabilitative programs designed to prevent the breakup of the Indian family and that these efforts have proved unsuccessful.

(e)   Foster care placement orders; evidence; determination of damage to child

No foster care placement may be ordered in such proceeding in the absence of a determination, supported by clear and convincing evidence, including testimony of qualified expert witnesses, that the continued custody of the child by the parent or Indian custodian is likely to result in serious emotional or physical damage to the child.

(f)   Parental rights termination orders; evidence; determination of damage to child

No termination of parental rights may be ordered in such proceeding in the absence of a determination, supported by evidence beyond a reasonable doubt, including testimony of qualified expert witnesses, that the continued custody of the child by the parent or Indian custodian is likely to result in serious emotional or physical damage to the child.

§ 1913. PARENTAL RIGHTS; VOLUNTARY TERMINATION

(a)   Consent; record; certification matters; invalid consents

Where any parent or Indian custodian voluntarily consents to a foster care placement or to termination of parental rights, such consent shall not be valid unless executed in writing and recorded before a judge of a court of competent jurisdiction and accompanied by the presiding judge's certificate that the terms and consequences of the consent were fully explained in detail and were fully understood by the parent or Indian custodian. The court shall also certify that either the parent or Indian custodian fully understood the explanation in English or that it was interpreted into a language that the parent or Indian custodian understood. Any consent given prior to, or within ten days after, birth of the Indian child shall not be valid.

(b) Foster care placement; withdrawal of consent

Any parent or Indian custodian may withdraw consent to a foster care placement under State law at any time and, upon such withdrawal, the child shall be returned to the parent or Indian custodian.

(c) Voluntary termination of parental rights or adoptive placement; withdrawal of consent; return of custody

In any voluntary proceeding for termination of parental rights to, or adoptive placement of, an Indian child, the consent of the parent may be withdrawn for any reason at any time prior to the entry of a final decree of termination or adoption, as the case may be, and the child shall be returned to the parent.

(d) Collateral attack; vacation of decree and return of custody; limitations

After the entry of a final decree of adoption of an Indian child in any State court, the parent may withdraw consent thereto upon the grounds that consent was obtained through fraud or duress and may petition the court to vacate such decree. Upon a finding that such consent was obtained through fraud or duress, the court shall vacate such decree and return the child to the parent. No adoption which has been effective for at least two years may be invalidated under the provisions of this subsection unless otherwise permitted under State law.

§ 1914. PETITION TO COURT OF COMPETENT JURISDICTION TO INVALIDATE ACTION UPON SHOWING OF CERTAIN VIOLATIONS

Any Indian child who is the subject of any action for foster care placement or termination of parental rights under State law, any parent or Indian custodian from whose custody such child was removed, and the Indian child's tribe may petition any court of competent jurisdiction to invalidate such action upon a showing that such action violated any provision of sections 1911, 1912, and 1913 of this title.

§ 1915. PLACEMENT OF INDIAN CHILDREN

(a) Adoptive placements; preferences

In any adoptive placement of an Indian child under State law, a preference shall be given, in the absence of good cause to the contrary, to a placement with (1) a member of the child's extended family; (2) other members of the Indian child's tribe; or (3) other Indian families.

(b) Foster care or preadoptive placements; criteria; preferences

Any child accepted for foster care or preadoptive placement shall be placed in the least restrictive setting which most approximates a family and in which his special needs, if any, may be met. The child shall also be placed within reasonable proximity to his or her home, taking into account any special needs of the child. In any foster care or preadoptive placement, a preference shall be given, in the absence of good cause to the contrary, to a placement with—

  (i) a member of the Indian child's extended family;

  (ii) a foster home licensed, approved, or specified by the Indian child's tribe;

  (iii) an Indian foster home licensed or approved by an authorized non-Indian licensing authority; or

  (iv) an institution for children approved by an Indian tribe or operated by an Indian organization which has a program suitable to meet the Indian child's needs.

(c) Tribal resolution for different order of preference; personal preference considered; anonymity in application of preferences

  In the case of a placement under subsection (a) or (b) of this section, if the Indian child's tribe shall establish a different order of preference by resolution, the agency or court effecting the placement shall follow such order so long as the placement is the least restrictive setting appropriate to the particular needs of the child, as provided in subsection (b) of this section. Where appropriate, the preference of the Indian child or parent shall be considered: *Provided*, That where a consenting parent evidences a desire for anonymity, the court or agency shall give weight to such desire in applying the preferences.

(d) Social and cultural standards applicable

  The standards to be applied in meeting the preference requirements of this section shall be the prevailing social and cultural standards of the Indian community in which the parent or extended family resides or with which the parent or extended family members maintain social and cultural ties.

(e) Record of placement; availability

  A record of each such placement, under State law, of an Indian child shall be maintained by the State in which the placement was made, evidencing the efforts to comply with the order of preference specified in this section. Such record shall be made available at any time upon the request of the Secretary or the Indian child's tribe.

§ 1916. RETURN OF CUSTODY

(a) Petition; best interests of child

  Notwithstanding State law to the contrary, whenever a final decree of adoption of an Indian child has been vacated or set aside or the adoptive parents voluntarily consent to the termination of their parental rights to the child, a biological parent or prior Indian custodian may petition for return of custody and the court shall grant such petition unless there is a showing, in a proceeding subject to the provisions of section 1912 of this title, that such return of custody is not in the best interests of the child.

(b) Removal from foster care home; placement procedure

Whenever an Indian child is removed from a foster care home or institution for the purpose of further foster care, preadoptive, or adoptive placement, such placement shall be in accordance with the provisions of this chapter, except in the case where an Indian child is being returned to the parent or Indian custodian from whose custody the child was originally removed.

§ 1917. TRIBAL AFFILIATION INFORMATION AND OTHER INFORMATION FOR PROTECTION OF RIGHTS FROM TRIBAL RELATIONSHIP; APPLICATION OF SUBJECT OF ADOPTIVE PLACEMENT; DISCLOSURE BY COURT

Upon application by an Indian individual who has reached the age of eighteen and who was the subject of an adoptive placement, the court which entered the final decree shall inform such individual of the tribal affiliation, if any, of the individual's biological parents and provide such other information as may be necessary to protect any rights flowing from the individual's tribal relationship.

§ 1918. REASSUMPTION OF JURISDICTION OVER CHILD CUSTODY PROCEEDINGS

(a) Petition; suitable plan; approval by Secretary

Any Indian tribe which became subject to State jurisdiction pursuant to the provisions of the Act of August 15, 1953 (67 Stat. 588), as amended by Title IV of the Act of April 11, 1968 (82 Stat. 73, 78), or pursuant to any other Federal law, may reassume jurisdiction over child custody proceedings. Before any Indian tribe may reassume jurisdiction over Indian child custody proceedings, such tribe shall present to the Secretary for approval a petition to reassume such jurisdiction which includes a suitable plan to exercise such jurisdiction.

(b) Criteria applicable to consideration by Secretary; partial retrocession

(1) In considering the petition and feasibility of the plan of a tribe under subsection (a) of this section, the Secretary may consider, among other things:

(i) whether or not the tribe maintains a membership roll or alternative provision for clearly identifying the persons who will be affected by the reassumption of jurisdiction by the tribe;

(ii) the size of the reservation or former reservation area which will be affected by retrocession and reassumption of jurisdiction by the tribe;

(iii) the population base of the tribe, or distribution of the population in homogeneous communities or geographic areas; and

(iv) the feasibility of the plan in cases of multitribal occupation of a single reservation or geographic area.

(2) In those cases where the Secretary determines that the jurisdictional provisions of section 1911(a) of this title are not feasible, he is authorized to accept partial retrocession which will enable tribes to exercise referral jurisdiction as provided in section 1911(b) of this title, or, where appropriate, will allow them to exercise exclusive jurisdiction as provided in section 1911(a) of this title over limited community or geographic areas without regard for the reservation status of the area affected.

(c) Approval of petition; publication in Federal Register; notice; reassumption period; correction of causes for disapproval

If the Secretary approves any petition under subsection (a) of this section, the Secretary shall publish notice of such approval in the Federal Register and shall notify the affected State or States of such approval. The Indian tribe concerned shall reassume jurisdiction sixty days after publication in the Federal Register of notice of approval. If the Secretary disapproves any petition under subsection (a) of this section, the Secretary shall provide such technical assistance as may be necessary to enable the tribe to correct any deficiency which the Secretary identified as a cause for disapproval.

(d) Pending actions or proceedings unaffected

Assumption of jurisdiction under this section shall not affect any action or proceeding over which a court has already assumed jurisdiction, except as may be provided pursuant to any agreement under section 1919 of this title.

§ 1919. AGREEMENTS BETWEEN STATES AND INDIAN TRIBES

(a) Subject coverage

States and Indian tribes are authorized to enter into agreements with each other respecting care and custody of Indian children and jurisdiction over child custody proceedings, including agreements which may provide for orderly transfer of jurisdiction on a case-by-case basis and agreements which provide for concurrent jurisdiction between States and Indian tribes.

(b)   Revocation; notice; actions or proceedings unaffected

Such agreements may be revoked by either party upon one hundred and eighty days' written notice to the other party. Such revocation shall not affect any action or proceeding over which a court has already assumed jurisdiction, unless the agreement provides otherwise.

§ 1920.   IMPROPER REMOVAL OF CHILD FROM CUSTODY; DECLINATION OF JURISDICTION; FORTHWITH RETURN OF CHILD: DANGER EXCEPTION

Where any petitioner in an Indian child custody proceeding before a State court has improperly removed the child from custody of the parent or Indian custodian or has improperly retained custody after a visit or other temporary relinquishment of custody, the court shall decline jurisdiction over such petition and shall forthwith return the child to his parent or Indian custodian unless returning the child to his parent or custodian would subject the child to a substantial and immediate danger or threat of such danger.

§ 1921.   HIGHER STATE OR FEDERAL STANDARD APPLICABLE TO PROTECT RIGHTS OF PARENT OR INDIAN CUSTODIAN OF INDIAN CHILD

In any case where State or Federal law applicable to a child custody proceeding under State or Federal law provides a higher standard of protection to the rights of the parent or Indian custodian of an Indian child than the rights provided under this subchapter, the State or Federal court shall apply the State or Federal standard.

§ 1922.   EMERGENCY REMOVAL OR PLACEMENT OF CHILD; TERMINATION; APPROPRIATE ACTION

Nothing in this subchapter shall be construed to prevent the emergency removal of an Indian child who is a resident of or is domiciled on a reservation, but temporarily located off the reservation, from his parent or Indian custodian or the emergency placement of such child in a foster home or institution, under applicable State law, in order to prevent imminent physical damage or harm to the child. The State authority, official, or agency involved shall insure that the emergency removal or placement terminates immediately when such removal or placement is no longer necessary to prevent imminent physical damage or harm to the child and shall expeditiously initiate a child custody proceeding subject to the provisions of this subchapter, transfer the child to the jurisdiction of the appropriate Indian tribe, or restore the child to the parent or Indian custodian, as may be appropriate.

§ 1923. Effective Date

None of the provisions of this subchapter, except sections 1911(a), 1918, and 1919 of this title, shall affect a proceeding under State law for foster care placement, termination of parental rights, preadoptive placement, or adoptive placement which was initiated or completed prior to one hundred and eighty days after November 8, 1978, but shall apply to any subsequent proceeding in the same matter or subsequent proceedings affecting the custody or placement of the same child.

INTERETHNIC ADOPTION

42 U.S.C.A. § 1996b (West 2016)

[EDITORS' INTRODUCTION: Katie Eyer, *Constitutional Colorblindness and the Family*, 162 U. PA. L. REV. 537 (2014); Barbara Fedders, *Race and Market Values in Domestic Infant Adoption*, 88 N.C. L. REV. 1687 (2010); Shani King, *The Family Law Canon in a (Post?) Racial Era*, 72 OHIO ST. L.J. 575 (2011); David Ray Papke, *Transracial Adoption in the United States: The Reflection and Reinforcement of Racial Hierarchy*, 15 J. L. & FAM. STUD. 57 (2013).]

§ 1996b. INTERETHNIC ADOPTION

(1) Prohibited conduct

A person or government that is involved in adoption or foster care placements may not—

(A) deny to any individual the opportunity to become an adoptive or a foster parent, on the basis of the race, color, or national origin of the individual, or of the child, involved; or

(B) delay or deny the placement of a child for adoption or into foster care, on the basis of the race, color, or national origin of the adoptive or foster parent, or the child, involved.

(2) Enforcement

Noncompliance with paragraph (1) is deemed a violation of title VI of the Civil Rights Act of 1964 [42 U.S.C.A. § 2000d et seq.].

(3) No effect on the Indian Child Welfare Act of 1978

This subsection shall not be construed to affect the application of the Indian Child Welfare Act of 1978 [25 U.S.C.A. § 1901 et seq.].

INTERNATIONAL CHILD ABDUCTION REMEDIES ACT

Pub. L. No. 100–300, 102 Stat. 437 (1988)
(codified as amended in scattered sections of 22 U.S.C.)

[EDITORS' INTRODUCTION: *Deference to the Executive—Hague Convention on the Civil Aspects of International Child Abduction*, 124 HARV. L. REV. 330 (2010); Noah L. Browne, *Relevance and Fairness: Protecting the Rights of Domestic-Violence Victims and Left-Behind Fathers Under the Hague Convention on International Child Abduction*, 60 DUKE L.J. 1193 (2011); Kevin O'Gorman & Efren C. Olivares, *The Hague Convention on the Civil Aspects of International Child Abduction: An Update after* Abbott, 33 HOUS. J. INT'L L. 39 (2010); Christina Piemonte, *International Child Abduction and Courts' Evolving Considerations in Evaluating the Hague Convention's Defenses to Return*, 22 TUL. J. INT'L & COMP. L. 191 (2013); Rhona Schuz & Benjamin Shmueli, *Between Tort Law, Contract Law, and Child Law: How to Compensate the Left-Behind Parent in International Child Abduction Cases*, 23 COLUM. J. GENDER & L. 65 (2012); Nicole Clark, Note, *Putting the "Remedy" Back in the International Child Abduction Remedies Act— Enforcing Visitation Rights for the Left Behind Parent*, 89 ST. JOHN'S L. REV. 997 (2015); Nicole Fontaine, Note, *Don't Stop the Clock: Why Equitable Tolling Should Not Be Read Into the Hague Convention on International Child Abduction*, 54 B.C. L. REV. 2091 (2013); Zadora M. Hightower, Comment, *Caught in the Middle: The Need for Uniformity in International Child Custody Dispute Cases*, 22 MICH. ST. INT'L. L. REV. 637 (2014).]

22 U.S.C. § 9001 ET SEQ.

§ 9001. FINDINGS AND DECLARATIONS

(a) Findings

The Congress makes the following findings:

(1) The international abduction or wrongful retention of children is harmful to their well-being.

(2) Persons should not be permitted to obtain custody of children by virtue of their wrongful removal or retention.

(3) International abductions and retentions of children are increasing, and only concerted cooperation pursuant to an international agreement can effectively combat this problem.

(4) The Convention on the Civil Aspects of International Child Abduction, done at The Hague on October 25, 1980, establishes legal rights and procedures for the prompt return of children who have been wrongfully removed or retained, as well as for securing the exercise of visitation rights. Children who are wrongfully removed or retained within the meaning of the Convention are to be promptly

returned unless one of the narrow exceptions set forth in the Convention applies. The Convention provides a sound treaty framework to help resolve the problem of international abduction and retention of children and will deter such wrongful removals and retentions.

(b) Declarations

The Congress makes the following declarations:

(1) It is the purpose of this chapter to establish procedures for the implementation of the Convention in the United States.

(2) The provisions of this chapter are in addition to and not in lieu of the provisions of the Convention.

(3) In enacting this chapter the Congress recognizes—

(A) the international character of the Convention; and

(B) the need for uniform international interpretation of the Convention.

(4) The Convention and this chapter empower courts in the United States to determine only rights under the Convention and not the merits of any underlying child custody claims.

§ 9002. DEFINITIONS

For the purposes of this chapter—

(1) the term "applicant" means any person who, pursuant to the Convention, files an application with the United States Central Authority or a Central Authority of any other party to the Convention for the return of a child alleged to have been wrongfully removed or retained or for arrangements for organizing or securing the effective exercise of rights of access pursuant to the Convention;

(2) the term "Convention" means the Convention on the Civil Aspects of International Child Abduction, done at The Hague on October 25, 1980;

(3) the term "Parent Locator Service" means the service established by the Secretary of Health and Human Services under section 653 of Title 42;

(4) the term "petitioner" means any person who, in accordance with this chapter, files a petition in court seeking relief under the Convention;

(5) the term "person" includes any individual, institution, or other legal entity or body;

(6) the term "respondent" means any person against whose interests a petition is filed in court, in accordance with this chapter, which seeks relief under the Convention;

(7) the term "rights of access" means visitation rights;

(8) the term "State" means any of the several States, the District of Columbia, and any commonwealth, territory, or possession of the United States; and

(9) the term "United States Central Authority" means the agency of the Federal Government designated by the President under section 9006(a) of this title.

§ 9003. JUDICIAL REMEDIES

(a) Jurisdiction of courts

The courts of the States and the United States district courts shall have concurrent original jurisdiction of actions arising under the Convention.

(b) Petitions

Any person seeking to initiate judicial proceedings under the Convention for the return of a child or for arrangements for organizing or securing the effective exercise of rights of access to a child may do so by commencing a civil action by filing a petition for the relief sought in any court which has jurisdiction of such action and which is authorized to exercise its jurisdiction in the place where the child is located at the time the petition is filed.

(c) Notice

Notice of an action brought under subsection (b) of this section shall be given in accordance with the applicable law governing notice in interstate child custody proceedings.

(d) Determination of case

The court in which an action is brought under subsection (b) of this section shall decide the case in accordance with the Convention.

(e) Burdens of proof

(1) A petitioner in an action brought under subsection (b) of this section shall establish by a preponderance of the evidence—

(A) in the case of an action for the return of a child, that the child has been wrongfully removed or retained within the meaning of the Convention; and

(B) in the case of an action for arrangements for organizing or securing the effective exercise of rights of access, that the petitioner has such rights.

(2) In the case of an action for the return of a child, a respondent who opposes the return of the child has the burden of establishing—

(A) by clear and convincing evidence that one of the exceptions set forth in article 13b or 20 of the Convention applies; and

(B) by a preponderance of the evidence that any other exception set forth in article 12 or 13 of the Convention applies.

(f)   Application of Convention

For purposes of any action brought under this chapter—

(1) the term "authorities", as used in article 15 of the Convention to refer to the authorities of the state of the habitual residence of a child, includes courts and appropriate government agencies;

(2) the terms "wrongful removal or retention" and "wrongfully removed or retained", as used in the Convention, include a removal or retention of a child before the entry of a custody order regarding that child; and

(3) the term "commencement of proceedings", as used in article 12 of the Convention, means, with respect to the return of a child located in the United States, the filing of a petition in accordance with subsection (b) of this section.

(g)   Full faith and credit

Full faith and credit shall be accorded by the courts of the States and the courts of the United States to the judgment of any other such court ordering or denying the return of a child, pursuant to the Convention, in an action brought under this chapter.

(h)   Remedies under Convention not exclusive

The remedies established by the Convention and this chapter shall be in addition to remedies available under other laws or international agreements.

§ 9004. PROVISIONAL REMEDIES

(a)   Authority of courts

In furtherance of the objectives of article 7(b) and other provisions of the Convention, and subject to the provisions of subsection (b) of this section, any court exercising jurisdiction of an action brought under section 9003(b) of this title may take or cause to be taken measures under Federal or State law, as appropriate, to protect the well-being of the child involved or to prevent the child's further removal or concealment before the final disposition of the petition.

(b)   Limitation on authority

No court exercising jurisdiction of an action brought under section 9003(b) of this title may, under subsection (a) of this section, order a child removed from a person having physical control of the child unless the applicable requirements of State law are satisfied.

§ 9005. ADMISSIBILITY OF DOCUMENTS

With respect to any application to the United States Central Authority, or any petition to a court under section 9003 of this title, which seeks relief under the Convention, or any other documents or information included with such application or petition or provided after such submission which relates to the application or petition, as the case may be, no authentication of such application, petition, document, or information shall be required in order for the application, petition, document, or information to be admissible in court.

§ 9006. UNITED STATES CENTRAL AUTHORITY

(a) Designation

The President shall designate a Federal agency to serve as the Central Authority for the United States under the Convention.

(b) Functions

The functions of the United States Central Authority are those ascribed to the Central Authority by the Convention and this chapter.

(c) Regulatory authority

The United States Central Authority is authorized to issue such regulations as may be necessary to carry out its functions under the Convention and this chapter.

(d) Obtaining information from Parent Locator Service

The United States Central Authority may, to the extent authorized by the Social Security Act, obtain information from the Parent Locator Service.

(e) Grant authority

The United States Central Authority is authorized to make grants to, or enter into contracts or agreements with, any individual, corporation, other Federal, State, or local agency, or private entity or organization in the United States for purposes of accomplishing its responsibilities under the Convention and this chapter.

(f) Limited liability of private entities acting under the direction of the United States Central Authority

(1) Limitation on liability

Except as provided in paragraphs (2) and (3), a private entity or organization that receives a grant from or enters into a contract or agreement with the United States Central Authority under subsection (e) of this section for purposes of assisting the United States Central Authority in carrying out its responsibilities and functions under the Convention and this chapter, including any director, officer, employee, or agent of such entity or organization, shall not be liable in any civil action sounding in tort for damages directly related to the performance of such responsibilities and functions as defined by the regulations issued under subsection (c) of this section that are in effect on October 1, 2004.

(2) Exception for intentional, reckless, or other misconduct

The limitation on liability under paragraph (1) shall not apply in any action in which the plaintiff proves that the private entity, organization, officer, employee, or agent described in paragraph (1), as the case may be, engaged in intentional misconduct or acted, or failed to act, with actual malice, with reckless disregard to a substantial risk of causing injury without legal justification, or for a purpose unrelated to the performance of responsibilities or functions under this chapter.

(3) Exception for ordinary business activities

The limitation on liability under paragraph (1) shall not apply to any alleged act or omission related to an ordinary business activity, such as an activity involving general administration or operations, the use of motor vehicles, or personnel management.

§ 9007. COSTS AND FEES

(a) Administrative costs

No department, agency, or instrumentality of the Federal Government or of any State or local government may impose on an applicant any fee in relation to the administrative processing of applications submitted under the Convention.

(b) Costs incurred in civil actions

(1) Petitioners may be required to bear the costs of legal counsel or advisors, court costs incurred in connection with their petitions, and travel costs for the return of the child involved and any accompanying persons, except as provided in paragraphs (2) and (3).

(2) Subject to paragraph (3), legal fees or court costs incurred in connection with an action brought under section 9003 of this title shall be borne by the petitioner unless they are covered by payments from Federal, State, or local legal assistance or other programs.

(3) Any court ordering the return of a child pursuant to an action brought under section 9003 of this title shall order the respondent to pay necessary expenses incurred by or on behalf of the petitioner, including court costs, legal fees, foster home or other care during the course of proceedings in the action, and transportation costs related to the return of the child, unless the respondent establishes that such order would be clearly inappropriate.

§ 9008. COLLECTION, MAINTENANCE, AND DISSEMINATION OF INFORMATION

(a) In general

In performing its functions under the Convention, the United States Central Authority may, under such conditions as the Central Authority prescribes by regulation, but subject to subsection (c) of this section, receive from or transmit to any department, agency, or instrumentality of the Federal Government or of any State or foreign government, and receive from or transmit to any applicant, petitioner, or respondent, information necessary to locate a child or for the purpose of otherwise implementing the Convention with respect to a child, except that the United States Central Authority—

(1) may receive such information from a Federal or State department, agency, or instrumentality only pursuant to applicable Federal and State statutes; and

(2) may transmit any information received under this subsection notwithstanding any provision of law other than this chapter.

(b) Requests for information

Requests for information under this section shall be submitted in such manner and form as the United States Central Authority may prescribe by regulation and shall be accompanied or supported by such documents as the United States Central Authority may require.

(c) Responsibility of government entities

Whenever any department, agency, or instrumentality of the United States or of any State receives a request from the United States Central Authority for information authorized to be provided to such Central Authority under subsection (a) of this section, the head of such department, agency, or instrumentality shall promptly cause a search to be made of the files and records maintained by such department, agency, or instrumentality in order to determine whether the information requested is contained in any such files or records. If such search discloses the information requested, the head of such department, agency, or instrumentality shall immediately transmit such information to the United States Central Authority, except that any such information the disclosure of which—

(1) would adversely affect the national security interests of the United States or the law enforcement interests of the United States or of any State; or

(2) would be prohibited by section 9 of Title 13;

shall not be transmitted to the Central Authority. The head of such department, agency, or instrumentality shall, immediately upon completion of the requested search, notify the Central Authority of the results of the search, and whether an exception set forth in paragraph (1) or (2) applies. In the event that the United States Central Authority receives information and the appropriate Federal or State department, agency, or instrumentality thereafter notifies the Central Authority that an exception set forth in paragraph (1) or (2) applies to that information, the Central Authority may not disclose that information under subsection (a) of this section.

(d) Information available from Parent Locator Service

To the extent that information which the United States Central Authority is authorized to obtain under the provisions of subsection (c) of this section can be obtained through the Parent Locator Service, the United States Central Authority shall first seek to obtain such information from the Parent Locator Service, before requesting such information directly under the provisions of subsection (c) of this section.

(e) Recordkeeping

The United States Central Authority shall maintain appropriate records concerning its activities and the disposition of cases brought to its attention.

§ 9009. OFFICE OF CHILDREN'S ISSUES

(a) Director requirements

The Secretary of State shall fill the position of Director of the Office of Children's Issues of the Department of State (in this section referred to as the "Office") with an individual of senior rank who can ensure long-term continuity in the management and policy matters of the Office and has a strong background in consular affairs.

(b) Case officer staffing

Effective April 1, 2000, there shall be assigned to the Office of Children's Issues of the Department of State a sufficient number of case officers to ensure that the average caseload for each officer does not exceed 75.

(c) Embassy contact

The Secretary of State shall designate in each United States diplomatic mission an employee who shall serve as the point of contact for matters relating to international abductions of children by parents. The Director of the Office shall regularly inform the designated employee of children of United States citizens abducted by parents to that country.

(d) Reports to parents

(1) In general

Except as provided in paragraph (2), beginning 6 months after November 29, 1999, and at least once every 6 months thereafter, the Secretary of State shall report to each parent who has requested assistance regarding an abducted child overseas. Each such report shall include information on the current status of the abducted child's case and the efforts by the Department of State to resolve the case.

(2) Exception

The requirement in paragraph (1) shall not apply in a case of an abducted child if—

(A) the case has been closed and the Secretary of State has reported the reason the case was closed to the parent who requested assistance; or

(B) the parent seeking assistance requests that such reports not be provided.

§ 9010. INTERAGENCY COORDINATING GROUP

The Secretary of State, the Secretary of Health and Human Services, and the Attorney General shall designate Federal employees and may, from time to time, designate private citizens to serve on an interagency coordinating group to monitor the operation of the Convention and to provide advice on its implementation to the United States Central Authority and other Federal agencies. This group shall meet from time to time at the request of the United States Central Authority. The agency in which the United States Central Authority is located is authorized to reimburse such private citizens for travel and other expenses incurred in participating at meetings of the interagency coordinating group at rates not to exceed those authorized under subchapter I of chapter 57 of Title 5 for employees of agencies.

§ 9011. AUTHORIZATION OF APPROPRIATIONS

There are authorized to be appropriated for each fiscal year such sums as may be necessary to carry out the purposes of the Convention and this chapter.

INTERNATIONAL PARENTAL KIDNAPPING CRIME ACT OF 1993

Pub. L. No. 103–173, 107 Stat. (1998)
(codified as amended in scattered sections of 18 U.S.C.)

[EDITORS' INTRODUCTION: Jason Nitz, Comment, *"Splitting the Baby" Internationally: Evaluating the Least "Restrictive Conundrum" When Protecting Children from International Parent Abduction*, 16 SCHOLAR 417 (2014); Maryl Sattler, Note, *The Problem of Parental Relocation: Closing the Loophole in the Law of International Child Abduction*, 67 WASH. & LEE L. REV. 1709 (2010).]

18 U.S.C. § 1204.

(a) Whoever removes a child from the United States, or attempts to do so, or retains a child (who has been in the United States) outside the United States with intent to obstruct the lawful exercise of parental rights shall be fined under this title or imprisoned not more than 3 years, or both.

(b) As used in this section—

(1) the term "child" means a person who has not attained the age of 16 years; and

(2) the term "parental rights", with respect to a child, means the right to physical custody of the child—

(A) whether joint or sole (and includes visiting rights); and

(B) whether arising by operation of law, court order, or legally binding agreement of the parties.

(c) It shall be an affirmative defense under this section that—

(1) the defendant acted within the provisions of a valid court order granting the defendant legal custody or visitation rights and that order was obtained pursuant to the Uniform Child Custody Jurisdiction Act or the Uniform Child Custody Jurisdiction and Enforcement Act and was in effect at the time of the offense;

(2) the defendant was fleeing an incidence or pattern of domestic violence; or

(3) the defendant had physical custody of the child pursuant to a court order granting legal custody or visitation rights and failed to return the child as a result of circumstances beyond the defendant's control, and the defendant notified or made reasonable attempts to notify the other parent or lawful custodian of the child of such circumstances within 24 hours after the visitation period had expired and returned the child as soon as possible.

(d)   This section does not detract from The Hague Convention on the Civil Aspects of International Parental Child Abduction, done at The Hague on October 25, 1980.

PARTIAL BIRTH ABORTION BAN ACT OF 2003

Pub. L. No. 108–105, 117 Stat. 1201, 18 U.S.C.A. § 1531 (West 2016)

[EDITORS' INTRODUCTION: Aziza Ahmed, *Medical Evidence and Expertise in Abortion Jurisprudence*, 41 AM. J.L. & MED. 85 (2015); Victoria Baranetsky, *Aborting Dignity: The Abortion Doctrine After Gonzales v. Carhart*, 36 HARV. J. L. & GENDER 123 (2013); Caitlin E. Borgmann, *Abortion, the Undue Burden Standard, and the Evisceration of Women's Privacy*, 16 WM. & MARY J. WOMEN & L. 291 (2010); Khiara M. Bridges, *"Life" in the Balance: Judicial Review of Abortion Regulations*, 46 U.C. DAVIS L. REV. 1285 (2013); Beth A. Burkstrand-Reid, *The Invisible Woman: Availability and Culpability in Reproductive Health Jurisprudence*, 81 U. COLO. L. REV. 97 (2010); Shea Leigh Line, *Twenty-Week Bans, New Medical Evidence, and the Effect on Current United States Supreme Court Abortion Law Precedent*, 50 IDAHO L. REV. 139 (2014); Maya Manian, *Lessons from Personhood's Defeat: Abortion Restrictions and Side Effects on Women's Health*, 74 OHIO ST. L.J. 75 (2013); Thomas J. Molony, Roe, Casey, *and Sex-Selection Abortion Bans*, 71 WASH. & LEE L. REV. 1089 (2014); Patricia J. Zettler, *Toward Coherent Federal Oversight of Medicine*, 52 SAN DIEGO L. REV. 427 (2015); Anthony Dutra, Note, *Men Come and Go, But* Roe *Abides: Why* Roe v. Wade *Will Not Be Overruled*, 90 B.U. L. REV. 1261 (2010).]

§ 1531. PARTIAL-BIRTH ABORTIONS PROHIBITED

(a) Any physician who, in or affecting interstate or foreign commerce, knowingly performs a partial-birth abortion and thereby kills a human fetus shall be fined under this title or imprisoned not more than 2 years, or both. This subsection does not apply to a partial-birth abortion that is necessary to save the life of a mother whose life is endangered by a physical disorder, physical illness, or physical injury, including a life-endangering physical condition caused by or arising from the pregnancy itself. This subsection takes effect 1 day after the enactment.

(b) As used in this section—

(1) the term "partial-birth abortion" means an abortion in which the person performing the abortion—

(A) deliberately and intentionally vaginally delivers a living fetus until, in the case of a head-first presentation, the entire fetal head is outside the body of the mother, or, in the case of breech presentation, any part of the fetal trunk past the navel is outside the body of the mother, for the purpose of performing an overt act that the person knows will kill the partially delivered living fetus; and

(B) performs the overt act, other than completion of delivery, that kills the partially delivered living fetus; and

(2) the term "physician" means a doctor of medicine or osteopathy legally authorized to practice medicine and surgery by the State in which the doctor performs such activity, or any other individual legally authorized by the State to perform abortions: *Provided, however,* That any individual who is not a physician or not otherwise legally authorized by the State to perform abortions, but who nevertheless directly performs a partial-birth abortion, shall be subject to the provisions of this section.

(c)(1)   The father, if married to the mother at the time she receives a partial-birth abortion procedure, and if the mother has not attained the age of 18 years at the time of the abortion, the maternal grandparents of the fetus, may in a civil action obtain appropriate relief, unless the pregnancy resulted from the plaintiff's criminal conduct or the plaintiff consented to the abortion.

(2) Such relief shall include—

(A) money damages for all injuries, psychological and physical, occasioned by the violation of this section; and

(B) statutory damages equal to three times the cost of the partial-birth abortion.

(d)(1)   A defendant accused of an offense under this section may seek a hearing before the State Medical Board on whether the physician's conduct was necessary to save the life of the mother whose life was endangered by a physical disorder, physical illness, or physical injury, including a life-endangering physical condition caused by or arising from the pregnancy itself.

(2) The findings on that issue are admissible on that issue at the trial of the defendant. Upon a motion of the defendant, the court shall delay the beginning of the trial for not more than 30 days to permit such a hearing to take place.

(e) A woman upon whom a partial-birth abortion is performed may not be prosecuted under this section, for a conspiracy to violate this section, or for an offense under section 2, 3, or 4 of this title based on a violation of this section.

VIOLENCE AGAINST WOMEN ACT

18 U.S.C.A. 2261–2266 (West 2016)

[EDITORS' INTRODUCTION: Camille Carey, *Domestic Violence Torts: Righting a Civil Wrong*, 62 U. KAN. L. REV. 695 (2014); Dr. Tracey B. Carter, *Local, State, and Federal Responses to Stalking: Are Anti-Stalking Laws Effective*, 22 WM. & MARY J. WOMEN & L. 333 (2016); Andrea L. Dennis & Carol E. Jordan, *Encouraging Victims: Responding to a Recent Study of Battered Women Who Commit Crimes*, 15 NEV. L.J. 1 (2014); Laura L. Dunn, *Addressing Sexual Violence in Higher Education: Ensuring Compliance with the Clery Act, Title IX and VAWA*, 15 GEO. J. GENDER & L. 563 (2014); Cheryl Hanna, *The Violence Against Women Act and Its Impact on the U.S. Supreme Court and International Law: A story of Vindication, Loss, and a New Human Rights Paradigm*, 52 DUQ. L. REV. 415 (2014); Rosie Hidalgo, *Advancing a Human Rights Framework to Reimagine the Movement to End Gender Violence*, 5 U. MIAMI RACE & SOC. JUST. L. REV. 559 (2015); Aaron Horth, *Toward a Comprehensive Gender-Based Violence Court System*, 24 B.U. PUB. INT. L.J. 221 (2015); Margaret E. Johnson, *Changing Course in the Anti-Domestic Violence Legal Movement: From Safety to Security*, 60 VILL. L. REV. 145 (2015); Tom Lininger, *An Ethical Duty to Charge Batterers Appropriately*, 22 DUKE J. GENDER L. & POL'Y 173 (2015); Jessica Miles, *We are Never Ever Getting Back Together: Domestic Violence Victims, Defendants, and Due Process*, 35 CARDOZO L. REV. 141 (2013); Robin R. Runge, *The Evolution of a National Response to Violence Against Women*, 24 HASTINGS WOMEN'S L.J. 429 (2013); Lawrence G. Sager, *Congress's Authority to Enact the Violence Against Women Act: One More Pass at the Missing Argument*, 121 YALE L.J. ONLINE 629 (2012); Jane K. Stoever, *Enjoining Abuse: The Case for Indefinite Domestic Violence Protection Orders*, 67 VAND. L. REV. 1015 (2014); Deborah M. Weissman, *Law, Social Movements, and the Political Economy of Domestic Violence*, 20 DUKE J. GENDER L. & POL'Y 221 (2013).]

§ 2261. INTERSTATE DOMESTIC VIOLENCE

(a) Offenses.—

(1) Travel or conduct of offender.—A person who travels in interstate or foreign commerce or enters or leaves Indian country or is present within the special maritime and territorial jurisdiction of the United States with the intent to kill, injure, harass, or intimidate a spouse, intimate partner, or dating partner, and who, in the course of or as a result of such travel or presence, commits or attempts to commit a crime of violence against that spouse, intimate partner, or dating partner, shall be punished as provided in subsection (b).

(2) Causing travel of victim.—A person who causes a spouse, intimate partner, or dating partner to travel in interstate or foreign

commerce or to enter or leave Indian country by force, coercion, duress, or fraud, and who, in the course of, as a result of, or to facilitate such conduct or travel, commits or attempts to commit a crime of violence against that spouse, intimate partner, or dating partner, shall be punished as provided in subsection (b).

(b) Penalties.—A person who violates this section or section 2261A shall be fined under this title, imprisoned—

(1) for life or any term of years, if death of the victim results;

(2) for not more than 20 years if permanent disfigurement or life threatening bodily injury to the victim results;

(3) for not more than 10 years, if serious bodily injury to the victim results or if the offender uses a dangerous weapon during the offense;

(4) as provided for the applicable conduct under chapter 109A if the offense would constitute an offense under chapter 109A (without regard to whether the offense was committed in the special maritime and territorial jurisdiction of the United States or in a Federal prison); and

(5) for not more than 5 years, in any other case, or both fined and imprisoned.

(6) Whoever commits the crime of stalking in violation of a temporary or permanent civil or criminal injunction, restraining order, no-contact order, or other order described in section 2266 of title 18, United States Code, shall be punished by imprisonment for not less than 1 year.

§ 2261A.   STALKING

Whoever—

(1) travels in interstate or foreign commerce or is present within the special maritime and territorial jurisdiction of the United States, or enters or leaves Indian country, with the intent to kill, injure, harass, intimidate, or place under surveillance with intent to kill, injure, harass, or intimidate another person, and in the course of, or as a result of, such travel or presence engages in conduct that—

(A) places that person in reasonable fear of the death of, or serious bodily injury to—

(i)   that person;

(ii) an immediate family member (as defined in section 115) of that person; or

(iii) a spouse or intimate partner of that person; or

(B) causes, attempts to cause, or would be reasonably expected to cause substantial emotional distress to a person described in clause (i), (ii), or (iii) of subparagraph (A); or

(2) with the intent to kill, injure, harass, intimidate, or place under surveillance with intent to kill, injure, harass, or intimidate another person, uses the mail, any interactive computer service or electronic communication service or electronic communication system of interstate commerce, or any other facility of interstate or foreign commerce to engage in a course of conduct that—

(A) places that person in reasonable fear of the death of or serious bodily injury to a person described in clause (i), (ii), or (iii) of paragraph (1)(A); or

(B) causes, attempts to cause, or would be reasonably expected to cause substantial emotional distress to a person described in clause (i), (ii), or (iii) of paragraph (1)(A), shall be punished as provided in section 2261(b) of this title.

§ 2262.   INTERSTATE VIOLATION OF PROTECTION ORDER

(a) Offenses.—

(1) Travel or conduct of offender.—A person who travels in interstate or foreign commerce, or enters or leaves Indian country or is present within the special maritime and territorial jurisdiction of the United States, with the intent to engage in conduct that violates the portion of a protection order that prohibits or provides protection against violence, threats, or harassment against, contact or communication with, or physical proximity to, another person, or that would violate such a portion of a protection order in the jurisdiction in which the order was issued, and subsequently engages in such conduct, shall be punished as provided in subsection (b).

(2) Causing travel of victim.—A person who causes another person to travel in interstate or foreign commerce or to enter or leave Indian country by force, coercion, duress, or fraud, and in the course of, as a result of, or to facilitate such conduct or travel engages in conduct that violates the portion of a protection order that prohibits or provides protection against violence, threats, or harassment against, contact or communication with, or physical proximity to, another person, or that would violate such a portion of a protection order in the jurisdiction in which the order was issued, shall be punished as provided in subsection (b).

(b) Penalties.—A person who violates this section shall be fined under this title, imprisoned—

(1)   for life or any term of years, if death of the victim results;

(2)   for not more than 20 years if permanent disfigurement or life threatening bodily injury to the victim results;

(3) for not more than 10 years, if serious bodily injury to the victim results or if the offender uses a dangerous weapon during the offense;

(4) as provided for the applicable conduct under chapter 109A if the offense would constitute an offense under chapter 109A (without regard to whether the offense was committed in the special maritime and territorial jurisdiction of the United States or in a Federal prison); and

(5) for not more than 5 years, in any other case, or both fined and imprisoned.

§ 2263. PRETRIAL RELEASE OF DEFENDANT

In any proceeding pursuant to section 3142 for the purpose of determining whether a defendant charged under this chapter shall be released pending trial, or for the purpose of determining conditions of such release, the alleged victim shall be given an opportunity to be heard regarding the danger posed by the defendant.

§ 2264. RESTITUTION

(a) In general.—Notwithstanding section 3663 or 3663A, and in addition to any other civil or criminal penalty authorized by law, the court shall order restitution for any offense under this chapter.

(b) Scope and nature of order.—

(1) Directions.—The order of restitution under this section shall direct the defendant to pay the victim (through the appropriate court mechanism) the full amount of the victim's losses as determined by the court pursuant to paragraph (2).

(2) Enforcement.—An order of restitution under this section shall be issued and enforced in accordance with section 3664 in the same manner as an order under section 3663A.

(3) Definition.—For purposes of this subsection, the term "full amount of the victim's losses" includes any costs incurred by the victim for—

(A) medical services relating to physical, psychiatric, or psychological care;

(B) physical and occupational therapy or rehabilitation;

(C) necessary transportation, temporary housing, and child care expenses;

(D) lost income;

(E) attorneys' fees, plus any costs incurred in obtaining a civil protection order; and

(F) any other losses suffered by the victim as a proximate result of the offense.

(4) Order mandatory.—(A) The issuance of a restitution order under this section is mandatory.

(B) A court may not decline to issue an order under this section because of—

(i)   the economic circumstances of the defendant; or

(ii) the fact that a victim has, or is entitled to, receive compensation for his or her injuries from the proceeds of insurance or any other source.

(c) Victim defined.—For purposes of this section, the term "victim" means the individual harmed as a result of a commission of a crime under this chapter, including, in the case of a victim who is under 18 years of age, incompetent, incapacitated, or deceased, the legal guardian of the victim or representative of the victim's estate, another family member, or any other person appointed as suitable by the court, but in no event shall the defendant be named as such representative or guardian.

§ 2265. FULL FAITH AND CREDIT GIVEN TO PROTECTION ORDERS

(a) Full Faith and Credit.—Any protection order issued that is consistent with subsection (b) of this section by the court of one State, Indian tribe, or territory (the issuing State, Indian tribe, or territory) shall be accorded full faith and credit by the court of another State, Indian tribe, or territory (the enforcing State, Indian tribe, or territory) and enforced by the court and law enforcement personnel of the other State, Indian tribal government or Territory as if it were the order of the enforcing State or tribe.

(b) Protection order.—A protection order issued by a State, tribal, or territorial court is consistent with this subsection if—

(1) such court has jurisdiction over the parties and matter under the law of such State, Indian tribe, or territory; and

(2) reasonable notice and opportunity to be heard is given to the person against whom the order is sought sufficient to protect that person's right to due process. In the case of ex parte orders, notice and opportunity to be heard must be provided within the time required by State, tribal, or territorial law, and in any event within a reasonable time after the order is issued, sufficient to protect the respondent's due process rights.

(c) Cross or counter petition.—A protection order issued by a State, tribal, or territorial court against one who has petitioned, filed a complaint, or otherwise filed a written pleading for protection against abuse by a spouse or intimate partner is not entitled to full faith and credit if—

(1) no cross or counter petition, complaint, or other written pleading was filed seeking such a protection order; or

(2) a cross or counter petition has been filed and the court did not make specific findings that each party was entitled to such an order.

(d) Notification and registration.—

(1) Notification.—A State, Indian tribe, or territory according full faith and credit to an order by a court of another State, Indian tribe, or territory shall not notify or require notification of the party against whom a protection order has been issued that the protection order has been registered or filed in that enforcing State, tribal, or territorial jurisdiction unless requested to do so by the party protected under such order.

(2) No prior registration or filing as prerequisite for enforcement.—Any protection order that is otherwise consistent with this section shall be accorded full faith and credit, notwithstanding failure to comply with any requirement that the order be registered or filed in the enforcing State, tribal, or territorial jurisdiction.

(3) Limits on Internet publication of registration information.—A State, Indian tribe, or territory shall not make available publicly on the Internet any information regarding the registration, filing of a petition for, or issuance of a protection order, restraining order or injunction, restraining order, or injunction in either the issuing or enforcing State, tribal or territorial jurisdiction, if such publication would be likely to publicly reveal the identity or location of the party protected under such order. A State, Indian tribe, or territory may share court-generated and law enforcement-generated information contained in secure, governmental registries for protection order enforcement purposes.

(e) Tribal court jurisdiction.—For purposes of this section, a court of an Indian tribe shall have full civil jurisdiction to issue and enforce protection orders involving any person, including the authority to enforce any orders through civil contempt proceedings, to exclude violators from Indian land, and to use other appropriate mechanisms, in matters arising anywhere in the Indian country of the Indian tribe (as defined in section 1151) or otherwise within the authority of the Indian tribe.

§ 2265A. REPEAT OFFENDERS

(a) Maximum term of imprisonment.—The maximum term of imprisonment for a violation of this chapter after a prior domestic violence or stalking offense shall be twice the term otherwise provided under this chapter.

(b) Definition.—For purposes of this section—

(1) the term "prior domestic violence or stalking offense" means a conviction for an offense—

(A) under section 2261, 2261A, or 2262 of this chapter; or

(B) under State or tribal law for an offense consisting of conduct that would have been an offense under a section referred to in subparagraph (A) if the conduct had occurred within the special maritime and territorial jurisdiction of the United States, or in interstate or foreign commerce; and

(2) the term "State" means a State of the United States, the District of Columbia, or any commonwealth, territory, or possession of the United States.

§ 2266. DEFINITIONS

In this chapter:

(1) Bodily injury.—The term "bodily injury" means any act, except one done in self-defense, that results in physical injury or sexual abuse.

(2) Course of conduct.—The term "course of conduct" means a pattern of conduct composed of 2 or more acts, evidencing a continuity of purpose.

(3) Enter or leave Indian country.—The term "enter or leave Indian country" includes leaving the jurisdiction of 1 tribal government and entering the jurisdiction of another tribal government.

(4) Indian country.—The term "Indian country" has the meaning stated in section 1151 of this title.

(5) Protection order.—The term "protection order" includes—

(A) any injunction, restraining order, or any other order issued by a civil or criminal court for the purpose of preventing violent or threatening acts or harassment against, sexual violence, or contact or communication with or physical proximity to, another person, including any temporary or final order issued by a civil or criminal court whether obtained by filing an independent action or as a pendente lite order in another proceeding so long as any civil or criminal order was issued in response to a complaint, petition, or motion filed by or on behalf of a person seeking protection; and

(B) any support, child custody or visitation provisions, orders, remedies or relief issued as part of a protection order, restraining order, or injunction pursuant to State, tribal, territorial, or local law authorizing the issuance of protection orders, restraining orders, or injunctions for the protection of victims of domestic violence, sexual assault, dating violence, or stalking.

(6) Serious bodily injury.—The term "serious bodily injury" has the meaning stated in section 2119(2).

(7) Spouse or intimate partner.—The term "spouse or intimate partner" includes—

(A) for purposes of—

(i) sections other than 2261A—

(I) a spouse or former spouse of the abuser, a person who shares a child in common with the abuser, and a person who cohabits or has cohabited as a spouse with the abuser; or

(II) a person who is or has been in a social relationship of a romantic or intimate nature with the abuser, as determined by the length of the relationship, the type of relationship, and the frequency of interaction between the persons involved in the relationship; and

(ii) section 2261A—

(I) a spouse or former spouse of the target of the stalking, a person who shares a child in common with the target of the stalking, and a person who cohabits or has cohabited as a spouse with the target of the stalking; or

(II) a person who is or has been in a social relationship of a romantic or intimate nature with the target of the stalking, as determined by the length of the relationship, the type of the relationship, and the frequency of interaction between the persons involved in the relationship.

(B) any other person similarly situated to a spouse who is protected by the domestic or family violence laws of the State or tribal jurisdiction in which the injury occurred or where the victim resides.

(8) State.—The term "State" includes a State of the United States, the District of Columbia, and a commonwealth, territory, or possession of the United States.

(9) Travel in interstate or foreign commerce.—The term "travel in interstate or foreign commerce" does not include travel from 1 State to another by an individual who is a member of an Indian tribe and who remains at all times in the territory of the Indian tribe of which the individual is a member.

(10) Dating partner.—The term "dating partner" refers to a person who is or has been in a social relationship of a romantic or intimate nature with the abuser. The existence of such a relationship is based on a consideration of—

(A) the length of the relationship; and

(B) the type of relationship; and

(C) the frequency of interaction between the persons involved in the relationship.

PART III

STATE STATUTES

ABA MODEL STANDARDS OF PRACTICE FOR FAMILY AND DIVORCE MEDIATION

N.D. R. Ct. App. I, Supp.

[EDITORS' INTRODUCTION: Rebecca Aviel, *Counsel for the Divorce*, 55 B.C. L. REV. 1099 (2014); Robert Kirkman Collins, *The Scrivener's Dilemma in Divorce Mediation: Promulgating Progressive Professional Parameters*, 17 CARDOZO J. CONFLICT RESOL. 691 (2016); Dafna Lavi, *Till Death Do Us Part?!: Online Mediation as an Answer to Divorce Cases Involving Violence*, 16 N.C. J. L. & TECH. 253 (2015); Kristine Paranica, *The Implications of Intimate Partner Violence on Ethical Mediation Practice*, 88 N.D. L. REV. 907 (2012); Sapna Kishnani, Note, *Working Towards the Welfare of Our Children: An Argument for a Rebuttable Presumption Against Awarding Abusers Custody and Other Non-Legislative Proposals*, 22 CARDOZO J.L. & GENDER 287 (2016); Caitlin Park Shin, Comment, *Drafting Agreements as an Attorney-Mediator: Revisiting Washington State Bar Association Advisory Opinion 2223*, 89 WASH. L. REV. 1035 (2014).]

OVERVIEW AND DEFINITIONS

Family and divorce mediation ("family mediation" or "mediation") is a process in which a mediator, an impartial third party, facilitates communication between people in family disputes and facilitates their voluntary and informed decision-making. The family mediator assists communication, encourages understanding and helps the participants to understand each other. The family mediator works with the participants to explore options, make decisions and reach their own decisions.

Family mediation is not a substitute for the need for family members to obtain independent legal advice or counseling or therapy. Nor is it appropriate for all families. However, experience has established that family mediation is a valuable option for many families because it can:

increase the self-determination of participants and their ability to communicate;

support decision making that is in the best interests of children; and

reduce the economic and emotional costs associated with the litigation of family disputes.

Effective mediation requires that the family mediator be qualified by training, experience and temperament; that the mediator be impartial; that the participants reach their decisions voluntarily; that their decisions be based on sufficient factual data; that the mediator be aware of the impact of culture and diversity; and that the best interests of children be taken into account. Further, the mediator should also be prepared to identify families whose history includes domestic abuse or child abuse.

THESE MODEL STANDARDS OF PRACTICE FOR FAMILY AND DIVORCE MEDIATION ("MODEL STANDARDS") AIM TO PERFORM THREE MAJOR FUNCTIONS:

(1) to serve as a guide for the conduct of family mediators;

(2) to inform the mediating participants of what they can expect; and

(3) to promote public confidence in mediation as a process for resolving family disputes.

The Model Standards are aspirational in character. They describe good practices for family mediators. They are not intended to create legal rules or standards of liability.

The Model Standards include different levels of guidance:

Use of the term "may" in a Standard is the lowest strength of guidance and indicates a practice that the family mediator should consider adopting but which can be deviated from in the exercise of good professional judgment. Most of the Standards employ the term "should" which indicates that the practice described in the Standard is highly desirable and should be departed from only with very strong reason. The rarer use of the term "shall" in a Standard is a higher level of guidance to the family mediator, indicating that the mediator should not have discretion to depart from the practice described.

STANDARD I: A FAMILY MEDIATOR SHALL RECOGNIZE THAT MEDIATION IS BASED ON THE PRINCIPLE OF SELF-DETERMINATION BY THE PARTICIPANTS.

(A) Self-determination is the fundamental principle of family mediation. The mediation process relies upon the ability of participants to make their own voluntary and informed decisions.

(B) The primary role of a family mediator is to assist the participants to gain a better understanding of their own needs and interests and the needs and interests of others and to facilitate discussion and decision-making among the participants.

(C) A family mediator should inform the participants that they may seek information and advice from a variety of sources during the mediation process.

(D) A family mediator shall inform the participants that they may withdraw from family mediation at any time and are not required to reach an agreement in mediation.

(E) The family mediator's commitment shall be to the participants and the process. Pressure from outside of the mediation process shall never influence the mediator to coerce participants to settle.

STANDARD II: A FAMILY MEDIATOR SHALL BE QUALIFIED BY EDUCATION AND TRAINING TO UNDERTAKE THE MEDIATION.

STANDARD III: A FAMILY MEDIATOR SHALL FACILITATE THE PARTICIPANTS' UNDERSTANDING OF WHAT MEDIATION IS AND ASSESS THEIR CAPACITY TO MEDIATE BEFORE THE PARTICIPANTS REACH AN AGREEMENT TO MEDIATE.

(A) Before family mediation begins a mediator should provide the participants with an overview of the process and its purposes, including:

(1) informing the participants that reaching an agreement in family mediation is consensual in nature, that a mediator is an impartial facilitator, and that a mediator may not give legal advice, evaluate the case, or impose or force any settlement on the parties;

(2) distinguishing family mediation from other processes designed to address family issues and disputes;

(3) informing the participants that any agreements reached will be reviewed by the court when court approval is required;

(4) informing the participants that they may obtain independent advice from attorneys, counsel, advocates, accountants, therapists or other professionals during the mediation process;

(5) advising the participants, in appropriate cases, that they can seek the advice of religious figures, elders or other significant persons in their community whose opinions they value;

(6) discussing, if applicable, the issue of separate sessions with the participants, a description of the circumstances in which the mediator may meet alone with any of the participants, or with any third party and the conditions of confidentiality concerning these separate sessions;

(7) informing the participants that the presence or absence of other persons at a mediation, including attorneys, counselors or advocates, depends on the agreement of the participants and the mediator, unless a statute or regulation otherwise requires or the mediator believes that the presence of another person is required or may be beneficial because of a history or threat of violence or other serious coercive activity by a participant;

(8) describing the obligations of the mediator to maintain the confidentiality of the mediation process and its results as well as any exceptions to confidentiality;

(9) advising the participants of the circumstances under which the mediator may suspend or terminate the mediation process and that a participant has a right to suspend or terminate mediation at any time.

(B) The participants should sign a written agreement to mediate their dispute and the terms and conditions thereof within a reasonable time after first consulting the family mediator.

(C) The family mediator should be alert to the capacity and willingness of the participants to mediate before proceeding with the mediation and throughout the process. A mediator should not agree to conduct the mediation if the mediator reasonably believes one or more of the participants is unable or unwilling to participate.

(D) Family mediators should not accept a dispute for mediation if they cannot satisfy the expectations of the participants concerning the timing of the process.

STANDARD IV: A FAMILY MEDIATOR SHALL CONDUCT THE MEDIATION PROCESS IN AN IMPARTIAL MANNER. A FAMILY MEDIATOR SHALL DISCLOSE ALL ACTUAL AND POTENTIAL GROUNDS OF BIAS AND CONFLICTS OF INTEREST REASONABLY KNOWN TO THE MEDIATOR. THE PARTICIPANTS SHALL BE FREE TO RETAIN THE MEDIATOR BY AN INFORMED, WRITTEN WAIVER OF THE CONFLICT OF INTEREST. HOWEVER, IF A BIAS OR CONFLICT OF INTEREST CLEARLY IMPAIRS A MEDIATOR'S IMPARTIALITY, THE MEDIATOR SHALL WITHDRAW REGARDLESS OF THE EXPRESS AGREEMENT OF THE PARTICIPANTS.

(A) Impartiality means freedom from favoritism or bias in word, action or appearance, and includes a commitment to assist all participants as opposed to any one individual.

(B) Conflict of interest means any relationship between the mediator, any participant or the subject matter of the dispute that compromises or appears to compromise the mediator's impartiality.

(C) A family mediator should not accept a dispute for mediation if the family mediator cannot be impartial.

(D) A family mediator should identify and disclose potential grounds of bias or conflict of interest upon which a mediator's impartiality might reasonably be questioned. Such disclosure should be made prior to the start of a mediation and in time to allow the participants to select an alternate mediator.

(E) A family mediator should resolve all doubts in favor of disclosure. All disclosures should be made as soon as practical after the mediator becomes aware of the bias or potential conflict of interest. The duty to disclose is a continuing duty.

(F) A family mediator should guard against bias or partiality based on the participants' personal characteristics, background or performance at the mediation.

(G) A family mediator should avoid conflicts of interest in recommending the services of other professionals.

(H) A family mediator shall not use information about participants obtained in a mediation for personal gain or advantage.

(I) A family mediator should withdraw pursuant to Standard IX if the mediator believes the mediator's impartiality has been compromised or a conflict of interest has been identified and has not been waived by the participants.

STANDARD V: A FAMILY MEDIATOR SHALL FULLY DISCLOSE AND EXPLAIN THE BASIS OF ANY COMPENSATION, FEES AND CHARGES TO THE PARTICIPANTS.

(A) The participants should be provided with sufficient information about fees at the outset of mediation to determine if they wish to retain the services of the mediator.

(B) The participants' written agreement to mediate their dispute should include a description of their fee arrangement with the mediator.

(C) A mediator should not enter into a fee agreement that is contingent upon the results of the mediation or the amount of the settlement.

(D) A mediator should not accept a fee for referral of a matter to another mediator or to any other person.

(E) Upon termination of mediation a mediator should return any unearned fee to the participants.

STANDARD VI: A FAMILY MEDIATOR SHALL STRUCTURE THE MEDIATION PROCESS SO THAT THE PARTICIPANTS MAKE DECISIONS BASED ON SUFFICIENT INFORMATION AND KNOWLEDGE.

(A) The mediator should facilitate full and accurate disclosure and the acquisition and development of information during mediation so that the participants can make informed decisions. This may be accomplished by encouraging participants to consult appropriate experts.

(B) Consistent with standards of impartiality and preserving participant self-determination, a mediator may provide the participants with basic information that the mediator is qualified by training or experience to provide. The mediator shall not provide therapy or legal advice.

(C) The mediator should recommend that the participants obtain independent legal representation before concluding an agreement.

(D) If the participants so desire, the mediator should allow attorneys, counsel or advocates for the participants to be present at the mediation sessions.

(E) With the agreement of the participants, the mediator may document the participants' decisions in the from of a decision summery (vs. a legal agreement). The mediator should inform the participants that any decision summary or agreement should be reviewed by an independent attorney before it is signed.

STANDARD VII: A FAMILY MEDIATOR SHALL MAINTAIN THE CONFIDENTIALITY OF ALL INFORMATION ACQUIRED IN THE MEDIATION PROCESS, UNLESS THE MEDIATOR IS PERMITTED OR REQUIRED TO REVEAL THE INFORMATION BY LAW OR AGREEMENT OF THE PARTICIPANTS.

(A) The mediator should discuss the participants' expectations of confidentiality with them prior to undertaking the mediation. The written agreement to mediate should include provisions concerning confidentiality.

(B) Prior to undertaking the mediation the mediator should inform the participants of the limitations of confidentiality such as statutory, judicially or ethically mandated reporting.

(C) As permitted by law, the mediator shall disclose a participant's threat of suicide or violence against any person to the threatened person and the appropriate authorities if the mediator believes such threat is likely to be acted upon, and use standard exit planning strategies with the parties.

(D) If the mediator holds private sessions with a participant, the obligations of confidentiality concerning those sessions should be discussed and agreed upon prior to the sessions.

(E) If subpoenaed or otherwise noticed to testify or to produce documents the mediator should inform the participants immediately. The mediator should not testify or provide documents in response to a subpoena without an order of the court if the mediator reasonably believes doing so would violate an obligation of confidentiality to the participants.

STANDARD VIII: A FAMILY MEDIATOR SHALL ASSIST PARTICIPANTS IN DETERMINING HOW TO PROMOTE THE BEST INTERESTS OF CHILDREN.

(A) The mediator should support the participants' exploration of the range of options available for separation or post divorce parenting arrangements and their respective costs and benefits. Referral to a specialist in child development or an attorney may be appropriate for these purposes. The parties may be given the following list of topics for discussion (this is not an exhaustive list and there may be other topics):

(1) information about community resources and programs that can help the participants and their children cope with the consequences of family reorganization and family violence;

(2) problems that continuing conflict creates for children's development and what steps might be taken to ameliorate the effects of conflict on the children;

(3) development of a parenting plan that covers the children's physical residence and decision-making responsibilities for the children, with appropriate levels of detail as agreed to by the participants;

(4) the possible need to revise parenting plans as the developmental needs of the children evolve over time; and

(5) encouragement to the participants to develop appropriate dispute resolution mechanisms to facilitate future revisions of the parenting plan.

(B) The mediator should be sensitive to the impact of culture and religion on parenting philosophy and other decisions.

(C) The local mediation administrator and/or the mediator shall inform any court-appointed representative for the children of the mediation. If a representative for the children participates, the mediator should, at the outset, discuss the effect of that participation on the mediation process and the confidentiality of the mediation with the participants. Whether the representative of the children participates or not, the mediator shall provide the representative with the resulting agreements insofar as they relate to the children.

(D) Except in extraordinary circumstances, the children should not participate in the mediation process without the consent of both parents and the children's court-appointed representative if one exists.

(E) Prior to including the children in the mediation process, the mediator should consult with the parents and the children's court-appointed representative about whether the children should participate in the mediation process and the form of that participation.

(F) The mediator should inform all concerned about the available options for the children's participation (which may include personal participation, an interview with a mental health professional, the mediator interviewing the child and reporting to the parents, or a videotaped statement by the child) and discuss the costs and benefits of each with the participants.

STANDARD IX: A FAMILY MEDIATOR SHALL RECOGNIZE A FAMILY SITUATION INVOLVING CHILD ABUSE OR NEGLECT AND TAKE APPROPRIATE STEPS TO SHAPE THE MEDIATION PROCESS ACCORDINGLY.

(A) As used in these Standards, child abuse or neglect is defined by applicable state law.

(B) A mediator shall not undertake a mediation in which the family situation has been assessed to involve child abuse or neglect without appropriate and adequate training.

(C) If the mediator has reasonable grounds to believe that a child of the participants is abused or neglected within the meaning of the jurisdiction's child abuse and neglect laws, the mediator shall comply with applicable child protection laws.

(1) The mediator should encourage the participants to explore appropriate services for the family.

(2) The mediator should consider the appropriateness of suspending or terminating the mediation process in light of the allegations.

STANDARD X: A FAMILY MEDIATOR SHALL RECOGNIZE A FAMILY SITUATION INVOLVING DOMESTIC ABUSE AND TAKE APPROPRIATE STEPS TO SHAPE THE MEDIATION PROCESS ACCORDINGLY.

(A) As used in these Standards, domestic abuse includes domestic violence as defined by applicable state law and issues of control and intimidation.

(B) A mediator shall not undertake a mediation in which the family situation has been assessed to involve domestic abuse without appropriate and adequate training.

(C) Some cases are not suitable for mediation because of safety, control or intimidation issues. A mediator should make a reasonable effort to screen for the existence of domestic abuse prior to entering into an agreement to mediate. The mediator should continue to assess for domestic abuse throughout the mediation process.

(D) If domestic abuse appears to be present the mediator shall consider taking measures to insure the safety of participants and the mediator including, among others:

(1) establishing appropriate security arrangements;

(2) holding separate sessions with the participants even without the agreement of all participants;

(3) allowing a friend, representative, advocate, counsel or attorney to attend the mediation sessions;

(4) encouraging the participants to be represented by an attorney, counsel or an advocate throughout the mediation process;

(5) referring the participants to appropriate community resources;

(6) suspending or terminating the mediation sessions, with appropriate steps to protect the safety of the participants.

STANDARD XI: A FAMILY MEDIATOR SHALL SUSPEND OR TERMINATE THE MEDIATION PROCESS WHEN THE MEDIATOR REASONABLY BELIEVES THAT A PARTICIPANT IS UNABLE TO EFFECTIVELY PARTICIPATE OR FOR OTHER COMPELLING REASON.

(A) Circumstances under which a mediator should consider suspending or terminating the mediation, may include, among others:

(1) the safety of a participant or well-being of a child is threatened;

(2) a participant has or is threatening to abduct a child;

(3) a participant is unable to participate due to the influence of drugs, alcohol, or physical or mental condition;

(4) the participants are about to enter into an agreement that the mediator reasonably believes to be unconscionable or violates public policy or law;

(5) a participant is using the mediation to further illegal conduct;

(6) a participant is using the mediation process to gain an unfair advantage;

(7) if the mediator believes the mediator's impartiality has been compromised in accordance with Standard IV.

(B) If the mediator does suspend or terminate the mediation, the mediator should take all reasonable steps to minimize prejudice or inconvenience to the participants which may result.

STANDARD XII: A FAMILY MEDIATOR SHALL BE TRUTHFUL IN THE ADVERTISEMENT AND SOLICITATION FOR MEDIATION.

(A) Mediators should refrain from promises and guarantees of results. A mediator should not advertise statistical settlement data or settlement rates.

(B) Mediators should accurately represent their qualifications. In an advertisement or other communication, a mediator may make reference to meeting state, national or private organizational qualifications only if the entity referred to has a procedure for qualifying mediators and the mediator has been duly granted the requisite status.

STANDARD XIII: A FAMILY MEDIATOR SHALL ACQUIRE AND MAINTAIN PROFESSIONAL COMPETENCE IN MEDIATION.

(A) Mediators should continuously improve their professional skills and abilities by, among other activities, participating in relevant continuing education programs and should regularly engage in self-assessment.

(B) Mediators should participate in programs of peer consultation and should help train and mentor the work of less experienced mediators.

(C) Mediators should continuously strive to understand the impact of culture and diversity on the mediator's practice.

SPECIAL POLICY CONSIDERATIONS FOR STATE REGULATION OF FAMILY MEDIATORS AND COURT AFFILIATED PROGRAMS

The Model Standards recognize the National Standards for Court Connected Dispute Resolution Programs (1992). There are also state and local regulations governing such programs and family mediators. The following principles of organization and practice, however, are especially important for regulation of mediators and court-connected family mediation programs. They are worthy of separate mention.

(A) Individual states or local courts should set standards and qualifications for family mediators including procedures for evaluations and handling grievances against mediators. In developing these standards and qualifications, regulators should consult with appropriate professional groups, including professional associations of family mediators.

(B) When family mediators are appointed by a court or other institution, the appointing agency should make reasonable efforts to insure that each mediator is qualified for the appointment. If a list of family mediators qualified for court appointment exists, the requirements for being included on the list should be made public and available to all interested persons.

(C) Confidentiality should not be construed to limit or prohibit the effective monitoring, research or evaluation of mediation programs by responsible individuals or academic institutions provided that no identifying information about any person involved in the mediation is disclosed without their prior written consent. Under appropriate circumstances, researchers may be permitted to obtain access to statistical data and, with the permission of the participants, to individual case files, observations of live mediations, and interviews with participants.

THESE MODEL STANDARDS WERE DEVELOPED BY THE ASSOCIATION FOR CONFLICT RESOLUTION AND WERE APPROVED BY THE AMERICAN BAR ASSOCIATION IN FEBRUARY 2001.

ABANDONMENT OF CHILDREN: SAFE HAVEN LAW

FLA. STAT. ANN. §§ 383.50–51 (West 2016)

[EDITORS' INTRODUCTION: Barbara A. Atwood, *Representing Children Who Can't or Won't Direct Counsel: Best Interests Lawyering or No Lawyer at All*, 53 ARIZ. L. REV. 381 (2011); Arielle Bardzell & Nicholas Bernard, *Adoption and Foster Care*, 16 GEO. J. GENDER & L. 3 (2015); Lynne Marie Kohm, Roe's *Effects on Family Law*, 71 WASH. & LEE L. REV. 1339 (2014); Lucinda Cornett, Note, *Remembering the Endangered "Child": Limiting the Definition of "Safe Haven" and Looking Beyond the Safe Haven Law Framework*, 98 KY. L.J. 833 (2010).]

§ 383.50. TREATMENT OF SURRENDERED NEWBORN INFANT

(1) As used in this section, the term "newborn infant" means a child who a licensed physician reasonably believes is approximately 7 days old or younger at the time the child is left at a hospital, emergency medical services station, or fire station.

(2) There is a presumption that the parent who leaves the newborn infant in accordance with this section intended to leave the newborn infant and consented to termination of parental rights.

(3) Each emergency medical services station or fire station staffed with full-time firefighters, emergency medical technicians, or paramedics shall accept any newborn infant left with a firefighter, emergency medical technician, or paramedic. The firefighter, emergency medical technician, or paramedic shall consider these actions as implied consent to and shall:

(a) Provide emergency medical services to the newborn infant to the extent he or she is trained to provide those services, and

(b) Arrange for the immediate transportation of the newborn infant to the nearest hospital having emergency services.

A licensee as defined in s. 401.23, a fire department, or an employee or agent of a licensee or fire department may treat and transport a newborn infant pursuant to this section. If a newborn infant is placed in the physical custody of an employee or agent of a licensee or fire department, such placement shall be considered implied consent for treatment and transport. A licensee, a fire department, or an employee or agent of a licensee or fire department is immune from criminal or civil liability for acting in good faith pursuant to this section. Nothing in this subsection limits liability for negligence.

(4) Each hospital of this state subject to s. 395.1041 shall, and any other hospital may, admit and provide all necessary emergency services and care, as defined in s. 395.002(9), to any newborn infant left with the hospital in accordance with this section. The hospital or any of its licensed health care professionals shall consider these actions as implied

consent for treatment, and a hospital accepting physical custody of a newborn infant has implied consent to perform all necessary emergency services and care. The hospital or any of its licensed health care professionals is immune from criminal or civil liability for acting in good faith in accordance with this section. Nothing in this subsection limits liability for negligence.

(5)   Except when there is actual or suspected child abuse or neglect, any parent who leaves a newborn infant with a firefighter, emergency medical technician, or paramedic at a fire station or emergency medical services station, or brings a newborn infant to an emergency room of a hospital and expresses an intent to leave the newborn infant and not return, has the absolute right to remain anonymous and to leave at any time and may not be pursued or followed unless the parent seeks to reclaim the newborn infant. When an infant is born in a hospital and the mother expresses intent to leave the infant and not return, upon the mother's request, the hospital or registrar shall complete the infant's birth certificate without naming the mother thereon.

(6)   A parent of a newborn infant left at a hospital, emergency medical services station, or fire station under this section may claim his or her newborn infant up until the court enters a judgment terminating his or her parental rights. A claim to the newborn infant must be made to the entity having physical or legal custody of the newborn infant or to the circuit court before whom proceedings involving the newborn infant are pending.

(7)   Upon admitting a newborn infant under this section, the hospital shall immediately contact a local licensed child-placing agency or alternatively contact the statewide central abuse hotline for the name of a licensed child-placing agency for purposes of transferring physical custody of the newborn infant. The hospital shall notify the licensed child-placing agency that a newborn infant has been left with the hospital and approximately when the licensed child-placing agency can take physical custody of the child. In cases where there is actual or suspected child abuse or neglect, the hospital or any of its licensed health care professionals shall report the actual or suspected child abuse or neglect in accordance with ss. 39.201 and 395.1023 in lieu of contacting a licensed child-placing agency.

(8)   Any newborn infant admitted to a hospital in accordance with this section is presumed eligible for coverage under Medicaid, subject to federal rules.

(9)   A newborn infant left at a hospital, emergency medical services station, or fire station in accordance with this section shall not be deemed abandoned and subject to reporting and investigation requirements under s. 39.201 unless there is actual or suspected child abuse or until the department takes physical custody of the child.

(10) A criminal investigation shall not be initiated solely because a newborn infant is left at a hospital under this section unless there is actual or suspected child abuse or neglect.

§ 383.51. CONFIDENTIALITY; IDENTIFICATION OF PARENT LEAVING NEWBORN INFANT AT HOSPITAL, EMERGENCY MEDICAL SERVICES STATION, OR FIRE STATION

The identity of a parent who leaves a newborn infant at a hospital, emergency medical services station, or fire station in accordance with s. 383.50 is confidential and exempt from s. 119.07(1) and s. 24(a), Art. I of the State Constitution. The identity of a parent leaving a child shall be disclosed to a person claiming to be a parent of the newborn infant.

ABUSE AND NEGLECT PROCEEDINGS: COURT-APPOINTED SPECIAL ADVOCATES

VIRGINIA COURT APPOINTED SPECIAL ADVOCATES (CASA)

Va. Code Ann. §§ 9.1–151 et seq. (West 2016)

[EDITORS' INTRODUCTION: MICHAEL T. FLANNERY & RAYMOND C. O'BRIEN, THE SEXUAL EXPLOITATION OF CHILDREN (2016); Barbara A. Atwood, *Representing Children Who Can't or Won't Direct Counsel: Best Interests Lawyering or No Lawyer At All*, 53 ARIZ. L. REV. 381 (2011); Marcia M. Boumil, Cristina F. Freitas & Debbie F. Freitas, *Legal and Ethical Issues Confronting Guardian Ad Litem Practice*, 13 J. L. & FAM. STUD. 43 (2011); Donald N. Duquettea & Julian Darwall, *Child Representation in America: Progress Report from the National Quality Improvement Center*, 46 FAM. L.Q. 87 (2012); Benjamin Good, *A Child's Right to Counsel in Removal Proceedings*, 10 STAN. J. CIV. RTS. & CIV. LIBERTIES 109 (2014); Suparna Malempati, *Beyond Paternalism: The Role of Counsel for Children in Abuse and Neglect Proceedings*, 11 U. N.H. L. REV. 97 (2013); Raymond C. O'Brien, *Reasonable Efforts and Parent-Child Reunification*, 2013 MICH. ST. L. REV. 1029 (2013); Brent Pattison, *When Children Object: Amplifying an Older Child's Objection to Termination of Parental Rights*, 49 U. MICH. J.L. REFORM 689 (2016); Jennifer K. Pokempner, Riya Saha Shah, Mark F. Houldin, Michal J. Dale & Robert G. Schwarz, *The Legal Significance of Adolescent Development on the Right to Counsel: Establishing the Constitutional Right to Counsel for Teens in Child Welfare Matters and Assuring a Meaningful Right to Counsel in Delinquency Matters*, 47 HARV. C.R.-C.L. L. REV. 529 (2012); Nicole A. Carnemolla, Note, *Raising the Bar for Child Advocates in Connecticut Family Court*, 33 QUINNIPIAC L. REV. 411 (2015); Ryan M. Rappa, Note, *Getting Abused and Neglected Children into Court: A Right of Access Under the Petition Clause of the First Amendment*, 2011 U. ILL. L. REV. 1419 (2011); Kasey L. Wassenaar, Comment, *Defenseless Children: Achieving Competent Representation for Children in Abuse and Neglect Proceedings Through Statutory Reform in South Dakota*, 56 S.D. L. Rev. 182 (2011).]

§ 9.1–151. COURT-APPOINTED SPECIAL ADVOCATE PROGRAM; APPOINTMENT OF ADVISORY COMMITTEE

A. There is established a Court-Appointed Special Advocate Program (the Program) that shall be administered by the Department. The Program shall provide services in accordance with this article to children who are subjects of judicial proceedings (i) involving allegations that the child is abused, neglected, in need of services, or in need of supervision or (ii) for the restoration of parental rights pursuant to § 16.1–283.2 and for whom the juvenile and domestic relations district court judge determines such services are appropriate. Court-Appointed Special Advocate volunteer appointments may continue for youth 18 years of age and older who are in foster care if the court has retained jurisdiction pursuant to § 16.1–242 and the juvenile and domestic relations district court judge determines such services are appropriate. The Department shall adopt regulations necessary and appropriate for the administration of the Program.

B. The Board shall appoint an Advisory Committee to the Court-Appointed Special Advocate Program, consisting of 15 members, knowledgeable of court matters, child welfare, and juvenile justice issues and representative of both state and local interests. The duties of the Advisory Committee shall be to advise the Board on all matters relating to the Program and the needs of the clients served by the Program, and to make such recommendations as it may deem desirable.

§ 9.1–152. LOCAL COURT-APPOINTED SPECIAL ADVOCATE PROGRAMS; POWERS AND DUTIES

A. The Department shall provide a portion of any funding appropriated for this purpose to applicants seeking to establish and operate a local court-appointed special advocate program in their respective judicial districts. Only local programs operated in accordance with this article shall be eligible to receive state funds.

B. Local programs may be established and operated by local boards created for this purpose. Local boards shall ensure conformance to regulations adopted by the Board and may:

1. Solicit and accept financial support from public and private sources.

2. Oversee the financial and program management of the local court- appointed special advocate program.

3. Employ and supervise a director who shall serve as a professional liaison to personnel of the court and agencies serving children.

4. Employ such staff as is necessary to the operation of the program.

§ 9.1–153. VOLUNTEER COURT-APPOINTED SPECIAL ADVOCATES; POWERS AND DUTIES; ASSIGNMENT; QUALIFICATIONS; TRAINING

A. Services in each local court-appointed special advocate program shall be provided by volunteer court-appointed special advocates, hereinafter referred to as advocates. The advocate's duties shall include:

1. Investigating the case to which he is assigned to provide independent factual information to the court.

2. Submitting to the court of a written report of his investigation in compliance with the provisions of § 16.1–274. The report may, upon request of the court, include recommendations as to the child's welfare.

3.   Monitoring the case to which he is assigned to ensure compliance with the court's orders.

4.   Assisting any appointed guardian ad litem to represent the child in providing effective representation of the child's needs and best interests.

5.   Reporting a suspected abused or neglected child pursuant to § 63.2–1509.

B.   The advocate is not a party to the case to which he is assigned and shall not call witnesses or examine witnesses. The advocate shall not, with respect to the case to which he is assigned, provide legal counsel or advice to any person, appear as counsel in court or in proceedings which are part of the judicial process, or engage in the unauthorized practice of law. The advocate may testify if called as a witness.

C.   The program director shall assign an advocate to a child when requested to do so by the judge of the juvenile and domestic relations district court having jurisdiction over the proceedings. The advocate shall continue his association with each case to which he is assigned until relieved of his duties by the court or by the program director.

D.   The Department shall adopt regulations governing the qualifications of advocates who for purposes of administering this subsection shall be deemed to be criminal justice employees. The regulations shall require that an advocate be at least twenty-one years of age and that the program director shall obtain with the approval of the court (i) a copy of his criminal history record or certification that no conviction data are maintained on him and (ii) a copy of information from the central registry maintained pursuant to § 63.2–1515 on any investigation of child abuse or neglect undertaken on him or certification that no such record is maintained on him. Advocates selected prior to the adoption of regulations governing qualifications shall meet the minimum requirements set forth in this article.

E.   An advocate shall have no associations which create a conflict of interests or the appearance of such a conflict with his duties as an advocate. No advocate shall be assigned to a case of a child whose family has a professional or personal relationship with the advocate. Questions concerning conflicts of interests shall be determined in accordance with regulations adopted by the Department.

F.   No applicant shall be assigned as an advocate until successful completion of a program of training required by regulations. The Department shall set standards for both basic and ongoing training.

§ 9.1–154. IMMUNITY

No staff of or volunteers participating in a program, whether or not compensated, shall be subject to personal liability while acting within the scope of their duties, except for gross negligence or intentional misconduct.

§ 9.1–155. NOTICE OF HEARINGS AND PROCEEDINGS

The provision of § 16.1–264 regarding notice to parties shall apply to ensure that an advocate is notified of hearings and other proceedings concerning the case to which he is assigned.

§ 9.1–156. INSPECTION AND COPYING OF RECORDS BY ADVOCATE; CONFIDENTIALITY OF RECORDS

A. Upon presentation by the advocate of the order of his appointment and upon specific court order, any state or local agency, department, authority, or institution, and any hospital, school, physician, or other health or mental health care provider shall permit the advocate to inspect and copy, without the consent of the child or his parents, any records relating to the child involved in the case. Upon the advocate presenting to the mental health provider the order of the advocate's appointment and, upon specific court order, in lieu of the advocate inspecting and copying any related records of the child involved, the mental health care provider shall be available within seventy-two hours to conduct for the advocate a review and an interpretation of the child's treatment records which are specifically related to the investigation.

B. An advocate shall not disclose the contents of any document or record to which he becomes privy, which is otherwise confidential pursuant to the provisions of this Code, except upon order of a court of competent jurisdiction.

§ 9.1–157. COOPERATION OF STATE AND LOCAL ENTITIES

All state and local departments, agencies, authorities, and institutions shall cooperate with the Department and with each local court-appointed special advocate program to facilitate its implementation of the Program.

ALIMONY

ILLINOIS

750 Ill. Comp. Stat. Ann. 5/504 (West 2016)

[EDITORS' INTRODUCTION: Llewellyn Joseph Gibbons, *Then, You Had It, Now, It's Gone: Interspousal or Community Property Transfer and Termination of an Illusory Ephemeral State Law Right or Interest in a Copyright*, 24 FORDHAM INTELL. PROP. MEDIA & ENT. L.J. 97 (2013); Judith G. McMullen, *Spousal Support in the 21st Century*, 29 WIS. J.L. GENDER & SOC'Y 1 (2014); Margaret Ryznar, *Alimony's Job Lock*, 49 AKRON L. REV. 91 (2016); Allison Anna Tait, *Divorce Equality*, 90 WASH. L. REV. 1245 (2015); Deborah A. Widiss, *Changing the Marriage Equation*, 89 WASH. U. L. REV. 721 (2012); Jill Bornstein, Note, *At a Cross-Road: Anti-Same-Sex Marriage Policies and Principles of Equity: The Effect of Same-Sex Cohabitation on Alimony Payments to an Ex-Spouse*, 84 CHI.-KENT L. REV. 1027 (2010); Katelin Eastman, Comment, *"Alimony for Your Eggs": Fertility Compensation in Divorce Proceedings*, 42 PEPP. L. REV. 293 (2015); Sarah Frances King, Comment, *Till Death Do Us Part or Otherwise Approved by the Court? Interpreting the Language Of § 510(C) of the IMDMA Regarding Post-Death Maintenance Obligations and Life Insurance*, 60 DEPAUL L. REV. 713 (2011); Emily M. May, Note, *Should Moving In Mean Losing Out? Making a Case to Clarify the Legal Effect of Cohabitation on Alimony*, 62 DUKE L.J. 403 (2012).]

§ 5/504. MAINTENANCE

(a) Entitlement to maintenance. In a proceeding for dissolution of marriage or legal separation or declaration of invalidity of marriage, or a proceeding for maintenance following dissolution of the marriage by a court which lacked personal jurisdiction over the absent spouse, the court may grant a maintenance award for either spouse in amounts and for periods of time as the court deems just, without regard to marital misconduct, and the maintenance may be paid from the income or property of the other spouse. The court shall first determine whether a maintenance award is appropriate, after consideration of all relevant factors, including:

(1) the income and property of each party, including marital property apportioned and non-marital property assigned to the party seeking maintenance as well as all financial obligations imposed on the parties as a result of the dissolution of marriage;

(2) the needs of each party;

(3) the realistic present and future earning capacity of each party;

(4) any impairment of the present and future earning capacity of the party seeking maintenance due to that party devoting time to

domestic duties or having forgone or delayed education, training, employment, or career opportunities due to the marriage;

(5) any impairment of the realistic present or future earning capacity of the party against whom maintenance is sought;

(6) the time necessary to enable the party seeking maintenance to acquire appropriate education, training, and employment, and whether that party is able to support himself or herself through appropriate employment or any parental responsibility arrangements and its effect on the party seeking employment;

(7) the standard of living established during the marriage;

(8) the duration of the marriage;

(9) the age, health, station, occupation, amount and sources of income, vocational skills, employability, estate, liabilities, and the needs of each of the parties;

(10) all sources of public and private income including, without limitation, disability and retirement income;

(11) the tax consequences of the property division upon the respective economic circumstances of the parties;

(12) contributions and services by the party seeking maintenance to the education, training, career or career potential, or license of the other spouse;

(13) any valid agreement of the parties; and

(14) any other factor that the court expressly finds to be just and equitable.

(b) (Blank).

(b–1) Amount and duration of maintenance. If the court determines that a maintenance award is appropriate, the court shall order maintenance in accordance with either paragraph (1) or (2) of this subsection (b–1):

(1) Maintenance award in accordance with guidelines. In situations when the combined gross income of the parties is less than $250,000 and the payor has no obligation to pay child support or maintenance or both from a prior relationship, maintenance payable after the date the parties' marriage is dissolved shall be in accordance with subparagraphs (A) and (B) of this paragraph (1), unless the court makes a finding that the application of the guidelines would be inappropriate.

(A) The amount of maintenance under this paragraph (1) shall be calculated by taking 30% of the payor's gross income minus 20% of the payee's gross income. The amount calculated as maintenance, however, when added to the gross income of the payee, may not result in the payee receiving an amount that is in excess of 40% of the combined gross income of the parties.

(B) The duration of an award under this paragraph (1) shall be calculated by multiplying the length of the marriage at the time the action was commenced by whichever of the following factors applies: 5 years or less (.20); more than 5 years but less than 10 years (.40); 10 years or more but less than 15 years (.60); or 15 years or more but less than 20 years (.80). For a marriage of 20 or more years, the court, in its discretion, shall order either permanent maintenance or maintenance for a period equal to the length of the marriage.

(2) Maintenance award not in accordance with guidelines. Any non-guidelines award of maintenance shall be made after the court's consideration of all relevant factors set forth in subsection (a) of this Section.

(b–2)   Findings. In each case involving the issue of maintenance, the court shall make specific findings of fact, as follows:

(1) the court shall state its reasoning for awarding or not awarding maintenance and shall include references to each relevant factor set forth in subsection (a) of this Section; and

(2) if the court deviates from otherwise applicable guidelines under paragraph (1) of subsection (b–1), it shall state in its findings the amount of maintenance (if determinable) or duration that would have been required under the guidelines and the reasoning for any variance from the guidelines.

(b–3)   Gross income. For purposes of this Section, the term "gross income" means all income from all sources, within the scope of that phase in Section 505 of this Act.

(b–4)   Unallocated maintenance. Unless the parties otherwise agree, the court may not order unallocated maintenance and child support in any dissolution judgment or in any post-dissolution order. In its discretion, the court may order unallocated maintenance and child support in any pre-dissolution temporary order.

(b–4.5) Fixed-term maintenance in marriages of less than 10 years. If a court grants maintenance for a fixed period under subsection (a) of this Section at the conclusion of a case commenced before the tenth anniversary of the marriage, the court may also designate the termination of the period during which this maintenance is to be paid as a "permanent termination". The effect of this designation is that maintenance is barred after the ending date of the period during which maintenance is to be paid.

(b–5)   Interest on maintenance. Any maintenance obligation including any unallocated maintenance and child support obligation, or any portion of any support obligation, that becomes due and remains unpaid shall accrue simple interest as set forth in Section 505 of this Act.

(b–7)   Maintenance judgments. Any new or existing maintenance order including any unallocated maintenance and child support order entered by the court under this Section shall be deemed to be a series of judgments against the person obligated to pay support thereunder. Each such judgment to be in the amount of each payment or installment of support and each such judgment to be deemed entered as of the date the corresponding payment or installment becomes due under the terms of the support order, except no judgment shall arise as to any installment coming due after the termination of maintenance as provided by Section 510 of the Illinois Marriage and Dissolution of Marriage Act or the provisions of any order for maintenance. Each such judgment shall have the full force, effect and attributes of any other judgment of this State, including the ability to be enforced. Notwithstanding any other State or local law to the contrary, a lien arises by operation of law against the real and personal property of the obligor for each installment of overdue support owed by the obligor.

(c)   Maintenance during an appeal. The court may grant and enforce the payment of maintenance during the pendency of an appeal as the court shall deem reasonable and proper.

(d)   Maintenance during imprisonment. No maintenance shall accrue during the period in which a party is imprisoned for failure to comply with the court's order for the payment of such maintenance.

(e)   Fees when maintenance is paid through the clerk. When maintenance is to be paid through the clerk of the court in a county of 1,000,000 inhabitants or less, the order shall direct the obligor to pay to the clerk, in addition to the maintenance payments, all fees imposed by the county board under paragraph (3) of subsection (u) of Section 27.1 of the Clerks of Courts Act. Unless paid in cash or pursuant to an order for withholding, the payment of the fee shall be by a separate instrument from the support payment and shall be made to the order of the Clerk.

(f)   Maintenance secured by life insurance. An award ordered by a court upon entry of a dissolution judgment or upon entry of an award of maintenance following a reservation of maintenance in a dissolution judgment may be reasonably secured, in whole or in part, by life insurance on the payor's life on terms as to which the parties agree, or, if they do not agree, on such terms determined by the court, subject to the following:

(1)   With respect to existing life insurance, provided the court is apprised through evidence, stipulation, or otherwise as to level of death benefits, premium, and other relevant data and makes findings relative thereto, the court may allocate death benefits, the right to assign death benefits, or the obligation for future premium payments between the parties as it deems just.

(2)   To the extent the court determines that its award should be secured, in whole or in part, by new life insurance on the payor's life, the court may only order:

(i)   that the payor cooperate on all appropriate steps for the payee to obtain such new life insurance; and

(ii)   that the payee, at his or her sole option and expense, may obtain such new life insurance on the payor's life up to a maximum level of death benefit coverage, or descending death benefit coverage, as is set by the court, such level not to exceed a reasonable amount in light of the court's award, with the payee or the payee's designee being the beneficiary of such life insurance.

In determining the maximum level of death benefit coverage, the court shall take into account all relevant facts and circumstances, including the impact on access to life insurance by the maintenance payor. If in resolving any issues under paragraph (2) of this subsection (f) a court reviews any submitted or proposed application for new insurance on the life of a maintenance payor, the review shall be in camera.

(3)   A judgment shall expressly set forth that all death benefits paid under life insurance on a payor's life maintained or obtained pursuant to this subsection to secure maintenance are designated as excludable from the gross income of the maintenance payee under Section 71(b)(1)(B) of the Internal Revenue Code, unless an agreement or stipulation of the parties otherwise provides.

ALLOCATION OF PARENTAL RESPONSIBILITY

ILLINOIS

750 Ill. Comp. Stat. Ann. 5/600 et seq. (West 2016)

[EDITORS' INTRODUCTION: Albertina Antognini, *From Citizenship to Custody: Unwed Fathers Abroad and at Home*, 36 HARV. J. L. & GENDER 405 (2013); J. Herbie DiFonzo, *Dilemmas of Shared Parenting in the 21st Century: How Law and Culture Shape Child Custody*, 43 HOFSTRA L. REV. 1003 (2015); Jeffrey A. Parness, *Survey of Illinois Law: Stepparent Childcare*, 38 S. ILL. U. L.J. 575 (2014); Jeffrey A. Parness, *Troxel Revisited: A New Approach to Third-Party Childcare*, 18 RICH. J.L. & PUB. INT. 227 (2015); Jeffrey A. Parness, *Federal Constitutional Childcare Interests and Superior Parental Rights in Illinois*, 33 N. ILL. U. L. REV. 305 (2013); Stacey Platt, *Set Another Place at the Table: Child Participation in Family Separation Cases*, 17 CARDOZO J. CONFLICT RESOL. 749 (2016); Ruth Zafran, *Children's Rights as Relational Rights: The Case of Relocation*, 18 AM. U. J. GENDER SOC. POL'Y & L. 163 (2010).]

§ 5/600. DEFINITIONS

(a) "Abuse" has the meaning ascribed to that term in Section 103 of the Illinois Domestic Violence Act of 1986.

(b) "Allocation judgment" means a judgment allocating parental responsibilities.

(c) "Caretaking functions" means tasks that involve interaction with a child or that direct, arrange, and supervise the interaction with and care of a child provided by others, or for obtaining the resources allowing for the provision of these functions. The term includes, but is not limited to, the following:

(1) satisfying a child's nutritional needs; managing a child's bedtime and wake-up routines; caring for a child when the child is sick or injured; being attentive to a child's personal hygiene needs, including washing, grooming, and dressing; playing with a child and ensuring the child attends scheduled extracurricular activities; protecting a child's physical safety; and providing transportation for a child;

(2) directing a child's various developmental needs, including the acquisition of motor and language skills, toilet training, self-confidence, and maturation;

(3) providing discipline, giving instruction in manners, assigning and supervising chores, and performing other tasks that attend to a child's needs for behavioral control and self-restraint;

(4) ensuring the child attends school, including remedial and special services appropriate to the child's needs and interests,

communicating with teachers and counselors, and supervising homework;

(5) helping a child develop and maintain appropriate interpersonal relationships with peers, siblings, and other family members;

(6) ensuring the child attends medical appointments and is available for medical follow-up and meeting the medical needs of the child in the home;

(7) providing moral and ethical guidance for a child; and

(8) arranging alternative care for a child by a family member, babysitter, or other child care provider or facility, including investigating such alternatives, communicating with providers, and supervising such care.

(d) "Parental responsibilities" means both parenting time and significant decision-making responsibilities with respect to a child.

(e) "Parenting time" means the time during which a parent is responsible for exercising caretaking functions and non-significant decision-making responsibilities with respect to the child.

(f) "Parenting plan" means a written agreement that allocates significant decision-making responsibilities, parenting time, or both.

(g) "Relocation" means:

(1) a change of residence from the child's current primary residence located in the county of Cook, DuPage, Kane, Lake, McHenry, or Will to a new residence within this State that is more than 25 miles from the child's current residence;

(2) a change of residence from the child's current primary residence located in a county not listed in paragraph (1) to a new residence within this State that is more than 50 miles from the child's current primary residence; or

(3) a change of residence from the child's current primary residence to a residence outside the borders of this State that is more than 25 miles from the current primary residence.

(h) "Religious upbringing" means the choice of religion or denomination of a religion, religious schooling, religious training, or participation in religious customs or practices.

(i) "Restriction of parenting time" means any limitation or condition placed on parenting time, including supervision.

(j) "Right of first refusal" has the meaning provided in subsection (b) of Section 602.3 of this Act.

(k) "Significant decision-making" means deciding issues of long-term importance in the life of a child.

(*l*) "Step-parent" means a person married to a child's parent, including a person married to the child's parent immediately prior to the parent's death.

(m) "Supervision" means the presence of a third party during a parent's exercise of parenting time.

§ 5/601.2.   JURISDICTION; COMMENCEMENT OF PROCEEDING

(a) A court of this State that is competent to allocate parental responsibilities has jurisdiction to make such an allocation in original or modification proceedings as provided in Section 201 of the Uniform Child-Custody Jurisdiction and Enforcement Act as adopted by this State.

(b) A proceeding for allocation of parental responsibilities with respect to a child is commenced in the court:

(1) by filing a petition for dissolution of marriage or legal separation or declaration of invalidity of marriage;

(2) by filing a petition for allocation of parental responsibilities with respect to the child in the county in which the child resides;

(3) by a person other than a parent, by filing a petition for allocation of parental responsibilities in the county in which the child is permanently resident or found, but only if he or she is not in the physical custody of one of his or her parents;

(4) by a step-parent, by filing a petition, if all of the following circumstances are met:

(A) the parent having the majority of parenting time is deceased or is disabled and cannot perform the duties of a parent to the child;

(B) the step-parent provided for the care, control, and welfare of the child prior to the initiation of proceedings for allocation of parental responsibilities;

(C) the child wishes to live with the step-parent; and

(D) it is alleged to be in the best interests and welfare of the child to live with the step-parent as provided in Section 602.5 of this Act; or

(5) when one of the parents is deceased, by a grandparent who is a parent or step-parent of a deceased parent, by filing a petition, if one or more of the following existed at the time of the parent's death:

(A) the surviving parent had been absent from the marital abode for more than one month without the spouse knowing his or her whereabouts;

(B) the surviving parent was in State or federal custody; or

(C) the surviving parent had: (i) received supervision for or been convicted of any violation of Section 11–1.20, 11–1.30, 11–1.40, 11–1.50, 11–1.60, 11–1.70, 12C–5, 12C–10, 12C–35, 12C–40, 12C–45, 18–6, 19–6, or Article 12 of the Criminal Code of 1961 or the Criminal Code of 2012 directed towards the deceased parent or the child; or (ii) received supervision or been convicted of violating an order of protection entered under Section 217, 218, or 219 of the Illinois Domestic Violence Act of 1986 for the protection of the deceased parent or the child.

(c) When a proceeding for allocation of parental responsibilities is commenced, the party commencing the action must, at least 30 days before any hearing on the petition, serve a written notice and a copy of the petition on the child's parent, guardian, person currently allocated parental responsibilities pursuant to subdivision (b)(4) or (b)(5) of Section 601.2, and any person with a pending motion for allocation of parental responsibilities with respect to the child. Nothing in this Section shall preclude a party in a proceeding for allocation of parental responsibilities from moving for a temporary order under Section 603.5.

§ 5/602.3.   CARE OF MINOR CHILDREN; RIGHT OF FIRST REFUSAL

(a) If the court awards parenting time to both parents under Section 602.7 or 602.8, the court may consider, consistent with the best interests of the child as defined in Section 602.7, whether to award to one or both of the parties the right of first refusal to provide child care for the minor child or children during the other parent's normal parenting time, unless the need for child care is attributable to an emergency.

(b) As used in this Section, "right of first refusal" means that if a party intends to leave the minor child or children with a substitute child-care provider for a significant period of time, that party must first offer the other party an opportunity to personally care for the minor child or children. The parties may agree to a right of first refusal that is consistent with the best interests of the minor child or children. If there is no agreement and the court determines that a right of first refusal is in the best interests of the minor child or children, the court shall consider and make provisions in its order for:

(1) the length and kind of child-care requirements invoking the right of first refusal;

(2) notification to the other parent and for his or her response;

(3) transportation requirements; and

(4) any other action necessary to protect and promote the best interest of the minor child or children.

(c) The right of first refusal may be enforced under Section 607.5 of this Act.

(d)   The right of first refusal is terminated upon the termination of the allocation of parental responsibilities or parenting time.

§ 5/602.5.   ALLOCATION OF PARENTAL RESPONSIBILITIES: DECISION-MAKING

(a)   Generally.   The   court   shall   allocate   decision-making responsibilities according to the child's best interests. Nothing in this Act requires that each parent be allocated decision-making responsibilities.

(b)   Allocation   of   significant   decision-making   responsibilities. Unless the parents otherwise agree in writing on an allocation of significant decision-making responsibilities, or the issue of the allocation of parental responsibilities has been reserved under Section 401, the court shall make the determination. The court shall allocate to one or both of the parents the significant decision-making responsibility for each significant issue affecting the child. Those significant issues shall include, without limitation, the following:

(1)   Education, including the choice of schools and tutors.

(2)   Health, including all decisions relating to the medical, dental, and psychological needs of the child and to the treatments arising or resulting from those needs.

(3)   Religion, subject to the following provisions:

(A)   The court shall allocate decision-making responsibility for the child's religious upbringing in accordance with any express or implied agreement between the parents.

(B)   The court shall consider evidence of the parents' past conduct as to the child's religious upbringing in allocating decision-making responsibilities consistent with demonstrated past conduct in the absence of an express or implied agreement between the parents.

(C)   The court shall not allocate any aspect of the child's religious upbringing if it determines that the parents do not or did not have an express or implied agreement for such religious upbringing or that there is insufficient evidence to demonstrate a course of conduct regarding the child's religious upbringing that could serve as a basis for any such order.

(4)   Extracurricular activities.

(c)   Determination of child's best interests. In determining the child's best interests for purposes of allocating significant decision-making responsibilities, the court shall consider all relevant factors, including, without limitation, the following:

(1)   the wishes of the child, taking into account the child's maturity and ability to express reasoned and independent preferences as to decision-making;

(2) the child's adjustment to his or her home, school, and community;

(3) the mental and physical health of all individuals involved;

(4) the ability of the parents to cooperate to make decisions, or the level of conflict between the parties that may affect their ability to share decision-making;

(5) the level of each parent's participation in past significant decision-making with respect to the child;

(6) any prior agreement or course of conduct between the parents relating to decision-making with respect to the child;

(7) the wishes of the parents;

(8) the child's needs;

(9) the distance between the parents' residences, the cost and difficulty of transporting the child, each parent's and the child's daily schedules, and the ability of the parents to cooperate in the arrangement;

(10) whether a restriction on decision-making is appropriate under Section 603.10;

(11) the willingness and ability of each parent to facilitate and encourage a close and continuing relationship between the other parent and the child;

(12) the physical violence or threat of physical violence by the child's parent directed against the child;

(13) the occurrence of abuse against the child or other member of the child's household;

(14) whether one of the parents is a sex offender, and if so, the exact nature of the offense and what, if any, treatment in which the parent has successfully participated; and

(15) any other factor that the court expressly finds to be relevant.

(d) A parent shall have sole responsibility for making routine decisions with respect to the child and for emergency decisions affecting the child's health and safety during that parent's parenting time.

(e) In allocating significant decision-making responsibilities, the court shall not consider conduct of a parent that does not affect that parent's relationship to the child.

§ 5/602.7.   ALLOCATION OF PARENTAL RESPONSIBILITIES: PARENTING TIME

(a) Best interests. The court shall allocate parenting time according to the child's best interests.

(b) Allocation of parenting time. Unless the parents present a mutually agreed written parenting plan and that plan is approved by the court, the court shall allocate parenting time. It is presumed both parents are fit and the court shall not place any restrictions on parenting time as defined in Section 600 and described in Section 603.10, unless it finds by a preponderance of the evidence that a parent's exercise of parenting time would seriously endanger the child's physical, mental, moral, or emotional health.

In determining the child's best interests for purposes of allocating parenting time, the court shall consider all relevant factors, including, without limitation, the following:

(1) the wishes of each parent seeking parenting time;

(2) the wishes of the child, taking into account the child's maturity and ability to express reasoned and independent preferences as to parenting time;

(3) the amount of time each parent spent performing caretaking functions with respect to the child in the 24 months preceding the filing of any petition for allocation of parental responsibilities or, if the child is under 2 years of age, since the child's birth;

(4) any prior agreement or course of conduct between the parents relating to caretaking functions with respect to the child;

(5) the interaction and interrelationship of the child with his or her parents and siblings and with any other person who may significantly affect the child's best interests;

(6) the child's adjustment to his or her home, school, and community;

(7) the mental and physical health of all individuals involved;

(8) the child's needs;

(9) the distance between the parents' residences, the cost and difficulty of transporting the child, each parent's and the child's daily schedules, and the ability of the parents to cooperate in the arrangement;

(10) whether a restriction on parenting time is appropriate;

(11) the physical violence or threat of physical violence by the child's parent directed against the child or other member of the child's household;

(12) the willingness and ability of each parent to place the needs of the child ahead of his or her own needs;

(13) the willingness and ability of each parent to facilitate and encourage a close and continuing relationship between the other parent and the child;

(14) the occurrence of abuse against the child or other member of the child's household;

(15) whether one of the parents is a convicted sex offender or lives with a convicted sex offender and, if so, the exact nature of the offense and what if any treatment the offender has successfully participated in; the parties are entitled to a hearing on the issues raised in this paragraph (15);

(16) the terms of a parent's military family-care plan that a parent must complete before deployment if a parent is a member of the United States Armed Forces who is being deployed; and

(17) any other factor that the court expressly finds to be relevant.

(c) In allocating parenting time, the court shall not consider conduct of a parent that does not affect that parent's relationship to the child.

(d) Upon motion, the court may allow a parent who is deployed or who has orders to be deployed as a member of the United States Armed Forces to designate a person known to the child to exercise reasonable substitute visitation on behalf of the deployed parent, if the court determines that substitute visitation is in the best interests of the child. In determining whether substitute visitation is in the best interests of the child, the court shall consider all of the relevant factors listed in subsection (b) of this Section and apply those factors to the person designated as a substitute for the deployed parent for visitation purposes. Visitation orders entered under this subsection are subject to subsections (e) and (f) of Section 602.9 and subsections (c) and (d) of Section 603.10.

(e) If the street address of a parent is not identified pursuant to Section 708 of this Act, the court shall require the parties to identify reasonable alternative arrangements for parenting time by the other parent including, but not limited to, parenting time of the minor child at the residence of another person or at a local public or private facility.

§ 5/602.8.   PARENTING   TIME   BY   PARENTS   NOT   ALLOCATED
            SIGNIFICANT DECISION-MAKING RESPONSIBILITIES

(a) A parent who has established parentage under the laws of this State and who is not granted significant decision-making responsibilities for a child is entitled to reasonable parenting time with the child, subject to subsections (d) and (e) of Section 603.10 of this Act, unless the court finds, after a hearing, that the parenting time would seriously endanger the child's mental, moral, or physical health or significantly impair the child's emotional development. The order setting forth parenting time shall be in the child's best interests pursuant to the factors set forth in subsection (b) of Section 602.7 of this Act.

(b) The court may modify an order granting or denying parenting time pursuant to Section 610.5 of this Act. The court may restrict parenting time, and modify an order restricting parenting time, pursuant to Section 603.10 of this Act.

(c) If the street address of the parent allocated parental responsibilities is not identified, pursuant to Section 708 of this Act, the court shall require the parties to identify reasonable alternative arrangements for parenting time by a parent not allocated parental responsibilities, including but not limited to parenting time of the minor child at the residence of another person or at a local public or private facility.

§ 5/602.9. VISITATION BY CERTAIN NON-PARENTS

(a) As used in this Section:

(1) "electronic communication" means time that a grandparent, great-grandparent, sibling, or step-parent spends with a child during which the child is not in the person's actual physical custody, but which is facilitated by the use of communication tools such as the telephone, electronic mail, instant messaging, video conferencing or other wired or wireless technologies via the Internet, or another medium of communication;

(2) "sibling" means a brother or sister either of the whole blood or the half blood, stepbrother, or stepsister of the minor child;

(3) "step-parent" means a person married to a child's parent, including a person married to the child's parent immediately prior to the parent's death; and

(4) "visitation" means in-person time spent between a child and the child's grandparent, great-grandparent, sibling, step-parent, or any person designated under subsection (d) of Section 602.7. In appropriate circumstances, visitation may include electronic communication under conditions and at times determined by the court.

(b) General provisions.

(1) An appropriate person, as identified in subsection (c) of this Section, may bring an action in circuit court by petition, or by filing a petition in a pending dissolution proceeding or any other proceeding that involves parental responsibilities or visitation issues regarding the child, requesting visitation with the child pursuant to this Section. If there is not a pending proceeding involving parental responsibilities or visitation with the child, the petition for visitation with the child must be filed in the county in which the child resides. Notice of the petition shall be given as provided in subsection (c) of Section 601.2 of this Act.

(2) This Section does not apply to a child:

(A) in whose interests a petition is pending under Section 2–13 of the Juvenile Court Act of 1987; or

(B) in whose interests a petition to adopt by an unrelated person is pending under the Adoption Act; or

(C) who has been voluntarily surrendered by the parent or parents, except for a surrender to the Department of Children and Family Services or a foster care facility; or

(D) who has been previously adopted by an individual or individuals who are not related to the biological parents of the child or who is the subject of a pending adoption petition by an individual or individuals who are not related to the biological parents of the child; or

(E) who has been relinquished pursuant to the Abandoned Newborn Infant Protection Act.

(3) A petition for visitation may be filed under this Section only if there has been an unreasonable denial of visitation by a parent and the denial has caused the child undue mental, physical, or emotional harm.

(4) There is a rebuttable presumption that a fit parent's actions and decisions regarding grandparent, great-grandparent, sibling, or step-parent visitation are not harmful to the child's mental, physical, or emotional health. The burden is on the party filing a petition under this Section to prove that the parent's actions and decisions regarding visitation will cause undue harm to the child's mental, physical, or emotional health.

(5) In determining whether to grant visitation, the court shall consider the following:

(A) the wishes of the child, taking into account the child's maturity and ability to express reasoned and independent preferences as to visitation;

(B) the mental and physical health of the child;

(C) the mental and physical health of the grandparent, great-grandparent, sibling, or step-parent;

(D) the length and quality of the prior relationship between the child and the grandparent, great-grandparent, sibling, or step-parent;

(E) the good faith of the party in filing the petition;

(F) the good faith of the person denying visitation;

(G) the quantity of the visitation time requested and the potential adverse impact that visitation would have on the child's customary activities;

(H) any other fact that establishes that the loss of the relationship between the petitioner and the child is likely to unduly harm the child's mental, physical, or emotional health; and

(I) whether visitation can be structured in a way to minimize the child's exposure to conflicts between the adults.

(6) Any visitation rights granted under this Section before the filing of a petition for adoption of the child shall automatically terminate by operation of law upon the entry of an order terminating parental rights or granting the adoption of the child, whichever is earlier. If the person or persons who adopted the child are related to the child, as defined by Section 1 of the Adoption Act, any person who was related to the child as grandparent, great-grandparent, or sibling prior to the adoption shall have standing to bring an action under this Section requesting visitation with the child.

(7) The court may order visitation rights for the grandparent, great-grandparent, sibling, or step-parent that include reasonable access without requiring overnight or possessory visitation.

(c) Visitation by grandparents, great-grandparents, step-parents, and siblings.

(1) Grandparents, great-grandparents, step-parents, and siblings of a minor child who is one year old or older may bring a petition for visitation and electronic communication under this Section if there is an unreasonable denial of visitation by a parent that causes undue mental, physical, or emotional harm to the child and if at least one of the following conditions exists:

(A) the child's other parent is deceased or has been missing for at least 90 days. For the purposes of this subsection a parent is considered to be missing if the parent's location has not been determined and the parent has been reported as missing to a law enforcement agency; or

(B) a parent of the child is incompetent as a matter of law; or

(C) a parent has been incarcerated in jail or prison for a period in excess of 90 days immediately prior to the filing of the petition; or

(D) the child's parents have been granted a dissolution of marriage or have been legally separated from each other or there is pending a dissolution proceeding involving a parent of the child or another court proceeding involving parental responsibilities or visitation of the child (other than an adoption proceeding of an unrelated child, a proceeding under Article II of the Juvenile Court Act of 1987, or an action for an order of protection under the Illinois Domestic Violence Act of 1986 or Article 112A of the Code of Criminal Procedure of 1963) and at least one parent does not object to the grandparent, great-grandparent, step-parent, or sibling having visitation with the child. The visitation of the grandparent, great-grandparent, step-parent, or sibling must not diminish the parenting time of the parent who is not related to the grandparent, great-grandparent, step-parent, or sibling seeking visitation; or

(E) the child is born to parents who are not married to each other, the parents are not living together, and the petitioner is a grandparent, great-grandparent, step-parent, or sibling of the child, and parentage has been established by a court of competent jurisdiction.

(2) In addition to the factors set forth in subdivision (b)(5) of this Section, the court should consider:

(A) whether the child resided with the petitioner for at least 6 consecutive months with or without a parent present;

(B) whether the child had frequent and regular contact or visitation with the petitioner for at least 12 consecutive months; and

(C) whether the grandparent, great-grandparent, sibling, or step-parent was a primary caretaker of the child for a period of not less than 6 consecutive months within the 24-month period immediately preceding the commencement of the proceeding.

(3) An order granting visitation privileges under this Section is subject to subsections (c) and (d) of Section 603.10.

(4) A petition for visitation privileges may not be filed pursuant to this subsection (c) by the parents or grandparents of a parent of the child if parentage between the child and the related parent has not been legally established.

(d) Modification of visitation orders.

(1) Unless by stipulation of the parties, no motion to modify a grandparent, great-grandparent, sibling, or step-parent visitation order may be made earlier than 2 years after the date the order was filed, unless the court permits it to be made on the basis of affidavits that there is reason to believe the child's present environment may endanger seriously the child's mental, physical, or emotional health.

(2) The court shall not modify an order that grants visitation to a grandparent, great-grandparent, sibling, or step-parent unless it finds by clear and convincing evidence, upon the basis of facts that have arisen since the prior visitation order or that were unknown to the court at the time of entry of the prior visitation order, that a change has occurred in the circumstances of the child or his or her parent, and that the modification is necessary to protect the mental, physical, or emotional health of the child. The court shall state in its decision specific findings of fact in support of its modification or termination of the grandparent, great-grandparent, sibling, or step-parent visitation. A child's parent may always petition to modify

visitation upon changed circumstances when necessary to promote the child's best interests.

(3) Notice of a motion requesting modification of a visitation order shall be provided as set forth in subsection (c) of Section 601.2 of this Act.

(4) Attorney's fees and costs shall be assessed against a party seeking modification of the visitation order if the court finds that the modification action is vexatious and constitutes harassment.

(e) No child's grandparent, great-grandparent, sibling, or step-parent, or any person to whom the court is considering granting visitation privileges pursuant to subsection (d) of Section 602.7, who was convicted of any offense involving an illegal sex act perpetrated upon a victim less than 18 years of age including, but not limited to, offenses for violations of Section 11–1.20, 11–1.30, 11–1.40, 11–1.50, 11–1.60, 11–1.70, or Article 12 of the Criminal Code of 1961 or the Criminal Code of 2012, is entitled to visitation while incarcerated or while on parole, probation, conditional discharge, periodic imprisonment, or mandatory supervised release for that offense, and upon discharge from incarceration for a misdemeanor offense or upon discharge from parole, probation, conditional discharge, periodic imprisonment, or mandatory supervised release for a felony offense. Visitation shall be denied until the person successfully completes a treatment program approved by the court. Upon completion of treatment, the court may deny visitation based on the factors listed in subdivision (b)(5) of Section 607 of this Act.

(f) No child's grandparent, great-grandparent, sibling, or step-parent, or any person to whom the court is considering granting visitation privileges pursuant to subsection (d) of Section 602.7, may be granted visitation if he or she has been convicted of first degree murder of a parent, grandparent, great-grandparent, or sibling of the child who is the subject of the visitation request. Pursuant to a motion to modify visitation, the court shall revoke visitation rights previously granted to any person who would otherwise be entitled to petition for visitation rights under this Section or granted visitation under subsection (d) of Section 602.7, if the person has been convicted of first degree murder of a parent, grandparent, great-grandparent, or sibling of the child who is the subject of the visitation order. Until an order is entered pursuant to this subsection, no person may visit, with the child present, a person who has been convicted of first degree murder of the parent, grandparent, great-grandparent, or sibling of the child without the consent of the child's parent, other than a parent convicted of first degree murder as set forth herein, or legal guardian.

§ 5/602.10. PARENTING PLAN

(a) Filing of parenting plan. All parents, within 120 days after service or filing of any petition for allocation of parental responsibilities, must file with the court, either jointly or separately, a proposed parenting plan. The time period for filing a parenting plan may be extended by the court for good cause shown.

(b) No parenting plan filed. In the absence of filing of one or more parenting plans, the court must conduct an evidentiary hearing to allocate parental responsibilities.

(c) Mediation. The court shall order mediation to assist the parents in formulating or modifying a parenting plan or in implementing a parenting plan unless the court determines that impediments to mediation exist. Costs under this subsection shall be allocated between the parties pursuant to the applicable statute or Supreme Court Rule.

(d) Parents' agreement on parenting plan. The parenting plan must be in writing and signed by both parents. The parents must submit the parenting plan to the court for approval within 120 days after service of a petition for allocation of parental responsibilities or the filing of an appearance, except for good cause shown. Notwithstanding the provisions above, the parents may agree upon and submit a parenting plan at any time after the commencement of a proceeding until prior to the entry of a judgment of dissolution of marriage. The agreement is binding upon the court unless it finds, after considering the circumstances of the parties and any other relevant evidence produced by the parties, that the agreement is unconscionable. If the court does not approve the parenting plan, the court shall make express findings of the reason or reasons for its refusal to approve the plan. The court, on its own motion, may conduct an evidentiary hearing to determine whether the parenting plan is in the child's best interests.

(e) Parents cannot agree on parenting plan. When parents fail to submit an agreed parenting plan, each parent must file and submit a written, signed parenting plan to the court within 120 days after the filing of an appearance, except for good cause shown. The court's determination of parenting time should be based on the child's best interests. The filing of the plan may be excused by the court if:

(1) the parties have commenced mediation for the purpose of formulating a parenting plan; or

(2) the parents have agreed in writing to extend the time for filing a proposed plan and the court has approved such an extension; or

(3) the court orders otherwise for good cause shown.

(f) Parenting plan contents. At a minimum, a parenting plan must set forth the following:

(1) an allocation of significant decision-making responsibilities;

(2) provisions for the child's living arrangements and for each parent's parenting time, including either:

(A) a schedule that designates in which parent's home the minor child will reside on given days; or

(B) a formula or method for determining such a schedule in sufficient detail to be enforced in a subsequent proceeding;

(3) a mediation provision addressing any proposed reallocation of parenting time or regarding the terms of allocation of parental responsibilities, except that this provision is not required if one parent is allocated all significant decision-making responsibilities;

(4) each parent's right of access to medical, dental, and psychological records (subject to the Mental Health and Developmental Disabilities Confidentiality Act), child care records, and school and extracurricular records, reports, and schedules, unless expressly denied by a court order or denied under subsection (g) of Section 602.5;

(5) a designation of the parent who will be denominated as the parent with the majority of parenting time for purposes of Section 606.10;

(6) the child's residential address for school enrollment purposes only;

(7) each parent's residence address and phone number, and each parent's place of employment and employment address and phone number;

(8) a requirement that a parent changing his or her residence provide at least 60 days prior written notice of the change to any other parent under the parenting plan or allocation judgment, unless such notice is impracticable or unless otherwise ordered by the court. If such notice is impracticable, written notice shall be given at the earliest date practicable. At a minimum, the notice shall set forth the following:

(A) the intended date of the change of residence; and

(B) the address of the new residence;

(9) provisions requiring each parent to notify the other of emergencies, health care, travel plans, or other significant child-related issues;

(10) transportation arrangements between the parents;

(11) provisions for communications, including electronic communications, with the child during the other parent's parenting time;

(12) provisions for resolving issues arising from a parent's future relocation, if applicable;

(13) provisions for future modifications of the parenting plan, if specified events occur;

(14) provisions for the exercise of the right of first refusal, if so desired, that are consistent with the best interests of the minor child; provisions in the plan for the exercise of the right of first refusal must include:

(i) the length and kind of child-care requirements invoking the right of first refusal;

(ii) notification to the other parent and for his or her response;

(iii) transportation requirements; and

(iv) any other provision related to the exercise of the right of first refusal necessary to protect and promote the best interests of the minor child; and

(15) any other provision that addresses the child's best interests or that will otherwise facilitate cooperation between the parents.

The personal information under items (6), (7), and (8) of this subsection is not required if there is evidence of or the parenting plan states that there is a history of domestic violence or abuse, or it is shown that the release of the information is not in the child's or parent's best interests.

(g) The court shall conduct a trial or hearing to determine a plan which maximizes the child's relationship and access to both parents and shall ensure that the access and the overall plan are in the best interests of the child. The court shall take the parenting plans into consideration when determining parenting time and responsibilities at trial or hearing.

(h) The court may consider, consistent with the best interests of the child as defined in Section 602.7 of this Act, whether to award to one or both of the parties the right of first refusal in accordance with Section 602.3 of this Act.

§ 5/602.11. ACCESS TO HEALTH CARE, CHILD CARE, AND SCHOOL RECORDS BY PARENTS

(a) Notwithstanding any other provision of law, access to records and information pertaining to a child including, but not limited to, medical, dental, child care, and school records shall not be denied to a parent for the reason that such parent has not been allocated parental responsibility. A parent who is not allocated parenting time (not denied parental responsibility) is not entitled to access to the child's school or health care records unless a court finds that it is in the child's best interests to provide those records to the parent.

(b) Health care professionals and health care providers shall grant access to health care records and information pertaining to a child to both parents, unless the health care professional or health care provider receives a court order or judgment that denies access to a specific individual. Except as may be provided by court order, no parent who is a named respondent in an order of protection issued pursuant to the Illinois Domestic Violence Act of 1986 or the Code of Criminal Procedure of 1963 shall have access to the health care records of a child who is a protected person under the order of protection provided the health care professional or health care provider has received a copy of the order of protection. Access to health care records is denied under this Section for as long as the order of protection remains in effect as specified in the order of protection or as otherwise determined by court order.

§ 5/603.5.   TEMPORARY ORDERS

(a) A court may order a temporary allocation of parental responsibilities in the child's best interests before the entry of a final allocation judgment. Any temporary allocation shall be made in accordance with the standards set forth in Sections 602.5 and 602.7: (i) after a hearing; or (ii) if there is no objection, on the basis of a parenting plan that, at a minimum, complies with subsection (f) of Section 602.10.

(b) A temporary order allocating parental responsibilities shall be deemed vacated when the action in which it was granted is dismissed, unless a parent moves to continue the action for allocation of parental responsibilities filed under Section 601.5.

§ 5/603.10.   RESTRICTION OF PARENTAL RESPONSIBILITIES

(a) After a hearing, if the court finds by a preponderance of the evidence that a parent engaged in any conduct that seriously endangered the child's mental, moral, or physical health or that significantly impaired the child's emotional development, the court shall enter orders as necessary to protect the child. Such orders may include, but are not limited to, orders for one or more of the following:

(1) a reduction, elimination, or other adjustment of the parent's decision-making responsibilities or parenting time, or both decision-making responsibilities and parenting time;

(2) supervision, including ordering the Department of Children and Family Services to exercise continuing supervision under Section 5 of the Children and Family Services Act;

(3) requiring the exchange of the child between the parents through an intermediary or in a protected setting;

(4) restraining a parent's communication with or proximity to the other parent or the child;

(5) requiring a parent to abstain from possessing or consuming alcohol or non-prescribed drugs while exercising parenting time with the child and within a specified period immediately preceding the exercise of parenting time;

(6) restricting the presence of specific persons while a parent is exercising parenting time with the child;

(7) requiring a parent to post a bond to secure the return of the child following the parent's exercise of parenting time or to secure other performance required by the court;

(8) requiring a parent to complete a treatment program for perpetrators of abuse, for drug or alcohol abuse, or for other behavior that is the basis for restricting parental responsibilities under this Section; and

(9) any other constraints or conditions that the court deems necessary to provide for the child's safety or welfare.

(b) The court may modify an order restricting parental responsibilities if, after a hearing, the court finds by a preponderance of the evidence that a modification is in the child's best interests based on (i) a change of circumstances that occurred after the entry of an order restricting parental responsibilities; or (ii) conduct of which the court was previously unaware that seriously endangers the child. In determining whether to modify an order under this subsection, the court must consider factors that include, but need not be limited to, the following:

(1) abuse, neglect, or abandonment of the child;

(2) abusing or allowing abuse of another person that had an impact upon the child;

(3) use of drugs, alcohol, or any other substance in a way that interferes with the parent's ability to perform caretaking functions with respect to the child; and

(4) persistent continuing interference with the other parent's access to the child, except for actions taken with a reasonable, good-faith belief that they are necessary to protect the child's safety pending adjudication of the facts underlying that belief, provided that the interfering parent initiates a proceeding to determine those facts as soon as practicable.

(c) An order granting parenting time to a parent or visitation to another person may be revoked by the court if that parent or other person is found to have knowingly used his or her parenting time or visitation to facilitate contact between the child and a parent who has been barred from contact with the child or to have knowingly used his or her parenting time or visitation to facilitate contact with the child that violates any restrictions imposed on a parent's parenting time by a court of competent jurisdiction. Nothing in this subsection limits a court's authority to enforce its orders in any other manner authorized by law.

(d) If parenting time of a parent is restricted, an order granting visitation to a non-parent with a child or an order granting parenting time to the other parent shall contain the following language:

"If a person granted parenting time or visitation under this order uses that time to facilitate contact between the child and a parent whose parenting time is restricted, or if such a person violates any restrictions placed on parenting time or visitation by the court, the parenting time or visitation granted under this order shall be revoked until further order of court."

(e)   A parent who, after a hearing, is determined by the court to have been convicted of any offense involving an illegal sex act perpetrated upon a victim less than 18 years of age, including but not limited to an offense under Article 11 of the Criminal Code of 2012, is not entitled to parenting time while incarcerated or while on parole, probation, conditional discharge, periodic imprisonment, or mandatory supervised release for a felony offense, until the parent complies with such terms and conditions as the court determines are in the child's best interests, taking into account the exact nature of the offense and what, if any, treatment in which the parent successfully participated.

(f)   A parent may not, while the child is present, visit any person granted visitation or parenting time who has been convicted of first degree murder, unless the court finds, after considering all relevant factors, including those set forth in subsection (b) of Section 602.7, that it would be in the child's best interests to allow the child to be present during such a visit.

§ 5/604.10.   INTERVIEWS; EVALUATIONS; INVESTIGATION

(a)   Court's interview of child. The court may interview the child in chambers to ascertain the child's wishes as to the allocation of parental responsibilities. Counsel shall be present at the interview unless otherwise agreed upon by the parties. The entire interview shall be recorded by a court reporter. The transcript of the interview shall be filed under seal and released only upon order of the court. The cost of the court reporter and transcript shall be paid by the court.

(b)   Court's professional. The court may seek the advice of any professional, whether or not regularly employed by the court, to assist the court in determining the child's best interests. The advice to the court shall be in writing and sent by the professional to counsel for the parties and to the court, under seal. The writing may be admitted into evidence without testimony from its author, unless a party objects. A professional consulted by the court shall testify as the court's witness and be subject to cross-examination. The court shall order all costs and fees of the professional to be paid by one or more of the parties, subject to reallocation in accordance with subsection (a) of Section 508.

The professional's report must, at a minimum, set forth the following:

> (1)   a description of the procedures employed during the evaluation;

> (2)   a report of the data collected;

> (3)   all test results;

(4)   any conclusions of the professional relating to the allocation of parental responsibilities under Sections 602.5 and 602.7;

(5)   any recommendations of the professional concerning the allocation of parental responsibilities or the child's relocation; and

(6)   an explanation of any limitations in the evaluation or any reservations of the professional regarding the resulting recommendations.

The professional shall send his or her report to all attorneys of record, and to any party not represented, at least 60 days before the hearing on the allocation of parental responsibilities. The court shall examine and consider the professional's report only after it has been admitted into evidence or after the parties have waived their right to cross-examine the professional.

(c)   Evaluation by a party's retained professional. In a proceeding to allocate parental responsibilities or to relocate a child, upon notice and motion made by a parent or any party to the litigation within a reasonable time before trial, the court shall order an evaluation to assist the court in determining the child's best interests unless the court finds that an evaluation under this Section is untimely or not in the best interests of the child. The evaluation may be in place of or in addition to any advice given to the court by a professional under subsection (b). A motion for an evaluation under this subsection must, at a minimum, identify the proposed evaluator and the evaluator's specialty or discipline. An order for an evaluation under this subsection must set forth the evaluator's name, address, and telephone number and the time, place, conditions, and scope of the evaluation. No person shall be required to travel an unreasonable distance for the evaluation. The party requesting the evaluation shall pay the evaluator's fees and costs unless otherwise ordered by the court.

The evaluator's report must, at a minimum, set forth the following:

(1)   a description of the procedures employed during the evaluation;

(2)   a report of the data collected;

(3)   all test results;

(4)   any conclusions of the evaluator relating to the allocation of parental responsibilities under Sections 602.5 and 602.7;

(5)   any recommendations of the evaluator concerning the allocation of parental responsibilities or the child's relocation; and

(6)   an explanation of any limitations in the evaluation or any reservations of the evaluator regarding the resulting recommendations.

A party who retains a professional to conduct an evaluation under this subsection shall cause the evaluator's written report to be sent to the attorneys of record no less than 60 days before the hearing on the allocation of parental responsibilities, unless otherwise ordered by the court; if a party fails to comply with this provision, the court may not admit the evaluator's report into evidence and may not allow the evaluator to testify.

The party calling an evaluator to testify at trial shall disclose the evaluator as a controlled expert witness in accordance with the Supreme Court Rules.

Any party to the litigation may call the evaluator as a witness. That party shall pay the evaluator's fees and costs for testifying, unless otherwise ordered by the court.

(d) Investigation. Upon notice and a motion by a parent or any party to the litigation, or upon the court's own motion, the court may order an investigation and report to assist the court in allocating parental responsibilities. The investigation may be made by any agency, private entity, or individual deemed appropriate by the court. The agency, private entity, or individual appointed by the court must have expertise in the area of allocation of parental responsibilities.

The court shall specify the purpose and scope of the investigation.

The investigator's report must, at a minimum, set forth the following:

(1) a description of the procedures employed during the investigation;

(2) a report of the data collected;

(3) all test results;

(4) any conclusions of the investigator relating to the allocation of parental responsibilities under Sections 602.5 and 602.7;

(5) any recommendations of the investigator concerning the allocation of parental responsibilities or the child's relocation; and

(6) an explanation of any limitations in the investigation or any reservations of the investigator regarding the resulting recommendations.

The investigator shall send his or her report to all attorneys of record, and to any party not represented, at least 60 days before the hearing on the allocation of parental responsibilities. The court shall examine and consider the investigator's report only after it has been admitted into evidence or after the parties have waived their right to cross-examine the investigator.

The investigator shall make available to all attorneys of record, and to any party not represented, the investigator's file, and the names and addresses of all persons whom the investigator has consulted, except that if such disclosure would risk abuse to the party or any member of the party's immediate family or household or reveal the confidential address of a shelter for domestic violence victims, that address may be omitted from the report. Any party to the proceeding may call the investigator, or any person consulted by the investigator as a court's witness, for cross-examination. No fees shall be paid for any investigation by a governmental agency. The fees incurred by any other investigator shall be allocated in accordance with Section 508.

§ 5/606.5.   HEARINGS

(a)   Proceedings to allocate parental responsibilities shall receive priority in being set for hearing.

(b)   The court, without a jury, shall determine questions of law and fact.

(c)   Previous statements made by the child relating to any allegations that the child is an abused or neglected child within the meaning of the Abused and Neglected Child Reporting Act, or an abused or neglected minor within the meaning of the Juvenile Court Act of 1987, shall be admissible in evidence in a hearing concerning allocation of parental responsibilities in accordance with Section 11.1 of the Abused and Neglected Child Reporting Act. No such statement, however, if uncorroborated and not subject to cross-examination, shall be sufficient in itself to support a finding of abuse or neglect.

(d)   If the court finds that a public hearing may be detrimental to the child's best interests, the court shall exclude the public from the hearing, but the court may admit any person having:

(1)   a direct and legitimate interest in the case; or

(2)   a legitimate educational or research interest in the work of the court, but only with the permission of both parties and subject to court approval.

(e)   The court may make an appropriate order sealing the records of any interview, report, investigation, or testimony.

§ 5/606.10.   DESIGNATION OF CUSTODIAN FOR PURPOSES OF OTHER STATUTES

Designation of custodian for purposes of other statutes. Solely for the purposes of all State and federal statutes that require a designation or determination of custody or a custodian, a parenting plan shall designate the parent who is allocated the majority of parenting time. This designation shall not affect parents' rights and responsibilities under the parenting plan. For purposes of Section 10–20.12b of the School Code only, the parent with the majority of parenting time is considered to have legal custody.

§ 5/607.5. ABUSE OF ALLOCATED PARENTING TIME

(a) The court shall provide an expedited procedure for the enforcement of allocated parenting time.

(b) An action for the enforcement of allocated parenting time may be commenced by a parent or a person appointed under Section 506 by filing a petition setting forth: (i) the petitioner's name and residence address or mailing address, except that if the petition states that disclosure of petitioner's address would risk abuse of petitioner or any member of petitioner's family or household or reveal the confidential address of a shelter for domestic violence victims, that address may be omitted from the petition; (ii) the respondent's name and place of residence, place of employment, or mailing address; (iii) the terms of the parenting plan or allocation judgment then in effect; (iv) the nature of the violation of the allocation of parenting time, giving dates and other relevant information; and (v) that a reasonable attempt was made to resolve the dispute.

(c) If the court finds by a preponderance of the evidence that a parent has not complied with allocated parenting time according to an approved parenting plan or a court order, the court, in the child's best interests, shall issue an order that may include one or more of the following:

(1) an imposition of additional terms and conditions consistent with the court's previous allocation of parenting time or other order;

(2) a requirement that either or both of the parties attend a parental education program at the expense of the non-complying parent;

(3) upon consideration of all relevant factors, particularly a history or possibility of domestic violence, a requirement that the parties participate in family or individual counseling, the expense of which shall be allocated by the court;

(4) a requirement that the non-complying parent post a cash bond or other security to ensure future compliance, including a provision that the bond or other security may be forfeited to the other parent for payment of expenses on behalf of the child as the court shall direct;

(5) a requirement that makeup parenting time be provided for the aggrieved parent or child under the following conditions:

(A) that the parenting time is of the same type and duration as the parenting time that was denied, including but not limited to parenting time during weekends, on holidays, and on weekdays and during times when the child is not in school;

(B) that the parenting time is made up within 6 months after the noncompliance occurs, unless the period of time or holiday cannot be made up within 6 months, in which case the parenting time shall be made up within one year after the noncompliance occurs;

(6) a finding that the non-complying parent is in contempt of court;

(7) an imposition on the non-complying parent of an appropriate civil fine per incident of denied parenting time;

(8) a requirement that the non-complying parent reimburse the other parent for all reasonable expenses incurred as a result of the violation of the parenting plan or court order; and

(9) any other provision that may promote the child's best interests.

(d) In addition to any other order entered under subsection (c), except for good cause shown, the court shall order a parent who has failed to provide allocated parenting time or to exercise allocated parenting time to pay the aggrieved party his or her reasonable attorney's fees, court costs, and expenses associated with an action brought under this Section. If the court finds that the respondent in an action brought under this Section has not violated the allocated parenting time, the court may order the petitioner to pay the respondent's reasonable attorney's fees, court costs, and expenses incurred in the action.

(e) Nothing in this Section precludes a party from maintaining any other action as provided by law.

(f) When the court issues an order holding a party in contempt for violation of a parenting time order and finds that the party engaged in parenting time abuse, the court may order one or more of the following:

(1) Suspension of a party's Illinois driving privileges pursuant to Section 7–703 of the Illinois Vehicle Code until the court determines that the party is in compliance with the parenting time order. The court may also order that a party be issued a family financial responsibility driving permit that would allow limited driving privileges for employment, for medical purposes, and to transport a child to or from scheduled parenting time in order to comply with a parenting time order in accordance with subsection (a–1) of Section 7–702.1 of the Illinois Vehicle Code.

(2) Placement of a party on probation with such conditions of probation as the court deems advisable.

(3) Sentencing of a party to periodic imprisonment for a period not to exceed 6 months; provided, that the court may permit the party to be released for periods of time during the day or night to:

(A) work; or

(B) conduct a business or other self-employed occupation.

(4)   Find that a party in engaging in parenting time abuse is guilty of a petty offense and should be fined an amount of no more than $500 for each finding of parenting time abuse.

(g)   When the court issues an order holding a party in contempt of court for violation of a parenting order, the clerk shall transmit a copy of the contempt order to the sheriff of the county. The sheriff shall furnish a copy of each contempt order to the Department of State Police on a daily basis in the form and manner required by the Department. The Department shall maintain a complete record and index of the contempt orders and make this data available to all local law enforcement agencies.

(h)   Nothing contained in this Section shall be construed to limit the court's contempt power.

§ 5/609.2.   PARENT'S RELOCATION

(a)   A parent's relocation constitutes a substantial change in circumstances for purposes of Section 610.5.

(b)   A parent who has been allocated a majority of parenting time or either parent who has been allocated equal parenting time may seek to relocate with a child.

(c)   A parent intending a relocation, as that term is defined in paragraph (1), (2), or (3) of subsection (g) of Section 600 of this Act, must provide written notice of the relocation to the other parent under the parenting plan or allocation judgment. A copy of the notice required under this Section shall be filed with the clerk of the circuit court. The court may waive or seal some or all of the information required in the notice if there is a history of domestic violence.

(d)   The notice must provide at least 60 days' written notice before the relocation unless such notice is impracticable (in which case written notice shall be given at the earliest date practicable) or unless otherwise ordered by the court. At a minimum, the notice must set forth the following:

(1)   the intended date of the parent's relocation;

(2)   the address of the parent's intended new residence, if known; and

(3)   the length of time the relocation will last, if the relocation is not for an indefinite or permanent period.

The court may consider a parent's failure to comply with the notice requirements of this Section without good cause (i) as a factor in determining whether the parent's relocation is in good faith; and (ii) as a basis for awarding reasonable attorney's fees and costs resulting from the parent's failure to comply with these provisions.

(e)   If the non-relocating parent signs the notice that was provided pursuant to subsection (c) and the relocating parent files the notice with the court, relocation shall be allowed without any further court action.

The court shall modify the parenting plan or allocation judgment to accommodate a parent's relocation as agreed by the parents, as long as the agreed modification is in the child's best interests.

(f)   If the non-relocating parent objects to the relocation, fails to sign the notice provided under subsection (c), or the parents cannot agree on modification of the parenting plan or allocation judgment, the parent seeking relocation must file a petition seeking permission to relocate.

(g)   The court shall modify the parenting plan or allocation judgment in accordance with the child's best interests. The court shall consider the following factors:

(1)   the circumstances and reasons for the intended relocation;

(2)   the reasons, if any, why a parent is objecting to the intended relocation;

(3)   the history and quality of each parent's relationship with the child and specifically whether a parent has substantially failed or refused to exercise the parental responsibilities allocated to him or her under the parenting plan or allocation judgment;

(4)   the educational opportunities for the child at the existing location and at the proposed new location;

(5)   the presence or absence of extended family at the existing location and at the proposed new location;

(6)   the anticipated impact of the relocation on the child;

(7)   whether the court will be able to fashion a reasonable allocation of parental responsibilities between all parents if the relocation occurs;

(8)   the wishes of the child, taking into account the child's maturity and ability to express reasoned and independent preferences as to relocation;

(9)   possible arrangements for the exercise of parental responsibilities appropriate to the parents' resources and circumstances and the developmental level of the child;

(10) minimization of the impairment to a parent-child relationship caused by a parent's relocation; and

(11) any other relevant factors bearing on the child's best interests.

(h)   If a parent moves with the child 25 miles or less from the child's current primary residence to a new primary residence outside Illinois, Illinois continues to be the home state of the child under subsection (c) of Section 202 of the Uniform Child-Custody Jurisdiction and Enforcement Act. Any subsequent move from the new primary residence outside Illinois greater than 25 miles from the child's original primary residence in Illinois must be in compliance with the provisions of this Section.

§ 5/609.5.   NOTIFICATION OF REMARRIAGE OR RESIDENCY WITH A SEX OFFENDER

Notification of remarriage or residency with a sex offender. A parent who intends to marry or reside with a sex offender, and knows or should know that the person with whom he or she intends to marry or reside is a sex offender, shall provide reasonable notice to the other parent with whom he or she has a minor child prior to the marriage or the commencement of the residency.

§ 5/610.5.   MODIFICATION

(a) Unless by stipulation of the parties or except as provided in subsection (b) of this Section or Section 603.10 of this Act, no motion to modify an order allocating parental responsibilities may be made earlier than 2 years after its date, unless the court permits it to be made on the basis of affidavits that there is reason to believe the child's present environment may endanger seriously his or her mental, moral, or physical health or significantly impair the child's emotional development.

(b) A motion to modify an order allocating parental responsibilities may be made at any time by a party who has been informed of the existence of facts requiring notice to be given under Section 609.5 of this Act.

(c) Except in a case concerning the modification of any restriction of parental responsibilities under Section 603.10, the court shall modify a parenting plan or allocation judgment when necessary to serve the child's best interests if the court finds, by a preponderance of the evidence, that on the basis of facts that have arisen since the entry of the existing parenting plan or allocation judgment or were not anticipated therein, a substantial change has occurred in the circumstances of the child or of either parent and that a modification is necessary to serve the child's best interests.

(d) The court shall modify a parenting plan or allocation judgment in accordance with a parental agreement, unless it finds that the modification is not in the child's best interests.

(e) The court may modify a parenting plan or allocation judgment without a showing of changed circumstances if (i) the modification is in the child's best interests; and (ii) any of the following are proven as to the modification:

     (1) the modification reflects the actual arrangement under which the child has been receiving care, without parental objection, for the 6 months preceding the filing of the petition for modification, provided that the arrangement is not the result of a parent's acquiescence resulting from circumstances that negated the parent's ability to give meaningful consent;

(2)   the modification constitutes a minor modification in the parenting plan or allocation judgment;

(3)   the modification is necessary to modify an agreed parenting plan or allocation judgment that the court would not have ordered or approved under Section 602.5 or 602.7 had the court been aware of the circumstances at the time of the order or approval; or

(4)   the parties agree to the modification.

(f)   Attorney's fees and costs shall be assessed against a party seeking modification if the court finds that the modification action is vexatious or constitutes harassment. If the court finds that a parent has repeatedly filed frivolous motions for modification, the court may bar the parent from filing a motion for modification for a period of time.

ASSISTED CONCEPTION AND SURROGACY: FLORIDA, MAINE AND VIRGINIA STATUTES

FLORIDA

ASSISTED CONCEPTION AND GESTATIONAL SURROGACY

Fla. Stat. Ann. §§ 742.11 et seq. (West 2016)

[EDITORS' INTRODUCTION: Katharine K. Baker, *Legitimate Families and Equal Protection*, 56 B.C. L. REV. 1647 (2015); Noah Baron & Jennifer Bazzell, *Assisted Reproductive Technologies*, 15 GEO. J. GENDER & L. 57 (2014); Michael D. Ellis, *A Need for Clarity: Assisted Reproduction and Embryo Adoption in Texas*, 66 BAYLOR L. REV. 164 (2014); Honorable William J. Giacomo & Angela DiBiasi, *Mommy Dearest: Determining Parental Rights and Enforceability of Surrogacy Agreements*, 36 PACE L. REV. 251 (2015); Morgan Holcomb & Mary Patricia Byrn, *When Your Body Is Your Business*, 85 WASH. L. REV. 647 (2010); Heather Kolinsky, *The Intended Parent: The Power and Problems Inherent in Designating and Determining Intent in the Context of Parental Rights*, 119 PENN ST. L. REV. (2015); Browne C. Lewis, *Due Date: Enforcing Surrogacy Promises in the Best Interest of the Child*, 87 ST. JOHN'S L. REV. 899 (2013); Browne Lewis, *"You Belong to Me": Unscrambling the Legal Ramifications of Recognizing a Property in Frozen Human Eggs*, 83 TENN. L. REV. 645 (2016); Lina Peng, *Surrogate Mothers: An Exploration of the Empirical and the Normative*, 21 AM. U. J. GENDER SOC. POL'Y & L. 555 (2013); Mark Strasser, *Traditional Surrogacy Contracts, Partial Enforcement, and the Challenge for Family Law*, 18 J. HEALTH CARE L. & POL'Y 85 (2015); Connor Cory, Note, *Access and Exploitation: Can Gay Men and Feminists Agree on Surrogacy Policy?*, 23 GEO. J. ON POVERTY L. & POL'Y 133 (2015); Amanda M. Herman, Comment, *The Regulation of Gestation: A Call for More Complete State Statutory Regulation of Gestational Surrogacy Contracts*, 18 CHAP. L. REV. 553 (2015); Michelle Elizabeth Holland, Comment, *Forbidding Gestational Surrogacy: Impending the Fundamental Right to Procreate*, 17 U.C. DAVIS J. JUV. L. & POL'Y 1 (2013); Chanel Vegh, Note, *My Body, My Property, My Baby? The Extension of Property Rights to Sexual Reproductive Cells and Embryos*, 14 CARDOZO PUB. L. POL'Y & ETHICS J. 649 (2016).]

§ 742.11. PRESUMED STATUS OF CHILD CONCEIVED BY MEANS OF ARTIFICIAL OR IN VITRO INSEMINATION OR DONATED EGGS OR PRE-EMBRYOS

(1) Except in the case of gestational surrogacy, any child born within wedlock who has been conceived by the means of artificial or in vitro insemination is irrebuttably presumed to be the child of the

husband and wife, provided that both husband and wife have consented in writing to the artificial or in vitro insemination.

(2) Except in the case of gestational surrogacy, any child born within wedlock who has been conceived by means of donated eggs or preembryos shall be irrebuttably presumed to be the child of the recipient gestating woman and her husband, provided that both parties have consented in writing to the use of donated eggs or preembryos.

§ 742.12.   SCIENTIFIC TESTING TO DETERMINE PATERNITY

(1) In any proceeding to establish paternity, the court on its own motion may require the child, mother, and alleged fathers to submit to scientific tests that are generally acceptable within the scientific community to show a probability of paternity. The court shall direct that the tests be conducted by a qualified technical laboratory.

(2) In any proceeding to establish paternity, the court may, upon request of a party providing a sworn statement or written declaration as provided by s. 92.525(2) alleging paternity and setting forth facts establishing a reasonable possibility of the requisite sexual contact between the parties or providing a sworn statement or written declaration denying paternity and setting forth facts establishing a reasonable possibility of the nonexistence of sexual contact between the parties, require the child, mother, and alleged fathers to submit to scientific tests that are generally acceptable within the scientific community to show a probability of paternity. The court shall direct that the tests be conducted by a qualified technical laboratory.

(3) The test results, together with the opinions and conclusions of the test laboratory, shall be filed with the court. Any objection to the test results must be made in writing and must be filed with the court at least 10 days prior to the hearing. If no objection is filed, the test results shall be admitted into evidence without the need for predicate to be laid or third-party foundation testimony to be presented. Nothing in this paragraph prohibits a party from calling an outside expert witness to refute or support the testing procedure or results, or the mathematical theory on which they are based. Upon the entry of the order for scientific testing, the court must inform each person to be tested of the procedure and requirements for objecting to the test results and of the consequences of the failure to object.

(4) Test results are admissible in evidence and should be weighed along with other evidence of the paternity of the alleged father unless the statistical probability of paternity equals or exceeds 95 percent. A statistical probability of paternity of 95 percent or more creates a rebuttable presumption, as defined by s. 90.304, that the alleged father is the biological father of the child. If a party fails to rebut the presumption of paternity which arose from the statistical probability of paternity of 95 percent or more, the court may enter a summary

judgment of paternity. If the test results show the alleged father cannot be the biological father, the case shall be dismissed with prejudice.

(5) Subject to the limitations in subsection (3), if the test results or the expert analysis of the inherited characteristics is disputed, the court, upon reasonable request of a party, shall order that an additional test be made by the same laboratory or an independent laboratory at the expense of the party requesting additional testing.

(6) Verified documentation of the chain of custody of the blood or other specimens is competent evidence to establish the chain of custody.

(7) The fees and costs for scientific tests shall be paid by the parties in proportions and at times determined by the court unless the parties reach a stipulated agreement which is adopted by the court.

§ 742.13. DEFINITIONS

As used in ss. 742.11–742.17, the term:

(1) "Assisted reproductive technology" means those procreative procedures which involve the laboratory handling of human eggs or preembryos, including, but not limited to, in vitro fertilization embryo transfer, gamete intrafallopian transfer, pronuclear stage transfer, tubal embryo transfer, and zygote intrafallopian transfer.

(2) "Commissioning couple" means the intended mother and father of a child who will be conceived by means of assisted reproductive technology using the eggs or sperm of at least one of the intended parents.

(3) "Egg" means the unfertilized female reproductive cell.

(4) "Fertilization" means the initial union of an egg and sperm.

(5) "Gestational surrogate" means a woman who contracts to become pregnant by means of assisted reproductive technology without the use of an egg from her body.

(6) "Gestational surrogacy" means a state that results from a process in which a commissioning couple's eggs or sperm, or both, are mixed in vitro and the resulting preembryo is implanted within another woman's body.

(7) "Gestational surrogacy contract" means a written agreement between the gestational surrogate and the commissioning couple.

(8) "Gamete intrafallopian transfer" means the direct transfer of eggs and sperm into the fallopian tube prior to fertilization.

(9) "Implantation" means the event that occurs when a fertilized egg adheres to the uterine wall for nourishment.

(10) "In vitro" refers to a laboratory procedure performed in an artificial environment outside a woman's body.

(11) "In vitro fertilization embryo transfer" means the transfer of an in vitro fertilized preembryo into a woman's uterus.

(12) "Preembryo" means the product of fertilization of an egg by a sperm until the appearance of the embryonic axis.

(13) "Pronuclear stage transfer" or "zygote intrafallopian transfer" means the transfer of an in vitro fertilized preembryo into the fallopian tube before cell division takes place.

(14) "Sperm" means the male reproductive cell.

(15) "Tubal embryo transfer" means the transfer of a dividing, in vitro fertilized preembryo into the fallopian tube.

§ 742.14.   DONATION OF EGGS, SPERM, OR PRE-EMBRYOS

The donor of any egg, sperm, or preembryo, other than the commissioning couple or a father who has executed a preplanned adoption agreement under s. 63.212, shall relinquish all maternal or paternal rights and obligations with respect to the donation or the resulting children. Only reasonable compensation directly related to the donation of eggs, sperm, and preembryos shall be permitted.

§ 742.15.   GESTATIONAL SURROGACY CONTRACT

(1) Prior to engaging in gestational surrogacy, a binding and enforceable gestational surrogacy contract shall be made between the commissioning couple and the gestational surrogate. A contract for gestational surrogacy shall not be binding and enforceable unless the gestational surrogate is 18 years of age or older and the commissioning couple are legally married and are both 18 years of age or older.

(2) The commissioning couple shall enter into a contract with a gestational surrogate only when, within reasonable medical certainty as determined by a physician licensed under chapter 458 or chapter 459:

(a) The commissioning mother cannot physically gestate a pregnancy to term;

(b) The gestation will cause a risk to the physical health of the commissioning mother; or

(c) The gestation will cause a risk to the health of the fetus.

(3) A gestational surrogacy contract must include the following provisions:

(a) The commissioning couple agrees that the gestational surrogate shall be the sole source of consent with respect to clinical intervention and management of the pregnancy.

(b) The gestational surrogate agrees to submit to reasonable medical evaluation and treatment and to adhere to reasonable medical instructions about her prenatal health.

(c) Except as provided in paragraph (e), the gestational surrogate agrees to relinquish any parental rights upon the child's birth and to proceed with the judicial proceedings prescribed under s. 742.16.

(d) Except as provided in paragraph (e), the commissioning couple agrees to accept custody of and to assume full parental rights and responsibilities for the child immediately upon the child's birth, regardless of any impairment of the child.

(e) The gestational surrogate agrees to assume parental rights and responsibilities for the child born to her if it is determined that neither member of the commissioning couple is the genetic parent of the child.

(4) As part of the contract, the commissioning couple may agree to pay only reasonable living, legal, medical, psychological, and psychiatric expenses of the gestational surrogate that are directly related to prenatal, intrapartal, and postpartal periods.

§ 742.16. EXPEDITED AFFIRMATION OF PARENTAL STATUS FOR GESTATIONAL SURROGACY

(1) Within 3 days after the birth of a child delivered of a gestational surrogate, the commissioning couple shall petition a court of competent jurisdiction for an expedited affirmation of parental status.

(2) After the petition is filed, the court shall fix a time and place for hearing the petition, which may be immediately after the filing of the petition. Notice of hearing shall be given as prescribed by the rules of civil procedure, and service of process shall be made as specified by law for civil actions.

(3) Upon a showing by the commissioning couple or the child or the gestational surrogate that privacy rights may be endangered, the court may order the names of the commissioning couple or the child or the gestational surrogate, or any combination thereof, to be deleted from the notice of hearing and from the copy of the petition attached thereto, provided the substantive rights of any person will not thereby be affected.

(4) Notice of the hearing shall be given by the commissioning couple to:

(a) The gestational surrogate.

(b) The treating physician of the assisted reproductive technology program.

(c) Any party claiming paternity.

(5) All hearings held in proceedings under this section shall be held in closed court without admittance of any person other than essential officers of the court, the parties, witnesses, and any persons who have received notice of the hearing.

(6) The commissioning couple or their legal representative shall appear at the hearing on the petition. At the conclusion of the hearing, after the court has determined that a binding and enforceable gestational surrogacy contract has been executed pursuant to s. 742.15 and that at least one member of the commissioning couple is the genetic parent of the child, the court shall enter an order stating that the commissioning couple are the legal parents of the child.

(7) When at least one member of the commissioning couple is the genetic parent of the child, the commissioning couple shall be presumed to be the natural parents of the child.

(8) Within 30 days after entry of the order, the clerk of the court shall prepare a certified statement of the order for the state registrar of vital statistics on a form provided by the registrar. The court shall thereupon enter an order requiring the Department of Health to issue a new birth certificate naming the commissioning couple as parents and requiring the department to seal the original birth certificate.

(9) All papers and records pertaining to the affirmation of parental status, including the original birth certificate, are confidential and exempt from the provisions of s. 119.07(1) and subject to inspection only upon order of the court. The court files, records, and papers shall be indexed only in the name of the petitioner, and the name of the child shall not be noted on any docket, index, or other record outside the court file.

§ 742.17.   DISPOSITION OF EGGS, SPERM, OR PRE-EMBRYOS; RIGHTS OF INHERITANCE

A commissioning couple and the treating physician shall enter into a written agreement that provides for the disposition of the commissioning couple's eggs, sperm, and preembryos in the event of a divorce, the death of a spouse, or any other unforeseen circumstance.

(1) Absent a written agreement, any remaining eggs or sperm shall remain under the control of the party that provides the eggs or sperm.

(2) Absent a written agreement, decisionmaking authority regarding the disposition of preembryos shall reside jointly with the commissioning couple.

(3) Absent a written agreement, in the case of the death of one member of the commissioning couple, any eggs, sperm, or preembryos shall remain under the control of the surviving member of the commissioning couple.

(4) A child conceived from the eggs or sperm of a person or persons who died before the transfer of their eggs, sperm, or preembryos to a woman's body shall not be eligible for a claim against the decedent's estate unless the child has been provided for by the decedent's will.

MAINE

Me. Stat. tit. 19–A, § 1931 (2016)

§ 1931.   ELIGIBILITY TO ENTER GESTATIONAL CARRIER AGREEMENT

1.   ELIGIBILITY OF GESTATIONAL CARRIER. In order to execute an agreement to act as a gestational carrier, a woman must:

A.   Be at least 21 years of age;

B.   Have previously given birth to at least one child;

C.   Have completed a medical evaluation that includes a mental health consultation;

D.   Have had independent legal representation of her own choosing and paid for by the intended parent or parents regarding the terms of the gestational carrier agreement and have been advised of the potential legal consequences of the gestational carrier agreement; and

E.   Not have contributed gametes that will ultimately result in an embryo that she will attempt to carry to term, unless the gestational carrier is entering into an agreement with a family member.

2.   ELIGIBILITY OF INTENDED PARENT OR PARENTS. Prior to executing a gestational carrier agreement, a person or persons intending to become a parent or parents, whether genetically related to the child or not, must:

A.   Complete a medical evaluation and mental health consultation; and

B.   Retain independent legal representation regarding the terms of the gestational carrier agreement and have been advised of the potential legal consequences of the gestational carrier agreement.

VIRGINIA

STATUS OF CHILDREN OF ASSISTED CONCEPTION

Va. Code Ann. §§ 20–156 et seq. (West 2016)

§ 20–156.   DEFINITIONS

As used in this chapter unless the context requires a different meaning:

"Assisted conception" means a pregnancy resulting from any intervening medical technology, whether in vivo or in vitro, which completely or partially replaces sexual intercourse as the means of conception. Such intervening medical technology includes, but is not limited to, conventional medical and surgical treatment as well as noncoital reproductive technology such as artificial insemination by donor, cryopreservation of gametes and embryos, in vitro fertilization, uterine embryo lavage, embryo transfer, gamete intrafallopian tube transfer, and low tubal ovum transfer.

"Compensation" means payment of any valuable consideration for services in excess of reasonable medical and ancillary costs.

"Cryopreservation" means freezing and storing of gametes and embryos for possible future use in assisted conception.

"Donor" means an individual, other than a surrogate, who contributes the sperm or egg used in assisted conception.

"Gamete" means either a sperm or an ovum.

"Genetic parent" means an individual who contributes a gamete resulting in a conception.

"Gestational mother" means the woman who gives birth to a child, regardless of her genetic relationship to the child.

"Embryo" means the organism resulting from the union of a sperm and an ovum from first cell division until approximately the end of the second month of gestation.

"Embryo transfer" means the placing of a viable embryo into the uterus of a gestational mother.

"Infertile" means the inability to conceive after one year of unprotected sexual intercourse.

"Intended parents" means a man and a woman, married to each other, who enter into an agreement with a surrogate under the terms of which they will be the parents of any child born to the surrogate through assisted conception regardless of the genetic relationships between the intended parents, the surrogate, and the child.

"In vitro" means any process that can be observed in an artificial environment such as a test tube or tissue culture plate.

"In vitro fertilization" means the fertilization of ova by sperm in an artificial environment.

"In vivo" means any process occurring within the living body.

"Ovum" means the female gamete or reproductive cell prior to fertilization.

"Reasonable medical and ancillary costs" means the costs of the performance of assisted conception, the costs of prenatal maternal health care, the costs of maternal and child health care for a reasonable post partum period, the reasonable costs for medications and maternity clothes, and any additional and reasonable costs for housing and other living expenses attributable to the pregnancy.

"Sperm" means the male gametes or reproductive cells which impregnate the ova.

"Surrogacy contract" means an agreement between intended parents, a surrogate, and her husband, if any, in which the surrogate agrees to be impregnated through the use of assisted conception, to carry any resulting fetus, and to relinquish to the intended parents the custody of and parental rights to any resulting child.

"Surrogate" means any adult woman who agrees to bear a child carried for intended parents.

§ 20–157.   VIRGINIA LAW TO CONTROL

The provisions of this chapter shall control, without exception, in any action brought in the courts of this Commonwealth to enforce or adjudicate any rights or responsibilities arising under this chapter.

§ 20–158.   PARENTAGE OF CHILD RESULTING FROM ASSISTED CONCEPTION

A.   Determination of parentage, generally.—Except as provided in subsections B, C, D, and E of this section, the parentage of any child resulting from the performance of assisted conception shall be determined as follows:

     1.   The gestational mother of a child is the child's mother.

     2.   The husband of the gestational mother of a child is the child's father, notwithstanding any declaration of invalidity or annulment of the marriage obtained after the performance of assisted conception, unless he commences an action in which the mother and child are parties within two years after he discovers or, in the exercise of due diligence, reasonably should have discovered the child's birth and in which it is determined that he did not consent to the performance of assisted conception.

     3.   A donor is not the parent of a child conceived through assisted conception, unless the donor is the husband of the gestational mother.

B.   Death of spouse.—Any child resulting from the insemination of a wife's ovum using her husband's sperm, with his consent, is the child of the husband and wife notwithstanding that, during the ten-month period immediately preceding the birth, either party died.

However, any person who dies before in utero implantation of an embryo resulting from the union of his sperm or her ovum with another gamete, whether or not the other gamete is that of the person's spouse, is not the parent of any resulting child unless (i) implantation occurs before notice of the death can reasonably be communicated to the physician performing the procedure or (ii) the person consents to be a parent in writing executed before the implantation.

C. Divorce.—Any child resulting from insemination of a wife's ovum using her husband's sperm, with his consent, is the child of the husband and wife notwithstanding that either party filed for a divorce or annulment during the ten-month period immediately preceding the birth. Any person who is a party to an action for divorce or annulment commenced by filing before in utero implantation of an embryo resulting from the union of his sperm or her ovum with another gamete, whether or not the other gamete is that of the person's spouse, is not the parent of any resulting child unless (i) implantation occurs before notice of the filing can reasonably be communicated to the physician performing the procedure or (ii) the person consents in writing to be a parent, whether the writing was executed before or after the implantation.

D. Birth pursuant to court approved surrogacy contract.—After approval of a surrogacy contract by the court and entry of an order as provided in subsection D of § 20–160, the intended parents are the parents of any resulting child. However, if the court vacates the order approving the agreement pursuant to subsection B of § 20–161, the surrogate is the mother of the resulting child and her husband is the father. The intended parents may only obtain parental rights through adoption as provided in Chapter 12 (§ 63.2–1200 et seq.) of Title 63.2.

E. Birth pursuant to surrogacy contract not approved by court.— In the case of a surrogacy contract that has not been approved by a court as provided in § 20–160, the parentage of any resulting child shall be determined as follows:

1. The gestational mother is the child's mother unless the intended mother is a genetic parent, in which case the intended mother is the mother.

2. If either of the intended parents is a genetic parent of the resulting child, the intended father is the child's father. However, if (i) the surrogate is married, (ii) her husband is a party to the surrogacy contract, and (iii) the surrogate exercises her right to retain custody and parental rights to the resulting child pursuant to § 20–162, then the surrogate and her husband are the parents.

3. If neither of the intended parents is a genetic parent of the resulting child, the surrogate is the mother and her husband is the child's father if he is a party to the contract. The intended parents may only obtain parental rights through adoption as provided in Chapter 12 (§ 63.2–1200 et seq.) of Title 63.2.

4. After the signing and filing of the surrogate consent and report form in conformance with the requirements of subsection A of § 20–162, the intended parents are the parents of the child and the surrogate and her husband, if any, shall not be the parents of the child.

§ 20–159. SURROGACY CONTRACTS PERMISSIBLE

A.   A surrogate, her husband, if any, and prospective intended parents may enter into a written agreement whereby the surrogate may relinquish all her rights and duties as parent of a child conceived through assisted conception, and the intended parents may become the parents of the child as provided in subsection D or E of § 20–158.

B.   Surrogacy contracts shall be approved by the court as provided in § 20–160. However, any surrogacy contract that has not been approved by the court shall be governed by the provisions of §§ 20–156 through 20–159 and §§ 20–162 through 20–165 including the provisions for reformation in conformance with this chapter as provided in § 20–162.

§ 20–160. PETITION AND HEARING FOR COURT APPROVAL OF SURROGACY CONTRACT; REQUIREMENTS; ORDERS

A.   Prior to the performance of assisted conception, the intended parents, the surrogate, and her husband shall join in a petition to the circuit court of the county or city in which at least one of the parties resides. The surrogacy contract shall be signed by all the parties and acknowledged before an officer or other person authorized by law to take acknowledgments.

A copy of the contract shall be attached to the petition. The court shall appoint a guardian ad litem to represent the interests of any resulting child and shall appoint counsel to represent the surrogate. The court shall order a home study by a local department of social services or welfare or a licensed child-placing agency, to be completed prior to the hearing on the petition.

All hearings and proceedings conducted under this section shall be held in camera, and all court records shall be confidential and subject to inspection only under the standards applicable to adoptions as provided in § 63.2–1245.

The court conducting the proceedings shall have exclusive and continuing jurisdiction of all matters arising under the surrogacy contract until all provisions of the contract are fulfilled.

B.   The court shall hold a hearing on the petition. The court shall enter an order approving the surrogacy contract and authorizing the performance of assisted conception for a period of twelve months after the date of the order, and may discharge the guardian ad litem and attorney for the surrogate upon finding that:

1.   The court has jurisdiction in accordance with § 20–157;

2.   A local department of social services or welfare or a licensed child-placing agency has conducted a home study of the intended parents, the surrogate, and her husband, if any, and has filed a report of this home study with the court;

3.   The intended parents, the surrogate, and her husband, if any, meet the standards of fitness applicable to adoptive parents;

4.   All the parties have voluntarily entered into the surrogacy contract and understand its terms and the nature, meaning, and effect of the proceeding and understand that any agreement between them for payment of compensation is void and unenforceable;

5.   The agreement contains adequate provisions to guarantee the payment of reasonable medical and ancillary costs either in the form of insurance, cash, escrow, bonds, or other arrangements satisfactory to the parties, including allocation of responsibility for such costs in the event of termination of the pregnancy, termination of the contract pursuant to § 20–161, or breach of the contract by any party;

6.   The surrogate has had at least one pregnancy, and has experienced at least one live birth, and bearing another child does not pose an unreasonable risk to her physical or mental health or to that of any resulting child. This finding shall be supported by medical evidence;

7.   Prior to signing the surrogacy contract, the intended parents, the surrogate, and her husband, if any, have submitted to physical examinations and psychological evaluations by practitioners licensed to perform such services pursuant to Title 54.1, and the court and all parties have been given access to the records of the physical examinations and psychological evaluations;

8.   The intended mother is infertile, is unable to bear a child, or is unable to do so without unreasonable risk to the unborn child or to the physical or mental health of the intended mother or the child. This finding shall be supported by medical evidence;

9.   At least one of the intended parents is expected to be the genetic parent of any child resulting from the agreement;

10. The husband of the surrogate, if any, is a party to the surrogacy agreement;

11. All parties have received counseling concerning the effects of the surrogacy by a qualified health care professional or social worker, and a report containing conclusions about the capacity of the parties to enter into and fulfill the agreement has been filed with the court; and

12. The agreement would not be substantially detrimental to the interests of any of the affected persons.

C.   Unless otherwise provided in the surrogacy contract, all court costs, counsel fees, and other costs and expenses associated with the hearing, including the costs of the home study, shall be assessed against the intended parents.

D. Within seven days of the birth of any resulting child, the intended parents shall file a written notice with the court that the child was born to the surrogate within 300 days after the last performance of assisted conception. Upon the filing of this notice and a finding that at least one of the intended parents is the genetic parent of the resulting child as substantiated by medical evidence, the court shall enter an order directing the State Registrar of Vital Records to issue a new birth certificate naming the intended parents as the parents of the child pursuant to § 32.1–261.

If evidence cannot be produced that at least one of the intended parents is the genetic parent of the resulting child, the court shall not enter an order directing the issuance of a new birth certificate naming the intended parents as the parents of the child, and the surrogate and her husband, if any, shall be the parents of the child. The intended parents may obtain parental rights only through adoption as provided in Chapter 12 (§ 63.2–1200 et seq.) of Title 63.2.

§ 20–161. TERMINATION OF COURT-APPROVED SURROGACY CONTRACT

A. Subsequent to an order entered pursuant to subsection B of § 20–160, but before the surrogate becomes pregnant through the use of assisted conception, the court for cause, or the surrogate, her husband, if any, or the intended parents may terminate the agreement by giving written notice of termination to all other parties and by filing notice of the termination with the court. Upon receipt of the notice, the court shall vacate the order entered under subsection B of § 20–160.

B. Within 180 days after the last performance of any assisted conception, a surrogate who is also a genetic parent may terminate the agreement by filing written notice with the court. The court shall vacate the order entered pursuant to subsection B of § 20–160 upon finding, after notice to the parties to the agreement and a hearing, that the surrogate has voluntarily terminated the agreement and that she understands the effects of the termination.

Unless otherwise provided in the contract as approved, the surrogate shall incur no liability to the intended parents for exercising her rights of termination pursuant to this section.

§ 20–162. CONTRACTS NOT APPROVED BY THE COURT; REQUIREMENTS

A. In the case of any surrogacy agreement for which prior court approval has not been obtained pursuant to § 20–160, the provisions of this section and §§ 20–156 through 20–159 and §§ 20–163 through 20–165 shall apply. Any provision in a surrogacy contract that attempts to reduce the rights or responsibilities of the intended parents, surrogate, or her husband, if any, or the rights of any resulting child shall be reformed to include the requirements set forth in this chapter. A provision in the contract providing for compensation to be paid to the surrogate is void and unenforceable. Such surrogacy contracts shall be enforceable and shall be construed only as follows:

1. The surrogate, her husband, if any, and the intended parents shall be parties to any such surrogacy contract.

2. The contract shall be in writing, signed by all the parties, and acknowledged before an officer or other person authorized by law to take acknowledgments.

3. Upon expiration of three days following birth of any resulting child, the surrogate may relinquish her parental rights to the intended parents, if at least one of the intended parents is the genetic parent of the child, by signing a surrogate consent and report form naming the intended parents as the parents of the child. The surrogate consent and report form shall be developed, furnished and distributed by the State Registrar of Vital Records. The surrogate consent and report form shall be signed and acknowledged before an officer or other person authorized by law to take acknowledgments. The surrogate consent and report form, a copy of the contract, and a statement from the physician who performed the assisted conception stating the genetic relationships between the child, the surrogate, and the intended parents, at least one of whom shall be the genetic parent of the child, shall be filed with the State Registrar within 180 days after the birth. The statement from the physician shall be signed and acknowledged before an officer or other person authorized by law to take acknowledgments. There shall be a rebuttable presumption that the statement from the physician accurately states the genetic relationships among the child, the surrogate and the intended parents. Where a physician's statement is not available, DNA testing establishing the genetic relationships between the child, the surrogate, and the intended parents may be substituted for the physician's statement.

4. Upon the filing of the surrogate consent and report form and the required attachments, including the physician's statement, within 180 days of the birth, a new birth certificate shall be established by the State Registrar for the child naming the intended parents as the parents of the child as provided in § 32.1–261.

B. Any contract governed by the provisions of this section shall include or, in the event such provisions are not explicitly covered in the contract or are included but are inconsistent with this section, shall be deemed to include the following provisions:

1. The intended parents shall be the parents of any resulting child only when the surrogate relinquishes her parental rights as provided in subdivision A 3 of this section and a new birth certificate

is established as provided in subdivision A 4 of this section and § 32.1–261;

2.   Incorporation of this chapter and a statement by each of the parties that they have read and understood the contract, they know and understand their rights and responsibilities under Virginia law, and the contract was entered into knowingly and voluntarily; and

3.   A guarantee by the intended parents for payment of reasonable medical and ancillary costs either in the form of insurance, cash, escrow, bonds, or other arrangements satisfactory to the parties, including allocation of responsibility for such costs in the event of termination of the pregnancy, termination of the contract, or breach of the contract by any party.

C.   Under any contract that does not include an allocation of responsibility for reasonable medical and ancillary costs in the event of termination of the pregnancy, termination of the contract, or breach of the contract by any party, the following provisions shall control:

1.   If the intended parents and the surrogate and her husband, if any, and if he is a party to the contract, consent in writing to termination of the contract, the intended parents are responsible for all reasonable medical and ancillary costs for a period of six weeks following the termination.

2.   If the surrogate voluntarily terminates the contract during the pregnancy, without consent of the intended parents, the intended parents shall be responsible for one-half of the reasonable medical and ancillary costs incurred prior to the termination.

3.   If, after the birth of any resulting child, the surrogate fails to relinquish parental rights to the intended parents pursuant to the contract, the intended parents shall be responsible for one-half of the reasonable medical and ancillary costs incurred prior to the birth.

§ 20–163.   MISCELLANEOUS   PROVISIONS   RELATED   TO   ALL SURROGACY CONTRACTS

A.   The surrogate shall be solely responsible for the clinical management of the pregnancy.

B.   After the entry of an order under subsection B of § 20–160 or upon the execution of a contract pursuant to § 20–162, the marriage of the surrogate shall not affect the validity of the order or contract, and her husband shall not be deemed a party to the contract in the absence of his explicit written consent.

C.   Following the entry of an order pursuant to subsection D of § 20–160 or upon the relinquishing of the custody of and parental rights to any resulting child and the filing of the surrogate consent and report form as provided in § 20–162, the intended parents shall have the custody of, parental rights to, and full responsibilities for any child resulting from the performance of assisted conception from a surrogacy agreement regardless of the child's health, physical appearance, any mental or physical handicap, and regardless of whether the child is born alive.

D.   A child born to a surrogate within 300 days after assisted conception pursuant to an order under subsection B of § 20–160 or a contract under § 20–162 is presumed to result from the assisted conception. This presumption is conclusive as to all persons who fail to file an action to test its validity within two years after the birth of the child. The child and the parties to the contract shall be named as parties in any such action. The action shall be filed in the court that issued or could have issued an order under § 20–160.

E.   Health care providers shall not be liable for recognizing the surrogate as the mother of the resulting child before receipt of a copy of an order entered under § 20–160 or a copy of the contract, or for recognizing the intended parents as the parents of the resulting child after receipt of such order or copy of the contract.

§ 20–164.   RELATION OF PARENT AND CHILD

A child whose status as a child is declared or negated by this chapter is the child only of his parent or parents as determined under this chapter, Title 64.2, and, when applicable, Chapter 3.1 (§ 20–49.1 et seq.) of this title for all purposes including, but not limited to, (i) intestate succession; (ii) probate law exemptions, allowances, or other protections for children in a parent's estate; and (iii) determining eligibility of the child or its descendants to share in a donative transfer from any person as an individual or as a member of a class determined by reference to the relationship. However, a child born more than ten months after the death of a parent shall not be recognized as such parent's child for the purposes of subdivisions (i), (ii) and (iii) of this section.

§ 20–165.   SURROGATE BROKERS PROHIBITED; PENALTY; LIABILITY OF SURROGATE BROKERS

A.   It shall be unlawful for any person, firm, corporation, partnership, or other entity to accept compensation for recruiting or procuring surrogates or to accept compensation for otherwise arranging or inducing intended parents and surrogates to enter into surrogacy contracts in this Commonwealth. A violation of this section shall be punishable as a Class 1 misdemeanor.

B.   Any person who acts as a surrogate broker in violation of this section shall, in addition, be liable to all the parties to the purported surrogacy contract in a total amount equal to three times the amount of compensation to have been paid to the broker pursuant to the contract. One-half of the damages under this subsection shall be due the surrogate and her husband, if any, and if he is a party to the contract, and one-half shall be due the intended parents. An action under this section shall be brought within five years of the date of the contract.

C.   The provisions of this section shall not apply to the services of an attorney in giving legal advice or in preparing a surrogacy contract.

CHILD ABUSE AND REPORTING STATUTE

VIRGINIA

VIRGINIA CHILD ABUSE REPORTING STATUTE

Va. Code Ann. §§ 63.2–1501–63.2–1530 (West 2016)

[EDITORS' INTRODUCTION: Brigid Benincasa, *Protecting Our Children: A Reformation of South Carolina's Homicide by Child Abuse Laws*, 65 S.C. L. REV. 735 (2014); Dale Margolin Cecka, *Abolish Anonymous Reporting to Child Abuse Hotlines*, 64 CATH. U. L. REV. 51 (2014); Jon M. Hogelin, *To Prevent and to Protect: The Reporting of Child Abuse by Educators*, 2013 B.Y.U. EDUC. & L.J. 225 (2013); Deseriee Kennedy, *From Collaboration to Consolidation: Developing a More Expansive Model for Responding to Family Violence*, 20 CARDOZO J.L. & GENDER 1 (2013); Tamara L. Kuennen, *Recognizing the Right to Petition for Victims of Domestic Violence*, 81 FORDHAM L. REV. 837 (2012); Megan M. Smith, *Causing Conflict: Indiana's Mandatory Reporting Laws in the Context of Juvenile Defense*, 81 FORDHAM L. REV. 837 (2012); Starla J. Williams, *Reforming Mandated Reporting Laws After Sandusky*, 22 KAN. J.L. & PUB. POL'Y 235 (2013); Matthew Johnson, Note, *Mandatory Child Abuse Reporting Laws in Georgia: Strengthening Protection for Georgia's Children*, 31 GA. ST. U. L. REV. 643 (2015); Erica M. Kelly, Note, *The Jerry Sandusky Effect: Child Abuse Reporting Laws Should No Longer Be "Don't Ask, Don't Tell"*, 75 U. PITT. L. REV. 209 (2013); David Manno, Comment, *How Dramatic Shifts in Perceptions of Parenting Have Exposed Families, Free-Range or Otherwise, to State Intervention: A Common Law Tort Approach to Redefining Child Neglect*, 65 AM. U. L. REV. 675 (2016); Breanna Trombley, Note, *Criminal Law—No Stiches for Snitches: The Need for a Duty-to-Report Law in Arkansas*, 34 U. ARK. LITTLE ROCK L. REV. 813 (2012).]

§ 63.2–1501. DEFINITIONS

As used in this chapter unless the context requires a different meaning: "Court" means the juvenile and domestic relations district court of the county or city. "Prevention" means efforts that (i) promote health and competence in people and (ii) create, promote and strengthen environments that nurture people in their development.

§ 63.2–1502. ESTABLISHMENT OF CHILD-PROTECTIVE SERVICES UNIT; DUTIES

There is created a Child-Protective Services Unit in the Department that shall have the following powers and duties:

    1. To evaluate and strengthen all local, regional and state programs dealing with child abuse and neglect.

2.   To assume primary responsibility for directing the planning and funding of child-protective services. This shall include reviewing and approving the annual proposed plans and budgets for protective services submitted by the local departments.

3.   To assist in developing programs aimed at discovering and preventing the many factors causing child abuse and neglect.

4.   To prepare and disseminate, including the presentation of, educational programs and materials on child abuse and neglect.

5.   To provide educational programs for professionals required by law to make reports under this chapter.

6.   To establish standards of training and provide educational programs to qualify workers in the field of child-protective services. Such standards of training shall include provisions regarding the legal duties of the workers in order to protect the constitutional and statutory rights and safety of children and families from the initial time of contact during investigation through treatment.

7.   To establish standards of training and educational programs to qualify workers to determine whether complaints of abuse or neglect of a child in a private or state-operated hospital, institution or other facility, or public school, are founded.

8.   To maintain staff qualified pursuant to Board regulations to assist local department personnel in determining whether an employee of a private or state-operated hospital, institution or other facility or an employee of a school board, abused or neglected a child in such hospital, institution, or other facility, or public school.

9.   To monitor the processing and determination of cases where an employee of a private or state-operated hospital, institution or other facility, or an employee of a school board, is suspected of abusing or neglecting a child in such hospital, institution, or other facility, or public school.

10. To help coordinate child-protective services at the state, regional, and local levels with the efforts of other state and voluntary social, medical and legal agencies.

11. To maintain a child abuse and neglect information system that includes all cases of child abuse and neglect within the Commonwealth.

12. To provide for methods to preserve the confidentiality of all records in order to protect the rights of the child, and his parents or guardians.

13. To establish minimum training requirements for workers and supervisors on family abuse and domestic violence, including the relationship between domestic violence and child abuse and neglect.

§ 63.2–1503. LOCAL DEPARTMENTS TO ESTABLISH CHILD-PROTECTIVE
SERVICES; DUTIES

A.   Each local department shall establish child-protective services under a departmental coordinator within such department or with one or more adjacent local departments that shall be staffed with qualified personnel pursuant to regulations adopted by the Board. The local department shall be the public agency responsible for receiving and responding to complaints and reports, except that (i) in cases where the reports or complaints are to be made to the court and the judge determines that no local department within a reasonable geographic distance can impartially respond to the report, the court shall assign the report to the court services unit for evaluation; and (ii) in cases where an employee at a private or state-operated hospital, institution or other facility, or an employee of a school board is suspected of abusing or neglecting a child in such hospital, institution or other facility, or public school, the local department shall request the Department and the relevant private or state-operated hospital, institution or other facility, or school board to assist in conducting a joint investigation in accordance with regulations adopted by the Board, in consultation with the Departments of Education, Health, Medical Assistance Services, Behavioral Health and Developmental Services, Juvenile Justice and Corrections.

B.   The local department shall ensure, through its own personnel or through cooperative arrangements with other local agencies, the capability of receiving reports or complaints and responding to them promptly on a 24-hours-a-day, seven-days-per-week basis.

C.   The local department shall widely publicize a telephone number for receiving complaints and reports.

D.   The local department shall notify the local attorney for the Commonwealth and the local law-enforcement agency of all complaints of suspected child abuse or neglect involving (i) any death of a child; (ii) any injury or threatened injury to the child in which a felony or Class 1 misdemeanor is also suspected; (iii) any sexual abuse, suspected sexual abuse or other sexual offense involving a child, including but not limited to the use or display of the child in sexually explicit visual material, as defined in § 18.2–374.1; (iv) any abduction of a child; (v) any felony or Class 1 misdemeanor drug offense involving a child; or (vi) contributing to the delinquency of a minor in violation of § 18.2–371, immediately, but in no case more than two hours of receipt of the complaint, and shall provide the attorney for the Commonwealth and the local law-enforcement agency with records and information of the local department, including records related to any complaints of abuse or neglect involving the victim or the alleged perpetrator, related to the investigation of the complaint. The local department shall not allow reports of the death of the victim from other local agencies to substitute for direct reports to the attorney for the Commonwealth and the local law-enforcement agency. The local department shall develop, when practicable, memoranda of understanding for responding to reports of child abuse and neglect with local law enforcement and the attorney for the Commonwealth.

In each case in which the local department notifies the local law-enforcement agency of a complaint pursuant to this subsection, the local department shall, within two business days of delivery of the notification, complete a written report, on a form provided by the Board for such purpose, which shall include (a) the name of the representative of the local department providing notice required by this subsection; (b) the name of the local law-enforcement officer who received such notice; (c) the date and time that notification was made; (d) the identity of the victim; (e) the identity of the person alleged to have abused or neglected the child, if known; (f) the clause or clauses in this subsection that describe the reasons for the notification; and (g) the signatures, which may be electronic signatures, of the representatives of the local department making the notification and the local law-enforcement officer receiving the notification. Such report shall be included in the record of the investigation and may be submitted either in writing or electronically.

E.   When abuse or neglect is suspected in any case involving the death of a child, the local department shall report the case immediately to the regional medical examiner and the local law-enforcement agency.

F.   The local department shall use reasonable diligence to locate (i) any child for whom a report of suspected abuse or neglect has been received and is under investigation, receiving family assessment, or for whom a founded determination of abuse and neglect has been made and a child-protective services case opened and (ii) persons who are the subject of a report that is under investigation or receiving family assessment, if the whereabouts of the child or such persons are unknown to the local department.

G.   When an abused or neglected child and the persons who are the subject of an open child-protective services case have relocated out of the jurisdiction of the local department, the local department shall notify the child-protective services agency in the jurisdiction to which such persons have relocated, whether inside or outside of the Commonwealth, and forward to such agency relevant portions of the case record. The receiving local department shall arrange protective and rehabilitative services as required by this section.

H.   When a child for whom a report of suspected abuse or neglect has been received and is under investigation or receiving family assessment and the child and the child's parents or other persons responsible for the child's care who are the subject of the report that is under investigation or family assessment have relocated out of the jurisdiction of the local department, the local department shall notify the child-protective services agency in the jurisdiction to which the child and such persons have relocated, whether inside or outside of the Commonwealth, and complete such investigation or family assessment by requesting such agency's assistance in completing the investigation or family assessment. The local department that completes the investigation or family assessment shall forward to the receiving agency relevant portions of the case record in order for the receiving agency to arrange protective and rehabilitative services as required by this section.

I.   Upon receipt of a report of child abuse or neglect, the local department shall determine the validity of such report and shall make a determination to conduct an investigation pursuant to § 63.2–1505 or, if designated as a child-protective services differential response agency by the Department according to § 63.2–1504, a family assessment pursuant to § 63.2–1506.

J.   The local department shall foster, when practicable, the creation, maintenance and coordination of hospital and community-based multidisciplinary teams that shall include where possible, but not be limited to, members of the medical, mental health, social work, nursing, education, legal and law-enforcement professions. Such teams shall assist the local departments in identifying abused and neglected children; coordinating medical, social, and legal services for the children and their families; developing innovative programs for detection and prevention of child abuse; promoting community concern and action in the area of child abuse and neglect; and disseminating information to the general public with respect to the problem of child abuse and neglect and the facilities and prevention and treatment methods available to combat child abuse and neglect. These teams may be the family assessment and planning teams established pursuant to § 2.2–5207. Multidisciplinary teams may develop agreements regarding the exchange of information among the parties for the purposes of the investigation and disposition of complaints of child abuse and neglect, delivery of services and child protection. Any information exchanged in accordance with the agreement shall not be considered to be a violation of the provisions of § 63.2–102, 63.2–104, or 63.2–105.

The local department shall also coordinate its efforts in the provision of these services for abused and neglected children with the judge and staff of the court.

K.   The local department may develop multidisciplinary teams to provide consultation to the local department during the investigation of selected cases involving child abuse or neglect, and to make recommendations regarding the prosecution of such cases. These teams may include, but are not limited to, members of the medical, mental health, legal and law-enforcement professions, including the attorney for the Commonwealth or his designee; a local child-protective services representative; and the guardian ad litem or other court-appointed advocate for the child. Any information exchanged for the purpose of such consultation shall not be considered a violation of § 63.2–102, 63.2–104, or 63.2–105.

L.   The local department shall report annually on its activities concerning abused and neglected children to the court and to the Child-Protective Services Unit in the Department on forms provided by the Department.

M.   Statements, or any evidence derived therefrom, made to local department child-protective services personnel, or to any person performing the duties of such personnel, by any person accused of the abuse, injury, neglect or death of a child after the arrest of such person, shall not be used in evidence in the case-in-chief against such person in the criminal proceeding on the question of guilt or innocence over the objection of the accused, unless the statement was made after such person was fully advised (i) of his right to remain silent, (ii) that anything he says may be used against him in a court of law, (iii) that he has a right to the presence of an attorney during any interviews, and (iv) that if he cannot afford an attorney, one will be appointed for him prior to any questioning.

N.   Notwithstanding any other provision of law, the local department, in accordance with Board regulations, shall transmit information regarding founded complaints or family assessments and may transmit other information regarding reports, complaints, family assessments and investigations involving active duty military personnel or members of their household to family advocacy representatives of the United States Armed Forces.

O.   The local department shall notify the custodial parent and make reasonable efforts to notify the noncustodial parent as those terms are defined in § 63.2–1900 of a report of suspected abuse or neglect of a child who is the subject of an investigation or is receiving family assessment, in those cases in which such custodial or noncustodial parent is not the subject of the investigation.

P.   The local department shall notify the Superintendent of Public Instruction when an individual holding a license issued by the Board of Education is the subject of a founded complaint of child abuse or neglect and shall transmit identifying information regarding such individual if the local department knows the person holds a license issued by the Board of Education and after all rights to any appeal provided by § 63.2–1526 have been exhausted.

Any information exchanged for the purpose of this subsection shall not be considered a violation of § 63.2–102, 63.2–104, or 63.2–105.

§ 63.2–1504. CHILD-PROTECTIVE SERVICES DIFFERENTIAL RESPONSE SYSTEM

The Department shall implement a child-protective services differential response system in all local departments. The differential response system allows local departments to respond to valid reports or complaints of child abuse or neglect by conducting either an investigation or a family assessment. The Department shall publish a plan to implement the child-protective services differential response system in local departments by July 1, 2000, and complete implementation in all local departments by July 1, 2003. The Department shall develop a training program for all staff persons involved in the differential response system, and all such staff shall receive this training.

§ 63.2–1505. INVESTIGATIONS BY LOCAL DEPARTMENTS

A.   An investigation requires the collection of information necessary to determine:

1.   The immediate safety needs of the child;

2.   The protective and rehabilitative services needs of the child and family that will deter abuse or neglect;

3.   Risk of future harm to the child;

4.   Alternative plans for the child's safety if protective and rehabilitative services are indicated and the family is unable or unwilling to participate in services;

5.   Whether abuse or neglect has occurred;

6.   If abuse or neglect has occurred, who abused or neglected the child; and

7.   A finding of either founded or unfounded based on the facts collected during the investigation.

B.   If the local department responds to the report or complaint by conducting an investigation, the local department shall:

1.   Make immediate investigation and, if the report or complaint was based upon one of the factors specified in subsection B of § 63.2–1509, the local department may file a petition pursuant to § 16.1–241.3;

2.   Complete a report and transmit it forthwith to the Department, except that no such report shall be transmitted in cases in which the cause to suspect abuse or neglect is one of the factors specified in subsection B of § 63.2–1509 and the mother sought substance abuse counseling or treatment prior to the child's birth;

3.   Consult with the family to arrange for necessary protective and rehabilitative services to be provided to the child and his family;

4.   Petition the court for services deemed necessary including, but not limited to, removal of the child or his siblings from their home;

5.   Determine within 45 days if a report of abuse or neglect is founded or unfounded and transmit a report to such effect to the Department and to the person who is the subject of the investigation.

However, upon written justification by the local department, the time for such determination may be extended not to exceed a total of 60 days or, in the event that the investigation is being conducted in cooperation with a law-enforcement agency and both parties agree that circumstances so warrant, as stated in the written justification, the time for such determination may be extended not to exceed 90 days. If through the exercise of reasonable diligence the local department is unable to find the child who is the subject of the report, the time the child cannot be found shall not be computed as part of the total time period allowed for the investigation and determination and documentation of such reasonable diligence shall be placed in the record. In cases involving the death of a child or alleged sexual abuse of a child who is the subject of the report, the time during which records necessary for the investigation of the complaint but not created by the local department, including autopsy or medical or forensic records or reports, are not available to the local department due to circumstances beyond the local department's control shall not be computed as part of the total time period allowed for the investigation and determination, and documentation of the circumstances that resulted in the delay shall be placed in the record. In cases in which the subject of the investigation is a full-time, part-time, permanent, or temporary employee of a school division who is suspected of abusing or neglecting a child in the course of his educational employment, the time period for determining whether a report is founded or unfounded and transmitting a report to that effect to the Department and the person who is the subject of the investigation shall be mandatory, and every local department shall make the required determination and report within the specified time period without delay;

6.   If a report of abuse or neglect is unfounded, transmit a report to such effect to the complainant and parent or guardian and the person responsible for the care of the child in those cases where such person was suspected of abuse or neglect; and

7.   If a report of child abuse and neglect is founded, and the subject of the report is a full-time, part-time, permanent, or temporary employee of a school division located within the Commonwealth, notify the relevant school board of the founded complaint.

Any information exchanged for the purposes of this subsection shall not be considered a violation of § 63.2–102, 63.2–104, or 63.2–105.

C.   Each local board may obtain and consider, in accordance with regulations adopted by the Board, statewide criminal history record information from the Central Criminal Records Exchange and results of a search of the child abuse and neglect central registry of any individual who is the subject of a child abuse or neglect investigation conducted under this section when there is evidence of child abuse or neglect and the local board is evaluating the safety of the home and whether removal will protect a child from harm. The local board also may obtain such a criminal records or registry search on all adult household members residing in the home where the individual who is the subject of the investigation resides and the child resides or visits. If a child abuse or neglect petition is filed in connection with such removal, a court may admit such information as evidence. Where the individual who is the subject of such information contests its accuracy through testimony under oath in hearing before the court, no court shall receive or consider the contested criminal history record information without certified copies of conviction. Further dissemination of the information provided to the local board is prohibited, except as authorized by law.

D. A person who has not previously participated in the investigation of complaints of child abuse or neglect in accordance with this chapter shall not participate in the investigation of any case involving a complaint of alleged sexual abuse of a child unless he (i) has completed a Board-approved training program for the investigation of complaints involving alleged sexual abuse of a child or (ii) is under the direct supervision of a person who has completed a Board-approved training program for the investigation of complaints involving alleged sexual abuse of a child. No individual may make a determination of whether a case involving a complaint of alleged sexual abuse of a child is founded or unfounded unless he has completed a Board-approved training program for the investigation of complaints involving alleged sexual abuse of a child.

§ 63.2–1506. FAMILY ASSESSMENTS BY LOCAL DEPARTMENTS

A. A family assessment requires the collection of information necessary to determine:

    1.   The immediate safety needs of the child;

    2.   The protective and rehabilitative services needs of the child and family that will deter abuse or neglect;

    3.   Risk of future harm to the child; and

    4.   Alternative plans for the child's safety if protective and rehabilitative services are indicated and the family is unable or unwilling to participate in services.

B. When a local department has been designated as a child-protective services differential response system participant by the Department pursuant to § 63.2–1504 and responds to the report or complaint by conducting a family assessment, the local department shall:

    1.   Conduct an immediate family assessment and, if the report or complaint was based upon one of the factors specified in subsection B of § 63.2–1509, the local department may file a petition pursuant to § 16.1–241.3;

2.   Immediately contact the subject of the report and the family of the child alleged to have been abused or neglected and give each a written and an oral explanation of the family assessment procedure. The family assessment shall be in writing and shall be completed in accordance with Board regulation;

3.   Complete the family assessment within forty-five days and transmit a report to such effect to the Department and to the person who is the subject of the family assessment. However, upon written justification by the local department, the family assessment may be extended, not to exceed a total of sixty days;

4.   Consult with the family to arrange for necessary protective and rehabilitative services to be provided to the child and his family. Families have the option of declining the services offered as a result of the family assessment. If the family declines the services, the case shall be closed unless the local department determines that sufficient cause exists to redetermine the case as one that needs to be investigated. In no instance shall a case be redetermined as an investigation solely because the family declines services;

5.   Petition the court for services deemed necessary;

6.   Make no disposition of founded or unfounded for reports in which a family assessment is completed. Reports in which a family assessment is completed shall not be entered into the central registry contained in § 63.2–1515; and

7.   Commence an immediate investigation, if at any time during the completion of the family assessment, the local department determines that an investigation is required.

C.   When a local department has been designated as a child-protective services differential response agency by the Department, the local department may investigate any report of child abuse or neglect, but the following valid reports of child abuse or neglect shall be investigated: (i) sexual abuse, (ii) child fatality, (iii) abuse or neglect resulting in serious injury as defined in § 18.2–371.1, (iv) child has been taken into the custody of the local department, or (v) cases involving a caretaker at a state-licensed child day center, religiously exempt child day center, licensed, registered or approved family day home, private or public school, hospital or any institution.

§ 63.2–1507. COOPERATION BY STATE ENTITIES

All law-enforcement departments and other state and local departments, agencies, authorities and institutions shall cooperate with each child-protective services coordinator of a local department and any multi- discipline teams in the detection and prevention of child abuse.

ARTICLE 2. COMPLAINTS

§ 63.2–1508. VALID REPORT OR COMPLAINT

A valid report or complaint means the local department has evaluated the information and allegations of the report or complaint and determined that the local department shall conduct an investigation or family assessment because the following elements are present:

1. The alleged victim child or children are under the age of eighteen at the time of the complaint or report;

2. The alleged abuser is the alleged victim child's parent or other caretaker;

3. The local department receiving the complaint or report has jurisdiction; and

4. The circumstances described allege suspected child abuse or neglect.

Nothing in this section shall relieve any person specified in § 63.2–1509 from making a report required by that section, regardless of the identity of the person suspected to have caused such abuse or neglect.

§ 63.2–1509. REQUIREMENT THAT CERTAIN INJURIES TO CHILDREN BE REPORTED BY PHYSICIANS, NURSES, TEACHERS, ETC.; PENALTY FOR FAILURE TO REPORT

A. The following persons who, in their professional or official capacity, have reason to suspect that a child is an abused or neglected child, shall report the matter immediately to the local department of the county or city wherein the child resides or wherein the abuse or neglect is believed to have occurred or to the Department's toll-free child abuse and neglect hotline:

1. Any person licensed to practice medicine or any of the healing arts;

2. Any hospital resident or intern, and any person employed in the nursing profession;

3. Any person employed as a social worker or family-services specialist;

4. Any probation officer;

5. Any teacher or other person employed in a public or private school, kindergarten or nursery school;

6. Any person providing full-time or part-time child care for pay on a regularly planned basis;

7. Any mental health professional;

8. Any law-enforcement officer or animal control officer;

9.   Any mediator eligible to receive court referrals pursuant to § 8.01–576.8;

10.   Any professional staff person, not previously enumerated, employed by a private or state-operated hospital, institution or facility to which children have been committed or where children have been placed for care and treatment;

11.   Any person 18 years of age or older associated with or employed by any public or private organization responsible for the care, custody or control of children;

12.   Any person who is designated a court-appointed special advocate pursuant to Article 5 (§ 9.1–151 et seq.) of Chapter 1 of Title 9.1;

13.   Any person 18 years of age or older who has received training approved by the Department of Social Services for the purposes of recognizing and reporting child abuse and neglect;

14.   Any person employed by a local department as defined in § 63.2–100 who determines eligibility for public assistance;

15.   Any emergency medical services provider certified by the Board of Health pursuant to § 32.1–111.5, unless such provider immediately reports the matter directly to the attending physician at the hospital to which the child is transported, who shall make such report forthwith;

16.   Any athletic coach, director or other person 18 years of age or older employed by or volunteering with a private sports organization or team;

17.   Administrators or employees 18 years of age or older of public or private day camps, youth centers and youth recreation programs; and

18.   Any person employed by a public or private institution of higher education other than an attorney who is employed by a public or private institution of higher education as it relates to information gained in the course of providing legal representation to a client.

This subsection shall not apply to any regular minister, priest, rabbi, imam, or duly accredited practitioner of any religious organization or denomination usually referred to as a church as it relates to (i) information required by the doctrine of the religious organization or denomination to be kept in a confidential manner or (ii) information that would be subject to § 8.01–400 or 19.2–271.3 if offered as evidence in court.

If neither the locality in which the child resides nor where the abuse or neglect is believed to have occurred is known, then such report shall be made to the local department of the county or city where the abuse or neglect was discovered or to the Department's toll-free child abuse and neglect hotline.

If an employee of the local department is suspected of abusing or neglecting a child, the report shall be made to the court of the county or city where the abuse or neglect was discovered. Upon receipt of such a report by the court, the judge shall assign the report to a local department that is not the employer of the suspected employee for investigation or family assessment. The judge may consult with the Department in selecting a local department to respond to the report or the complaint.

If the information is received by a teacher, staff member, resident, intern or nurse in the course of professional services in a hospital, school or similar institution, such person may, in place of said report, immediately notify the person in charge of the institution or department, or his designee, who shall make such report forthwith. If the initial report of suspected abuse or neglect is made to the person in charge of the institution or department, or his designee, pursuant to this subsection, such person shall notify the teacher, staff member, resident, intern or nurse who made the initial report when the report of suspected child abuse or neglect is made to the local department or to the Department's toll-free child abuse and neglect hotline, and of the name of the individual receiving the report, and shall forward any communication resulting from the report, including any information about any actions taken regarding the report, to the person who made the initial report.

The initial report may be an oral report but such report shall be reduced to writing by the child abuse coordinator of the local department on a form prescribed by the Board. Any person required to make the report pursuant to this subsection shall disclose all information that is the basis for his suspicion of abuse or neglect of the child and, upon request, shall make available to the child-protective services coordinator and the local department, which is the agency of jurisdiction, any information, records, or reports that document the basis for the report. All persons required by this subsection to report suspected abuse or neglect who maintain a record of a child who is the subject of such a report shall cooperate with the investigating agency and shall make related information, records and reports available to the investigating agency unless such disclosure violates the federal Family Educational Rights and Privacy Act (20 U.S.C. § 1232g). Provision of such information, records, and reports by a health care provider shall not be prohibited by § 8.01–399. Criminal investigative reports received from law-enforcement agencies shall not be further disseminated by the investigating agency nor shall they be subject to public disclosure.

B. For purposes of subsection A, "reason to suspect that a child is abused or neglected" shall include (i) a finding made by a health care provider within six weeks of the birth of a child that the results of toxicology studies of the child indicate the presence of a controlled substance not prescribed for the mother by a physician; (ii) a finding made by a health care provider within six weeks of the birth of a child that the child was born dependent on a controlled substance which was not prescribed by a physician for the mother and has demonstrated withdrawal symptoms; (iii) a diagnosis made by a health care provider at any time following a child's birth that the child has an illness, disease or condition which, to a reasonable degree of medical certainty, is attributable to in utero exposure to a controlled substance which was not prescribed by a physician for the mother or the child; or (iv) a diagnosis made by a health care provider at any time following a child's birth that the child has a fetal alcohol spectrum disorder attributable to in utero exposure to alcohol. When "reason to suspect" is based upon this subsection, such fact shall be included in the report along with the facts relied upon by the person making the report.

C.   Any person who makes a report or provides records or information pursuant to subsection A or who testifies in any judicial proceeding arising from such report, records, or information shall be immune from any civil or criminal liability or administrative penalty or sanction on account of such report, records, information, or testimony, unless such person acted in bad faith or with malicious purpose.

D.   Any person required to file a report pursuant to this section who fails to do so as soon as possible, but not longer than 24 hours after having reason to suspect a reportable offense of child abuse or neglect, shall be fined not more than $500 for the first failure and for any subsequent failures not less than $1,000. In cases evidencing acts of rape, sodomy, or object sexual penetration as defined in Article 7 (§ 18.2–61 et seq.) of Chapter 4 of Title 18.2, a person who knowingly and intentionally fails to make the report required pursuant to this section shall be guilty of a Class 1 misdemeanor.

E.   No person shall be required to make a report pursuant to this section if the person has actual knowledge that the same matter has already been reported to the local department or the Department's toll-free child abuse and neglect hotline.

§ 63.2–1510. COMPLAINTS BY OTHERS OF CERTAIN INJURIES TO CHILDREN

Any person who suspects that a child is an abused or neglected child may make a complaint concerning such child, except as hereinafter provided, to the local department of the county or city wherein the child resides or wherein the abuse or neglect is believed to have occurred or to the Department's toll-free child abuse and neglect hotline. If an employee of the local department is suspected of abusing or neglecting a child, the complaint shall be made to the court of the county or city where the abuse or neglect was discovered. Upon receipt of such a report by the court, the judge shall assign the report to a local department that is not the employer of the suspected employee for investigation or family assessment; or, if the judge believes that no local department in a reasonable geographic distance can be impartial in responding to the reported case, the judge shall assign the report to the court service unit of his court for evaluation. The judge may consult with the Department in selecting a local department to respond to the report or complaint. Such a complaint may be oral or in writing and shall disclose all information which is the basis for the suspicion of abuse or neglect of the child.

§ 63.2–1511. COMPLAINTS OF ABUSE AND NEGLECT AGAINST SCHOOL PERSONNEL; INTERAGENCY AGREEMENT

A. If a teacher, principal or other person employed by a local school board or employed in a school operated by the Commonwealth is suspected of abusing or neglecting a child in the course of his educational employment, the complaint shall be investigated in accordance with §§ 63.2–1503, 63.2–1505 and 63.2–1516.1. Pursuant to § 22.1–279.1, no teacher, principal or other person employed by a school board or employed in a school operated by the Commonwealth shall subject a student to corporal punishment. However, this prohibition of corporal punishment shall not be deemed to prevent (i) the use of incidental, minor or reasonable physical contact or other actions designed to maintain order and control; (ii) the use of reasonable and necessary force to quell a disturbance or remove a student from the scene of a disturbance that threatens physical injury to persons or damage to property; (iii) the use of reasonable and necessary force to prevent a student from inflicting physical harm on himself; (iv) the use of reasonable and necessary force for self-defense or the defense of others; or (v) the use of reasonable and necessary force to obtain possession of weapons or other dangerous objects or controlled substances or paraphernalia that are upon the person of the student or within his control. In determining whether the actions of a teacher, principal or other person employed by a school board or employed in a school operated by the Commonwealth are within the exceptions provided in this section, the local department shall examine whether the actions at the time of the event that were made by such person were reasonable.

B. For purposes of this section, "corporal punishment," "abuse," or "neglect" shall not include physical pain, injury or discomfort caused by the use of incidental, minor or reasonable physical contact or other actions designed to maintain order and control as permitted in clause (i) of subsection A or the use of reasonable and necessary force as permitted by clauses (ii), (iii), (iv), and (v) of subsection A, or by participation in practice or competition in an interscholastic sport, or participation in physical education or an extracurricular activity.

C. If, after an investigation of a complaint under this section, the local department determines that the actions or omissions of a teacher, principal, or other person employed by a local school board or employed in a school operated by the Commonwealth were within such employee's scope of employment and were taken in good faith in the course of supervision, care, or discipline of students, then the standard in determining if a report of abuse or neglect is founded is whether such acts or omissions constituted gross negligence or willful misconduct.

D.   Each local department and local school division shall adopt a written interagency agreement as a protocol for investigating child abuse and neglect reports. The interagency agreement shall be based on recommended procedures for conducting investigations developed by the Departments of Education and Social Services.

§ 63.2–1512. IMMUNITY OF PERSON MAKING REPORT, ETC., FROM LIABILITY

Any person making a report pursuant to § 63.2–1509, a complaint pursuant to § 63.2–1510, or who takes a child into custody pursuant to § 63.2–1517, or who participates in a judicial proceeding resulting therefrom shall be immune from any civil or criminal liability in connection therewith, unless it is proven that such person acted in bad faith or with malicious intent.

§ 63.2–1513. KNOWINGLY MAKING FALSE REPORTS; PENALTIES

A.   Any person fourteen years of age or older who makes or causes to be made a report of child abuse or neglect pursuant to this chapter that he knows to be false shall be guilty of a Class 1 misdemeanor. Any person fourteen years of age or older who has been previously convicted under this subsection and who is subsequently convicted under this subsection shall be guilty of a Class 6 felony.

B.   The child-protective services records regarding the person who was alleged to have committed abuse or neglect that result from a report for which a conviction is obtained under this section shall be purged immediately by any custodian of such records upon presentation to the custodian of a certified copy of such conviction. After purging the records, the custodian shall notify the person in writing that such records have been purged.

ARTICLE 3. RECORDS

§ 63.2–1514. RETENTION OF RECORDS IN ALL REPORTS; PROCEDURES REGARDING UNFOUNDED REPORTS ALLEGED TO BE MADE IN BAD FAITH OR WITH MALICIOUS INTENT

A.   The local department shall retain the records of all reports or complaints made pursuant to this chapter, in accordance with regulations adopted by the Board. However, all records related to founded cases of child sexual abuse involving injuries or conditions, real or threatened, that result in or were likely to have resulted in serious harm to a child shall be maintained by the local department for a period of 25 years from the date of the complaint.

B.   The Department shall maintain a child abuse and neglect information system that includes a central registry of founded complaints, pursuant to § 63.2–1515. The Department shall maintain all (i) unfounded investigations, (ii) family assessments, and (iii) reports or complaints determined to be not valid in a record which is separate from the central registry and accessible only to the Department and to local departments for child-protective services. The purpose of retaining these complaints or reports is to provide local departments with information regarding prior complaints or reports. In no event shall the mere existence of a prior complaint or report be used to determine that a subsequent complaint or report is founded. The subject of the complaint or report is the person who is alleged to have committed abuse or neglect. The subject of the complaint or report shall have access to his own record. The record of unfounded investigations and complaints and reports determined to be not valid shall be purged one year after the date of the complaint or report if there are no subsequent complaints or reports regarding the same child or the person who is the subject of the complaint or report in that one year. The local department shall retain such records for an additional period of up to two years if requested in writing by the person who is the subject of such complaint or report. The record of family assessments shall be purged three years after the date of the complaint or report if there are no subsequent complaints or reports regarding the same child or the person who is the subject of the report in that three-year period. The child-protective services records regarding the petitioner which result from such complaint or report shall be purged immediately by any custodian of such records upon presentation to the custodian of a certified copy of a court order that there has been a civil action that determined that the complaint or report was made in bad faith or with malicious intent. After purging the records, the custodian shall notify the petitioner in writing that the records have been purged.

C.   At the time the local department notifies a person who is the subject of a complaint or report made pursuant to this chapter that such complaint or report is either an unfounded investigation or a completed family assessment, it shall notify him how long the record will be retained and of the availability of the procedures set out in this section regarding reports or complaints alleged to be made in bad faith or with malicious intent. Upon request, the local department shall advise the person who was the subject of an unfounded investigation if the complaint or report was made anonymously. However, the identity of a complainant or reporter shall not be disclosed.

D.   Any person who is the subject of an unfounded report or complaint made pursuant to this chapter who believes that such report or complaint was made in bad faith or with malicious intent may petition the circuit court in the jurisdiction in which the report or complaint was made for the release to such person of the records of the investigation or family assessment. Such petition shall specifically set forth the reasons such person believes that such report or complaint was made in bad faith or with malicious intent. Upon the filing of such petition, the circuit court shall request and the local department shall provide to the circuit court its records of the investigation or family assessment for the circuit court's in camera review. The petitioner shall be entitled to present evidence to support his petition. If the circuit court determines that there is a reasonable question of fact as to whether the report or complaint was made in bad faith or with malicious intent and that disclosure of the identity of the complainant would not be likely to endanger the life or safety of the complainant, it shall provide to the petitioner a copy of the records of the investigation or family assessment. The original records shall be subject to discovery in any subsequent civil action regarding the making of a complaint or report in bad faith or with malicious intent.

§ 63.2–1515. CENTRAL REGISTRY; DISCLOSURE OF INFORMATION

The central registry shall contain such information as shall be prescribed by Board regulation; however, when the founded case of abuse or neglect does not name the parents or guardians of the child as the abuser or neglector, and the abuse or neglect occurred in a licensed or unlicensed child day center, a licensed, registered or approved family day home, a private or public school, or a children's residential facility, the child's name shall not be entered on the registry without consultation with and permission of the parents or guardians. If a child's name currently appears on the registry without consultation with and permission of the parents or guardians for a founded case of abuse and neglect that does not name the parents or guardians of the child as the abuser or neglector, such parents or guardians may have the child's name removed by written request to the Department. The information contained in the central registry shall not be open to inspection by the public. However, appropriate disclosure may be made in accordance with Board regulations.

The Department shall respond to requests for a search of the central registry made by (i) local departments and (ii) local school boards regarding applicants for employment, pursuant to § 22.1–296.4, in cases where there is no match within the central registry within 10 business days of receipt of such requests. In cases where there is a match within the central registry regarding applicants for employment, the Department shall respond to requests made by local departments and local school boards within 30 business days of receipt of such requests. The response may be by first-class mail or facsimile transmission.

Any central registry check of a person who has applied to be a volunteer with a (a) Virginia affiliate of Big Brothers/Big Sisters of America, (b) Virginia affiliate of Compeer, (c) Virginia affiliate of Childhelp USA, (d) volunteer fire company or volunteer emergency medical services agency, or (e) court-appointed special advocate program pursuant to § 9.1–153 shall be conducted at no charge.

ARTICLE 4. PROCEDURES

§ 63.2–1516. TAPE RECORDING CHILD ABUSE INVESTIGATIONS

Any person who is suspected of abuse or neglect of a child and who is the subject of an investigation or family assessment pursuant to this chapter may tape record any communications between him and child-protective services personnel that take place during the course of such investigation or family assessment, provided all parties to the conversation are aware the conversation is to be recorded. The parties' knowledge of the recording shall be demonstrated by a declaration at the beginning of the recorded portion of the conversation that the recording is to be made. If a person who is suspected of abuse or neglect of a child and who is the subject of an investigation or family assessment pursuant to this chapter elects to make a tape recording as provided in this section, the child-protective services personnel may also make such a recording.

§ 63.2–1516.01. INVESTIGATION PROCEDURES INVOLVING PERSON WHO IS THE SUBJECT OF COMPLAINT

The local department shall, at the initial time of contact with the person subject to a child abuse and neglect investigation, advise such person of the complaints or allegations made against the person, in a manner that is consistent with laws protecting the rights of the person making the report or complaint. In cases where a child is alleged to have been abused or neglected by a teacher, principal or other person employed by a local school board or employed in a school operated by the Commonwealth, in the course of such employment in a nonresidential setting, the provisions of § 63.2–1516.1 shall also apply.

§ 63.2–1516.1. INVESTIGATION PROCEDURES WHEN SCHOOL EMPLOYEE IS SUBJECT OF THE COMPLAINT OR REPORT; RELEASE OF INFORMATION IN JOINT INVESTIGATIONS

A. Except as provided in subsection B of this section, in cases where a child is alleged to have been abused or neglected by a teacher, principal or other person employed by a local school board or employed in a school operated by the Commonwealth, in the course of such employment in a nonresidential setting, the local department conducting the investigation shall comply with the following provisions in conducting its investigation:

1. The local department shall conduct a face-to-face interview with the person who is the subject of the complaint or report.

2. At the onset of the initial interview with the alleged abuser or neglector, the local department shall notify him in writing of the general nature of the complaint and the identity of the alleged child victim regarding the purpose of the contacts.

3.   The written notification shall include the information that the alleged abuser or neglector has the right to have an attorney or other representative of his choice present during his interviews. However, the failure by a representative of the Department of Social Services to so advise the subject of the complaint shall not cause an otherwise voluntary statement to be inadmissible in a criminal proceeding.

4.   Written notification of the findings shall be submitted to the alleged abuser or neglector. The notification shall include a summary of the investigation and an explanation of how the information gathered supports the disposition.

5.   The written notification of the findings shall inform the alleged abuser or neglector of his right to appeal.

6.   The written notification of the findings shall inform the alleged abuser or neglector of his right to review information about himself in the record with the following exceptions:

a.   The identity of the person making the report.

b.   Information provided by any law-enforcement official.

c.   Information that may endanger the well-being of the child.

d.   The identity of a witness or any other person if such release may endanger the life or safety of such witness or person.

B.   In all cases in which an alleged act of child abuse or neglect is also being criminally investigated by a law-enforcement agency, and the local department is conducting a joint investigation with a law-enforcement officer in regard to such an alleged act, no information in the possession of the local department from such joint investigation shall be released by the local department except as authorized by the investigating law-enforcement officer or his supervisor or the local attorney for the Commonwealth.

C.   Failure to comply with investigation procedures does not preclude a finding of abuse or neglect if such a finding is warranted by the facts.

§ 63.2–1517. AUTHORITY TO TAKE CHILD INTO CUSTODY

A.   A physician or child-protective services worker of a local department or law-enforcement official investigating a report or complaint of abuse and neglect may take a child into custody for up to 72 hours without prior approval of parents or guardians provided:

1.   The circumstances of the child are such that continuing in his place of residence or in the care or custody of the parent, guardian, custodian or other person responsible for the child's care, presents an imminent danger to the child's life or health to the

extent that severe or irremediable injury would be likely to result or if evidence of abuse is perishable or subject to deterioration before a hearing can be held;

2. A court order is not immediately obtainable;

3. The court has set up procedures for placing such children;

4. Following taking the child into custody, the parents or guardians are notified as soon as practicable. Every effort shall be made to provide such notice in person;

5. A report is made to the local department; and

6. The court is notified and the person or agency taking custody of such child obtains, as soon as possible, but in no event later than 72 hours, an emergency removal order pursuant to § 16.1–251; however, if a preliminary removal order is issued after a hearing held in accordance with § 16.1–252 within 72 hours of the removal of the child, an emergency removal order shall not be necessary. Any person or agency petitioning for an emergency removal order after four hours have elapsed following taking custody of the child shall state the reasons therefor pursuant to § 16.1–251.

B. If the 72-hour period for holding a child in custody and for obtaining a preliminary or emergency removal order expires on a Saturday, Sunday, or legal holiday or day on which the court is lawfully closed, the 72 hours shall be extended to the next day that is not a Saturday, Sunday, or legal holiday or day on which the court is lawfully closed.

§ 63.2–1518. AUTHORITY TO TALK TO CHILD OR SIBLING

Any person required to make a report or conduct an investigation or family assessment, pursuant to this chapter may talk to any child suspected of being abused or neglected or to any of his siblings without consent of and outside the presence of his parent, guardian, legal custodian, or other person standing in loco parentis, or school personnel.

§ 63.2–1519. PHYSICIAN-PATIENT AND HUSBAND-WIFE PRIVILEGES INAPPLICABLE

In any legal proceeding resulting from the filing of any report or complaint pursuant to this chapter, the physician-patient and husband-wife privileges shall not apply.

§ 63.2–1520. PHOTOGRAPHS AND X-RAYS OF CHILD; USE AS EVIDENCE

In any case of suspected child abuse, photographs and X-rays of the child may be taken without the consent of the parent or other person responsible for such child as a part of the medical evaluation. Photographs of the child may also be taken without the consent of the parent or other person responsible for such child as a part of the investigation or family assessment of the case by the local department or the court; however, such photographs shall not be used in lieu of medical evaluation. Such photographs and X-rays may be introduced into evidence in any subsequent proceeding.

The court receiving such evidence may impose such restrictions as to the confidentiality of photographs of any minor as it deems appropriate.

§ 63.2–1521. TESTIMONY BY CHILD USING TWO-WAY CLOSED-CIRCUIT TELEVISION

A. In any civil proceeding involving alleged abuse or neglect of a child pursuant to this chapter or pursuant to §§ 16.1–241, 16.1–251, 16.1–252, 16.1–253, 16.1–283 or § 20–107.2, the child's attorney or guardian ad litem or, if the child has been committed to the custody of a local department, the attorney for the local department may apply for an order from the court that the testimony of the alleged victim or of a child witness be taken in a room outside the courtroom and be televised by two-way closed-circuit television. The person seeking such order shall apply for the order at least seven days before the trial date.

B. The provisions of this section shall apply to the following:

1. An alleged victim who was fourteen years of age or under on the date of the alleged offense and is sixteen or under at the time of the trial; and

2. Any child witness who is fourteen years of age or under at the time of the trial.

C. The court may order that the testimony of the child be taken by closed-circuit television as provided in subsections A and B if it finds that the child is unavailable to testify in open court in the presence of the defendant, the jury, the judge, and the public, for any of the following reasons:

1. The child's persistent refusal to testify despite judicial requests to do so;

2. The child's substantial inability to communicate about the offense; or

3. The substantial likelihood, based upon expert opinion testimony, that the child will suffer severe emotional trauma from so testifying.

Any ruling on the child's unavailability under this subsection shall be supported by the court with findings on the record or with written findings in a court not of record.

D. In any proceeding in which closed-circuit television is used to receive testimony, the attorney for the child and the defendant's attorney and, if the child has been committed to the custody of a local board, the attorney for the local board shall be present in the room with the child, and the child shall be subject to direct and cross examination. The only other persons allowed to be present in the room with the child during his testimony shall be the guardian ad litem, those persons necessary to operate the closed-circuit equipment, and any other person whose presence is determined by the court to be necessary to the welfare and well-being of the child.

E. The child's testimony shall be transmitted by closed-circuit television into the courtroom for the defendant, jury, judge and public to view. The defendant shall be provided with a means of private, contemporaneous communication with his attorney during the testimony.

§ 63.2–1522. ADMISSION OF EVIDENCE OF SEXUAL ACTS WITH CHILDREN

A. In any civil proceeding involving alleged abuse or neglect of a child pursuant to this chapter or pursuant to §§ 16.1–241, 16.1–251, 16.1–252, 16.1–253, 16.1–283 or § 20–107.2, an out-of-court statement made by a child the age of twelve or under at the time the statement is offered into evidence, describing any act of a sexual nature performed with or on the child by another, not otherwise admissible by statute or rule, may be admissible in evidence if the requirements of subsection B are met.

B. An out-of-court statement may be admitted into evidence as provided in subsection A if:

1. The child testifies at the proceeding, or testifies by means of a videotaped deposition or closed-circuit television, and at the time of such testimony is subject to cross examination concerning the out-of-court statement or the child is found by the court to be unavailable to testify on any of these grounds:

a. The child's death;

b. The child's absence from the jurisdiction, provided such absence is not for the purpose of preventing the availability of the child to testify;

c. The child's total failure of memory;

d. The child's physical or mental disability;

e. The existence of a privilege involving the child;

f. The child's incompetency, including the child's inability to communicate about the offense because of fear or a similar reason; and

g. The substantial likelihood, based upon expert opinion testimony, that the child would suffer severe emotional trauma from testifying at the proceeding or by means of a videotaped deposition or closed-circuit television.

2.   The child's out-of-court statement is shown to possess particularized guarantees of trustworthiness and reliability.

C.   A statement may not be admitted under this section unless the proponent of the statement notifies the adverse party of his intention to offer the statement and the substance of the statement sufficiently in advance of the proceedings to provide the adverse party with a reasonable opportunity to prepare to meet the statement, including the opportunity to subpoena witnesses.

D.   In determining whether a statement possesses particularized guarantees of trustworthiness and reliability under subdivision B 2, the court shall consider, but is not limited to, the following factors:

1.   The child's personal knowledge of the event;

2.   The age and maturity of the child;

3.   Certainty that the statement was made, including the credibility of the person testifying about the statement and any apparent motive such person may have to falsify or distort the event including bias, corruption or coercion;

4.   Any apparent motive the child may have to falsify or distort the event, including bias, corruption, or coercion;

5.   The timing of the child's statement;

6.   Whether more than one person heard the statement;

7.   Whether the child was suffering pain or distress when making the statement;

8.   Whether the child's age makes it unlikely that the child fabricated a statement that represents a graphic, detailed account beyond the child's knowledge and experience;

9.   Whether the statement has internal consistency or coherence, and uses terminology appropriate to the child's age;

10. Whether the statement is spontaneous or directly responsive to questions;

11. Whether the statement is responsive to suggestive or leading questions; and

12. Whether extrinsic evidence exists to show the defendant's opportunity to commit the act complained of in the child's statement.

E.   The court shall support with findings on the record, or with written findings in a court not of record, any rulings pertaining to the child's unavailability and the trustworthiness and reliability of the out-of-court statement.

§ 63.2–1523. USE OF VIDEOTAPED STATEMENTS OF COMPLAINING WITNESSES AS EVIDENCE

A.   In any civil proceeding involving alleged abuse or neglect of a child pursuant to this chapter or pursuant to §§ 16.1–241, 16.1–251, 16.1–252, 16.1–253, 16.1–283 or § 20–107.2, a recording of a statement of the alleged victim of the offense, made prior to the proceeding, may be admissible as evidence if the requirements of subsection B are met and the court determines that:

    1.   The alleged victim is the age of twelve or under at the time the statement is offered into evidence;

    2.   The recording is both visual and oral, and every person appearing in, and every voice recorded on, the tape is identified;

    3.   The recording is on videotape or was recorded by other electronic means capable of making an accurate recording;

    4.   The recording has not been altered;

    5.   No attorney for any party to the proceeding was present when the statement was made;

    6.   The person conducting the interview of the alleged victim was authorized to do so by the child-protective services coordinator of the local department;

    7.   All persons present at the time the statement was taken, including the alleged victim, are present and available to testify or be cross examined at the proceeding when the recording is offered; and

    8.   The parties or their attorneys were provided with a list of all persons present at the recording and were afforded an opportunity to view the recording at least ten days prior to the scheduled proceedings.

B.   A recorded statement may be admitted into evidence as provided in subsection A if:

    1.   The child testifies at the proceeding, or testifies by means of closed-circuit television, and at the time of such testimony is subject to cross examination concerning the recorded statement or the child is found by the court to be unavailable to testify on any of these grounds:

        a.   The child's death;

        b.   The child's absence from the jurisdiction, provided such absence is not for the purpose of preventing the availability of the child to testify;

        c.   The child's total failure of memory;

        d.   The child's physical or mental disability;

        e.   The existence of a privilege involving the child;

      f.   The child's incompetency, including the child's inability to communicate about the offense because of fear or a similar reason;

      g.   The substantial likelihood, based upon expert opinion testimony, that the child would suffer severe emotional trauma from testifying at the proceeding or by means of closed-circuit television; and

      2.   The child's recorded statement is shown to possess particularized guarantees of trustworthiness and reliability.

      C.   A recorded statement may not be admitted under this section unless the proponent of the statement notifies the adverse party of his intention to offer the statement and the substance of the statement sufficiently in advance of the proceedings to provide the adverse party with a reasonable opportunity to prepare to meet the statement, including the opportunity to subpoena witnesses.

      D.   In determining whether a recorded statement possesses particularized guarantees of trustworthiness and reliability under subdivision B 2, the court shall consider, but is not limited to, the following factors:

      1.   The child's personal knowledge of the event;

      2.   The age and maturity of the child;

      3.   Any apparent motive the child may have to falsify or distort the event, including bias, corruption, or coercion;

      4.   The timing of the child's statement;

      5.   Whether the child was suffering pain or distress when making the statement;

      6.   Whether the child's age makes it unlikely that the child fabricated a statement that represents a graphic, detailed account beyond the child's knowledge and experience;

      7.   Whether the statement has a "ring of verity," has internal consistency or coherence, and uses terminology appropriate to the child's age;

      8.   Whether the statement is spontaneous or directly responsive to questions;

      9.   Whether the statement is responsive to suggestive or leading questions; and

      10.   Whether extrinsic evidence exists to show the defendant's opportunity to commit the act complained of in the child's statement.

      E.   The court shall support with findings on the record, or with written findings in a court not of record, any rulings pertaining to the child's unavailability and the trustworthiness and reliability of the recorded statement.

§ 63.2–1524. COURT MAY ORDER CERTAIN EXAMINATIONS

The court may order psychological, psychiatric and physical examinations of the child alleged to be abused or neglected and of the parents, guardians, caretakers or siblings of a child suspected of being neglected or abused.

§ 63.2–1525. PRIMA FACIE EVIDENCE FOR REMOVAL OF CHILD CUSTODY

In the case of a petition in the court for removal of custody of a child alleged to have been abused or neglected, competent evidence by a physician that a child is abused or neglected shall constitute prima facie evidence to support such petition.

§ 63.2–1526. APPEALS OF CERTAIN ACTIONS OF LOCAL DEPARTMENTS

A. A person who is suspected of or is found to have committed abuse or neglect may, within thirty days of being notified of that determination, request the local department rendering such determination to amend the determination and the local department's related records. Upon written request, the local department shall provide the appellant all information used in making its determination. Disclosure of the reporter's name or information which may endanger the well-being of a child shall not be released. The identity of a collateral witness or any other person shall not be released if disclosure may endanger his life or safety. Information prohibited from being disclosed by state or federal law or regulation shall not be released. The local department shall hold an informal conference or consultation where such person, who may be represented by counsel, shall be entitled to informally present testimony of witnesses, documents, factual data, arguments or other submissions of proof to the local department. With the exception of the local director, no person whose regular duties include substantial involvement with child abuse and neglect cases shall preside over the informal conference. If the local department refuses the request for amendment or fails to act within forty-five days after receiving such request, the person may, within thirty days thereafter, petition the Commissioner, who shall grant a hearing to determine whether it appears, by a preponderance of the evidence, that the determination or record contains information which is irrelevant or inaccurate regarding the commission of abuse or neglect by the person who is the subject of the determination or record and therefore shall be amended. A person who is the subject of a report who requests an amendment to the record, as provided above, has the right to obtain an extension for an additional specified period of up to sixty days by requesting in writing that the forty-five days in which the local department must act be extended. The extension period, which may be up to sixty days, shall begin at the end of the forty-five days in which the local department must act. When there is an extension period, the thirty-day period to request an administrative hearing shall begin on the termination of the extension period.

B.   The Commissioner shall designate and authorize one or more members of his staff to conduct such hearings. The decision of any staff member so designated and authorized shall have the same force and effect as if the Commissioner had made the decision. The hearing officer shall have the authority to issue subpoenas for the production of documents and the appearance of witnesses. The hearing officer is authorized to determine the number of depositions that will be allowed and to administer oaths or affirmations to all parties and witnesses who plan to testify at the hearing. The Board shall adopt regulations necessary for the conduct of such hearings. Such regulations shall include provisions stating that the person who is the subject of the report has the right (i) to submit oral or written testimony or documents in support of himself and (ii) to be informed of the procedure by which information will be made available or withheld from him. In case of any information withheld, such person shall be advised of the general nature of such information and the reasons, for reasons of privacy or otherwise, that it is being withheld. Upon giving reasonable notice, either party at his own expense may depose a nonparty and submit such deposition at the hearing pursuant to Board regulation. Upon good cause shown, after a party's written motion, the hearing officer may issue subpoenas for the production of documents or to compel the attendance of witnesses at the hearing, except that alleged child victims of the person and their siblings shall not be subpoenaed, deposed or required to testify. The person who is the subject of the report may be represented by counsel at the hearing. Upon petition, the court shall have the power to enforce any subpoena that is not complied with or to review any refusal to issue a subpoena. Such decisions may not be further appealed except as part of a final decision that is subject to judicial review. Such hearing officers are empowered to order the amendment of such determination or records as is required to make them accurate and consistent with the requirements of this chapter or the regulations adopted hereunder. If, after hearing the facts of the case, the hearing officer determines that the person who is the subject of the report has presented information that was not available to the local department at the time of the local conference and which if available may have resulted in a different determination by the local department, he may remand the case to the local department for reconsideration. The local department shall have fourteen days in which to reconsider the case. If, at the expiration of fourteen days, the local department fails to act or fails to amend the record to the satisfaction of the appellant, the case shall be returned to the hearing officer for a determination. If aggrieved by the decision of the hearing officer, such person may obtain further review of the decision in accordance with Article 5 (§ 2.2–4025 et seq.) of the Administrative Process Act (§ 2.2–4000 et seq.).

C.   Whenever an appeal of the local department's finding is made and a criminal charge is also filed against the appellant for the same conduct involving the same victim as investigated by the local department, the appeal process shall automatically be stayed until the criminal prosecution in circuit court is completed. During such stay, the appellant's right of access to the records of the local department regarding the matter being appealed shall also be stayed. Once the criminal prosecution in circuit court has been completed, the local department shall advise the appellant in writing of his right to resume his appeal within the time frames provided by law and regulation.

ARTICLE 5. OVERSIGHT AND EVALUATION OF PROGRAM

§ 63.2–1527. BOARD OVERSIGHT DUTIES; OUT-OF-FAMILY INVESTIGATIONS ADVISORY COMMITTEE

A. The Board shall be responsible for establishing standards for out-of-family investigations and for the implementation of the family assessment track of the differential response system.

B. The Out-of-Family Investigations Advisory Committee (the Committee) is hereby established as an advisory committee in the executive branch of state government.

C. The Committee shall consist of 15 members as follows: one representative of public school employees, one representative of a hospital for children, one representative of a licensed child care center, one representative of a juvenile detention home, one representative of a public or private residential facility for children, one representative of a family day care home, one representative of a local department of Social Services, one representative of a religious organization with a program for children, one representative of Virginians for Child Abuse Prevention and six citizens of the Commonwealth at large. The Chairman of the Board shall appoint such persons for terms established by the Board.

D. The Committee shall advise the Board on the effectiveness of the policies and standards governing out-of-family investigations.

E. The Committee shall elect a chairman and vice-chairman from among its membership. A majority of the members shall constitute a quorum. The meetings of the Committee shall be held at the call of the chairman or whenever the majority of the voting members so request.

F. Members shall receive no compensation for their services nor be reimbursed for expenses incurred in the discharge of their duties as provided in §§ 2.2–2813 and 2.2–2825.

G. The Department of Social Services shall provide staff support to the Committee. All agencies of the Commonwealth shall provide assistance to the Committee, upon request.

ARTICLE 6. VIRGINIA CHILD PROTECTION ACCOUNTABILITY SYSTEM

§ 63.2–1530. VIRGINIA CHILD PROTECTION ACCOUNTABILITY SYSTEM

A.   The Virginia Child Protection Accountability System (the System) is created to collect and make available to the public information on the response to reported cases of child abuse and neglect in the Commonwealth. The Department shall establish and maintain the System. The Board shall promulgate regulations to implement the provisions of this section.

B.   The following information shall, notwithstanding any state law regarding privacy or confidentiality of records, be included in the System and made available to the public via a website maintained by the Department and in print format:

1.   From the Department: (i) the total number of complaints alleging child abuse, neglect, or a combination thereof received; (ii) the total number of complaints deemed valid pursuant to § 63.2–1508; (iii) the total number of complaints investigated by the Department pursuant to subsection I of §§ 63.2–1503 and 63.2–1505; (iv) the total number of cases determined to be founded cases of abuse or neglect; and (v) the total number of cases resulting in a finding that the complaint was founded resulting in administrative appeal. Information reported pursuant to clause (v) shall be reported by total number of appeals to the local department, total number of appeals to the Department, and total number of appeals by outcome of the appeal. For each category of information required by this subdivision, the Department shall also report the total number of cases by type of abuse; by gender, age, and race of the alleged victim; and by the nature of the relationship between the alleged victim and alleged abuser.

2.   From the Department of State Police, annually, in a format approved by the Department of Social Services, arrest and disposition statistics for violations of §§ 18.2–48, 18.2–61, 18.2–63, 18.2–64.1, 18.2–67.1, 18.2–67.2, 18.2–67.3, 18.2–67.4, 18.2–355, 18.2–361, 18.2–366, 18.2–370 through 18.2–370.2, 18.2–371, 18.2–371.1, 18.2–374.1, 18.2–374.1:1, 18.2–374.3, 18.2–387, and 40.1–103 for inclusion in the Child Protection Accountability System.

3.   From every circuit court in the Commonwealth for which data is available through the statewide Case Management System: (i) the total number of (a) misdemeanor convictions appealed from the district court to the circuit court, (b) felony charges certified from the district court to the circuit court, and (c) charges brought by direct indictment in the circuit court that involve a violation of any Code section set forth in subdivision 2; (ii) the total number of cases appealed, certified, or transferred to the court or brought by direct

indictment in the circuit court involving a violation of any Code section set forth in subdivision 2 that result in a trial, including the number of bench trials and the number of jury trials; and (iii) the total number of trials involving a violation of any Code section set forth in subdivision 2 resulting in (a) a plea agreement, (b) transfer to another court, (c) a finding of not guilty, (d) conviction on a lesser included offense, or (e) conviction on all charges, by type of trial.

4. From the Virginia Criminal Sentencing Commission, information on sentences imposed for offenses listed in subdivision 2, including (i) the name of the sentencing judge, (ii) the offense or offenses for which a sentence was imposed, (iii) the age of the victim and offender, (iv) the relationship between the victim and the offender, (v) the locality in which the offense occurred, (vi) the sentence imposed and the actual time served, (vii) whether the sentence was an upward or downward departure from the sentencing guidelines or within the sentencing guidelines, and (viii) the reasons given for the departure, if any, from the sentencing guidelines.

5. From the Office of the Executive Secretary of the Supreme Court of Virginia, information by locality on cases from the Juvenile and Domestic Relations District Courts' Case Management System involving (i) children alleged to be abused or neglected, including (a) the number of petitions filed, (b) the number of cases in which an emergency removal order was issued, (c) the number of cases in which a preliminary removal order was issued prior to an adjudicatory hearing, (d) the number of cases in which a preliminary removal order or a preliminary child protective order or both were issued at a preliminary hearing, and (e) the number of cases in which a preliminary child protective order or a child protective order was issued other than at a preliminary hearing; and (ii) family abuse cases, including (a) the number of family abuse emergency protective orders issued by magistrates and juvenile and domestic relations district courts pursuant to § 16.1–253.4, (b) the number of family abuse protective petitions filed, and (c) the number of family abuse protective orders issued pursuant to § 16.1–279.1.

Information required to be reported pursuant to subdivisions 1 through 5 shall be reported annually in a format approved by the Department of Social Services and aggregated by locality.

C. Data collected pursuant to subsection B shall be made available to the public on a website established and maintained by the Department and shall also be made readily available to the public in print format. Information included in the System shall be presented in such a manner that no individual identifying information shall be included.

CHILD CUSTODY STATUTES

CALIFORNIA AND WEST VIRGINIA STATUTES

CALIFORNIA CHILD CUSTODY STATUTE

Cal. Fam. Code §§ 3000–3011, 3060, 3064, 3080–3089, 3100–3105, 3120, 3200–3204 (West 2016)

[EDITORS' INTRODUCTION: Ariel Ayanna, *From Children's Interests to Parental Responsibility: Degendering Parenthood Through Custodial Obligation*, 19 UCLA WOMEN'S L.J. 1 (2015); J. Herbie DiFonzo, *Dilemmas of Shared Parenting in the 21st Century: How Law and Culture Shape Child Custody*, 43 HOFSTRA L. REV. 1003 (2015); Mary Jean Dolan & Daniel J. Hynan, *Fighting Over Bedtime Stories: An Empirical Study of the Risks of Valuing Quantity Over Quality in Child Custody Decisions*, 38 LAW & PSYCHOL. REV. 45 (2014); Samantha Godwin, *Against Parental Rights*, 47 COLUM. HUM. RTS. L. REV. 1 (2015); Pamela Laufer-Ukelesa & Ayelet Blecher-Prigat, *Between Function and Form: Towards a Differentiated Model of Functional Parenthood*, 20 GEO. MASON L. REV. 419 (2013); Mary Ann Mason, *The Roller Coaster of Child Custody Law Over the Last Half Century*, 24 J. AM. ACAD. MATRIM. LAW. 451 (2012); Rebecca N. Morrow, *Mediating Parental Relocation Cases Behind a Veil of Ignorance*, 49 WAKE FOREST L. REV. 771 (2014); Ruth Sovronsky, *The Relocation Dilemma: In Search of "Best Interests"*, 75 ALB. L. REV. 1075 (2012); Gargi Sen & Tiffanie Tam, *Child Custody, Visitation, & Termination of Parental Rights*, 16 GEO. J. GENDER & L. 41 (2015); Lindsey A. Waits, *For Better or for Worse: Joint Custody Should Be the Presumption in South Carolina*, 9 CHARLESTON L. REV. 473 (2015); Stephen J. Yanni, Note, *Experts as Final Arbiters: State Law and Problematic Expert Testimony on Domestic Violence in Child Custody Cases*, 116 COLUM. L. REV. 533 (2016).]

§ 3000. CONSTRUCTION OF DIVISION

Unless the provision or context otherwise requires, the definitions in this chapter govern the construction of this division.

* * *

§ 3002. JOINT CUSTODY

"Joint custody" means joint physical custody and joint legal custody.

§ 3003. JOINT LEGAL CUSTODY

"Joint legal custody" means that both parents shall share the right and the responsibility to make the decisions relating to the health, education, and welfare of a child.

§ 3004. JOINT PHYSICAL CUSTODY

"Joint physical custody" means that each of the parents shall have significant periods of physical custody. Joint physical custody shall be shared by the parents in such a way so as to assure a child of frequent and continuing contact with both parents, subject to Sections 3011 and 3020.

* * *

§ 3006. SOLE LEGAL CUSTODY

"Sole legal custody" means that one parent shall have the right and the responsibility to make the decisions relating to the health, education, and welfare of a child.

§ 3007. SOLE PHYSICAL CUSTODY

"Sole physical custody" means that a child shall reside with and be under the supervision of one parent, subject to the power of the court to order visitation.

* * *

§ 3010. CUSTODY OF UNEMANCIPATED MINOR CHILDREN

(a) The mother of an unemancipated minor child and the father, if presumed to be the father under Section 7611, are equally entitled to the custody of the child.

(b) If one parent is dead, is unable or refuses to take custody, or has abandoned the child, the other parent is entitled to custody of the child.

§ 3011. BEST INTEREST OF CHILD; CONSIDERATIONS

In making a determination of the best interest of the child in a proceeding described in Section 3021, the court shall, among any other factors it finds relevant, consider all of the following:

(a) The health, safety, and welfare of the child.

(b) Any history of abuse by one parent or any other person seeking custody against any of the following:

(1) Any child to whom he or she is related by blood or affinity or with whom he or she has had a caretaking relationship, no matter how temporary.

(2) The other parent.

(3) A parent, current spouse, or cohabitant, of the parent or person seeking custody, or a person with whom the parent or person seeking custody has a dating or engagement relationship.

As a prerequisite to considering allegations of abuse, the court may require substantial independent corroboration, including, but not limited to, written reports by law enforcement agencies, child protective services or other social welfare agencies, courts, medical facilities, or other public agencies or private nonprofit organizations providing services to victims of sexual assault or domestic violence. As used in this subdivision, "abuse against a child" means "child abuse" as defined in Section 11165.6 of the Penal Code and abuse against any of the other persons described in paragraph (2) or (3) means "abuse" as defined in Section 6203 of this code.

(c)   The nature and amount of contact with both parents, except as provided in Section 3046.

(d)   The habitual or continual illegal use of controlled substances, the habitual or continual abuse of alcohol, or the habitual or continual abuse of prescribed controlled substances by either parent. Before considering these allegations, the court may first require independent corroboration, including, but not limited to, written reports from law enforcement agencies, courts, probation departments, social welfare agencies, medical facilities, rehabilitation facilities, or other public agencies or nonprofit organizations providing drug and alcohol abuse services. As used in this subdivision, "controlled substances" has the same meaning as defined in the California Uniform Controlled Substances Act, Division 10 (commencing with Section 11000) of the Health and Safety Code.

(e)(1)   Where allegations about a parent pursuant to subdivision (b) or (d) have been brought to the attention of the court in the current proceeding, and the court makes an order for sole or joint custody to that parent, the court shall state its reasons in writing or on the record. In these circumstances, the court shall ensure that any order regarding custody or visitation is specific as to time, day, place, and manner of transfer of the child as set forth in subdivision (b) of Section 6323.

(2)   The provisions of this subdivision shall not apply if the parties stipulate in writing or on the record regarding custody or visitation.

§ 3060. PETITION FOR TEMPORARY CUSTODY ORDER

A petition for a temporary custody order, containing the statement required by Section 3409, may be included with the initial filing of the petition or action or may be filed at any time after the initial filing.

§ 3064. RESTRICTIONS ON EX PARTE ORDERS GRANTING OR MODIFYING CUSTODY ORDER

(a) The court shall refrain from making an order granting or modifying a custody order on an ex parte basis unless there has been a showing of immediate harm to the child or immediate risk that the child will be removed from the State of California.

(b) "Immediate harm to the child" includes, but is not limited to, the following:

(1) Having a parent who has committed acts of domestic violence, where the court determines that the acts of domestic violence are of recent origin or are a part of a demonstrated and continuing pattern of acts of domestic violence.

(2) Sexual abuse of the child, where the court determines that the acts of sexual abuse are of recent origin or are a part of a demonstrated and continuing pattern of acts of sexual abuse.

§ 3080. PRESUMPTION OF JOINT CUSTODY

There is a presumption, affecting the burden of proof, that joint custody is in the best interest of a minor child, subject to Section 3011, where the parents have agreed to joint custody or so agree in open court at a hearing for the purpose of determining the custody of the minor child.

§ 3081. APPLICATION BY PARENTS; CUSTODY INVESTIGATION

On application of either parent, joint custody may be ordered in the discretion of the court in cases other than those described in Section 3080, subject to Section 3011. For the purpose of assisting the court in making a determination whether joint custody is appropriate under this section, the court may direct that an investigation be conducted pursuant to Chapter 6 (commencing with Section 3110).

§ 3082. STATEMENT OF REASONS FOR GRANT OR DENIAL

When a request for joint custody is granted or denied, the court, upon the request of any party, shall state in its decision the reasons for granting or denying the request. A statement that joint physical custody is, or is not, in the best interest of the child is not sufficient to satisfy the requirements of this section.

§ 3083. CONTENTS AND CONSTRUCTION OF JOINT LEGAL CUSTODY ORDER

In making an order of joint legal custody, the court shall specify the circumstances under which the consent of both parents is required to be obtained in order to exercise legal control of the child and the consequences of the failure to obtain mutual consent. In all other circumstances, either parent acting alone may exercise legal control of the child. An order of joint legal custody shall not be construed to permit an action that is inconsistent with the physical custody order unless the action is expressly authorized by the court.

§ 3084. RIGHTS OF PARENTS TO PHYSICAL CONTROL OF CHILD

In making an order of joint physical custody, the court shall specify the rights of each parent to physical control of the child in sufficient detail to enable a parent deprived of that control to implement laws for relief of child snatching and kidnapping.

§ 3085. GRANT OF JOINT LEGAL CUSTODY WITHOUT JOINT PHYSICAL CUSTODY.

In making an order for custody with respect to both parents, the court may grant joint legal custody without granting joint physical custody.

§ 3086. ORDERS OF JOINT PHYSICAL CUSTODY OR JOINT LEGAL CUSTODY; DESIGNATION OF PRIMARY CARETAKER AND PRIMARY HOME OF CHILD

In making an order of joint physical custody or joint legal custody, the court may specify one parent as the primary caretaker of the child and one home as the primary home of the child, for the purposes of determining eligibility for public assistance.

§ 3087. MODIFICATION OR TERMINATION OF JOINT CUSTODY ORDER; STATEMENT OF REASONS

An order for joint custody may be modified or terminated upon the petition of one or both parents or on the court's own motion if it is shown that the best interest of the child requires modification or termination of the order. If either parent opposes the modification or termination order, the court shall state in its decision the reasons for modification or termination of the joint custody order.

§ 3088. MODIFICATION OF CUSTODY ORDER TO JOINT CUSTODY ORDER

An order for the custody of a minor child entered by a court in this state or any other state may, subject to the jurisdictional requirements in Sections 3403 and 3414, be modified at any time to an order for joint custody in accordance with this chapter.

§ 3089. CONCILIATION COURT; CONSULTATION BY COURT OR PARTIES

In counties having a conciliation court, the court or the parties may, at any time, pursuant to local rules of court, consult with the conciliation court for the purpose of assisting the parties to formulate a plan for implementation of the custody order or to resolve a controversy which has arisen in the implementation of a plan for custody.

§ 3100. JOINT CUSTODY ORDERS; VISITATION RIGHTS; DOMESTIC VIOLENCE PREVENTION ORDERS; TRANSFER OF CHILDREN; DETAIL SPECIFIC ORDERS; CONFIDENTIALITY OF SHELTER LOCATIONS

(a) In making an order pursuant to Chapter 4 (commencing with Section 3080), the court shall grant reasonable visitation rights to a parent unless it is shown that the visitation would be detrimental to the best interest of the child. In the discretion of the court, reasonable visitation rights may be granted to any other person having an interest in the welfare of the child.

(b) If a protective order, as defined in Section 6218, has been directed to a parent, the court shall consider whether the best interest of the child requires that any visitation by that parent be limited to situations in which a third person, specified by the court, is present, or whether visitation shall be suspended or denied. The court shall include in its deliberations a consideration of the nature of the acts from which the parent was enjoined and the period of time that has elapsed since that order. A parent may submit to the court the name of a person that the parent deems suitable to be present during visitation.

(c) If visitation is ordered in a case in which domestic violence is alleged and an emergency protective order, protective order, or other restraining order has been issued, the visitation order shall specify the time, day, place, and manner of transfer of the child, so as to limit the child's exposure to potential domestic conflict or violence and to ensure the safety of all family members. If a criminal protective order has been issued pursuant to Section 136.2 of the Penal Code, the visitation order shall make reference to, and, unless there is an emergency protective order that has precedence in enforcement pursuant to paragraph (1) of subdivision (c) of Section 136.2 of the Penal Code or a no-contact order, as described in Section 6320, acknowledge the precedence of enforcement of, an appropriate criminal protective order.

(d) If the court finds a party is staying in a place designated as a shelter for victims of domestic violence or other confidential location, the court's order for time, day, place, and manner of transfer of the child for visitation shall be designed to prevent disclosure of the location of the shelter or other confidential location.

§ 3101. STEPPARENT'S VISITATION RIGHTS

(a) Notwithstanding any other provision of law, the court may grant reasonable visitation to a stepparent, if visitation by the stepparent is determined to be in the best interest of the minor child.

(b) If a protective order, as defined in Section 6218, has been directed to a stepparent to whom visitation may be granted pursuant to this section, the court shall consider whether the best interest of the child requires that any visitation by the stepparent be denied.

(c) Visitation rights may not be ordered under this section that would conflict with a right of custody or visitation of a birth parent who is not a party to the proceeding.

(d) As used in this section:

(1) "Birth parent" means "birth parent" as defined in Section 8512.

(2) "Stepparent" means a person who is a party to the marriage that is the subject of the proceeding, with respect to a minor child of the other party to the marriage.

§ 3102. DECEASED PARENT; VISITATION RIGHTS OF CLOSE RELATIVES; ADOPTION OF CHILD

(a) If either parent of an unemancipated minor child is deceased, the children, siblings, parents, and grandparents of the deceased parent may be granted reasonable visitation with the child during the child's minority upon a finding that the visitation would be in the best interest of the minor child.

(b) In granting visitation pursuant to this section to a person other than a grandparent of the child, the court shall consider the amount of personal contact between the person and the child before the application for the visitation order.

(c) This section does not apply if the child has been adopted by a person other than a stepparent or grandparent of the child. Any visitation rights granted pursuant to this section before the adoption of the child automatically terminate if the child is adopted by a person other than a stepparent or grandparent of the child.

§ 3103. GRANDPARENT'S RIGHTS; CUSTODY PROCEEDING

(a) Notwithstanding any other provision of law, in a proceeding described in Section 3021, the court may grant reasonable visitation to a grandparent of a minor child of a party to the proceeding if the court determines that visitation by the grandparent is in the best interest of the child.

(b) If a protective order as defined in Section 6218 has been directed to the grandparent during the pendency of the proceeding, the court shall consider whether the best interest of the child requires that visitation by the grandparent be denied.

(c) The petitioner shall give notice of the petition to each of the parents of the child, any stepparent, and any person who has physical custody of the child, by certified mail, return receipt requested, postage prepaid, to the person's last known address, or to the attorneys of record of the parties to the proceeding.

(d) There is a rebuttable presumption affecting the burden of proof that the visitation of a grandparent is not in the best interest of a minor child if the child's parents agree that the grandparent should not be granted visitation rights.

(e) Visitation rights may not be ordered under this section if that would conflict with a right of custody or visitation of a birth parent who is not a party to the proceeding.

(f) Visitation ordered pursuant to this section shall not create a basis for or against a change of residence of the child, but shall be one of the factors for the court to consider in ordering a change of residence.

(g)   When a court orders grandparental visitation pursuant to this section, the court in its discretion may, based upon the relevant circumstances of the case:

(1)   Allocate the percentage of grandparental visitation between the parents for purposes of the calculation of child support pursuant to the statewide uniform guideline (Article 2 (commencing with Section 4050) of Chapter 2 of Part 2 of Division 9).

(2)   Notwithstanding Sections 3930 and 3951, order a parent or grandparent to pay to the other, an amount for the support of the child or grandchild. For purposes of this paragraph, "support" means costs related to visitation such as any of the following:

(A)   Transportation.

(B)   Provision of basic expenses for the child or grandchild, such as medical expenses, day care costs, and other necessities.

(h)   As used in this section, "birth parent" means "birth parent" as defined in Section 8512.

§ 3104.   GRANDPARENT'S RIGHTS; PETITION BY GRANDPARENT; NOTICE; PROTECTIVE ORDER DIRECTED TO GRANDPARENT; REBUTTABLE PRESUMPTIONS; CONFLICT WITH RIGHTS OF NON-PARTY BIRTH PARENT; CHANGE OF RESIDENCE OF THE CHILD; DISCRETION OF COURT

(a)   On petition to the court by a grandparent of a minor child, the court may grant reasonable visitation rights to the grandparent if the court does both of the following:

(1)   Finds that there is a preexisting relationship between the grandparent and the grandchild that has engendered a bond such that visitation is in the best interest of the child.

(2)   Balances the interest of the child in having visitation with the grandparent against the right of the parents to exercise their parental authority.

(b)   A petition for visitation under this section shall not be filed while the natural or adoptive parents are married, unless one or more of the following circumstances exist:

(1)   The parents are currently living separately and apart on a permanent or indefinite basis.

(2)   One of the parents has been absent for more than one month without the other spouse knowing the whereabouts of the absent spouse.

(3)   One of the parents joins in the petition with the grandparents.

(4)   The child is not residing with either parent.

(5)   The child has been adopted by a stepparent.

(6) One of the parents is incarcerated or involuntarily institutionalized.

At any time that a change of circumstances occurs such that none of these circumstances exist, the parent or parents may move the court to terminate grandparental visitation and the court shall grant the termination.

(c) The petitioner shall give notice of the petition to each of the parents of the child, any stepparent, and any person who has physical custody of the child, by personal service pursuant to Section 415.10 of the Code of Civil Procedure.

(d) If a protective order as defined in Section 6218 has been directed to the grandparent during the pendency of the proceeding, the court shall consider whether the best interest of the child requires that any visitation by that grandparent should be denied.

(e) There is a rebuttable presumption that the visitation of a grandparent is not in the best interest of a minor child if the natural or adoptive parents agree that the grandparent should not be granted visitation rights.

(f) There is a rebuttable presumption affecting the burden of proof that the visitation of a grandparent is not in the best interest of a minor child if the parent who has been awarded sole legal and physical custody of the child in another proceeding, or the parent with whom the child resides if there is currently no operative custody order objects to visitation by the grandparent.

(g) Visitation rights may not be ordered under this section if that would conflict with a right of custody or visitation of a birth parent who is not a party to the proceeding.

(h) Visitation ordered pursuant to this section shall not create a basis for or against a change of residence of the child, but shall be one of the factors for the court to consider in ordering a change of residence.

(i) When a court orders grandparental visitation pursuant to this section, the court in its discretion may, based upon the relevant circumstances of the case:

(1) Allocate the percentage of grandparental visitation between the parents for purposes of the calculation of child support pursuant to the statewide uniform guideline (Article 2 (commencing with Section 4050) of Chapter 2 of Part 2 of Division 9).

(2) Notwithstanding Sections 3930 and 3951, order a parent or grandparent to pay to the other, an amount for the support of the child or grandchild. For purposes of this paragraph, "support" means costs related to visitation such as any of the following:

(A) Transportation.

(B) Provision of basic expenses for the child or grandchild, such as medical expenses, day care costs, and other necessities.

(j) As used in this section, "birth parent" means "birth parent" as defined in Section 8512.

§ 3105. FORMER LEGAL GUARDIANS; VISITATION RIGHTS

(a) The Legislature finds and declares that a parent's fundamental right to provide for the care, custody, companionship, and management of his or her children, while compelling, is not absolute. Children have a fundamental right to maintain healthy, stable relationships with a person who has served in a significant, judicially approved parental role.

(b) The court may grant reasonable visitation rights to a person who previously served as the legal guardian of a child, if visitation is determined to be in the best interest of the minor child.

(c) In the absence of a court order granting or denying visitation between a former legal guardian and his or her former minor ward, and if a dependency proceeding is not pending, a former legal guardian may maintain an independent action for visitation with his or her former minor ward. If the child does not have at least one living parent, visitation shall not be determined in a proceeding under the Family Code, but shall instead be determined in a guardianship proceeding which may be initiated for that purpose.

§ 3120. ACTION FOR EXCLUSIVE CUSTODY; ORDER

Without filing a petition for dissolution of marriage or legal separation of the parties, a spouse may bring an action for the exclusive custody of the children of the marriage. The court may, during the pendency of the action, or at the final hearing thereof, or afterwards, make such order regarding the support, care, custody, education, and control of the children of the marriage as may be just and in accordance with the natural rights of the parents and the best interest of the children. The order may be modified or terminated at any time thereafter as the natural rights of the parties and the best interest of the children may require.

§ 3200. SUPERVISED VISITATION PROVIDER STANDARDS; GUIDELINES

The Judicial Council shall develop standards for supervised visitation providers in accordance with the guidelines set forth in this section. For the purposes of the development of these standards, the term "provider" shall include any individual who functions as a visitation monitor, as well as supervised visitation centers. Provisions shall be made within the standards to allow for the diversity of supervised visitation providers.

(a) When developing standards, the Judicial Council shall consider all of the following issues:

(1) The provider's qualifications, experience, and education.

(2) Safety and security procedures, including ratios of children per supervisor.

(3) Any conflict of interest.

(4) Maintenance and disclosure of records, including confidentiality policies.

(5) Procedures for screening, delineation of terms and conditions, and termination of supervised visitation services.

(6) Procedures for emergency or extenuating situations.

(7) Orientation to and guidelines for cases in which there are allegations of domestic violence, child abuse, substance abuse, or special circumstances.

(8) The legal obligations and responsibilities of supervisors.

(b) The Judicial Council shall consult with visitation centers, mothers' groups, fathers' groups, judges, the State Bar of California, children's advocacy groups, domestic violence prevention groups, Family Court Services, and other groups it regards as necessary in connection with these standards.

(c) It is the intent of the Legislature that the safety of children, adults, and visitation supervisors be a precondition to providing visitation services. Once safety is assured, the best interest of the child is the paramount consideration at all stages and particularly in deciding the manner in which supervision is provided.

§ 3201. ADMINISTRATION OF SUPERVISED VISITATION [SECTION AS ADDED BY STATS. 1999, C. 985 (S.B. 792), § 2. SEE, ALSO, ANOTHER SECTION OF THE SAME NUMBER, ADDED BY STATS. 1999, C. 1004 (A.B. 673), § 2.]

Any supervised visitation maintained or imposed by the court shall be administered in accordance with Section 26.2 of the California Standards of Judicial Administration recommended by the Judicial Council.

§ 3201.5. ADMINISTRATION OF PROGRAMS; EDUCATION ABOUT PROTECTING CHILDREN DURING FAMILY DISRUPTION [SECTION AS ADDED BY STATS. 1999, C. 1004 (A.B. 673), § 2. SEE, ALSO,

ANOTHER SECTION OF THE SAME NUMBER, ADDED BY STATS. 1999, C. 985 (S.B. 792), § 2.]

(a) The programs described in this chapter shall be administered by the family law division of the superior court in the county.

(b) For purposes of this chapter, "education about protecting children during family disruption" includes education on parenting skills and the impact of parental conflict on children, how to put a parenting agreement into effect, and the responsibility of both parents to comply with custody and visitation orders.

§ 3202. UNIFORM STANDARDS OF PRACTICE FOR PROVIDERS OF SUPERVISED VISITATION; ELIGIBLE PROVIDERS

(a) All supervised visitation and exchange programs funded pursuant to this chapter shall comply with all requirements of the Uniform Standards of Practice for Providers of Supervised Visitation set forth in Standard 5.20 of the Standards of Judicial Administration as amended. The family law division of the superior court may contract with eligible providers of supervised visitation and exchange services, education, and group counseling to provide services under this chapter.

(b) As used in this section, "eligible provider" means:

(1) For providers of supervised visitation and exchange services, a local public agency or nonprofit entity that satisfies the Uniform Standards of Practice for Providers of Supervised Visitation.

(2) For providers of group counseling, a professional licensed to practice psychotherapy in this state, including, but not limited to, a licensed psychiatrist, licensed psychologist, licensed clinical social worker, licensed marriage and family therapist, or licensed professional clinical counselor; or a mental health intern working under the direct supervision of a professional licensed to practice psychotherapy.

(3) For providers of education, a professional with a bachelor's or master's degree in human behavior, child development, psychology, counseling, family-life education, or a related field, having specific training in issues relating to child and family development, substance abuse, child abuse, domestic violence, effective parenting, and the impact of divorce and interparental conflict on children; or an intern working under the supervision of that professional.

§ 3203. ESTABLISHMENT AND ADMINISTRATION OF PROGRAMS BY FAMILY LAW DIVISION OF COUNTY SUPERIOR COURTS

Subject to the availability of federal funding for the purposes of this chapter, the family law division of the superior court in each county may establish and administer a supervised visitation and exchange program, programs for education about protecting children during family disruption, and group counseling programs for parents and children under this chapter. The programs shall allow parties and children to participate in supervised visitation between a custodial party and a noncustodial party or joint custodians, and to participate in the education and group counseling programs, irrespective of whether the parties are or are not married to each other or are currently living separately and apart on a permanent or temporary basis.

§ 3204. JUDICIAL COUNCIL; APPLICATION FOR GRANTS FROM THE FEDERAL ADMINISTRATION FOR CHILDREN AND FAMILIES; LEGISLATIVE INTENT, REPORTS

(a) The Judicial Council shall annually submit an application to the federal Administration for Children and Families, pursuant to Section 669B of the "1996 Federal Personal Responsibility and Work Opportunity Recovery Act" (PRWORA), for a grant to fund child custody and visitation programs pursuant to this chapter. The Judicial Council shall be charged with the administration of the grant funds.

(b)(1)   It is the intention of the Legislature that, effective October 1, 2000, the grant funds described in subdivision (a) shall be used to fund the following three types of programs: supervised visitation and exchange services, education about protecting children during family disruption, and group counseling for parents and children, as set forth in this chapter. Contracts shall follow a standard request for proposal procedure, that may include multiple year funding. Requests for proposals shall meet all state and federal requirements for receiving access and visitation grant funds.

(2) The grant funds shall be awarded with the intent of approving as many requests for proposals as possible while assuring that each approved proposal would provide beneficial services and satisfy the overall goals of the program under this chapter. The Judicial Council shall determine the final number and amount of grants. Requests for proposals shall be evaluated based on the following criteria:

(A) Availability of services to a broad population of parties.

(B) The ability to expand existing services.

(C) Coordination with other community services.

(D) The hours of service delivery.

(E) The number of counties or regions participating.

(F) Overall cost-effectiveness.

(G) The purpose of the program to promote and encourage healthy parent and child relationships between noncustodial parents and their children, while ensuring the health, safety, and welfare of the children.

(3) Special consideration for grant funds shall be given to proposals that coordinate supervised visitation and exchange services, education, and group counseling with existing court-based programs and services.

(c)   The family law division of the superior court in each county shall approve sliding scale fees that are based on the ability to pay for all parties, including low-income families, participating in a supervised visitation and exchange, education, and group counseling programs under this chapter.

(d)   The Judicial Council shall, on March 1, 2002, and on the first day of March of each subsequent even-numbered year, report to the Legislature on the programs funded pursuant to this chapter and whether and to what extent those programs are achieving the goal of promoting and encouraging healthy parent and child relationships between noncustodial or joint custodial parents and their children while ensuring the health, safety, and welfare of children, and the other goals described in this chapter.

WEST VIRGINIA CHILD CUSTODY STATUTE

W. Va. Code Ann. §§ 48–9–102, 48–9–206, 48–9–207 (West 2016)

§ 48–9–102. OBJECTIVES; BEST INTERESTS OF THE CHILD

(a)   The primary objective of this article is to serve the child's best interests, by facilitating:

(1)   Stability of the child;

(2)   Parental planning and agreement about the child's custodial arrangements and upbringing;

(3)   Continuity of existing parent-child attachments;

(4)   Meaningful contact between a child and each parent;

(5)   Caretaking relationships by adults who love the child, know how to provide for the child's needs, and who place a high priority on doing so;

(6)   Security from exposure to physical or emotional harm; and

(7)   Expeditious, predictable decision-making and avoidance of prolonged uncertainty respecting arrangements for the child's care and control.

(b)   A secondary objective of article is to achieve fairness between the parents.

§ 48–9–206. ALLOCATION OF CUSTODIAL RESPONSIBILITY

(a)   Unless otherwise resolved by agreement of the parents under section 9–201 or unless manifestly harmful to the child, the court shall allocate custodial responsibility so that the proportion of custodial time the child spends with each parent approximates the proportion of time each parent spent performing caretaking functions for the child prior to the parents' separation or, if the parents never lived together, before the filing of the action, except to the extent required under section 9–209 or necessary to achieve any of the following objectives:

(1)   To permit the child to have a relationship with each parent who has performed a reasonable share of parenting functions;

(2)   To accommodate the firm and reasonable preferences of a child who is fourteen years of age or older, and with regard to a child under fourteen years of age, but sufficiently matured that he or she can intelligently express a voluntary preference for one parent, to give that preference such weight as circumstances warrant;

(3)   To keep siblings together when the court finds that doing so is necessary to their welfare;

(4)   To protect the child's welfare when, under an otherwise appropriate allocation, the child would be harmed because of a gross disparity in the quality of the emotional attachments between each parent and the child or in each parent's demonstrated ability or availability to meet a child's needs;

(5)   To take into account any prior agreement of the parents that, under the circumstances as a whole including the reasonable expectations of the parents in the interest of the child, would be appropriate to consider;

(6)   To avoid an allocation of custodial responsibility that would be extremely impractical or that would interfere substantially with the child's need for stability in light of economic, physical or other circumstances, including the distance between the parents' residences, the cost and difficulty of transporting the child, the parents' and child's daily schedules, and the ability of the parents to cooperate in the arrangement;

(7)   To apply the principles set forth in 9–403(d) of this article if one parent relocates or proposes to relocate at a distance that will impair the ability of a parent to exercise the amount of custodial responsibility that would otherwise be ordered under this section; and

(8)   To consider the stage of a child's development.

(b)   In determining the proportion of caretaking functions each parent previously performed for the child under subsection (a) of this section, the court shall not consider the divisions of functions arising from temporary arrangements after separation, whether those arrangements are consensual or by court order. The court may take into account information relating to the temporary arrangements in determining other issues under this section.

(c) If the court is unable to allocate custodial responsibility under subsection (a) of this section because the allocation under that subsection would be manifestly harmful to the child, or because there is no history of past performance of caretaking functions, as in the case of a newborn, or because the history does not establish a pattern of caretaking sufficiently dispositive of the issues of the case, the court shall allocate custodial responsibility based on the child's best interest, taking into account the factors in considerations that are set forth in this section and in section two hundred nine and 9–403(d) of this article and preserving to the extent possible this section's priority on the share of past caretaking functions each parent performed.

(d) In determining how to schedule the custodial time allocated to each parent, the court shall take account of the economic, physical and other practical circumstances such as those listed in subdivision (6), subsection (a) of this section.

§ 48–9–207. ALLOCATION   OF   SIGNIFICANT   DECISION-MAKING RESPONSIBILITY

(a) Unless otherwise resolved by agreement of the parents under section 9–201, the court shall allocate responsibility for making significant life decisions on behalf of the child, including the child's education and health care, to one parent or to two parents jointly, in accordance with the child's best interest, in light of:

(1) The allocation of custodial responsibility under section 9–206 of this article;

(2) The level of each parent's participation in past decision-making on behalf of the child;

(3) The wishes of the parents;

(4) The level of ability and cooperation the parents have demonstrated in decision-making on behalf of the child;

(5) Prior agreements of the parties; and

(6) The existence of any limiting factors, as set forth in section 9–209 of this article.

(b) If each of the child's legal parents has been exercising a reasonable share of parenting functions for the child, the court shall presume that an allocation of decision-making responsibility to both parents jointly is in the child's best interests. The presumption is overcome if there is a history of domestic abuse, or by a showing that joint allocation of decision-making responsibility is not in the child's best interest.

(c) Unless otherwise provided or agreed by the parents, each parent who is exercising custodial responsibility shall be given sole responsibility for day-to-day decisions for the child, while the child is in that parent's care and control, including emergency decisions affecting the health and safety of the child.

Consent to Medical Care for Minors

Arkansas and California Statutes

Arkansas

Ark. Code Ann. §§ 20–9–601 et seq. (West 2016)

[EDITORS' INTRODUCTION: Shawna Benston, *Not of Minor Consequence?: Medical Decision-Making Autonomy and the Mature Minor Doctrine*, 13 IND. HEALTH L. REV. 1 (2016); Jason Potter Burda, *Prep and Our Youth: Implications in Law and Policy*, 30 COLUM. J. GENDER & L. 295 (2016); James G. Dwyer, *Equality Between Adults and Children: Its Meaning, Implications, and Opposition*, 2013 MICH. ST. L. REV. 1007 (2013); Martin R. Gardner, *The Categorical Distinction Between Adolescents and Adults: The Supreme Court's Juvenile Punishment Cases—Constitutional Implications for Regulating Teenage Sexual Activity*, 28 BYU J. PUB. L. 1 (2013); Michele Goodwin & Naomi Duke, *Capacity and Autonomy: A Thought Experiment on Minors' Access to Assisted Reproductive Technology*, 34 HARV. J. L. & GENDER 503 (2011); B. Jessie Hill, *Medical Decision Making by and on Behalf of Adolescents: Reconsidering First Principles*, 15 J. HEALTH CARE L. & POL'Y 37 (2012); B. Jessie Hill, *Whose Body? Whose Soul? Medical Decision-Making on Behalf of Children and the Free Exercise Clause Before and After* Employment Division v. Smith, 32 CARDOZO L. REV. 1857 (2011); Nicole Phillis, *When Sixteen Ain't So Sweet: Rethinking the Regulation of Adolescent Sexuality*, 17 MICH. J. GENDER & L. 271 (2011); Cheryl B. Preston & Brandon T. Crowther, *Minor Restrictions: Adolescence Across Legal Disciplines, the Infancy Doctrine, and the Restatement (Third) of Restitution and Unjust Enrichment*, 61 U. KAN. L. REV. 343 (2012).]

§ 20–9–601. DEFINITION

(a) As used in this subchapter, "of unsound mind" means the inability to perceive all relevant facts related to one's condition and proposed treatment so as to make an intelligent decision based thereon, whether or not the inability is:

(1) Only temporary, has existed for an extended period of time, or occurs or has occurred only intermittently; or

(2) Due to natural state, age, shock or anxiety, illness, injury, drugs or sedation, intoxication, or other cause of whatever nature.

(b) An individual shall not be considered to be of unsound mind based solely upon his or her refusal of medical care or treatment.

§ 20–9–602. CONSENT GENERALLY

It is recognized and established that, in addition to other authorized persons, any one (1) of the following persons may consent, either orally or otherwise, to any surgical or medical treatment or procedure not prohibited by law that is suggested, recommended, prescribed, or directed by a licensed physician:

(1) Any adult, for himself or herself;

(2)(A)   Any parent, whether an adult or a minor, for his or her minor child or for his or her adult child of unsound mind whether the child is of the parent's blood, an adopted child, a stepchild, a foster child not in custody of the Department of Human Services, or a preadoptive child not in custody of the Department of Human Services.

(B) However, the father of an illegitimate child cannot consent for the child solely on the basis of parenthood;

(3) Any married person, whether an adult or a minor, for himself or herself;

(4) Any female, regardless of age or marital status, for herself when given in connection with pregnancy or childbirth, except the unnatural interruption of a pregnancy;

(5) Any person standing in loco parentis, whether formally serving or not, and any guardian, conservator, or custodian, for his or her ward or other charge under disability;

(6) Any emancipated minor, for himself or herself;

(7) Any unemancipated minor of sufficient intelligence to understand and appreciate the consequences of the proposed surgical or medical treatment or procedures, for himself or herself;

(8) Any adult, for his or her minor sibling or his or her adult sibling of unsound mind;

(9) During the absence of a parent so authorized and empowered, any maternal grandparent and, if the father is so authorized and empowered, any paternal grandparent, for his or her minor grandchild or for his or her adult grandchild of unsound mind;

(10) Any married person, for a spouse of unsound mind;

(11) Any adult child, for his or her mother or father of unsound mind;

(12) Any minor incarcerated in the Department of Correction or the Department of Community Correction, for himself or herself; and

(13)(A)   Any foster parent or preadoptive parent for a child in custody of the Department of Human Services in:

(i)(a)   Emergency situations.

(b) As used in this subdivision (13)(A)(i), "emergency situation" means a situation in which, in competent medical judgment, the proposed surgical or medical treatment or procedures are immediately or imminently necessary and any delay occasioned by an attempt to obtain a consent would reasonably be expected to jeopardize the life, health, or safety of the person affected or would reasonably be expected to result in disfigurement or impaired faculties;

(ii) Routine medical treatment;

(iii) Ongoing medical treatment;

(iv) Nonsurgical procedures by a primary care provider; and

(v) Nonsurgical procedures by a specialty care provider.

(B) The Department of Human Services shall be given timely notice of all admissions and discharges consented to by a foster parent or preadoptive parent for a child in custody of the Department of Human Services.

(C) The consent of a representative of the Department of Human Services is required for:

(i) Nonemergency surgical procedures;

(ii) Nonemergency invasive procedures;

(iii) "End-of-life" nonemergency procedures such as do-not-resuscitate orders, withdrawal of life support, and organ donation; and

(iv) Nonemergency medical procedures relating to a criminal investigation or judicial proceeding that involves gathering forensic evidence.

§ 20–9–603. IMPLIED CONSENT; CIRCUMSTANCES

In addition to any other instances in which consent is excused or implied at law, consent to surgical or medical treatment or procedures suggested, recommended, prescribed, or directed by a licensed physician will be implied in the following circumstances:

(1)(A) When an emergency exists and there is no one immediately available who is authorized, empowered to, or capable of consent.

(B) "Emergency" means a situation in which, in competent medical judgment, the proposed surgical or medical treatment or procedures are immediately or imminently necessary and any delay occasioned by an attempt to obtain a consent would reasonably be expected to jeopardize the life, health, or safety of the person affected or would reasonably be expected to result in disfigurement or impaired faculties; and

(2) When any emergency exists, there has been a protest or refusal of consent by a person authorized and empowered to do so, and there is no other person immediately available who is authorized, empowered, or capable of consenting but there has been

a subsequent material and morbid change in the condition of the affected person.

§ 20–9–604. EMERGENCY CONSENT BY COURTS

(a)(1)   Except as provided in subsection (e) of this section, consent may be given by a court when:

(A) An emergency exists;

(B) There has been a protest or refusal of consent by a person authorized and empowered to do so; and

(C) There is no other person immediately available who is authorized, empowered, or capable of consent.

(2) The consent shall be given upon the presentation of a petition accompanied by the written advice or certificate of one (1) or more licensed physicians that in their professional opinion there is an immediate or imminent necessity for medical or surgical treatment or procedures.

(3) Any circuit judge may summarily grant injunctive and declaratory relief ordering and directing that the necessary surgical or medical treatment or procedures be rendered, provided that the affected person is:

(A) A pregnant female in the last trimester of pregnancy;

(B) A person of insufficient age or mental capacity to understand and appreciate the nature of the proposed surgical or medical treatment and the probable consequences of refusal of the treatment; or

(C) A parent of a minor child, provided that the court in its discretion finds that the life or health of the parent is essential to the child's financial support or physical or emotional well-being.

(b) Any circuit judge granting the declaratory and injunctive relief directing the provision of surgical or medical treatment or procedures pursuant to this section shall be immune from liability based on any claim that the surgical or medical treatment or procedures for the affected person should not have been administered.

(c) The reasonable expense incurred for emergency surgical or medical treatment or procedures administered pursuant to this section shall be borne by:

(1) The estate of the person affected;

(2) Any person liable at law for the necessities of the person affected; or

(3) If the estate or person is unable to pay, the county of residence of the person receiving the surgical or medical care.

(d) Upon request of an attending physician, any other licensed physician, or a representative of a hospital to which a patient has been admitted or presented for treatment, it shall be the duty of the prosecuting attorney, or his or her designee, of the county in which the surgical or medical care is proposed to be rendered to give his or her assistance in the presentation of the petition, with medical advice or certificate, and in obtaining an order from the court of proper jurisdiction.

(e)(1) Consent may be given by a court when an emergency exists and there is no one immediately available who is authorized, empowered to, or capable of consent for a person of unsound mind or there has been a subsequent material and morbid change in the condition of the affected person who is in the custody of the Department of Correction or the Department of Community Correction.

(2) The consent shall be given upon the presentation of a petition accompanied by the written advice or certificate of one (1) or more licensed physicians that in their professional opinion there is an immediate or imminent necessity for medical or surgical treatment or procedures.

(3) Any circuit judge may summarily grant injunctive and declaratory relief ordering and directing that the necessary surgical or medical treatment or procedures be rendered.

CALIFORNIA

Cal. Fam. Code §§ 6900 et seq. (West 2016)

§ 6900. CONSTRUCTION OF PART

Unless the provision or context otherwise requires, the definitions in this chapter govern the construction of this part.

§ 6901. "DENTAL CARE" DEFINED

"Dental care" means X-ray examination, anesthetic, dental or surgical diagnosis or treatment, and hospital care by a dentist licensed under the Dental Practice Act.[1]

§ 6902. "MEDICAL CARE" DEFINED

"Medical care" means X-ray examination, anesthetic, medical or surgical diagnosis or treatment, and hospital care under the general or special supervision and upon the advice of or to be rendered by a physician and surgeon licensed under the Medical Practice Act.[2]

---

[1] See Business and Professions Code § 1600 et seq.
[2] See Business and Professions Code § 2000 et seq.

§ 6903. "PARENT OR GUARDIAN" DEFINED

"Parent or guardian" means either parent if both parents have legal custody, or the parent or person having legal custody, or the guardian, of a minor.

CHAPTER 2. CONSENT BY PERSON HAVING CARE OF MINOR OR BY COURT

§ 6910. MEDICAL TREATMENT OF MINOR; ADULT ENTRUSTED WITH CONSENSUAL POWER

The parent, guardian, or caregiver of a minor who is a relative of the minor and who may authorize medical care and dental care under Section 6550, may authorize in writing an adult into whose care a minor has been entrusted to consent to medical care or dental care, or both, for the minor.

§ 6911. CONSENT BY COURT; CONDITIONS

(a) Upon application by a minor, the court may summarily grant consent for medical care or dental care or both for the minor if the court determines all of the following:

(1) The minor is 16 years of age or older and resides in this state.

(2) The consent of a parent or guardian is necessary to permit the medical care or dental care or both, and the minor has no parent or guardian available to give the consent.

(b) No fee may be charged for proceedings under this section.

CHAPTER 3. CONSENT BY MINOR

§ 6920. CAPACITY OF MINOR TO CONSENT

Subject to the limitations provided in this chapter, notwithstanding any other provision of law, a minor may consent to the matters provided in this chapter, and the consent of the minor's parent or guardian is not necessary.

§ 6921. EFFECT OF MINORITY UPON CONSENT

A consent given by a minor under this chapter is not subject to disaffirmance because of minority.

§ 6922. CONDITIONS FOR CONSENT OF MINOR; LIABILITY OF PARENTS OR GUARDIANS; NOTIFICATION OF MINOR'S PARENTS OR GUARDIANS

(a) A minor may consent to the minor's medical care or dental care if all of the following conditions are satisfied:

(1) The minor is 15 years of age or older.

(2) The minor is living separate and apart from the minor's parents or guardian, whether with or without the consent of a parent or guardian and regardless of the duration of the separate residence.

(3) The minor is managing the minor's own financial affairs, regardless of the source of the minor's income.

(b) The parents or guardian are not liable for medical care or dental care provided pursuant to this section.

(c) A physician and surgeon or dentist may, with or without the consent of the minor patient, advise the minor's parent or guardian of the treatment given or needed if the physician and surgeon or dentist has reason to know, on the basis of the information given by the minor, the whereabouts of the parent or guardian.

§ 6924. MENTAL HEALTH TREATMENT OR COUNSELING SERVICES; INVOLVEMENT OF PARENTS OR GUARDIANS; LIABILITY OF PARENTS OR GUARDIANS

(a) As used in this section:

(1) "Mental health treatment or counseling services" means the provision of mental health treatment or counseling on an outpatient basis by any of the following:

(A) A governmental agency.

(B) A person or agency having a contract with a governmental agency to provide the services.

(C) An agency that receives funding from community united funds.

(D) A runaway house or crisis resolution center.

(E) A professional person, as defined in paragraph (2).

(2) "Professional person" means any of the following:

(A) A person designated as a mental health professional in Sections 622 to 626, inclusive, of Article 8 of Subchapter 3 of Chapter 1 of Title 9 of the California Code of Regulations.

(B) A marriage and family therapist as defined in Chapter 13 (commencing with Section 4980) of Division 2 of the Business and Professions Code.

(C) A licensed educational psychologist as defined in Article 5 (commencing with Section 4986) of Chapter 13 of Division 2 of the Business and Professions Code.

(D) A credentialed school psychologist as described in Section 49424 of the Education Code.

(E) A clinical psychologist as defined in Section 1316.5 of the Health and Safety Code.

(F) The chief administrator of an agency referred to in paragraph (1) or (3).

(G) A person registered as a marriage and family therapist intern, as defined in Chapter 13 (commencing with Section 4980) of Division 2 of the Business and Professions Code, while working under the supervision of a licensed professional specified in subdivision (g) of Section 4980.03 of the Business and Professions Code.

(H) A licensed professional clinical counselor, as defined in Chapter 16 (commencing with Section 4999.10) of Division 2 of the Business and Professions Code.

(I) A person registered as a clinical counselor intern, as defined in Chapter 16 (commencing with Section 4999.10) of Division 2 of the Business and Professions Code, while working under the supervision of a licensed professional specified in subdivision (h) of Section 4999.12 of the Business and Professions Code.

(3) "Residential shelter services" means any of the following:

(A) The provision of residential and other support services to minors on a temporary or emergency basis in a facility that services only minors by a governmental agency, a person or agency having a contract with a governmental agency to provide these services, an agency that receives funding from community funds, or a licensed community care facility or crisis resolution center.

(B) The provision of other support services on a temporary or emergency basis by any professional person as defined in paragraph (2).

(b) A minor who is 12 years of age or older may consent to mental health treatment or counseling on an outpatient basis, or to residential shelter services, if both of the following requirements are satisfied:

(1) The minor, in the opinion of the attending professional person, is mature enough to participate intelligently in the outpatient services or residential shelter services.

(2) The minor (A) would present a danger of serious physical or mental harm to self or to others without the mental health treatment or counseling or residential shelter services, or (B) is the alleged victim of incest or child abuse.

(c) A professional person offering residential shelter services, whether as an individual or as a representative of an entity specified in paragraph (3) of subdivision (a), shall make his or her best efforts to notify the parent or guardian of the provision of services.

(d) The mental health treatment or counseling of a minor authorized by this section shall include involvement of the minor's parent or guardian unless, in the opinion of the professional person who is treating or counseling the minor, the involvement would be inappropriate. The professional person who is treating or counseling the minor shall state in the client record whether and when the person attempted to contact the minor's parent or guardian, and whether the attempt to contact was successful or unsuccessful, or the reason why, in the professional person's opinion, it would be inappropriate to contact the minor's parent or guardian.

(e)   The minor's parents or guardian are not liable for payment for mental health treatment or counseling services provided pursuant to this section unless the parent or guardian participates in the mental health treatment or counseling, and then only for services rendered with the participation of the parent or guardian. The minor's parents or guardian are not liable for payment for any residential shelter services provided pursuant to this section unless the parent or guardian consented to the provision of those services.

(f)   This section does not authorize a minor to receive convulsive therapy or psychosurgery as defined in subdivisions (f) and (g) of Section 5325 of the Welfare and Institutions Code, or psychotropic drugs without the consent of the minor's parent or guardian.

§ 6925.   PREVENTION OR TREATMENT OF PREGNANCY

(a)   A minor may consent to medical care related to the prevention or treatment of pregnancy.

(b)   This section does not authorize a minor:

(1)   To be sterilized without the consent of the minor's parent or guardian.

(2)   To receive an abortion without the consent of a parent or guardian other than as provided in Section 123450 of the Health and Safety Code.

§ 6926.   DIAGNOSIS OR TREATMENT OF INFECTIOUS, CONTAGIOUS, OR COMMUNICABLE DISEASES; CONSENT BY MINOR TO CERTAIN MEDICAL CARE; LIABILITY OF PARENTS OR GUARDIANS

(a)   A minor who is 12 years of age or older and who may have come into contact with an infectious, contagious, or communicable disease may consent to medical care related to the diagnosis or treatment of the disease, if the disease or condition is one that is required by law or regulation adopted pursuant to law to be reported to the local health officer, or is a related sexually transmitted disease, as may be determined by the State Public Health Officer.

(b)   A minor who is 12 years of age or older may consent to medical care related to the prevention of a sexually transmitted disease.

(c) The minor's parents or guardian are not liable for payment for medical care provided pursuant to this section.

§ 6927. DIAGNOSIS OR TREATMENT FOR RAPE

A minor who is 12 years of age or older and who is alleged to have been raped may consent to medical care related to the diagnosis or treatment of the condition and the collection of medical evidence with regard to the alleged rape.

§ 6928. DIAGNOSIS OR TREATMENT FOR SEXUAL ASSAULT

(a) "Sexually assaulted" as used in this section includes, but is not limited to, conduct coming within Section 261, 286, or 288a of the Penal Code.

(b) A minor who is alleged to have been sexually assaulted may consent to medical care related to the diagnosis and treatment of the condition, and the collection of medical evidence with regard to the alleged sexual assault.

(c) The professional person providing medical treatment shall attempt to contact the minor's parent or guardian and shall note in the minor's treatment record the date and time the professional person attempted to contact the parent or guardian and whether the attempt was successful or unsuccessful. This subdivision does not apply if the professional person reasonably believes that the minor's parent or guardian committed the sexual assault on the minor.

§ 6929. DIAGNOSIS OR TREATMENT OF DRUG AND ALCOHOL ABUSE; LIABILITY FOR COST OF SERVICES; DISCLOSURE OF MEDICAL INFORMATION

(a) As used in this section:

(1) "Counseling" means the provision of counseling services by a provider under a contract with the state or a county to provide alcohol or drug abuse counseling services pursuant to Part 2 (commencing with Section 5600) of Division 5 of the Welfare and Institutions Code or pursuant to Division 10.5 (commencing with Section 11750) of the Health and Safety Code.

(2) "Drug or alcohol" includes, but is not limited to, any substance listed in any of the following:

(A) Section 380 or 381 of the Penal Code.

(B) Division 10 (commencing with Section 11000) of the Health and Safety Code.

(C) Subdivision (f) of Section 647 of the Penal Code.

(3) "LAAM" means levoalphacetylmethadol as specified in paragraph (10) of subdivision (c) of Section 11055 of the Health and Safety Code.

(4) "Professional person" means a physician and surgeon, registered nurse, psychologist, clinical social worker, professional clinical counselor, marriage and family therapist, registered marriage and family therapist intern when appropriately employed and supervised pursuant to Section 4980.43 of the Business and Professions Code, psychological assistant when appropriately employed and supervised pursuant to Section 2913 of the Business and Professions Code, associate clinical social worker when appropriately employed and supervised pursuant to Section 4996.18 of the Business and Professions Code, or registered clinical counselor intern when appropriately employed and supervised pursuant to Section 4999.42 of the Business and Professions Code.

(b) A minor who is 12 years of age or older may consent to medical care and counseling relating to the diagnosis and treatment of a drug- or alcohol-related problem.

(c) The treatment plan of a minor authorized by this section shall include the involvement of the minor's parent or guardian, if appropriate, as determined by the professional person or treatment facility treating the minor. The professional person providing medical care or counseling to a minor shall state in the minor's treatment record whether and when the professional person attempted to contact the minor's parent or guardian, and whether the attempt to contact the parent or guardian was successful or unsuccessful, or the reason why, in the opinion of the professional person, it would not be appropriate to contact the minor's parent or guardian.

(d) The minor's parent or guardian is not liable for payment for any care provided to a minor pursuant to this section, except that if the minor's parent or guardian participates in a counseling program pursuant to this section, the parent or guardian is liable for the cost of the services provided to the minor and the parent or guardian.

(e) This section does not authorize a minor to receive replacement narcotic abuse treatment, in a program licensed pursuant to Article 3 (commencing with Section 11875) of Chapter 1 of Part 3 of Division 10.5 of the Health and Safety Code, without the consent of the minor's parent or guardian.

(f) It is the intent of the Legislature that the state shall respect the right of a parent or legal guardian to seek medical care and counseling for a drug- or alcohol-related problem of a minor child when the child does not consent to the medical care and counseling, and nothing in this section shall be construed to restrict or eliminate this right.

(g) Notwithstanding any other provision of law, in cases where a parent or legal guardian has sought the medical care and counseling for a drug- or alcohol-related problem of a minor child, the physician and surgeon shall disclose medical information concerning the care to the minor's parent or legal guardian upon his or her request, even if the minor child does not consent to disclosure, without liability for the disclosure.

COURT ORDERED PARENTING PLAN

Or. Rev. Stat. Ann. § 107.102 (West 2016)

[EDITORS' INTRODUCTION: Margaret F. Brinig, *Result Inequality in Family Law*, 49 AKRON L. REV. 471 (2016); Leslie Joan Harris, *Failure to Protect from Exposure to Domestic Violence in Private Custody Contests*, 44 FAM. L.Q. 169 (2010); Jan Jeske, *Custody Mediation Within the Context of Domestic Violence*, 31 HAMLINE J. PUB. L. & POL'Y Y657 (2010); Patrick Parkinson, *When is Parenthood Dissoluble?*, 26 BYU J. PUB. L. 147 (2012); Jessica Pearson, *Establishing Parenting Time in Child Support Cases: New Opportunities and Challenges*, 53 FAM. CT. REV. 246 (2015).]

§ 107.102. WHEN PARENTING PLAN REQUIRED; CONTENTS

(1) In any proceeding to establish or modify a judgment providing for parenting time with a child, except for matters filed under ORS 107.700 to 107.735, there shall be developed and filed with the court a parenting plan to be included in the judgment. A parenting plan may be either general or detailed.

(2) A general parenting plan may include a general outline of how parental responsibilities and parenting time will be shared and may allow the parents to develop a more detailed agreement on an informal basis. However, a general parenting plan must set forth the minimum amount of parenting time and access a noncustodial parent is entitled to have.

(3) A detailed parenting plan may include, but need not be limited to, provisions relating to:

    (a) Residential schedule;

    (b) Holiday, birthday and vacation planning;

    (c) Weekends, including holidays, and school in-service days preceding or following weekends;

    (d) Decision-making and responsibility;

    (e) Information sharing and access;

    (f) Relocation of parents;

    (g) Telephone access;

    (h) Transportation; and

    (i) Methods for resolving disputes.

(4) (a) The court shall develop a detailed parenting plan when:

    (A) So requested by either parent; or

    (B) The parent or parents are unable to develop a parenting plan.

(b) In developing a parenting plan under this subsection, the court may consider only the best interests of the child and the safety of the parties.

COVENANT MARRIAGE

LOUISIANA

La. Rev. Stat. Ann. § 9:273 (2016)

[EDITORS' INTRODUCTION: Barbara A. Atwood, *Marital Contracts and the Meaning of Marriage*, 54 ARIZ. L. REV. 11 (2012); Lauren Brown & Jena Shoaf, *Marriage and Divorce*, 12 GEO. J. GENDER & L. 493 (2011); Adam Candeub & Mae Kuykendall, *Modernizing Marriage*, 44 U. MICH. J.L. REFORM 735 (2011); William N. Eskridge, Jr., *Family Law Pluralism: The Guided-Choice Regime of Menus, Default Rules, and Override Rules*, 100 GEO. L.J. 1881 (2012); Jessica Feinberg, *Exposing the Traditional Marriage Agenda*, 7 NW J. L. & SOC. POL'Y 301 (2012); Alan J. Hawkins, *A Proposal for a Feasible, First-Step, Legislative Agenda for Divorce Reform*, 26 BYU J. PUB. L. 215 (2012); John A. Lovett, *Love, Loyalty and the Louisiana Civil Code: Rules, Standards and Hybrid Discretion in a Mixed Jurisdiction*, 72 LA. L. REV. 923 (2012); Ali Kunen, Note, *Divorce and Domestic Violence in the United States: A Focus on New York State's Adoption of No-Fault Legislation and Its Impact on the Incidence of Domestic Violence*, 11 CARDOZO PUB. L. POL'Y & ETHICS J. 353 (2013).]

§ 273.   COVENANT MARRIAGE; CONTENTS OF DECLARATION OF INTENT

A.   A declaration of intent to contract a covenant marriage shall contain all of the following:

(1)   A recitation signed by both parties to the following effect:

"A COVENANT MARRIAGE

We do solemnly declare that marriage is a covenant between a man and a woman who agree to live together as husband and wife for so long as they both may live. We have chosen each other carefully and disclosed to one another everything which could adversely affect the decision to enter into this marriage. We have received premarital counseling on the nature, purposes, and responsibilities of marriage. We have read the Covenant Marriage Act, and we understand that a Covenant Marriage is for life. If we experience marital difficulties, we commit ourselves to take all reasonable efforts to preserve our marriage, including marital counseling.

With full knowledge of what this commitment means, we do hereby declare that our marriage will be bound by Louisiana law on Covenant Marriages and we promise to love, honor, and care for one another as husband and wife for the rest of our lives."

(2)(a)   An affidavit by the parties attesting they have received premarital counseling from a priest, minister, rabbi, clerk of the Religious Society of Friends, any clergyman of any religious sect, or a professional marriage counselor, which counseling shall include a discussion of the seriousness of covenant marriage, communication of the fact that a covenant marriage is a commitment for life, a discussion of the obligation to seek marital counseling in times of marital difficulties, and that they have received and read the informational pamphlet developed and promulgated by the office of the attorney general entitled "Covenant Marriage Act" which provides a full explanation of the terms and conditions of a covenant marriage.

(b) An attestation, signed by the counselor and attached to or included in the parties' affidavit, confirming that the parties were counseled as to the nature and purpose of the marriage.

(3)(a)   The signature of both parties witnessed by a notary.

(b) If one or both of the parties are minors, the written consent or authorization of those persons required under the Children's Code to consent to or authorize the marriage of minors.

B.   The declaration shall contain two separate documents, the recitation and the affidavit, the latter of which shall include the attestation either included therein or attached thereto. The recitation shall be prepared in duplicate originals, one of which shall be retained by the parties and the other, together with the affidavit and attestation, shall be filed as provided in R.S. 9:272(B).

DOMESTIC VIOLENCE

MASSACHUSETTS

Mass. Gen. Laws Ann. ch. 209A, §§ 1–10 (2016)

[EDITORS' INTRODUCTION: Hannah Brenner, *Transcending the Criminal Law's "One Size Fits All" Response to Domestic Violence*, 19 WM. & MARY J. WOMEN & L. 301 (2013); Camille Carey, *Domestic Violence Torts: Righting a Civil Wrong*, 62 U. KAN. L. REV. 695 (2014); Erin R. Collins, *The Evidentiary Rules of Engagement in the War Against Domestic Violence*, 90 N.Y.U. L. REV. 397 (2015); Justine A. Dunlap, *Soft Misogyny: The Subtle Perversion of Domestic Violence "Reform"*, 46 SETON HALL L. REV. 775 (2016); Rona Kaufman Kitchen, *Constrained Choice: Mothers, the State, and Domestic Violence*, 24 TEMP. POL. & CIV. RTS. L. REV. 375 (2015); Elizabeth L. MacDowell, *Domestic Violence and the Politics of Self-Help*, 22 WM. & MARY J. WOMEN & L. 203 (2016); Caitlin Mahserjian, *We're All in This Together: A Global Comparison on Domestic Violence and the Means Necessary to Combat It*, 79 ALB. L. REV. 297 (2016); Caitlin Valiulis, *Domestic Violence*, 15 GEO. J. GENDER & L. 123 (2014); Kathryn Gillespie Wellman, *Taking the Next Step in the Legal Response to Domestic Violence: The Need to Reexamine Specialized Domestic Violence Courts from a Victim Perspective*, 24 COLUM. J. GENDER & L. 444 (2013); Deborah M. Weissman, *Rethinking a New Domestic Violence Pedagogy*, 5 U. MIAMI RACE & SOC. JUST. L. REV. 635 (2015); Talley Wood, *Relocation Law and Survivors of Domestic Violence*, 22 DUKE J. GENDER L. & POL'Y 263 (2015); Anna Kastner, Comment, *The Other War at Home: Chronic Nuisance Laws and the Revictimization of Survivors of Domestic Violence*, 103 CAL. L. REV. 1047 (2015); Suraji R. Wagage, Note, *When the Consequences Are Life and Death: Pretrial Detention for Domestic Violence Offenders*, 7 DREXEL L. REV. 195 (2014).]

§ 1. DEFINITIONS

As used in this chapter the following words shall have the following meanings:

"Abuse", the occurrence of one or more of the following acts between family or household members:

(a) attempting to cause or causing physical harm;

(b) placing another in fear of imminent serious physical harm;

(c) causing another to engage involuntarily in sexual relations by force, threat or duress.

"Court", the superior, probate and family, district or Boston municipal court departments of the trial court, except when the petitioner is in a dating relationship when "Court" shall mean district, probate, or Boston municipal courts.

"Family or household members", persons who:

(a)   are or were married to one another;

(b)   are or were residing together in the same household;

(c)   are or were related by blood or marriage;

(d)   having a child in common regardless of whether they have ever married or lived together; or

(e)   are or have been in a substantive dating or engagement relationship, which shall be adjudged by district, probate or Boston municipal courts consideration of the following factors:

(1)   the length of time of the relationship; (2) the type of relationship; (3) the frequency of interaction between the parties; and (4) if the relationship has been terminated by either person, the length of time elapsed since the termination of the relationship.

"Law officer", any officer authorized to serve criminal process.

"Protection order issued by another jurisdiction", any injunction or other order issued by a court of another state, territory or possession of the United States, the Commonwealth of Puerto Rico, or the District of Columbia, or tribal court that is issued for the purpose of preventing violent or threatening acts or harassment against, or contact or communication with or physical proximity to another person, including temporary and final orders issued by civil and criminal courts filed by or on behalf of a person seeking protection.

"Vacate order", court order to leave and remain away from a premises and surrendering forthwith any keys to said premises to the plaintiff. The defendant shall not damage any of the plaintiff's belongings or those of any other occupant and shall not shut off or cause to be shut off any utilities or mail delivery to the plaintiff. In the case where the premises designated in the vacate order is a residence, so long as the plaintiff is living at said residence, the defendant shall not interfere in any way with the plaintiff's right to possess such residence, except by order or judgment of a court of competent jurisdiction pursuant to appropriate civil eviction proceedings, a petition to partition real estate, or a proceeding to divide marital property. A vacate order may include in its scope a household, a multiple family dwelling and the plaintiff's workplace. When issuing an order to vacate the plaintiff's workplace, the presiding justice must consider whether the plaintiff and defendant work in the same location or for the same employer.

§ 2. VENUE

Proceedings under this chapter shall be filed, heard and determined in the superior court department or the Boston municipal court department or respective divisions of the probate and family or district court departments having venue over the plaintiff's residence. If the plaintiff has left a residence or household to avoid abuse, such plaintiff shall have the option of commencing an action in the court having venue over such prior residence or household, or in the court having venue over the present residence or household.

§ 3. REMEDIES; PERIOD OF RELIEF

A person suffering from abuse from an adult or minor family or household member may file a complaint in the court requesting protection from such abuse, including, but not limited to, the following orders:

(a) ordering the defendant to refrain from abusing the plaintiff, whether the defendant is an adult or minor;

(b) ordering the defendant to refrain from contacting the plaintiff, unless authorized by the court, whether the defendant is an adult or minor;

(c) ordering the defendant to vacate forthwith and remain away from the household, multiple family dwelling, and workplace. Notwithstanding the provisions of section thirty-four B of chapter two hundred and eight, an order to vacate shall be for a fixed period of time, not to exceed one year, at the expiration of which time the court may extend any such order upon motion of the plaintiff, with notice to the defendant, for such additional time as it deems necessary to protect the plaintiff from abuse;

(d) awarding the plaintiff temporary custody of a minor child; provided, however, that in any case brought in the probate and family court a finding by such court by a preponderance of the evidence that a pattern or serious incident of abuse, as defined in section 31A of chapter 208, toward a parent or child has occurred shall create a rebuttable presumption that it is not in the best interests of the child to be placed in sole custody, shared legal custody or shared physical custody with the abusive parent. Such presumption may be rebutted by a preponderance of the evidence that such custody award is in the best interests of the child. For the purposes of this section, an "abusive parent" shall mean a parent who has committed a pattern of abuse or a serious incident of abuse;

For the purposes of this section, the issuance of an order or orders under chapter 209A shall not in and of itself constitute a pattern or serious incident of abuse; nor shall an order or orders entered ex parte under said chapter 209A be admissible to show whether a pattern or serious incident of abuse has in fact occurred; provided, however, that an order or orders entered ex parte under said chapter 209A may be admissible for other purposes as the court may determine, other than showing whether a pattern or serious incident of abuse has in fact occurred; provided further, that the underlying facts upon which an order or orders under said chapter 209A was based may also form the basis for a finding by the probate and family court that a pattern or serious incident of abuse has occurred.

If the court finds that a pattern or serious incident of abuse has occurred and issues a temporary or permanent custody order, the court shall within 90 days enter written findings of fact as to the effects of the abuse on the child, which findings demonstrate that such order is in the furtherance of the child's best interests and provides for the safety and well-being of the child.

If ordering visitation to the abusive parent, the court shall provide for the safety and well-being of the child and the safety of the abused parent. The court may consider:

(a) ordering an exchange of the child to occur in a protected setting or in the presence of an appropriate third party;

(b) ordering visitation supervised by an appropriate third party, visitation center or agency;

(c) ordering the abusive parent to attend and complete, to the satisfaction of the court, a certified batterer's treatment program as a condition of visitation;

(d) ordering the abusive parent to abstain from possession or consumption of alcohol or controlled substances during the visitation and for 24 hours preceding visitation;

(e) ordering the abusive parent to pay the costs of supervised visitation;

(f) prohibiting overnight visitation;

(g) requiring a bond from the abusive parent for the return and safety of the child;

(h) ordering an investigation or appointment of a guardian ad litem or attorney for the child; and

(i) imposing any other condition that is deemed necessary to provide for the safety and well-being of the child and the safety of the abused parent.

Nothing in this section shall be construed to affect the right of the parties to a hearing under the rules of domestic relations procedure or to affect the discretion of the probate and family court in the conduct of such hearing.

(e) ordering the defendant to pay temporary support for the plaintiff or any child in the plaintiff's custody or both, when the defendant has a legal obligation to support such a person. In determining the amount to be paid, the court shall apply the standards established in the child support guidelines. Each judgment or order of support which is issued, reviewed or modified pursuant to this chapter shall conform to and shall be enforced in accordance with the provisions of section 12 of chapter 119A;

(f) ordering the defendant to pay the person abused monetary compensation for the losses suffered as a direct result of such abuse. Compensatory losses shall include, but not be limited to, loss of earnings or support, costs for restoring utilities, out-of-pocket losses for injuries sustained, replacement costs for locks or personal property removed or destroyed, medical and moving expenses and reasonable attorney's fees;

(g) ordering information in the case record to be impounded in accordance with court rule;

(h) ordering the defendant to refrain from abusing or contacting the plaintiff's child, or child in plaintiff's care or custody, unless authorized by the court;

(i) the judge may recommend to the defendant that the defendant attend a batterer's intervention program that is certified by the department of public health.

No filing fee shall be charged for the filing of the complaint. Neither the plaintiff nor the plaintiff's attorney shall be charged for certified copies of any orders entered by the court, or any copies of the file reasonably required for future court action or as a result of the loss or destruction of plaintiff's copies.

Any relief granted by the court shall be for a fixed period of time not to exceed one year. Every order shall on its face state the time and date the order is to expire and shall include the date and time that the matter will again be heard. If the plaintiff appears at the court at the date and time the order is to expire, the court shall determine whether or not to extend the order for any additional time reasonably necessary to protect the plaintiff or to enter a permanent order. When the expiration date stated on the order is on a weekend day or holiday, or a date when the court is closed to business, the order shall not expire until the next date that the court is open to business. The plaintiff may appear on such next court business day at the time designated by the order to request that the order be extended. The court may also extend the order upon motion of the plaintiff, for such additional time as it deems necessary to protect from abuse the plaintiff or any child in the plaintiff's care or custody. The fact that abuse has not occurred during the pendency of an order shall not, in itself, constitute sufficient ground for denying or failing to extend the order, of allowing an order to expire or be vacated, or for refusing to issue a new order.

The court may modify its order at any subsequent time upon motion by either party. When the plaintiff's address is inaccessible to the defendant as provided in section 8 of this chapter and the defendant has filed a motion to modify the court's order, the court shall be responsible for notifying the plaintiff. In no event shall the court disclose any such inaccessible address.

No order under this chapter shall in any manner affect title to real property.

No court shall compel parties to mediate any aspect of their case. Although the court may refer the case to the family service office of the probation department or victim/witness advocates for information gathering purposes, the court shall not compel the parties to meet together in such information gathering sessions.

A court shall not deny any complaint filed under this chapter solely because it was not filed within a particular time period after the last alleged incident of abuse.

A court may issue a mutual restraining order or mutual no-contact order pursuant to any abuse prevention action only if the court has made specific written findings of fact. The court shall then provide a detailed order, sufficiently specific to apprise any law officer as to which party has violated the order, if the parties are in or appear to be in violation of the order.

Any action commenced under the provisions of this chapter shall not preclude any other civil or criminal remedies. A party filing a complaint under this chapter shall be required to disclose any prior or pending actions involving the parties for divorce, annulment, paternity, custody or support, guardianship, separate support or legal separation, or abuse prevention.

If there is a prior or pending custody support order from the probate and family court department of the trial court, an order issued in the superior, district or Boston municipal court departments of the trial court pursuant to this chapter may include any relief available pursuant to this chapter including orders for custody or support; provided, however, that upon issuing an order for custody or support, the superior, district or Boston municipal court shall provide a copy of the order to the probate and family court department of the trial court that issued the prior or pending custody or support order immediately; provided further, that such order for custody or support shall be for a fixed period of time, not to exceed 30 days; and provided further, that such order may be superseded by a subsequent custody or support order issued by the probate and family court department, which shall retain final jurisdiction over any custody or support order. This section shall not be interpreted to mean that superior, district or Boston municipal court judges are prohibited or discouraged from ordering all other necessary relief or issuing the custody and support provisions of orders pursuant to this chapter for the full duration permitted under subsection (c).

If the parties to a proceeding under this chapter are parties in a subsequent proceeding in the probate and family court department for divorce, annulment, paternity, custody or support, guardianship or separate support, any custody or support order or judgment issued in the subsequent proceeding shall supersede any prior custody or support order under this chapter.

§ 3A. NATURE OF PROCEEDINGS AND AVAILABILITY OF OTHER CRIMINAL PROCEEDINGS; INFORMATION REQUIRED TO BE GIVEN TO COMPLAINANT UPON FILING

Upon the filing of a complaint under this chapter, a complainant shall be informed that the proceedings hereunder are civil in nature and that violations of orders issued hereunder are criminal in nature. Further, a complainant shall be given information prepared by the appropriate district attorney's office that other criminal proceedings may be available and such complainant shall be instructed by such district attorney's office relative to the procedures required to initiate criminal proceedings including, but not limited to, a complaint for a violation of section forty-three of chapter two hundred and sixty-five. Whenever possible, a complainant shall be provided with such information in the complainant's native language.

§ 3B. ORDER FOR SUSPENSION AND SURRENDER OF FIREARMS LICENSE; SURRENDER OF FIREARMS; PETITION FOR REVIEW; HEARING

Upon issuance of a temporary or emergency order under section four or five of this chapter, the court shall, if the plaintiff demonstrates a substantial likelihood of immediate danger of abuse, order the immediate suspension and surrender of any license to carry firearms and or firearms identification card which the defendant may hold and order the defendant to surrender all firearms, rifles, shotguns, machine guns and ammunition which he then controls, owns or possesses in accordance with the provisions of this chapter and any license to carry firearms or firearms identification cards which the defendant may hold shall be surrendered to the appropriate law enforcement officials in accordance with the provisions of this chapter and, said law enforcement official may store, transfer or otherwise dispose of any such weapon in accordance with the provisions of section 129D of chapter 140; provided however, that nothing herein shall authorize the transfer of any weapons surrendered by the defendant to anyone other than a licensed dealer. Notice of such suspension and ordered surrender shall be appended to the copy of abuse prevention order served on the defendant pursuant to section seven. Law enforcement officials, upon the service of said orders, shall immediately take possession of all firearms, rifles, shotguns, machine guns, ammunition, any license to carry firearms and any firearms identification cards in the control, ownership, or possession of said defendant. Any violation of such orders shall be punishable by a fine of not more than five thousand dollars, or by imprisonment for not more than two and one-half years in a house of correction, or by both such fine and imprisonment.

Any defendant aggrieved by an order of surrender or suspension as described in the first sentence of this section may petition the court which issued such suspension or surrender order for a review of such action and such petition shall be heard no later than ten court business days after the receipt of the notice of the petition by the court. If said license to carry firearms or firearms identification card has been suspended upon the issuance of an order issued pursuant to section four or five, said petition may be heard contemporaneously with the hearing specified in the second sentence of the second paragraph of section four. Upon the filing of an affidavit by the defendant that a firearm, rifle, shotgun, machine gun or ammunition is required in the performance of the defendant's employment, and upon a request for an expedited hearing, the court shall order said hearing within two business days of receipt of such affidavit and request but only on the issue of surrender and suspension pursuant to this section.

§ 3C. CONTINUATION OR MODIFICATION OF ORDER FOR SURRENDER OR SUSPENSION

Upon the continuation or modification of an order issued pursuant to section 4 or upon petition for review as described in section 3B, the court shall also order or continue to order the immediate suspension and surrender of a defendant's license to carry firearms, including a Class A or Class B license, and firearms identification card and the surrender of all firearms, rifles, shotguns, machine guns or ammunition which such defendant then controls, owns or possesses if the court makes a determination that the return of such license to carry firearms, including a Class A or Class B license, and firearm identification card or firearms, rifles, shotguns, machine guns or ammunition presents a likelihood of abuse to the plaintiff. A suspension and surrender order issued pursuant to this section shall continue so long as the restraining order to which it relates is in effect; and, any law enforcement official to whom such weapon is surrendered may store, transfer or otherwise dispose of any such weapon in accordance with the provisions of section 129D of chapter 140; provided, however, that nothing herein shall authorize the transfer of any weapons surrendered by the defendant to anyone other than a licensed dealer. Any violation of such order shall be punishable by a fine of not more than $5,000 or by imprisonment for not more than two and one-half years in a house of correction or by both such fine and imprisonment.

§ 3D. TRANSMISSION OF REPORT CONTAINING DEFENDANT'S NAME AND IDENTIFYING INFORMATION AND STATEMENT DESCRIBING DEFENDANT'S ALLEGED CONDUCT AND RELATIONSHIP TO PLAINTIFF TO DEPARTMENT OF CRIMINAL JUSTICE INFORMATION SERVICES UPON ORDER FOR SUSPENSION OR SURRENDER

Upon an order for suspension or surrender issued pursuant to sections 3B or 3C, the court shall transmit a report containing the defendant's name and identifying information and a statement describing the defendant's alleged conduct and relationship to the plaintiff to the department of criminal justice information services. Upon the expiration, cancellation or revocation of the order, the court shall transmit a report containing the defendant's name and identifying information, a statement describing the defendant's alleged conduct and relationship to the plaintiff and an explanation that the order is no longer current or valid to the department of criminal justice information services who shall transmit the report, pursuant to paragraph (h) of section 167A of chapter 6, to the attorney general of the United States to be included in the National Instant Criminal Background Check System.

§ 4. TEMPORARY ORDERS; NOTICE; HEARING

Upon the filing of a complaint under this chapter, the court may enter such temporary orders as it deems necessary to protect a plaintiff from abuse, including relief as provided in section three. Such relief shall not be contingent upon the filing of a complaint for divorce, separate support, or paternity action.

If the plaintiff demonstrates a substantial likelihood of immediate danger of abuse, the court may enter such temporary relief orders without notice as it deems necessary to protect the plaintiff from abuse and shall immediately thereafter notify the defendant that the temporary orders have been issued. The court shall give the defendant an opportunity to be heard on the question of continuing the temporary order and of granting other relief as requested by the plaintiff no later than ten court business days after such orders are entered.

Notice shall be made by the appropriate law enforcement agency as provided in section seven.

If the defendant does not appear at such subsequent hearing, the temporary orders shall continue in effect without further order of the court.

§ 5. GRANTING OF RELIEF WHEN COURT CLOSED; CERTIFICATION

When the court is closed for business or the plaintiff is unable to appear in court because of severe hardship due to the plaintiff's physical condition, any justice of the superior, probate and family, district or Boston municipal court departments may grant relief to the plaintiff as provided under section four if the plaintiff demonstrates a substantial likelihood of immediate danger of abuse. In the discretion of the justice, such relief may be granted and communicated by telephone to an officer or employee of an appropriate law enforcement agency, who shall record such order on a form of order promulgated for such use by the chief justice of the trial court and shall deliver a copy of such order on the next court day to the clerk-magistrate of the court having venue and jurisdiction over the matter.

If relief has been granted without the filing of a complaint pursuant to this section of this chapter, then the plaintiff shall appear in court on the next available business day to file said complaint. If the plaintiff in such a case is unable to appear in court without severe hardship due to the plaintiff's physical condition, then a representative may appear in court on the plaintiff's behalf and file the requisite complaint with an affidavit setting forth the circumstances preventing the plaintiff from appearing personally. Notice to the plaintiff and defendant and an opportunity for the defendant to be heard shall be given as provided in said section four.

Any order issued under this section and any documentation in support thereof shall be certified on the next court day by the clerk-magistrate or register of the court issuing such order to the court having venue and jurisdiction over the matter. Such certification to the court shall have the effect of commencing proceedings under this chapter and invoking the other provisions of this chapter but shall not be deemed necessary for an emergency order issued under this section to take effect.

§ 5A. PROTECTION ORDER ISSUED BY ANOTHER JURISDICTION; ENFORCEMENT; FILING; PRESUMPTION OF VALIDITY

Any protection order issued by another jurisdiction, as defined in section one, shall be given full faith and credit throughout the commonwealth and enforced as if it were issued in the commonwealth for as long as the order is in effect in the issuing jurisdiction.

A person entitled to protection under a protection order issued by another jurisdiction may file such order in the superior court department or the Boston municipal court department or any division of the probate and family or district court departments by filing with the court a certified copy of such order which shall be entered into the statewide domestic violence record keeping system established pursuant to the provisions of section seven of chapter one hundred and eighty-eight of the acts of nineteen hundred and ninety-two and maintained by the office of the commissioner of probation. Such person shall swear under oath in an affidavit, to the best of such person's knowledge, that such order is presently in effect as written. Upon request by a law enforcement agency, the register or clerk of such court shall provide a certified copy of the protection order issued by the other jurisdiction.

A law enforcement officer may presume the validity of, and enforce in accordance with section six, a copy of a protection order issued by another jurisdiction which has been provided to the law enforcement officer by any source; provided, however, that the officer is also provided with a statement by the person protected by the order that such order remains in effect. Law enforcement officers may rely on such statement by the person protected by such order.

§ 6. POWERS OF POLICE

Whenever any law officer has reason to believe that a family or household member has been abused or is in danger of being abused, such officer shall use all reasonable means to prevent further abuse. The officer shall take, but not be limited to the following action:

(1)   remain on the scene of where said abuse occurred or was in danger of occurring as long as the officer has reason to believe that at least one of the parties involved would be in immediate physical danger without the presence of a law officer. This shall include, but not be limited to remaining in the dwelling for a reasonable period of time;

(2)   assist the abused person in obtaining medical treatment necessitated by an assault, which may include driving the victim to the emergency room of the nearest hospital, or arranging for appropriate transportation to a health care facility, notwithstanding any law to the contrary;

(3)   assist the abused person in locating and getting to a safe place; including but not limited to a designated meeting place for a shelter or a family member's or friend's residence. The officer shall consider the victim's preference in this regard and what is reasonable under all the circumstances;

(4)   give such person immediate and adequate notice of his or her rights. Such notice shall consist of handing said person a copy of the statement which follows below and reading the same to said person. Where said person's native language is not English, the statement shall be then provided in said person's native language whenever possible.

"You have the right to appear at the Superior, Probate and Family, District or Boston Municipal Court, if you reside within the appropriate jurisdiction, and file a complaint requesting any of the following applicable orders: (a) an order restraining your attacker from abusing you; (b) an order directing your attacker to leave your household, building or workplace; (c) an order awarding you custody of a minor child; (d) an order directing your attacker to pay support for you or any minor child in your custody, if the attacker has a legal obligation of support; and (e) an order directing your attacker to pay you for losses suffered as a result of abuse, including medical and moving expenses, loss of earnings or support, costs for restoring utilities and replacing locks, reasonable attorney's fees and other out-of-pocket losses for injuries and property damage sustained.

For an emergency on weekends, holidays, or weeknights the police will refer you to a justice of the superior, probate and family, district, or Boston municipal court departments.

You have the right to go to the appropriate district court or the Boston municipal court and seek a criminal complaint for threats, assault and battery, assault with a deadly weapon, assault with intent to kill or other related offenses.

If you are in need of medical treatment, you have the right to request that an officer present drive you to the nearest hospital or otherwise assist you in obtaining medical treatment.

If you believe that police protection is needed for your physical safety, you have the right to request that the officer present remain at the scene until you and your children can leave or until your safety is otherwise ensured. You may also request that the officer assist you in locating and taking you to a safe place, including but not limited to a designated meeting place for a shelter or a family member's or a friend's residence, or a similar place of safety.

You may request a copy of the police incident report at no cost from the police department."

The officer shall leave a copy of the foregoing statement with such person before leaving the scene or premises.

(5) assist such person by activating the emergency judicial system when the court is closed for business;

(6) inform the victim that the abuser will be eligible for bail and may be promptly released; and

(7) arrest any person a law officer witnesses or has probable cause to believe has violated a temporary or permanent vacate, restraining, or no-contact order or judgment issued pursuant to section eighteen, thirty-four B or thirty-four C of chapter two hundred and eight, section thirty-two of chapter two hundred and nine, section three, three B, three C, four or five of this chapter, or sections fifteen or twenty of chapter two hundred and nine C or similar protection order issued by another jurisdiction. When there are no vacate, restraining, or no-contact orders or judgments in effect, arrest shall be the preferred response whenever an officer witnesses or has probable cause to believe that a person:

(a) has committed a felony;

(b) has committed a misdemeanor involving abuse as defined in section one of this chapter;

(c) has committed an assault and battery in violation of section thirteen A of chapter two hundred and sixty-five.

The safety of the victim and any involved children shall be paramount in any decision to arrest. Any officer arresting both parties must submit a detailed, written report in addition to an incident report, setting forth the grounds for dual arrest.

No law officer investigating an incident of domestic violence shall threaten, suggest, or otherwise indicate the arrest of all parties for the purpose of discouraging requests for law enforcement intervention by any party.

No law officer shall be held liable in any civil action regarding personal injury or injury to property brought by any party to a domestic violence incident for an arrest based on probable cause when such officer acted reasonably and in good faith and in compliance with this chapter and the statewide policy as established by the secretary of public safety.

Whenever any law officer investigates an incident of domestic violence, the officer shall immediately file a written incident report in accordance with the standards of the officer's law enforcement agency and, wherever possible, in the form of the National Incident-Based Reporting System, as defined by the Federal Bureau of Investigation. The latter information may be submitted voluntarily by the local police on a monthly basis to the crime reporting unit of the department of criminal justice information services.

The victim shall be provided a copy of the full incident report at no cost upon request to the appropriate law enforcement department.

When a judge or other person authorized to take bail bails any person arrested under the provisions of this chapter, he shall make reasonable efforts to inform the victim of such release prior to or at the time of said release.

When any person charged with or arrested for a crime involving abuse under this chapter is released from custody, the court or the emergency response judge shall issue, upon the request of the victim, a written no-contact order prohibiting the person charged or arrested from having any contact with the victim and shall use all reasonable means to notify the victim immediately of release from custody. The victim shall be given at no cost a certified copy of the no-contact order.

§ 7. ABUSE PREVENTION ORDERS; DOMESTIC VIOLENCE RECORD SEARCH; SERVICE OF ORDER; ENFORCEMENT; VIOLATIONS

When considering a complaint filed under this chapter, a judge shall cause a search to be made of the records contained within the statewide domestic violence record keeping system maintained by the office of the commissioner of probation and shall review the resulting data to determine whether the named defendant has a civil or criminal record involving domestic or other violence. Upon receipt of information that an outstanding warrant exists against the named defendant, a judge shall order that the appropriate law enforcement officials be notified and shall order that any information regarding the defendant's most recent whereabouts shall be forwarded to such officials. In all instances where an outstanding warrant exists, a judge shall make a finding, based upon all of the circumstances, as to whether an imminent threat of bodily injury exists to the petitioner. In all instances where such an imminent threat of bodily injury is found to exist, the judge shall notify the appropriate law enforcement officials of such finding and such officials shall take all necessary actions to execute any such outstanding warrant as soon as is practicable.

Whenever the court orders under sections eighteen, thirty-four B, and thirty-four C of chapter two hundred and eight, section thirty-two of chapter two hundred and nine, sections three, four and five of this chapter, or sections fifteen and twenty of chapter two hundred and nine C, the defendant to vacate, refrain from abusing the plaintiff or to have no contact with the plaintiff or the plaintiff's minor child, the register or clerk-magistrate shall transmit two certified copies of each such order and one copy of the complaint and summons forthwith to the appropriate law enforcement agency which, unless otherwise ordered by the court, shall serve one copy of each order upon the defendant, together with a copy of the complaint, order and summons and notice of any suspension or surrender ordered pursuant to section three B of this chapter. Law enforcement agencies shall establish adequate procedures to ensure that, when effecting service upon a defendant pursuant to this paragraph, a law enforcement officer shall, to the extent practicable: (i) fully inform the defendant of the contents of the order and the available penalties for any violation of an order or terms thereof and (ii) provide the defendant with informational resources, including, but not limited to, a list of certified batterer intervention programs, substance abuse counseling, alcohol abuse counseling and financial counseling programs located within or near the court's jurisdiction. The law enforcement agency shall promptly make its return of service to the court.

Law enforcement officers shall use every reasonable means to enforce such abuse prevention orders. Law enforcement agencies shall establish procedures adequate to insure that an officer on the scene of an alleged violation of such order may be informed of the existence and terms of such order. The court shall notify the appropriate law enforcement agency in writing whenever any such order is vacated and shall direct the agency to destroy all record of such vacated order and such agency shall comply with that directive.

Each abuse prevention order issued shall contain the following statement:

VIOLATION OF THIS ORDER IS A CRIMINAL OFFENSE.

Any violation of such order or a protection order issued by another jurisdiction shall be punishable by a fine of not more than five thousand dollars, or by imprisonment for not more than two and one-half years in a house of correction, or by both such fine and imprisonment. In addition to, but not in lieu of, the forgoing penalties and any other sentence, fee or assessment, including the victim witness assessment in section 8 of chapter 258B, the court shall order persons convicted of a crime under this statute to pay a fine of $25 that shall be transmitted to the treasurer for deposit into the General Fund. For any violation of such order, or as a condition of a continuance without a finding, the court shall order the defendant to complete a certified batterer's intervention program unless, upon good cause shown, the court issues specific written findings describing the reasons that batterer's intervention should not be ordered or unless the batterer's intervention program determines that the defendant is not suitable for intervention. The court shall not order substance abuse or anger management treatment or any other form of treatment as a substitute for certified batterer's intervention. If a defendant ordered to undergo treatment has received a suspended sentence, the original sentence shall be reimposed if the defendant fails to participate in said program as required by the terms of his probation. If the court determines that the violation was in retaliation for the defendant being reported by the plaintiff to the department of revenue for failure to pay child support payments or for the establishment of paternity, the defendant shall be punished by a fine of not less than one thousand dollars and not more than ten thousand dollars and by imprisonment for not less than sixty days; provided, however, that the sentence shall not be suspended, nor shall any such person be eligible for probation, parole, or furlough or receive any deduction from his sentence for good conduct until he shall have served sixty days of such sentence.

When a defendant has been ordered to participate in a treatment program pursuant to this section, the defendant shall be required to regularly attend a certified or provisionally certified batterer's treatment program. To the extent permitted by professional requirements of confidentiality, said program shall communicate with local battered women's programs for the purpose of protecting the victim's safety. Additionally, it shall specify the defendant's attendance requirements and keep the probation department informed of whether the defendant is in compliance.

In addition to, but not in lieu of, such orders for treatment, if the defendant has a substance abuse problem, the court may order appropriate treatment for such problem. All ordered treatment shall last until the end of the probationary period or until the treatment program decides to discharge the defendant, whichever comes first. When the defendant is not in compliance with the terms of probation, the court shall hold a revocation of probation hearing. To the extent possible, the defendant shall be responsible for paying all costs for court ordered treatment.

Where a defendant has been found in violation of an abuse prevention order under this chapter or a protection order issued by another jurisdiction, the court may, in addition to the penalties provided for in this section after conviction, as an alternative to incarceration and, as a condition of probation, prohibit contact with the victim through the establishment of court defined geographic exclusion zones including, but not limited to, the areas in and around the complainant's residence, place of employment, and the complainant's child's school, and order that the defendant to wear a global positioning satellite tracking device designed to transmit and record the defendant's location data. If the defendant enters a court defined exclusion zone, the defendant's location data shall be immediately transmitted to the complainant, and to the police, through an appropriate means including, but not limited to, the telephone, an electronic beeper or a paging device. The global positioning satellite device and its tracking shall be administered by the department of probation. If a court finds that the defendant has entered a geographic exclusion zone, it shall revoke his probation and the defendant shall be fined, imprisoned or both as provided in this section. Based on the defendant's ability to pay, the court may also order him to pay the monthly costs or portion thereof for monitoring through the global positioning satellite tracking system.

In each instance where there is a violation of an abuse prevention order or a protection order issued by another jurisdiction, the court may order the defendant to pay the plaintiff for all damages including, but not limited to, cost for shelter or emergency housing, loss of earnings or support, out-of-pocket losses for injuries sustained or property damaged, medical expenses, moving expenses, cost for obtaining an unlisted telephone number, and reasonable attorney's fees.

Any such violation may be enforced in the superior, the district or Boston municipal court departments. Criminal remedies provided herein are not exclusive and do not preclude any other available civil or criminal remedies. The superior, probate and family, district and Boston municipal court departments may each enforce by civil contempt procedure a violation of its own court order.

The provisions of section eight of chapter one hundred and thirty-six shall not apply to any order, complaint or summons issued pursuant to this section.

§ 8. Confidentiality of Records

The records of cases arising out of an action brought under the provisions of this chapter where the plaintiff or defendant is a minor shall be withheld from public inspection except by order of the court; provided, that such records shall be open, at all reasonable times, to the inspection of the minor, said minor's parent, guardian, attorney, and to the plaintiff and the plaintiff's attorney, or any of them.

The plaintiff's residential address, residential telephone number and workplace name, address and telephone number, contained within the court records of cases arising out of an action brought by a plaintiff under the provisions of this chapter, shall be confidential and withheld from public inspection, except by order of the court, except that the plaintiff's residential address and workplace address shall appear on the court order and accessible to the defendant and the defendant's attorney unless the plaintiff specifically requests that this information be withheld from the order. All confidential portions of the records shall be accessible at all reasonable times to the plaintiff and plaintiff's attorney, to others specifically authorized by the plaintiff to obtain such information, and to prosecutors, victim-witness advocates as defined in section 1 of chapter 258B, domestic violence victim's counselors as defined in section 20K of chapter 233, sexual assault counselors as defined in section 20J of chapter 233, and law enforcement officers, if such access is necessary in the performance of their duties. The provisions of this paragraph shall apply to any protection order issued by another jurisdiction, as defined in section 1, that is filed with a court of the commonwealth pursuant to section 5A. Such confidential portions of the court records shall not be deemed to be public records under the provisions of clause twenty-sixth of section 7 of chapter 4.

§ 9. Form of Complaint; Promulgation

The administrative justices of the superior court, probate and family court, district court, and the Boston municipal court departments shall jointly promulgate a form of complaint for use under this chapter which shall be in such form and language to permit a plaintiff to prepare and file such complaint *pro se*.

§ 10. Assessments Against Persons Referred to Certified Batterers' Treatment Program as Condition of Probation

The court shall impose an assessment of three hundred and fifty dollars against any person who has been referred to a certified batterers' treatment program as a condition of probation. Said assessment shall be in addition to the cost of the treatment program. In the discretion of the court, said assessment may be reduced or waived when the court finds that the person is indigent or that payment of the assessment would cause the person, or the dependents of such person, severe financial hardship. Assessments made pursuant to this section shall be in addition to any other fines, assessments, or restitution imposed in any disposition. All funds collected by the court pursuant to this section shall be transmitted monthly to the state treasurer, who shall deposit said funds in the General Fund.

ELDER ABUSE AND DEPENDENT ADULT CIVIL PROTECTION ACT

Cal. Welf. & Inst. Code § 15656(c)–(d) (West 2016)

[EDITORS' INTRODUCTION: RAYMOND C. O'BRIEN & MICHAEL T. FLANNERY, THE FUNDAMENTALS OF ELDER LAW (2015); Jane K. Stoever, *Mirandizing Family Justice*, 39 HARV. J. L. & GENDER 189 (2016); Priscilla Vargas Wrosch, *What More Can Congress Do About the Elder Abuse Epidemic? A Proposal for National Movement*, 23 TEMP. POL. & CIV. RTS. L. REV. 1 (2013); Linda K. Chen, Comment, *Eradicating Elder Abuse in California Nursing Homes*, 52 SANTA CLARA L. REV. 213 (2012); Kerry Koehler, Note, *Comparative Shopping in Nursing Homes*, 11 J. HEALTH & BIOMEDICAL L. 439 (2016); Katherine B. Ledden, Comment, *A Nudge in the Right Direction with a Stick the Size of CMS: Physician-Patient Communication at the End of Life*, 6 ST. LOUIS U. J. HEALTH L. & POL'Y 389 (2013); Daniel L. Madow, Comment, *Why Many Meritorious Elder Abuse Cases in California are Not Litigated*, 47 U.S.F. L. REV. 619 (2013); Courtney A. Martin, Comment, *Hoarding in California: Stop Our Elders from Being Buried Alive*, 41 SW. L. REV. 149 (2011).]

§ 15656. SUBJECTING ELDER OR DEPENDENT ADULTS TO GREAT BODILY HARM OR DEATH; UNJUSTIFIABLE PHYSICAL PAIN OR MENTAL SUFFERING; THEFT OR EMBEZZLEMENT; PENALTIES

* * *

(c) Any caretaker of an elder or a dependent adult who violates any provision of law prescribing theft or embezzlement, with respect to the property of that elder or dependent adult, is punishable by imprisonment in the county jail not exceeding one year, or in the state prison for two, three, or four years when the money, labor, or real or personal property taken is of a value exceeding nine hundred fifty dollars ($950), and by a fine not exceeding one thousand dollars ($1,000), or by imprisonment in the county jail not exceeding one year, or by both that imprisonment and fine, when the money, labor, or real or personal property taken is of a value not exceeding nine hundred fifty dollars ($950).

(d) As used in this section, "caretaker" means any person who has the care, custody, or control of or who stands in a position of trust with, an elder or a dependent adult.

* * *

EMANCIPATION OF MINORS

CALIFORNIA

Cal. Fam. Code §§ 7000 et seq. (West 2016)

[EDITORS' INTRODUCTION: Dane S. Ciolino & Monica Hof Wallace, *Recodifying Emancipation: A Précis of the 2009 Revision of Louisiana Emancipation Law*, 56 LOY. L. REV. 135 (2010); Lauren C. Barnett, Comment, *Having Their Cake and Eating It Too? Post-Emancipation Child Support as a Valid Judicial Option*, 80 U. CHI. L. REV. 1799 (2013); Mayra Alicia Cataldo, Note, *Safe Haven: Granting Support to Victims of Child Abuse Who Have Been Judicially Emancipated*, 52 FAM. CT. REV. 592 (2014); Dana M. Dohn & Amy Pimer, Note, *Child Labor Laws and the Impossibility of Statutory Emancipation*, 33 HOFSTRA LAB. & EMP. L.J. 121 (2015); Samantha Godwin, *Against Parental Rights*, 47 COLUM. HUM. RTS. L. REV. 1 (2015).]

§ 7000. SHORT TITLE

This part may be cited as the Emancipation of Minors Law.

§ 7001. PURPOSE OF PART

It is the purpose of this part to provide a clear statement defining emancipation and its consequences and to permit an emancipated minor to obtain a court declaration of the minor's status. This part is not intended to affect the status of minors who may become emancipated under the decisional case law that was in effect before the enactment of Chapter 1059 of the Statutes of 1978.

§ 7002. EMANCIPATED MINOR; DESCRIPTION

A person under the age of 18 years is an emancipated minor if any of the following conditions is satisfied:

(a) The person has entered into a valid marriage, whether or not the marriage has been dissolved.

(b) The person is on active duty with the armed forces of the United States.

(c) The person has received a declaration of emancipation pursuant to Section 7122.

§ 7050. PURPOSES FOR WHICH EMANCIPATED MINORS ARE CONSIDERED AN ADULT

An emancipated minor shall be considered as being an adult for the following purposes:

(a) The minor's right to support by the minor's parents.

(b)   The right of the minor's parents to the minor's earnings and to control the minor.

(c)   The application of Sections 300 and 601 of the Welfare and Institutions Code.

(d)   Ending all vicarious or imputed liability of the minor's parents or guardian for the minor's torts. Nothing in this section affects any liability of a parent, guardian, spouse, or employer imposed by the Vehicle Code, or any vicarious liability that arises from an agency relationship.

(e)   The minor's capacity to do any of the following:

(1)   Consent to medical, dental, or psychiatric care, without parental consent, knowledge, or liability.

(2)   Enter into a binding contract or give a delegation of power.

(3)   Buy, sell, lease, encumber, exchange, or transfer an interest in real or personal property, including, but not limited to, shares of stock in a domestic or foreign corporation or a membership in a nonprofit corporation.

(4)   Sue or be sued in the minor's own name.

(5)   Compromise, settle, arbitrate, or otherwise adjust a claim, action, or proceeding by or against the minor.

(6)   Make or revoke a will.

(7)   Make a gift, outright or in trust.

(8)   Convey or release contingent or expectant interests in property, including marital property rights and any right of survivorship incident to joint tenancy, and consent to a transfer, encumbrance, or gift of marital property.

(9)   Exercise or release the minor's powers as donee of a power of appointment unless the creating instrument otherwise provides.

(10) Create for the minor's own benefit or for the benefit of others a revocable or irrevocable trust.

(11) Revoke a revocable trust.

(12) Elect to take under or against a will.

(13) Renounce or disclaim any interest acquired by testate or intestate succession or by inter vivos transfer, including exercise of the right to surrender the right to revoke a revocable trust.

(14) Make an election referred to in Section 13502 of, or an election and agreement referred to in Section 13503 of, the Probate Code.

(15) Establish the minor's own residence.

(16) Apply for a work permit pursuant to Section 49110 of the Education Code without the request of the minor's parents.

(17) Enroll in a school or college.

§ 7051. INSURANCE CONTRACTS

An insurance contract entered into by an emancipated minor has the same effect as if it were entered into by an adult and, with respect to that contract, the minor has the same rights, duties, and liabilities as an adult.

§ 7052. POWERS OF EMANCIPATED MINOR WITH RESPECT TO SHARES OF STOCK AND SIMILAR PROPERTY

With respect to shares of stock in a domestic or foreign corporation held by an emancipated minor, a membership in a nonprofit corporation held by an emancipated minor, or other property held by an emancipated minor, the minor may do all of the following:

(a) Vote in person, and give proxies to exercise any voting rights, with respect to the shares, membership, or property.

(b) Waive notice of any meeting or give consent to the holding of any meeting.

(c) Authorize, ratify, approve, or confirm any action that could be taken by shareholders, members, or property owners.

§ 7110. LEGISLATIVE INTENT; MINIMUM EXPENSE; FORMS

It is the intent of the Legislature that proceedings under this part be as simple and inexpensive as possible. To that end, the Judicial Council is requested to prepare and distribute to the clerks of the superior courts appropriate forms for the proceedings that are suitable for use by minors acting as their own counsel.

§ 7111. ISSUANCE OF DECLARATION OF EMANCIPATION; EFFECT ON PUBLIC SOCIAL SERVICE BENEFITS

The issuance of a declaration of emancipation does not entitle the minor to any benefits under Division 9 (commencing with Section 10000) of the Welfare and Institutions Code which would not otherwise accrue to an emancipated minor.

§ 7120. PETITIONS FOR DECLARATION OF EMANCIPATION; CONTENTS

(a) A minor may petition the superior court of the county in which the minor resides or is temporarily domiciled for a declaration of emancipation.

(b) The petition shall set forth with specificity all of the following facts:

(1) The minor is at least 14 years of age.

(2) The minor willingly lives separate and apart from the minor's parents or guardian with the consent or acquiescence of the minor's parents or guardian.

(3) The minor is managing his or her own financial affairs. As evidence of this, the minor shall complete and attach a declaration of income and expenses as provided in Judicial Council form FL–150.

(4) The source of the minor's income is not derived from any activity declared to be a crime by the laws of this state or the laws of the United States.

§ 7121. NOTICE OF DECLARATION PROCEEDINGS

(a) Before the petition for a declaration of emancipation is heard, notice the court determines is reasonable shall be given to the minor's parents, guardian, or other person entitled to the custody of the minor, or proof shall be made to the court that their addresses are unknown or that for other reasons the notice cannot be given.

(b) The clerk of the court shall also notify the local child support agency of the county in which the matter is to be heard of the proceeding. If the minor is a ward of the court, notice shall be given to the probation department. If the child is a dependent child of the court, notice shall be given to the county welfare department.

(c) The notice shall include a form whereby the minor's parents, guardian, or other person entitled to the custody of the minor may give their written consent to the petitioner's emancipation. The notice shall include a warning that a court may void or rescind the declaration of emancipation and the parents may become liable for support and medical insurance coverage pursuant to Chapter 2 (commencing with Section 4000) of Part 2 of Division 9 and Sections 17400, 17402, 17404, and 17422.

§ 7122. FINDINGS OF COURT; ISSUANCE OF DECLARATION OF EMANCIPATION

(a) The court shall sustain the petition if it finds that the minor is a person described by Section 7120 and that emancipation would not be contrary to the minor's best interest.

(b) If the petition is sustained, the court shall forthwith issue a declaration of emancipation, which shall be filed by the clerk of the court.

(c) A declaration is conclusive evidence that the minor is emancipated.

§ 7123. GRANT OR DENIAL OF PETITION; FILING OF PETITION FOR WRIT OF MANDATE

(a) If the petition is denied, the minor has a right to file a petition for a writ of mandate.

(b) If the petition is sustained, the parents or guardian have a right to file a petition for a writ of mandate if they have appeared in the proceeding and opposed the granting of the petition.

§ 7130. GROUNDS FOR VOIDING OR RESCINDING DECLARATION

(a) A declaration of emancipation obtained by fraud or by the withholding of material information is voidable.

(b) A declaration of emancipation of a minor who is indigent and has no means of support is subject to rescission.

§ 7131. FILING OF PETITIONS TO VOID DECLARATIONS

A petition to void a declaration of emancipation on the ground that the declaration was obtained by fraud or by the withholding of material information may be filed by any person or by any public or private agency. The petition shall be filed in the court that made the declaration.

§ 7132. FILING OF PETITIONS TO RESCIND DECLARATIONS

(a) A petition to rescind a declaration of emancipation on the ground that the minor is indigent and has no means of support may be filed by the minor declared emancipated, by the minor's conservator, or by the district attorney of the county in which the minor resides. The petition shall be filed in the county in which the minor or the conservator resides.

(b) The minor may be considered indigent if the minor's only source of income is from public assistance benefits. The court shall consider the impact of the rescission of the declaration of emancipation on the minor and shall find the rescission of the declaration of emancipation will not be contrary to the best interest of the minor before granting the order to rescind.

§ 7133. NOTICE OF PETITION TO VOID OR RESCIND DECLARATION

(a) Before a petition under this article is heard, notice the court determines is reasonable shall be given to the minor's parents or guardian, or proof shall be made to the court that their addresses are unknown or that for other reasons the notice cannot be given.

(b) The notice to parents shall state that if the declaration of emancipation is voided or rescinded, the parents may be liable to provide support and medical insurance coverage for the child pursuant to Chapter 2 (commencing with Section 4000) of Part 2 of Division 9 of this code and Sections 11350, 11350.1, 11475.1, and 11490 of the Welfare and Institutions Code.

(c) No liability accrues to a parent or guardian not given actual notice, as a result of voiding or rescinding the declaration of emancipation, until that parent or guardian is given actual notice.

§ 7134. ISSUANCE OF ORDER

If the petition is sustained, the court shall forthwith issue an order voiding or rescinding the declaration of emancipation, which shall be filed by the clerk of the court.

§ 7135. EFFECT UPON CONTRACTUAL AND PROPERTY OBLIGATIONS

Voiding or rescission of the declaration of emancipation does not alter any contractual obligation or right or any property right or interest that arose during the period that the declaration was in effect.

§ 7140. ENTRY OF IDENTIFYING INFORMATION INTO DEPARTMENT OF MOTOR VEHICLES RECORDS SYSTEMS; STATEMENT OF EMANCIPATION UPON IDENTIFICATION CARD

On application of a minor declared emancipated under this chapter, the Department of Motor Vehicles shall enter identifying information in its law enforcement computer network, and the fact of emancipation shall be stated on the department's identification card issued to the emancipated minor.

§ 7141. RELIANCE ON REPRESENTATION OF EMANCIPATION; EFFECT

A person who, in good faith, has examined a minor's identification card and relies on a minor's representation that the minor is emancipated, has the same rights and obligations as if the minor were in fact emancipated at the time of the representation.

§ 7142. LIABILITY OF PUBLIC ENTITIES OR EMPLOYEES

No public entity or employee is liable for any loss or injury resulting directly or indirectly from false or inaccurate information contained in the Department of Motor Vehicles records system or identification cards as provided in this part.

§ 7143. NOTIFICATION OF MOTOR VEHICLES DEPARTMENT UPON VOIDING OR RESCISSION OF DECLARATION OF EMANCIPATION; INVALIDATION OF IDENTIFICATION CARDS

If a declaration of emancipation is voided or rescinded, notice shall be sent immediately to the Department of Motor Vehicles which shall remove the information relating to emancipation in its law enforcement computer network. Any identification card issued stating emancipation shall be invalidated.

FAMILY LAW MEDIATION

Or. Rev. Stat. Ann. § 107.755 (West 2016)

[EDITORS' INTRODUCTION: Deborah Thompson Eisenberg, *What We Know and Need to Know About Court-Annexed Dispute Resolution*, 67 S.C. L. REV. 245 (2016); William J. Howe, III & Elizabeth Potter Scully, *Redesigning the Family Law System to Promote Healthy Families*, 53 FAM. CT. REV. 361 (2015); Susan Landrum, *The Ongoing Debate About Mediation in the Context of Domestic Violence: A Call for Empirical Studies of Mediation Effectiveness*, 12 CARDOZO J. CONFLICT RESOL. 425 (2011); Jane C. Murphy, *Revitalizing the Adversary System in Family Law*, 78 U. CIN. L. REV. 891 (2010); Sandra J. Perry, Tanya M. Marcum, & Charles R. Stoner, *Stumbling Down the Courthouse Steps: Mediators' Perceptions of the Stumbling Blocks to Successful Mandated Mediation in Child Custody and Visitation*, 11 PEPP. DISP. RESOL. L.J. 441 (2011); Melinda Taylor et al., *The Resource Center for Separating and Divorcing Families: Interdisciplinary Perspectives On a Collaborative and Child-Focused Approach to Alternative Dispute Resolution*, 53 FAM. CT. REV. 7 (2015).]

§ 107.755. MEDIATION REQUIRED IN CERTAIN CASES; GUIDELINES FOR MEDIATION INVOLVING DOMESTIC VIOLENCE ISSUES

(1) Each judicial district shall:

(a) Provide a mediation orientation session for all parties in cases in which child custody, parenting time or visitation is in dispute, and in any other domestic relations case in which mediation has been ordered. The orientation session may be structured in any way the circuit court determines best meets the needs of the parties. The orientation session should be designed to make the parties aware of:

(A) What mediation is;

(B) Mediation options available to them; and

(C) The advantages and disadvantages of each method of dispute resolution.

(b) Except in matters tried under ORS 107.097 and 107.138 or upon a finding of good cause, require parties in all cases described in paragraph (a) of this subsection to attend a mediation orientation session prior to any judicial determination of the issues.

(c) Provide mediation under ORS 107.755 to 107.795 in any case in which child custody, parenting time and visitation are in dispute.

(d) Have developed a plan that addresses domestic violence issues and other power imbalance issues in the context of mediation orientation sessions and mediation of any issue in accordance with the following guidelines:

(A) All mediation programs and mediators must recognize that mediation is not an appropriate process for all cases and that agreement is not necessarily the appropriate outcome of all mediation;

(B) Neither the existence of nor the provisions of a restraining order issued under ORS 107.718 may be mediated;

(C) All mediation programs and mediators must develop and implement:

(i) A screening and ongoing evaluation process of domestic violence issues for all mediation cases;

(ii) A provision for opting out of mediation that allows a party to decline mediation after the party has been informed of the advantages and disadvantages of mediation or at any time during the mediation; and

(iii) A set of safety procedures intended to minimize the likelihood of intimidation or violence in the orientation session, during mediation or on the way in or out of the building in which the orientation or mediation occurs;

(D) When a mediator explains the process to the parties, the mediator shall include in the explanation the disadvantages of mediation and the alternatives to mediation;

(E) All mediators shall obtain continuing education regarding domestic violence and related issues; and

(F) Mediation programs shall collect appropriate data. Mediation programs shall be sensitive to domestic violence issues when determining what data to collect.

(e) In developing the plan required by paragraph (d) of this subsection, consult with one or more of the following:

(A) A statewide or local multidisciplinary domestic violence coordinating council.

(B) A nonprofit private organization funded under ORS 409.292.

(2) Notwithstanding any other provision of law, mediation under ORS 107.755 to 107.795, including the mediation orientation session described in subsection (1)(a) of this section, may not be encouraged or provided in proceedings under ORS 30.866, 107.700 to 107.735, 124.005 to 124.040 or 163.738.

(3) The court, as provided in ORS 3.220, may make rules consistent with ORS 107.755 to 107.795 to govern the operation and procedure of mediation provided under this section.

(4) If a court provides mediation of financial issues, it shall develop a list of mediators who meet the minimum education and experience qualifications established by rules adopted under ORS 1.002. The rules

must require demonstrated proficiency in mediation of financial issues. Once the list is developed, the judicial district shall maintain the list. Mediation of financial issues is subject to the plan developed under subsection (1)(d) of this section and to the limitations imposed by subsection (2) of this section.

(5) A circuit court may provide mediation in connection with its exercise of conciliation jurisdiction under ORS 107.510 to 107.610, but a circuit court need not provide conciliation services in order to provide mediation under ORS 107.755 to 107.795.

FOSTER CARE

VIRGINIA FOSTER CARE STATUTE

Va. Code Ann. §§ 63.2–900–63.2–912 (West 2016)

[EDITORS' INTRODUCTION: Arielle Bardzell & Nicholas Bernard, *Adoption and Foster Care*, 16 GEO. J. GENDER & L. 3 (2015); Richard R. Carlson, *A Child's Right to a Family Versus a State's Discretion to Institutionalize the Child*, 47 GEO. J. INT'L L. 937 (2016); Tanya Asim Cooper, *Racial Bias in American Foster Care: The National Debate*, 97 MARQ. L. REV. 215 (2013); Ramesh Kasarabada, *Fostering the Human Rights of Youth in Foster Care: Defining Reasonable Efforts to Improve Consequences of Aging Out*, 17 CUNY L. REV. 145 (2013); Randi Mandelbaum, *Re-Examining and Re-Defining Permanency from a Youth's Perspective*, 43 CAP. U. L. REV. 259 (2015); The Honorable Christopher K. Peace & Amy L. Woolard, *Recent Children's Policy and Legislative Developments in Virginia: A Brief History, a Bright Future*, 19 RICH. J.L. & PUB. INT. 17 (2015); Shardé Armstrong, Note, *The Foster Care System Looking Forward: The Growing Fiscal and Policy Rationale for the Elimination of the "AFDC Look-Back"*, 17 N.Y.U. J. LEGIS. & PUB. POL'Y 193 (2014); Aimee Corbin, Comment, *Decreasing Disproportionality Through Kinship Care*, 18 SCHOLAR 73 (2016).]

§ 63.2–900. ACCEPTING CHILDREN FOR PLACEMENT IN HOMES, FACILITIES, ETC., BY LOCAL BOARDS

A. Pursuant to § 63.2–319, a local board shall have the right to accept for placement in suitable family homes, children's residential facilities or independent living arrangements, subject to the supervision of the Commissioner and in accordance with regulations adopted by the Board, such persons under 18 years of age as may be entrusted to it by the parent, parents or guardian, committed by any court of competent jurisdiction, or placed through an agreement between it and the parent, parents or guardians where legal custody remains with the parent, parents, or guardians.

The Board shall adopt regulations for the provision of foster care services by local boards, which shall be directed toward the prevention of unnecessary foster care placements and towards the immediate care of and permanent planning for children in the custody of or placed by local boards and that shall achieve, as quickly as practicable, permanent placements for such children. The local board shall first seek out kinship care options to keep children out of foster care and as a placement option for those children in foster care, if it is in the child's best interests, pursuant to § 63.2–900.1. In cases in which a child cannot be returned to his prior family or placed for adoption and kinship care is not currently in the best interests of the child, the local board shall consider the placement and services that afford the best alternative for protecting the child's welfare. Placements may include but are not limited to family foster care, treatment foster care and residential care. Services may include but are not limited to assessment and stabilization, diligent family search, intensive in-home, intensive wraparound, respite, mentoring, family mentoring, adoption support, supported adoption, crisis stabilization or other community-based services. The Board shall also approve in foster care policy the language of the agreement required in § 63.2–902. The agreement shall include at a minimum a Code of Ethics and mutual responsibilities for all parties to the agreement.

Within 30 days of accepting for foster care placement a person under 18 years of age whose father is unknown, the local board shall request a search of the Putative Father Registry established pursuant to Article 7 (§ 63.2–1249 et seq.) of Chapter 12 to determine whether any man has registered as the putative father of the child. If the search results indicate that a man has registered as the putative father of the child, the local board shall contact the man to begin the process to determine paternity.

The local board shall, in accordance with the regulations adopted by the Board and in accordance with the entrustment agreement or other order by which such person is entrusted or committed to its care, have custody and control of the person so entrusted or committed to it until he is lawfully discharged, has been adopted or has attained his majority.

Whenever a local board places a child where legal custody remains with the parent, parents or guardians, the board shall enter into an agreement with the parent, parents or guardians. The agreement shall specify the responsibilities of each for the care and control of the child.

The local board shall have authority to place for adoption, and to consent to the adoption of, any child properly committed or entrusted to its care when the order of commitment or entrustment agreement between the parent or parents and the agency provides for the termination of all parental rights and responsibilities with respect to the child for the purpose of placing and consenting to the adoption of the child.

The local board shall also have the right to accept temporary custody of any person under 18 years of age taken into custody pursuant to subdivision B of § 16.1–246 or § 63.2–1517. The placement of a child in a foster home, whether within or without the Commonwealth, shall not be for the purpose of adoption unless the placement agreement between the foster parents and the local board specifically so stipulates.

B.   Prior to the approval of any family for placement of a child, a home study shall be completed and the prospective foster or adoptive parents shall be informed that information about shaken baby syndrome, its effects, and resources for help and support for caretakers is available on a website maintained by the Department as prescribed in regulations adopted by the Board.

C.   Prior to placing any such child in any foster home or children's residential facility, the local board shall enter into a written agreement with the foster parents, pursuant to § 63.2–902, or other appropriate custodian setting forth therein the conditions under which the child is so placed pursuant to § 63.2–902. However, if a child is placed in a children's residential facility licensed as a temporary emergency shelter, and a verbal agreement for placement is secured within eight hours of the child's arrival at the facility, the written agreement does not need to be entered into prior to placement, but shall be completed and signed by the local board and the facility representative within 24 hours of the child's arrival or by the end of the next business day after the child's arrival.

D.   Within 72 hours of placing a child of school age in a foster care placement, as defined in § 63.2–100, the local social services agency making such placement shall, in writing, (i) notify the principal of the school in which the student is to be enrolled and the superintendent of the relevant school division or his designee of such placement, and (ii) inform the principal of the status of the parental rights.

If the documents required for enrollment of the foster child pursuant to § 22.1–3.1, 22.1–270 or 22.1–271.2, are not immediately available upon taking the child into custody, the placing social services agency shall obtain and produce or otherwise ensure compliance with such requirements for the foster child within 30 days after the child's enrollment.

§ 63.2–900.1.   KINSHIP FOSTER CARE

A.   The local board shall, in accordance with regulations adopted by the Board, determine whether the child has a relative who is eligible to become a kinship foster parent.

B.   Kinship foster care placements pursuant to this section shall be subject to all requirements of, and shall be eligible for all services related to, foster care placement contained in this chapter. However, the Commissioner may grant a variance from the requirements of this chapter pursuant to 42 U.S.C. § 671(a)(10) and allow the placement of a child in with a kinship foster care provider when he determines that (i) the requirement would impose a substantial hardship on the kinship foster care provider and (ii) the variance would not adversely affect the safety and well-being of the child to be placed in an arrangement for kinship care as defined in § 63.2–100 or with the kinship foster care provider. Variances granted pursuant to this subsection shall be considered and, if appropriate, granted on a case-by-case basis and shall include consideration of the unique needs of each child to be placed.

C.   The kinship foster parent shall be eligible to receive payment at the full foster care rate for the care of the child.

D.   A child placed in kinship foster care pursuant to this section shall not be removed from the physical custody of the kinship foster parent, provided the child has been living with the kinship foster parent for six consecutive months and the placement continues to meet approval standards for foster care, unless (i) the kinship foster parent consents to the removal; (ii) removal is agreed upon at a family partnership meeting as defined by the Department; (iii) removal is ordered by a court of competent jurisdiction; or (iv) removal is warranted pursuant to § 63.2–1517.

§ 63.2–900.2.   PLACEMENT OF SIBLING GROUPS; VISITATION

All reasonable steps shall be taken to place siblings entrusted to the care of a local board or licensed child-placing agency, committed to the care of a local board or agency by any court of competent jurisdiction, or placed with a local board or public agency through an agreement between a local board or a public agency and the parent, parents, or guardians, where legal custody remains with the parent, parents, or guardian, together in the same foster home.

Where siblings are placed in separate foster homes, the local department, child-placing agency, or public agency shall develop a plan to encourage frequent and regular visitation or communication between the siblings. The visitation or communication plan shall take into account the wishes of the child, and shall specify the frequency of visitation or communication, identify the party responsible for encouraging that visits or communication occur, and state any other requirements or restrictions related to such visitation or communication as may be determined necessary by the local department, child-placing agency, or public agency.

§ 63.2–900.3.   SCHOOL PLACEMENT OF CHILDREN IN FOSTER CARE

When placing a child of school age in a foster care placement, as defined in § 63.2–100, the local social services agency making such placement shall, in writing, determine jointly with the local school division whether it is in the child's best interests to remain enrolled at the school in which he was enrolled prior to the most recent foster care placement, pursuant to § 22.1–3.4.

§ 63.2–901. SUPERVISION OF PLACEMENT OF CHILDREN IN HOMES

The local director shall supervise the placement in suitable homes of children placed through an agreement with the parents or guardians or entrusted or committed to the local board pursuant to §§ 63.2–900, 63.2–902 and 63.2–903.

§ 63.2–901.1.   CRIMINAL HISTORY AND CENTRAL REGISTRY CHECK FOR PLACEMENTS OF CHILDREN

A.   Each local board and licensed child-placing agency shall obtain, in accordance with regulations adopted by the Board, criminal history record information from the Central Criminal Records Exchange and the Federal Bureau of Investigation through the Central Criminal Records Exchange and the results of a search of the child abuse and neglect central registry of any individual with whom the local board or licensed child-placing agency is considering placing a child on an emergency, temporary or permanent basis, including the birth parent of a child in foster care placement, unless the birth parent has revoked an entrustment agreement pursuant to § 63.2–1223 or 63.2–1817 or a local board or birth parent revokes a placement agreement while legal custody remains with the parent, parents, or guardians pursuant to § 63.2–900. The local board or licensed child-placing agency shall also obtain such background checks on all adult household members residing in the home of the individual with whom the child is to be placed pursuant to subsection B. Such state criminal records or registry search shall be at no cost to the individual. The local board or licensed child-placing agency shall pay for the national fingerprint criminal history record check or may require such individual to pay the cost of the fingerprinting or the national fingerprinting criminal history record check or both. In addition to the fees assessed by the Federal Bureau of Investigation, the designated state agency may assess a fee for responding to requests required by this section.

B. Background checks pursuant to this section require the following:

1. A sworn statement or affirmation disclosing whether or not the individual has a criminal conviction or is the subject of any pending criminal charges within or outside the Commonwealth and whether or not the individual has been the subject of a founded complaint of child abuse or neglect within or outside the Commonwealth;

2. That the individual submit to fingerprinting and provide personal descriptive information to be forwarded along with the individual's fingerprints through the Central Criminal Records Exchange to the Federal Bureau of Investigation for the purpose of obtaining criminal history record information. The local board or licensed child-placing agency shall inform the individual that he is entitled to obtain a copy of any background check report and to challenge the accuracy and completeness of any such report and obtain a prompt resolution before a final decision is made of the individual's fitness to have responsibility for the safety and well-being of children.

The Central Criminal Records Exchange, upon receipt of an individual's record or notification that no record exists, shall forward it to the designated state agency. The state agency shall, upon receipt of an individual's record lacking disposition data, conduct research in whatever state and local recordkeeping systems are available in order to obtain complete data. The state agency shall report to the local board or licensed child-placing agency whether the individual meets the criteria for having responsibility for the safety and well-being of children based on whether or not the individual has ever been convicted of or is the subject of pending charges set forth in § 63.2–1719 or an equivalent set forth in another state. Copies of any information received by a local board or licensed child-placing agency pursuant to this section shall be available to the state agency that regulates or operates such a child-placing agency but shall not be disseminated further; and

3.   A search of the central registry maintained pursuant to § 63.2–1515 for any founded complaint of child abuse or neglect. In addition, a search of the child abuse and neglect registry maintained by any other state pursuant to the Adam Walsh Child Protection and Safety Act of 2006, Pub. L. 109–248, in which a prospective parent or other adult in the home has resided in the preceding five years.

C.   In emergency circumstances, each local board may obtain, from a criminal justice agency, criminal history record information from the Central Criminal Records Exchange and the Federal Bureau of Investigation through the Virginia Criminal Information Network (VCIN) for the criminal records search authorized by this section. Within three days of placing a child, the local board shall require the individual for whom a criminal history record information check was requested to submit to fingerprinting and provide personal descriptive information to be forwarded along with the fingerprints through the Central Criminal Records Exchange to the Federal Bureau of Investigation for the purpose of obtaining criminal record history information, pursuant to subsection B. The child shall be removed from the home immediately if any adult resident fails to provide such fingerprints and written permission to perform a criminal history record check when requested.

D.   Any individual with whom the local board is considering placing a child on an emergency basis shall submit to a search of the central registry maintained pursuant to § 63.2–1515 and the Adam Walsh Child Protection and Safety Act of 2006, Pub. L. 109–248 for any founded complaint of child abuse or neglect. The search of the central registry must occur prior to emergency placement. Such central registry search shall be at no cost to the individual. Prior to emergency placement, the individual shall provide a written statement of affirmation disclosing whether he has ever been the subject of a founded case of child abuse or neglect within or outside the Commonwealth. Child-placing agencies shall not approve individuals with a founded complaint of child abuse as foster or adoptive parents.

E.   The child-placing agency shall not approve a foster or adoptive home if any individual has a record of an offense defined in § 63.2–1719 or a founded complaint of abuse or neglect as maintained in registries pursuant to § 63.2–1515 and 42 U.S.C.S. 16901 et seq. A child-placing agency may approve as a foster parent an applicant convicted of not more than one misdemeanor as set out in § 18.2–57, not involving the abuse, neglect, or moral turpitude of a minor, provided 10 years have elapsed following the conviction.

F. A local board or child-placing agency may approve as a kinship foster care parent an applicant convicted of the following offenses, provided that 10 years have elapsed from the date of the conviction and the local board or child-placing agency makes a specific finding that approving the kinship foster care placement would not adversely affect the safety and well-being of the child: (i) a felony conviction for possession of drugs as set out in Article 1 (§ 18.2–247 et seq.) of Chapter 7 of Title 18.2, but not including a felony conviction for possession of drugs with the intent to distribute; (ii) a misdemeanor conviction for arson as set out in Article 1 (§ 18.2–77 et seq.) of Chapter 5 of Title 18.2; or (iii) an equivalent offense in another state.

§ 63.2–902. AGREEMENTS WITH PERSONS TAKING CHILDREN

Every local board and licensed child-placing agency shall, with respect to each child placed by it in a foster home or children's residential facility, enter into a written agreement contained in an approved foster care policy with the head of such home or facility, which agreement shall provide that the authorized representatives of the local board or agency shall have access at all times to such child and to the home or facility, and that the head of the home or facility will release custody of the child so placed to the authorized representatives of the local board or agency whenever, in the opinion of the local board or agency, or in the opinion of the Commissioner, it is in the best interests of the child.

§ 63.2–903. ENTRUSTMENT AGREEMENTS; ADOPTION

A. Whenever a local board accepts custody of a child pursuant to an entrustment agreement entered into under the authority of § 63.2–900, or a licensed child-placing agency accepts custody of a child pursuant to an entrustment agreement entered into under the authority of § 63.2–1817, in the city or county juvenile and domestic relations district court a petition for approval of the entrustment agreement (i) shall be filed within a reasonable period of time, not to exceed 89 days after the execution of an entrustment agreement for less than 90 days, if the child is not returned to his home within that period; (ii) shall be filed within a reasonable period of time, not to exceed 30 days after the execution of an entrustment agreement for 90 days or longer or for an unspecified period of time, if such entrustment agreement does not provide for the termination of all parental rights and responsibilities with respect to the child; and (iii) may be filed in the case of a permanent entrustment agreement which provides for the termination of all parental rights and responsibilities with respect to the child.

B. For purposes of §§ 63.2–900, 63.2–1817 and this section, a parent who is less than 18 years of age shall be deemed fully competent and shall have legal capacity to execute a valid entrustment agreement, including an agreement that provides for the termination of all parental rights and responsibilities, and shall be as fully bound thereby as if such parent had attained the age of 18 years. An entrustment agreement for the termination of all parental rights and responsibilities shall be executed in writing and notarized. An entrustment agreement for the termination of all parental rights and responsibilities with respect to the child shall be valid notwithstanding that it is not signed by the father of a child born out of wedlock if the identity of the father is not reasonably ascertainable, or if such father is given notice of the entrustment by registered or certified mail to his last known address and fails to object to the entrustment within 15 days of mailing of such notice. An affidavit of the mother that the identity of the father is not reasonably ascertainable shall be sufficient evidence of this fact, provided there is no other evidence that would refute such an affidavit. The absence of such an affidavit shall not be deemed evidence that the identity of the father is reasonably ascertainable. For purposes of determining whether the identity of the father is reasonably ascertainable, the standard of what is reasonable under the circumstances shall control, taking into account the relative interests of the child, the mother and the father.

C. An entrustment agreement for the termination of parental rights and responsibilities with respect to the child shall be valid notwithstanding that it is not signed by the birth father of a child when such father has been convicted of a violation of subsection A of § 18.2–61, § 18.2–63, subsection B of § 18.2–366, or an equivalent offense of another state, the United States, or any foreign jurisdiction, and the child was conceived as a result of such violation.

D. A child may be placed for adoption by a licensed child-placing agency or a local board, in accordance with the provisions of § 63.2–1221.

§ 63.2–904. INVESTIGATION; VISITATION AND SUPERVISION OF FOSTER HOMES OR INDEPENDENT LIVING ARRANGEMENT; REMOVAL OF CHILD

A. Before placing or arranging for the placement of any such child in a foster home or independent living arrangement, a local board or licensed child-placing agency shall cause a careful study to be made to determine the suitability of such home or independent living arrangement, and after placement shall cause such home or independent living arrangement and child to be visited as often as necessary to protect the interests of such child.

B. Every local board or licensed child-placing agency that places a child in a foster home or independent living arrangement shall maintain such supervision over such home or independent living arrangement as shall be required by the standards and policies established by the Board.

C.   Whenever any child placed by a local board or licensed child-placing agency and still under its control or supervision is subject, in the home in which he is placed, to unwholesome influences or to neglect or mistreatment, or whenever the Commissioner shall so order, such local board or agency shall cause the child to be removed from such home and shall make for him such arrangements as may be approved by the Commissioner.

§ 63.2–905.   FOSTER CARE SERVICES

Foster care services are the provision of a full range of casework, treatment and community services, including but not limited to independent living services, for a planned period of time to a child who is abused or neglected as defined in § 63.2–100 or in need of services as defined in § 16.1–228 and his family when the child (i) has been identified as needing services to prevent or eliminate the need for foster care placement, (ii) has been placed through an agreement between the local board or the public agency designated by the community policy and management team and the parents or guardians where legal custody remains with the parents or guardians, or (iii) has been committed or entrusted to a local board or licensed child placing agency. Foster care services also include the provision and restoration of independent living services to a person who is over the age of 18 years but who has not yet reached the age of 21 years, in accordance with § 63.2–905.1.

§ 63.2–905.1.   INDEPENDENT LIVING SERVICES

Local departments and licensed child-placing agencies shall provide independent living services to any person between 18 and 21 years of age who is in the process of transitioning from foster care to self-sufficiency. Any person who was committed or entrusted to a local board or licensed child-placing agency may choose to discontinue receiving independent living services any time before his twenty-first birthday in accordance with regulations adopted by the Board. The local board or licensed child-placing agency shall restore independent living services at the request of that person provided that (i) the person has not yet reached 21 years of age and (ii) the person has entered into a written agreement, less than 60 days after independent living services have been discontinued, with the local board or licensed child-placing agency regarding the terms and conditions of his receipt of independent living services.

Local departments and licensed child-placing agencies shall provide independent living services to any person between 18 and 21 years of age who (a) was in the custody of the local department of social services immediately prior to his commitment to the Department of Juvenile Justice, (b) is in the process of transitioning from a commitment to the Department of Juvenile Justice to self-sufficiency, and (c) provides written notice of his intent to receive independent living services and enters into a written agreement for the provision of independent living services, which sets forth the terms and conditions of the provision of independent living services, with the local board or licensed child-placing agency within 60 days of his release from commitment to the Department of Juvenile Justice.

Local departments shall provide any person who chooses to leave foster care or terminate independent living services before his twenty-first birthday written notice of his right to request restoration of independent living services in accordance with this section by including such written notice in the person's transition plan. Such transition plan shall be created within 90 days prior to the person's discharge from foster care. Local departments and licensed child-placing agencies may provide independent living services as part of the foster care services provided to any child 14 years of age or older. All independent living services shall be provided in accordance with regulations adopted by the Board.

§ 63.2–905.2. ANNUAL CREDIT CHECKS FOR CHILDREN IN FOSTER CARE

Local departments shall conduct annual credit checks on children aged 16 years and older who are in foster care to identify cases of identity theft or misuse of personal identifying information of such children. Local departments shall resolve, to the greatest extent possible, cases of identity theft or misuse of personal identifying information of foster care children identified pursuant to this section.

§ 63.2–906. FOSTER CARE PLANS; PERMISSIBLE PLAN GOALS; COURT REVIEW OF FOSTER CHILDREN

A.   Each child who is committed or entrusted to the care of a local board or to a licensed child-placing agency or who is placed through an agreement between a local board and the parent, parents or guardians, where legal custody remains with the parent, parents or guardians, shall have a foster care plan prepared by the local department, the child welfare agency, or the family assessment and planning team established pursuant to § 2.2–5207, as specified in § 16.1–281. The representatives of such department, child welfare agency, or team shall involve the child's parent(s) in the development of the plan, except when parental rights have been terminated or the local department of social services or child welfare agency has made diligent efforts to locate the parent(s) and such parent(s) cannot be located, and any other person or persons standing in loco parentis at the time the board or child welfare agency obtained custody or the board or the child welfare agency placed the child. The representatives of such department, child welfare agency, or team shall involve the child in the development of the plan, if such involvement is consistent with the best interests of the child. In cases where either the parent(s) or child is not involved in the development of the plan, the department, child welfare agency, or team shall include in the plan a full description of the reasons therefor.

A court may place a child in the care and custody of (i) a public agency in accordance with § 16.1–251 or 16.1–252, and (ii) a public or licensed private child-placing agency in accordance with § 16.1–278.2, 16.1–278.4, 16.1–278.5, 16.1–278.6, or 16.1–278.8. Children may be placed by voluntary relinquishment in the care and custody of a public or private agency in accordance with § 16.1–277.01 or §§ 16.1–277.02 and 16.1–278.3. Children may be placed through an agreement where legal custody remains with the parent, parents or guardians in accordance with §§ 63.2–900 and 63.2–903, or § 2.2–5208.

B.   Each child in foster care shall be assigned a permanent plan goal to be reviewed and approved by the juvenile and domestic relations district court having jurisdiction of the child's case. Permissible plan goals are to:

1.   Transfer custody of the child to his prior family;

2.   Transfer custody of the child to a relative other than his prior family;

3.   Finalize an adoption of the child;

4.   Place the child in permanent foster care;

5.   Transition to independent living if, and only if, the child is admitted to the United States as a refugee or asylee; or

6.   Place the child in another planned permanent living arrangement in accordance with subsection A2 of § 16.1–282.1.

C.   Each child in foster care shall be subject to the permanency planning and review procedures established in §§ 16.1–281, 16.1–282, and 16.1–282.1.

§ 63.2–907. ADMINISTRATIVE REVIEW OF CHILDREN IN FOSTER CARE

Each local board shall establish and keep current a social service plan with service objectives and shall provide the necessary social services for achievement of a permanent home for each child for whom it has care and custody or has an agreement with the parents or guardians to place in accordance with regulations adopted by the Board. Each local board shall review the cases of children placed through an agreement or in its custody in accordance with the regulations adopted by the Board. Each local board shall review the cases of children placed through an agreement or in its custody on a planned basis to evaluate the current status and effectiveness (i) of the service plan's objectives and (ii) of the services being provided for each child in custody, which are directed toward the immediate care of and planning for permanency for the child, in accordance with policies of the Board.

The Department shall establish and maintain (a) a system to review and monitor compliance by local boards with the policies adopted by the Board and (b) a tracking system of every child in the care and custody of or placed by local boards in order to monitor the effectiveness of service planning, service objectives and service delivery by the local boards that shall be directed toward the achievement of permanency for children in foster care.

The Board shall adopt regulations necessary to implement the procedures and policies set out in this section. The Board shall establish as a goal that at any point in time the number of children who are in foster care for longer than twenty-four months shall not exceed 5,500 children.

* * *

§ 63.2–909. CHILD SUPPORT FOR CHILD PLACED IN FOSTER CARE BY COURT

Pursuant to § 16.1–290, responsible persons shall pay child support for a child placed in foster care from the date that custody was awarded to the local department. The court order shall state the names of the responsible persons obligated to pay support, and either specify the amount of the support obligation pursuant to §§ 20–108.1 and 20–108.2 or indicate that the Division of Child Support Enforcement will establish the amount of the support obligation. In fixing the amount of support, the court or the Division of Child Support Enforcement shall consider the extent to which the payment of support by the responsible person may affect the ability of such responsible person to implement a foster care plan developed pursuant to § 16.1–281.

§ 63.2–910. CHILD SUPPORT FOR CHILD PLACED IN FOSTER CARE WHERE LEGAL CUSTODY REMAINS WITH PARENT OR GUARDIAN

Responsible persons shall pay child support for a child placed in foster care through an agreement where legal custody remains with the parent or guardian pursuant to subdivision A 4 of § 16.1–278.2 or § 63.2–900, from the date that the child was placed in foster care. The agreement between the parents and the local board shall include provisions for the payment of child support. In fixing the amount of support, the court, the Division of Child Support Enforcement, and the local board shall consider the extent to which the payment of support by the responsible person may affect the ability of such responsible person to implement a foster care plan. If the responsible person fails or refuses to pay such sum on a timely basis, the local board may petition the juvenile court to order such payment.

§ 63.2–910.1. ACCEPTANCE OF CHILDREN BY LOCAL DEPARTMENTS OF SOCIAL SERVICES

A local department of social services has the authority to take custody of abandoned children, to arrange appropriate placements for abandoned children, including foster care, and to institute proceedings for the termination of parental rights of abandoned children as provided in this title and Title 16.1.

§ 63.2–911. LIABILITY INSURANCE FOR FOSTER PARENTS

The Department may provide liability insurance for civil matters for persons providing basic foster care services in foster homes, as defined in §§ 63.2–100 and 63.2–905, that are approved by local boards for children in their custody or children who the board has entered into an agreement to place where legal custody remains with the parents or guardians.

§ 63.2–912. VISITATION OF CHILD PLACED IN FOSTER CARE.

The circuit courts and juvenile and domestic relations district courts shall have the authority to grant visitation rights to the natural parents, siblings, and grandparents of any child entrusted or committed to foster care if the court finds (i) that the parent, sibling, or grandparent had an ongoing relationship with the child prior to his being placed in foster care and (ii) it is in the best interests of the child that the relationship continue. The order of the court committing the child to foster care shall state the nature and extent of any visitation rights granted as provided in this section.

* * *

INTERSTATE COMPACT ON PLACEMENT OF CHILDREN

VIRGINIA

Va. Code Ann. §§ 63.2–1000 et seq. (West 2016)

[EDITORS' INTRODUCTION: Matthew E. Christoph, *Why Massachusetts Should Not Relegate Parents to "Legal Strangers": A Survey Of The Myriad Interpretations of the ICPC*, 35 W. NEW ENG. L. REV. 77 (2013); Rebecca Miller, Note, *The Parental Kidnapping Prevention Act: Thirty Years Later and of No Effect? Where Can the Unwed Father Turn?*, 40 PEPP. L. REV. 735 (2013); C. Nneka Nzekwu, Note, *The Lost Ones of the Interstate Compact on the Placement of Children*, 44 HOFSTRA L. REV. 1001 (2016); S. Megan Testerman, Note, *A World Wide Web of Unwanted Children: The Practice, the Problem, and the Solution to Private Re-Homing*, 67 FLA. L. REV. 2103 (2015).]

§ 63.2–1000. INTERSTATE COMPACT ON THE PLACEMENT OF CHILDREN; FORM OF COMPACT

The Governor of Virginia is hereby authorized and requested to execute, on behalf of the Commonwealth of Virginia, with any other state or states legally joining therein, a compact which shall be in form substantially as follows:

The contracting states solemnly agree that:

ARTICLE I.

Purpose and Policy.

It is the purpose and policy of the party states to cooperate with each other in the interstate placement of children to the end that:

(a) Each child requiring placement shall receive the maximum opportunity to be placed in a suitable environment and with persons or institutions having appropriate qualifications and facilities to provide a necessary and desirable degree and type of care.

(b) The appropriate authorities in a state where a child is to be placed may have full opportunity to ascertain the circumstances of the proposed placement, thereby promoting full compliance with applicable requirements for the protection of the child.

(c) The proper authorities of the state from which the placement is made may obtain the most complete information on the basis of which to evaluate a projected placement before it is made.

(d) Appropriate jurisdictional arrangements for the care of children will be promoted.

ARTICLE II.

Definitions.

As used in this compact:

(a) "Child" means a person who, by reason of minority, is legally subject to parental, guardianship or similar control.

(b) "Sending agency" means a party state, officer or employee thereof; a subdivision of a party state, or officer or employee thereof; a court of a party state; a person, corporation, association, charitable agency or other entity which sends, brings, or causes to be sent or brought any child to another party state.

(c) "Receiving state" means the state to which a child is sent, brought, or caused to be sent or brought, whether by public authorities or private persons or agencies, and whether for placement with state or local public authorities or for placement with private agencies or persons.

(d) "Placement" means the arrangement for the care of a child in a family free or boarding home or in a child-caring agency or institution but does not include any institution caring for individuals with mental illness, intellectual disability, or epilepsy or any institution primarily educational in character, and any hospital or other medical facility.

ARTICLE III.

Conditions for Placement.

(a) No sending agency shall send, bring, or cause to be sent or brought into any other party state any child for placement in foster care or as a preliminary to a possible adoption unless the sending agency shall comply with each and every requirement set forth in this article and with the applicable laws of the receiving state governing the placement of children therein.

(b) Prior to sending, bringing or causing any child to be sent or brought into a receiving state for placement in foster care or as a preliminary to a possible adoption, the sending agency shall furnish the appropriate public authorities in the receiving state written notice of the intention to send, bring, or place the child in the receiving state. The notice shall contain:

(1) The name, date and place of birth of the child.

(2) The identity and address or addresses of the parents or legal guardian.

(3) The name and address of the person, agency or institution to or with which the sending agency proposes to send, bring, or place the child.

(4) A full statement of the reasons for such proposed action and evidence of the authority pursuant to which the placement is proposed to be made.

(c) Any public officer or agency in a receiving state which is in receipt of a notice pursuant to paragraph (b) of this article may request of the sending agency, or any other appropriate officer or agency of or in the sending agency's state, and shall be entitled to receive therefrom, such supporting or additional information as it may deem necessary under the circumstances to carry out the purpose and policy of this compact.

(d) The child shall not be sent, brought or caused to be sent or brought into the receiving state until the appropriate public authorities in the receiving state shall notify the sending agency, in writing, to the effect that the proposed placement does not appear to be contrary to the interests of the child.

ARTICLE IV.

Penalty for Illegal Placement.

The sending, bringing, or causing to be sent or brought into any receiving state of a child in violation of the terms of this compact shall constitute a violation of the laws respecting the placement of children of both the state in which the sending agency is located or from which it sends or brings the child and of the receiving state. Such violation may be punished or subjected to penalty in either jurisdiction in accordance with its laws. In addition to liability for any such punishment or penalty, any such violation shall constitute full and sufficient grounds for the suspension or revocation of any license, permit, or other legal authorization held by the sending agency which empowers or allows it to place, or care for children.

ARTICLE V.

Retention of Jurisdiction.

(a) The sending agency shall retain jurisdiction over the child sufficient to determine all matters in relation to the custody, supervision, care, treatment and disposition of the child which it would have had if the child had remained in the sending agency's state, until the child is adopted, reaches majority, becomes self-supporting or is discharged with the concurrence of the appropriate authority in the receiving state. Such jurisdiction shall also include the power to effect or cause the return of the child or its transfer to another location and custody pursuant to law. The sending agency shall continue to have financial responsibility for support and maintenance of the child during the period of the placement. Nothing contained herein shall defeat a claim of jurisdiction by a receiving state sufficient to deal with an act of delinquency or crime committed therein.

(b) When the sending agency is a public agency, it may enter into an agreement with an authorized public or private agency in the receiving state providing for the performance of one or more services in respect of such cases by the latter as agent for the sending agency.

(c) Nothing in this compact shall be construed to prevent a private charitable agency authorized to place children in the receiving state from performing services or acting as agent in that state for a private charitable agency of the sending state; nor to prevent the agency in the receiving state from discharging financial responsibility for the support and maintenance of a child who has been placed on behalf of the sending agency without relieving the responsibility set forth in paragraph (a) hereof.

ARTICLE VI.

Institutional Care of Delinquent Children.

A child adjudicated delinquent may be placed in an institution in another party jurisdiction pursuant to this compact but no such placement shall be made unless the child is given a court hearing on notice to the parent or guardian with opportunity to be heard, prior to his being sent to such other party jurisdiction for institutional care and the court finds that:

1. Equivalent facilities for the child are not available in the sending agency's jurisdiction; and

2. Institutional care in the other jurisdiction is in the best interest of the child and will not produce undue hardship.

ARTICLE VII.

Compact Administrator.

The executive head of each jurisdiction party to this compact shall designate an officer who shall be general coordinator of activities under this compact in his jurisdiction and who, acting jointly with like officers of other party jurisdictions, shall have the power to promulgate rules and regulations to carry out more effectively the terms and provisions of this compact.

ARTICLE VIII.

Limitations.

This compact shall not apply to:

(a) The sending or bringing of a child into a receiving state by his parent, step-parent, grandparent, adult brother or sister, adult uncle or aunt, or his guardian and leaving the child with any such relative or nonagency guardian in the receiving state.

(b) Any placement, sending or bringing of a child into a receiving state pursuant to any other interstate compact to which both the state from which the child is sent or brought and the receiving state are party, or to any other agreement between said states which has the force of law.

ARTICLE IX.

Enactment and Withdrawal.

This compact shall be open to joinder by any state, territory or possession of the United States, the District of Columbia, the Commonwealth of Puerto Rico, and, with the consent of Congress, the Government of Canada or any province thereof. It shall become effective with respect to any such jurisdiction when such jurisdiction has enacted the same into law. Withdrawal from this compact shall be by the enactment of a statute repealing the same, but shall not take effect until two years after the effective date of such statute and until written notice of the withdrawal has been given by the withdrawing state to the Governor of each other party jurisdiction. Withdrawal of a party state shall not affect the rights, duties and obligations under this compact of any sending agency therein with respect to a placement made prior to the effective date of withdrawal.

ARTICLE X.

Construction and Severability.

The provisions of this compact shall be liberally construed to effectuate the purposes thereof. The provisions of this compact shall be severable and if any phrase, clause, sentence or provision of this compact is declared to be contrary to the constitution of any party state or of the United States or the applicability thereof to any government, agency, person or circumstance is held invalid, the validity of the remainder of this compact and the applicability thereof to any government, agency, person or circumstance shall not be affected thereby. If this compact shall be held contrary to the constitution of any state party thereto, the compact shall remain in full force and effect as to the remaining states and in full force and effect as to the state affected as to all severable matters.

§ 63.2–1100. DEFINITIONS

For the purposes of Chapter 10 (§ 63.2–1000 et seq.) of this title, the following words shall have the meaning ascribed to them by this section:

A. "Appropriate public authorities" as used in Article III of the compact means, with reference to this Commonwealth, the Department.

B. "Appropriate authority in the receiving state" as used in subdivision (a) of Article V of the compact means, with reference to this Commonwealth, the Commissioner.

§ 63.2–1105. CHILDREN PLACED OUT OF COMMONWEALTH

A.   Any child-placing agency, licensed pursuant to Subtitle IV (§ 63.2–1700 et seq.), local board or court that takes or sends, or causes to be taken or sent, any resident child out of the Commonwealth for the purpose of an interstate or intercountry placement shall comply with the appropriate provisions of the Interstate Compact on the Placement of Children (§ 63.2–1000 et seq.) or shall first obtain the consent of the Commissioner, given in accordance with regulations of the Board relating to resident children so taken or sent out of the Commonwealth.

B.   The Board is authorized to adopt regulations for the placement of children out of the Commonwealth by licensed child-placing agencies, local boards or courts as are reasonably conducive to the welfare of such children and as comply with the Interstate Compact on the Placement of Children (§ 63.2–1000 et seq.). Provided, however, notwithstanding the provisions of subdivision (d) of Article II of the compact that exclude from the definition of "placement" those institutions that care for individuals with mental illness, intellectual disability, or epilepsy or any institution primarily educational in character and any hospital or other medical facility, the Board shall prescribe procedures and regulations to govern such placements out of the Commonwealth by licensed child-placing agencies, local boards or courts.

OPEN ADOPTION

NEW MEXICO

N.M. Stat. Ann. § 32A–5–35 (West 2016)

[EDITORS' INTRODUCTION: Cynthia Godsoe, *Permanency Puzzle*, 2013 MICH. ST. L. REV. 1113 (2013); Randi Mandelbaum, *Delicate Balances: Assessing the Needs and Rights of Siblings in Foster Care to Maintain Their Relationships Post-Adoption*, 41 N.M. L. REV. 1 (2011); Carol Sanger, *Bargaining for Motherhood: Postadoption Visitation Agreements*, 41 HOFSTRA L. REV. 309 (2012); Kristina V. Foehrkolb, Comment, *When the Child's Best Interest Calls for It: Post-Adoption Contact by Court Order in Maryland*, 71 MD. L. REV. 490 (2012).]

§ 32A–5–35. OPEN ADOPTIONS

A.   The parents of the adoptee and the petitioner may agree to contact between the parents and the petitioner or contact between the adoptee and one or more of the parents or contact between the adoptee and relatives of the parents. An agreement shall, absent a finding to the contrary, be presumed to be in the best interests of the child and shall be included in the decree of adoption. The agreement may also include contact between siblings and the adoptee based on a finding that it is in the best interests of the adoptee and the adoptee's siblings and a determination that the siblings' parent, guardian or custodian has consented to the agreement. The contact may include exchange of identifying or nonidentifying information or visitation between the parents or the parents' relatives or the adoptee's siblings and the petitioner or visitation between the parents or the parents' relatives or the adoptee's siblings and the adoptee. An agreement entered into pursuant to this section shall be considered an open adoption.

B.   The court may appoint a guardian ad litem for the adoptee. The court shall adopt a presumption in favor of appointing a guardian ad litem for the adoptee when visitation between the biological family and the adoptee is included in an agreement; however, this requirement may be waived by the court for good cause shown. When an adoptive placement is made voluntarily through an agency or pursuant to Section 32A–5–13 NMSA 1978, the court may, in its discretion, appoint a guardian ad litem. If the child is fourteen years of age or older, the court may appoint an attorney for the child. In all adoptions other than those in which the child is placed by the department, the court may assess the parties for the cost of services rendered by the guardian ad litem or the child's attorney. The duties of the guardian ad litem or child's attorney end upon the filing of the decree, unless otherwise ordered by the court.

C.   In determining whether the agreement is in the adoptee's best interests, the court shall consider the adoptee's wishes, but the wishes of the adoptee shall not control the court's findings as to the best interests of the adoptee.

D.   Every agreement entered into pursuant to provisions of this section shall contain a clause stating that the parties agree to the continuing jurisdiction of the court and to the agreement and understand and intend that any disagreement or litigation regarding the terms of the agreement shall not affect the validity of the relinquishment of parental rights, the adoption or the custody of the adoptee.

E.   The court shall retain jurisdiction after the decree of adoption is entered, if the decree contains an agreement for contact, for the purpose of hearing motions brought to enforce or modify an agreement entered into pursuant to the provisions of this section. The court shall not grant a request to modify the agreement unless the moving party establishes that there has been a change of circumstances and the agreement is no longer in the adoptee's best interests.

OREGON DEATH WITH DIGNITY ACT (1999)

Or. Rev. Stat. Ann. § 127.800 et seq. (West 2016)

[EDITORS' INTRODUCTION: Janet L. Dolgin, *Dying Discourse: Contextualizing Advance Care Planning*, 34 QUINNIPIAC L. REV. 235 (2016); Shara M. Johnson et al., *What Patient and Psychologist Characteristics are Important in Competency for Physician-Assisted Suicide Evaluations?*, 21 PSYCHOL. PUB. POL'Y & L. 420 (2015); Browne C. Lewis, *A Graceful Exit: Redefining Terminal to Expand the Availability of Physician-Facilitated Suicide*, 91 OR. L. REV. 457 (2012); Steve Perlmutter, *Physician-Assisted Suicide - A Medicolegal Inquiry*, 15 MICH. ST. U. J. MED. & L. 203 (2011); Timothy E. Quill, *Physicians Should "Assist in Suicide" When it is Appropriate*, 40 J.L. MED. & ETHICS 57 (2012); Mark L. Rienzi, *The Constitutional Right Not to Kill*, 62 EMORY L.J. 121 (2012); Nicole F. Dailo, Note, *"Give Me Dignity by Giving Me Death": Using Balancing to Uphold Death Row Volunteers' Dignity Interests Amidst Executive Clemency*, 23 S. CAL. REV. L. & SOC. JUST. 249 (2014); Christina White, Comment, *Physician Aid-in-Dying*, 53 HOUS. L. REV. 595 (2015).]

§ 1.01. DEFINITIONS

The following words and phrases, whenever used in ORS 127.800 to 127.897, have the following meanings:

(1) "Adult" means an individual who is 18 years of age or older.

(2) "Attending physician" means the physician who has primary responsibility for the care of the patient and treatment of the patient's terminal disease.

(3) "Capable" means that in the opinion of a court or in the opinion of the patient's attending physician or consulting physician, psychiatrist or psychologist, a patient has the ability to make and communicate health care decisions to health care providers, including communication through persons familiar with the patient's manner of communicating if those persons are available.

(4) "Consulting physician" means a physician who is qualified by specialty or experience to make a professional diagnosis and prognosis regarding the patient's disease.

(5) "Counseling" means one or more consultations as necessary between a state licensed psychiatrist or psychologist and a patient for the purpose of determining that the patient is capable and not suffering from a psychiatric or psychological disorder or depression causing impaired judgment.

(6) "Health care provider" means a person licensed, certified or otherwise authorized or permitted by the law of this state to administer health care or dispense medication in the ordinary course

of business or practice of a profession, and includes a health care facility.

(7) "Informed decision" means a decision by a qualified patient, to request and obtain a prescription to end his or her life in a humane and dignified manner, that is based on an appreciation of the relevant facts and after being fully informed by the attending physician of:

(a) His or her medical diagnosis;

(b) His or her prognosis;

(c) The potential risks associated with taking the medication to be prescribed;

(d) The probable result of taking the medication to be prescribed; and

(e) The feasible alternatives, including, but not limited to, comfort care, hospice care and pain control.

(8) "Medically confirmed" means the medical opinion of the attending physician has been confirmed by a consulting physician who has examined the patient and the patient's relevant medical records.

(9) "Patient" means a person who is under the care of a physician.

(10) "Physician" means a doctor of medicine or osteopathy licensed to practice medicine by the Oregon Medical Board.

(11) "Qualified patient" means a capable adult who is a resident of Oregon and has satisfied the requirements of ORS 127.800 to 127.897 in order to obtain a prescription for medication to end his or her life in a humane and dignified manner.

(12) "Terminal disease" means an incurable and irreversible disease that has been medically confirmed and will, within reasonable medical judgment, produce death within six months.

§ 3.01. RESPONSIBILITIES OF THE ATTENDING PHYSICIAN

(1) The attending physician shall:

(a) Make the initial determination of whether a patient has a terminal disease, is capable, and has made the request voluntarily;

(b) Request that the patient demonstrate Oregon residency pursuant to ORS 127.860;

(c) To ensure that the patient is making an informed decision, inform the patient of:

(A) His or her medical diagnosis;

(B) His or her prognosis;

(C) The potential risks associated with taking the medication to be prescribed;

(D) The probable result of taking the medication to be prescribed; and

(E) The feasible alternatives, including, but not limited to, comfort care, hospice care and pain control;

(d) Refer the patient to a consulting physician for medical confirmation of the diagnosis, and for a determination that the patient is capable and acting voluntarily;

(e) Refer the patient for counseling if appropriate pursuant to ORS 127.825;

(f) Recommend that the patient notify next of kin;

(g) Counsel the patient about the importance of having another person present when the patient takes the medication prescribed pursuant to ORS 127.800 to 127.897 and of not taking the medication in a public place;

(h) Inform the patient that he or she has an opportunity to rescind the request at any time and in any manner, and offer the patient an opportunity to rescind at the end of the 15-day waiting period pursuant to ORS 127.840;

(i) Verify, immediately prior to writing the prescription for medication under ORS 127.800 to 127.897, that the patient is making an informed decision;

(j) Fulfill the medical record documentation requirements of ORS 127.855;

(k) Ensure that all appropriate steps are carried out in accordance with ORS 127.800 to 127.897 prior to writing a prescription for medication to enable a qualified patient to end his or her life in a humane and dignified manner; and

(*l*)(A) Dispense medications directly, including ancillary medications intended to facilitate the desired effect to minimize the patient's discomfort, provided the attending physician is registered as a dispensing physician with the Oregon Medical Board, has a current Drug Enforcement Administration certificate and complies with any applicable administrative rule; or

(B) With the patient's written consent:

(i) Contact a pharmacist and inform the pharmacist of the prescription; and

(ii) Deliver the written prescription personally or by mail to the pharmacist, who will dispense the medications to either the patient, the attending physician or an expressly identified agent of the patient.

(2) Notwithstanding any other provision of law, the attending physician may sign the patient's report of death.

§ 3.08.   WAITING PERIODS

No less than fifteen (15) days shall elapse between the patient's initial oral request and the writing of a prescription under ORS 127.800 to 127.897. No less than 48 hours shall elapse between the patient's written request and the writing of a prescription under ORS 127.800 to 127.897.

§ 6.01.   FORM OF THE REQUEST

A request for a medication as authorized by ORS 127.800 to 127.897 shall be in substantially the following form:

REQUEST FOR MEDICATION TO END MY LIFE IN A HUMANE AND DIGNIFIED MANNER

I, _____, am an adult of sound mind.

I am suffering from, which my attending physician has determined is a terminal disease and which has been medically confirmed by a consulting physician.

I have been fully informed of my diagnosis, prognosis, the nature of medication to be prescribed and potential associated risks, the expected result, and the feasible alternatives, including comfort care, hospice care and pain control.

I request that my attending physician prescribe medication that will end my life in a humane and dignified manner.

INITIAL ONE:

_____ I have informed my family of my decision and taken their opinions into consideration.

_____ I have decided not to inform my family of my decision.

_____ I have no family to inform of my decision.

I understand that I have the right to rescind this request at any time.

I understand the full import of this request and I expect to die when I take the medication to be prescribed. I further understand that although most deaths occur within three hours, my death may take longer and my physician has counseled me about this possibility.

I make this request voluntarily and without reservation, and I accept full moral responsibility for my actions.

Signed: _____

Dated: _____

DECLARATION OF WITNESSES

We declare that the person signing this request:

(a) Is personally known to us or has provided proof of identity;

(b) Signed this request in our presence;

(c) Appears to be of sound mind and not under duress, fraud or undue influence;

(d) Is not a patient for whom either of us is attending physician.

_____ Witness 1/Date

_____ Witness 2/Date

NOTE: One witness shall not be a relative (by blood, marriage or adoption) of the person signing this request, shall not be entitled to any portion of the person's estate upon death and shall not own, operate or be employed at a health care facility where the person is a patient or resident. If the patient is an inpatient at a health care facility, one of the witnesses shall be an individual designated by the facility.

PATERNITY AND SCIENTIFIC PROOF

FLORIDA AND NEW YORK STATUTES

FLORIDA

Fla. Stat. Ann. §§ 742.12, 760.40(2)(a) (West 2016)

[EDITORS' INTRODUCTION: Leslie Joan Harris, *Reforming Paternity Law to Eliminate Gender, Status, and Class Inequality*, 2013 MICH. ST. L. REV. 1295 (2013); Kristen K. Jacobs, *If the Genes Don't Fit: An Overview of Paternity Disestablishment Statutes*, 24 J. AM. ACAD. MATRIM. LAW. 249 (2011); Solangel Maldonado, *Illegitimate Harm: Law, Stigma, and Discrimination Against Nonmarital Children*, 63 FLA. L. REV. 345 (2011); Alycia Kennedy, Note, *Social Security Survivor Benefits: Why Congress Must Create a Uniform Standard of Eligibility for Posthumously Conceived Children*, 54 B.C. L. REV. 821 (2013); Elan Renee-Guerin Longstreet, Comment, *Who's My Real Daddy? Reducing the Prevalence of False Paternity in Texas*, 1 TEX. A&M L. REV. 183 (2013); Morgan Quigley, Comment, *Are You My Dad? The Pitfalls of Ohio's Paternity Rescission Statutes: Comparing Ohio's Law to Other Jurisdictions*, 83 U. CIN. L. REV. 969 (2015).]

§ 742.12.   SCIENTIFIC TESTING TO DETERMINE PATERNITY

(1) In any proceeding to establish paternity, the court on its own motion may require the child, mother, and alleged fathers to submit to scientific tests that are generally acceptable within the scientific community to show a probability of paternity. The court shall direct that the tests be conducted by a qualified technical laboratory.

(2) In any proceeding to establish paternity, the court may, upon request of a party providing a sworn statement or written declaration as provided by s. 92.525(2) alleging paternity and setting forth facts establishing a reasonable possibility of the requisite sexual contact between the parties or providing a sworn statement or written declaration denying paternity and setting forth facts establishing a reasonable possibility of the nonexistence of sexual contact between the parties, require the child, mother, and alleged fathers to submit to scientific tests that are generally acceptable within the scientific community to show a probability of paternity. The court shall direct that the tests be conducted by a qualified technical laboratory.

(3) The test results, together with the opinions and conclusions of the test laboratory, shall be filed with the court. Any objection to the test results must be made in writing and must be filed with the court at least 10 days prior to the hearing. If no objection is filed, the test results shall be admitted into evidence without the need for predicate to be laid or third-party foundation testimony to be presented. Nothing in this paragraph prohibits a party from calling an outside expert witness to

refute or support the testing procedure or results, or the mathematical theory on which they are based. Upon the entry of the order for scientific testing, the court must inform each person to be tested of the procedure and requirements for objecting to the test results and of the consequences of the failure to object.

(4) Test results are admissible in evidence and should be weighed along with other evidence of the paternity of the alleged father unless the statistical probability of paternity equals or exceeds 95 percent. A statistical probability of paternity of 95 percent or more creates a rebuttable presumption, as defined by s. 90.304, that the alleged father is the biological father of the child. If a party fails to rebut the presumption of paternity which arose from the statistical probability of paternity of 95 percent or more, the court may enter a summary judgment of paternity. If the test results show the alleged father cannot be the biological father, the case shall be dismissed with prejudice.

(5) Subject to the limitations in subsection (3), if the test results or the expert analysis of the inherited characteristics is disputed, the court, upon reasonable request of a party, shall order that an additional test be made by the same laboratory or an independent laboratory at the expense of the party requesting additional testing.

(6) Verified documentation of the chain of custody of the blood or other specimens is competent evidence to establish the chain of custody.

(7) The fees and costs for scientific tests shall be paid by the parties in proportions and at times determined by the court unless the parties reach a stipulated agreement which is adopted by the court.

§ 760.40.   GENETIC TESTING; INFORMED CONSENT; CONFIDENTIALITY; PENALTIES; NOTICE OF USE OF RESULTS

(1) As used in this section, the term "DNA analysis" means the medical and biological examination and analysis of a person to identify the presence and composition of genes in that person's body. The term includes DNA typing and genetic testing.

(2)(a)   Except for purposes of criminal prosecution, except for purposes of determining paternity as provided in s. 409.256 or s. 742.12(1), and except for purposes of acquiring specimens as provided in s. 943.325, DNA analysis may be performed only with the informed consent of the person to be tested, and the results of such DNA analysis, whether held by a public or private entity, are the exclusive property of the person tested, are confidential, and may not be disclosed without the consent of the person tested. Such information held by a public entity is exempt from the provisions of s. 119.07(1) and s. 24(a), Art. I of the State Constitution.

(b) A person who violates paragraph (a) is guilty of a misdemeanor of the first degree, punishable as provided in s. 775.082 or s. 775.083.

(3) A person who performs DNA analysis or receives records, results, or findings of DNA analysis must provide the person tested with notice that the analysis was performed or that the information was received. The notice must state that, upon the request of the person tested, the information will be made available to his or her physician. The notice must also state whether the information was used in any decision to grant or deny any insurance, employment, mortgage, loan, credit, or educational opportunity. If the information was used in any decision that resulted in a denial, the analysis must be repeated to verify the accuracy of the first analysis, and if the first analysis is found to be inaccurate, the denial must be reviewed.

NEW YORK

N.Y. Fam. Ct. Act § 532 (McKinney 2016)

§ 532. GENETIC MARKER AND DNA TESTS; ADMISSIBILITY OF RECORDS OR REPORTS OF TEST RESULTS; COSTS OF TESTS

(a) The court shall advise the parties of their right to one or more genetic marker tests or DNA tests and, on the court's own motion or the motion of any party, shall order the mother, her child and the alleged father to submit to one or more genetic marker or DNA tests of a type generally acknowledged as reliable by an accreditation body designated by the secretary of the federal department of health and human services and performed by a laboratory approved by such an accreditation body and by the commissioner of health or by a duly qualified physician to aid in the determination of whether the alleged father is or is not the father of the child. No such test shall be ordered, however, upon a written finding by the court that it is not in the best interests of the child on the basis of res judicata, equitable estoppel, or the presumption of legitimacy of a child born to a married woman. The record or report of the results of any such genetic marker or DNA test ordered pursuant to this section or pursuant to section one hundred eleven-k of the social services law shall be received in evidence by the court pursuant to subdivision (e) of rule forty-five hundred eighteen of the civil practice law and rules where no timely objection in writing has been made thereto and that if such timely objections are not made, they shall be deemed waived and shall not be heard by the court. If the record or report of the results of any such genetic marker or DNA test or tests indicate at least a ninety-five percent probability of paternity, the admission of such record or report shall create a rebuttable presumption of paternity, and shall establish, if unrebutted, the paternity of and liability for the support of a child pursuant to this article and article four of this act.

(b) Whenever the court directs a genetic marker or DNA test pursuant to this section, a report made as provided in subdivision (a) of this section may be received in evidence pursuant to rule forty-five hundred eighteen of the civil practice law and rules if offered by any party.

(c) The cost of any test ordered pursuant to subdivision (a) of this section shall be, in the first instance, paid by the moving party. If the moving party is financially unable to pay such cost, the court may direct any qualified public health officer to conduct such test, if practicable; otherwise, the court may direct payment from the funds of the appropriate local social services district. In its order of disposition, however, the court may direct that the cost of any such test be apportioned between the parties according to their respective abilities to pay or be assessed against the party who does not prevail on the issue of paternity, unless such party is financially unable to pay.

PLACEMENT OF CHILDREN LONG-TERM OR PERMANENT FOSTER CARE

VIRGINIA

Va. Code Ann. § 63.2–908 (West 2016)

[EDITORS' INTRODUCTION: Lacey Mickleburgh, *A Special Case for Children with Special Needs*, 14 WHITTIER J. CHILD & FAM. ADVOC. 113 (2015); Janet L. Wallace & Lisa R Pruitt, *Judging Parents, Judging Place: Poverty, Rurality, and Termination of Parental Rights*, 77 MO. L. REV. 95 (2012); Meredith L. Alexander, Note, *Harming Vulnerable Children: The Injustice of California's Kinship Foster Care Policy*, 7 HASTINGS RACE & POVERTY L. J. 381 (2010).]

§ 63.2–908. PERMANENT FOSTER HOME CARE PLACEMENT

A. Permanent foster care placement means the place in which a child has been placed pursuant to the provisions of §§ 63.2–900, 63.2–903 and this section with the expectation and agreement between the placing agency and the place of permanent foster care that the child shall remain in the placement until he reaches the age of majority unless modified by court order or unless removed pursuant to § 16.1–251 or § 63.2–1517. A permanent foster care placement may be a place of residence of any natural person or persons deemed appropriate to meet a child's needs on a long-term basis.

B. A local department or a licensed child-placing agency shall have authority pursuant to a court order to place a child over whom it has legal custody in a permanent foster care placement where the child shall remain until attaining majority or thereafter, until the age of twenty-one years, if such placement is a requisite to providing funds for the care of such child, so long as the child is a participant in an educational, treatment or training program approved pursuant to regulations of the Board. No such child shall be removed from the physical custody of the foster parents in the permanent care placement except upon order of the court or pursuant to § 16.1–251 or § 63.2–1517. The department or agency so placing a child shall retain legal custody of the child. A court shall not order that a child be placed in permanent foster care unless it finds that (i) diligent efforts have been made by the local department to place the child with his natural parents and such efforts have been unsuccessful, and (ii) diligent efforts have been made by the local department to place the child for adoption and such efforts have been unsuccessful or adoption is not a reasonable alternative for a long-term placement for the child under the circumstances.

C. Unless modified by the court order, the foster parent in the permanent foster care placement shall have the authority to consent to surgery, entrance into the armed services, marriage, application for a motor vehicle and driver's license, application for admission into college and any other such activities that require parental consent and shall have the responsibility for informing the placing department or agency of any such actions.

D.   Any child placed in a permanent foster care placement by a local department shall, with the cooperation of the foster parents with whom the permanent foster care placement has been made, receive the same services and benefits as any other child in foster care pursuant to §§ 63.2–319, 63.2–900 and 63.2–903 and any other applicable provisions of law.

E.   The Board shall establish minimum standards for the utilization, supervision and evaluation of permanent foster care placements.

F.   The rate of payment for permanent foster care placements by a local department shall be in accordance with standards and rates established by the Board. The rate of payment for such placements by other licensed child-placing agencies shall be in accordance with standards and rates established by the individual agency.

G.   If the child has a continuing involvement with his natural parents, the natural parents should be involved in the planning for a permanent placement. The court order placing the child in a permanent placement shall include a specification of the nature and frequency of visiting arrangements with the natural parents.

H.   Any change in the placement of a child in permanent foster care or the responsibilities of the foster parents for that child shall be made only by order of the court which ordered the placement pursuant to a petition filed by the foster parents, local department, licensed child-placing agency or other appropriate party.

STANDBY GUARDIANSHIP

MARYLAND

Md. Code Ann., Est. & Trusts §§ 13–901 et seq. (West 2016)

§ 13–901.   DEFINITIONS

In general

(a)   In this subtitle the following words have the meanings indicated.

Attending physician

(b)(1)   "Attending physician" means a physician who has primary responsibility for the treatment and care of a parent described under this subtitle.

(2)   If more than one physician shares the responsibility for the treatment and care of a parent or if another physician is acting on the attending physician's behalf, any physician described in this paragraph may act as the attending physician under this subtitle.

(3)   If no physician has responsibility for the treatment and care of a parent, any physician who is familiar with the parent's medical condition may act as the attending physician under this subtitle.

Debilitation

(c)(1)   "Debilitation" means a person's chronic and substantial inability, as a result of a physically incapacitating illness, disease, or injury, to care for the person's dependent minor child.

(2)   "Debilitated" means the state of having a debilitation.

Incapacity

(d)(1)   "Incapacity" means a person's chronic and substantial inability, as a result of mental impairment, to understand the nature and consequences of decisions concerning the care of the person's dependent minor child, and a consequent inability to care for the child.

(2)   "Incapacitated" means the state of having an incapacity.

Standby guardian

(e)   "Standby guardian" means a person:

(1)   Appointed by a court under § 13–903 of this subtitle as standby guardian of the person or property of a minor, whose authority becomes effective on the incapacity or death of the minor's parent, or on the consent of the parent;

or

(2)   Designated under § 13–904 of this subtitle as standby guardian of the person or property of a minor, whose authority becomes effective on the incapacity of the minor's parent, or on the debilitation and consent of the parent.

§ 13–902.   Application of title to standby guardians

Except as otherwise provided in this subtitle, the provisions of this title concerning a guardian of the person or property of a minor shall apply to standby guardians.

§ 13–903.   Petition for appointment of standby guardian

Petition filed by parent of minor

(a)(1)   Subject to the provisions of paragraphs (2) and (3) of this subsection, a petition for the judicial appointment of a standby guardian of the person or property of a minor under this section may be filed only by a parent of the minor, and if filed, shall be joined by each person having parental rights over the minor.

(2)   If a person who has parental rights cannot be located after reasonable efforts have been made to locate the person, the parent may file a petition for the judicial appointment of a standby guardian.

(3)   If the petitioner submits documentation, satisfactory to the court, of the reasonable efforts to locate the person who has parental rights, the court may issue a decree under this section.

Contents of petition

(b)   A petition for the judicial appointment of a standby guardian shall state:

(1)   The duties of the standby guardian;

(2)   Whether the authority of the standby guardian is to become effective on the petitioner's incapacity, on the petitioner's death, or on whichever occurs first; and

(3)   That there is a significant risk that the petitioner will become incapacitated or die, as applicable, within 2 years of the filing of the petition, and the basis for this statement.

Appearance of petitioner in court

(c)   If the petitioner is medically unable to appear, the petitioner's appearance in court may not be required, except on a motion and for good cause shown.

Finding of court and contents of decree

(d)(1)   If the court finds that there is a significant risk that the petitioner will become incapacitated or die within 2 years of the filing of the petition and that the interests of the minor will be promoted by the appointment of a standby guardian of the person or property of the minor, the court shall issue a decree accordingly.

(2) A decree under this subsection shall:

(i) Specify whether the authority of the standby guardian is effective on the receipt of a determination of the petitioner's incapacity, on the receipt of the certificate of the petitioner's death, or on whichever occurs first; and

(ii) Provide that the authority of the standby guardian may become effective earlier on written consent of the petitioner in accordance with subsection (e)(3) of this section.

(3) If at any time before the beginning of the authority of the standby guardian the court finds that the requirements of paragraph (1) of this subsection are no longer satisfied, the court may rescind the decree.

Beginning of standby guardian's authority

(e)(1)(i) If a decree under subsection (d) of this section provides that the authority of the standby guardian is effective on receipt of a determination of the petitioner's incapacity, the standby guardian's authority shall begin on the standby guardian's receipt of a copy of a determination of incapacity made under § 13–906 of this subtitle.

(ii) A standby guardian shall file a copy of the determination of incapacity with the court that issued the decree within 90 days of the date of receipt of the determination.

(iii) If a standby guardian fails to comply with subparagraph (ii) of this paragraph, the court may rescind the standby guardian's authority.

(2)(i) If a decree under subsection (d) of this section provides that the authority of the standby guardian is effective on receipt of a certificate of the petitioner's death, the standby guardian's authority shall begin on the standby guardian's receipt of a certificate of death.

(ii) The standby guardian shall file a copy of the certificate of death with the court that issued the decree within 90 days of the date of the petitioner's death.

(iii) If the standby guardian fails to comply with subparagraph (ii) of this paragraph, the court may rescind the standby guardian's authority.

(3)(i) Notwithstanding paragraphs (1) and (2) of this subsection, a standby guardian's authority shall begin on the standby guardian's receipt of the petitioner's written consent to the beginning of the standby guardian's authority signed by:

> 1.   The petitioner in the presence of two witnesses at least 18 years of age, neither of whom may be the standby guardian; and
>
> 2.   The standby guardian.

(ii) 1.   If the petitioner is physically unable to sign a written consent to the beginning of the standby guardian's authority, another person may sign the consent on the petitioner's behalf and at the petitioner's direction.

> 2.   A consent under this subparagraph to the beginning of the standby guardian's authority shall be signed in the presence of the petitioner and two witnesses at least 18 years of age, neither of whom may be the standby guardian.
>
> 3.   A standby guardian also shall sign a written consent to the beginning of the standby guardian's authority under this subparagraph.

(iii) The standby guardian shall file the written consent with the court that issued the decree within 90 days of the date of receipt of the written consent.

(iv) If the standby guardian fails to comply with subparagraph (iii) of this paragraph, the court may rescind the standby guardian's authority.

Revocation of standby guardian by petitioner

(f)   The petitioner may revoke a standby guardianship created under this section by:

(1)   Executing a written revocation;

(2)   Filing the revocation with the court that issued the decree; and

(3)   Promptly notifying the standby guardian of the revocation.

Renunciation of authority by standby guardian

(g)   A person who is judicially appointed as a standby guardian under this section may at any time before the beginning of the person's authority renounce the appointment by:

(1)   Executing a written renunciation;

(2)   Filing the renunciation with the court that issued the decree; and

(3)   Promptly notifying in writing the petitioner of the revocation.

§ 13–904.   Designation of standby guardian

Designation by parent

(a)(1)   A parent may designate a standby guardian by means of a written designation:

(i)   Signed in the presence of two witnesses, at least 18 years old, neither of whom is the standby guardian; and

(ii)   Signed by the standby guardian.

(2)(i)   If a parent is physically unable to sign a written designation, another person may sign the designation on the parent's behalf and at the parent's direction.

(ii) 1.   A designation under this paragraph shall be signed in the presence of the parent and two witnesses at least 18 years of age, neither of whom may be the standby guardian.

2.   The standby guardian also shall sign a designation under this paragraph.

Form and contents of designation and alternate standby guardian

(b)(1)   A designation of a standby guardian shall identify the parent, the minor, and the person designated to be the standby guardian, state the duties of the standby guardian, and indicate that the parent intends for the standby guardian to become the minor's guardian in the event the parent either:

(i)   Becomes incapacitated; or

(ii)   Becomes debilitated and consents to the beginning of the standby guardian's authority.

(2)   A parent may designate an alternate standby guardian in the same writing and by the same manner as the designation of a standby guardian.

(3)   A designation may, but need not, be in the following form:

Designation of Standby Guardian

I (name of parent) hereby designate (name, home address, and telephone number of standby guardian) as standby guardian of the person and property of my child(ren)(name of child(ren)).

(You may, if you wish, provide that the standby guardian's authority shall extend only to the person, or only to the property, of your child, by crossing out "person" or "property", whichever is inapplicable, above.)

The standby guardian's authority shall take effect if and when either:

(1)   My doctor concludes I am mentally incapacitated, and thus unable to care for my child(ren); or

(2) My doctor concludes that I am physically debilitated, and thus unable to care for my child(ren) and I consent in writing, before two witnesses, to the standby guardian's authority taking effect.

If the person I designate above is unable or unwilling to act as guardian for my child(ren), I hereby designate (name, home address, and telephone number of alternate standby guardian), as standby guardian of my child(ren).

I also understand that my standby guardian's authority will cease 180 days after beginning unless by that date my standby guardian petitions the court for appointment as guardian.

I understand that I retain full parental rights even after the beginning of the standby guardian's authority, and may revoke the standby guardianship at any time.

Parent's Signature:

_____

Address:

_____

Date:

_____

     I declare that the person whose name appears above signed this document in my presence, or was physically unable to sign and asked another to sign this document, who did so in my presence. I further declare that I am at least 18 years old and am not the person designated as standby guardian.

Witness's Signature:

_____

Address:

_____

Date:

_____

Witness's Signature:

_____

Address:

_____

Date:

_____

Standby Guardian's Signature:

_____

Address:

_____

Date:

_____

    (4) A consent by another person with parental rights to a designation of a standby guardian by a parent may, but need not be, in the following form:

Consent to Designation of Standby Guardian

    I (name of person with parental rights) agree with the designation by (name of parent) of (name, home address, and telephone number of standby guardian) as standby guardian of the person and property of my child(ren)(name of child(ren)).

    I agree also to the terms stated above and understand that I retain full parental rights even after the beginning of the standby guardian's authority, and may revoke my consent to the standby guardianship at any time.

Signature of Person with Parental Rights:

_____

Address:

_____

Date:

_____

    I declare that the person whose name appears above signed this document in my presence, or was physically unable to sign and asked another to sign this document, who did so in my presence. I further declare that I am at least 18 years old and am not the person designated as standby guardian.

Witness's Signature:

_____

Address:

_____

Date:

_____

Witness's Signature:

_____

Address:

_____

Date:

_____

Standby Guardian's Signature:

_____

Address:

_____

Date:

_____

When authority of standby guardian begins

(c)   The authority of the standby guardian under a designation shall begin on:

(1) The standby guardian's receipt of a copy of a determination of incapacity under § 13–906 of this subtitle; or

(2)   The standby guardian's receipt of:

(i)   A copy of a determination of debilitation under § 13–906 of this subtitle;

(ii) A copy of the parent's written consent to the beginning of the standby guardianship, signed by the parent in the presence of two witnesses at least 18 years of age, neither of whom is the standby guardian, and signed by the standby guardian; and

(iii) A copy of the birth certificate for each child for whom the standby guardian is designated.

Written consent to beginning of standby guardianship

(d)(1)   If a parent is physically unable to sign a written consent to the beginning of the standby guardianship, another person may sign the written consent to the beginning of the standby guardianship on the parent's behalf and at the parent's direction.

(2)   A consent under this subsection to the beginning of the standby guardianship shall be signed in the presence of the parent and two witnesses at least 18 years of age, neither of whom may be the standby guardian.

(3)   The standby guardian also shall sign a consent to the beginning of the standby guardianship under this subsection.

Petition for judicial appointment

(e)(1)   A standby guardian shall file a petition for judicial appointment within 180 days of the date of the beginning of the standby guardianship under this section.

(2)   If the standby guardian fails to file the petition within the time specified in this subsection, the standby guardian's authority shall terminate 180 days from the date of the beginning of the standby guardianship.

(3) The standby guardian's authority shall begin again on the filing of the petition.

Documents needed to file petition for judicial appointment

(f)(1)   A standby guardian shall file a petition for appointment as guardian after receipt of:

(i) A copy of a determination of incapacity made under § 13–906 of this subtitle; or

(ii) Copies of:

1.   A determination of debilitation made under § 13–906 of this subtitle; and

2.   The parent's written consent to the beginning of the standby guardianship under this section.

(2) Subject to the provisions of paragraphs (3) and (4) of this subsection, the petition shall be accompanied by:

(i) The written designation of the standby guardian signed, or consented to, by each person having parental rights over the child;

(ii) A copy of:

1.   The determination of incapacity of the parent; or

2.   The determination of debilitation and the parental consent to the beginning of the standby guardianship; and

(iii) If the petition is filed by a person designated as alternate standby guardian, a statement that the person designated as standby guardian is unwilling or unable to act as standby guardian, and the basis for the statement.

(3) If a person who has parental rights cannot be located after reasonable efforts have been made to locate the person, the standby guardian may file a petition under this section without the consent of the person to the designation of the standby guardian.

(4) If the standby guardian submits documentation, satisfactory to the court, of the reasonable efforts to locate the person who has parental rights, the court may appoint a standby guardian under this section.

Factors considered by court

(g) The court shall appoint a person to be a standby guardian under this section if the court finds that:

(1) The person was duly designated as standby guardian;

(2) A determination of incapacity, or a determination of debilitation and parental consent to the beginning of the standby guardianship, has been made under this section;

(3) The interests of the minor will be promoted by the appointment of a standby guardian of the person or property of the minor; and

(4) If the petition is by a person designated as alternate standby guardian, the person designated as standby guardian is unwilling or unable to act as standby guardian.

Revocation of standby guardianship

(h) A parent may revoke a standby guardianship created under this section:

(1) Before the filing of a petition, by notifying the standby guardian verbally or in writing or by any other act that is evidence of a specific intent to revoke the standby guardianship; and

(2) If a petition has been filed by:

(i) Executing a written revocation;

(ii) Filing the revocation with the court in which the petition was filed; and

(iii) Promptly notifying the standby guardian of the revocation.

Renunciation of appointment

(i) A person who is judicially appointed as a standby guardian under this section may at any time before the beginning of the person's authority renounce the appointment by:

(1) Executing a written renunciation;

(2) Filing the renunciation with the court that issued the decree; and

(3) Promptly notifying in writing the parent of the revocation.

§ 13–905.   ALTERNATIVE METHODS OF GUARDIAN APPOINTMENT

A standby guardian may also file a petition for appointment as guardian in any other manner permitted by this title, on notice to the parent, and may append a designation of a standby guardian to the petition for consideration by the court in the determination of the petition.

§ 13–906.   DETERMINATION OF INCAPACITY OR DEBILITATION

In general

(a)(1)   A determination of incapacity or debilitation under this subtitle shall:

(i)   Be made by the attending physician to a reasonable degree of medical certainty;

(ii)   Be in writing; and

(iii) Contain the attending physician's opinion regarding the cause and nature of the parent's incapacity or debilitation, and the extent and probable duration of the incapacity or debilitation.

(2)   If a standby guardian's identity is known to an attending physician, the attending physician shall provide a copy of a determination of incapacity or debilitation to the standby guardian.

Request for determination by standby guardian

(b)   If requested by a standby guardian, an attending physician shall make a determination regarding the parent's incapacity or debilitation for purposes of this subtitle.

Notification and rights of parent

(c)   If the parent is able to comprehend the information, a standby guardian shall inform the parent of:

(1)   The beginning of the standby guardian's authority as a result of a determination of incapacity; and

(2)   The parent's right to revoke the authority promptly after receipt of the determination of incapacity.

§ 13–907.   AUTHORITY OF STANDBY GUARDIAN

Effect on parental or guardianship rights

(a)   The beginning of a standby guardian's authority in accordance with a determination of incapacity, determination of debilitation, or consent may not, itself, divest a parent of any parental or guardianship rights.

Authority limited by court order

(b)   The authority of a standby guardian with respect to the minor is limited to the express authority granted to the standby guardian by a court under this subtitle.

§ 13–908.   BOND REQUIREMENTS

The furnishing of a bond by a standby guardian shall be governed by the provisions of § 13–208 of this title.

STATUTORY CUSTODIAL CLAIM (FOR INCAPACITATED RELATIVE'S CARE)

755 Ill. Comp. Stat. Ann. § 5/18–1.1 (West 2016)

[EDITORS' INTRODUCTION: RAYMOND C. O'BRIEN & MICHAEL T. FLANNERY, DECEDENTS' ESTATES (3d ed. 2016); RAYMOND C. O'BRIEN & MICHAEL T. FLANNERY, THE FUNDAMENTALS OF ELDER LAW (2015); Linda S. Whitton & Lawrence A. Frolik, *Surrogate Decision-Making Standards for Guardians: Theory and Reality*, 2012 UTAH L. REV. 1491 (2012); Lawrence A. Frolik & Linda S. Whitton, *The UPC Substituted Judgment/Best Interest Standard for Guardian Decisions: A Proposal for Reform*, 45 U. MICH. J.L. REFORM 739 (2012).]

§ 5/18–1.1. STATUTORY CUSTODIAL CLAIM

§ 18–1.1.Statutory custodial claim. Any spouse, parent, brother, sister, or child of a person with a disability who dedicates himself or herself to the care of the person with a disability by living with and personally caring for the person with a disability for at least 3 years shall be entitled to a claim against the estate upon the death of the person with a disability. The claim shall take into consideration the claimant's lost employment opportunities, lost lifestyle opportunities, and emotional distress experienced as a result of personally caring for the person with a disability. Notwithstanding the statutory claim amounts stated in this Section, a court may reduce an amount to the extent that the living arrangements were intended to and did in fact also provide a physical or financial benefit to the claimant. The factors a court may consider in determining whether to reduce a statutory custodial claim amount may include but are not limited to: (i) the free or low cost of housing provided to the claimant; (ii) the alleviation of the need for the claimant to be employed full time; (iii) any financial benefit provided to the claimant; (iv) the personal care received by the claimant from the decedent or others; and (v) the proximity of the care provided by the claimant to the decedent to the time of the decedent's death. The claim shall be in addition to any other claim, including without limitation a reasonable claim for nursing and other care. The claim shall be based upon the nature and extent of the person's disability and, at a minimum but subject to the extent of the assets available, shall be in the amounts set forth below:

1. 100% disability, $180,000

2. 75% disability, $135,000

3. 50% disability, $90,000

4. 25% disability, $45,000

Subsidized Adoptions: Assistance for Children with Special Needs

Virginia Statute for Adoption Assistance for Children with Special Needs

Va. Code Ann. §§ 63.2–1300–63.2–1304 (West 2016)

§ 63.2–1300. Purpose and Intent of Adoption Assistance; Eligibility

The purpose of adoption assistance is to facilitate adoptive placements and ensure permanency for children with special needs. Adoption assistance may include Title IV-E maintenance payments, state-funded maintenance payments, state special services payments and nonrecurring expense payments made pursuant to requirements set forth in this chapter.

A child with special needs is a child who is a citizen or legal resident of the United States who is unlikely to be adopted within a reasonable period of time due to one or more of the following factors:

 1. Physical, mental or emotional condition existing prior to adoption;

 2. Hereditary tendency, congenital problem or birth injury leading to substantial risk of future disability; or

 3. Individual circumstances of the child related to age, racial or ethnic background or close relationship with one or more siblings.

A child with special needs will be eligible for adoption assistance if (i) the child cannot or should not be returned to the home of his parents and (ii) reasonable efforts to place the child in an appropriate adoptive home without the provision of adoption assistance have been unsuccessful. An exception may be made to the requirement that efforts be made to place the child in an adoptive home without the provision of adoption assistance when the child has developed significant emotional ties with his foster parents while in their care and that the foster parents wish to adopt the child.

§ 63.2–1301. Types of Adoption Assistance Payments

 A. Title IV-E maintenance payments shall be made to the adoptive parents on behalf of an adopted child placed if it is determined that the child is a child with special needs and the child meets the requirements set forth in § 473 of Title IV-E of the Social Security Act (42 U.S.C. § 673).

 B. State-funded maintenance payments shall be made to the adoptive parents on behalf of an adopted child if it is determined that the child does not meet the requirements set forth in § 473 of Title IV-E of the Social Security Act (42 U.S.C. § 673) but the child is a child with special needs. For this purpose of state-funded maintenance payments only, a child with special needs may include:

1.   A child for whom the factors set forth in subdivision 1 or 2 of § 63. 2–1300 are present at the time of adoption but are not diagnosed until after the final order of adoption, when no more than one year has elapsed from the date of diagnosis; or

2.   A child who has lived with his foster parents for at least 12 months and has developed significant emotional ties with his foster parents while in their care, when the foster parents wish to adopt the child and state-funded maintenance payments are necessary to enable the adoption.

C.   State special services payments shall be made to the adoptive parents and other persons on behalf of a child in the custody of the local board or in the custody of a licensed child-placing agency and placed for adoption, pursuant to this chapter, if it is determined that:

1.   The child is a child with special needs; and

2.   The adoptive parents are capable of providing the permanent family relationships needed by the child in all respects except financial.

D.   Nonrecurring expense payments shall be made to the adoptive parents for expenses related to the adoption including reasonable and necessary adoption fees, court costs, attorney fees and other legal service fees, as well as any other expenses that are directly related to the legal adoption of a child with special needs including costs related to the adoption study, any health and psychological examinations, supervision of the placement prior to adoption and any transportation costs and reasonable costs of lodging and food for the child and the adoptive parents when necessary to complete the placement or adoption process for which the adoptive parents carry ultimate liability for payment and that have not been reimbursed from any other source, as set forth in 45 C.F.R. § 1356.41. However, the total amount of nonrecurring expense payments made to adoptive parents for the adoption of a child shall not exceed $2,000 or an amount established by federal law.

§ 63.2–1302. ADOPTION   ASSISTANCE   PAYMENTS;   MAINTENANCE; SPECIAL   NEEDS;   PAYMENT   AGREEMENTS;   CONTINUATION   OF PAYMENTS   WHEN   ADOPTIVE   PARENTS   MOVE   TO   ANOTHER JURISDICTION; PROCEDURAL REQUIREMENTS

A.   Adoption assistance payments may include:

1.   Title IV-E or state-funded maintenance payments that shall be payable monthly to provide for the support and care of the child; however, Title IV-E or state-funded maintenance payments shall not exceed the foster care payment that would otherwise be made for the child; and

2.   State special services payments to provide special services to the child that the adoptive parents cannot afford and that are not covered by insurance or otherwise, including, but not limited to:

a.   Medical, surgical and dental care;

b.   Hospitalization;

c.   Individual remedial educational services;

d.   Psychological and psychiatric treatment;

e.   Speech and physical therapy; and

f.   Special services, equipment, treatment and training for physical and mental handicaps.

State special services payments may be paid to the vendor of the goods or services directly or to the adoptive parents.

B.   Adoption assistance payments shall cease when the child with special needs reaches the age of 18 years. If it is determined that the child has a mental or physical handicap, or an educational delay resulting from such handicap, warranting the continuation of assistance, adoption assistance payments may be made until the child reaches the age of 21 years.

C.   Adoption assistance payments shall be made on the basis of an adoption assistance agreement entered into by the local board and the adoptive parents or, in cases in which the child is in the custody of a licensed child-placing agency, an agreement between the local board, the licensed child-placing agency and the adoptive parents.

Prior to entering into an adoption assistance agreement, the local board or licensed child-placing agency shall ensure that adoptive parents have received information about their child's eligibility for adoption assistance; about their child's special needs and, to the extent possible, the current and potential impact of those special needs. The local board or licensed child-placing agency shall also ensure that adoptive parents receive information about the process for appeal in the event of a disagreement between the adoptive parent and the local board or the adoptive parent and the child-placing agency and information about the procedures for revising the adoption assistance agreement.

Adoptive parents shall submit annually to the local board within thirty days of the anniversary date of the approved agreement an affidavit which certifies that (i) the child on whose behalf they are receiving adoption assistance payments remains in their care, (ii) the child's condition requiring adoption assistance continues to exist, and (iii) whether or not changes to the adoption assistance agreement are requested.

Title IV-E and state-funded maintenance payments made pursuant to this section shall be changed only in accordance with the provisions of § 473 of Title IV-E of the Social Security Act (42 U.S.C. § 673).

D. Responsibility for adoption assistance payments for a child placed for adoption shall be continued by the local board that initiated the agreement in the event that the adoptive parents live in or move to another jurisdiction.

E. Payments may be made under this chapter from appropriations for foster care services for the maintenance and medical or other services for children who have special needs in accordance with § 63.2–1301. Within the limitations of the appropriations to the Department, the Commissioner shall reimburse any agency making payments under this chapter. Any such agency may seek and accept funds from other sources, including federal, state, local, and private sources, to carry out the purposes of this chapter.

§ 63.2–1303. QUALIFICATION FOR ADOPTION ASSISTANCE PAYMENTS

Qualification for adoption assistance payments shall be determined by the local board in response to an application for adoption assistance submitted in accordance with regulations adopted by the Board.

§ 63.2–1304. APPEAL TO COMMISSIONER REGARDING ADOPTION ASSISTANCE

Any applicant for or recipient of adoption assistance aggrieved by any decision of a local board or licensed child-placing agency in granting, denying, changing or discontinuing adoption assistance, may, within 30 days after receiving written notice of such decision, appeal therefrom to the Commissioner. Any applicant or recipient aggrieved by the failure of the local board or licensed child-placing agency to make a decision within a reasonable time may ask for review by the Commissioner. The Commissioner may delegate the duty and authority to duly qualified hearing officers to consider and make determinations on any appeal or review. The Commissioner shall provide an opportunity for a hearing, reasonable notice of which shall be given in writing to the applicant or recipient and to the proper local board in such manner and form as the Commissioner may prescribe. The Commissioner may make or cause to be made an investigation of the facts. The Commissioner shall give fair and impartial consideration to the testimony of witnesses, or other evidence produced at the hearing, reports of investigation of the local board and local director or licensed child-placing agency or of investigations made or caused to be made by the Commissioner, or any facts that the Commissioner may deem proper to enable him to decide fairly the appeal or review. The decision of the Commissioner shall be binding and considered a final agency action for purposes of judicial review of such action pursuant to the provisions of the Administrative Process Act (§ 2.2–4000 et seq.).

PART IV

INTERNATIONAL TREATIES

HAGUE CONVENTION ON THE CIVIL ASPECTS OF INTERNATIONAL CHILD ABDUCTION

19 I.L.M. 1501 (October 25, 1980)

[EDITORS' INTRODUCTION: Sam F. Halabi, *Abstention, Parity, and Treaty Rights: How Federal Courts Regulate Jurisdiction Under the Hague Convention on the Civil Aspects of International Child Abduction*, 32 BERKELEY J. INT'L L. 144 (2014); Tracy Jones, *A Ne Exeat Right is a "Right Of Custody" for the Purposes of the Hague Convention:* Abbott v. Abbott, 49 DUQ. L. REV. 523 (2011); Rhona Schuz, *The Doctrine of Comity in the Age of Globalization: Between International Child Abduction and Cross-Border Insolvency*, 40 BROOK. J. INT'L L. 31 (2014); Linda J. Silberman, *The Hague Convention on Child Abduction and Unilateral Relocations by Custodial Parents: A Perspective from the United States and Europe* - Abbott, Neulinger, Zarraga, 63 OKLA. L. REV. 733 (2011); Karen Brown Williams, *Fleeing Domestic Violence: A Proposal to Change the Inadequacies of the Hague Convention on the Civil Aspects of International Child Abduction in Domestic Violence Cases*, 4 J. MARSHALL L.J. 39 (2011); Caitlin M. Bannon, Note, *The Hague Convention on the Civil Aspects of International Child Abduction: The Need for Mechanisms to Address Noncompliance*, 31 B.C. THIRD WORLD L.J. 129 (2011); Farsheed Fozouni, Note, *International Child Abduction—Second Circuit Finds Federal Right of Action for Visitation Rights Under Federal Law Implementing the Hague Convention on Civil Aspects of International Child Abduction*, 67 SMU L. REV. 195 (2014); Yoko Konno, Comment, *A Haven for International Child Abduction: Will the Hague Convention Shape Japanese Family Law?*, 46 CAL. W. INT'L L.J. 39 (2015); Monique Vieites, Note, Chafin v. Chafin: *Protecting a U.S. Parent's Power to Litigate International Abductions*, 45 U. MIAMI INTER-AM. L. REV. 269 (2013); Antoinette A. Newberry Wood, Note, *Hey Uncle Sam! Maybe It's Time to Stop Condoning Child Abductions to Mexico*, 42 GA. J. INT'L & COMP. L. 217 (2013).]

The States signatory to the present Convention,

Firmly convinced that the interests of children are of paramount importance in matters relating to their custody,

Desiring to protect children internationally from the harmful effects of their wrongful removal or retention and to establish procedures to ensure their prompt return to the State of their habitual residence, as well as to secure protection for rights of access,

Have resolved to conclude a Convention to this effect, and have agreed upon the following provisions—

CHAPTER I—SCOPE OF THE CONVENTION

ARTICLE 1

The objects of the present Convention are—

a)   to secure the prompt return of children wrongfully removed to or retained in any Contracting State; and

b)   to ensure that rights of custody and of access under the law of one Contracting State are effectively respected in the other Contracting States.

ARTICLE 2

Contracting States shall take all appropriate measures to secure within their territories the implementation of the objects of the Convention. For this purpose they shall use the most expeditious procedures available.

ARTICLE 3

The removal or the retention of a child is to be considered wrongful where—

a)   it is in breach of rights of custody attributed to a person, an institution or any other body, either jointly or alone, under the law of the State in which the child was habitually resident immediately before the removal or retention; and

b)   at the time of removal or retention those rights were actually exercised, either jointly or alone, or would have been so exercised but for the removal or retention.

The rights of custody mentioned in sub-paragraph a above, may arise in particular by operation of law or by reason of a judicial or administrative decision, or by reason of an agreement having legal effect under the law of that State.

ARTICLE 4

The Convention shall apply to any child who was habitually resident in a Contracting State immediately before any breach of custody or access rights. The Convention shall cease to apply when the child attains the age of 16 years.

ARTICLE 5

For the purposes of this Convention—

a)   'rights of custody' shall include rights relating to the care of the person of the child and, in particular, the right to determine the child's place of residence;

b)   'rights of access' shall include the right to take a child for a limited period of time to a place other than the child's habitual residence.

CHAPTER II—CENTRAL AUTHORITIES

ARTICLE 6

A Contracting State shall designate a Central Authority to discharge the duties which are imposed by the Convention upon such authorities.

Federal States, States with more than one system of law or States having autonomous territorial organizations shall be free to appoint more than one Central Authority and to specify the territorial extent of their powers. Where a State has appointed more than one Central Authority, it shall designate the Central Authority to which applications may be addressed for transmission to the appropriate Central Authority within that State.

ARTICLE 7

Central Authorities shall co-operate with each other and promote co-operation amongst the competent authorities in their respective States to secure the prompt return of children and to achieve the other objects of this Convention.

In particular, either directly or through any intermediary, they shall take all appropriate measures—

a) to discover the whereabouts of a child who has been wrongfully removed or retained;

b) to prevent further harm to the child or prejudice to interested parties by taking or causing to be taken provisional measures;

c) to secure the voluntary return of the child or to bring about an amicable resolution of the issues;

d) to exchange, where desirable, information relating to the social background of the child;

e) to provide information of a general character as to the law of their State in connection with the application of the Convention;

f) to initiate or facilitate the institution of judicial or administrative proceedings with a view to obtaining the return of the child and, in a proper case, to make arrangements for organizing or securing the effective exercise of rights of access;

g) where the circumstances so require, to provide or facilitate the provision of legal aid and advice, including the participation of legal counsel and advisers;

h) to provide such administrative arrangements as may be necessary and appropriate to secure the safe return of the child;

i) to keep each other informed with respect to the operation of this Convention and, as far as possible, to eliminate any obstacles to its application.

CHAPTER III—RETURN OF CHILDREN

ARTICLE 8

Any person, institution or other body claiming that a child has been removed or retained in breach of custody rights may apply either to the Central Authority of the child's habitual residence or to the Central Authority of any other Contracting State for assistance in securing the return of the child.

The application shall contain—

a)   information concerning the identity of the applicant, of the child and of the person alleged to have removed or retained the child;

b)   where available, the date of birth of the child;

c)   the grounds on which the applicant's claim for return of the child is based;

d)   all available information relating to the whereabouts of the child and the identity of the person with whom the child is presumed to be.

The application may be accompanied or supplemented by—

e)   an authenticated copy of any relevant decision or agreement;

f)   a certificate or an affidavit emanating from a Central Authority, or other competent authority of the State of the child's habitual residence, or from a qualified person, concerning the relevant law of that State;

g)   any other relevant document.

ARTICLE 9

If the Central Authority which receives an application referred to in Article 8 has reason to believe that the child is in another Contracting State, it shall directly and without delay transmit the application to the Central Authority of that Contracting State and inform the requesting Central Authority, or the applicant, as the case may be.

ARTICLE 10

The Central Authority of the State where the child is shall take or cause to be taken all appropriate measures in order to obtain the voluntary return of the child.

ARTICLE 11

The judicial or administrative authorities of Contracting States shall act expeditiously in proceedings for the return of children.

If the judicial or administrative authority concerned has not reached a decision within six weeks from the date of commencement of the proceedings, the applicant or the Central Authority of the requested State, on its own initiative or if asked by the Central Authority of the requesting State, shall have the right to request a statement of the reasons for the delay. If a reply is received by the Central Authority of the requested State, that Authority shall transmit the reply to the Central Authority of the requesting State, or to the applicant, as the case may be.

ARTICLE 12

Where a child has been wrongfully removed or retained in terms of Article 3 and, at the date of the commencement of the proceedings before the judicial or administrative authority of the Contracting State where the child is, a period of less than one year has elapsed from the date of the wrongful removal or retention, the authority concerned shall order the return of the child forthwith.

The judicial or administrative authority, even where the proceedings have been commenced after the expiration of the period of one year referred to in the preceding paragraph, shall also order the return of the child, unless it is demonstrated that the child is now settled in its new environment.

Where the judicial or administrative authority in the requested State has reason to believe that the child has been taken to another State, it may stay the proceedings or dismiss the application for the return of the child.

ARTICLE 13

Notwithstanding the provisions of the preceding Article, the judicial or administrative authority of the requested State is not bound to order the return of the child if the person, institution or other body which opposes its return establishes that —

a)   the person, institution or other body having the care of the person of the child was not actually exercising the custody rights at the time of removal or retention, or had consented to or subsequently acquiesced in the removal or retention; or

b)   there is a grave risk that his or her return would expose the child to physical or psychological harm or otherwise place the child in an intolerable situation.

The judicial or administrative authority may also refuse to order the return of the child if it finds that the child objects to being returned and has attained an age and degree of maturity at which it is appropriate to take account of its views.

In considering the circumstances referred to in this Article, the judicial and administrative authorities shall take into account the information relating to the social background of the child provided by the

Central Authority or other competent authority of the child's habitual residence.

ARTICLE 14

In ascertaining whether there has been a wrongful removal or retention within the meaning of Article 3, the judicial or administrative authorities of the requested State may take notice directly of the law of, and of judicial or administrative decisions, formally recognized or not in the State of the habitual residence of the child, without recourse to the specific procedures for the proof of that law or for the recognition of foreign decisions which would otherwise be applicable.

ARTICLE 15

The judicial or administrative authorities of a Contracting State may, prior to the making of an order for the return of the child, request that the applicant obtain from the authorities of the State of the habitual residence of the child a decision or other determination that the removal or retention was wrongful within the meaning of Article 3 of the Convention, where such a decision or determination may be obtained in that State. The Central Authorities of the Contracting States shall so far as practicable assist applicants to obtain such a decision or determination.

ARTICLE 16

After receiving notice of a wrongful removal or retention of a child in the sense of Article 3, the judicial or administrative authorities of the Contracting State to which the child has been removed or in which it has been retained shall not decide on the merits of rights of custody until it has been determined that the child is not to be returned under this Convention or unless an application under this Convention is not lodged within a reasonable time following receipt of the notice.

ARTICLE 17

The sole fact that a decision relating to custody has been given in or is entitled to recognition in the requested State shall not be a ground for refusing to return a child under this Convention, but the judicial or administrative authorities of the requested State may take account of the reasons for that decision in applying this Convention.

ARTICLE 18

The provisions of this Chapter do not limit the power of a judicial or administrative authority to order the return of the child at any time.

ARTICLE 19

A decision under this Convention concerning the return of the child shall not be taken to be a determination on the merits of any custody issue.

ARTICLE 20

The return of the child under the provisions of Article 12 may be refused if this would not be permitted by the fundamental principles of the requested State relating to the protection of human rights and fundamental freedoms.

CHAPTER IV—RIGHTS OF ACCESS

ARTICLE 21

An application to make arrangements for organizing or securing the effective exercise of rights of access may be presented to the Central Authorities of the Contracting States in the same way as an application for the return of a child.

The Central Authorities are bound by the obligations of co-operation which are set forth in Article 7 to promote the peaceful enjoyment of access rights and the fulfilment of any conditions to which the exercise of those rights may be subject. The Central Authorities shall take steps to remove, as far as possible, all obstacles to the exercise of such rights.

The Central Authorities, either directly or through intermediaries, may initiate or assist in the institution of proceedings with a view to organizing or protecting these rights and securing respect for the conditions to which the exercise of these rights may be subject.

CHAPTER V—GENERAL PROVISIONS

ARTICLE 22

No security, bond or deposit, however described, shall be required to guarantee the payment of costs and expenses in the judicial or administrative proceedings falling within the scope of this Convention.

ARTICLE 23

No legalization or similar formality may be required in the context of this Convention.

ARTICLE 24

Any application, communication or other document sent to the Central Authority of the requested State shall be in the original language, and shall be accompanied by a translation into the official language or one of the official languages of the requested State or, where that is not feasible, a translation into French or English.

However, a Contracting State may, by making a reservation in accordance with Article 42, object to the use of either French or English, but not both, in any application, communication or other document sent to its Central Authority.

ARTICLE 25

Nationals of the Contracting States and persons who are habitually resident within those States shall be entitled in matters concerned with the application of this Convention to legal aid and advice in any other Contracting State on the same conditions as if they themselves were nationals of and habitually resident in that State.

ARTICLE 26

Each Central Authority shall bear its own costs in applying this Convention.

Central Authorities and other public services of Contracting States shall not impose any charges in relation to applications submitted under this Convention. In particular, they may not require any payment from the applicant towards the costs and expenses of the proceedings or, where applicable, those arising from the participation of legal counsel or advisers. However, they may require the payment of the expenses incurred or to be incurred in implementing the return of the child.

However, a Contracting State may, by making a reservation in accordance with Article 42, declare that it shall not be bound to assume any costs referred to in the preceding paragraph resulting from the participation of legal counsel or advisers or from court proceedings, except insofar as those costs may be covered by its system of legal aid and advice.

Upon ordering the return of a child or issuing an order concerning rights of access under this Convention, the judicial or administrative authorities may, where appropriate, direct the person who removed or retained the child, or who prevented the exercise of rights of access, to pay necessary expenses incurred by or on behalf of the applicant, including travel expenses, any costs incurred or payments made for locating the child, the costs of legal representation of the applicant, and those of returning the child.

ARTICLE 27

When it is manifest that the requirements of this Convention are not fulfilled or that the application is otherwise not well founded, a Central Authority is not bound to accept the application. In that case, the Central Authority shall forthwith inform the applicant or the Central Authority through which the application was submitted, as the case may be, of its reasons.

ARTICLE 28

A Central Authority may require that the application be accompanied by a written authorization empowering it to act on behalf of the applicant, or to designate a representative so to act.

ARTICLE 29

This Convention shall not preclude any person, institution or body who claims that there has been a breach of custody or access rights within the meaning of Article 3 or 21 from applying directly to the judicial or administrative authorities of a Contracting State, whether or not under the provisions of this Convention.

ARTICLE 30

Any application submitted to the Central Authorities or directly to the judicial or administrative authorities of a Contracting State in accordance with the terms of this Convention, together with documents and any other information appended thereto or provided by a Central Authority, shall be admissible in the courts or administrative authorities of the Contracting States.

ARTICLE 31

In relation to a State which in matters of custody of children has two or more systems of law applicable in different territorial units—

a)   any reference to habitual residence in that State shall be construed as referring to habitual residence in a territorial unit of that State;

b)   any reference to the law of the State of habitual residence shall be construed as referring to the law of the territorial unit in that State where the child habitually resides.

ARTICLE 32

In relation to a State which in matters of custody of children has two or more systems of law applicable to different categories of persons, any reference to the law of that State shall be construed as referring to the legal system specified by the law of that State.

ARTICLE 33

A State within which different territorial units have their own rules of law in respect of custody of children shall not be bound to apply this Convention where a State with a unified system of law would not be bound to do so.

ARTICLE 34

This Convention shall take priority in matters within its scope over the Convention of 5 October 1961 concerning the powers of authorities and the law applicable in respect of the protection of minors, as between Parties to both Conventions. Otherwise the present Convention shall not restrict the application of an international instrument in force between the State of origin and the State addressed or other law of the State addressed for the purposes of obtaining the return of a child who has been wrongfully removed or retained or of organizing access rights.

ARTICLE 35

This Convention shall apply as between Contracting States only to wrongful removals or retentions occurring after its entry into force in those States.

Where a declaration has been made under Article 39 or 40, the reference in the preceding paragraph to a Contracting State shall be taken to refer to the territorial unit or units in relation to which this Convention applies.

ARTICLE 36

Nothing in this Convention shall prevent two or more Contracting States, in order to limit the restrictions to which the return of the child may be subject, from agreeing among themselves to derogate from any provisions of this Convention which may imply such a restriction.

CHAPTER VI—FINAL CLAUSES

ARTICLE 37

The Convention shall be open for signature by the States which were Members of the Hague Conference on Private International Law at the time of its Fourteenth Session.

It shall be ratified, accepted or approved and the instruments of ratification, acceptance or approval shall be deposited with the Ministry of Foreign Affairs of the Kingdom of the Netherlands.

ARTICLE 38

Any other State may accede to the Convention.

The instrument of accession shall be deposited with the Ministry of Foreign Affairs of the Kingdom of the Netherlands.

The Convention shall enter into force for a State acceding to it on the first day of the third calendar month after the deposit of its instrument of accession.

The accession will have effect only as regards the relations between the acceding State and such Contracting States as will have declared their acceptance of the accession. Such a declaration will also have to be made by any Member State ratifying, accepting or approving the Convention after an accession. Such declaration shall be deposited at the Ministry of Foreign Affairs of the Kingdom of the Netherlands; this Ministry shall forward, through diplomatic channels, a certified copy to each of the Contracting States.

The Convention will enter into force as between the acceding State and the State that has declared its acceptance of the accession on the first day of the third calendar month after the deposit of the declaration of acceptance.

ARTICLE 39

Any State may, at the time of signature, ratification, acceptance, approval or accession, declare that the Convention shall extend to all the territories for the international relations of which it is responsible, or to one or more of them. Such a declaration shall take effect at the time the Convention enters into force for that State.

Such declaration, as well as any subsequent extension, shall be notified to the Ministry of Foreign Affairs of the Kingdom of the Netherlands.

ARTICLE 40

If a Contracting State has two or more territorial units in which different systems of law are applicable in relation to matters dealt with in this Convention, it may at the time of signature, ratification, acceptance, approval or accession declare that this Convention shall extend to all its territorial units or only to one or more of them and may modify this declaration by submitting another declaration at any time.

Any such declaration shall be notified to the Ministry of Foreign Affairs of the Kingdom of the Netherlands and shall state expressly the territorial units to which the Convention applies.

ARTICLE 41

Where a Contracting State has a system of government under which executive, judicial and legislative powers are distributed between central and other authorities within that State, its signature or ratification, acceptance or approval of, or accession to this Convention, or its making of any declaration in terms of Article 40 shall carry no implication as to the internal distribution of powers within that State.

ARTICLE 42

Any State may, not later than the time of ratification, acceptance, approval or accession, or at the time of making a declaration in terms of Article 39 or 40, make one or both of the reservations provided for in

Article 24 and Article 26, third paragraph. No other reservation shall be permitted.

Any State may at any time withdraw a reservation it has made. The withdrawal shall be notified to the Ministry of Foreign Affairs of the Kingdom of the Netherlands.

The reservation shall cease to have effect on the first day of the third calendar month after the notification referred to in the preceding paragraph.

ARTICLE 43

The Convention shall enter into force on the first day of the third calendar month after the deposit of the third instrument of ratification, acceptance, approval or accession referred to in Articles 37 and 38.

Thereafter the Convention shall enter into force—

(1) for each State ratifying, accepting, approving or acceding to it subsequently, on the first day of the third calendar month after the deposit of its instrument of ratification, acceptance, approval or accession;

(2) for any territory or territorial unit to which the Convention has been extended in conformity with Article 39 or 40, on the first day of the third calendar month after the notification referred to in that Article.

ARTICLE 44

The Convention shall remain in force for five years from the date of its entry into force in accordance with the first paragraph of Article 43 even for States which subsequently have ratified, accepted, approved it or acceded to it.

If there has been no denunciation, it shall be renewed tacitly every five years.

Any denunciation shall be notified to the Ministry of Foreign Affairs of the Kingdom of the Netherlands at least six months before the expiry of the five year period. It may be limited to certain of the territories or territorial units to which the Convention applies.

The denunciation shall have effect only as regards the State which has notified it. The Convention shall remain in force for the other Contracting States.

ARTICLE 45

The Ministry of Foreign Affairs of the Kingdom of the Netherlands shall notify the States Members of the Conference, and the States which have acceded in accordance with Article 38, of the following—

(1)   the signatures and ratifications, acceptances and approvals referred to in Article 37;

(2)   the accessions referred to in Article 38;

(3)   the date on which the Convention enters into force in accordance with Article 43;

(4)   the extensions referred to in Article 39;

(5)   the declarations referred to in Articles 38 and 40;

(6)   the reservations referred to in Article 24 and Article 26, third paragraph, and the withdrawals referred to in Article 42;

(7)   the denunciations referred to in Article 44.

HAGUE CONVENTION ON THE PROTECTION OF CHILDREN AND COOPERATION IN RESPECT OF INTERCOUNTRY ADOPTION

32 I.L.M. 1134 (May 29, 1993)

[EDITORS' INTRODUCTION: Nila Bala, *The Children in Families First Act: Overlooking International Law and the Best Interests of the Child*, 66 STAN. L. REV. ONLINE 135 (2014); James G. Dwyer, *Inter-Country Adoption and the Special Rights Fallacy*, 35 U. PA. J. INT'L L. 189 (2013); Marie A. Failinger, *Moving Toward Human Rights Principles for Intercountry Adoption*, 39 N.C. J. INT'L L. & COM. REG. 523 (2014); Ann Laquer Estin, *Global Child Welfare: The Challenges for Family Law*, 63 OKLA. L. REV. 691 (2011); Maria LoPiccolo, *You Don't Have to Go Home, But You Can't Stay Here: Problems Arising When SIJS Meets International Adoption*, 33 WIS. INT'L L.J. 194 (2015); Seema Mohapatra, *Adopting an International Convention on Surrogacy—A Lesson from Intercountry Adoption*, 13 LOY. U. CHI. INT'L L. REV. 25 (2015); Malinda L. Seymore, *Openness in International Adoption*, 46 COLUM. HUM. RTS. L. REV. 163 (2015); Chad Turner, *The History of the Subsidiarity Principle in the Hague Convention on Intercountry Adoption*, 16 CHI.-KENT J. INT'L & COMP. L. 95 (2016); Jessica Alexander, Comment, *Why the United States Should Define Illegal Adoption Practices as Human Trafficking*, 36 HOUS. J. INT'L L. 715 (2014); Jade Gary, Comment, *Understanding the Decline in Transnational Adoption Channels: Whether the Children in Families First Act is an Effective Response to the Exploitation Of Orphans*, 11 LOY. U. CHI. INT'L L. REV. 141 (2014); Elizabeth Long, Note, *Where Are They Coming From, Where Are They Going: Demanding Accountability in International Adoption*, 18 CARDOZO J.L. & GENDER 827 (2012); Sean McIntyre, Note, *A Proposal to Eliminate a Black Market for Children*, 66 CASE W. RES. L. REV. 1117 (2016); Colin Joseph Troy, Comment, *Members Only: The Need for Reform in U.S. Intercountry Adoption Policy*, 35 SEATTLE U. L. REV. 1525 (2012).]

The States signatory to the present Convention,

Recognizing that the child, for the full and harmonious development of his or her personality, should grow up in a family environment, in an atmosphere of happiness, love and understanding,

Recalling that each State should take, as a matter of priority, appropriate measures to enable the child to remain in the care of his or her family of origin,

Recognizing that intercountry adoption may offer the advantage of a permanent family to a child for whom a suitable family cannot be found in his or her State of origin,

Convinced of the necessity to take measures to ensure that intercountry adoptions are made in the best interests of the child and with respect for his or her fundamental rights, and to prevent the abduction, the sale of, or traffic in children,

Desiring to establish common provisions to this effect, taking into account the principles set forth in international instruments, in particular the United Nations Convention on the Rights of the Child, of 20 November 1989, and the United Nations Declaration on Social and Legal Principles relating to the Protection and Welfare of Children, with Special Reference to Foster Placement and Adoption Nationally and Internationally (General Assembly Resolution 41/85, of 3 December 1986),

Have agreed upon the following provisions—

CHAPTER I—SCOPE OF THE CONVENTION

ARTICLE 1

The objects of the present Convention are—

a) to establish safeguards to ensure that intercountry adoptions take place in the best interests of the child and with respect for his or her fundamental rights as recognized in international law;

b) to establish a system of co-operation amongst Contracting States to ensure that those safeguards are respected and thereby prevent the abduction, the sale of, or traffic in children;

c) to secure the recognition in Contracting States of adoptions made in accordance with the Convention.

ARTICLE 2

(1) The Convention shall apply where a child habitually resident in one Contracting State ('the State of origin') has been, is being, or is to be moved to another Contracting State ('the receiving State') either after his or her adoption in the State of origin by spouses or a person habitually resident in the receiving State, or for the purposes of such an adoption in the receiving State or in the State of origin.

(2) The Convention covers only adoptions which create a permanent parent-child relationship.

ARTICLE 3

The Convention ceases to apply if the agreements mentioned in Article 17, sub-paragraph c, have not been given before the child attains the age of eighteen years.

CHAPTER II—REQUIREMENTS FOR INTERCOUNTRY ADOPTIONS

ARTICLE 4

An adoption within the scope of the Convention shall take place only if the competent authorities of the State of origin—

a)   have established that the child is adoptable;

b)   have determined, after possibilities for placement of the child within the State of origin have been given due consideration, that an intercountry adoption is in the child's best interests;

c)   have ensured that

(1)   the persons, institutions and authorities whose consent is necessary for adoption, have been counselled as may be necessary and duly informed of the effects of their consent, in particular whether or not an adoption will result in the termination of the legal relationship between the child and his or her family of origin,

(2)   such persons, institutions and authorities have given their consent freely, in the required legal form, and expressed or evidenced in writing,

(3)   the consents have not been induced by payment or compensation of any kind and have not been withdrawn, and

(4)   the consent of the mother, where required, has been given only after the birth of the child; and

d)   have ensured, having regard to the age and degree of maturity of the child, that

(1)   he or she has been counselled and duly informed of the effects of the adoption and of his or her consent to the adoption, where such consent is required,

(2)   consideration has been given to the child's wishes and opinions,

(3)   the child's consent to the adoption, where such consent is required, has been given freely, in the required legal form, and expressed or evidenced in writing, and

(4)   such consent has not been induced by payment or compensation of any kind.

ARTICLE 5

An adoption within the scope of the Convention shall take place only if the competent authorities of the receiving State—

a)   have determined that the prospective adoptive parents are eligible and suited to adopt;

b)   have ensured that the prospective adoptive parents have been counselled as may be necessary; and

c)   have determined that the child is or will be authorized to enter and reside permanently in that State.

CHAPTER III—CENTRAL AUTHORITIES AND ACCREDITED BODIES

ARTICLE 6

(1) A Contracting State shall designate a Central Authority to discharge the duties which are imposed by the Convention upon such authorities.

(2) Federal States, States with more than one system of law or States having autonomous territorial units shall be free to appoint more than one Central Authority and to specify the territorial or personal extent of their functions. Where a State has appointed more than one Central Authority, it shall designate the Central Authority to which any communication may be addressed for transmission to the appropriate Central Authority within that State.

ARTICLE 7

(1) Central Authorities shall co-operate with each other and promote co-operation amongst the competent authorities in their States to protect children and to achieve the other objects of the Convention.

(2) They shall take directly all appropriate measures to—

a)   provide information as to the laws of their States concerning adoption and other general information, such as statistics and standard forms;

b)   keep one another informed about the operation of the Convention and, as far as possible, eliminate any obstacles to its application.

ARTICLE 8

Central Authorities shall take, directly or through public authorities, all appropriate measures to prevent improper financial or other gain in connection with an adoption and to deter all practices contrary to the objects of the Convention.

ARTICLE 9

Central Authorities shall take, directly or through public authorities or other bodies duly accredited in their State, all appropriate measures, in particular to—

a)   collect, preserve and exchange information about the situation of the child and the prospective adoptive parents, so far as is necessary to complete the adoption;

b)   facilitate, follow and expedite proceedings with a view to obtaining the adoption;

c)   promote the development of adoption counselling and post-adoption services in their States;

d)   provide each other with general evaluation reports about experience with intercountry adoption;

e)   reply, in so far as is permitted by the law of their State, to justified requests from other Central Authorities or public authorities for information about a particular adoption situation.

ARTICLE 10

Accreditation shall only be granted to and maintained by bodies demonstrating their competence to carry out properly the tasks with which they may be entrusted.

ARTICLE 11

An accredited body shall—

a)   pursue only non-profit objectives according to such conditions and within such limits as may be established by the competent authorities of the State of accreditation;

b)   be directed and staffed by persons qualified by their ethical standards and by training or experience to work in the field of intercountry adoption; and

c)   be subject to supervision by competent authorities of that State as to its composition, operation and financial situation.

ARTICLE 12

A body accredited in one Contracting State may act in another Contracting State only if the competent authorities of both States have authorized it to do so.

ARTICLE 13

The designation of the Central Authorities and, where appropriate, the extent of their functions, as well as the names and addresses of the accredited bodies shall be communicated by each Contracting State to the Permanent Bureau of the Hague Conference on Private International Law.

CHAPTER IV—PROCEDURAL REQUIREMENTS
IN INTERCOUNTRY ADOPTION

ARTICLE 14

Persons habitually resident in a Contracting State, who wish to adopt a child habitually resident in another Contracting State, shall apply to the Central Authority in the State of their habitual residence.

ARTICLE 15

(1) If the Central Authority of the receiving State is satisfied that the applicants are eligible and suited to adopt, it shall prepare a report including information about their identity, eligibility and suitability to adopt, background, family and medical history, social environment, reasons for adoption, ability to undertake an intercountry adoption, as well as the characteristics of the children for whom they would be qualified to care.

(2) It shall transmit the report to the Central Authority of the State of origin.

ARTICLE 16

(1) If the Central Authority of the State of origin is satisfied that the child is adoptable, it shall—

a) prepare a report including information about his or her identity, adoptability, background, social environment, family history, medical history including that of the child's family, and any special needs of the child;

b) give due consideration to the child's upbringing and to his or her ethnic, religious and cultural background;

c) ensure that consents have been obtained in accordance with Article 4; and

d) determine, on the basis in particular of the reports relating to the child and the prospective adoptive parents, whether the envisaged placement is in the best interests of the child.

(2) It shall transmit to the Central Authority of the receiving State its report on the child, proof that the necessary consents have been obtained and the reasons for its determination on the placement, taking care not to reveal the identity of the mother and the father if, in the State of origin, these identities may not be disclosed.

ARTICLE 17

Any decision in the State of origin that a child should be entrusted to prospective adoptive parents may only be made if—

a) the Central Authority of that State has ensured that the prospective adoptive parents agree;

b)   the Central Authority of the receiving State has approved such decision, where such approval is required by the law of that State or by the Central Authority of the State of origin;

c)   the Central Authorities of both States have agreed that the adoption may proceed; and

d)   it has been determined, in accordance with Article 5, that the prospective adoptive parents are eligible and suited to adopt and that the child is or will be authorized to enter and reside permanently in the receiving State.

ARTICLE 18

The Central Authorities of both States shall take all necessary steps to obtain permission for the child to leave the State of origin and to enter and reside permanently in the receiving State.

ARTICLE 19

(1) The transfer of the child to the receiving State may only be carried out if the requirements of Article 17 have been satisfied.

(2) The Central Authorities of both States shall ensure that this transfer takes place in secure and appropriate circumstances and, if possible, in the company of the adoptive or prospective adoptive parents.

(3) If the transfer of the child does not take place, the reports referred to in Articles 15 and 16 are to be sent back to the authorities who forwarded them.

ARTICLE 20

The Central Authorities shall keep each other informed about the adoption process and the measures taken to complete it, as well as about the progress of the placement if a probationary period is required.

ARTICLE 21

(1) Where the adoption is to take place after the transfer of the child to the receiving State and it appears to the Central Authority of that State that the continued placement of the child with the prospective adoptive parents is not in the child's best interests, such Central Authority shall take the measures necessary to protect the child, in particular—

a)   to cause the child to be withdrawn from the prospective adoptive parents and to arrange temporary care;

b)   in consultation with the Central Authority of the State of origin, to arrange without delay a new placement of the child with a view to adoption or, if this is not appropriate, to arrange alternative long-term care; an adoption shall not take place until the Central

Authority of the State of origin has been duly informed concerning the new prospective adoptive parents;

c) as a last resort, to arrange the return of the child, if his or her interests so require.

(2) Having regard in particular to the age and degree of maturity of the child, he or she shall be consulted and, where appropriate, his or her consent obtained in relation to measures to be taken under this Article.

ARTICLE 22

(1) The functions of a Central Authority under this Chapter may be performed by public authorities or by bodies accredited under Chapter III, to the extent permitted by the law of its State.

(2) Any Contracting State may declare to the depositary of the Convention that the functions of the Central Authority under Articles 15 to 21 may be performed in that State, to the extent permitted by the law and subject to the supervision of the competent authorities of that State, also by bodies or persons who—

a) meet the requirements of integrity, professional competence, experience and accountability of that State; and

b) are qualified by their ethical standards and by training or experience to work in the field of intercountry adoption.

(3) A Contracting State which makes the declaration provided for in paragraph 2 shall keep the Permanent Bureau of the Hague Conference on Private International Law informed of the names and addresses of these bodies and persons.

(4) Any Contracting State may declare to the depositary of the Convention that adoptions of children habitually resident in its territory may only take place if the functions of the Central Authorities are performed in accordance with paragraph 1.

(5) Notwithstanding any declaration made under paragraph 2, the reports provided for in Articles 15 and 16 shall, in every case, be prepared under the responsibility of the Central Authority or other authorities or bodies in accordance with paragraph 1.

CHAPTER V—RECOGNITION AND EFFECTS OF THE ADOPTION

ARTICLE 23

(1) An adoption certified by the competent authority of the State of the adoption as having been made in accordance with the Convention shall be recognized by operation of law in the other Contracting States. The certificate shall specify when and by whom the agreements under Article 17, sub-paragraph c, were given.

(2) Each Contracting State shall, at the time of signature, ratification, acceptance, approval or accession, notify the depositary of the Convention of the identity and the functions of the authority or the authorities which, in that State, are competent to make the certification. It shall also notify the depositary of any modification in the designation of these authorities.

ARTICLE 24

The recognition of an adoption may be refused in a Contracting State only if the adoption is manifestly contrary to its public policy, taking into account the best interests of the child.

ARTICLE 25

Any Contracting State may declare to the depositary of the Convention that it will not be bound under this Convention to recognize adoptions made in accordance with an agreement concluded by application of Article 39, paragraph 2.

ARTICLE 26

(1) The recognition of an adoption includes recognition of

a)   the legal parent-child relationship between the child and his or her adoptive parents;

b)   parental responsibility of the adoptive parents for the child;

c)   the termination of a pre-existing legal relationship between the child and his or her mother and father, if the adoption has this effect in the Contracting State where it was made.

(2) In the case of an adoption having the effect of terminating a pre-existing legal parent-child relationship, the child shall enjoy in the receiving State, and in any other Contracting State where the adoption is recognized, rights equivalent to those resulting from adoptions having this effect in each such State.

(3) The preceding paragraphs shall not prejudice the application of any provision more favourable for the child, in force in the Contracting State which recognizes the adoption.

ARTICLE 27

(1) Where an adoption granted in the State of origin does not have the effect of terminating a pre-existing legal parent-child relationship, it may, in the receiving State which recognizes the adoption under the Convention, be converted into an adoption having such an effect—

a)   if the law of the receiving State so permits; and

b)   if the consents referred to in Article 4, subparagraphs c and d, have been or are given for the purpose of such an adoption.

(2) Article 23 applies to the decision converting the adoption.

CHAPTER VI—GENERAL PROVISIONS

ARTICLE 28

The Convention does not affect any law of a State of origin which requires that the adoption of a child habitually resident within that State take place in that State or which prohibits the child's placement in, or transfer to, the receiving State prior to adoption.

ARTICLE 29

There shall be no contact between the prospective adoptive parents and the child's parents or any other person who has care of the child until the requirements of Article 4, sub-paragraphs a to c, and Article 5, subparagraph a, have been met, unless the adoption takes place within a family or unless the contact is in compliance with the conditions established by the competent authority of the State of origin.

ARTICLE 30

(1) The competent authorities of a Contracting State shall ensure that information held by them concerning the child's origin, in particular information concerning the identity of his or her parents, as well as the medical history, is preserved.

(2) They shall ensure that the child or his or her representative has access to such information, under appropriate guidance, in so far as is permitted by the law of that State.

ARTICLE 31

Without prejudice to Article 30, personal data gathered or transmitted under the Convention, especially data referred to in Articles 15 and 16, shall be used only for the purposes for which they were gathered or transmitted.

ARTICLE 32

(1) No one shall derive improper financial or other gain from an activity related to an intercountry adoption.

(2) Only costs and expenses, including reasonable professional fees of persons involved in the adoption, may be charged or paid.

(3) The directors, administrators and employees of bodies involved in an adoption shall not receive remuneration which is unreasonably high in relation to services rendered.

ARTICLE 33

A competent authority which finds that any provision of the Convention has not been respected or that there is a serious risk that it may not be respected, shall immediately inform the Central Authority of its State. This Central Authority shall be responsible for ensuring that appropriate measures are taken.

ARTICLE 34

If the competent authority of the State of destination of a document so requests, a translation certified as being in conformity with the original must be furnished. Unless otherwise provided, the costs of such translation are to be borne by the prospective adoptive parents.

ARTICLE 35

The competent authorities of the Contracting States shall act expeditiously in the process of adoption.

ARTICLE 36

In relation to a State which has two or more systems of law with regard to adoption applicable in different territorial units—

a) any reference to habitual residence in that State shall be construed as referring to habitual residence in a territorial unit of that State;

b) any reference to the law of that State shall be construed as referring to the law in force in the relevant territorial unit;

c) any reference to the competent authorities or to the public authorities of that State shall be construed as referring to those authorized to act in the relevant territorial unit;

d) any reference to the accredited bodies of that State shall be construed as referring to bodies accredited in the relevant territorial unit.

ARTICLE 37

In relation to a State which with regard to adoption has two or more systems of law applicable to different categories of persons, any reference to the law of that State shall be construed as referring to the legal system specified by the law of that State.

ARTICLE 38

A State within which different territorial units have their own rules of law in respect of adoption shall not be bound to apply the Convention where a State with a unified system of law would not be bound to do so.

ARTICLE 39

(1) The Convention does not affect any international instrument to which Contracting States are Parties and which contains provisions on

matters governed by the Convention, unless a contrary declaration is made by the States Parties to such instrument.

(2)   Any Contracting State may enter into agreements with one or more other Contracting States, with a view to improving the application of the Convention in their mutual relations. These agreements may derogate only from the provisions of Articles 14 to 16 and 18 to 21. The States which have concluded such an agreement shall transmit a copy to the depositary of the Convention.

ARTICLE 40

No reservation to the Convention shall be permitted.

ARTICLE 41

The Convention shall apply in every case where an application pursuant to Article 14 has been received after the Convention has entered into force in the receiving State and the State of origin.

ARTICLE 42

The Secretary General of the Hague Conference on Private International Law shall at regular intervals convene a Special Commission in order to review the practical operation of the Convention.

CHAPTER VII—FINAL CLAUSES

ARTICLE 43

(1)   The Convention shall be open for signature by the States which were Members of the Hague Conference on Private International Law at the time of its Seventeenth Session and by the other States which participated in that Session.

(2)   It shall be ratified, accepted or approved and the instruments of ratification, acceptance or approval shall be deposited with the Ministry of Foreign Affairs of the Kingdom of the Netherlands, depositary of the Convention.

ARTICLE 44

(1)   Any other State may accede to the Convention after it has entered into force in accordance with Article 46, paragraph 1.

(2)   The instrument of accession shall be deposited with the depositary.

(3)   Such accession shall have effect only as regards the relations between the acceding State and those Contracting States which have not raised an objection to its accession in the six months after the receipt of the notification referred to in sub-paragraph b of Article 48. Such an objection may also be raised by States at the time when they ratify,

accept or approve the Convention after an accession. Any such objection shall be notified to the depositary.

ARTICLE 45

(1) If a State has two or more territorial units in which different systems of law are applicable in relation to matters dealt with in the Convention, it may at the time of signature, ratification, acceptance, approval or accession declare that this Convention shall extend to all its territorial units or only to one or more of them and may modify this declaration by submitting another declaration at any time.

(2) Any such declaration shall be notified to the depositary and shall state expressly the territorial units to which the Convention applies.

(3) If a State makes no declaration under this Article, the Convention is to extend to all territorial units of that State.

ARTICLE 46

(1) The Convention shall enter into force on the first day of the month following the expiration of three months after the deposit of the third instrument of ratification, acceptance or approval referred to in Article 43.

(2) Thereafter the Convention shall enter into force—

a) for each State ratifying, accepting or approving it subsequently, or acceding to it, on the first day of the month following the expiration of three months after the deposit of its instrument of ratification, acceptance, approval or accession;

b) for a territorial unit to which the Convention has been extended in conformity with Article 45, on the first day of the month following the expiration of three months after the notification referred to in that Article.

ARTICLE 47

(1) A State Party to the Convention may denounce it by a notification in writing addressed to the depositary.

(2) The denunciation takes effect on the first day of the month following the expiration of twelve months after the notification is received by the depositary. Where a longer period for the denunciation to take effect is specified in the notification, the denunciation takes effect upon the expiration of such longer period after the notification is received by the depositary.

ARTICLE 48

The depositary shall notify the States Members of the Hague Conference on Private International Law, the other States which participated in the Seventeenth Session and the States which have acceded in accordance with Article 44, of the following—

    a)   the signatures, ratifications, acceptances and approvals referred to in Article 43;

    b)   the accessions and objections raised to accessions referred to in Article 44;

    c)   the date on which the Convention enters into force in accordance with Article 46;

    d)   the declarations and designations referred to in Articles 22, 23, 25 and 45;

    e)   the agreements referred to in Article 39;

    f)   the denunciations referred to in Article 47.

UNITED NATIONS: CONVENTION ON THE RIGHTS OF THE CHILD

ADOPTED AND OPENED FOR SIGNATURE, RATIFICATION, AND ACCESSION BY GENERAL ASSEMBLY RESOLUTION 44/25 OF 20 NOVEMBER 1989

28 I.L.M. 1448 (1989)

[EDITORS' INTRODUCTION: Tamar R. Birckhead, *Children in Isolation: The Solitary Confinement of Youth*, 50 WAKE FOREST L. REV. 1 (2015); Kathleen Boumans, Note, *Filling the Gaps: New Proposals for the Convention on the Rights of a Child*, 43 SYRACUSE J. INT'L. L. & COM. 191 (2015); Lynne Marie Kohm, *A Brief Assessment of the 25-Year Effect of the Convention on the Rights of the Child*, 23 CARDOZO J. INT'L & COMP. L. 323 (2015); Sheila Menz, *Statelessness and Child Marriage as Intersectional Phenomena: Instability, Inequality, and the Role of the International Community*, 104 CAL. L. REV. 497 (2016); Violeta K. Haralampieva, Note, *The U.S. Asylum Pro Se-Dures for Unaccompanied and Undocumented Children: Cost and Fear v. Child's Best Interest*, 25 B.U. PUB. INT. L.J. 43 (2016); Katelyn A. Horne, Note, *Navigating Nationality: The Rights to Birth Registration and Nationality in Refugee Magnet States*, 53 COLUM. J. TRANSNAT'L L. 114 (2014).]

PREAMBLE

The States Parties to the present Convention,

Considering that, in accordance with the principles proclaimed in the Charter of the United Nations, recognition of the inherent dignity and of the equal and inalienable rights of all members of the human family is the foundation of freedom, justice and peace in the world,

Bearing in mind that the peoples of the United Nations have, in the Charter, reaffirmed their faith in fundamental human rights and in the dignity and worth of the human person, and have determined to promote social progress and better standards of life in larger freedom,

Recognizing that the United Nations has, in the Universal Declaration of Human Rights and in the International Covenants on Human Rights, proclaimed and agreed that everyone is entitled to all the rights and freedoms set forth therein, without distinction of any kind, such as race, colour, sex, language, religion, political or other opinion, national or social origin, property, birth or other status,

Recalling that, in the Universal Declaration of Human Rights, the United Nations has proclaimed that childhood is entitled to special care and assistance,

Convinced that the family, as the fundamental group of society and the natural environment for the growth and well-being of all its members and particularly children, should be afforded the necessary protection and assistance so that it can fully assume its responsibilities within the community,

Recognizing that the child, for the full and harmonious development of his or her personality, should grow up in a family environment, in an atmosphere of happiness, love and understanding,

Considering that the child should be fully prepared to live an individual life in society, and brought up in the spirit of the ideals proclaimed in the Charter of the United Nations, and in particular in the spirit of peace, dignity, tolerance, freedom, equality and solidarity,

Bearing in mind that the need to extend particular care to the child has been stated in the Geneva Declaration of the Rights of the Child of 1924 and in the Declaration of the Rights of the Child adopted by the General Assembly on 20 November 1959 and recognized in the Universal Declaration of Human Rights, in the International Covenant on Civil and Political Rights (in particular in articles 23 and 24), in the International Covenant on Economic, Social and Cultural Rights (in particular in article 10) and in the statutes and relevant instruments of specialized agencies and international organizations concerned with the welfare of children,

Bearing in mind that, as indicated in the Declaration of the Rights of the Child, "the child, by reason of his physical and mental immaturity, needs special safeguards and care, including appropriate legal protection, before as well as after birth",

Recalling the provisions of the Declaration on Social and Legal Principles relating to the Protection and Welfare of Children, with Special Reference to Foster Placement and Adoption Nationally and Internationally; the United Nations Standard Minimum Rules for the Administration of Juvenile Justice (The Beijing Rules); and the Declaration on the Protection of Women and Children in Emergency and Armed Conflict, Recognizing that, in all countries in the world, there are children living in exceptionally difficult conditions, and that such children need special consideration,

Taking due account of the importance of the traditions and cultural values of each people for the protection and harmonious development of the child,

Recognizing the importance of international co-operation for improving the living conditions of children in every country, in particular in the developing countries,

Have agreed as follows:

PART I

ARTICLE 1

For the purposes of the present Convention, a child means every human being below the age of eighteen years unless, under the law applicable to the child, majority is attained earlier.

ARTICLE 2

1.   States Parties shall respect and ensure the rights set forth in the present Convention to each child within their jurisdiction without discrimination of any kind, irrespective of the child's or his or her parent's or legal guardian's race, colour, sex, language, religion, political or other opinion, national, ethnic or social origin, property, disability, birth or other status.

2.   States Parties shall take all appropriate measures to ensure that the child is protected against all forms of discrimination or punishment on the basis of the status, activities, expressed opinions, or beliefs of the child's parents, legal guardians, or family members.

ARTICLE 3

1.   In all actions concerning children, whether undertaken by public or private social welfare institutions, courts of law, administrative authorities or legislative bodies, the best interests of the child shall be a primary consideration.

2.   States Parties undertake to ensure the child such protection and care as is necessary for his or her well-being, taking into account the rights and duties of his or her parents, legal guardians, or other individuals legally responsible for him or her, and, to this end, shall take all appropriate legislative and administrative measures.

3.   States Parties shall ensure that the institutions, services and facilities responsible for the care or protection of children shall conform with the standards established by competent authorities, particularly in the areas of safety, health, in the number and suitability of their staff, as well as competent supervision.

ARTICLE 4

States Parties shall undertake all appropriate legislative, administrative, and other measures for the implementation of the rights recognized in the present Convention. With regard to economic, social and cultural rights, States Parties shall undertake such measures to the maximum extent of their available resources and, where needed, within the framework of international co-operation.

ARTICLE 5

States Parties shall respect the responsibilities, rights and duties of parents or, where applicable, the members of the extended family or community as provided for by local custom, legal guardians or other persons legally responsible for the child, to provide, in a manner consistent with the evolving capacities of the child, appropriate direction and guidance in the exercise by the child of the rights recognized in the present Convention.

ARTICLE 6

1.   States Parties recognize that every child has the inherent right to life.

2.   States Parties shall ensure to the maximum extent possible the survival and development of the child.

ARTICLE 7

1.   The child shall be registered immediately after birth and shall have the right from birth to a name, the right to acquire a nationality and, as far as possible, the right to know and be cared for by his or her parents.

2.   States Parties shall ensure the implementation of these rights in accordance with their national law and their obligations under the relevant international instruments in this field, in particular where the child would otherwise be stateless.

ARTICLE 8

1.   States Parties undertake to respect the right of the child to preserve his or her identity, including nationality, name and family relations as recognized by law without unlawful interference.

2.   Where a child is illegally deprived of some or all of the elements of his or her identity, States Parties shall provide appropriate assistance and protection, with a view to speedily re-establishing his or her identity.

ARTICLE 9

1.   States Parties shall ensure that a child shall not be separated from his or her parents against their will, except when competent authorities subject to judicial review determine, in accordance with applicable law and procedures, that such separation is necessary for the best interests of the child. Such determination may be necessary in a particular case such as one involving abuse or neglect of the child by the parents, or one where the parents are living separately and a decision must be made as to the child's place of residence.

2.   In any proceedings pursuant to paragraph 1 of the present article, all interested parties shall be given an opportunity to participate in the proceedings and make their views known.

3.   States Parties shall respect the right of the child who is separated from one or both parents to maintain personal relations and direct contact with both parents on a regular basis, except if it is contrary to the child's best interests.

4.   Where such separation results from any action initiated by a State Party, such as the detention, imprisonment, exile, deportation or death (including death arising from any cause while the person is in the custody of the State) of one or both parents or of the child, that State Party shall, upon request, provide the parents, the child or, if appropriate, another member of the family with the essential information concerning the whereabouts of the absent member(s) of the family unless the provision of the information would be detrimental to the well-being of the child. States Parties shall further ensure that the submission of such a request shall of itself entail no adverse consequences for the person(s) concerned.

ARTICLE 10

1.   In accordance with the obligation of States Parties under article 9, paragraph 1, applications by a child or his or her parents to enter or leave a State Party for the purpose of family reunification shall be dealt with by States Parties in a positive, humane and expeditious manner. States Parties shall further ensure that the submission of such a request shall entail no adverse consequences for the applicants and for the members of their family.

2.   A child whose parents reside in different States shall have the right to maintain on a regular basis, save in exceptional circumstances personal relations and direct contacts with both parents. Towards that end and in accordance with the obligation of States Parties under article 9, paragraph 2, States Parties shall respect the right of the child and his or her parents to leave any country, including their own, and to enter their own country. The right to leave any country shall be subject only to such restrictions as are prescribed by law and which are necessary to protect the national security, public order (ordre public), public health or morals or the rights and freedoms of others and are consistent with the other rights recognized in the present Convention.

ARTICLE 11

1.   States Parties shall take measures to combat the illicit transfer and non-return of children abroad.

2.   To this end, States Parties shall promote the conclusion of bilateral or multilateral agreements or accession to existing agreements.

ARTICLE 12

1.   States Parties shall assure to the child who is capable of forming his or her own views the right to express those views freely in all matters affecting the child, the views of the child being given due weight in accordance with the age and maturity of the child.

2.   For this purpose, the child shall in particular be provided the opportunity to be heard in any judicial and administrative proceedings affecting the child, either directly, or through a representative or an appropriate body, in a manner consistent with the procedural rules of national law.

ARTICLE 13

1.   The child shall have the right to freedom of expression; this right shall include freedom to seek, receive and impart information and ideas of all kinds, regardless of frontiers, either orally, in writing or in print, in the form of art, or through any other media of the child's choice.

2.   The exercise of this right may be subject to certain restrictions, but these shall only be such as are provided by law and are necessary:

(a) For respect of the rights or reputations of others; or

(b) For the protection of national security or of public order (ordre public), or of public health or morals.

ARTICLE 14

1.   States Parties shall respect the right of the child to freedom of thought, conscience and religion.

2.   States Parties shall respect the rights and duties of the parents and, when applicable, legal guardians, to provide direction to the child in the exercise of his or her right in a manner consistent with the evolving capacities of the child.

3.   Freedom to manifest one's religion or beliefs may be subject only to such limitations as are prescribed by law and are necessary to protect public safety, order, health or morals, or the fundamental rights and freedoms of others.

ARTICLE 15

1.   States Parties recognize the rights of the child to freedom of association and to freedom of peaceful assembly.

2.   No restrictions may be placed on the exercise of these rights other than those imposed in conformity with the law and which are necessary in a democratic society in the interests of national security or public safety, public order (ordre public), the protection of public health or morals or the protection of the rights and freedoms of others.

ARTICLE 16

1.   No child shall be subjected to arbitrary or unlawful interference with his or her privacy, family, home or correspondence, nor to unlawful attacks on his or her honour and reputation.

2.   The child has the right to the protection of the law against such interference or attacks.

ARTICLE 17

States Parties recognize the important function performed by the mass media and shall ensure that the child has access to information and material from a diversity of national and international sources, especially those aimed at the promotion of his or her social, spiritual and moral well-being and physical and mental health.

To this end, States Parties shall:

(a)   Encourage the mass media to disseminate information and material of social and cultural benefit to the child and in accordance with the spirit of article 29;

(b)   Encourage international co-operation in the production, exchange and dissemination of such information and material from a diversity of cultural, national and international sources;

(c)   Encourage the production and dissemination of children's books;

(d)   Encourage the mass media to have particular regard to the linguistic needs of the child who belongs to a minority group or who is indigenous;

(e)   Encourage the development of appropriate guidelines for the protection of the child from information and material injurious to his or her well-being, bearing in mind the provisions of articles 13 and 18.

ARTICLE 18

1.   States Parties shall use their best efforts to ensure recognition of the principle that both parents have common responsibilities for the upbringing and development of the child. Parents or, as the case may be, legal guardians, have the primary responsibility for the upbringing and development of the child. The best interests of the child will be their basic concern.

2.   For the purpose of guaranteeing and promoting the rights set forth in the present Convention, States Parties shall render appropriate assistance to parents and legal guardians in the performance of their child-rearing responsibilities and shall ensure the development of institutions, facilities and services for the care of children.

3.   States Parties shall take all appropriate measures to ensure that children of working parents have the right to benefit from child-care services and facilities for which they are eligible.

ARTICLE 19

1.   States Parties shall take all appropriate legislative, administrative, social and educational measures to protect the child from all forms of physical or mental violence, injury or abuse, neglect or negligent treatment, maltreatment or exploitation, including sexual abuse, while in the care of parent(s), legal guardian(s) or any other person who has the care of the child.

2.   Such protective measures should, as appropriate, include effective procedures for the establishment of social programmes to provide necessary support for the child and for those who have the care of the child, as well as for other forms of prevention and for identification, reporting, referral, investigation, treatment and follow-up of instances of child maltreatment described heretofore, and, as appropriate, for judicial involvement.

ARTICLE 20

1.   A child temporarily or permanently deprived of his or her family environment, or in whose own best interests cannot be allowed to remain in that environment, shall be entitled to special protection and assistance provided by the State.

2.   States Parties shall in accordance with their national laws ensure alternative care for such a child.

3.   Such care could include, inter alia, foster placement, kafalah of Islamic law, adoption or if necessary placement in suitable institutions for the care of children. When considering solutions, due regard shall be paid to the desirability of continuity in a child's upbringing and to the child's ethnic, religious, cultural and linguistic background.

ARTICLE 21

States Parties that recognize and/or permit the system of adoption shall ensure that the best interests of the child shall be the paramount consideration and they shall:

(a)   Ensure that the adoption of a child is authorized only by competent authorities who determine, in accordance with applicable law and procedures and on the basis of all pertinent and reliable information, that the adoption is permissible in view of the child's status concerning parents, relatives and legal guardians and that, if required, the persons concerned have given their informed consent to the adoption on the basis of such counselling as may be necessary;

(b)   Recognize that inter-country adoption may be considered as an alternative means of child's care, if the child cannot be placed in a foster or an adoptive family or cannot in any suitable manner be cared for in the child's country of origin;

(c)   Ensure that the child concerned by inter-country adoption enjoys safeguards and standards equivalent to those existing in the case of national adoption,

(d)   Take all appropriate measures to ensure that, in inter-country adoption, the placement does not result in improper financial gain for those involved in it;

(e)   Promote, where appropriate, the objectives of the present article by concluding bilateral or multilateral arrangements or agreements, and endeavour, within this framework, to ensure that the placement of the child in another country is carried out by competent authorities or organs.

ARTICLE 22

1.   States Parties shall take appropriate measures to ensure that a child who is seeking refugee status or who is considered a refugee in accordance with applicable international or domestic law and procedures shall, whether unaccompanied or accompanied by his or her parents or by any other person, receive appropriate protection and humanitarian assistance in the enjoyment of applicable rights set forth in the present Convention and in other international human rights or humanitarian instruments to which the said States are Parties.

2.   For this purpose, States Parties shall provide, as they consider appropriate, co-operation in any efforts by the United Nations and other competent intergovernmental organizations or non-governmental organizations co-operating with the United Nations to protect and assist such a child and to trace the parents or other members of the family of any refugee child in order to obtain information necessary for reunification with his or her family. In cases where no parents or other members of the family can be found, the child shall be accorded the same protection as any other child permanently or temporarily deprived of his or her family environment for any reason, as set forth in the present Convention.

ARTICLE 23

1.   States Parties recognize that a mentally or physically disabled child should enjoy a full and decent life, in conditions which ensure dignity, promote self-reliance and facilitate the child's active participation in the community.

2.   States Parties recognize the right of the disabled child to special care and shall encourage and ensure the extension, subject to available resources, to the eligible child and those responsible for his or her care, of assistance for which application is made and which is appropriate to

the child's condition and to the circumstances of the parents or others caring for the child.

3. Recognizing the special needs of a disabled child, assistance extended in accordance with paragraph 2 of the present article shall be provided free of charge, whenever possible, taking into account the financial resources of the parents or others caring for the child, and shall be designed to ensure that the disabled child has effective access to and receives education, training, health care services, rehabilitation services, preparation for employment and recreation opportunities in a manner conducive to the child's achieving the fullest possible social integration and individual development, including his or her cultural and spiritual development.

4. States Parties shall promote, in the spirit of international co-operation, the exchange of appropriate information in the field of preventive health care and of medical, psychological and functional treatment of disabled children, including dissemination of and access to information concerning methods of rehabilitation, education and vocational services, with the aim of enabling States Parties to improve their capabilities and skills and to widen their experience in these areas. In this regard, particular account shall be taken of the needs of developing countries.

ARTICLE 24

1. States Parties recognize the right of the child to the enjoyment of the highest attainable standard of health and to facilities for the treatment of illness and rehabilitation of health. States Parties shall strive to ensure that no child is deprived of his or her right of access to such health care services.

2. States Parties shall pursue full implementation of this right and, in particular, shall take appropriate measures:

(a) To diminish infant and child mortality;

(b) To ensure the provision of necessary medical assistance and health care to all children with emphasis on the development of primary health care;

(c) To combat disease and malnutrition, including within the framework of primary health care, through, inter alia, the application of readily available technology and through the provision of adequate nutritious foods and clean drinking-water, taking into consideration the dangers and risks of environmental pollution;

(d) To ensure appropriate pre-natal and post-natal health care for mothers;

(e) To ensure that all segments of society, in particular parents and children, are informed, have access to education and are supported in the use of basic knowledge of child health and nutrition, the advantages of breast-feeding, hygiene and environmental sanitation and the prevention of accidents;

(f)   To develop preventive health care, guidance for parents and family planning education and services.

3.   States Parties shall take all effective and appropriate measures with a view to abolishing traditional practices prejudicial to the health of children.

4.   States Parties undertake to promote and encourage international co-operation with a view to achieving progressively the full realization of the right recognized in the present article. In this regard, particular account shall be taken of the needs of developing countries.

ARTICLE 25

States Parties recognize the right of a child who has been placed by the competent authorities for the purposes of care, protection or treatment of his or her physical or mental health, to a periodic review of the treatment provided to the child and all other circumstances relevant to his or her placement.

ARTICLE 26

1.   States Parties shall recognize for every child the right to benefit from social security, including social insurance, and shall take the necessary measures to achieve the full realization of this right in accordance with their national law.

2.   The benefits should, where appropriate, be granted, taking into account the resources and the circumstances of the child and persons having responsibility for the maintenance of the child, as well as any other consideration relevant to an application for benefits made by or on behalf of the child.

ARTICLE 27

1.   States Parties recognize the right of every child to a standard of living adequate for the child's physical, mental, spiritual, moral and social development.

2.   The parent(s) or others responsible for the child have the primary responsibility to secure, within their abilities and financial capacities, the conditions of living necessary for the child's development.

3.   States Parties, in accordance with national conditions and within their means, shall take appropriate measures to assist parents and others responsible for the child to implement this right and shall in case of need provide material assistance and support programmes, particularly with regard to nutrition, clothing and housing.

4.   States Parties shall take all appropriate measures to secure the recovery of maintenance for the child from the parents or other persons

having financial responsibility for the child, both within the State Party and from abroad. In particular, where the person having financial responsibility for the child lives in a State different from that of the child, States Parties shall promote the accession to international agreements or the conclusion of such agreements, as well as the making of other appropriate arrangements.

ARTICLE 28

1.   States Parties recognize the right of the child to education, and with a view to achieving this right progressively and on the basis of equal opportunity, they shall, in particular:

(a) Make primary education compulsory and available free to all;

(b) Encourage the development of different forms of secondary education, including general and vocational education, make them available and accessible to every child, and take appropriate measures such as the introduction of free education and offering financial assistance in case of need;

(c) Make higher education accessible to all on the basis of capacity by every appropriate means;

(d) Make educational and vocational information and guidance available and accessible to all children;

(e) Take measures to encourage regular attendance at schools and the reduction of drop-out rates.

2.   States Parties shall take all appropriate measures to ensure that school discipline is administered in a manner consistent with the child's human dignity and in conformity with the present Convention.

3.   States Parties shall promote and encourage international co-operation in matters relating to education, in particular with a view to contributing to the elimination of ignorance and illiteracy throughout the world and facilitating access to scientific and technical knowledge and modern teaching methods. In this regard, particular account shall be taken of the needs of developing countries.

ARTICLE 29

1.   States Parties agree that the education of the child shall be directed to:

(a) The development of the child's personality, talents and mental and physical abilities to their fullest potential;

(b) The development of respect for human rights and fundamental freedoms, and for the principles enshrined in the Charter of the United Nations;

(c) The development of respect for the child's parents, his or her own cultural identity, language and values, for the national values of the country in which the child is living, the country from which he or she may originate, and for civilizations different from his or her own;

(d) The preparation of the child for responsible life in a free society, in the spirit of understanding, peace, tolerance, equality of sexes, and friendship among all peoples, ethnic, national and religious groups and persons of indigenous origin;

(e) The development of respect for the natural environment.

2.   No part of the present article or article 28 shall be construed so as to interfere with the liberty of individuals and bodies to establish and direct educational institutions, subject always to the observance of the principles set forth in paragraph 1 of the present article and to the requirements that the education given in such institutions shall conform to such minimum standards as may be laid down by the State.

ARTICLE 30

In those States in which ethnic, religious or linguistic minorities or persons of indigenous origin exist, a child belonging to such a minority or who is indigenous shall not be denied the right, in community with other members of his or her group, to enjoy his or her own culture, to profess and practise his or her own religion, or to use his or her own language.

ARTICLE 31

1.   States Parties recognize the right of the child to rest and leisure, to engage in play and recreational activities appropriate to the age of the child and to participate freely in cultural life and the arts.

2.   States Parties shall respect and promote the right of the child to participate fully in cultural and artistic life and shall encourage the provision of appropriate and equal opportunities for cultural, artistic, recreational and leisure activity.

ARTICLE 32

1.   States Parties recognize the right of the child to be protected from economic exploitation and from performing any work that is likely to be hazardous or to interfere with the child's education, or to be harmful to the child's health or physical, mental, spiritual, moral or social development.

2.   States Parties shall take legislative, administrative, social and educational measures to ensure the implementation of the present article. To this end, and having regard to the relevant provisions of other international instruments, States Parties shall in particular:

(a)   Provide for a minimum age or minimum ages for admission to employment;

(b)   Provide for appropriate regulation of the hours and conditions of employment;

(c)   Provide for appropriate penalties or other sanctions to ensure the effective enforcement of the present article.

ARTICLE 33

States Parties shall take all appropriate measures, including legislative, administrative, social and educational measures, to protect children from the illicit use of narcotic drugs and psychotropic substances as defined in the relevant international treaties, and to prevent the use of children in the illicit production and trafficking of such substances.

ARTICLE 34

States Parties undertake to protect the child from all forms of sexual exploitation and sexual abuse. For these purposes, States Parties shall in particular take all appropriate national, bilateral and multilateral measures to prevent:

(a)   The inducement or coercion of a child to engage in any unlawful sexual activity;

(b)   The exploitative use of children in prostitution or other unlawful sexual practices;

(c)   The exploitative use of children in pornographic performances and materials.

ARTICLE 35

States Parties shall take all appropriate national, bilateral and multilateral measures to prevent the abduction of, the sale of or traffic in children for any purpose or in any form.

ARTICLE 36

States Parties shall protect the child against all other forms of exploitation prejudicial to any aspects of the child's welfare.

ARTICLE 37

States Parties shall ensure that:

(a)   No child shall be subjected to torture or other cruel, inhuman or degrading treatment or punishment. Neither capital punishment nor life imprisonment without possibility of release shall be imposed for offences committed by persons below eighteen years of age;

(b) No child shall be deprived of his or her liberty unlawfully or arbitrarily. The arrest, detention or imprisonment of a child shall be in conformity with the law and shall be used only as a measure of last resort and for the shortest appropriate period of time;

(c) Every child deprived of liberty shall be treated with humanity and respect for the inherent dignity of the human person, and in a manner which takes into account the needs of persons of his or her age. In particular, every child deprived of liberty shall be separated from adults unless it is considered in the child's best interest not to do so and shall have the right to maintain contact with his or her family through correspondence and visits, save in exceptional circumstances;

(d) Every child deprived of his or her liberty shall have the right to prompt access to legal and other appropriate assistance, as well as the right to challenge the legality of the deprivation of his or her liberty before a court or other competent, independent and impartial authority, and to a prompt decision on any such action.

ARTICLE 38

1.   States Parties undertake to respect and to ensure respect for rules of international humanitarian law applicable to them in armed conflicts which are relevant to the child.

2.   States Parties shall take all feasible measures to ensure that persons who have not attained the age of fifteen years do not take a direct part in hostilities.

3.   States Parties shall refrain from recruiting any person who has not attained the age of fifteen years into their armed forces. In recruiting among those persons who have attained the age of fifteen years but who have not attained the age of eighteen years, States Parties shall endeavour to give priority to those who are oldest.

4.   In accordance with their obligations under international humanitarian law to protect the civilian population in armed conflicts, States Parties shall take all feasible measures to ensure protection and care of children who are affected by an armed conflict.

ARTICLE 39

States Parties shall take all appropriate measures to promote physical and psychological recovery and social reintegration of a child victim of: any form of neglect, exploitation, or abuse; torture or any other form of cruel, inhuman or degrading treatment or punishment; or armed conflicts. Such recovery and reintegration shall take place in an environment which fosters the health, self-respect and dignity of the child.

ARTICLE 40

1.   States Parties recognize the right of every child alleged as, accused of, or recognized as having infringed the penal law to be treated in a manner consistent with the promotion of the child's sense of dignity and worth, which reinforces the child's respect for the human rights and fundamental freedoms of others and which takes into account the child's age and the desirability of promoting the child's reintegration and the child's assuming a constructive role in society.

2.   To this end, and having regard to the relevant provisions of international instruments, States Parties shall, in particular, ensure that:

(a)   No child shall be alleged as, be accused of, or recognized as having infringed the penal law by reason of acts or omissions that were not prohibited by national or international law at the time they were committed;

(b)   Every child alleged as or accused of having infringed the penal law has at least the following guarantees:

(i)   To be presumed innocent until proven guilty according to law;

(ii)   To be informed promptly and directly of the charges against him or her, and, if appropriate, through his or her parents or legal guardians, and to have legal or other appropriate assistance in the preparation and presentation of his or her defence;

(iii) To have the matter determined without delay by a competent, independent and impartial authority or judicial body in a fair hearing according to law, in the presence of legal or other appropriate assistance and, unless it is considered not to be in the best interest of the child, in particular, taking into account his or her age or situation, his or her parents or legal guardians;

(iv) Not to be compelled to give testimony or to confess guilt; to examine or have examined adverse witnesses and to obtain the participation and examination of witnesses on his or her behalf under conditions of equality;

(v)   If considered to have infringed the penal law, to have this decision and any measures imposed in consequence thereof reviewed by a higher competent, independent and impartial authority or judicial body according to law;

(vi) To have the free assistance of an interpreter if the child cannot understand or speak the language used;

(vii) To have his or her privacy fully respected at all stages of the proceedings.

3.   States Parties shall seek to promote the establishment of laws, procedures, authorities and institutions specifically applicable to children alleged as, accused of, or recognized as having infringed the penal law, and, in particular:

(a) The establishment of a minimum age below which children shall be presumed not to have the capacity to infringe the penal law;

(b) Whenever appropriate and desirable, measures for dealing with such children without resorting to judicial proceedings, providing that human rights and legal safeguards are fully respected.

4.   A variety of dispositions, such as care, guidance and supervision orders; counselling; probation; foster care; education and vocational training programmes and other alternatives to institutional care shall be available to ensure that children are dealt with in a manner appropriate to their well-being and proportionate both to their circumstances and the offence.

ARTICLE 41

Nothing in the present Convention shall affect any provisions which are more conducive to the realization of the rights of the child and which may be contained in:

(a) The law of a State Party; or

(b) International law in force for that State.

PART II

ARTICLE 42

States Parties undertake to make the principles and provisions of the Convention widely known, by appropriate and active means, to adults and children alike.

ARTICLE 43

1.   For the purpose of examining the progress made by States Parties in achieving the realization of the obligations undertaken in the present Convention, there shall be established a Committee on the Rights of the Child, which shall carry out the functions hereinafter provided.

2.   The Committee shall consist of ten experts of high moral standing and recognized competence in the field covered by this Convention. The members of the Committee shall be elected by States Parties from among their nationals and shall serve in their personal capacity, consideration being given to equitable geographical distribution, as well as to the principal legal systems.

3.   The members of the Committee shall be elected by secret ballot from a list of persons nominated by States Parties. Each State Party may nominate one person from among its own nationals.

4.   The initial election to the Committee shall be held no later than six months after the date of the entry into force of the present Convention and thereafter every second year. At least four months before the date of each election, the Secretary-General of the United Nations shall address a letter to States Parties inviting them to submit their nominations within two months. The Secretary-General shall subsequently prepare a list in alphabetical order of all persons thus nominated, indicating States Parties which have nominated them, and shall submit it to the States Parties to the present Convention.

5.   The elections shall be held at meetings of States Parties convened by the Secretary-General at United Nations Headquarters. At those meetings, for which two thirds of States Parties shall constitute a quorum, the persons elected to the Committee shall be those who obtain the largest number of votes and an absolute majority of the votes of the representatives of States Parties present and voting.

6.   The members of the Committee shall be elected for a term of four years. They shall be eligible for re-election if renominated. The term of five of the members elected at the first election shall expire at the end of two years; immediately after the first election, the names of these five members shall be chosen by lot by the Chairman of the meeting.

7.   If a member of the Committee dies or resigns or declares that for any other cause he or she can no longer perform the duties of the Committee, the State Party which nominated the member shall appoint another expert from among its nationals to serve for the remainder of the term, subject to the approval of the Committee.

8.   The Committee shall establish its own rules of procedure.

9.   The Committee shall elect its officers for a period of two years.

10.   The meetings of the Committee shall normally be held at United Nations Headquarters or at any other convenient place as determined by the Committee. The Committee shall normally meet annually. The duration of the meetings of the Committee shall be determined, and reviewed, it necessary, by a meeting of the States Parties to the present Convention, subject to the approval of the General Assembly.

11.   The Secretary-General of the United Nations shall provide the necessary staff and facilities for the effective performance of the functions of the Committee under the present Convention.

12.   With the approval of the General Assembly, the members of the Committee established under the present Convention shall receive emoluments from United Nations resources on such terms and conditions as the Assembly may decide.

ARTICLE 44

1.   States Parties undertake to submit to the Committee, through the Secretary-General of the United Nations, reports on the measures they have adopted which give effect to the rights recognized herein and on the progress made on the enjoyment of those rights:

(a) Within two years of the entry into force of the Convention for the State Party concerned;

(b) Thereafter every five years.

2.   Reports made under the present article shall indicate factors and difficulties, if any, affecting the degree of fulfilment of the obligations under the present Convention. Reports shall also contain sufficient information to provide the Committee with a comprehensive understanding of the implementation of the Convention in the country concerned.

3.   A State Party which has submitted a comprehensive initial report to the Committee need not, in its subsequent reports submitted in accordance with paragraph 1 (b) of the present article, repeat basic information previously provided.

4.   The Committee may request from States Parties further information relevant to the implementation of the Convention.

5.   The Committee shall submit to the General Assembly, through the Economic and Social Council, every two years, reports on its activities.

6.   States Parties shall make their reports widely available to the public in their own countries.

ARTICLE 45

In order to foster the effective implementation of the Convention and to encourage international co-operation in the field covered by the Convention:

(a) The specialized agencies, the United Nations Children's Fund, and other United Nations organs shall be entitled to be represented at the consideration of the implementation of such provisions of the present Convention as fall within the scope of their mandate. The Committee may invite the specialized agencies, the United Nations Children's Fund and other competent bodies as it may consider appropriate to provide expert advice on the implementation of the Convention in areas falling within the scope of their respective mandates. The Committee may invite the specialized agencies, the United Nations Children's Fund, and other United Nations organs to submit reports on the implementation of the Convention in areas falling within the scope of their activities;

(b) The Committee shall transmit, as it may consider appropriate, to the specialized agencies, the United Nations Children's Fund and other competent bodies, any reports from States Parties that contain a request, or indicate a need, for technical advice or assistance, along with the Committee's observations and suggestions, if any, on these requests or indications;

(c) The Committee may recommend to the General Assembly to request the Secretary-General to undertake on its behalf studies on specific issues relating to the rights of the child;

(d) The Committee may make suggestions and general recommendations based on information received pursuant to articles 44 and 45 of the present Convention. Such suggestions and general recommendations shall be transmitted to any State Party concerned and reported to the General Assembly, together with comments, if any, from States Parties.

PART III

ARTICLE 46

The present Convention shall be open for signature by all States.

ARTICLE 47

The present Convention is subject to ratification. Instruments of ratification shall be deposited with the Secretary-General of the United Nations.

ARTICLE 48

The present Convention shall remain open for accession by any State. The instruments of accession shall be deposited with the Secretary-General of the United Nations.

ARTICLE 49

1. The present Convention shall enter into force on the thirtieth day following the date of deposit with the Secretary-General of the United Nations of the twentieth instrument of ratification or accession.

2. For each State ratifying or acceding to the Convention after the deposit of the twentieth instrument of ratification or accession, the Convention shall enter into force on the thirtieth day after the deposit by such State of its instrument of ratification or accession.

ARTICLE 50

1. Any State Party may propose an amendment and file it with the Secretary-General of the United Nations. The Secretary-General shall thereupon communicate the proposed amendment to States Parties, with

a request that they indicate whether they favour a conference of States Parties for the purpose of considering and voting upon the proposals. In the event that, within four months from the date of such communication, at least one third of the States Parties favour such a conference, the Secretary-General shall convene the conference under the auspices of the United Nations. Any amendment adopted by a majority of States Parties present and voting at the conference shall be submitted to the General Assembly for approval.

2.   An amendment adopted in accordance with paragraph 1 of the present article shall enter into force when it has been approved by the General Assembly of the United Nations and accepted by a two-thirds majority of States Parties.

3.   When an amendment enters into force, it shall be binding on those States Parties which have accepted it, other States Parties still being bound by the provisions of the present Convention and any earlier amendments which they have accepted.

ARTICLE 51

1.   The Secretary-General of the United Nations shall receive and circulate to all States the text of reservations made by States at the time of ratification or accession.

2.   A reservation incompatible with the object and purpose of the present Convention shall not be permitted.

3.   Reservations may be withdrawn at any time by notification to that effect addressed to the Secretary-General of the United Nations, who shall then inform all States. Such notification shall take effect on the date on which it is received by the Secretary-General.

ARTICLE 52

A State Party may denounce the present Convention by written notification to the Secretary-General of the United Nations. Denunciation becomes effective one year after the date of receipt of the notification by the Secretary-General.

ARTICLE 53

The Secretary-General of the United Nations is designated as the depositary of the present Convention.

ARTICLE 54

The original of the present Convention, of which the Arabic, Chinese, English, French, Russian and Spanish texts are equally authentic, shall be deposited with the Secretary-General of the United Nations. In witness thereof the undersigned plenipotentiaries, being duly authorized thereto by their respective Governments, have signed the present Convention.

United Nations Declaration on the Elimination of Discrimination Against Women

G.A. Res. 2263 (November 7, 1967)

[EDITORS' INTRODUCTION: Alice Edwards, *Violence Against Women as Sex Discrimination: Judging the Jurisprudence of the United Nations Human Rights Treaty Bodies*, 18 TEX. J. WOMEN & L. 1 (2008); Darren Rosenblum, *Unsex CEDAW, or What's Wrong with Women's Rights*, 20 COLUM. J. GENDER & L. 98 (2011); Elizabeth Sepper, *Confronting the "Sacred and Unchangeable": The Obligation to Modify Cultural Patterns Under the Women's Discrimination Treaty*, 30 U. PA. J. INT'L L. 585 (2008).]

The General Assembly,

Considering that the peoples of the United Nations have, in the Charter, reaffirmed their faith in fundamental human rights, in the dignity and worth of the human person and in the equal rights of men and women,

Considering that the Universal Declaration of Human Rights asserts the principle of non-discrimination and proclaims that all human beings are born free and equal in dignity and rights and that everyone is entitled to all the rights and freedoms set forth therein without distinction of any kind, including any distinction as to sex,

Taking into account the resolutions, declarations, conventions and recommendations of the United Nations and the specialized agencies designed to eliminate all forms of discrimination and to promote equal rights for men and women,

Concerned that, despite the Charter of the United Nations, the Universal Declaration of Human Rights, the International Covenants on Human Rights and other instruments of the United Nations and the specialized agencies and despite the progress made in the matter of equality of rights, there continues to exist considerable discrimination against women,

Considering that discrimination against women is incompatible with human dignity and with the welfare of the family and of society, prevents their participation, on equal terms with men, in the political, social, economic and cultural life of their countries and is an obstacle to the full development of the potentialities of women in the service of their countries and of humanity,

Bearing in mind the great contribution made by women to social, political, economic and cultural life and the part they play in the family and particularly in the rearing of children,

Convinced that the full and complete development of a country, the welfare of the world and the cause of peace require the maximum participation of women as well as men in all fields,

Considering that it is necessary to ensure the universal recognition in law and in fact of the principle of equality of men and women,

Solemnly proclaims this Declaration:

ARTICLE 1

Discrimination against women, denying or limiting as it does their equality of rights with men, is fundamentally unjust and constitutes an offence against human dignity.

ARTICLE 2

All appropriate measures shall be taken to abolish existing laws, customs, regulations and practices which are discriminatory against women, and to establish adequate legal protection for equal rights of men and women, in particular:

(a) The principle of equality of rights shall be embodied in the constitution or otherwise guaranteed by law;

(b) The international instruments of the United Nations and the specialized agencies relating to the elimination of discrimination against women shall be ratified or acceded to and fully implemented as soon as practicable.

ARTICLE 3

All appropriate measures shall be taken to educate public opinion and to direct national aspirations towards the eradication of prejudice and the abolition of customary and all other practices which are based on the idea of the inferiority of women.

ARTICLE 4

All appropriate measures shall be taken to ensure to women on equal terms with men, without any discrimination:

(a) The right to vote in all elections and be eligible for election to all publicly elected bodies;

(b) The right to vote in all public referenda;

(c) The right to hold public office and to exercise all public functions.

Such rights shall be guaranteed by legislation.

ARTICLE 5

Women shall have the same rights as men to acquire, change or retain their nationality. Marriage to an alien shall not automatically affect the nationality of the wife either by rendering her stateless or by forcing upon her the nationality of her husband.

ARTICLE 6

1.   Without prejudice to the safeguarding of the unity and the harmony of the family, which remains the basic unit of any society, all appropriate measures, particularly legislative measures, shall be taken to ensure to women, married or unmarried, equal rights with men in the field of civil law, and in particular:

(a)   The right to acquire, administer, enjoy, dispose of and inherit property, including property acquired during marriage;

(b)   The right to equality in legal capacity and the exercise thereof;

(c)   The same rights as men with regard to the law on the movement of persons.

2.   All appropriate measures shall be taken to ensure the principle of equality of status of the husband and wife, and in particular:

(a)   Women shall have the same right as men to free choice of a spouse and to enter into marriage only with their free and full consent;

(b)   Women shall have equal rights with men during marriage and at its dissolution. In all cases the interest of the children shall be paramount;

(c)   Parents shall have equal rights and duties in matters relating to their children. In all cases the interest of the children shall be paramount.

3.   Child marriage and the betrothal of young girls before puberty shall be prohibited, and effective action, including legislation, shall be taken to specify a minimum age for marriage and to make the registration of marriages in an official registry compulsory.

ARTICLE 7

All provisions of penal codes which constitute discrimination against women shall be repealed.

ARTICLE 8

All appropriate measures, including legislation, shall be taken to combat all forms of traffic in women and exploitation of prostitution of women.

ARTICLE 9

All appropriate measures shall be taken to ensure to girls and women, married or unmarried, equal rights with men in education at all levels, and in particular:

(a) Equal conditions of access to, and study in, educational institutions of all types, including universities and vocational, technical and professional schools;

(b) The same choice of curricula, the same examinations, teaching staff with qualifications of the same standard, and school premises and equipment of the same quality, whether the institutions are co-educational or not;

(c) Equal opportunities to benefit from scholarships and other study grants;

(d) Equal opportunities for access to programmes of continuing education, including adult literacy programmes;

(e) Access to educational information to help in ensuring the health and well-being of families.

ARTICLE 10

1. All appropriate measures shall be taken to ensure to women, married or unmarried, equal rights with men in the field of economic and social life, and in particular:

(a) The right, without discrimination on grounds of marital status or any other grounds, to receive vocational training, to work, to free choice of profession and employment, and to professional and vocational advancement;

(b) The right to equal remuneration with men and to equality of treatment in respect of work of equal value;

(c) The right to leave with pay, retirement privileges and provision for security in respect of unemployment, sickness, old age or other incapacity to work;

(d) The right to receive family allowances on equal terms with men.

2. In order to prevent discrimination against women on account of marriage or maternity and to ensure their effective right to work, measures shall be taken to prevent their dismissal in the event of marriage or maternity and to provide paid maternity leave, with the guarantee of returning to former employment, and to provide the necessary social services, including child-care facilities.

3. Measures taken to protect women in certain types of work, for reasons inherent in their physical nature, shall not be regarded as discriminatory.

ARTICLE 11

1. The principle of equality of rights of men and women demands implementation in all States in accordance with the principles of the

Charter of the United Nations and of the Universal Declaration of Human Rights.

2.   Governments, non-governmental organizations and individuals are urged, therefore, to do all in their power to promote the implementation of the principles contained in this Declaration.

United Nations Declaration on Social and Legal Principles Relating to the Protection and Welfare of Children, with Special Reference to Foster Placement and Adoption Nationally and Internationally

G.A. Res. 41/85 of December 3, 1986, 26 I.L.M. 1096 (1987)

[EDITORS' INTRODUCTION: Richard R. Carlson, *A Child's Right to a Family Versus a State's Discretion to Institutionalize the Child*, 47 Geo. J. Int'l L. 937 (2016); Eric Engle, *The Convention on the Rights of the Child*, 29 QUINNIPIAC L. REV. 793 (2011); Malinda L. Seymore, *Openness in International Adoption*, 46 COLUM. HUM. RTS. L. REV. 163 (2015); Rachel J. Wechsler, *Giving Every Child a Chance: The Need for Reform and Infrastructure in Intercountry Adoption Policy*, 22 PACE INT'L L. REV. 1 (2010).]

The General Assembly,

Recalling the Universal Declaration of Human Rights, the International Covenant on Economic, Social and Cultural Rights, the International Covenant on Civil and Political Rights, the International Convention on the Elimination of All Forms of Racial Discrimination and the Convention on the Elimination of All Forms of Discrimination against Women,

Recalling also the Declaration of the Rights of the Child, which it proclaimed by its resolution 1386 (XIV) of 20 November 1959,

Reaffirming principle 6 of that Declaration, which states that the child shall, wherever possible, grow up in the care and under the responsibility of his parents and, in any case, in an atmosphere of affection and of moral and material security,

Concerned at the large number of children who are abandoned or become orphans owing to violence, internal disturbance, armed conflicts, natural disasters, economic crises or social problems,

Bearing in mind that in all foster placement and adoption procedures the best interests of the child should be the paramount consideration,

Recognizing that under the principal legal systems of the world, various valuable alternative institutions exist, such as the Kafala of Islamic Law, which provide substitute care to children who cannot be cared for by their own parents,

Recognizing further that only where a particular institution is recognized and regulated by the domestic law of a State would the provisions of this Declaration relating to that institution be relevant and that such provisions would in no way affect the existing alternative institutions in other legal systems,

Conscious of the need to proclaim universal principles to be taken into account in cases where procedures are instituted relating to foster placement or adoption of a child, either nationally or internationally,

Bearing in mind, however, that the principles set forth hereunder do not impose on States such legal institutions as foster placement or adoption,

Proclaims the following principles:

A.   GENERAL FAMILY AND CHILD WELFARE

ARTICLE 1

Every State should give a high priority to family and child welfare.

ARTICLE 2

Child welfare depends upon good family welfare.

ARTICLE 3

The first priority for a child is to be cared for by his or her own parents.

ARTICLE 4

When care by the child's own parents is unavailable or inappropriate, care by relatives of the child's parents, by another substitute - foster or adoptive - family or, if necessary, by an appropriate institution should be considered.

ARTICLE 5

In all matters relating to the placement of a child outside the care of the child's own parents, the best interests of the child, particularly his or her need for affection and right to security and continuing care, should be the paramount consideration.

ARTICLE 6

Persons responsible for foster placement or adoption procedures should have professional or other appropriate training.

ARTICLE 7

Governments should determine the adequacy of their national child welfare services and consider appropriate actions.

ARTICLE 8

The child should at all times have a name, a nationality and a legal representative. The child should not, as a result of foster placement, adoption or any alternative regime, be deprived of his or her name, nationality or legal representative unless the child thereby acquires a new name, nationality or legal representative.

ARTICLE 9

The need of a foster or an adopted child to know about his or her background should be recognized by persons responsible for the child's care, unless this is contrary to the child's best interests.

B. FOSTER PLACEMENT

ARTICLE 10

Foster placement of children should be regulated by law.

ARTICLE 11

Foster family care, though temporary in nature, may continue, if necessary, until adulthood but should not preclude either prior return to the child's own parents or adoption.

ARTICLE 12

In all matters of foster family care, the prospective foster parents and, as appropriate, the child and his or her own parents should be properly involved. A competent authority or agency should be responsible for supervision to ensure the welfare of the child.

C. ADOPTION

ARTICLE 13

The primary aim of adoption is to provide the child who cannot be cared for by his or her own parents with a permanent family.

ARTICLE 14

In considering possible adoption placements, persons responsible for them should select the most appropriate environment for the child.

ARTICLE 15

Sufficient time and adequate counselling should be given to the child's own parents, the prospective adoptive parents and, as appropriate, the child in order to reach a decision on the child's future as early as possible.

ARTICLE 16

The relationship between the child to be adopted and the prospective adoptive parents should be observed by child welfare agencies or services prior to the adoption. Legislation should ensure that the child is recognized in law as a member of the adoptive family and enjoys all the rights pertinent thereto.

ARTICLE 17

If a child cannot be placed in a foster or an adoptive family or cannot in any suitable manner be cared for in the country of origin, intercountry adoption may be considered as an alternative means of providing the child with a family.

ARTICLE 18

Governments should establish policy, legislation and effective supervision for the protection of children involved in intercountry adoption. Intercountry adoption should, wherever possible, only be undertaken when such measures have been established in the States concerned.

ARTICLE 19

Policies should be established and laws enacted, where necessary, for the prohibition of abduction and of any other act for illicit placement of children.

ARTICLE 20

In intercountry adoption, placements should, as a rule, be made through competent authorities or agencies with application of safeguards and standards equivalent to those existing in respect of national adoption. In no case should the placement result in improper financial gain for those involved in it.

ARTICLE 21

In intercountry adoption through persons acting as agents for prospective adoptive parents, special precautions should be taken in order to protect the child's legal and social interests.

ARTICLE 22

No intercountry adoption should be considered before it has been established that the child is legally free for adoption and that any pertinent documents necessary to complete the adoption, such as the consent of competent authorities, will become available. It must also be established that the child will be able to migrate and to join the prospective adoptive parents and may obtain their nationality.

ARTICLE 23

In intercountry adoption, as a rule, the legal validity of the adoption should be assured in each of the countries involved.

ARTICLE 24

Where the nationality of the child differs from that of the prospective adoptive parents, all due weight shall be given to both the law of the State of which the child is a national and the law of the State of which the prospective adoptive parents are nationals. In this connection due regard shall be given to the child's cultural and religious background and interests.

UNITED NATIONS: OPTIONAL PROTOCOL TO THE CONVENTION ON THE RIGHTS OF THE CHILD ON THE INVOLVEMENT OF CHILDREN IN ARMED CONFLICT

ADOPTED AND OPENED FOR SIGNATURE, RATIFICATION, AND ACCESSION BY GENERAL ASSEMBLY RESOLUTION

May 25, 2000, U.N. GAOR, 54th Sess., U.N. Doc. A/54/RES/263

[EDITORS' INTRODUCTION: Heather L. Carmody, *The Child Soldiers Prevention Act: How the Act's Inadequacy Leaves the World's Children Vulnerable*, 43 CAL. W. INT'L L.J. 233 (2012); Caroline Davidson, *Explaining Inhumanity: The Use of Crime-Definition Experts at International Criminal Courts*, 48 VAND. J. TRANSNAT'L L. 359 (2015); Diane A. Desierto, *Leveraging International Economic Tools to Confront Child Soldiering*, 43 N.Y.U. J. INT'L L. & POL. 337 (2011); Erin Lafayette, *The Prosecution of Child Soldiers: Balancing Accountability with Justice*, 63 SYRACUSE L. REV. 297 (2013); Luz E. Nagle, *Child Soldiers and the Duty of Nations to Protect Children from Participation in Armed Conflict*, 19 CARDOZO J. INT'L & COMP. L. 1 (2011); *Elizabeth A. Rossi, A "Special Track" for Former Child Soldiers: Enacting a "Child Soldier Visa" as an Alternative to Asylum Protection*, 31 BERKELEY J. INT'L L. 392 (2013); Addison L. Boyland, Comment, *Sending Mixed Messages on Combatting the Use of Child Soldiers through Unilateral Economic Sanctions: The U.S.'s Manipulation of the Child Soldiers Prevention Act of 2008*, 22 MICH. ST. INT'L. L. REV. 669 (2014); Cristina Martinez Squiers, Comment, *How the Law Should View Voluntary Child Soldiers: Does Terrorism Pose a Different Dilemma?*, 68 SMU L. REV. 567 (2015).]

The States Parties to the present Protocol,

Encouraged by the overwhelming support for the Convention on the Rights of the Child, demonstrating the widespread commitment that exists to strive for the promotion and protection of the rights of the child,

Reaffirming that the rights of children require special protection, and calling for continuous improvement of the situation of children without distinction, as well as for their development and education in conditions of peace and security,

Disturbed by the harmful and widespread impact of armed conflict on children and the long-term consequences it has for durable peace, security and development,

Condemning the targeting of children in situations of armed conflict and direct attacks on objects protected under international law, including places that generally have a significant presence of children, such as schools and hospitals,

Noting the adoption of the Rome Statute of the International Criminal Court, in particular, the inclusion therein as a war crime, of conscripting or enlisting children under the age of 15 years or using them to participate actively in hostilities in both international and non-international armed conflict,

Considering therefore that to strengthen further the implementation of rights recognized in the Convention on the Rights of the Child there is a need to increase the protection of children from involvement in armed conflict,

Noting that article 1 of the Convention on the Rights of the Child specifies that, for the purposes of that Convention, a child means every human being below the age of 18 years unless, under the law applicable to the child, majority is attained earlier,

Convinced that an optional protocol to the Convention that raises the age of possible recruitment of persons into armed forces and their participation in hostilities will contribute effectively to the implementation of the principle that the best interests of the child are to be a primary consideration in all actions concerning children,

Noting that the twenty-sixth International Conference of the Red Cross and Red Crescent in December 1995 recommended, inter alia, that parties to conflict take every feasible step to ensure that children below the age of 18 years do not take part in hostilities,

Welcoming the unanimous adoption, in June 1999, of International Labour Organization Convention No. 182 on the Prohibition and Immediate Action for the Elimination of the Worst Forms of Child Labour, which prohibits, inter alia, forced or compulsory recruitment of children for use in armed conflict,

Condemning with the gravest concern the recruitment, training and use within and across national borders of children in hostilities by armed groups distinct from the armed forces of a State, and recognizing the responsibility of those who recruit, train and use children in this regard,

Recalling the obligation of each party to an armed conflict to abide by the provisions of international humanitarian law,

Stressing that the present Protocol is without prejudice to the purposes and principles contained in the Charter of the United Nations, including Article 51, and relevant norms of humanitarian law,

Bearing in mind that conditions of peace and security based on full respect of the purposes and principles contained in the Charter and observance of applicable human rights instruments are indispensable for the full protection of children, in particular during armed conflict and foreign occupation,

Recognizing the special needs of those children who are particularly vulnerable to recruitment or use in hostilities contrary to the present Protocol owing to their economic or social status or gender,

Mindful of the necessity of taking into consideration the economic, social and political root causes of the involvement of children in armed conflict,

Convinced of the need to strengthen international cooperation in the implementation of the present Protocol, as well as the physical and psychosocial rehabilitation and social reintegration of children who are victims of armed conflict,

Encouraging the participation of the community and, in particular, children and child victims in the dissemination of informational and educational programmes concerning the implementation of the Protocol,

Have agreed as follows:

ARTICLE 1

States Parties shall take all feasible measures to ensure that members of their armed forces who have not attained the age of 18 years do not take a direct part in hostilities.

ARTICLE 2

States Parties shall ensure that persons who have not attained the age of 18 years are not compulsorily recruited into their armed forces.

ARTICLE 3

1. States Parties shall raise the minimum age for the voluntary recruitment of persons into their national armed forces from that set out in article 38, paragraph 3, of the Convention on the Rights of the Child, taking account of the principles contained in that article and recognizing that under the Convention persons under the age of 18 years are entitled to special protection.

2. Each State Party shall deposit a binding declaration upon ratification of or accession to the present Protocol that sets forth the minimum age at which it will permit voluntary recruitment into its national armed forces and a description of the safeguards it has adopted to ensure that such recruitment is not forced or coerced.

3. States Parties that permit voluntary recruitment into their national armed forces under the age of 18 years shall maintain safeguards to ensure, as a minimum, that:

(a) Such recruitment is genuinely voluntary;

(b) Such recruitment is carried out with the informed consent of the person's parents or legal guardians;

(c) Such persons are fully informed of the duties involved in such military service;

(d) Such persons provide reliable proof of age prior to acceptance into national military service.

4. Each State Party may strengthen its declaration at any time by notification to that effect addressed to the Secretary-General of the United Nations, who shall inform all States Parties. Such notification

shall take effect on the date on which it is received by the Secretary-General.

5.   The requirement to raise the age in paragraph 1 of the present article does not apply to schools operated by or under the control of the armed forces of the States Parties, in keeping with articles 28 and 29 of the Convention on the Rights of the Child.

ARTICLE 4

1.   Armed groups that are distinct from the armed forces of a State should not, under any circumstances, recruit or use in hostilities persons under the age of 18 years.

2.   States Parties shall take all feasible measures to prevent such recruitment and use, including the adoption of legal measures necessary to prohibit and criminalize such practices.

3.   The application of the present article shall not affect the legal status of any party to an armed conflict.

ARTICLE 5

Nothing in the present Protocol shall be construed as precluding provisions in the law of a State Party or in international instruments and international humanitarian law that are more conducive to the realization of the rights of the child.

ARTICLE 6

1.   Each State Party shall take all necessary legal, administrative and other measures to ensure the effective implementation and enforcement of the provisions of the present Protocol within its jurisdiction.

2.   States Parties undertake to make the principles and provisions of the present Protocol widely known and promoted by appropriate means, to adults and children alike.

3.   States Parties shall take all feasible measures to ensure that persons within their jurisdiction recruited or used in hostilities contrary to the present Protocol are demobilized or otherwise released from service. States Parties shall, when necessary, accord to such persons all appropriate assistance for their physical and psychological recovery and their social reintegration.

ARTICLE 7

1.   States Parties shall cooperate in the implementation of the present Protocol, including in the prevention of any activity contrary thereto and in the rehabilitation and social reintegration of persons who are victims of acts contrary thereto, including through technical cooperation and financial assistance. Such assistance and cooperation

will be undertaken in consultation with the States Parties concerned and the relevant international organizations.

2.   States Parties in a position to do so shall provide such assistance through existing multilateral, bilateral or other programmes or, inter alia, through a voluntary fund established in accordance with the rules of the General Assembly.

ARTICLE 8

1.   Each State Party shall, within two years following the entry into force of the present Protocol for that State Party, submit a report to the Committee on the Rights of the Child providing comprehensive information on the measures it has taken to implement the provisions of the Protocol, including the measures taken to implement the provisions on participation and recruitment.

2.   Following the submission of the comprehensive report, each State Party shall include in the reports it submits to the Committee on the Rights of the Child, in accordance with article 44 of the Convention, any further information with respect to the implementation of the Protocol. Other States Parties to the Protocol shall submit a report every five years.

3.   The Committee on the Rights of the Child may request from States Parties further information relevant to the implementation of the present Protocol.

ARTICLE 9

1.   The present Protocol is open for signature by any State that is a party to the Convention or has signed it.

2.   The present Protocol is subject to ratification and is open to accession by any State. Instruments of ratification or accession shall be deposited with the Secretary-General of the United Nations.

3.   The Secretary-General, in his capacity as depositary of the Convention and the Protocol, shall inform all States Parties to the Convention and all States that have signed the Convention of each instrument of declaration pursuant to article 3.

ARTICLE 10

1.   The present Protocol shall enter into force three months after the deposit of the tenth instrument of ratification or accession.

2.   For each State ratifying the present Protocol or acceding to it after its entry into force, the Protocol shall enter into force one month after the date of the deposit of its own instrument of ratification or accession.

ARTICLE 11

1.   Any State Party may denounce the present Protocol at any time by written notification to the Secretary- General of the United Nations, who shall thereafter inform the other States Parties to the Convention and all States that have signed the Convention. The denunciation shall take effect one year after the date of receipt of the notification by the Secretary-General. If, however, on the expiry of that year the denouncing State Party is engaged in armed conflict, the denunciation shall not take effect before the end of the armed conflict.

2.   Such a denunciation shall not have the effect of releasing the State Party from its obligations under the present Protocol in regard to any act that occurs prior to the date on which the denunciation becomes effective. Nor shall such a denunciation prejudice in any way the continued consideration of any matter that is already under consideration by the Committee on the Rights of the Child prior to the date on which the denunciation becomes effective.

ARTICLE 12

1.   Any State Party may propose an amendment and file it with the Secretary-General of the United Nations. The Secretary-General shall thereupon communicate the proposed amendment to States Parties with a request that they indicate whether they favour a conference of States Parties for the purpose of considering and voting upon the proposals. In the event that, within four months from the date of such communication, at least one third of the States Parties favour such a conference, the Secretary-General shall convene the conference under the auspices of the United Nations. Any amendment adopted by a majority of States Parties present and voting at the conference shall be submitted to the General Assembly of the United Nations for approval.

2.   An amendment adopted in accordance with paragraph 1 of the present article shall enter into force when it has been approved by the General Assembly and accepted by a two-thirds majority of States Parties.

3.   When an amendment enters into force, it shall be binding on those States Parties that have accepted it, other States Parties still being bound by the provisions of the present Protocol and any earlier amendments they have accepted.

ARTICLE 13

1.   The present Protocol, of which the Arabic, Chinese, English, French, Russian and Spanish texts are equally authentic, shall be deposited in the archives of the United Nations.

2.   The Secretary-General of the United Nations shall transmit certified copies of the present Protocol to all States Parties to the Convention and all States that have signed the Convention.

United Nations: Optional Protocol to the Convention on the Rights of the Child on the Sale of Children, Child Prostitution and Child Pornography

Adopted and Opened for Signature, Ratification, and Accession by General Assembly Resolution

May 25, 2000, U.N. GAOR, 54th Sess., U.N. Doc. A/RES/54/263

[EDITORS' INTRODUCTION: Eric Engle, *The Convention on the Rights of the Child*, 29 QUINNIPIAC L. REV. 793 (2011); John A. Hall, *Sex Offenders and Child Sex Tourism: The Case for Passport Revocation*, 18 VA. J. SOC. POL'Y & L. 153 (2011); Carole J. Petersen & Susan M. Chandler, *Sex Offender Registration and the Convention on the Rights of the Child: Legal and Policy Implications of Registering Juvenile Sex Offenders*, 3 WM. & MARY POL'Y REV. 1 (2011); David M. Smolin, *Surrogacy as the Sale of Children: Applying Lessons Learned from Adoption to the Regulation of the Surrogacy Industry's Global Marketing of Children*, 43 PEPP. L. REV. 265 (2016); Jonathan Todres, *A Child Rights Framework for Addressing Trafficking of Children*, 22 MICH. ST. INT'L. L. REV. 557 (2014); Gregory Van Houten, Note, *Testing Congress's Foreign Commerce and Treaty Powers: A New, (Un)Constitutional Tool for Combating American Child Sex Tourists?*, 53 AM. CRIM. L. REV. 177 (2016).]

The States Parties to the present Protocol,

Considering that, in order further to achieve the purposes of the Convention on the Rights of the Child and the implementation of its provisions, especially articles 1, 11, 21, 32, 33, 34, 35 and 36, it would be appropriate to extend the measures that States Parties should undertake in order to guarantee the protection of the child from the sale of children, child prostitution and child pornography,

Considering also that the Convention on the Rights of the Child recognizes the right of the child to be protected from economic exploitation and from performing any work that is likely to be hazardous or to interfere with the child's education, or to be harmful to the child's health or physical, mental, spiritual, moral or social development,

Gravely concerned at the significant and increasing international traffic in children for the purpose of the sale of children, child prostitution and child pornography,

Deeply concerned at the widespread and continuing practice of sex tourism, to which children are especially vulnerable, as it directly promotes the sale of children, child prostitution and child pornography,

Recognizing that a number of particularly vulnerable groups, including girl children, are at greater risk of sexual exploitation and that girl children are disproportionately represented among the sexually exploited,

Concerned about the growing availability of child pornography on the Internet and other evolving technologies, and recalling the International Conference on Combating Child Pornography on the Internet, held in Vienna in 1999, in particular its conclusion calling for the worldwide criminalization of the production, distribution, exportation, transmission, importation, intentional possession and advertising of child pornography, and stressing the importance of closer cooperation and partnership between Governments and the Internet industry,

Believing that the elimination of the sale of children, child prostitution and child pornography will be facilitated by adopting a holistic approach, addressing the contributing factors, including underdevelopment, poverty, economic disparities, inequitable socio-economic structure, dysfunctioning families, lack of education, urban-rural migration, gender discrimination, irresponsible adult sexual behaviour, harmful traditional practices, armed conflicts and trafficking in children,

Believing also that efforts to raise public awareness are needed to reduce consumer demand for the sale of children, child prostitution and child pornography, and believing further in the importance of strengthening global partnership among all actors and of improving law enforcement at the national level,

Noting the provisions of international legal instruments relevant to the protection of children, including the Hague Convention on Protection of Children and Cooperation in Respect of Intercountry Adoption, the Hague Convention on the Civil Aspects of International Child Abduction, the Hague Convention on Jurisdiction, Applicable Law, Recognition, Enforcement and Cooperation in Respect of Parental Responsibility and Measures for the Protection of Children, and International Labour Organization Convention No. 182 on the Prohibition and Immediate Action for the Elimination of the Worst Forms of Child Labour,

Encouraged by the overwhelming support for the Convention on the Rights of the Child, demonstrating the widespread commitment that exists for the promotion and protection of the rights of the child,

Recognizing the importance of the implementation of the provisions of the Programme of Action for the Prevention of the Sale of Children, Child Prostitution and Child Pornography and the Declaration and Agenda for Action adopted at the World Congress against Commercial Sexual Exploitation of Children, held in Stockholm from 27 to 31 August 1996, and the other relevant decisions and recommendations of pertinent international bodies,

Taking due account of the importance of the traditions and cultural values of each people for the protection and harmonious development of the child, Have agreed as follows:

ARTICLE 1

States Parties shall prohibit the sale of children, child prostitution and child pornography as provided for by the present Protocol.

ARTICLE 2

For the purposes of the present Protocol:

(a) Sale of children means any act or transaction whereby a child is transferred by any person or group of persons to another for remuneration or any other consideration;

(b) Child prostitution means the use of a child in sexual activities for remuneration or any other form of consideration;

(c) Child pornography means any representation, by whatever means, of a child engaged in real or simulated explicit sexual activities or any representation of the sexual parts of a child for primarily sexual purposes.

ARTICLE 3

1. Each State Party shall ensure that, as a minimum, the following acts and activities are fully covered under its criminal or penal law, whether such offences are committed domestically or transnationally or on an individual or organized basis:

(a) In the context of sale of children as defined in article 2:

(i) Offering, delivering or accepting, by whatever means, a child for the purpose of:

    a. Sexual exploitation of the child;

    b. Transfer of organs of the child for profit;

    c. Engagement of the child in forced labour;

(ii) Improperly inducing consent, as an intermediary, for the adoption of a child in violation of applicable international legal instruments on adoption;

(b) Offering, obtaining, procuring or providing a child for child prostitution, as defined in article 2;

(c) Producing, distributing, disseminating, importing, exporting, offering, selling or possessing for the above purposes child pornography as defined in article 2.

2. Subject to the provisions of the national law of a State Party, the same shall apply to an attempt to commit any of the said acts and to complicity or participation in any of the said acts.

3. Each State Party shall make such offences punishable by appropriate penalties that take into account their grave nature.

4. Subject to the provisions of its national law, each State Party shall take measures, where appropriate, to establish the liability of legal persons for offences established in paragraph 1 of the present article. Subject to the legal principles of the State Party, such liability of legal persons may be criminal, civil or administrative.

5. States Parties shall take all appropriate legal and administrative measures to ensure that all persons involved in the adoption of a child act in conformity with applicable international legal instruments.

ARTICLE 4

1. Each State Party shall take such measures as may be necessary to establish its jurisdiction over the offences referred to in article 3, paragraph 1, when the offences are committed in its territory or on board a ship or aircraft registered in that State.

2. Each State Party may take such measures as may be necessary to establish its jurisdiction over the offences referred to in article 3, paragraph 1, in the following cases:

(a) When the alleged offender is a national of that State or a person who has his habitual residence in its territory;

(b) When the victim is a national of that State.

3. Each State Party shall also take such measures as may be necessary to establish its jurisdiction over the aforementioned offences when the alleged offender is present in its territory and it does not extradite him or her to another State Party on the ground that the offence has been committed by one of its nationals.

4. The present Protocol does not exclude any criminal jurisdiction exercised in accordance with internal law.

ARTICLE 5

1. The offences referred to in article 3, paragraph 1, shall be deemed to be included as extraditable offences in any extradition treaty existing between States Parties and shall be included as extraditable offences in every extradition treaty subsequently concluded between them, in accordance with the conditions set forth in such treaties.

2. If a State Party that makes extradition conditional on the existence of a treaty receives a request for extradition from another State Party with which it has no extradition treaty, it may consider the present Protocol to be a legal basis for extradition in respect of such offences. Extradition shall be subject to the conditions provided by the law of the requested State.

3.　States Parties that do not make extradition conditional on the existence of a treaty shall recognize such offences as extraditable offences between themselves subject to the conditions provided by the law of the requested State.

4.　Such offences shall be treated, for the purpose of extradition between States Parties, as if they had been committed not only in the place in which they occurred but also in the territories of the States required to establish their jurisdiction in accordance with article 4.

5.　If an extradition request is made with respect to an offence described in article 3, paragraph 1, and the requested State Party does not or will not extradite on the basis of the nationality of the offender, that State shall take suitable measures to submit the case to its competent authorities for the purpose of prosecution.

ARTICLE 6

1.　States Parties shall afford one another the greatest measure of assistance in connection with investigations or criminal or extradition proceedings brought in respect of the offences set forth in article 3, paragraph 1, including assistance in obtaining evidence at their disposal necessary for the proceedings.

2.　States Parties shall carry out their obligations under paragraph 1 of the present article in conformity with any treaties or other arrangements on mutual legal assistance that may exist between them. In the absence of such treaties or arrangements, States Parties shall afford one another assistance in accordance with their domestic law.

ARTICLE 7

States Parties shall, subject to the provisions of their national law:

(a)　Take measures to provide for the seizure and confiscation, as appropriate, of:

(i)　Goods, such as materials, assets and other instrumentalities used to commit or facilitate offences under the present protocol;

(ii)　Proceeds derived from such offences;

(b)　Execute requests from another State Party for seizure or confiscation of goods or proceeds referred to in subparagraph (a);

(c)　Take measures aimed at closing, on a temporary or definitive basis, premises used to commit such offences.

ARTICLE 8

1.　States Parties shall adopt appropriate measures to protect the rights and interests of child victims of the practices prohibited under the present Protocol at all stages of the criminal justice process, in particular by:

(a) Recognizing the vulnerability of child victims and adapting procedures to recognize their special needs, including their special needs as witnesses;

(b) Informing child victims of their rights, their role and the scope, timing and progress of the proceedings and of the disposition of their cases;

(c) Allowing the views, needs and concerns of child victims to be presented and considered in proceedings where their personal interests are affected, in a manner consistent with the procedural rules of national law;

(d) Providing appropriate support services to child victims throughout the legal process;

(e) Protecting, as appropriate, the privacy and identity of child victims and taking measures in accordance with national law to avoid the inappropriate dissemination of information that could lead to the identification of child victims;

(f) Providing, in appropriate cases, for the safety of child victims, as well as that of their families and witnesses on their behalf, from intimidation and retaliation;

(g) Avoiding unnecessary delay in the disposition of cases and the execution of orders or decrees granting compensation to child victims.

2.   States Parties shall ensure that uncertainty as to the actual age of the victim shall not prevent the initiation of criminal investigations, including investigations aimed at establishing the age of the victim.

3.   States Parties shall ensure that, in the treatment by the criminal justice system of children who are victims of the offences described in the present Protocol, the best interest of the child shall be a primary consideration.

4.   States Parties shall take measures to ensure appropriate training, in particular legal and psychological training, for the persons who work with victims of the offences prohibited under the present Protocol.

5.   States Parties shall, in appropriate cases, adopt measures in order to protect the safety and integrity of those persons and/or organizations involved in the prevention and/or protection and rehabilitation of victims of such offences.

6.   Nothing in the present article shall be construed to be prejudicial to or inconsistent with the rights of the accused to a fair and impartial trial.

ARTICLE 9

1.   States Parties shall adopt or strengthen, implement and disseminate laws, administrative measures, social policies and programmes to prevent the offences referred to in the present Protocol. Particular attention shall be given to protect children who are especially vulnerable to such practices.

2.   States Parties shall promote awareness in the public at large, including children, through information by all appropriate means, education and training, about the preventive measures and harmful effects of the offences referred to in the present Protocol. In fulfilling their obligations under this article, States Parties shall encourage the participation of the community and, in particular, children and child victims, in such information and education and training programmes, including at the international level.

3.   States Parties shall take all feasible measures with the aim of ensuring all appropriate assistance to victims of such offences, including their full social reintegration and their full physical and psychological recovery.

4.   States Parties shall ensure that all child victims of the offences described in the present Protocol have access to adequate procedures to seek, without discrimination, compensation for damages from those legally responsible.

5.   States Parties shall take appropriate measures aimed at effectively prohibiting the production and dissemination of material advertising the offences described in the present Protocol.

ARTICLE 10

1.   States Parties shall take all necessary steps to strengthen international cooperation by multilateral, regional and bilateral arrangements for the prevention, detection, investigation, prosecution and punishment of those responsible for acts involving the sale of children, child prostitution, child pornography and child sex tourism. States Parties shall also promote international cooperation and coordination between their authorities, national and international non-governmental organizations and international organizations.

2.   States Parties shall promote international cooperation to assist child victims in their physical and psychological recovery, social reintegration and repatriation.

3.   States Parties shall promote the strengthening of international cooperation in order to address the root causes, such as poverty and underdevelopment, contributing to the vulnerability of children to the sale of children, child prostitution, child pornography and child sex tourism.

4.   States Parties in a position to do so shall provide financial, technical or other assistance through existing multilateral, regional, bilateral or other programmes.

ARTICLE 11

Nothing in the present Protocol shall affect any provisions that are more conducive to the realization of the rights of the child and that may be contained in:

(a) The law of a State Party;

(b) International law in force for that State.

ARTICLE 12

1.   Each State Party shall, within two years following the entry into force of the present Protocol for that State Party, submit a report to the Committee on the Rights of the Child providing comprehensive information on the measures it has taken to implement the provisions of the Protocol.

2.   Following the submission of the comprehensive report, each State Party shall include in the reports they submit to the Committee on the Rights of the Child, in accordance with article 44 of the Convention, any further information with respect to the implementation of the present Protocol. Other States Parties to the Protocol shall submit a report every five years.

3.   The Committee on the Rights of the Child may request from States Parties further information relevant to the implementation of the present Protocol.

ARTICLE 13

1.   The present Protocol is open for signature by any State that is a party to the Convention or has signed it.

2.   The present Protocol is subject to ratification and is open to accession by any State that is a party to the Convention or has signed it. Instruments of ratification or accession shall be deposited with the Secretary- General of the United Nations.

ARTICLE 14

1.   The present Protocol shall enter into force three months after the deposit of the tenth instrument of ratification or accession.

2.   For each State ratifying the present Protocol or acceding to it after its entry into force, the Protocol shall enter into force one month after the date of the deposit of its own instrument of ratification or accession.

ARTICLE 15

1.   Any State Party may denounce the present Protocol at any time by written notification to the Secretary- General of the United Nations, who shall thereafter inform the other States Parties to the Convention and all States that have signed the Convention. The denunciation shall take effect one year after the date of receipt of the notification by the Secretary-General.

2.   Such a denunciation shall not have the effect of releasing the State Party from its obligations under the present Protocol in regard to any offence that occurs prior to the date on which the denunciation becomes effective. Nor shall such a denunciation prejudice in any way the continued consideration of any matter that is already under consideration by the Committee on the Rights of the Child prior to the date on which the denunciation becomes effective.

ARTICLE 16

1.   Any State Party may propose an amendment and file it with the Secretary-General of the United Nations. The Secretary-General shall thereupon communicate the proposed amendment to States Parties with a request that they indicate whether they favour a conference of States Parties for the purpose of considering and voting upon the proposals. In the event that, within four months from the date of such communication, at least one third of the States Parties favour such a conference, the Secretary-General shall convene the conference under the auspices of the United Nations. Any amendment adopted by a majority of States Parties present and voting at the conference shall be submitted to the General Assembly of the United Nations for approval.

2.   An amendment adopted in accordance with paragraph 1 of the present article shall enter into force when it has been approved by the General Assembly and accepted by a two-thirds majority of States Parties.

3.   When an amendment enters into force, it shall be binding on those States Parties that have accepted it, other States Parties still being bound by the provisions of the present Protocol and any earlier amendments they have accepted.

ARTICLE 17

1.   The present Protocol, of which the Arabic, Chinese, English, French, Russian and Spanish texts are equally authentic, shall be deposited in the archives of the United Nations.

2.   The Secretary-General of the United Nations shall transmit certified copies of the present Protocol to all States Parties to the Convention and all States that have signed the Convention.